Spiro, Edward.
940.548   Set Europe ablaze [by] E. H. Cookridge. New York,
c. 1   Crowell [1967]

            vii, 410 p. illus., ports. 24 cm.

            First ed. published in 1966 under title: Inside S. O. E.
            Bibliography: p. 385–393.

            1. Gt. Brit. Special Operations Executive.   2. World War, 1939–
        1945—Secret service—Gt. Brit.   I. Title.

        D810.S7S57 1967   940.548'6'42   67–12308

                                            Cookridge, E. H., Pseud.

Set Europe Ablaze

Books by E. H. Cookridge

Secrets of the British Secret Service
Soviet Spy Net
The Net That Covers the World
Sisters of Delilah
Traitor Betrayed
They Came from the Sky
The Baron of Arizona
From Battenberg to Mountbatten
Set Europe Ablaze

E. H. COOKRIDGE

Set Europe Ablaze

THOMAS Y. CROWELL COMPANY

New York, Established 1834

First published in the United States of America in 1967.

Originally published in Great Britain
under the title
Inside S.O.E.

Preface and Acknowledgments

W H E N I first submitted the manuscript of this book to the British Security authorities, more than four years ago, I was told that my story could never be published. I was warned that the Official Secrets Act (which protects all classified material under threat of imprisonment) would be invoked, and that an unauthorized publication would result in "repercussions for other heads besides the author's." My SOE friends, who had provided much information, and I had signed the Official Secrets Act during the war. We were thus open to indictment, and so were the publishers and printers, should the warning be disregarded.

The story of SOE—the Special Operations Executive, precursor and later opposite number of the American OSS—is an important part of the secret history of World War II. The story of OSS and its founder and chief, General "Big Bill" Donovan has been told and retold many times. British authorities, however, believed that the twenty-five-year-old-secrets of SOE must be kept from the British public, even though any potential enemy could seek them out in official archives abroad.

Determined, nevertheless, to publish my story, I continued my research, which altogether took six years. During this time I traveled in seven countries in Europe, interviewed some six hundred men and women involved in the secret work of SOE, and made tape recordings and took signed statements, including many from former officers of the *Abwehr* and Gestapo.

Eventually, after protracted negotiations and the intervention of high-placed personalities, British Security agreed to the publication of my book in Britain on the understanding that a number of deletions would be made. They mainly concerned passages in which I disclosed some of the gravest blunders of the British Secret Service and named the men responsible. In the American edition of *Set Europe Ablaze* no such deletions have been made, and this is the full and unvarnished story. The same applies to several editions in foreign languages, which are being published during the spring of 1967 in Paris, The Hague, Munich, and Rome.

Lacking the cooperation of British authorities, I discovered early in my research that most relevant SOE files were available in the archives of other nations. General Dwight D. Eisenhower, the Allied Supreme Commander, had arranged at the end of the war that many SOE and OSS reports to SHAEF should be incorporated into the vast collection at the Historical Records Center and other archives of the Department of the Army at the Pentagon in Washington, D.C. There, as well as in several European capitals, I was able to obtain all the official material I wanted.

Unauthorized by British authorities, yet fortified with official British material gathered from legitimate sources abroad, I was able to check, corroborate, and, if need be, reject eyewitness accounts obtained from surviving SOE leaders, agents, and members of the Resistance. In Paris I was given access to all official sources. Government departments in the Netherlands, Denmark, Norway, and Germany were equally helpful.

At the risk of involving some of my friends in Great Britain in officious inquiries—which they assured me, they would not mind—I was able to add to my narrative quite a few of their own copies of signals exchanged with SOE headquarters, and reports and instructions never published before. I can and do claim that all material in *Set Europe Ablaze* is fully authentic.

Sometimes I was able to write from my own experience, particularly of Gestapo treatment, having been a prisoner at Dachau and Buchenwald. For everything recounted I accept full responsibility, and all opinions and comments, except where specifically quoted, are entirely my own.

Expressing thanks individually to all my SOE friends for their help would involve repeating many of the names listed in the Index of this book. They know of my gratitude. But I want to single out just a few who have given me much of their time and provided invaluable information and advice: Colonel Maurice J. Buckmaster, Vera Atkins, Professor H. A. Rée, Lieutenant-Colonel Francis Cammaerts, Major Roger Landes, and Captains Francis Basin, Denis Rake, and Cyril Watney.

For their assistance in obtaining French material, I am particularly indebted to Professor Henri Michel, secretary general of the Comité d'histoire de la Deuxième Guerre Mondiale (Office of the Prime Minister of the French Republic) and Monsieur Constantin Melnik, formarly Councellor for Intelligence and Security to the French Prime Minister; and in the Netherlands, Dr. Louis de Jong, Director of the State Institute for War Documentation, who generously made important material available. To the many government officials, archivists, and intelligence officers in several foreign countries upon whose time and kindness I have greatly imposed I desire to express my sincere gratitude.

I wish to thank also Captain Peter Churchill, D.S.O., Dr. Jorge Haestrup, Colonel H. Montgomery-Hyde, Major Peter Kemp, James Leasor, Bruce Marshall, Dr. H. C. P. Meyjes, R. J. Minney, and Dame Irene Ward, M.P. and to remember the late Lord Dalton, the late Lord Ismay, the late Professor Sverre Kjeldstadli, and the late Commander F. N. Stagg, RN for their kind permission to quote from their books, or for the use of unpublished material they gave me.

I want to pay special tribute to Morland Lee, who gave me unstinted help in research, particularly in the earlier stages, to the translators of Dutch, Danish, and Norwegian documents, and to my secretary. Last but not least, I want to mention my wife Fina, who for years had to endure my concern with the story of SOE, and without whose tender support I would have succumbed to the often felt desire for a silence as deep as that of a good secret agent.

E.H.C.

Contents

Illustrations

SS Sturmbann-Führer Joseph Schreieder
Lt. Col. Hermann J. Giskes
Professor George Louis Jambroes
Theological College at Haaren, North Brabant
Lofoten raid, March 1941
Lorens Duus Hansen
Major Flemming Muus

Maps

Set Europe Ablaze

One spy in the right place
is worth
twenty thousand men on the battlefield.

NAPOLEON BONAPARTE

Sweet is war for those who know it not.

ERASMUS OF ROTTERDAM

I

No War for Gentlemen

THE ORGANIZATION called Special Operations Executive was born on 19 July 1940. On that day Winston Churchill drafted a brief memorandum for his War Cabinet. A few strokes of his pen, and a body was created "to coordinate all action by way of subversion and sabotage against the enemy overseas." Or, as the Prime Minister later put it, "to set Europe ablaze."

On that very day, Hitler addressed the German Reichstag in Berlin. The hour of Britain's total defeat was at hand, he said, and Churchill would shortly take refuge in Canada. France, Belgium, Holland, Denmark, and Norway had fallen. The conquest had been easy. On the following day, through diplomatic channels in Sweden, the United States, and the Vatican, the führer of the Third Reich that was to last a thousand years offered to end hostilities. Hitler said he was making this offer "as a victor, speaking in the name of reason."

On 22 July the British War Cabinet decided to dismiss Hitler's gesture. That evening the foreign secretary, Lord Halifax, in a broadcast to the nation "brushed aside Hitler's summons to capitulate to his will." In doing so, he compared Europe, subjugated by the Nazis, with the Europe for which Britain was fighting. "We shall not stop fighting until freedom is secure," he concluded.

It was at the War Cabinet meeting the same morning that the Prime Minister's memorandum was approved and the Special Operations Executive officially established under the responsibility of the minister of economic warfare, Dr. Hugh Dalton.

Throughout his life Winston Churchill was interested in the problems of irregular warfare. It had been his idea, when first lord of the Admiralty in the Chamberlain cabinet, to raise the Striking Companies who later accomplished daring exploits during the campaign in Norway. In the summer of 1940, when Britain "stood alone and at bay," he knew that the only hope for offensive action against the enemy was by air bombardment, by raiding the coasts of the occupied countries, and by sabotage and subversion inside Europe. The handful of aircraft Britain had, insufficient even for the defense of the island, precluded the pursuit of the first objective on a large scale for a long time. So the idea of sending small raiding forces to the coasts of Europe and parachuting secret agents behind the enemy lines to work as saboteurs and to help create guerilla units appears to have been in his mind quite early in the war.

At the end of May 1940, a fortnight after the German attack on the Low Countries and when the situation in France had become desperate, Churchill had a memorable meeting with the chiefs of staff. He put to them a blunt question: What was, in their opinion, the prospect of Britain being able to continue the war alone? On 27 May the chiefs of staff submitted to the Prime Minister a joint memorandum. It contained thirteen paragraphs, and dealt particularly with the problems of superiority in the air and with the possibilities of putting pressure upon Hitler's war potential. The memorandum continued:

The only other method of bringing about the downfall of Germany is by stimulating the seeds of revolt within the conquered territories. The occupied countries are likely to prove a fruitful ground for these operations, particularly when economic conditions begin to deteriorate. In the circumstances we regard this form of activity as of the very highest importance.[1]

At a later meeting it was agreed that a special organization would be required to put sabotage operations and subversive activities into effect, and it was decided to form such a unit and to begin training special agents as quickly as possible.

Even before the war the British Secret Service and Military Intelligence had sections concerned with planning sabotage and subversive activities. But Churchill must have had serious doubts about their efficacy.

On 4 June he wrote in a memorandum to General Hastings Lionel Ismay: "The completely defensive habit of mind which has ruined France must not be allowed to ruin all our initiative . . . . How wonderful it would be if the Germans could be made to wonder where they were going to be struck next, instead of forcing us to try to wall in the Island and roof it over!"

And on 6 June he sent a minute to Ismay urgently asking: "What arrangements are being made for good agents in Denmark, Holland, Belgium and along the French coast?" demanding from the chiefs of staff proposals for "a proper system of espionage and intelligence along the whole coasts." He wanted to see "enterprises prepared with specially trained men . . . who can develop a reign of terror," so that "the lives of the German troops in occupied Europe be made an intense torment." [2]

[1] *History of the Second World War, Grand Strategy,* Vol. 2, Ed. J. R. M. Butler, H.M.S.O., 1957.
[2] Churchill, W. S., *The Second World War,* Vol. 2, Cassell, London, 1949.

In spite of the importance attached by the chiefs of staff in their report in May to subversive action in enemy-occupied Europe, it seems that no initiative was taken by them during the succeeding few weeks. On 1 July a meeting took place with Lord Halifax in the chair and several ministers present at which plans were drafted for a new organization, Special Operations Executive, to coordinate all subversive and sabotage actions against the enemy.

When SOE was to be established, a wrangle immediately ensued as to which government department it should be subordinated. The War Office demanded to assume control, and so did the Foreign Office. The chiefs of staff lodged their claim, while the head of SIS (Secret Intelligence Service), Colonel (later Major General Sir Stewart) Menzies, could naturally expect that the new organization would, in one or another form, be subordinated to him. Within his department were sections—(to which I shall conveniently refer as the D department)—that were already engaged in tasks to be assigned to SOE.

The chiefs of staff suggested to the Prime Minister that SOE should be controlled by a committee on which representatives of the service departments, the SIS, the Foreign Office, the Ministry of Information, and the Ministry of Economic Warfare should sit. Such a committee would have had complete preponderance of the three services and the secret service.

The matter came before the Cabinet. Dr. Hugh Dalton, the head of MEW (Ministry of Economic Warfare), suggested that Clement Attlee, the Lord Privy Seal and deputy Prime Minister, who had no departmental duties, should take charge, while he—Dr. Dalton—would become Attlee's chief of staff, SOE being administratively part of his Ministry of Economic Warfare.

When Lord Halifax put the claim for the Foreign Office, Lord Lloyd, the colonial secretary, told him: "You should never be consulted, because you would never consent to anything. You will never make a gangster!" [3] When a Cabinet member observer that the War Office had the strongest claim, or that alternatively SOE should be put under Colonel Menzies, Dr. Dalton strongly objected and stressed that "the War Office had more than enough on their plate already," and that "branches of MI were proliferating everywhere." He and the Labour party ministers insisted that what they had in mind was not primarily a military job at all. "Sabotage and subversion in Europe," they said, "would concern trade unionists and Socialists in enemy and enemy-occupied territories, the creation of Fifth Columns, of explosions, chaos and revolution." [4]

Dalton put his ideas before Churchill in great detail and he wrote to Lord

[3] Dalton, H., *The Fateful Years,* Muller, London, 1957, p. 367.
[4] Dalton, *ibid.,* p. 368.

Halifax, knowing the foreign secretary's great influence upon the Conservative ministers:

We must organize movements in enemy-occupied territory comparable to the Sinn Fein in Ireland, to the Chinese guerillas now operating against Japan, to Spanish Irregulars . . . in Wellington's campaign, or, one might as well admit it, to the organizations the Nazis themselves have developed in almost every country in the world. We must use many different methods, including industrial and military sabotage, labour agitation and strikes, continuous propaganda, terrorists acts against traitors and German leaders, boycotts and riots.[5]

The Ministry of Economic Warfare was much better equipped for such work than its name implied. Churchill himself called it the "Ministry of Ungentlemanly Warfare." A revival of the Ministry of Blockade of the First World War, MEW was organized on a very much broader basis, had already an important intelligence department of its own, and was engaged in propaganda and subversive activities. Some of its activities, such as the plan in the late autumn of 1939 to sabotage by the use of explosives the Swedish port of Oxelsund in order to prevent shipments of iron ore to Germany, were known to only a handful of people including, of course, Churchill and his close friend Major (now Sir Desmond) Morton, former head of the Industrial Intelligence Centre, who had become one of the directors of the Ministry of Economic Warfare.

Following the 1 July meeting at which plans for SOE were drafted, Churchill gave Dalton control of the new organization. Dalton kept this post until February 1942, when he became president of the Board of Trade. He was succeeded at SOE by Lord Wolmer (later Lord Selborne).

Churchill never fully disclosed why he did not entrust direct control over SOE to the eagerly outstretched hands of the top brass. But in many of his minutes and memoranda to his closest assistant, General Ismay, one can find illuminating pointers to the reasons for his decision. In the summer of 1940 the Prime Minister wrote:

I am not satisfied with the volume or quality of information received . . . . We seem to be as much cut off from these territories as from Germany . . . . Further, I await proposals for improving and extending our information about France and for keeping a continued flow of agents moving to and fro . . . . So far as the Vichy Government is concerned, it is not creditable that we have so little information. To what extent are American, Swiss and Spanish agents being used? [6]

General Ismay on his part briefly assessed the situation thus: "The War Office struck me as hidebound, unimaginative and overpopulated" [7]

[5] Dalton, *ibid.,* p. 368.
[6] Churchill, *op. cit.*
[7] Lord Ismay, *Memoirs,* Heinemann, London, 1958.

In any case, Churchill was not prepared to leave a matter so dear to his heart entirely to other people. He must have decided from the very beginning of SOE to keep a fatherly eye on his brainchild and he watched its progress closely. On the day following the Cabinet approval for the establishment of SOE he sent a minute to Anthony Eden (now Lord Avon), the war secretary:

It is of course urgent and indispensable that every effort should be made to obtain secretly the best possible information about the German forces in the various countries overrun, and to establish intimate contacts with local people, and to plant agents. This, I hope, will be done on the largest scale, as opportunity services, by the new organization under the Ministry of Economic Warfare.[8]

Thus the Prime Minister assigned to SOE a role that went beyond the initially intended task of spreading subversion and carrying out sabotage in enemy-occupied territories. That SOE agents were supposed to obtain information and convey it to the Cabinet, thus acting in competition with SIS and Military Intelligence, was resented by the chiefs of the departments so recently and sharply reproved and finally bypassed. Professor J. R. M. Butler, the chief historian of the Official War Histories, sums it up neatly thus: "In its early months SOE suffered from the suspicions of an upstart felt by older organizations and embittered by personal animosities." [9]

The tasks of SOE were only vaguely defined by its creators and had to be discovered only as the organization developed. Churchill's minute to Eden —and many subsequent orders by the chiefs of staff and later by SHAEF (Supreme Headquarters, Allied Expeditionary Force)—show, however, that SOE agents in the field were expected to provide intelligence information and play a part in the complex political intrigues and ideological discords which rent some of Europe's Resistance movements. The aim of SOE to create or assist nationwide Resistance organizations in the Nazi-subjugated countries was often frustrated by problems of political allegiance. Resistance groups were torn by political conflicts and by jealousies among their leaders, as for instance in Greece and Yugoslavia between monarchists and Communists, and in France among Gaullists, right-wing officers, and Communist *francs-tireurs*.

Even the primary tasks of SOE were, as General Sir Colin Gubbins later stated,[10] often fundamentally incompatible: To divert attention from the creation of secret armies meant avoiding any activities that would attract German attention; to act offensively by carrying out sabotage entailed at-

[8] Churchill, *op. cit.*
[9] Butler, *op. cit.*
[10] *Cf.* Lecture at the Royal United Services Association in London on 28 January 1948.

tracting the special attention and efforts of the Gestapo and SS and the redoubling of vigilance on their part.

Also, the various departments, whose chiefs believed that they should have participated in managing SOE, disagreed on its objectives. Field Marshal Lord Wilson of Libya, under whose supreme command SOE Mediterranean headquarters functioned from 1943 onward, said:

> In the early days there were a lot of heated bearings because so many people were implicated in what was called 'putting it across.' The Air Force was interested because aircraft were taken off other jobs to do the work, although there were never enough to go round; the Special Operations Executive had its own Directorates which wanted special things; the Foreign Office also had its own ideas, which were often contrary to the ideas of the Special Operations Executive; and the Commanders-in-Chief had their strategy to carry out. So there were times when there were many heated bearings upon which oil had to be poured.[11]

Oil was in short supply and the bearings often became overheated. The War Office of course had to play a vital role in the inauguration because SOE personnel had to be recruited mainly through the Army. But the whole conception of a clandestine organization, controlled by a Socialist minister and infiltrated by Churchill with businessmen, university dons, and journalists, was anathema to the generals and brigadiers. Their antagonism found expression in a tendency to administer petty pinpricks to the handful of men bent on putting the new organization on its feet. This was not particularly surprising; the War Office had been compelled to dissolve one of its own intelligence departments, the MI(R), and give it to SOE.

The British Secret Service

At the beginning of the war there existed several departments within whose orbits the tasks envisaged for SOE could have fallen. One was MI(R)— Research—at the War Office, headed by Colonel John Holland, an engineer, who served in Ireland during the Troubles and was keenly interested in irregular warfare. One of his chief assistants was Lieutenant Colonel Colin Gubbins, the future head of SOE. Another department was the Industrial Intelligence Centre created by Major Morton in 1931 as a private enterprise, becoming in 1935 a department conducting studies on behalf of the Imperial Defence Committee on industrial resources and mobilization in certain foreign countries. Early in 1939 the Foreign Office had organized a section concerned with propaganda in potential enemy countries.

Above all, there was that legendary body—SIS—vaguely referred to in newspapers and books as "the British Secret Service," whose history goes

[11] Presiding at the Gubbins lecture at the RUSA on 28 January 1948.

[6]

back to the beginning of the century or, indeed, to Cardinal Wolsey, Walsingham, and Thurloe. It had, in times past, employed such personalities as Rudyard Kipling, Baden-Powell, Somerset Maugham, and Compton Mackenzie. Its chief for many years had been Vice Admiral Sir Hugh Sinclair, always referred to by the initiated as "C." After his death, in October 1939, he was succeeded by his deputy, Colonel Menzies.

Within the complex structure of SIS was the D department, consisting of two sections; the department was headed by Colonel Menzies' deputy, Lieutenant Colonel (later Major General) Laurence Douglas Grand. One of D department's sections had been concerned with the study of methods of industrial sabotage, irregular warfare, and the training of a small number of potential saboteurs. Another concentrated on political and economic subversive propaganda against the enemy in wartime. First the War Office's, MI(R) and then the two D sections were put under the new Special Operations Executive; the propaganda section becoming SO1, the sabotage section SO2. Later, SO1 became the Political Warfare Executive, detached from the parent organization. The SIS continued, however, to gather political, economic, and military information overseas, although the number of its agents in Nazi-subjugated Europe had greatly diminished. The activities of SIS agents were often necessarily involved with the newly formed Resistance movements, and thus SIS and SOE duplicated and overlapped on occasion.

To some degree SIS exercised influence over certain SOE activities, having its own national sections that maintained liaison with the secret service organizations of the various Allied exile governments in London. The French section of SIS was by far more prominent and influential than the French section of SOE in dealing with General de Gaulle's BCRA.[12] This was mainly because the two chiefs of this section, Commander Kenneth Cohen (Duncan) and Colonel Sir Claude Dansey, were able to establish cordial personal relations with the head of de Gaulle's secret service, Colonel Passy (André Dewavrin), and his assistants.

When SOE began operations, however, SIS was able to provide little or no help. After the war Major General Sir Colin Gubbins described SOE tasks thus:

> The problem and the plan was to encourage and enable the peoples of the occupied countries to harass the German war effort at every possible point by sabotage, subversion, go-slow practices, *coup de main* raids, etc., and at the same time to build up secret forces therein, organized, armed and trained to take their part only when the final assault began . . . . In its simplest terms, this plan involved the ultimate delivery to occupied territory of large numbers of personnel and quantities of arms and explosives. But the first problem was to make contact with those countries, to get information of the possibilities, to

[12] BCRA—Bureau Central de Renseignements et d'Action (of the French Committee of National Liberation in London).

find out the prospects of getting local help, and an even more immediate task was to find someone suitable and willing to undertake the first hazardous trip, then to train him and fit him for the job and ensure communications with him when he had landed. But all contacts with occupied territories closed when the last British forces returned to Great Britain in 1940, so the first man to go back to any country had to be parachuted "blind" as we say, i.e. there was no one waiting to receive him on the dropping ground, no household ready to give him shelter, conceal his kit, and arrange his onward passage . . . .[13]

This statement by the former head of SOE, while bearing out Churchill's lament that the Secret Intelligence Service was cut off from its sources of information, correctly assessed the situation in 1940. SIS had very few agents left on the Continent.

The Venlo Incident

One reason for the breakdown of the Secret Intelligence Service in Nazi-occupied Western Europe was the disaster that had overtaken one of its main outposts situated in Holland in 1939.

The Continental center of operations of SIS, set up before the war by Admiral Sinclair, was at 15 Nieuwe Uitweg in The Hague, next door to the house where Mata Hari lived in 1915. Chief of this European office was Major H. R. Stevens, with Captain S. Payne Best as his deputy.

In the late summer of 1939 these two officers were lured to a series of meetings with Germans who posed as anti-Nazis, offering to supply secret military and political information. During the course of these meetings at the Central Hotel in Amsterdam, the two British officers were introduced by a certain Dr. Franz Fischer, who pretended to be a refugee from Nazi Germany, to a "Captain Solm of the Luftwaffe." This man produced plausible credentials that he was acting on behalf of a group of anti-Hitler generals, including General Gerd von Rundstedt, General von Fritsch (whom Hitler had dismissed from his post as chief of the general staff), and General von Wietersheim.

In fact Captain Solm was Captain Johannes Travaglio of the German Abwehr counterespionage department. He acted in concert with Himmler's *Reichssicherheitshauptamt* (RSHA) and on orders of Dr. Helmuth Knochen (who later became Gestapo chief in Paris and after the war was sentenced to death by the French, but reprieved). Solm told Major Stevens and Captain Payne Best that General von Wietersheim would be prepared to meet them at the Hotel Wilhelmina at Venlo, on the German–Dutch frontier. The general would give them top-secret information about mobilization plans of the high command of the Wehrmacht and about the armament industry in the Ruhr.

[13] In the lecture at the Royal United Services Association, 28 January, 1948.

After several more meetings at the Parkzicht Hotel in Amsterdam, it was agreed that the meeting between the two British intelligence officers and General von Wietersheim and other German officers should take place at Venlo in September. The negotiations continued after the outbreak of the war on 3 September 1939. The British officers naturally reported to their superiors in London and were instructed—in order to avoid any embarrassment to the authorities of neutral Holland—to inform in strict confidence the chief of the Dutch secret service of their movements. This was done, and the head of the Dutch Military Intelligence, Major General J. W. van Oorschot, somewhat unwillingly gave his consent to the Anglo–German parleys taking place on Dutch soil. He made a condition that the two British officers should be accompanied by a Dutch intelligence officer, Lieutenant Daniel Klop.

The meeting with the general was arranged for 19 October at Dinxperlo. But when Major Stevens, Captain Payne Best, and Lieutenant Klop arrived there, they were confronted by Captain Solm and two Germans who introduced themselves as "Colonel von Salisch" and "Major Christensen" and explained that General von Wietersheim had been unable to come. A new rendezvous was agreed upon for 30 October at The Hague. On this occasion two more Germans arrived, but not the general. One of the Germans was introduced to the British officers as "Dr. Schemmel," and both were described as high officials of German intelligence. This was quite true, with the difference that Dr. Schemmel was certainly no anti-Nazi. In fact he was SS Group Leader Walter Schellenberg of the *Reichssicherheitshauptamt,* a trusted henchman of Himmler, who four years later was to become the chief of all German secret services. The other was introduced as "Colonel Martin" of the German general staff and a spokesman for the anti-Hitler generals. They told the British officers that plans were ready for the arrest of Hitler and the overthrow of the Nazi regime by the German army. Following the *coup d'état,* the German generals would immediately ask the British and French governments to open peace negotiations. The war was then six weeks old.

Having reported to London, Major Stevens and Captain Payne Best were ordered to go to the momentous meeting at which, at last, the German generals were to be present. This was arranged for 7 November at Venlo.

The Germans, led by Dr. Schemmel, met the British officers and Lieutenant Klop at the Café Backus on the following day. Dr. Schemmel told them that General von Wietersheim and "some even more important German generals" would arrive on the frontier at 4 P.M. on 9 November. They met on that afternoon again at the Café Backus, which was only a few yards from the German frontier post. They drove to the frontier and stood there in a group waiting. Dr. Schemmel explained that he would give a wave with his arms, which was the signal for the generals to come over. When he gave the sign a large black van came across the frontier, several armed men jumped out, surrounded the group, and forced Major Stevens and Captain Payne Best at gun point to enter the van. Lieutenant Klop ran away and fired several shots from his revolver, perhaps in the hope of alerting Dutch frontier guards. Several Germans opened fire and Klop was severely wounded. He, too, was bundled into the van, which sped into Germany.

The kidnapped British officers and the Dutch lieutenant were taken to Düsseldorf, where Klop died from his injuries in a military prison hospital. The two British officers spent the war years in German prisons and concentration camps, much of the time in solitary confinement.

This kidnapping of the two chiefs of the Secret Intelligence Service in Europe was aggravated by another event. After the invasion of Holland, one of their agents left a suitcase behind when he escaped from The Hague in May 1940. In the suitcase were secret files on all his contact addresses.[14]

After the war Lieutenant Colonel Hermann Giskes, the chief of section III-F of the Abwehr in Holland, revealed, following his release from Allied captivity, that the Germans had been continuously watching the British Secret Service officers at Scheveningen and The Hague since 1935. He wrote:

I have myself seen a film produced by the German counter-espionage before the war, in which the entire staff, associates, and visitors of the British espionage organization operating against Germany appeared. A couple of cold-blooded sportsmen had taken this film, quite undisturbed, through a porthole of a large canal barge, which from time to time spent days or even weeks secured alongside a jetty not thirty yards from the street in which the British Secret Service headquarters stood. Unfortunately it was only a silent film, but the captions recorded with complete accuracy the names, cover-names, assigned duties, activities and contacts of every single one of the involuntary film stars. It scarcely needs saying that the British agents in Germany who operated from this headquarters received a warm reception . . . .[15]

In France, where German agents succeeded in infiltrating government and police authorities, the Secret Intelligence Service fared little better, indeed in many respects even worse. The Venlo affair and other previous incidents, compelled SIS to withdraw hurriedly from France, the Low Countries, and Germany almost all British agents who had become identified by the German counterespionage or were in dire danger of discovery. The fact was that none of the British Secret Service departments was really prepared for the situation created by the German conquest of Western Europe. Before the war and until the fall of France, Military Intelligence cooperated to some

[14] De Jong, Dr. Louis, director of the Netherlands State Institute for War Documentation, *Britain and Dutch Resistance,* No. 109, p. 7, Amsterdam, 1961.
[15] Giskes, H., *Abwehr III-F* (German counterespionage in Holland), De Bezige Bij, Amsterdam, 1949.

degree with the French *Deuxième Bureau*. This link was broken by the Pétain armistice, when the *Bureau* temporarily disappeared. Contact with some French intelligence officers who had remained loyal to the Allied cause while serving under Pétain in Vichy was only slowly restored. As a result, the military services and the Foreign Office began to lean heavily upon SOE for information, although they had watched its creation with skepticism.

As soon as the first SOE agents were landed in Europe every possible pressure was exercised upon SOE chiefs to provide military and political information. But this was not at all in the line of duty of the brave men and women who had volunteered to go across the Channel "to set Europe ablaze." They were not professionally trained spies, nor should they have been exposed to even graver risks than their perilous assignments ordinarily involved.

Owing to these demands for military and political intelligence reports, SOE officers, often unaware of what they were supposed to supply, were compelled to overstep the limits of their own security. In day-to-day work as leaders and instructors of sabotage groups, as liaison officers to Resistance movements, as commanders of networks organizing secret militant units, as distributors of arms received by air from Britain, as wireless operators and couriers, the SOE officers in the field were already exposed to danger and treachery, particularly when the Germans had succeeded in infiltrating many Resistance groups.

The additional strain of collecting the communicating intelligence reports was enormous. Surely, to be asked to discover the progress of German research in V-rockets, the pace of German armament production, the location of German warships in western ports, were tall orders indeed. Yet, just such inquiries were insistently and regularly put to the SOE men on behalf of the War Office and other service departments, although these matters were strictly the business of Military, Naval, or Air Intelligence. Involved in such assignments, SOE officers became exceedingly vulnerable. This often caused capture and tragic loss of life.

This situation prevailed for a long time, even after SOE came under the control of SHAEF and almost fused with the American OSS at the end of 1943. Colonel Sir Geoffrey Vickers, who served with SOE, sat on the Joint Intelligence Committee [16] as its representative, and was deputy director-general of the Ministry of Economic Warfare from 1942 to 1944, stated after the war:

The Enemy Branch of the Ministry of Economic Warfare was engaged from 1942 to 1944 almost exclusively on Intelligence work which the Services needed

[16] Members of the Joint Intelligence Committee were V. F. W. Cavendish-Bentinck, of the Foreign Office, Vice Admiral J. H. Godfrey, director of Naval Intelligence, Major General F. H. N. Davidson, director of Military Intelligence, Air Vice Marshal C. E. H. Midhurst, director of Air Intelligence, and Colonel G. S. Vickers, VC.

for strategical and operational planning, but which their own Intelligence Directorates were not organized to supply. We had to do the work almost entirely with civilian personnel. It is highly abnormal that the Services should go outside their own Intelligence Directorates for information and advice needed to plan operations.[17]

Political Warfare

In addition to its rivalry with SIS and the military, SOE had to contend with the Political Warfare Executive. PWE's origin went back to one of the mysterious bodies founded by the omniscient and omnipresent Sir Campbell Stuart, director of *The Times,* who played an important role in British intelligence and organized British propaganda against Germany during the First World War. An expert in telecommunications, press, and propaganda, he became an adviser to successive Conservative governments, and, as chairman of the Imperial Communications Advisory Council, created a private study group that met at Electra House on London's Embankment. With his friends Sir Robert Bruce Lockhart, the famous British agent in Russia during the Bolshevik Revolution, and Rex (later Sir Reginald) Leeper, then a counselor at the Foreign Office, and with a thirty-three-year-old Royal Marines officer, Major (now General Sir Dallas) Brooks, Sir Campbell Stuart conducted an exhaustive study of the art and science of radio propaganda, of which untried medium Dr. Goebbels was proving himself an undisputed master.

The EH group, as it was called after its meeting place, devised plans for countering Nazi propaganda and for preparing a British organization that, in an armed conflict with Hitler, could embark upon political warfare.

In 1939 Sir Campbell became director of propaganda in enemy countries at the Ministry of Information; Bruce Lockhart was head of the propaganda department at the Foreign Office, while Colonel Menzies had in SO1 his own propaganda and subversion section within the Secret Intelligence Service. When SO1 was transferred to MEW, Dr. Dalton appointed several EH members to his SO1 section. Leeper became its director (and continued with Political Warfare Executive), operating from the Duke of Bedford's Woburn Abbey. Brigadier Dallas Brooks became its liaison officer to the chiefs of staff.

The staff recruited by Dr. Dalton for SO1-PWE was, as he put it, "A mixed lot, with much talent and much temperament; their Whitehall name was 'Leeper's sleepers,' but this was undeserved. Most of them were continually active, and some were sleepless prima donnas. I often found the atmosphere (at Woburn) highly charged with personal rivalries, and with apprehensive jealousy, often fully reciprocated, of other departments." [18]

[17] Medlicott, W. N., *The Economic Blockade,* Vol. 2, Appendix IV, p. 675 ff.
[18] Dalton, *op. cit.,* p. 378.

The Political Warfare Executive grew into a powerful weapon, under-mining German morale and stiffening the spirit of Resistance throughout Europe. Its tactics ranged from producing enormous quantities of leaflets dropped by RAF into enemy-occupied territories and Germany itself, to operating "black" radio stations, purporting to broadcast inside Europe and Germany. The fake *Soldaten Sender* (soldiers' radios of the German army) were Richard Crossman's particular pigeons; Patrick Gordon Walker directed the German workers programs to undermine morale in German factories. Italian anti-Fascists were employed for similar radio propaganda, which was broadcast in almost every language and round the clock. PWE also cooperated with BBC's foreign programs, prepared by the various free governments and national committees in exile in London. The Germans were completely foxed by these radio stations; at one time they carried out house-to-house searches in Bucharest to locate a Rumanian Freedom Station, which in fact emanated from Woburn Abbey.

Ideally, the Political Warfare Executive should have worked in close harmony with SOE, the SIS, the service departments, the Foreign Office, and the Ministry of Information. In fact, there was much overlapping and rivalry. Cooperation improved after a great struggle, when Dalton had to yield and PWE was transferred from his control to that of Anthony Eden at the Foreign Office. Dalton himself admitted that his relations with Duff Cooper (who was minister of information until July 1941) "were sometimes rough, with his successor Brendan Bracken they were often stormy." [19] Hugh Gaitskell, who had become Dalton's principal private secretary was sometimes called upon to conciliate between the officials.

Sometimes the arguments were over almost farcical happenings. Once Brendan Bracken found out that the PWE had bought a newspaper in a neutral country in order to disseminate anti-German and pro-British news and comment. This, he said, was an admirable thing to do, the only trouble was that he had already bought the same newspaper through a middleman for the Ministry of Information. On another occasion SOE headquarters in Cairo, at that time headed by Lord Glenconner, devised a scheme by which SOE officers could induce Italian prisoners of war in Egypt to write letters home, saying how well they were treated in captivity and urging their rela-tives and friends in Italy to behave in the same way toward Allied prisoners and escapees. As soon as PWE chiefs heard of it, they lodged strong protests at highest level. This, they said, was political propaganda and therefore their business. Cabinet ministers were alerted, and conferences took place with Sir Alexander Cadogan of the Foreign Office, the chiefs of staff, and the heads of the two warring organizations. In the end, as no agreement could be reached, the whole scheme was abandoned. Nevertheless, SOE continued to

[19] Dalton, *op. cit. Cf.* Lockhart, Sir Robert Bruce, *Comes the Reckoning,* Putnam, London, 1947.

compose "sibs," anti-German stories and slogans, which were disseminated by its agents, particularly in France.

SOE and the Resistance

Another and much more serious malady that bedeviled the work of SOE was the strained relations between the British and the exiled governments and national committees in London. Quite apart from problems of high policy, the British held very different views of the role and tasks of the Resistance movements in Europe from those held by the national leaders in exile.

Even the Norwegians, Britain's most loyal friends, found that the British were acting too independently and arbitrarily in Norway. The exiled Norwegian government bitterly complained that raids on the coast of Norway provoked German reprisals against the civilian population and made it difficult for the Norwegian Resistance movement to work. The British insisted that *Milorg,* the secret patriotic organization inside Norway, accept orders from the SIS, which by the end of 1941 led to a bitter controversy and made it difficult to continue the cooperation between *Milorg* and SOE. After many months of strain and frustration, Colonel John Wilson, head of SOE Norwegian section, established happy relations with the Norwegian exile government.

The exiled Dutch government had set up its own secret service in London but was told that all Dutch agents must be vetted, trained, and directed by the British authorities. When subsequently almost every one of these agents —all of them Dutch subjects—was caught by the Germans, who had succeeded in infiltrating SOE radio posts in Holland, the Dutch blamed the British for the disaster; some of the Dutch secret service chiefs in London even accused officers of the SOE Dutch section of treachery.

The British, and later to a much greater degree the Americans, refused to regard the Resistance in Europe as a simple revolt against the Nazi occupation. They saw it—as history proved, quite rightly— in terms of political movements. Leaders of the Resistance, where it was divided by differing shades of political opinion, aimed at asserting their positions with an eye on the future. Whoever controlled the underground movements would evidently be in the strongest position to control the nation when liberation came.

This applied especially to France. Churchill made it clear, early in the war, that "de Gaulle and his handful of followers could not claim to be an effective alternative French Goverment," [20] and he continued relations with the Vichy government. It was only much later, when in May 1943 the French Resistance groups formed the National Committee under the presidency of Georges Bidault, and this body recognized General de Gaulle as

[20] Churchill, *op. cit.,* Vol. 2, p. 405.

the leader and trustee of the French nation, that the British attitude changed somewhat. But President Roosevelt never accepted de Gaulle as the inevitable leader of France.

At times the strained personal relations between General de Gaulle and the British war leaders precluded any fruitful collaboration between his secret service organization in London and SOE. Churchill said in his memoirs that

de Gaulle felt it to be essential to his position before the French people that he should maintain a proud and haughty demeanour towards 'perfidious Albion,' although an exile, dependent upon our protection and dwelling in our midst. He had to be rude to the British to prove to French eyes that he was not a British puppet. He certainly carried out this policy with perseverance.[21]

On the other hand, in de Gaulle's view, the British did not fail in attempts at making his secret agents their puppets and at gaining control of at least some of the Resistance groups.

General de Gaulle felt the British were trying to wreck or minimize the efforts of his own secret service, the BCRA, whose agents had to be approved by the British authorities, whose radio signals were controlled by the British, and whose information was frequently disregarded by the British. De Gaulle accused the British government and, without justification, the SOE and British intelligence chiefs, of trying by such measures to weaken the French Resistance.

On at least two occasions the general broke off all relations with British departments and forbade his secret service officers to talk to their counterparts in SOE.

Matters improved after Churchill appointed Major Morton to the post of chairman of the Committee on Allied Resistance. He was a gifted and amiable man who could calm tempers and smooth over differences where lesser men would have given up in despair. Another happy appointment was that of Sir Claude Dansey as deputy director of SIS French section and chief British liaison officer to the Gaullist secret service in London.

It is not surprising that a man of such patriotic fervor and opinionated convictions as General de Gaulle was impatient for the liberation of his country and thirsty for action. Neither is it surprising that, seeing France beaten, humiliated by the terms of the armistice, and betrayed by many of his own countrymen, de Gaulle felt great pride that millions of Frenchmen had nevertheless rallied to challenge the invaders. What is surprising is that as a professional soldier and strategist he seemed to have overestimated the role that the Resistance was able to play before 1943 and underestimated the ruthless German reaction to its challenge.

De Gaulle's BCRA, under Colonel Passy, worked with Resistance leaders

21 Churchill, *op. cit.*

[15]

for two years, from 1941 to the spring of 1943, to amalgamate the many organizations and groups in France. In this, Colonel Passy was assisted by SOE's RF section. After the National Committee of the Resistance was formed, Jean Moulin, former prefect of Chartres, who had arrived in London September 1941 and had returned to France the following January, was appointed de Gaulle's personal representative. The various militant organizations, supplied with arms by SOE, were organized into the *Armée Secrète* under the command of General Charles Delestraint (known to the underground as General Vidal). The secret army was organized on a regional basis and under regional commanders, with whom SOE liaison officers and instructors cooperated on good terms in many parts of the country.

However, much of the success of this first nationwide Gaullist organization soon became illusory. The Germans were aware of its progress. The Gestapo had infiltrated V-men [22] into a number of the command staffs and was only waiting for the completion of the organization before striking. After the capture of Moulton and Hardy (chief of the sabotage section of the National Committee of the Resistance) in June 1943, mass arrests took place among the leaders of the Resistance and the *Armée Secrète*. Jean Moulin died under torture; General Delestraint was shot, the leadership decimated. A similar disaster overtook several SOE networks, including the large PROSPER circuit in Paris. The national organization was shattered and Resistance groups throughout the country suffered heavy losses.

At about the same time the Gestapo struck in Holland. The National Committee was rounded up and all its members, including several former cabinet ministers and the chairmen of the Conservative, Liberal, Roman Catholic, and Socialist parties, arrested.

In the widespread catastrophe, however, there were some encouraging facts. By tipping their hand in the summer of 1943, apparently expecting that Allied landings were imminent, the Germans revealed to London the fatal weakness of the highly centralized underground organizations in time to permit the establishment of a new system before D day.

A memorandum prepared by SOE chiefs for SHAEF [23] provided an assessment of the situation that subsequently proved to be correct. Although the underground organizations had suffered severe losses, and although many agents dispatched from London had been caught, the second line of the leadership and the hard core of local and regional groups had survived. Surprisingly, only a small percentage of supplies was lost. Elated by the capture of many prominent Resistance leaders, the Germans had failed to

[22] V-Mann (*Vertrauensmann*)—a trusted informer. In France the V-men were mainly recruited from among members of pro-Nazi and pro-Fascist organizations of Marcel Déat, Darnand, and Doriot.
[23] Present Value and Tempo of Resistance, SOE report to SHAEF, dated 9 October 1943.

find the hideouts and dumps of arms, ammunition, and explosives, which SOE had been delivering on an increasing scale. In many areas reception committees, reorganized and led by local leaders, continued to welcome new supplies and new SOE instructors, liaison officers, and radio operators from Britain.

Secret Armies

Despite grievous losses, Resistance groups evinced remarkable resilience and many thousands of new recruits joined the paramilitary organizations, such as the *Armée Secrète* in France, the *Orde Dienst* in Holland, and the *Milorg* in Norway. The reorganization did away with the formerly rigid centralized system. Though a nominal national unity through national committees was preserved, paramilitary training and equipment, sabotage actions, and radio communications were from then on controlled regionally. The Germans continued to make arrests, but damage to the underground movements was now much more localized.

The lesson had been learned at a high price. It might have been less costly if some of the national leaders of European Resistance, both in London and on the Continent, had paid greater attention to the advice given by SOE chiefs.

In August 1941 Dr. Hugh Dalton formulated the aims in terms that held good for SOE policy and its relations with the Resistance movements over the next two years:

The underground fighters should show sufficient active resistance to cause constant embarrassment to the occupying forces, and prevent any reduction in their numbers. But they should keep their main organizations underground and avoid any attempt at large-scale risings or ambitious paramilitary operations which could only result in severe oppression and the loss of our key men. They should do all they can to prepare a widespread underground organization ready to strike hard later, when we give the signal.

The British were anxious to restrain the Resistance leaders from actions that would lead to the destruction of their secret military organizations. Their role, according to SOE instructions, was rather to organize a common front and a disciplined force whose operations could be connected at a later stage directly with those of the Allied armies. SOE objects were thus to reconcile the political groups upon which the Resistance concentrated, and which were often hostile to each other, and to bring them effectively under the common authority—at first of a British command and later of SHAEF.[24]

These tenets were, however, not easily acceptable to the exile govern-

[24] Cf. *The History of the Second World War, Grand Strategy,* Vol. 5, H.M.S.O., London, 1956.

ments in London. They resented the British tutelage of the Resistance and suspected that the British pursued some hidden and ulterior political aims. This is not the place to examine the complex problems of high policy—for instance, Britain's and America's delicate relations with the Soviet Union, the Russian pressure for a second front, the understandable resentment of General de Gaulle and French leaders after the British attack (3 July 1940) on the French fleet in the harbor of Mers-el-Kebir, the British and American negotiations with Admiral Darlan and Pétainist authorities after the Allied landings in North Africa, or the attempts at replacing de Gaulle with General Giraud.

All these problems were, of course, far removed from any influence SOE chiefs could exercise, and they were hardly known or understood by SOE officers in the field. The political quarrels among the leaders of the Allied governments, however, caused repercussions on the day-to-day work of SOE. Problems of politics and diplomacy constantly interfered with matters that would have seemed to be quite straightforward, such as recruiting and training of agents, the supply of arms, the control of radio reception stations, and the exchange of information received from agents in the field.

Churchill's order in July 1940 had been brief and to the point: "Set Europe ablaze!" But before the new SOE organization could take its first toddling steps toward this target, Britain, threatened by invasion and standing alone in the defense of freedom, was herself set ablaze by the blitz of the German Luftwaffe.

Many months passed before even elementary preparations could be realized for recruiting and training of the men who were to execute this order. During 1941 SOE grew into maturity only slowly and laboriously, and the handful of men who had assembled at the cramped, blacked-out offices in Baker Street wondered if they would ever get a chance to kindle the torch.

2

"The Racket"

BAKER STREET, the home of Sherlock Holmes, seemed to exert a magnetic attraction to the men entrusted to organize the cloak-and-dagger activities of the war. Emerging from the D department, the new Special Operations Executive at first occupied a suite of rooms at the government-requisitioned St. Ermin's Hotel in Caxton Street, halfway between the Houses of Parliament and Victoria Station. In the autumn of 1940, when accommodations became too cramped, every service department in turn declined to provide better premises. They pointed out that SOE was under a civilian minister and that it was for the Ministry of Economic Warfare to supply required offices.

Hence it was through some of the businessmen associated with SOE that a new home was found, after many frustrating attempts, at 62-64 Baker Street. Soon afterward this building was left mainly to the French section and a few other departments, and the top brass moved to offices secured by courtesy of Messrs. Marks & Spencer. These were at 82 Baker Street, St. Michael House, a name adopted by that firm as a trademark for their underwear known to every housewife. In 1940 it was one of the world's most secret addresses. The building, which housed the SOE headquarters and directorates, was converted some years after the war, and Messrs. Marks & Spencer moved across the road to a new, functional edifice.

Later other departments of SOE were moved to Norgeby House, 83 Baker Street, a bleak, red-brick building, today populated by battalions of HM Inspectors of Taxes and eager Inland Revenue collectors. As it grew, SOE spread to many other requisitioned houses and apartments in the Baker Street area, in Marylebone Street, Berkeley Court, Bickenhall Mansions, Chiltern Court (where the Scandinavian sections, among others, were housed), Dorset Square, Portman Square, Oxford Square, Wimpole Street. This had the advantage of greater security, as centralization under a single roof would have attracted too much attention.

St. Michael House had a back entrance from a narrow lane of dilapidated mews, and the top brass entered and departed discreetly, as did other SOE officers, rarely wearing uniform, along with secretaries, code clerks, and typists. At the door of Norgeby House only a small black metal plaque with the inscription INTER-SERVICES RESEARCH BUREAU indicated its official use. The existence of SOE remained for a long time unknown even to high-ranking service personnel. Officers and clerks attached to the directorates and various sections were discouraged from referring to its official name in private conversation and were bound by the Official Secrets Act not to mention it to anybody outside. They referred to SOE among themselves as "The Org" or "The Old Firm" or "The Racket."

The service departments and their intelligence directorates observed a studied aloofness, although the War Office insisted on supervising the recruitment, and secret service departments on conducting security examinations of all SOE recruits. Interviews with candidates were held in a small room at the Ministry of Pensions at Sanctuary Buildings, Westminster; later two dark back rooms were allocated for this purpose at the War Office annex in Northumberland Avenue—the old Victoria Hotel—where several intelligence departments also were housed.

When the question of the appointment of the first chiefs of SOE arose, one of those consulted was the "grand old man" of the British Secret Service, Sir Claude Marjoribank Dansey, "Uncle Claude," as he was affectionately and respectfully called by his friends, superiors, and subordinates alike. Churchill greatly esteemed him; they had been friends for half a century. Dansey had fought in every campaign of the British Empire: as a young officer in Matabeleland in the 1890s; against Mahamed Salleh, chieftain of the headhunters of North Borneo; against the Zulus; and in the Boer War he was on Field Marshal Roberts' staff when young Winston Churchill gained his first spurs. He served in the intelligence during the 1914–18 war and retired in 1938, living as Lord of the Manor at Bathampton in Somerset and never dreaming of receiving another call to duty in 1940. He became deputy chief of SIS French section, and the troubleshooter of the Secret Intelligence Service in its dealings with General de Gaulle and BCRA. That even de Gaulle and his Colonel Passy could refer to Sir Claude as their "very dear friend" must be regarded as the highest testimonial to Dansey's wisdom and kindliness, as well as proof of his supreme skill in dealing with the Free French in London.

Dansey recommended Sir Frank Nelson, a former Indian army officer, secret intelligence man, and Conservative Member of Parliament, as head of SOE. It was at first intended that Nelson would share the responsibilities with Colonel Grand of the defunct D department. Grand, however, departed within days for unexplained reasons and returned to the War Office, leaving Nelson in sole command. But several officers who had arrived with Colonel Grand from D department stayed on. Among them were Colonel F. T.

Davies, who was given charge of training the would-be secret agents (a mere handful was recruited during the first few months); Major (later Colonel) George Taylor, an Australian, who had done important work for D in Yugoslavia and Rumania before these countries were overrun by the Nazis and was now entrusted with organizing the first country sections and planning operations; Captain (later Colonel) Bickham Sweet-Escott, in charge of the first Balkans and Middle East sections; Captain George Courtauld and Captain Leslie Sheridan. Last, but not least, Colonel Colin Gubbins was put in charge of the Eastern European sections, which were given priority at this early stage owing to the desire of the Poles of General Sikorski's army in Britain and the Czechs around Dr. Eduard Beneš to take revenge for the attacks on their countries. By late autumn Colonel Gubbins was appointed director of operations to supervise all country sections; soon he was the real moving spirit of "The Racket."

Sir Frank Nelson, although nearly sixty, was a prodigious worker who for weeks could spend sixteen hours a day at his desk. He accomplished the difficult and delicate task of establishing the initial administration of SOE headquarters. To look after finance, he called in a chartered accountant, Mr. John Venner, who gained the almost unique distinction of remaining in the same post during the entire existence of SOE. Major Taylor became chief of staff to Sir Frank, and Captain Sweet-Escott later gave up the Balkans section and became Taylor's personal assistant, looking after the Western European sections.

Another early arrival was Charles Hambro. Head of the merchant bankers firm and a notable figure of the City of London, he had been Churchill's intimate and his business and financial adviser for many years. His family was of Scandinavian origin and he had a wide circle of personal and business friends abroad. In 1928 he became, at the age of thirty, the youngest director of the Bank of England. Entrenched in Britain's Establishment, he was acceptable to the military chiefs: he had been at Eton, captaining the cricket eleven in 1915, served in the Coldstream Guards and won the MC. He advised Churchill during the 1940 Norwegian campaign, performed remarkable exploits in Sweden at the outset of the war, was at first given the task of establishing the Scandinavian sections of SOE, and soon became Sir Frank's deputy.

When in February 1942, after Dr. Dalton's departure to the Board of Trade, Lord Selborne became minister of economic warfare, one of his first actions was to ask Mr. (later Sir John) Hanbury-Williams, a director and later chairman of the Courtaulds textile firm, to investigate the organization of SOE. At that time SOE had suffered a series of setbacks and the secret report, which Mr. Hanbury-Williams and his assistant, Mr. (later Sir Edward) Playfair of the Treasury, submitted to Lord Selborne, must have been critical of SOE direction in 1941. The search for a scape-goat ended at the top. Sir Frank Nelson's not entirely voluntary resignation was accepted.

Great changes took place at Baker Street in May 1942. Sir Charles Hambro (knighted in 1941) became head of SOE, with Brigadier Colin Gubbins as his deputy. That spring there was a great shake-up in SOE directorates and many section chiefs were replaced. Sir Charles Hambro possessed great knowledge of the world, shrewd perception, and a genial but forceful personality. For more than a year he somehow managed to divide his energy and talents between the command of SOE and the chairmanship of the Great Western Railway, which involved extremely difficult problems of wartime transport.

Many able men contributed to the creation of SOE, but without Colonel (later Major General Sir Colin) Gubbins The Racket would not have survived its birth pangs. Gubbins, who had organized and commanded the Striking Companies that covered the retreat of the British Expeditionary Force in Norway in 1940, came to SOE from MI(R). In September 1943 he moved to the top, and how it came about I have directly from Dr. Dalton.

One evening in November 1939 Dr. Dalton, then the Labour opposition's front-bench spokesman for the Air Ministry and the new Ministry of Economic Warfare, attended a dinner given by Count Raczynski, the Polish ambassador in London. It was a sad occasion; only a few weeks earlier Poland had been crushed. At the dinner Dalton sat next to a British colonel whose name he did not catch at the introduction, but from whom he learned during the conversation that he had been with the British military mission and had narrowly escaped capture in Warsaw in September. Dalton did not easily warm to colonels, but he found this officer "most intelligent and extremely well informed." Colonel Gubbins told him that if the Polish army, instead of displaying romantic heroism, had retreated to the rivers Vistula and Bug, this line might have been held at least for some time. He also told Dalton that in August Britain had sent 120 Hurricanes to Poland; on the 28th they reached Denmark. There they were stopped because of a squabble with the British Treasury as to who should pay £4,000 toward the cost of transport. The aircraft never arrived in Poland and were sent back from Denmark. Had they arrived, history might have taken a different turn. Gubbins also knew a lot about irregular warfare and Dr. Dalton made a mental note to consult this "very intelligent colonel" if he ever wanted information on this subject.

When Brigadier Gubbins arrived at SOE headquarters he was forty-five years old, a wiry man of medium height, with dark hair and a clipped, military mustache. He looked one straight in the eye and spoke in short,

[22]

staccato sentences. A casual observer might have described him as a typical British colonel. His whole bearing was deceptively orthodox. This veneer of the professional soldier belied a man of high intelligence and culture, possessing the gift of leadership and a sense of humor. He needed these qualities in good measure when dealing with the motley collection of bankers, dons, lawyers, journalists, film directors, schoolmasters, playboys, adventurers, and "foreigners" from a dozen European countries who were to serve under him. Applying his boundless energy, Brigadier Gubbins gave SOE spirit and substance; and in his subordinates roused the enthusiasm so direly needed in adversity. He was not an easy man to serve, but he set an example of hard work, determination, and integrity, which not all the men at Baker Street could follow.

The Making of an Agent

The perplexities confronting the men charged with setting up the new organization and with recruiting and training SOE agents were almost insuperable. Their activities had no precedent in any war or conflict the British had ever fought. They had to improvise against staggering odds.

In peacetime a professional intelligence officer received full military training, graduated from one of the military academies, and was hand-picked after he had completed long courses of special instruction. When abroad he would be attached or at least in contact with the diplomatic or consular offices, and could bank on the protection and advice of reliable friends. The few professional agents who remained in enemy territory in wartime were supposed to be well established and to have the necessary secret connections.

The new would-be SOE agents, who were to act as saboteurs and instructors to partisan units and secret armies, were amateurs almost to a man when the recruiting officers received them.

As General Gubbins put it, the first man to go back to any enemy-occupied country had to use his native wit to establish himself safely and open up communication. The lone and intrusive agent was in great danger of discovery or betrayal, for his very first whispered inquiries might reach the Gestapo.

The man who volunteered to accept the perils, and who could survive and fulfill his tasks in spite of them, had to be of exceptional character. The crafts in which he had to become expert, the crafts of clandestine warfare, were many and varied: establishing his headquarters, enlisting and instructing helpers and couriers, organizing the reception of new agents and supplies dropped from aircraft, recruiting and training patriots to be formed into paramilitary units, planning and executing sabotage actions, which included the use of explosives. In most cases he would be expected to operate a wireless transmitter, which involved some technical knowledge and skill in coding and deciphering.

The above list contains routine operations, but soon after the inception of SOE its chiefs had to consider more unexpected tasks that placed their agents in a wider setting. The SOE officer in the field often had to act as a mediator between warring Resistance factions, smoothing over political or personal rivalries that involved him in a complex web of intrigue. Then came assignments of more conventional espionage: the collecting, sifting, and conveying of military, political, and economic information, which the various departments demanded.

The first condition for an agent in the field merely to survive, let alone to fulfill any of his tasks, was to have thorough knowledge of the required language. Also, he had to behave as a native to avoid attention. This meant learning the items of trivia one normally acquires from having lived in a country—the popular songs, folklore, personalities, and so forth—as well as showing an awareness of the community's attitudes, which reflect class and regional differences in such things as food and drink, religion, customs, mores. And, of course, the agent had to be provided with a background, an occupation, and a full identity of his own.

General Gubbins' personnel came almost entirely from the armed forces of the Allies, mostly British officers and other ranks and men from the dominions. In the case of agents required for the Dutch, Norwegian, Polish, or Czech sections the procedure was simple, since almost all of them were nationals of those countries. They had been seconded by their exile governments and recommended by their secret service offices in London. As a rule, those who had not come to Britain with their military units in 1940 but who had arrived as refugees or escapees after that date went through the Patriotic School, a holding camp in the requisitioned buildings of the Royal Victoria Patriotic School on Wandsworth Common in London, where they passed through a thorough screening by British officers, supervised by SOE's director of security, Mr. (now Sir) John Senter. The recruitment of agents from the ranks of Allied armed forces and screened patriots did, as General Gubbins has emphasized, largely obviate the risk of penetration of the organization bv German spies.

On the other hand, nearly all SOE agents sent to Southeastern Europe—Yugoslavia, Albania, Greece—were British, and the same applied to most of the agents dispatched to Italy. However, these were not agents in the strict sense of the term but members of military missions to be attached to guerilla units or headquarters of partisan armies.

The French section, which required the largest number of agents, had particular problems of recruiting, which will be described in detail in the next chapter.

The candidate interviewed was not told initially what was required of him. He was told only that he would be employed on some secret work, and sometimes it was hinted that he might have to serve abroad. Relevant passages of the Official Secrets Act were read to each candidate. He had to sign this; and he was bound on his word of honor not to speak to anybody of what he had been told. Several interviews followed, and if the recruiting officer was impressed by his personality and knowledge of the language, the candidate was told that he would have to undergo a preliminary course of training. He was also warned that the training might not result in his special employment with the organization, in which case he would be returned to his unit. This was not to be taken as a reflection on his character or courage; he just might not be the right person for this work. In fact, despite the dire need for agents, quite a number of candidates were rejected outright, and others did not survive the preliminary training.

Special Training Schools

At the beginning of the war there were no training schools that could produce many men to be employed as secret agents, saboteurs, and raiders behind the enemy's rear. But a select group of potential instructors for such schools existed.

When the Red Army invaded Finland on 30 November 1939, preparations were made to send a British volunteer force to help the Finns. It must be remembered that Stalin had a friendship treaty with Hitler. The Russians had occupied half of Poland after the lightning German attack on that country. The sending of the "volunteers" was backed by Churchill and Anthony Eden, then secretary for war, though the Cabinet was not unanimously in favor of this enterprise.

A composite ski battalion, 600 strong, composed to a large extent of officers from every corps and regiment, was hurriedly assembled. Almost every one of the volunteers was an experienced skier and mountaineer. Some, like Lieutenant Frederick Spencer Chapman, a housemaster at Gordonstoun School, had taken part in Himalayan or Arctic expeditions; three of them, Quintin Riley, J. M. Scott, and Martin Lindsay (later MP for Solihull), had been with Chapman on the Gino Watkins' Greenland expedition. The volunteers took a hectic training course at Bordon Camp, Aldershot, for though they were all tough, very few could handle a rifle. Then they went to Chamonix in the Savoy Alps to continue their training with the French Chasseurs Alpins, who were also earmarked for embarkation to Finland. In the end the whole scheme came to nought. The Finns signed a peace treaty with Russia, accepting the harsh conditions of the surrender of 16,000 square miles of their territory to the Soviet Union. The volunteers' battalion was recalled and disbanded.

However, it was a nucleus of a paramilitary force and a symbol of a more imaginative approach to war. Subsequently, Colonel Mayfield and Captain Bill Stirling, Scots Guards, were entrusted by MI(R) to start a training course, mainly for junior officers who would themselves become instructors for other men to be "specially employed." This first Special Training School was given a home at Inverailort House, some twenty-five miles west of Fort William at the head of Loch Ailort. This STS later gave great service in training of many SOE agents.

"Inverailort House was a large square building of plain grey stone, situated at the Head of Loch Ailort, on the south shore, where the gloom of its natural surroundings matches the chill austerity of its design," recalls Major Peter Kemp, who was there as an instructor and assistant to Lord Lovat, then senior instructor in fieldcraft, in the early days of this school, from which so many men of the commandos and SOE were to graduate. "The front of the house faces north to the sea loch, whose sombre waters, alternately wrapped in mist and whipped by rainstorms, blend with the leaden tones of walls and roof. The back is overshadowed by a grim black cliff surmounted by a thick, forbidding growth of trees, which rises from the back door to well above the height of the roof, blotting out the light of the sun at all times except high noon in summer. The rainfall at Glenfinnan, ten miles to the east, is the highest in the British Isles . . . ." [1]

When one considers the modest and haphazard beginnings of the training in these Macbethian surroundings, it is surprising that by 1944 SOE had no less than sixty Special Training Schools, including a number in North Africa and Italy, to serve the special purposes of the separate SOE HQ in the Mediterranean. The figure does not include many more established in conjunction with other special forces and the American OSS in such far-flung places as Haifa, Khartoum, Burma, Ceylon, India, Australia, Timor, Siam, and Chungking. An SOE school established in December 1941 at Oshawa, near Toronto, later became a model for American OSS training schools, for which British instructors were recruited.

From the SOE training schools 7,500 men and women were graduated and sent from Britain to Western Europe; 4,000 more were sent from the Mediterranean bases to Italy, Yugoslavia, Greece, Albania, Poland, Czechoslovakia, Hungary, Rumania, and so on.[2]

These figures, however, include members of the Jedburgh teams dropped into France shortly before and after the 1944 Allied invasions in Normandy and in the south of France. Jedburgh teams consisted of uniformed

[1] Cf. Kemp, P., No Colours or Crest, Cassell, London, 1958.
[2] Cf. Major General R. H. Barry in European Resistance Movements, Pergamon Press, Oxford, 1960.

[26]

and heavily armed groups of three or more Allied officers and men who were dropped into semi-liberated areas to help mop up fleeing German units.

The hard core of officers sent to Europe during the first three years of SOE operations (until the spring of 1944) did not exceed about 2,000.

The first director of training was Colonel George Taylor, who came from the D department. He was succeeded by Colonel J. S. Wilson, whose long experience in the Indian Police and the Scout movement well qualified him for training men to "set Europe ablaze." While the training was conducted along military lines, it was to Colonel Wilson's credit that the STS resembled scouting camps rather than military establishments. The atmosphere was fresh and informal. Instructors were bent on teaching new tricks they themselves evolved, whether in the handling of explosives or in the crafts of clandestine work, rather than trying to inculcate traditional but useless disciplines. Among these early instructors were men such as Captain Mike Calvert, the famous "Mad Mike," who three years later, at the age of twenty-five, was one of Orde Wingate's brigadiers in the jungles of Burma; and Major James Gavin, an engineer and famous mountaineer, who conducted a very special course in demolition and explosives. When Colonel Wilson left the training directorate in 1942 to assume command of the Scandinavian sections, there flourished a well-organized training scheme with a syllabus that provided all that could possibly be devised to make the work of secret agents in the field efficient and successful.

In the course of its expansion SOE acquired the use of a large number of England's stately homes. The task of finding suitable premises for training and administration was entrusted to Lieutenant Colonel D. T. Wallace, an architect in civilian life. He acted as liaison officer with the Ministry of Works, which appealed to owners to put their country houses at its disposal for a special war effort. Most of these tenancies were concluded amicably, although in a few cases requisition procedure was applied.

One of the first preliminary STS was Wanborough Manor, on the Hog's Back near Guildford in Surrey, close to the ancient Pilgrim's Way. Built in 1527, it has been owned by the Earls of Onslow since the 17th century. The setting for great soirées in the 18th century, when the lavish lounges and fine park (where Queen Victoria and Mr. Gladstone planted trees a century later) were added, was inhabited in the 20th century by young men and women on strange business.

Like all the STS, Wanborough Manor was serviced by the FANYs.[3] These young and sometimes not so young women, many from titled families, acted as hostesses, guardian angels, and friends of the somewhat bewildered recruits. They also did all the chores: cooking meals, cleaning

[3] FANY—First Aid Nursing Yeomanry, founded in 1907, mainly as an ambulance service.

rooms, and looking after the men's clothes and washing. To some they were a cross between their public school matrons and glorified house-keepers, others no doubt regarded them rather differently.

From their initial role the FANYs soon graduated to many other SOE jobs. A large number were trained as secretaries, typists, code clerks, W/T operators, and teleprinter telegraphists. In 1943, when the Royal Signal Corps handled the reception and transmission of signals from and to agents in the field, the FANYs provided most of the personnel at the W/T stations. They were sometimes considered casually by soldiers, civilians, and by the other women's services, as "that posh but rather idle corps," because only few knew of the secret work the FANYs were performing. In fact, as in 1914–18, the war galvanized a considerable number of the upper-class women out of their rut of pleasure and lethargy.

Indeed, some of the great SOE heroines, such as Marie Le Chêne, Mary Herbert, Peggy Knight, Andrée Borrel, Denise Bloch, Madeleine Damerment, Vera Leigh, Eliane Plewman, Diana Rowden, Yvonne Rudelatt, Violette Szabo—who gave their lives—and Lise de Baissac, Eileen and Jacqueline Nearne, Nancy Wake, and Odette Sansom joined SOE as members of FANY. The part the FANYs played in SOE operations was vital; it is no exaggeration to say that the organization would hardly have survived without them.

By necessity their service and achievements had to be secret, and these women have never received the public acclaim they deserved. In a letter written to their commandant, Hope Gamwell, after the war Major General Gubbins expressed the general feeling in SOE:

I am tongue-tied when I try to tell what the FANYs have meant to the organization and me . . . . To the organization they were everything, and without them we just could not have done it. They have become a household word for efficiency, guts, cheerfulness, persistence, tenacity and comradeship in difficulty, and I am proud to have been the means of their proving their great qualities. They have been magnificent and invaluable.[4]

Education for Cloak and Dagger

At Wanborough Manor Roger de Wesslow, Coldstream Guards, was in command. In the words of Section Officer Vera Atkins (then chief assistant in F section of SOE, and at the end of the war in charge of that section), "He always remained a guardee, but he got on well with people from all walks of life." Although a disciplinarian, he knew how to cope with the very mixed bag of his students; a confirmed gourmet, he would discuss at length the merits of a *coq au vin* or an Italian *pasta* dish with his wards, most of whom had spent their lives on the Continent.

[4] *Cf.* Ward, I., *FANY Invicta*, p. 189, Hutchinson, London, 1955.

[28]

Although the students had to endure some military drill and attend interminable lectures on the crafts of a secret agent, the atmosphere resembled a country house party more than a sojourn in a military establishment. It was, of course, a very secret house party, and the STS were strictly guarded by Field Security Police. The students and the FANYs were not allowed to leave the compounds or even to communicate with their families. Home or Sunday leaves were granted only exceptionally, and not at all during the initial period.

Among the first students were Poles and Norwegians; then came Britons, Canadians, Danes, Dutch, men from the Commonwealth, and others recruited by the various sections. The students were instructed by officers from various units: guardsmen, Military Intelligence men, sappers, engineers, Service and Ordnance Corps men, and Scotland Yard detectives. In addition they were watched by officers from their respective sections, who often visited the training schools, and were also interviewed and examined by army psychiatrists. During the preliminary course their behavior and reactions were closely watched. For instance, they were offered strong drink, indeed tempted to take more whisky, gin, or brandy than they might normally desire; then their behavior under the influence was noted. Would they be boisterous, talkative, or quarrelsome and aggressive? Would they give away secrets? They were watched in their bedrooms, too, to see if they talked in their sleep; and if so, in what language. Headquarters officers would mix with them in leisure hours, in the guise of students, to see if they talked too much. All this might sound a bit too clever and severe, but these were the best methods of discovering what a student would be like in the field, because the best man at an interview might live carelessly in day-to-day circumstances, with his guard down.

Not all the recruits, however great their enthusiasm, survived this preliminary training—even in a situation where recruits were desperately needed. Those who passed the initial course, after about four weeks, were sent to other training schools to learn the skills they would use in the field. Those who achieved this could be fairly sure of special employment.

The next step was a course in physical toughening. Although SOE chiefs—sometimes at variance with the military instructors—quite rightly did not put too great an emphasis on the physical abilities of their men (they were not being trained as commandos, though they had to have some of their capabilities), a course in physical training was necessary if only to give the men an idea of possible hardships they might have to endure. Accordingly, students were sent to camps in Scotland. The SOE was allowed to use the very first commando school at Loch Ailort, and several others were established later, such as STS No. 26 at Arisaig.

The STS at Meoble not far from Arisaig was in one of the wildest and most inaccessible parts of the highlands. To get there one had to walk to Loch Beoraid over a mountain track from Glenfinnan, and though one might go lilting along in sunlit summer or autumn when rowan and heather were warm and rich, or in spring when the gorse was startling yellow and the sky and mountains delicately clear and precise, more often than not the weather was appalling. The denim-clad students had to learn to cross rough country, avoiding the skyline and hiding from imaginary German patrols; to creep silently through undergrowth, wade across rock-strewn streams, and pretend to blow up bridges with dummy explosives. There were forced marches with heavy rucksacks when some faltered under the strain and were asked to make one more effort to prove their perseverance. There were organized games of Resistance fighters and SS men, hunting and hiding by turns.

Some relished such exertion as goats on a mountain. Others, who had spent years in cloistered common rooms or newspaper offices, and whose most strenuous exercise had been persistent elbow-bending, hardly survived this part of the training. Yet they all took it in good humor. I can remember only a few who tendered resignations, only to withdraw them the next morning after a good night's sleep. Some even had gumption for private amusement, such as poaching salmon with charges of gelignite. Instructors ignored such irregularities because they indicated the kind of initiative they were trying to inculcate.

After the formidable Scottish training the students were distributed among other STS, which later developed a high degree of specialization. A course of parachute jumping was obligatory.

At first this was given at Dunham Massey House, between Altrincham and Knutsford in Cheshire, but the number of trainees soon greatly increased, and the Airborne Troops Parachute School at Tatton Park, Ringway, near Manchester, was substituted. Many thousands of secret agents, including nearly a hundred women, learned to jump there.

Commanding the school was Group Captain Maurice Newnham, who went to Ringway when it was first opened in October 1940. Newnham had been a flyer in the First World War, and had rejoined the RAF in 1939 in the hope of being able to fly again. He was then forty-four years old and managing director of Triumph Motorcar Company, and instead of a return to wings he was given a desk job at the Air Ministry—much to his chagrin. One day an air marshal telephoned an offer: "I don't know whether this is your line, but it's a job which might prove more exciting. . . ." This was the appointment to the command of the new parachute school; the tone of the telephone conversation illustrates the degree of improvisation which military leaders then adopted. Newnham had never made a parachute jump in his life, but he accepted. In the course of time he made thirty-one jumps, and on one occasion broke his leg when his parachute did not open properly.

Ringway started from scratch, with three professional parachute "artistes" from Sir Alan Cobham's famous prewar air circus. Their techniques were found to be rather useless, and instruction had to start afresh. Like a smoke screen in the sky, Ringway training grew to unpredictable proportions. By the end of the war 60,000 airborne troops had been trained there, including the British Airborne Commandos, the famous Red Berets, whose deeds became epics.

Many secret agents had to practice landing in water. A lake is a good landmark for a navigator in search of a DZ (dropping zone), and because a parachute is sometimes deflected by wind and lands far from the intended target, the landing might be in a lake, a river, or a tree. Quite a few of the future agents had to be fished out of the lake at Tatton Park, their tangled parachutes actually saving them from drowning.

Before jumping, the students were given a series of lectures, usually by Warrant Officer Joe Sutherland, a natural comedian. He ponderously explained the technical difficulties, first the parachute, the eighty yards of silk on which a man's life literally depended. He reassured them as to its strength, reliability, and perfection, but invariably remarked afterward that all this would count "for nought," because a safe landing depended on a jumper's skill and presence of mind. So, "you're a dead loss all of you, and the quicker you give up and go home the better. . . ." This is an unmistakably English trick, an oblique and paradoxical way of raising morale. I remember one of Sutherland's stories, of a "body" who was bracing himself for a leap and suddenly snatched his dental plate out of his mouth and stuffed it into his pocket. Asked after his jump and safe landing why he did it, the man replied: "I had to . . . those bloody teeth were chattering!"

Never Kill a German

Some students started the second part of training at Brockhall, between Daventry and Northampton, for generations the home of the Thornton family, which Colonel T. A. Thornton had offered to SOE. Others went to Belasis, near Dorking in Surrey, or to Chorley Wood in Hertfordshire. Many of the Danish and Norwegian agents trained at STS No. 45 at Hatherop Castle in Gloucestershire, a beautiful house in the Cotswolds, now a finishing school for young ladies. Perhaps this gratifies the *genius loci* after the indignities during the war years.

At these schools pupils received instruction in cloak-and-dagger work. These hackneyed words are not chosen at random, for here, among many other skills, the intricacies of unarmed combat were taught, worthy of present-day fiction spies of the film and TV screens. At Aston House in Hertfordshire two former Shanghai policemen (promoted to Captains), Sykes and Fairburn, imparted their skill in silent killing. Sykes explained to his pupils that "a knife should be used as delicately as an artist uses his paint brush," but also advised his bewildered pupils "to kick the fellow in the balls as hard as you can."

At Brockhall, Sergeant Harry Court, who trained more than a thousand SOE and special forces men, favored a different approach: "Never kill a German. Put him in hospital for six months. He is more bother alive than dead. A wounded soldier has to be looked after, wasting German manpower. A dead soldier is buried and forgotten. . . ." He produced a selection of examples of how to deal with a German sentry: suddenly, silently, ruthlessly. To learn how to attack, the pupil had to learn two things: the principles of leverage, and the most vulnerable parts of the body. Court told his pupils: "Forget any fistfights you have seen in gangster films, and any boxing lessons you might have had at your schools or sports clubs. Never bother with your fists; it would be a pity if you damaged your knuckles by punching." He showed them how to hit upward with the heel of the open hand to smash a man's jaw, or to strike brutal blows with the side of the hand against vulnerable parts of the neck and body. A walking stick or umbrella could, after Court's instruction, become as lethal as a sword. A man always has a weapon in his pockets, he used to say—a nail file, comb, or fountain pen. Judo training was given to most students, and they were taught how to throw a man from behind and in the dark.

STS No. 17 at Hatfield, Hertfordshire, was used both for preliminary training and for a special course in industrial sabotage, while STS No. 40 near Bedford was at one time the center for the training of W/T operators. Hatfield, too, produced excellent "pianists" (radio operators).

Every student was supposed to go through rifle and revolver practice, and to become a fairly good shot. He was taught to use, dismantle, and assemble various types of arms, including rifles, pistols, Sten guns, Bren guns, bazookas, and Piats; from 1942 onward these were dropped in increasing quantities to Resistance fighters. He was told that he would have to instruct others in the handling of these weapons, and this, of course, in conditions of secrecy imposed by danger in the field. He took a comprehensive course in the use of various explosives. At Hatfield and other schools quite realistic demolition actions were carried out, including the destruction of concrete pylons, walls, stretches of railway track specially laid for the purpose, and even small buildings. Sappers and engineers initiated future saboteurs into this particular branch of the trade.

Eventually the students were transferred to one of the finishing schools. The most famous, though top secret during the war, was the SOE security school at Beaulieu, the ancestral home of the Lords Montagu in the New Forest. There Colonel Frank Spooner, a former Indian army officer, was in command, assisted by many instructors, including several Scotland Yard officers.

An American intelligence officer, Colonel Farago, said that the British had produced some exceptional intelligence officers as a result of an educational system that stimulates intellectual skill needed for this particular work. He added that in the lives of Britain's most outstanding intelligence officers—and his opinion includes SOE officers—there was "that combination of public school education and Coldstream Guards, of Cambridge and Oxford and Cameron Highlanders." Although it can be accepted as a compliment, this statement is not entirely correct. Many of the SOE agents did not have such an advantageous background. However, it is true that the influence of officers who had the background described by the American colonel was felt at the finishing and security schools.

At Beaulieu the agents were housed in cottages on the estate, romantically named The House by the Shore or The House in the Woods. In the great hall, where Sunday trippers now pay 2s. 6d. (35 cents) to inspect the museum of vintage motorcars, hundreds of SOE agents were given their final grooming. To mentally mold themselves into their new identities required many hours of assimilation. They met their conducting officers— the men who would assist the agents most closely as the time for their departure on missions drew near. Many of the conducting officers had already been in the field and could impart advice from firsthand experience. The students became proficient in map reading, coding, microphotography, and in the hundred and one ways of guarding their own and their future comrades' security.

They learned how to find a safe house, establish contacts, use mail drops at accommodation addresses, employ couriers, arrange dates, communicate with friends in the Resistance, prepare dropping grounds and receptions of other agents and material, and use false documents. Above all, they learned what not to do in order to avoid detection and capture. They were given microfilms and told to hide them on their bodies, in the rectum and elsewhere, or in personal articles. Then they were searched by experienced instructors, most of them Scotland Yard detectives. Some students achieved great skill and could have become peerless smugglers.

There were sessions of simulated Gestapo *Verhör* (interrogation). Short of being actually brutally manhandled, the "prisoner" received somewhat rough treatment that had all the genuine flavor. *"Raus Du Schweinehund!"* the pseudo-Gestapo men would shout, and wield steel rods or rifle butts, snarl commands, and question the "prisoner" under blazing lights to frighten and bewilder him into telling something he should have kept secret. Afterward, over a drink, he was told of mistakes he made and how he should behave if he ever had to face the real thing.

[33]

In particular the would-be agents had to be impressed with the cardinal importance of communications. Everything the agent was expected to accomplish in the field depended on his maintaining a regular contact with headquarters. Cut off from headquarters, without instructions, without the possibility of reporting back, he would be in a vacuum and even his best exploits would be of little value. He could, as a lone wolf, perhaps harass the enemy by some daring sabotage action—blowing up a railway track or a power station—but even such action would be a mere pinprick if it were not part of a pattern of planned strategy.

The main task of an SOE agent was to organize and instruct Resistance groups, from which the secret armies would emerge to assist the Allied invasion forces by sabotaging enemy communications, by disrupting railway and road systems, by hampering his supplies, and finally by open attack at his rear and flanks. The lone agent in the field depended on instructions as well as on supplies by air of arms, explosives, and money. He had to keep headquarters informed of what he was doing. In many ways his own survival depended on a regular contact by radio with headquarters. If his group network or his own safety was endangered, he could ask for help—for instance, for a pickup or for the direction to another agent in a neighboring area, or to an escape route. The majority of the agents were, therefore, trained in the operation of a wireless transmitter. Those given a special task as organizers, liaison officers, or sabotage instructors were provided with a "pianist."

There was a possibility of sending messages and instructions to an agent who had no direct radio contact or had lost it temporarily, by BBC broadcasts. Prearranged code phrases broadcast as personal messages on the various foreign programs from Bush House in London (there were continuous day and night transmissions in every language and to every occupied country) could usually reach him, because the agent was expected to find friends who had a radio set (even though listening to the BBC was forbidden by the Germans). But this was, of course, an extremely risky contact and, in any case, a solely one-sided one, as the agent could only receive a brief, and sometimes incomprehensive message, and could not reply.

Another method of contact was by couriers, who could convey and collect messages, by way of neutral countries. This was often used in Norway and Denmark via neutral Sweden, and to some extent in France and Italy via Switzerland. But, again, this was risky and sporadic communication.

The only really worthwhile regular contact was by establishing radio posts inside the enemy-occupied territory, with all the perils involved. The agent or his "pianist" had to be well trained in working the transmitter, using Morse signals that were elaborately coded, so that the Germans, if picking them up, could not easily understand them.

Each transmitter, by using specially ground crystals, was tuned to one of the reception stations, of which a large number were established in various parts of Britain. Usually the radio operators worked at regular "skeds"—scheduled times—for instance every Tuesday, Thursday, Saturday, and Sunday at 7 P.M. Messages, of course, were elaborately coded and included one or more security checks. In addition, test questions were asked, and test answers given. The answer was not a logical one but a pre-arranged short phrase. For instance, if the test question was: IS YOUR SHIRT CLEAN? the answer might have been: THE SUN IS SHINING.

There were, unfortunately, occasions when an agent under interrogation by the Gestapo had to reveal his security checks, or at least one of them. The code might have still remained unbroken if the test question and answer were not given away. There were also other possibilities to discover at the receiving end whether a message had come from a genuine radio post or one taken over or infiltrated by the enemy. Usually the signals from an agent in the field were received at the scheduled time by the same FANY telegraphist. Thus the operator had his distant godmother at the W/T station, somewhere in a stately home in Oxfordshire or Gloucestershire. As every operator has an individual touch on the Morse key, she would get to know his "fist" and, if the touch was different, could detect an impostor.

However, in many cases all these security precautions proved useless. Some operators omitted to give security checks, because they worked either in a great hurry or under a great strain. For the same reasons their touch on the Morse key varied greatly. Fragmentary messages arrived, or messages with scrambled letters and figures. In many cases all was disregarded and signals were accepted as genuine. Sometimes this had tragic results, as we shall see.

Although laxity or disregard of security rules cannot be excused where lives are at stake, one must remember that up to two million words a week passed through the SOE signal stations.

Finally, quite apart from the enormous difficulties and dangers of operating a transmitter in enemy territory—with German radio direction-finding service (*Funkpeildienst*) constantly on the trail of the operators—there was atmospheric and other interference, which made the transmission and reception often difficult. Nevertheless, the radio link with individual agents, as long as it lasted, provided the lifeblood of all activities.

Many operators acquired great skill and surpassed all expectations of their instructors. At the Home stations hundreds of men and women of the Royal Corps of Signals, FANY, and Women's Services worked as code clerks, and wireless, teleprinter, perforator, and switchboard operators. At some stations the coding sections were entirely manned by FANYs. For example, in the spring of 1942 Signal Station No. 53A at Bicester started with three W/T operators and four FANY coders. Within a year, the establishment was increased to 125. In February 1943 Station 53B was opened at Aylesbury to relieve traffic from the overloaded channels of the Bicester station. At first 83 FANYs were transferred to it; by October 1943 the personnel was increased to 200, including 60 FANY coders.

Into the Field

The final stage of the agent's education was the holding camp, where the graduates went before being sent into the field. One was at Fawley Court near Henley-on-Thames, where the commander was Major Thomas Lindsay, Irish Guards. Another at Tempsford House, Bedfordshire, near the airfield where a Moon Squadron was stationed, shipped the agents into Europe. Here Major Archibald Rose, a young officer of the Argyll and Sutherlands, was in command. Beaulieu, the security school, was also used as a holding camp.

The agent's time in a holding camp depended on the weather and the availability of aircraft. If he arrived a few days before a moon period and the weather was bad, he had to wait three or four weeks. Many agents had the nerve-shattering, anticlimactic experience of crossing the Channel or the North Sea two or three times before they could be dropped. They had to be returned to base, usually because of bad weather en route or lack of visibility on the dropping ground, sometimes because of attack by enemy aircraft or AA fire. Only in exceptional cases was an agent dropped "blind," that is without the reception committee on the ground directing the aircraft with patterns of lights. The time of arrival was signaled to the radio operator in the field, and he received and confirmed the message— provided the time and place of the drop were right at his end. On occasions a sortie had to be canceled or an aircraft recalled at the last moment because some sudden emergency precluded reception.

Apart from contact between Home and Out stations, signals of aircraft departures were given at the very last moment in personal messages broadcast by the BBC during ordinary programs. Many strange messages puzzled uninitiated listeners during the war years: "Jean did not shave this morning," might have indicated postponing a secret agent's flight.

SOE sections were allocated a small number of RAF aircraft for the dispatch of agents and the dropping of supplies but never enough. Until 1943 this caused a perpetual battle between the chiefs of SOE and the chiefs of staff and the Air Ministry. SOE had to explain not only the strategic use they could make of aircraft, but also some expensive losses, which could be crippling, for instance, on flights to distant Poland.

Before North Africa and Italy were involved in 1943 and 1944, most SOE agents were dispatched via the special duties squadrons' base at Tempsford airfield. Submarines were too expensive to risk very often, and the swift motor gunboats sometimes used to carry a man across the Channel to the Continent, or perhaps bring one back, were for emergencies only. Like submarines, they were too easily detected from the air and especially near the bristling German shore defenses of the Channel and Dutch coasts. Sea transport was, however, quite widely used to carry agents to Norway. To the Mediterranean coasts, a sea approach was much more feasible, sometimes by submarine and thence by dinghy, more often by the picturesque feluccas, small, dirty, swift sardine fishing boats that plied between Gibraltar and the Côte d'Azur.

Air routes are the least detected, and most SOE transport was the special responsibility of the Tempsford Moon Squadron. Here a tremendous *esprit de corps* developed, especially among the pilots of 138 Squadron who bore the early burden. Their work became intimately associated with the Joes they dropped over the dark fields of Europe, men to whom they hardly spoke and would never know by name. They often flew under great pressure, and faced numerous dangers.

One development of the specialization of Special Duties 161 Squadron was the landing of planes in occupied Europe. For the pilots this was the most hazardous operation of all, for the runways were fields which the Resistance organizers had prepared for their reception, often under the noses of the Gestapo. The pilot could never be certain who would receive him, for Germans fervently aspired to capture a British plane intact. At least once a careful trap was laid, when the Gestapo learned of the time, place, and prearranged signals for a landing. Forewarned at the last moment, the plane barely touched down before it was in the air again, though sprayed with machine-gun bullets.

Tiny Lysander aircraft, painted black or silver, were used for these moonlit landings and pickups. Compared with other planes they could land on a pocket handkerchief, and could be pushed and pulled by teams of villagers if their wheels became stuck in heavy ground. Of course landings might be perfect, but it was impossible to be sure. Very often the Lysanders returned with their wings and fuselages cut up by flak, or with the branches of treetops and hedgerows or wire from high-tension cables twined round their wheels.

The agent ready to go at the holding camp had his own conducting officer sent from his respective section. These officers were much more than official escorts; they tendered the final advice during the agent's last days and hours in Britain, double-checked his equipment, and tried to make the agent feel and act his assumed role.

At the holding camps the agent's false identity and his processed *curriculum vitae* were checked once again. Lieutenant John Smith had now become Jacques Dupont, an agronomist from the Auvergne or a traveling salesman from Bordeaux. He was provided with a complete new identity and an imaginary family, including Oncle Jean and Tante Geneviève. He had to know by heart—even if awakened in the middle of the night by Gestapo men—the names of his schoolteachers at Mauriac, or the street where he was supposed to have been born in the Bordeaux suburb of Bacalan. Sometimes his cover story, or legend, coincided with the truth, for many agents had spent much of their lives abroad; and for agents dispatched anywhere but France, much of the identity of their real lives could be used.

Scientists and Forgers

The metamorphosis of the agent into his new identity included minute details; some of the legends filled several closely typed pages. But all this inventive effort would go to waste if the Gestapo examined his clothes after arrest, and found that he was wearing new shoes with the label of a Northampton factory, or had a ticket stub from the Kensington theater in his pocket. It was the duty of the conducting officer to ferret out any such details. Sometimes he was assisted by Scotland Yard detectives seconded to SOE. They scrutinized the clothes of the agent literally with a toothbrush; pockets and trouser cuffs were examined for traces of Virginia tobacco; a British-made pencil or a scrap of paper watermarked "Bond" would immediately be confiscated.

The agent was, of course, provided with a complete set of identity papers, which had to be genuine or well forged, for the bureaucratic controls, always strong in Europe, had run riot under the Nazi regime. Frenchmen, Dutchmen, Norwegians, Belgians, or Danes carried identity cards, passes, curfew permits, working and ration cards. These were the first things examined when a man was stopped by German security police.

The first agents sent to Europe in 1941 were equipped with poorly forged documents; indeed, on arrival they were warned by Resistance friends that the papers were death warrants.

However, SOE, in cooperation with the Scientific Research Department, headed by Professor Dudley Maurice Newitt of the Imperial College of Science in Kensington, created a sequence of laboratories that soon supplied a fantastic variety of special equipment needed by the agents to survive—and in certain circumstances, to die. The SOE's documentation section enlisted the help of printing experts, including a works manager, foremen, and compositors of a famous printing works that manufactured British postage stamps and security paper for banknotes and shares. A specially equipped printing works and a block-process department produced thousands of French *cartes d'identité, feuilles sémestrelles* (for food rations), Dutch *paaspoorts,* German military *Passierscheine,* and other credentials. An SOE agent wanted to be free from the curfew and traveling restrictions that burdened the civilian population, so the special passes issued by local *Feld Kommandantur* for the exemption of power station workers and officials of public utilities (such as hospitals and transport) were forged.

In addition to the forged documents, every agent was given the option of carrying the "L" pill, because of the possibility of torture greater than he or she could bear, and the determination not to betray comrades under such torture. The L pill contained potassium cyanide. The pill covering was insoluble and if held in the mouth and swallowed, the pill would pass through the body without causing harm. If the pill were crushed between the teeth, the poison would kill instantly.

But for the most part the scientific section was concerned with means of survival. In this respect it was helped enormously by the genius of one man, who at the outbreak of war, at the age of forty, had the ripe experience of a working life in the world of disguise and make-believe.

Elder Wills had served in the RAF during the First World War; after studying architecture he became a scenic artist at the Drury Lane Theatre. Later he turned to films, as art director, producer, and director. In 1939 Wills went to France with the British Expeditionary Force as a camouflage officer and returned from Dunkirk with a leg injury. For a year he was employed camouflaging buildings and aerodromes, designing cardboard tanks and aircraft to mystify the Luftwaffe and to help deter Hitler from invasion. In November 1941 he was asked to see Professor Newitt, and soon afterward Captain (later Lieutenant Colonel) Wills became the boss of one of the strangest businesses in the world.

His first important task was to provide a satisfactory suitcase for the W/T sets dropped with agents into Europe, for these were, horrifyingly, a general issue. If the Germans had captured several such cases, all agents carrying identical models would have been endangered. Wills sought old Continental suitcases, begging and borrowing from friends and acquaintances and visiting London junk shops. On such models many cases were artificially battered to make them look well-worn, and equipped with concealed double bottoms and secret compartments.

The next problem to which he turned his attention was the concealing of codes. Wills invented a new invisible ink which would show only under

[39]

infrared light, and he constructed small flashlights with concealed infrared disks. Nobody would be suspicious of a flashlight in itself, for they were indispensable articles in the blackout that reigned over Europe.

Colonel Wills' laboratory produced microfilmed documents so minute that they could be sealed in tiny containers, which in turn were hidden in various parts of the body, for instance, in the navel or the rectum. A matchstick was made to hold a microfilm containing the equivalent of nine sheets of foolscap paper, and put into a box with other matches from which it was distinguishable only by a tiny nick. Scores of other conventional articles were used: toothpaste tubes with special compartments; shoelaces with a soft tube inside; microdots, which could be placed on the lens of spectacles or the glass of a watch, no bigger than a speck of dust, but when developed by special photographic process would reveal codes or instructions up to five hundred words in length.

The problem of codes and wireless transmission was solved in Operation Lavatory. Agents were advised to hide their W/T sets, once they reached a safe house, in lavatory cisterns, and were given a specially designed pulling chain to provide an aerial. The codes were written with the invisible ink on men's shirttails and pants, and on women's underwear. Thus on visiting the lavatory agents were all set for radio transmission.

It is said that, next to his voice, nothing gives a man away so much as his clothes. With this in mind, Colonel Wills enlisted the help of a tailor, a Jewish refugee from Vienna, as his chief adviser on fashions. The style of French clothes in particular is very different from English, and details had to be correct down to the underwear. The tailor spoke English very haltingly, but he ended the war as a captain in the British Army, through his services to this special haberdashery. He managed a small secret factory in Margaret Street near Oxford Circus, where a number of tailors and seamstresses made the full range of garments according to his specifications. He also made the rounds of London synagogues to find refugees, relieving them of a few old clothes or perhaps just the label from a jacket or shirt that bore the name of a Paris or Amsterdam firm, without giving the game away. Later such labels were manufactured in his workshops and sewn into the clothes, which had to be frayed. A Northampton firm made Continental shoes and boots, which were then given sliding heels in Wills' laboratories to conceal a cavity for microfilms or codes.

Under his military superior, Colonel F. T. Davies, Wills established a number of workshops and laboratories in and near London. The first was in a disused carpenter's shop at the Albert and Victoria Museum, where he was assisted by some of his former workers from Elstree film studios: wardrobe masters, makeup artists, plasterers—all experts in make-believe.

As quantity and diversity increased, Lieutenant Colonel Wills added many more workshops—at the Natural History Museum, at offices in Queens Gate, Kensington—until eventually a new large laboratory was installed at the Thatched Barn, the well-known roadhouse of prewar days on the Barnett By-pass.

The scientific research section, however, did not confine itself to saving lives. British engineering ingenuity was, in fact, turned to many offensive projects.

Explosive devices for sabotage actions produced at the Thatched Barn and secret factories included hundreds of types. Any German soldier, if he had ever learned the secrets, would have wondered what articles of everyday use, if any, were safe to touch. The common virtue was that they were small, easy to carry, and ordinary. There were milk bottles that could be placed in a Gestapo office and which would explode if the cap was removed, loaves of bread that would cause devastation if broken or cut in half, fountain pens that squirted death.

In the bitter winter of 1942–43, tons of artificial coal lumps and timber logs (looking like those used for electric fires) were filled with high explosives. Dropped in specially insulated containers to SOE officers and their Resistance helpers, the coal and logs could be carried openly on the roads of occupied Europe. Their destination would be German barracks or Gestapo offices, with death and pandemonium to follow.

Perhaps the most ingenious of all the booby traps invented by Colonel Wills were the horse, mule, camel, and elephant droppings. To imitate them successfully, such distinguished experts as Professor Julian Huxley, then secretary of the London Zoological Society, and keepers of the Natural History Museum were enlisted as advisers. The droppings were made of plastic and painted by hand, closely simulating the real thing. They were sent to appropriate countries: horse droppings to Western and Northern Europe, horse and mule droppings to the Southeast, camel droppings to North Africa, elephant droppings to the Far East. So a Resistance fighter could set out in his cart in front of a German staff car or a marching squad of the SS, and surreptitiously drop a few of these lethal excrements in the midst of the real ones. When he looked back some hundred yards up the road, it might be to see the car and the men blown into the air.

Some 14,000 "cigarettes" containing incendiary and explosive materials were distributed from the Thatched Barn by courtesy of SOE officers in France, Holland, Belgium, Norway, Italy, and other enemy-occupied territory. They caused enormous damage to German stores, fuel tanks, and armament establishments.

French railwaymen and factory workers became very fond of, and adept in, using certain nuts and bolts devised by Wills and his imaginative helpers. They were hollow and filled with high explosive, and they could be attached to railway engines in shunting yards or machine tools in factories, with disastrous results. The full story of Colonel Wills' industrial activities makes fascinating reading.[5]

Wills was also concerned with the production of many escape aid devices. But in this field the special communications section at the War Office excelled. It was headed by Colonel (later Sir John) Russell, a distinguished London lawyer in civilian life. Major Clayton Hutton, an ex-film director like Wills, produced for this section some of the most ingenious escape aids. They were first made to help bailed-out airmen and escapees from German POW camps, but many SOE agents found them extremely useful in their hide-and-seek game with the Gestapo.

Among escape aids invented by Major Hutton were tiny compasses concealed in buttons, signet rings, pencils, and tobacco pipes; maps printed on silk, outlining the escape routes, such as extremely detailed ones of the Pyrenees for the Spanish escape route, easily concealed in the lining of a jacket or inside boots; and even escape saws—to cope with prison bars—made of the thinnest leaf steel and only five inches long.

Among the many ramifications of SOE one of obviously vital importance was finance. To keep an agent and his network in funds, to enable him to make bulk purchases of food and other commodities on the black market to sustain the Resistance groups and armed units of the secret armies in hiding, was a considerable task. Usually agents were sent into the field with fairly large sums in foreign currency, provided by the British Treasury from prewar deposits. But money had to be replenished if an agent remained in the field for months.

Very large sums, without much regard to safety, had to be dropped in containers. Eventually, a complex scheme of financial barter deals was devised by SOE finance section, headed by Colonel John Venner. SOE agents approached individual bankers, businessmen, or just wealthy people who were sympathetic to the Resistance, and asked them to lend them money, on the promise that the loans were in fact made to the British government and would be repaid—with interest if required—after the war. An agent who made such a request of a rich man was unable to prove his real identity, not to speak of offering security for the loan. He could have been a clever con man for all the financier knew. To overcome this difficulty, the SOE agent agreed with the lender that a personal message would be broadcast by the BBC to confirm the loan deal. The financier made up the phrase himself and, after the agent had sent a radio signal to Baker Street, the phrase was broadcast several times on the respective national program a day or two later. This was confirmation enough; and, indeed,

[5] Bell, L., *Sabotage, the Story of Lt.-Col. J. Elder Wills,* Laurie, London, 1957.

[42]

many people in France, Holland, and other countries willingly gave large sums to SOE men without even asking for a receipt or any safeguard. All such loans made to SOE officers were fully repaid by the British Treasury after the liberation of Europe.

For SOE very large sums in dollars and other foreign currencies had to be obtained in the United States in order to provide agents with suitable funds in Europe. The additional difficulty was that this money had to be obtained in banknotes of small denominations—five- and ten-dollar bills. SOE needed dollars particularly for its secret agents sent to Poland and other Eastern European countries. Between February and June 1943, over $10,000,000 was sent to Britain as a result of secret arrangements made between the U.S. Treasury and British Security Co-ordination (BSC), headed by Sir William Stephenson, which handled intelligence activities in the Western Hemisphere. Quite apart from the difficulty of accumulating such vast quantities of small banknotes without arousing unwanted attention, there was the problem of transport. Although a million dollars in large bills could be packed into one bag and sent to London by air, the same amount in small-denomination banknotes required forty or more bags. Between May and September 1944 a further consignment of $8,000,000 in small notes was sent to SOE.

Large quantities of equipment for SOE agents—radio transmitters, cameras, rubber dinghies, and many gadgets for sabotage— were procured by BSC in the United States, particularly in the earlier stages of the war, when production of such articles was very limited in Britain. The most extraordinary request from Baker Street, duly granted, was for a small quantity of curare, the arrow poison used by Orinoco and Amazon Indians which paralyzes the motor nerves. The poison, obtained after much effort by one of Stephenson's agents from Indians in Venezuela, was sent to London in the original bamboo *"tubos."*

When OSS got into stride, large quantities of American-made sabotage "toys" were dispatched to Europe, particularly during the months before D day.

Cardinal assistance was rendered by BSC to the SOE Norwegian section. Until the summer of 1943 the Shetland Bus, that unique ferry service between Lerwick in Scotland and the Norwegian fjords, carrying agents and arms to, and bringing volunteers and refugees from, Norway (as well as occasional cargoes of Swedish ball bearings), was heroically managed by small fishing boats. In May 1943 Stephenson obtained three U.S. Navy submarine chasers, which greatly improved this service. In many other ways SOE and BSC cooperated successfully, particularly after the close link between SOE and OSS was established at the end of 1943. BSC assisted the Ministry of Economic Warfare even more when its ramifications spread around the world after Hitler's attack on Russia and after Japan entered the war. The Ministry, as well as SOE, maintained missions in Russia, in China, and in neutral countries.

Thus the complex organization of SOE headquarters and its many sections fell into order and operation, not with methodical and ruthless Teutonic dynamism—for it had to prove itself before it was given rope—but with British ingenuity and effectiveness, once results were obtained.

The virtue of the SOE recruiting and training and the scientific equipping of agents was a strength akin to the state of the individual SOE man himself: a fruitful combination of amateur and professional. Nobody had been trained for this particular work, but everyone contributed something. In some cases this was a genius or expertise in a particular sphere; more often it was enthusiasm, determination, and hard work.

SOE organization was typical of a nation that is not military-minded, does not win first battles, and learns by trial and error. Schoolmasters and accountants became saboteurs and instructors of secret armies. Whatever setbacks had to be endured and overcome, somehow the transformation occurred. That was the final proof of the success of SOE.

3

First Agents Across
the Channel

AT NOON on 17 June 1940, a group of French officers were sitting in a restaurant in the rue du Fort d'Octville near the railway station at Cherbourg. They had orders to proceed to the new seat of the French government at Bordeaux. They were discussing what they believed to be the latest news.

They had witnessed the disintegration of the French forces. The Germans had entered Paris on the 14th. The tenth, seventh, sixth, fourth, second, third, and fifth French armies, deployed in that order from the coast at Le Havre to the Maginot Line and the Swiss frontier, were surrendering. Almost the whole of the British Expeditionary Force had been withdrawn from the Dunkirk beaches a fortnight earlier. During the past four days the Germans had reached Orléans and the Loire.

But the officers at the small restaurant at Cherbourg did not admit to themselves that France was defeated. They discussed the latest rumors that several French army corps in the north were regrouping; that the British 8th Division under Major General Montgomery, saved at Dunkirk, was on its way back from England to Normandy; that the French fleet was steaming from Toulon to the Channel ports.

Of course they did not know that on the previous evening, the 16th, Winston Churchill, accompanied by Clement Attlee and Sir Archibald Sinclair, was driven with the British chiefs of staff to Waterloo Station in London to board a train to Southampton, where they were to embark on a British cruiser for Concarneau, a small seaside place near Quimper in Brittany.

There they were to meet Paul Reynaud, the French premier, who after the fall of Paris had set up his government at Bordeaux. Mr. Churchill carried with him the draft of the "Proclamation of the Union of Great Britain and France." Its introductory sentence was:

At this most fateful moment in history of the modern world the governments of the United Kingdom and the French Republic make this declaration of indissoluble union and unyielding resolution in their common defense of justice and freedom against subjection to a system which reduces mankind to a life of robots and slaves.

The plan was to sail all units of the French navy to ports in North Africa and Britain, to fly all airworthy French aircraft to African and British airfields, and to extricate as many French, Belgian, Polish, and Czech troops present in France to similar destinations. France, in union with Britain, would then continue the war against Hitler from North Africa.

But no sooner had Churchill's party taken their seats in the special train at Waterloo than a breathless official from Downing Street handed a message to the Prime Minister. It was a telegram from Sir Ronald Campbell, the British ambassador at Bordeaux. He reported that Reynaud had been defeated by his own cabinet when presenting the plan for a union with Britain and a withdrawal to North Africa, that he was forced into resignation, and that Marshal Pétain had taken over the government and had decided to ask Hitler for "an honourable armistice."

Churchill and his colleagues alighted from the train and returned to Downing Street. What remained of Free France was the handful of French soldiers who had come to Britain after Dunkirk.

The few French officers at the Cherbourg restaurant sat around a radio set waiting impatiently for the news bulletin. All morning only records of classical music were played. Suddenly there was an interruption: "Attention, attention," said the announcer. "There will be an important statement by the chief of the government, Marshal Pétain . . . ."

Over the air came the solemn voice of the old and now toothless Lion of Verdun, telling his people that he had sent emissaries to the German high command, requesting an armistice.

For some moments the officers sat tense and silent. The first to speak was Captain Pierre de Vomécourt.

"I do not accept this shameful surrender. I am going to England. Britain will continue to fight, and I shall go there to help to free France!"

The other officers were undecided. They thought of their families, of the uncertain future in England now threatened by invasion. After much argument most of them decided to obey orders and go to Bordeaux.

Pierre de Vomécourt was the son of an old and proud family that for generations had paid *la dette du sang* to France. In the war of 1870 his great-grandfather had been tortured and killed by the Prussian invaders. In the 1914 war his father joined as a volunteer at the age of forty-five and was killed in his first battle. His elder brother, Jean, attending school in England in 1917, lied about his age and joined the Royal Flying Corps.

[46]

Key to Map of France

1 First agent parachuted, May 1941
2 Philippe de Vomécourt's château
3 First Lysander landing (Morel, de Guélis)
4 Cowburn and five agents parachuted, September 1941
5 The Cat and de Vomécourt embark for England
6 First Cannes circuit: Basin, Carte, later Peter Churchill
7 Lyons: Dubourdin, Virginia Hall, Denis Rake
8 Lyonnais circuits: Brooks, Boiteux, R. Lyon
9 Sologne: Gaspard, Culioli, Jacqueline, Clech; later St. Paul
10 PROSPER: Suttill, Norman, Andrée Borrel
11 Sarthe-Le Mans: Garry; radio posts (Hércule, Phono).
12 ROBIN: Worms, Weil, Cohen
13 The three racing drivers: Benoist, Grover-Williams, Wimille
14 Gisors: George Darling
15 Lille: Michel Trotobas
16 St. Quentin: Guy Bieler
17 Rouen: Liewer (Staunton), Violette Szabo
18 Troyes-Marne: Cowburn, Mulsant
19 Angers: Déricourt's main Lysander grounds
20 Bleicher and Eckert's fake réseaux
21 Rennes-Vendée: Floegge, Vallée, Garel, Rousset
22 Poitiers: Lise de Baissac
23 Bordeaux: Claude de Baissac and Roger Landes
24 Tarbes: Charles Rechenmann
25 Toulouse: Pertschuk, Bloch, later George Starr's large circuit
     in the Gascogne
26 Marseilles: various circuits, later MONK and Boiteux-Cohen
27 South and southeast: Francis Cammaerts' large circuit
28 Jura, Franche-Comté: Harry Rée
29 Capture of Peter Churchill at St. Jorioz
30 Central France: Rafferty, G. D. Jones, later Southgate's large circuit;
     Pearl Witherington, Maingard
31 Corrèze: Harry Peulevé, later Poirier
32 Lot: VENY, Hiller, and Watney
33 Jura-Ain: Heslop's large circuit
34 Frager's DONKEYMAN in the Yonne
35 Angoulême: Corbin and Sirois
36 Auvergne: Nancy Wake, Denis Rake, and John Farmer
37 Miranda de Ebro, Spanish internment camp

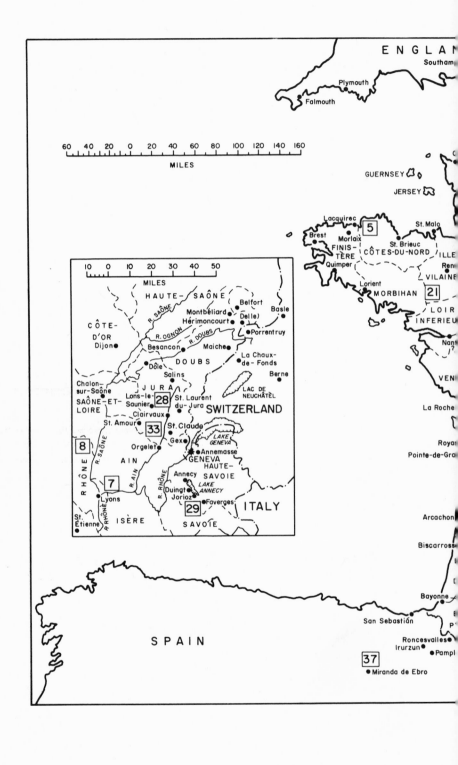

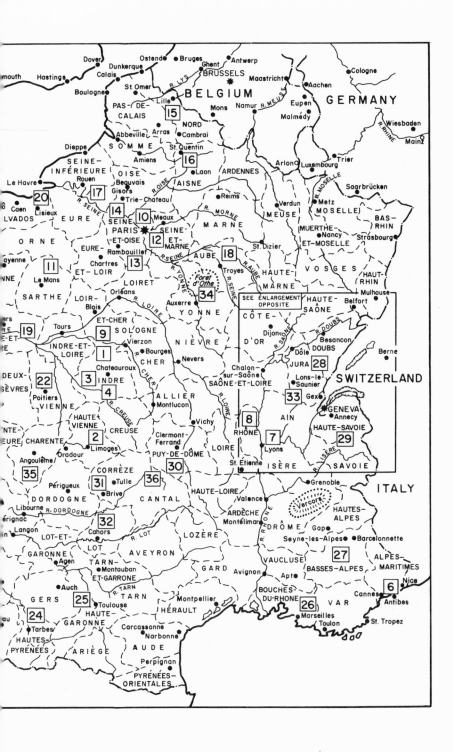

He was badly wounded when his canvas-and-string plane was shot down, and he was given a British RAF commission. His other brother, Philippe, had been too young to fight, but in 1918 he had completed his OCTU training at the famous Roman Catholic school, Beaumont College, at Old Windsor, and held a British Territorial commission.

On the evening of that momentous 17th of June, Pierre de Vomécourt, who had been a French liaison officer with one of the BEF units, sailed aboard a British warship from Cherbourg to England. With him were men of the remainder of the British 157th Brigade, which had been extricated from the collapsed front and after hard fighting had reached Cherbourg. Other scattered British units, a handful of French soldiers, and nearly 20,000 Polish troops, who had refused to capitulate, were also taken aboard British ships at Cherbourg, Brest, St. Malo, and St. Nazaire.

The voyage from Brittany to England normally requires a few hours. On this occasion it lasted two days. Some of the transports, old cargo vessels, had not sufficient fuel for even this short journey. On the *Meknes,* which was the last ship to leave Brest on 18 June, troops were set to work cutting up the wooden superstructure for fuel. Escaping aboard this ship was another valiant Frenchman, Captain André Dewavrin, subsequently Colonel Passy, chief of de Gaulle's secret service, and on many occasions a bitter rival of SOE.

When Pierre de Vomécourt arrived at Southampton he was conveyed with other foreign soldiers to Trentham Park, where British military police led them through pouring rain to a hastily erected camp. There de Vomécourt encountered old comrades, men of the 6th and 12th battalions of the Chasseurs. They too had come to continue the fight. But they were treated almost as if they were prisoners of war.

The War Office appeared to be most unhappy about the arrival of so many foreign warriors. Previously more than 100,000 French and Polish soldiers had reached Britain from Dunkirk and most of them had been moved to Scotland. Understandably, the latest arrivals were viewed with deeper suspicion. British Military Intelligence, remembering the lessons of Norway where many German soldiers had been found wearing Norwegian uniforms, believed that the latest contingent of foreigners must include German spies.

After the armistice Marshal Pétain ordered all French troops in the United Kingdom to proceed to North Africa. Hitler had given him permission to retain a small army with strictly limited armament to serve in Algeria and the unoccupied Vichy zone of France. Many of the French officers and men eventually accepted the British offer to board French ships at Barry Docks for passage to Casablanca. They decided that for them the war was over.

[50]

Pierre de Vomécourt, however, decided that for him the war had only just begun.

The same evening de Vomécourt had left Cherbourg, another French officer had left Bordeaux for England. He was Major General Charles de Gaulle, undersecretary for National Defense in the fallen Reynaud cabinet. He had escaped by air and, as Churchill phrased it, "he carried with him, in that small aeroplane, the honour of France."

On the evening of his arrival in London, de Gaulle delivered his memorable broadcast to the French people: "France is not alone. She has a vast empire behind her. She can unite with the British Empire, which holds the seas, and continue the struggle!"

Within days General de Gaulle had formed the Free French Committee in London and installed himself with a handful of supporters at St. Stephen's House. Pierre de Vomécourt at once decided to offer his service to the leader of Free France. But access to the general's presence proved difficult, and when at last he succeeded in seeing de Gaulle the young officer was received coolly.

De Gaulle was at that time surrounded by a handful of general staff officers, products, like himself, of St. Cyr, the French West Point, and they were inclined to be somewhat disdainful toward a reserve officer educated in England, such as Pierre de Vomécourt.

When Captain de Vomécourt evolved a plan for clandestine resistance and sabotage actions in France and volunteered to return and organize them, de Gaulle told him that such activities would only provoke reprisals on the part of the Germans and thus create hostility against his own freedom movement among many Frenchmen. De Gaulle also told him that his National Committee had already installed a secret service department that was for the time being concerned only with collecting intelligence reports, work that had to be done by experts.

Sadly de Vomécourt turned to the British. But at the War Office his reception was even cooler. He was told there were no plans for sending secret agents and saboteurs to France. The only alternative open to him was enlisting as a private in the British army, with a prospect of having a commission awarded at a later date.

For some months de Vomécourt cooled his heels in London, until he learned of a secret organization established by the British just for the purpose that he had discussed with General de Gaulle. During his many abortive visits to the War Office he had been treated kindly by Lieutenant General Templer, who eventually gave him an introduction to Brigadier Gubbins, the newly appointed chief of operations of SOE.

That was how the French Captain Pierre de Vomécourt became Lucas, the first secret agent of SOE's F section.

A few steps across Baker Street from Norgeby House, the HQ of the Inter-Services Research Bureau, and St. Michael House, where the high brass of SOE was pitched on the upper floors between heaven and Marks & Spencer, were the offices of the French sections.

No. 64 Baker Street, or, to be exact, Nos. 62–64—although the door of No. 62 entrance was permanently locked—is no more. Those who have known that gray, five-story building, with its dark narrow hall, the briefing room, the map room and its benches and blackboards, and the wobbly lift hesitantly ascending to the small plainly furnished office rooms, will remember it with nostalgia.

The early history of the French section, or rather sections, was extremely checkered. The D department of SIS had a section concerned with France. Its outpost in Paris was headed by a professional intelligence officer, Major Leslie Humphreys, who had a narrow escape from Bordeaux late in June 1940. When SOE was created, he moved with Colonel Grand and other D officers to the new organization to establish its first French section, which became known as the DF section. Its initial tasks were to arrange escapes of British agents and officers stranded in France, to extract French VIPs ready to come to Britain, and to organize small-scale raiding parties against the Channel Islands and the French coast.

There were some eccentric enterprises, such as the landing of Gaullist volunteers (including a tough Breton, Marcel Clech, who later became one of SOE's most astute radio operators) from little boats on the Channel coast or sending a few *pétroleurs,* without defined orders, to blow up docks at Brest or Cherbourg. No attempt was made to make contact with Resistance groups that were springing up, and these heroic but picaresque actions went on into 1941, mere pinpricks, hardly noticed by the Germans. DF section developed in the course of time into a useful organization for arranging escape routes. One of its chief agents, Victor Gerson, and his friends established the first and for a long time most effective escape route. Later DF agents included Captain Ian Garrow, Virginia Hall, and the famous Pat, Dr. Albert Guérisse (better known as Lieutenant Commander Pat O'Leary).

While building up DF section, Humphreys began to organize a parallel F section, destined to set up regional circuits, establish radio posts, provide liaison with Resistance groups, and train saboteurs and fighters for future mass uprisings. This work proceeded extremely slowly. The main handicap was shortage of recruits. Training facilities were almost nonexistent. The men who had been put in charge had only a vague idea of what they were supposed to do. Other SOE sections, particularly the Scandinavian, which enjoyed Sir Charles Hambro's special interest, were soon in their stride.

De Gaulle's secret service had its first secret agent sent to France on 25 July 1940. In August he was followed by Maurice Duclos, who achieved fame as St. Jacques, and by the legendary Colonel Rémy, founder and chief of the great *réseau* CONFRÉRIE DE NOTRE-DAME. I consider Rémy the greatest secret agent of the war, and am proud to call him a friend. From Nancy to Bayonne, and particularly along the Channel coast, he established forty effective underground networks, or *réseaux;* he rendered unique and invaluable service to the Allies.

It was the Secret Intelligence Service, not SOE, that established the initial networks in France. The very first was set up by a few Polish officers and soon made contact with London. It was called INTERALLÉ (also known as FAMILLE) and it gave good service to the British until its lamentable destruction.[1] Subsequently the British intelligence controlled several other networks founded by French patriots, after a sort of gentleman's agreement had been concluded with de Gaulle's BCRA. They included ALLIANCE, MARIE MADELEINE, and GILBERT. Eventually Humphreys devoted all his energy to DF section. At F section he was succeeded by Major Harry Marriott, who had worked for Courtaulds in France before the war. His subordinates knew him by his initials, "H. M." It was under Marriott's command, in the spring of 1941, that Captain (later Lieutenant Colonel) Maurice Buckmaster, who became Marriott's successor, joined F section as its information officer.

When Buckmaster first visited Baker Street in March 1941 he wondered what his duties would be. He had been given no clue about his own tasks or those of the fledgling organization itself.

"The fact is, Buckmaster," the commanding officer told him, "everything is highly embryonic here."

The bare office and the deserted atmosphere of the place confirmed this gloomy observation. The man on the other side of the desk seemed rather dispirited. In fact, Marriott was soon to retire.

"The general idea," H. M. explained, "is to see what we can do about getting information about occupied France. We want to find out what's going on there, what sort of targets we should concentrate on attacking . . . when we're in a position to attack them."

To Buckmaster it seemed that the man was either being cryptic or rather vague.

"What sort of information is available?" he asked.

H. M. shrugged. "Very little. There's hardly anything to go on."

"What about secret service reports?" Buckmaster inquired.

"Oh, no, we don't get those. Can't get hold of them," replied the commanding officer.

Buckmaster's elation at his new job was fast disappearing. He tele-

[1] See chapter 4.

[53]

phoned a colonel in the intelligence department, using the scrambler, and asked him what the whole setup was about.

"Subversive activities," the colonel explained.

"I've gathered that, sir, but what kind of subversive activities?"

"I'm not too clear myself, but I think the idea is to sabotage industrial installations in France," the colonel said.

"This isn't a secret service affair then?" Buckmaster asked.

"Heavens no, old boy; Special Operations . . . !"

The colonel was probably annoyed that anybody should suggest that SOE had anything to do with secret service work.

Thus Maurice Buckmaster started work with F section.

In the bare office he sat staring into the out-tray. There was no in-tray, and it seemed to him that the best thing he could do was to try and remember what he could about French factories he had visited when working from 1932 to 1936 for the Ford Company in France. He drew up a pile of typing paper. Day after day, for three weeks, he dredged his brain, noting down everything he could about the potential, the staff, and the layout of French industry.

He remembered the *Bottin*. This is a series of fat volumes of reference directories, listing in great detail, and by department and town, all industrial and commercial enterprises of France. But there was no *Bottin* at Baker Street. No bookseller in wartime London had it in stock. Buckmaster turned to the War Office. It took several visits and many phone calls until, and only through General Templer's help, Buckmaster found a colonel who had a *Bottin* at his office. But Colonel Denvers had never heard of SOE and he was not prepared to lend the *Bottin* to Buckmaster.

"We're not allowed to release any of our secret material," he said firmly.

"Why should the *Bottin* be secret material?" Buckmaster asked in astonishment. "The Germans in France have got as many copies of it as they want. What's the point of keeping material from your own side that is freely available to the enemy?"

"Look, old man, that's not my worry," was the colonel's reply. "My instructions are not to let my copy of the *Bottin* out of my sight."

In the end, after a long interview, Colonel Denvers melted and allowed Buckmaster to see his precious *Bottin*. But there was no question of taking the volumes away.

"I can't have you working actually in the room with me, Buckmaster," the colonel said. "I've put you in the little office my secretary uses for keeping her coat."

In this cloakroom about the size of a wardrobe, the new information officer of the French section of SOE began laboriously to select the potential industrial targets to be sabotaged by intrepid secret agents who had not yet been recruited.

One night in May 1941, when he was night duty officer, Buckmaster had his first chance meeting with Sir Charles Hambro.

"What is our job, sir?" Buckmaster ventured. "I've never been told."

Sir Charles looked up and blinked mildly. "To set Europe ablaze," he said.

"I see, sir; but what's being done?"

"Well," Sir Charles said, "we're very much in the first stages still . . . we've got a small nucleus in training already, including about ten men preparing to get back into France and see what it's all about. I know it seems slow, but there would be little point in encouraging rashness on the part of the French. We don't want a lot of people shot and repressive measures taken by the Germans until the reasons for them are a sufficient compensation for the fall in French civil morale that would result. What we want is coordinated action, and coordination takes a long time. All the same, the sooner we get someone into France to take the temperature of the French, so to speak, the better we'll be able to plan future action."

"Has anyone gone yet?" Buckmaster asked.

"They're in training," Sir Charles Hambro replied.

"Good Lord," Buckmaster exclaimed. "It's nearly a year since we were chucked out of France . . . !"

"Now look here," said Sir Charles. "If SOE is to have any justification it must be as a military operation, properly planned with a definite object. We must build up an organization and have it ready for use when it's most needed."

That made sense, in fact Hambro was making an understatement. In May 1941 the first agents of the French section had reached France. They were Captain Pierre de Vomécourt, Commandant Georges Begué, and Roger Cottin.

Their dispatch was arranged by Marriott's deputy, Thomas Cadett, a former Paris correspondent of *The Times*.

Although Cadett's spell at the French section was brief—he left SOE in September to join BBC—the dispatch of the first agents of SOE to France goes to his credit. Cadett did not hesitate to infringe on the order that only British and Commonwealth citizens must be employed. Both Begué and de Vomécourt were, of course, French, but he could not have found better and braver men.

Buckmaster Section

In July 1941 Sir Charles Hambro asked Buckmaster to temporarily take over command of the Belgian section. Two months later Sir Charles, obviously impressed by his inquiring mind and impatience for action, asked Buckmaster to return to F section as its commanding officer.

For almost four years Maurice Buckmaster held the reins of F section, which became the largest and most important of SOE. Under his command 480 men and women were dispatched to France, by parachute, Lysander aircraft, submarines, and small fishing boats. That mistakes and errors of judgment were made at Baker Street, no one will deny. But to emphasize only failures and conceal great accomplishments is not the way a dispassionate and unprejudiced observer should report. Several years after the war Colonel Buckmaster was attacked by a writer who admitted she had never even heard of the existence of SOE until five years after the end of the war, when she began research for a book.

I hold no brief for Colonel Buckmaster and his assistants, but I know of their work during four war years, under almost superhuman difficulties. To attacks against himself by writers whose books of exposés sold very well, Colonel Buckmaster replied in a dignified manner, not because he wanted to defend himself, but because he rightly felt that the unsubstantiated accusations (many emanating from either anonymous Germans or convicted war criminals) "were efforts to discredit the achievements of the agents who worked for the French section of SOE and the officers in London responsible for the conduct of operations." He reluctantly replied to the attacks on himself and his comrades, because, as he said, he would have preferred to have left the dead to sleep in peace and to have allowed the results of their bravery to speak for themselves.

Maurice Buckmaster is certainly not the kind of man, as accusers implied, who would deliberately send comrades into the hands of the Gestapo. Shortly before this book was completed I attended the celebrations of the 20th anniversary of D day, together with several friends who had served under Buckmaster and had been parachuted into France, each on at least two missions. In Paris and Normandy we had reunions with hundreds of old comrades of the Resistance and the maquis. Reminiscences were naturally voiced, and, without exception, every former agent recalled the personal kindness Colonel Buckmaster had shown. One told me that at the airfield, mere minutes before takeoff, Buckmaster again asked if he was quite decided to go, and averred that it would not be held against him if he wished to change his mind at the last moment.

Perhaps Buckmaster was too gentle and fair-minded, not tough enough for a job that required the ruthlessness a general must exercise in battle when he decides to sacrifice three central battalions to secure a strategic advance on one flank. Perhaps, as Pierre de Vomécourt said after the war, he was not the ideal man for the job, because he had to combat the stubborn prejudices of military minds steeped in conventional concepts of obsolete warfare—and, perhaps, he was not quite successful in this. In conducting my research for this book I spoke to many former agents of F section. I am confident that the 375 survivors who served under Colonel Buckmaster respect him and with very few exceptions, admire and like him.

When Buckmaster took over, his staff at Baker Street numbered eight. During the following year it increased to twenty-four, but his assistants were not mere pen-pushers. Nearly all of them had been in the field in France at least once, and some had been severely wounded or had suffered privation in Vichy or Gestapo prisons.

Of the men who worked with Buckmaster I can mention only a few. There was his chief recruiting officer, Captain (later Lieutenant Colonel) Lewis Gielgud, brother of John, the actor. Another recruiting officer was Captain Selwyn Jepson, a well-known author of thrillers with such captivating titles as *I Met Murder* and *Keep Murder Quiet,* and of many films, such as *The Riverside Murders* and *The Scarab Murder,* all prewar box office hits. There was Nicholas Bodington, former Paris correspondent of the *Daily Express,* who was twice dropped into France when matters had become dangerously chaotic and many networks had been destroyed by the Germans. Lieutenant Colonel R. A. Bourne-Paterson, a Scottish chartered accountant in civilian life, was the planning officer; he knew the topography of France so well he could point to a village on a Michelin map without looking twice. Major Jacques de Guélis, the briefing officer, made three missions to France, and Major Gerard Morel, who plotted operations for agents in the field, twice went into the field himself.

Discord with de Gaulle

Buckmaster and his officers at Baker Street had the unenviable task of recruiting agents against the constant opposition of the Free French National Committee and its secret service. For two years they were desperately short of suitable recruits. Not only was the supply short, its pipeline was often choked by the interference of other departments. In theory Buckmaster and his recruiting officers had to find men who were not French citizens. General de Gaulle had insisted, and had received Churchill's assurance, that French men and women who arrived in Britain from abroad, whether as refugees from France, or from a French colony, or from any other country, were barred from joining SOE. In practice—at least during the initial period—quite a few French citizens volunteered to join SOE instead of Colonel Passy's BCRA. One French citizen, Maurice Dufour, suffered terribly at the hands of his countrymen for daring to volunteer for SOE.

Dufour, a former French officer who had arrived in London in 1942 after having worked for a Resistance group in southern France, was waiting to be accepted into SOE when he was invited on some pretext to visit the head-

[57]

quarters of Colonel Passy's BCRA at 10 Duke Street. What happened there has never been fully disclosed, but I can quote the following passages from Dufour's statement to Scotland Yard on 6 August 1942, when he took out a summons for assault and battery against Colonel Passy and his two deputies, Captain Wybot and Captain Girard:

At 10:30 P.M., after I have been taken by force to the basement, I was ordered to take off my shirt and vest. I obeyed. Then Captain Wybot (whose real name is Captain Roger Wavrin) and Captain Girard hit me with their fists several times in my face and body. They also beat me with a leather-covered steel rod on the small of my back, taking care to hit me on the spot of my wound which I sustained in France, which caused me extreme pain.

They threatened to kill me and also threatened to kidnap and rape a young girl [Andrée Borrel], the daughter of one of my friends, who had come with me from France and was now serving with the FANY at the SOE office in Baker Street. They told me: "We have arrested Mademoiselle Borrel [2] and we shall make her talk using every means, even if we have to rape her one after another." They asked me what orders I have received from SOE and they beat and tortured me until 3 A.M.

I was then put into a small room, like a cell, in the basement of 10 Duke Street, and kept there from May 19th until May 29th. Because of the beating, which was repeated almost every night, I was unable to lie down, neither could I stand, and spent many days and nights crouching and whimpering.

What was Dufour's crime for which his Gaullist compatriots meted out punishment worthy of Gestapo thugs? It was nothing more than his desire to join SOE instead of Colonel Passy's French secret service. The chiefs at Baker Street learned belatedly of his kidnapping, and it required the personal intervention of Winston Churchill—who was told about the incident by Lord Selborne, the minister of economic warfare—with General de Gaulle before Dufour was freed.

The Prime Minister sent de Gaulle a stern official note, stating that the British authorities would not tolerate torture chambers in London. The scandal was hushed up, Dufour was persuaded to withdraw his summons against the chiefs of de Gaulle's secret service, and (it has been said) was paid a substantial sum as compensation by the Free French authorities. He enlisted in the Royal Canadian Air Force and became an airman.

SOE also recruited a considerable number of French-speaking Canadians, a few South Africans, Britons who had lived in French colonies, inhabitants of the British colonies of Mauritius (from this little island more than a dozen were enlisted) and the Seychelles, where French is spoken, and a few men of nondescript nationality who had lived in Indochina or North Africa. Finally, when SOE and OSS were integrated under SHAEF, a num-

[2] This was untrue.

ber of French-speaking Americans joined F section, and an American officer, Major Huot, worked at the office.

On the whole, however, F section depended on Britons who were bilingual and knew France. Recruitment at first was conducted on a rather haphazard basis. The War Office was not very helpful, although it did supply lists of officers and other ranks whose knowledge of French, on paper at least, justified an interview. Commanding officers of various army units were asked to recommend men who knew French. Schoolboy French was not sufficient and many of the French-speaking Canadians had never been in France and had only the vaguest idea of the atmosphere of the country and the ways of her people. Although many doubtful recruits proved themselves in the field, their enlistment constituted a great risk.

Some sources closer at hand were fully used: Britons, of one French parent, for instance, who spoke both languages effortlessly; others who had spent their childhood or their working lives in France. Major Roger Landes, who led the SOE network in southwest France for almost three years, was born in Paris of English parents. When he joined up in 1941 as a private in the Royal Signal Corps, he became the mascot of his unit— the only soldier who could not speak proper English. Captain Cyril Watney, born in Calais, where his father had been the president of the French Lace Manufacturers' Association, had learned English only at the age of twelve. Such men volunteered in various ways; quite a few of them, serving officers or soldiers, heard rumors of a secret organization wanting people who could be sent to France. Craving something more exciting than drilling and polishing brass, they sought that organization. Sergeant (later Captain) Harry Rée applied four times before he was summoned for an interview.

General de Gaulle and his secret service men at Duke Street watched the efforts of the French section with a jaundiced eye. The fact that a British secret organization was recruiting, training, and sending agents to France, and setting up networks there, under British control and with the cooperation of French Resistance members, deeply offended the Free French in London. De Gaulle told Churchill that the presence of these British agents in France, no matter what their individual merits and achievements, "infringed on the sovereignty of France." Moreover the Gaullists in London, who were sending their own agents and setting up networks much earlier and more efficiently than SOE during the first two years, found it galling to be left in complete ignorance of British SOE agents in France.

Some shocking incidents in France precipitated the already poisoned relations between de Gaulle's headquarters and Baker Street. On one occasion Gaullists occupied dropping grounds in the Gironde, which had been prepared by SOE agents, and insisted on encroaching the containers dropped from SOE aircraft. Sometimes fistfights ensued between Resistance men (belonging to a *réseau* under control of de Gaulle's secret service) and SOE men over dropped arms and ammunition. Fortunately such incidents were rare. Later the comradeship between Gaullist and SOE men in the field was established and many different *réseaux* cooperated harmoniously.

During early stages SOE officers found that dropping grounds that they had scouted and reported to Baker Street, and which were consequently incorporated on the operational maps, became subject of dispute because the Gaullist headquarters in London considered that they had a right to them. There was also constant rivalry in regard to the supply of aircraft and armament. But it must be said that the de Gaulle secret service was treated by British authorities in charge of the supplies like poor relations to be satisfied with crumbs from the table. Alas, the table was not richly provided for the French section either. Buckmaster battled incessantly for more aircraft and material to supply his own networks.

The French in London, not unnaturally, saw it all in a very different light. As General de Gaulle recalls in his memoirs: "The British would have liked us to simply send over agents with instructions to gather, in isolation, information about the enemy." This information the French were supposed to deliver to the British intelligence. The general had, of course, other ideas about the role his agents should play.

Since the action in France would be carried on in the midst of a population which would be teeming with [Gaullist] well-wishers, we meant to set up networks. By binding together handpicked elements and communicating with us through centralized means, these would give us the best return.

Our action was to grow wider and to include the armed groups within the country and the resistance movements with their multiple activities.[3]

It was quite natural and legitimate for the general to aim in a political direction. To him the secret networks of BCRA, the Resistance movements, and the maquis were instruments for restoring France's freedom and sovereignty under his leadership. At that time neither the British nor—even more definitely—the United States government was prepared to recognize de Gaulle as the sole and unchallenged leader of Free France. In any case, SOE and its French section were in no way involved in the complex political maneuvers and intrigues. They were exclusively concerned with carrying out their tasks of harassing the enemy by carefully planned sabotage and by preparing the training and arming of units, which were to fight in the open when Allied invasion came.

General de Gaulle forbade his secret service officers to have any truck

[3] General de Gaulle, *Mémoires de guerre*, Vol. *L'Appel*, Librairie Plon, Paris, 1953–56.

with the French section. Strangely enough, relations between the French and SIS and Military Intelligence were almost cordial by comparison.

RF Section

In an attempt to establish some sort of coexistence with the Free French National Committee and its secret service in London, the chiefs of the Western directorate of SOE decided to set up a separate section to maintain direct liaison with Colonel Passy, This section was incepted in the early summer of 1941, mainly through the efforts of Colonel Harry Sporborg and Sir Claude Dansey, and named French section, RF. Its first commanding officer was Captain Eric Piquet-Wicks, of the Royal Inniskilling Fusiliers who was half-French, had lived and studied in France, and had fought during the campaign in Norway beside French Chasseurs Alpins. The RF section had hardly any contact with the Buckmaster section; indeed, it was not supposed to. Housed in a smallish terrace house at 1 Dorset Square, Marylebone, it was just across the road from Baker Street. This had been the office of Bertram Mills' Circus, which had been closed down for the duration.

Until September 1939, lion tamers, trapeze artists, jugglers, and clowns used the little door. After the war Queen Elizabeth, the Queen Mother, unveiled a little plaque on the wall of the building. Under a Cross of Lorraine is the following inscription:

THIS PLAQUE IS ERECTED TO COMMEMORATE
THE DEEDS OF MEN AND WOMEN OF THE
FREE FRENCH FORCES
AND THEIR BRITISH COMRADES
WHO LEFT FROM THIS HOUSE ON SPECIAL MISSIONS
TO ENEMY-OCCUPIED FRANCE
AND TO HONOUR THOSE WHO DID NOT RETURN
1941–1944

These simple words, evincing the real comradeship between French and British men and women, contain a better epitaph than any account of the activities of the RF section I could possibly offer. At first Captain Piquet-Wicks became the buffer for numerous complaints, often substantial, that flowed from Colonel Passy's office. Nevertheless, despite many thunderstorms, the RF section managed to cooperate with Passy and particularly with his deputy, Captain Raymond Lagier (Bienvenue), who had become head of the *départment d'action* of BCRA. The British and French officers slowly created an atmosphere of mutual respect and confidence, so different from the haze of suspicion and antagonism that seemed to hold sway in the higher strata of Anglo–French relations.

The RF section, which was exclusively concerned with the activities of Gaullist agents and *réseaux,* had one or two problems that were similar to those of Colonel Buckmaster and his officers.

One of Passy's continual and justified complaints was that recruiting officers of the French sections were allowed to see Frenchmen passing through the Patriotic School, whereas the Free French were not allowed similar access. Passy accused the French sections of filching Frenchmen on the pretext that they would serve de Gaulle, and enrolling them in SOE. This had been firmly denied by officers of the F section; but Captain Piquet-Wicks said that it did happen that a few officers of the RF section in the field, canvassing the support of local Resistance men, had used de Gaulle's name.

Piquet-Wicks did all the spade work when he started the RF section under most difficult conditions. Until the autumn of 1942 he was responsible for the liaison with BCRA, and for all arrangements for parachuting arms and equipment to Gaullist *réseaux* and the dispatch of Passy's agents.

How difficult his task was, in view of the French attitude, can be judged from the fact that the British controlled all the material means—aircraft for parachuting or pickup operations, sea operations, wireless communications, provision of containers, arms, ammunition, sabotage material, and money. All this was outside Free French control. The British also insisted that a common code should be used for all radio transmissions on military and technical subjects, so that de Gaulle's secret service could not communicate with its own agents without the British knowing, if they wished, of all such communications.

Only much later, after Piquet-Wicks had left SOE and was replaced by Colonel James Hutchison as head of the RF section, did the Free French gain many concessions from the British government, enabling them to operate their secret service and *réseaux* in France almost entirely independently.

The Making of a Frenchman

Though it was understandable that the Free French National Committee and its BCRA wished to secure the services of their compatriots for their own use, this put the French section into a difficult position. Other SOE sections relied almost exclusively upon nationals of the countries in question; Buckmaster had to produce Frenchmen of his own making.

The complex task of devising and supervising the transformation of John Smith into Jacques Dupont was meticulously and brilliantly executed by Vera Atkins, a WAAF squadron officer, who had joined F section soon after Buckmaster assumed command. She was Buckmaster's intelligence officer, a designation covering a multitude of duties. This young and highly intelligent woman has been described by some as cool, extremely competent, and analytical, by others as the real brain of the French section. To this it may be added that she was also the heart of the section.

She collected every scrap of current information about life in wartime France. In her orderly mind she stored an encyclopedic knowledge of all regulations concerning work, travel, curfew, food rationing, police registration, and so on. The forged documents were supplied by SOE secret laboratories, but Vera always managed to add a few most useful credentials: some "family" photographs, old visiting cards, a letter from a friend or an old flame—things a man might carry in his wallet and which would enhance his imaginary identity when his pockets were searched. She produced these items from her own private and mysterious sources, along with French tailors' tabs, Metro tickets, French matches, and other theatrical props.

But above all, she was a perpetual fount of information, which she presented "with a smile as remote, as it was seraphic." Vera Atkins participated in the agents' briefing sessions on the last day or two before dispatch. Every agent had his or her conducting officer who kept a fatherly eye on the candidate during the training, and usually spent the last few days with the fledgling agent at the finishing school and the holding camp. In addition to her many other duties, Vera Atkins also fulfilled such assignments.

How did the would-be agent behave at the dinner table? Did he, as would a Frenchman, wipe the gravy with a piece of bread and eat it with gusto, or did he, in proper English manner, leave a few *petits pois* on the plate and carefully align his knife and fork at "half-past six"? Of course most of the students had some experience of French manners, but refreshers had to be offered in such realms as French cuisine and wines. On occasion the conducting officers would take their wards to Soho restaurants; a favorite was the Coquille, where even the wartime French cuisine reminded them how to behave like Frenchmen.

Final briefing sessions were held at Buckmaster's private apartment at Orchard Court in Portman Square. This was not his home but a small flat provided by SOE for this special purpose. The few modestly but tastefully furnished rooms had a convivial atmosphere that soothed agents on the eve of perilous journeys. Here Colonel Buckmaster and his top assistants talked with the agents, not as their superior officers, but as friends proffering last bits of advice.

This apartment at Orchard Court contained two features especially memorable to all visiting SOE agents: a butler named Park and a black-tiled bathroom, complete with an onyx bidet.

Park had been a bank messenger in the Paris branch of the Westminster Bank, and he had a prodigious memory. He knew every agent by his pseudonym and made each one personally welcome on arrival. His cheerful countenance was beloved by all. His tact averted many awkward meetings between men who were not supposed to see each other. Buckmaster discouraged agents from meeting each other in the field, and the best way to do that was to avoid possible encounters in England. Park would spirit people from room to room.

"Of course people did meet each other," Buckmaster recalls, "and we were not silly about forbidding it—our agents were far too intelligent to need petty regulations of that kind—but there was one thing which was absolutely against order—that was to tell anyone where one was going. There was particular danger of this when two agents met in the apartment and knew that they were due to be sent off at the same time."

This was an important security precaution that worked well in practice. Even agents who were dropped by parachute from the same aircraft, or landed from a Lysander or a boat, did not know each other's ultimate destination. If one of them was unlucky enough to be caught, he could not, even under torture, reveal the whereabouts of the man at large.

One of the most popular conducting officers was André Simon, a well-known wine merchant and gourmet and himself a veteran agent. Those tense trips to Soho restaurants, made easier by comforting and illuminating anecdotes about life in France, were just his *métier*. Of course it was not mere frivolity. The conducting officer, who had been largely responsible for the supervision of the training of the agent and had to compile the final report on his accomplishments, escorted him to the airfield and stayed with him until the very moment he boarded the aircraft.

He made the final check of the agent's equipment, even went through his pockets for British cigarettes, money, or a forgotten bus ticket. And his final duty was to give the agent the tiny poison pill, his own personal emotion concealed by a casual "Well, old boy, I'm sure you won't ever have to use it." Colonel Buckmaster, whenever his time allowed, accompanied his agents to the airfield. He often gave them a personal memento, a pair of cuff links or a cigarette case.

But the meticulous care with which the section officers had arranged his training, supervised his progress, briefed him for his mission, was not at an end. Indeed, once the radio link had been established, a flow of instructions and advice emanated from Baker Street to the man or woman in the field.

Of course, mistakes were made at Baker Street, some with terrible results, as when signals were sent to radio posts infiltrated by the Germans, leading to the capture of agents. None of these incidents have been omitted from this book. But one must realize that SOE was continually faced with such risks.

Vera Atkins played a prominent part in maintaining contact with agents in the field. At the height of the activity, signals from the radio posts in France were handled by a large team of FANYs at the W/T station near Sevenoaks. The coded messages usually were brought by dispatch riders to Baker Street. There they were decoded, with Vera Atkins checking every incoming and outgoing message. Often signals arrived badly scrambled and even hopelessly undecipherable. But even if the decoding officers threw up their hands in despair, Vera Atkins, applying her razor-sharp intellect and knowledge of agents and operators and their personal foibles, would try again and usually succeed in making sense of a fragmentary or seemingly incomprehensible signal.

For instance, what did this mean: HAVE PREPARED UNION WITH FERMNAN? The name could be ascertained quickly as that of an agent with the code name Fernand. But the agent Armand, who sent the signal, was under no circumstances supposed to arrange a meeting with Fernand. Vera Atkins soon found out that UNION should read ONION and that it was the code name for a dropping zone, which Armand had prepared, a fact that the decoding officer knew nothing about. That one was easy. But what could be gleaned from a signal that read:

IMI THRMY SAYG ABLE TAKE TWHGVE CONTTT?S G??U?D AFFLY BBBR
MASSAGE MIEUW TORT KUE ???IIS

And this was the text after careful decoding. The question marks denoted letters the FANY signaler at the reception station had been unable to take down, apparently because of atmospheric interference.

After nerve-racking toil, Vera triumphantly produced a signal that made sense:

IMI TOMMY SAYS ABLE TAKE TWELVE CONTAINERS GROUND APPLE
B B C MESSAGE MIEUX TARD QUE JAMAIS[4]

The last four words in French indicated the phrase which the agent suggested should be broadcast on the BBC French program among the daily personal messages. When this prearranged phrase was actually broadcast, it meant that Baker Street had approved the operation and that an aircraft was on the way to drop the containers and a reception had to be arranged that night.

Voici quelques Messages Personnels

Wartime listeners of the numerous BBC French programs were puzzled by seemingly idiotic phrases announced at dictating speed and often repeated four or five times at every broadcast or even for two consecutive days. To listeners at home they were nonsense, but to a solitary agent in a

[4] Better late than never.

village in the Massif Central, or a group of railwaymen huddled together on a frosty night in a darkened backroom at St. Quentin, the phrases "Josephine wears a blue dress," "Uncle Jacques has lost his umbrella," or "The cow will jump over the moon tonight," were sometimes matters of life and death.

Although listening to BBC broadcasts was forbidden by the Germans, under threat of severe punishment, innumerable Frenchmen hid radios, listened regularly, and wrote down the news bulletins and talks. These were printed in hundreds of clandestine journals and broadsheets.

SOE agents and Resistance leaders always tried to listen to the programs, in France or any enemy-occupied country, because the system of personal messages had been adopted on overseas programs to Norway, Holland, Denmark, Belgium, and many other countries. If occupied with something that could not wait, the SOE agents entrusted some friend to listen and take down all the messages. It was always possible that one of the messages would be directed to the particular agent or members of his circuit and might inform him of an impending drop of material or the cancellation of an operation.

Vera Atkins introduced a special sideline to the official system of personal messages. From time to time she used this means to inform an agent about his home life and family. Such messages had to be prearranged either before the agent left or by preceding radio signals. Some of the agents' wives were expecting when their husbands had to leave; most agents had close relatives serving in the armed forces. When Vera Atkins received news from an agent's family (the relatives were, of course, never told of the agent's whereabouts) she would relay it by means of a personal message. Thus Vera preserved the sanity of many SOE men often cut off from home and families for a year or more. Not for nothing did men in the field call Vera Atkins their guardian angel.

Of course such private personal messages were exceptions. The BBC system was almost exclusively used for business, and although it operated, in only one direction, it was vital. In the spring of 1944, for example, all radio posts were warned to stand by at least twice a month, on the 1st and 15th at 7:30 and 9:15 P.M. Then, when D day approached, SOE operators in France were alerted. During the night of 5 June, in addition to some five hundred radio signals sent to more than fifty SOE operators, a stream of "personal messages," all of course prearranged phrases, gave the call for action. This triggered an epidemic of explosions, attacks on railway junctions, dectruction of telecommunications, and assorted sabotage operations throughout France, Holland, and Belgium.

However, in 1941 and 1942 the French section was still at its heroic stage: only a handful of agents in the field, poor communications, sometimes none whatsoever, battling an enemy who seemed to hold all the trump cards.

[66]

The first agent of F section to be parachuted into France was Georges Begué, alias George Noble, who was dropped with his large and rather inefficient transmitter in the Dordogne on 5 May 1941. He proceeded to the region of Châteauroux where he was to go to an address given him in London—the house of Max Hymans, former Socialist member of the Chamber of Deputies for the Indre constituency. On 10 May Pierre de Vomécourt and on 13 May Roger Cottin were dropped, also "blind," not far from Châteauroux. If all went well, Pierre was to visit his brother Philippe, who lived on his estate at Brignac, near Limoges. Cottin was to go to Paris, where he had worked before the war, and Pierre was to join him in Paris. Then, with the "pianist" Begué they would set up the first radio post and try to establish the first *réseau.*

The F agents had been preceded by several sent by BCRA and DF section, including a party of five French officers and NCOs led by Captain Bergé, who were dropped on 15 March in Brittany. Among them was Joel Letac, who subsequently established the important RF circuit OVERCLOUD.

Roger Cottin was a big, sturdy man nicknamed "Roger les cheveux blancs" because of his prematurely white hair. He was born in France of British parents and had traveled the world as the representative of a famous Paris perfume firm. Like Pierre de Vomécourt, he had escaped from France to England in 1940, with one of the last units of the BEF, after Dunkirk.

Pierre de Vomécourt reached his brother's house safely. He learned with relief that his wife and children, whom he had left behind almost a year ago, were well and living in his Paris apartment. His brother Philippe immediately offered to work with him for SOE and told him that their eldest brother, Jean, the RAF pilot of the First World War, would also join them. Within a few days the three brothers and two of Philippe's friends, the Marquis de Moustier and Henri Sevenet, began to organize the first SOE network, AUTOGIRO.

They decided that their first meeting with Begué and Cottin should be in Châteauroux rather than in Paris, and the two SOE officers came south. They all agreed that Jean de Vomécourt should operate a *réseau* at Pontarlier in the German-occupied zone, where he had an estate; Philippe would stay in the unoccupied Vichy zone, building up his network based in Limoges, where he could count on many local helpers. Pierre, Roger Cottin, and George One [5] (Begué) would go to Paris, where Pierre could use his house near the Bois de Boulogne as a temporary foothold.

Thus the original SOE networks were set up in France in the early sum-

---

[5] Subsequent radio operators were referred to by the code name George (or Georges) with an appropriate number.

mer of 1941. They consisted of the three brothers de Vomécourt, Georges Begué, and Roger Cottin, helped by several friends of the de Vomécourts. The very first signals that George One sent to London asked for "stuff," so that they could begin serious business. It was agreed that the moon period in June should be used for the first drop of containers, and that Philippe would mark the dropping grounds in a field about a quarter of a mile from his château, Bas Soleil.

Four times Baker Street signaled that an aircraft had left, but for two nights Philippe and four helpers waited in vain. On the third night they saw a plane circle overhead and return. At last, on the fourth night, when the small reception committee had diminished to two—Philippe and Gabie, a young man from the Lorraine—the flight succeeded. Two containers were dropped, but one fell outside the marked ground, more than a mile away into a chestnut wood near the hamlet of Chabeau. The two men dragged the heavy loads across a stream, up a steep hill, and over six fences to the house. They hid the buckets in the cellar and covered them with straw and apples. This, as far as I know, was the first drop of SOE material into France.

Early in the morning Philippe de Vomécourt went into the village. He was soon surrounded by excited peasants. They had heard aircraft circling during the night, not one but two . . . no, three . . . five . . . six! Anxiously they asked him if the British would bomb the locality. He drove to the gendarmerie post at St. Léonard-de-Noblat and reported that he, too, saw planes flying during the night over the district and that he believed that men had been dropped by parachute.

"You'd better come and investigate," he told the gendarmes.

They visited the estate, plodded over the fields, and found nothing. They left satisfied that it was just gossip.

The ruse had been successful, and Philippe and his friends could now unpack the containers. They looked at the few tommy guns, revolvers, knives, and packets with explosives, as children look at gaily wrapped presents under a Christmas tree.

For the next few weeks the activities of the little band of SOE men developed quickly and satisfactorily. In August Major Jacques de Guélis, Buckmaster's briefing officer, came from London to see for himself how things were going. He met the first agents of F section at Châteauroux, and told them that many more agents would soon arrive and that the supplies of arms, explosives, and money would be stepped up.

During the night of 6 September six agents were dropped from a Whitley bomber near Argenton-sur-Creuse. They were Ben Cowburn (Benoit); Michel Trotobas (Sylvestre); Victor Gerson (Vic), who later was to accomplish five other dangerous missions; George Langelaan; Comte Maurice du Puy; and André Bloch (Draftsman), their "pianist."

They were received by Begué, Hymans, and Octave Chantraine,[6] the mayor of Tendu, who provided their first safe house. Cowburn was an oil mining engineer, thirty-three years old, born at Leigh in Lancashire, who had spent many years in France.

Cowburn, or Benoit as he now was, went to Paris where he met Pierre de Vomécourt and Roger Cottin in a small office the two had rented in the building of the Lido nightclub on the Champs Elysées. Pierre, believing it wiser to leave his own home, shared a small apartment with Roger; Cowburn took a studio at Neuilly. They found a safe house for André Bloch's radio post but later decided there would be less risk if he were to work outside Paris, and the George IX station was set up in the house of a Resistance friend at Le Mans. For several weeks the radio link with Baker Street functioned satisfactorily, and the SOE agents sent encouraging reports about their work.

They traveled to many French districts. Pierre set up several *réseaux* in the north, while his brother Jean was in Besançon organizing networks in the Franche-Comté and arranging an escape route for British pilots to Switzerland. Cowburn traveled south and recruited helpers as far as Montauban and Toulouse.

Langelaan's orders were to find Édouard Herriot, former premier of France, and persuade him to come to Britain—another attempt at replacing de Gaulle—but Herriot refused. Langelaan was caught a month later by the Vichy police.

Two more teams arrived on 19 September and 10 October. The first, by sea, disembarked north of Perpignan from the *Fidelity*. It consisted of a French merchant sailor, Robert Leroy (who after sabotage work at Bordeaux docks returned five months later to England), Raymond Roche (destined for Marseilles), Georges Dubourdin, and Francis Basin. The second party was parachuted in the Dordogne, north of Bergerac, and received by Pierre Bloch, a former Socialist deputy recruited by de Guélis. Code-named CORSICA, its members were Jack Hayes, Claude Jumeau (who on his second mission was to die from wounds incurred on landing), Jean Le Harivel, a radio operator, and Denis Turberville, who landed a mile away from his comrades, lost contact, and was picked up by Vichy gendarmes the next day. Baker Street had given the CORSICA team and several agents already in the field the address of Christophe (Georges Turck, a French architect who had been dropped with de Guélis) at the Villa des Bois in Marseilles as a safe house. Turberville carried a note with this address when he was arrested, and Vichy police were waiting there when the three others arrived.

[6] Chantraine rendered great service to the SOE for more than three years. In 1944 he was finally caught and put to death.

One by one the agents were trapped at the villa—Robert Lyon, Pierre Bloch, and finally, on 24 October, Georges Begué. The debacle was complete when radio operator André Bloch and Michel Trotobas also were arrested—Bloch at Le Mans and Trotobas at Châteauroux. Despite torture André Bloch kept silent and was shot a few weeks later.

With the capture of Begué and André Bloch the radio link was gone and all SOE agents were cut off from Baker Street.

Of the score of agents in France, most were now in various prisons, soon to be reunited at the Vichy concentration camp of Mauzac on the Dordogne. They stayed there until July 1942, when they managed an extraordinary escape made possible by smuggling duplicate keys to the prisoners. Two women played a remarkable role in this daring feat: Madame Bloch, the wife of the French deputy, and Virginia Hall.

Miss Hall, later famous as Marie of Lyon, had worked for D department early in the war. An American citizen and correspondent of the New York *Post,* she was a woman of great intelligence and energy, not at all handicapped by an artificial leg, which she affectionaly called "Cuthbert." She arrived in the Vichy zone in August 1941, from Madrid, quite legitimately as an accredited American newspaper correspondent to the Pétain regime, and immediately became immersed in SOE work. She looked after Turck at Marseilles, introduced Langelaan to Herriot at Lyons, was in regular contact with Philippe de Vomécourt, Ben Cowburn, and the agents in the south, such as Robert Lyon and Philippe Liewer. For many months she guided, rescued, and hid agents, provided them with money and radio transmitters, arranged escape routes, and remained a vital communication link with Baker Street. She will appear again.

In Paris, Pierre de Vomécourt and Roger Cottin tried desperately to convey a message to London, urging the dispatch of another radio operator. For many weeks their efforts were fruitless. Then Pierre heard from Michel Brault, a distinguished lawyer who had become a Resistance leader soon after the fall of France, of the existence of a group of former Polish intelligence officers. Maître Brault told him they had set up several radio posts and were in regular contact with British intelligence in London.

Eagerly but cautiously, Pierre de Vomécourt, giving only his code name Lucas, contacted the woman Maître Brault said was one of the leaders of the Polish network. Her real name was Mathilde Carré; her friends called her Lily or sometimes *la petite chatte,* the little cat.

A most pressing problem to the stranded SOE men was money. They were all broke. When Ben Cowburn had left England he had been given only 26,000 francs, worth about $500 and this for a stay of indefinite length. Pierre de Vomécourt and Roger Cottin had brought not much more; and all their work had been financed since May mainly from the pockets of the brothers de Vomécourt. When Lucas first met the Cat he told her of his troubles and asked her to transmit a message to London asking for money. He did so to learn if the new contact was reliable. Two days later the woman came back and told him that an agent of British intelligence was ordered to give him a sum of money at Vichy. Lucas went to Vichy, met the man, and was handed the sum.

When the first messages reached Baker Street, Buckmaster and his officers were jubilant. At last they had good news! Although the two radio operators had been caught, the three chief agents were safe and well.

The messages had come to Baker Street via British Military Intelligence. Neither Buckmaster nor MI suspected that the messages had been transmitted from a German-controlled radio post and cunningly fabricated by officers of the German Abwehr.

4

The Bedraggled Cat

AFTER the fall of France in June 1940 British secret service relied almost entirely upon reports from agents in Switzerland and Spain, until contact was established with some officers of the former deuxième bureau, who now worked at Vichy. Luckily, late in 1940 help came from an unexpected source.

Within weeks of the armistice in France a handful of Polish officers, who had missed the evacuation of the Polish army units, established intelligence cells in several French cities. Two of the chiefs of these Franco–Polish organizations were Colonel Vincent Zarembski, a former general staff officer to General Sikorski, the Polish commander in chief in France in 1940 (later the head of the Polish exile government in London), and my friend Captain (later Wing Commander) Roman Czerniawski.

A young intelligence officer in the Polish air force, Czerniawski escaped from Poland in November 1939. Disguised as a peasant, he made his way through Rumania, Yugoslavia, and Italy to France, where he joined the Polish army. With the Polish First Division he was fighting in Alsace when Marshal Pétain signed France's surrender.

Colonel Zarembski set up his first cell at Toulouse. His organization, TUDOR, established a regular radio link with London.

When the front collapsed in Alsace, Roman Czerniawski decided to dive under. A young French widow, Renée Borni, with whom he had been billeted at Lunéville before his division moved into action, gave him shelter and some of her late husband's clothes and, most important of all, his birth certificate and documents. Thus Czerniawski, almost the same age as the dead man and speaking fluent French, overnight became Armand Borni. After many adventures he reached Toulouse and Colonel Zarembski. Soon to TUDOR's secret network, which had spread to Marseilles, Clermont-Ferrand, Lyons, Limoges, and even Vichy, another important cell was added: Czerniawski, alias Armand, set up his headquarters in Paris. From this cell grew the INTERALLIÉ network. Its history is one of courage and tragedy, and it is closely connected with the events in which Pierre de Vomécourt, Roger Cottin, and Ben Cowburn became deeply involved.

Czerniawski—or Armand, as I shall call him hereafter—had met by chance, in a café at Toulouse, a young French woman, Mathilde Carré. She came from a military family and her father had won the Legion of Honor in the First World War. She had been working with the Red Cross, expressed her hatred of the Germans, and appeared to be trustworthy. Armand enrolled her in his organization. Mathilde Carré, who was called Lily, soon became his most dependable and enthusiastic helper. They set up their first clandestine headquarters in a top-floor studio on the rue du Faubourg St. Jacques in Paris. Their work for London began on 16 November 1940, and the first radio post started transmitting soon after Christmas. Several Polish officers made up the staff, helped by a number of French patriots, including René Aubertin, a former captain in a tank regiment; George Bourcier, a pilot; Lucien de Roquigny, a journalist; and Charles Lejeune, an inspector of the Paris police who provided the members with false documents.

In due course INTERALLIÉ grew into a mighty network with circuits in fourteen sectors covering the whole of German-occupied France. Armand's agents at Brest, Cherbourg, Calais, and Boulogne kept the Channel ports and German naval installations under constant observation. Other agents at Bordeaux, Biarritz, and Hendaye helped his couriers maintain regular communication with the British embassy in Madrid; still others were placed in strategic points on the "green border" between the occupied and unoccupied zones. Agents in industrial centers such as Lille, Lyons, Nantes, and Reims sent reports, destined to reach RAF Bomber Command, of German-controlled armament works.

By the summer of 1941 Armand had established four radio posts in Paris; one near the Trocadero transmitted four times daily to London. He had contacts with a number of highly placed Frenchmen who professed to collaborate with the Germans but who secretly supported the Resistance. One such man was Monsieur Marc Marchal, the president of the Institute of Chemical Engineers; another was an official of the French railways, who passed on secret reports on transport communications.

It was at about this time that Armand gave Lily the nickname by which she became notorious. While Armand sifted reports from his agents, Lily typed others, preparing them to be microphotographed. She often entered his room so quietly that he did not notice it.

"You know, Lily, you walk like a cat, so softly," he told her.

"And I can scratch as well, if I wish," she replied.

"You know, I shall call you *ma petite chatte*—my little cat," he said. "It's a good code name, too; we shall use it for our radio signals. . . . The Cat reports—that sounds interesting and it's easy to send in Morse. Just dash dot dash dot . . . dot dash . . . dash."

Lily also brought some contacts to INTERALLIE, including Maître Brault. Within a few months INTERALLIE had grown from a handful of brave amateurs to an intelligence network with more than 120 members, agents, and couriers, covering, in conjunction with TUDOR, the whole of France.

The counterespionage sections of the Paris Abwehr and the Gestapo soon became aware of an efficient organization working for London, but despite many efforts failed to locate it, or to capture even one of its members. Searching for the elusive radio posts, detection vans of the *Funkpeildienst* cruised the streets of Paris, and on at least one occasion almost caught Armand, Lily, and their helpers at their headquarters in a house on the rue du Colonel Moll. They had to abandon some of their hideouts, and in October 1941 the work was concentrated at Villa Léandre on Avenue Junot in Montmartre.

At the end of September the chiefs of the SIS asked Armand to come to London for consultations. Through the French section of SOE it was arranged that he would be picked up by an RAF Lysander from a field near Estrées-St. Denis. Armand arrived in Britain on 1 October and spent nine days in London. He had meetings with British officers at the intelligence headquarters at St. James' and in Bayswater, was complimented by the War Office, and spent several days in conferences with Polish general staff officers in Kensington. General Sikorski decorated him with the highest Polish gallantry award, the Order of Virtuti Militari.

During the night of 9 October he was dropped near Tours and the following day was back in Paris. From London he brought important instructions and the news that several SOE officers would soon arrive by parachute to cooperate with INTERALLIÉ. During his London stay Armand had been told at Baker Street that some SOE agents in France had got into trouble and that the French section had lost contact with their radio operators. The SOE chiefs hoped, however, that one of their agents, Benoit (Cowburn), would manage to get in touch with INTERALLIÉ, and Armand was asked to accept messages from him and relay them over his transmitters to SIS.

They were all in high spirits at Villa Léandre, where a little champagne party was held to celebrate Armand's safe return and his award. And they waited impatiently for the visit of British agent Benoit.

It was at this juncture that Lucas (Pierre de Vomécourt) heard from Maître Brault, whom he knew from prewar days, of Mathilde Carré and the Polish organization, which had a regular radio link with London. De Vomécourt at first hesitated to get in touch with this unknown group, even though the news of an existing radio contact was extremely tempting. But after nearly six months of his and Roger Cottin's frustrating stay in France, he was running out of money. So at Christmas, de Vomécourt asked Brault to arrange a meeting with the woman who was apparently in a position to solve all his problems.

Neither he nor Brault knew anything of the events that had taken place in the meantime concerning INTERALLIÉ and its chief, Armand.

Sergeant Hugo Bleicher

Sector D of INTERALLIÉ was based in Cherbourg and Lisieux. It comprised six departments of northern France, covering the whole of Brittany and the western areas of Normandy. Armand had appointed in the spring of 1941, a young French ex-pilot, Raoul Kiffer, as chief of this sector. Kiffer had been providing reports on German installations in the Channel ports, which Armand conveyed to London and which were highly commended by British intelligence.

At the beginning of October a Luftwaffe corporal reported to the *Geheime Feldpolizei* station in Cherbourg that a French woman had been approaching workers at a Luftwaffe fuel depot for information. It seemed, the corporal suggested, that this woman was working for a British spy. The report was sent by Sergeant Hugo Bleicher of the Cherbourg station to the Paris headquarters of the Abwehr, as a matter of routine. There it was treated with great urgency and a counterespionage investigations officer, Captain Erich Borchers, was ordered to go to Cherbourg.

When Captain Borchers arrived at the Cherbourg field police station, the NCO on duty was Sergeant Bleicher. He seemed intelligent and knew French well, so Captain Borchers asked him to assist on the case. Next day they arrested the woman, Charlotte Bouffet, and she admitted working for a British agent, saying she knew only his code name, Paul.

The hunt for Paul was now on, and Bleicher devised a trap. On 3 November Bleicher arrested Paul outside the station at Cherbourg, on his arrival from Paris. In his pocket were notes on German military installations in the Calvados Department and some coded instructions. Paul was none other than Raoul Kiffer. The two Germans took him to Paris and then to the Abwehr headquarters at St. Germain-en-Laye. Kiffer at first refused to talk, but after Bleicher told him that he had been betrayed and that the names of his friends were known, he broke down.

From the information extracted from Kiffer, it was not particularly difficult to pick up the trail to Villa Léandre and the hideout of INTERALLIÉ. The Abwehr officers found Sergeant Hugo Bleicher a useful man, and he was told that he would stay in Paris to work for Abwehr HQ.

This was the beginning of Hugo Bleicher's career as the ace of the Abwehr. The humble, forty-two-year-old NCO, who had been assigned to the field police because poor eyesight made him unfit for combat duty, became the star spy-catcher of the German counterespionage. Under many disguises—as Monsieur Henri Castell, a Belgian businessman; as Monsieur Jean; as the anti-Nazi Colonel Henri of the Luftwaffe—he succeeded in infiltrating and destroying many French and Belgian Resistance groups and several SOE networks, and in capturing a large number of French and SOE agents.

After Kiffer's confession, in Bleicher's words, "It was plain sailing from now on." Bleicher had given him a choice between telling everything or being handed over to the Gestapo. Kiffer not only accepted this offer but also accepted Bleicher's suggestion to work for him as a V-man. From then on, endearingly called Kiki by Bleicher, he became one of the Germans' most useful informers, as enthusiastic a traitor as he had been a Resistance agent.

First, twenty-one of the members of the D Sector in Brittany were arrested and put in prison; then Bleicher, using Kiki as a stool pigeon, arrested several members of Armand's staff in Paris. Finally, on 17 November Bleicher pounced on the headquarters at Villa Léandre. At 3 A.M. four black cars with soldiers of the secret field police drove up at the two ends of the little street. A few minutes later Armand was led out from the house in handcuffs. Two radio operators, who were in the attic, managed to escape. Bleicher left several guards at the house; and when at 9 A.M. Mathilde Carré, who lived in an apartment near by, arrived, she was taken too.

Armand admitted that he really was Captain Roman Czerniawski and that he worked for the Allies. That was about all he told his interrogators. Neither threats nor manhandling could prompt him to provide any information about INTERALLIÉ and its contact with London. He was taken to Fresnes prison and held in solitary confinement.

Bleicher decided to work on the two women captured—Renée Borni, the young widow from Lunéville, who had come on Armand's invitation to work for INTERALLIÉ in Paris, and Mathilde Carré, the Cat.

At Santé prison Bleicher held long interviews with Madame Borni, who proved ready to tell all she knew. Unfortunately for Bleicher this was little. Even leading figures of INTERALLIÉ had registered in her mind only as "that handsome middle-aged man with graying temples," or "the young man who is always making jokes." So Bleicher decided to concentrate on the Cat. He had her removed from prison to the Hotel Edouard VII on the Avenue de l'Opera, which the Abwehr had commandeered for its Paris offices. She was given one of the elegant bedrooms, with bath and dressing room, and although there was a guard at her door, she was made quite comfortable.

Bleicher came to visit her and they had a sumptuous meal together. He told her he had found all the documents he needed; a word from him could send her and all her friends to the firing squad.

"We know everything and there is no point in being foolishly brave," Bleicher said. "You cannot save anybody by remaining silent. But if you help me, I shall try my best to save you and your friends from the Gestapo. You will be free and well looked after; they will be treated as prisoners of war, and one day they will return home. If you don't help me the Gestapo will take over and then God help you all.

"From the papers I found at the Villa Léandre I see you have a rendez-vous with one of your agents at the Café Pam-Pam. Let's go together. If you work for us I shall arrange that you are paid sixty thousand francs a month, which is much more than you get from the British. You'll be free and the others will be safe. Do you understand?" he asked.

"I understand," the Cat replied.

During the next few days Bleicher and the Cat drove around Paris, fol-lowed by a carload of secret field police. Mathilde Carré knew all the ad-dresses of the INTERALLIÉ members by heart. One by one they were picked up. Within three days Armand's fine organization was destroyed.

The Cattery

Besides prisoners, documents, and codes, the Germans also captured four radio transmitters tuned to the London wavelengths. Bleicher went to see his chief at the Paris Abwehr office, Colonel Oscar Reile, and put to him a proposition that at first seemed fantastic.

"Herr Oberst," he said, "we have four transmitters. If we can keep quiet about the arrests, we can play the radio posts and make London believe that INTERALLIÉ functions as before. In this way we can get all the signals and instructions from British intelligence, all news about the dispatch of secret agents from London, and we can send them some fake reports in exchange. In short, we can run the INTERALLIÉ as a network of the British under German control, without London discovering it, at least for a time, if we do it cleverly . . . ."

Colonel Reile was doubtful. The problem was to get at least a few of the former INTERALLIÉ members to cooperate. Bleicher was certain that the Cat would. He succeeded in winning over French radio operator Henri Tabet. All the Poles, when propositioned by Bleicher, refused to become traitors, but Renée Borni, that rather stupid young woman, agreed to work for the Germans when she saw that the Cat, whom she hated, was given special treatment as a result of her treachery.

The radio transmitters were removed to the home of a wealthy business-man at St. Germain-en-Laye. One of the Abwehr officers, Baron von Hoeffel, was put in charge of the fake INTERALLIÉ stations. Captain Borchers, Major Eschig, Dr. Kaiser, Sergeant Tritsch, and a radio operator, Sergeant Probst, made up his staff. Bleicher took the Cat, Renée Borni, and Henri Tabet with him to the house, which he aptly named *La Chatterie,* the cattery.

There was hardly any interruption in the radio link with British Military Intelligence. The Cat knew all the codes, the "skeds" for the transmissions, the prearranged security checks for signals. She was now collaborating wholeheartedly with the Germans. Within hours of their removal the transmitters were sending bogus messages to London.

In the early stages the Germans took care to send nothing that would excite London unduly, just reports about movements of troops, railway stock, military installations. Some were even true. Bleicher suggested that London should be informed that some of the INTERALLIÉ agents had been arrested, and by mid-December a signal was sent to London stating that Armand had been taken by the Germans, but that most of the other members were safe and work was to continue. London was also informed that the Cat was now in charge and would in future sign the signals under the code name of Victoire—victory. London lapped it all up and went on to inquire whether the missing SOE officers had now got in touch with INTERALLIÉ.

The Germans decided not to arrest Maître Brault, correctly assuming that through Brault they eventually would get on to the trail of the SOE agents. The Cat saw Maître Brault occasionally and she told him of the arrests of Armand and some other members of the INTERALLIÉ network. Bleicher ordered her to do this because he knew that Brault was connected with the Allied secret services and he wanted to forestall any suspicion that might have arisen in London.

For his part, Brault had mentioned to the Cat that he might need her help on a matter concerning some British agents. On 26 December they met for dinner at the Café Georges V in the Champs Elysées. Brault brought with him Pierre de Vomécourt, whom he introduced to the Cat as Monsieur Lucas.

De Vomécourt told her he was a British agent and asked her if she would transmit some radio messages to London for him. She immediately reported the meeting to Bleicher, and was ordered to see Lucas again and promise him that his messages would be sent.

The first of Lucas' messages to London, via the cattery, caused even more of a stir in Baker Street than might be expected. At 4 P.M. on 1 January 1942 Colonel Buckmaster received a telephone call from a colonel in the Military Intelligence department of the War Office, who said, "We've had a message on our line from one of your chaps. The whole thing's a bit peculiar, because strictly speaking your chaps shouldn't know that our chaps exist at all."[1]

Ironically, this message through the fake INTERALLIÉ transmitters came as a welcome relief to Baker Street. Colonel Buckmaster recalls: "From September to the end of December 1941 we were completely cut off from our

[1] Buckmaster, M., *They Fought Alone*, pp. 42–43, Odhams, London, 1958.

agents in France. By then, none of us at headquarters in Baker Street was in a very Christmasy mood. I was continually being asked by inquisitive generals what I was doing, and my persistent reply that Rome wasn't built in a day became more and more hollow . . . ." [2]

After an exchange of a series of radio signals, Pierre de Vomécourt was ordered to go on 16 January to Laas, a village near Le Mans, where he would be picked up by a Lysander. With the assistance of Benier, a schoolteacher and member of the Le Mans Resistance group, Roger Cottin found a suitable field.

In the meantime the Cat had several meetings with de Vomécourt and Cottin. She also visited their office, bringing along Bleicher, whom she introduced as Monsieur Jean Castell, a Belgian Resistance leader. Bleicher had obtained Colonel Reile's permission to send Lucas to London. Bleicher believed the SOE officer would report favorably on the services rendered by INTERALLIÉ, and his superiors agreed it would strengthen their position and enable them to use the fake transmitters for a considerable period. On the day fixed for the Lysander pickup, de Vomécourt, Roger Cottin, the Cat, and Monsieur Castell went by car to Laas. It was driven by Monsieur Severin, another "Belgian Resistance man" who also was a sergeant of the Abwehr. They spent the night huddled together in the car, near the field, waiting for the Lysander. The aircraft never arrived and, half-frozen, they drove back to Paris. De Vomécourt gave the Cat a strongly worded message for transmission to London, demanding an explanation.

The reply from the French section informed de Vomécourt that the plane had been grounded because of weather conditions and that he would be picked up on 30 January in a field near Estrées-St. Denis. So once again de Vomécourt, Cottin, M. Castell, and the Cat went to the rendezvous with the Lysander and once again spent a night, this time in thickly falling snow, waiting for the aircraft, which failed to arrive.

By this time de Vomécourt, Cottin, and Brault were apprehensive. They doubted the Cat's sincerity and began to wonder whether they were getting into a trap. Their suspicion changed to certainty through an incident that finally compromised the Cat in their eyes. They had asked her whether she could procure some forged identity documents. The next day she arrived with an altogether too impressive collection of passes and identity cards, supplied by Bleicher and Dr. Kaiser. She also produced a photograph and asked Lucas and Cottin if they knew the man, remarking, "I believe he works for Commandant Paillole of the Vichy secret service." It was a photo of Trotobas (Sylvestre), the agent who had parachuted with Ben Cowburn and whom the Abwehr was anxious to identify.

It had now become clear to the stranded SOE agents that the Abwehr was using the Cat. They decided to warn London. Ben Cowburn managed

[2] *Op. cit.*

[79]

to convey the warning to Switzerland. But it never reached Baker Street. In their perilous position, de Vomécourt and Cottin could do nothing but wait and redouble their vigilance.

The anxiety of the Germans concerning London's attitude toward their fake INTERALLIÉ messages also increased following the two abortive assignations with the Lysander. The Germans suspected that it was not just bad weather but London's suspicions that had grounded the plane. They also began to suspect the Cat of playing a double game. Captain Borchers had been replaced at the Abwehr HQ by Major Eschig, who put a bold plan before Colonel Reile: Why not send the Cat with Lucas to London? If she was genuinely working for the Germans, she would find out all she could about the organization of the French section and then return, by asking the SOE chiefs to send her back and let her work for INTERALLIÉ or a new SOE circuit. Colonel Reile agreed.

Bleicher worked hard on the Cat to persuade her to accept it. She may have feared that London would not give her quite the enthusiastic reception the Germans expected for her. On the other hand, she may have hoped to put an end to her sordid dealings and to cross once again to the other side. At her treason trial after the war she insisted that she intended to confess her betrayals and throw herself on the mercy of the Allied authorities in London.

An Odd Party

She was now meeting Lucas and Roger daily, and she sensed that they were suspicious of her. One evening Lucas challenged her with a direct question: "How did you get all those genuine passes and identity cards? Are you working for the Germans?"

Tearfully the Cat confessed. She told the truth about what had happened to INTERALLIÉ in November and how she had been forced by Bleicher to work for the Abwehr. It was a very dramatic account that bore little resemblance to the real role she had played. She did not admit that she had become Bleicher's mistress. The two agents were faced with the decision of either breaking off all contacts with the Cat and going into hiding, or accepting the situation in the hope that with German help they would reach England. They chose the second solution, although realizing its grave risk.

At the beginning of February 1942 the Germans sent signals to London, urgently demanding a pickup for Lucas and the Cat, saying that the Gestapo was on their trail and that their lives were in danger. Baker Street replied that an air pickup was impossible, but that a Royal Navy motor torpedo boat would be sent. It was agreed that Benoit (Ben Cowburn) should prepare the rendezvous at a place on the Brittany coast, which he knew from his previous work.

On 10 February signals were exchanged arranging for the arrival of a British MTB off the Point-du-Moulin-de-la-Rive, about a mile from Locquirec beach, during the night of 11–12.

Bleicher told the Cat he would not come along this time, but that Captain Heinz Eckert and Sergeant Tritsch of the Abwehr would go with her, Lucas, and Benoit. He assured her that German coastal guards had been warned to stay away and that the two Germans would disappear as soon as the British vessel came in sight. The party left Paris by the Brest express. De Vomécourt, Cowburn, and the Cat traveled in one compartment, Captain Eckert and Sergeant Tritsch in an adjacent one. At 7 P.M. the escapees were dining in a deserted seaside hotel. They drank two bottles of wine and Ben Cowburn said, "What a party! A French spy, a British spy, and a German spy . . . all we need now is a chap from the Russian OGPU!"

Captain Eckert had left the train at Morlaix and had gone to the local field police station to make sure that all German sentries would be withdrawn from the area where the British boat was to arrive. Then he went with Sergeant Meier, of the local field station, to a small shelter overlooking the beach.

Soon after midnight de Vomécourt, Cowburn, and the Cat arrived at the beach. A short time later the muffled noise of an engine was heard from the sea. After light signals came from the boat, the Cat answered with her flashlight three times in reply.

Two dinghies set out from the small MTB, which stopped some 400 yards from the beach. In the first dinghy was an RN officer and two civilians; in the second, two sailors in uniform. The Cat and Lucas ran toward the first boat. The three men scrambled ashore while the sailors of the other boat began to throw out pieces of luggage.

The arrivals were Lieutenant Commander Ivan Black, RN, and two SOE agents, Claude Redding, a former English teacher in Paris, and G. W. Abbott, a travel agent, who spoke fluent French and Italian and was a trained radio operator. They had been sent by Colonel Buckmaster to assist Cowburn and Cottin during Lucas' visit to London, and to set up the long-awaited radio post. Abbott's transmitters were being unloaded from the second dinghy.

De Vomécourt told the Royal Navy officer that he and his female companion should be taken immediately to the MTB. As the Cat tried to board the little boat in the rough sea, dragging her heavy suitcase after her, she suddenly lost her balance and fell. The dinghy immediately overturned, the Cat disappeared in the dark and muddy water, and de Vomécourt and Commander Black went to her rescue. It was a very bedraggled Cat that was eventually pulled ashore.

The dripping figures held a brief council of war with Coburn, while the

Cat, who had cut her leg on a rock while struggling in the sea, lay exhausted on the beach.

De Vomécourt, knowing their German escort must be somewhere near by, urged that they make for the MTB. Commander Black produced a flashlight and began signaling to his ship. Suddenly some shadowy figures emerged from the bushes in the background. They were Captain Eckert and Sergeant Meier, to whom the evening's performance must have seemed farcical. Some German field policemen, whom Eckert had placed at strategical points, had also moved forward.

Major Ben Cowburn recalls: "It was all over. The MTB had to leave in order to be out of sight of land. . . . We gathered together. Lucas decided that the two SOE agents and the naval officer should hide in the woods, and that the old trio should stay in the neighborhood so that the Cat could contact the Germans first thing in the morning, and that all six should meet again at the same spot the next night, in the hope that the MTB would return."

So the group parted. The Cat, supported by de Vomécourt and Cowburn, made her way to Locquirec and the seaside hotel. Agents Redding and Abbott headed for a barn, where they hoped to hide, while Commander Black, the most conspicuous figure in his Royal Navy uniform, made for the bushes.

Eckert left the trio alone and approached the RN officer, revolver in hand. Telling him that he was a German officer, Eckert asked him to surrender. There was little Black could do. He went with Eckert to the shelter, now alive with field policemen. A posse was sent out to look for the two civilians, whom Eckert naturally suspected were British secret agents. They were captured early in the morning at a nearby farm.

Eckert had his men fetch the suitcases from the beach. Inside them he found two radio transmitters, 600,000 francs, a pile of forged French and German documents, passes and identity cards, 25 Sten guns, several boxes with ammunition, cartons with explosives and limpet bombs, several revolvers, and other material.

In the morning the Cat went to the German station at Locquirec, met Captain Eckert, and tried to telephone Bleicher in Paris. She came back to the little hotel and told de Vomémourt and Cowburn that the Germans had watched the whole operation and "were quite thrilled." Eckert had promised to alert Bleicher and ask him to arrange by radio another pickup on the same spot for the next night. The three spent the day ambling through the villages, and when night came they trudged back to the beach for another vigil. They signaled with their flashlight for hours, but nothing happened. Eventually they walked to Lanmeur, took a bus to Morlaix, and boarded a train for Paris. During the journey the Cat fell asleep and de Vomécourt insisted on Cowburn making his escape. Cowburn left the train at a small station and took another for Tours. He spent several weeks in France, hunted by the Gestapo all the time, yet, always lucky and resourceful, was never caught. He visited Limoges and contacted Pierre's brother Philippe (Gauthier), who advised him to go to Lyons and see a trusted friend, Virginia Hall. With her help Cowburn finally reached Spain, after an arduous crossing of the Pyrenees during the height of winter.

British embassy officials in Madrid took him to Lisbon, and he was put aboard an aircraft for London. At Baker Street Ben Cowburn found, to his great relief, his friend Lucas, who had in the meantime safely arrived with the Cat.

Third Time Lucky

After Cowburn had left the Paris train, the Cat and Pierre de Vomécourt continued their journey. In Paris the Cat went to Bleicher and bitterly complained about her misadventures. With some justification Bleicher told her that it was not entirely the fault of the Germans. De Vomécourt, anxious to get away, made a new offer to Bleicher. He told him that once he and the Cat had reached England, they would return to France and bring with them "a general of the British Military Intelligence." De Vomécourt had played out the joker in this strange game, and the Germans swallowed his bluff.

Another series of radio messages was exchanged between London and the German-controlled INTERALLIÉ transmitters. London was now alarmed by the disaster at Locquirec. The naval officers of the MTB had, of course, made a full report and the SOE chiefs were now worried about what had happened, not only to de Vomécourt and Cowburn but also to Redding and Abbott. However, good news arrived from Paris: After long conferences at the Abwehr HQ the Germans decided to tell London that everything was under control and that the two new arrivals were safe. London was urgently requested to provide another pickup for Lucas and the Cat.

Another MTB was dispatched during the night of 19-20 February to the Brittany coast. Once again Bleicher instructed Captain Eckert to keep the coast clear. This time the meeting place was the Point de Bihit. The MTB duly arrived, flashed signals, and cruised off the coast for nearly an hour. But de Vomécourt and the Cat had taken a wrong turn coming from Morlaix and never reached the arranged spot. The final date was made with London for the night of 26-27 February, and a message of confirmation was broadcast by the BBC after the MTB had left the English port. The rendezvous was again the Point de Bihit. Bleicher and Eckert accompanied the couple and made sure that they found the stretch of the foreshore at the Rock Mignon, where the boat was to land.

Colonel Buckmaster sent Major Nicholas Bodington aboard the MTB to supervise the embarkation so that this time nothing untoward should happen. Bodington led a landing party of eight armed Royal Navy seamen, with hand grenades at the ready. They surrounded the couple and hustled them into the boat and aboard ship without mishap. Four hours later de Vomécourt and the Cat disembarked at Dartmouth, where Colonel Buckmaster waited for them on the jetty. They traveled together to London. During the train journey, de Vomécourt told Buckmaster the truth about the Cat.

Mme Mathilde Carré, as she was now addressed politely by the British officers who interrogated her, was treated as a welcomed and honored friend. The intelligence officers decided she should be left under the impression that they believed her when she said she had not actually betrayed Armand and his INTERALLIÉ network. They wanted to gain a little time and, indeed, they continued to exchange signals with the fake INTERALLIÉ—now fully aware that it was under Abwehr control—informing the Germans that Lucas and Victoire had safely arrived and would soon return to France, accompanied by a high-ranking British intelligence officer.

In fact, the Cat proved of some use. Talkative as she was, she told all she knew about the German Abwehr organization at St. Germain-en-Laye, gave the names of all the officers she had met at the cattery, and produced a German code, which Bleicher had given her. The British now turned the tables on the Germans, who were slow to realize that the Cat had once again changed sides.

This game went on for several months. One reason why it was played by British intelligence was that Pierre de Vomécourt had asked to be allowed to return to France as soon as possible. He considered it his duty to help his two brothers and his friend Cottin, who was living precariously in Paris. He had conferences with Major General Gubbins and Colonel Buckmaster, was introduced to Lord Selborne, the new minister of economic warfare, and received by Anthony Eden and General Sir Alan Brooke, chief of the imperial general staff. His escape brought much more important results than merely the deception of the Abwehr. He gave the British leaders a lucid and detailed picture of the situation in France, the growing strength of the Resistance, and an outline for SOE reorganization in the field.

De Vomécourt returned to France on 1 April 1942. He was dropped "blind," as on his first mission one year before, but this time it was almost dead on target: his parachute came down in a tree a few hundred yards from the Brignac estate of his brother Philippe. His departure was, of course, kept secret from both the Cat and the Abwehr men at the cattery in France.

The Germans patiently waited for his return with the British intelligence general. Although Bleicher suspected the Cat was a bad risk, some of his superiors were quite happy to continue the radio play with London, and still hoped that the British were in the dark.

From Limoges de Vomécourt went to Paris, where he found Roger Cottin still free. The Germans had left him alone; they considered him a valuable pawn in their game. By the end of April, however, an SD official SS Sturmbann-Führer Hans Josef Kieffer, who had been kept informed by his counterpart at the Paris Abwehr about the events concerning INTERALLIÉ and the Cat, had become restive. He had been keeping Cottin under surveillance without telling the Abwehr about it.

One of the Gestapo's many French V-men, Claude Jouffret,[3] had been shadowing Cottin. On 20 April he told Kieffer that Cottin had a visitor whose description tallied with that of the missing Lucas. Jouffret's discovery was correct. Although Cottin lived under various aliases and changed his address frequently, he was unable to escape the pursuit.

Bleicher traced de Vomécourt to a flat he shared with his Belgian-born agent, Léon Wolters. First the Germans arrested Cottin, then Wolters, and finally, on 25 April, Pierre de Vomécourt was lured to a rendezvous and also taken. Their arrest led to the capture of Noël Burdeyron (Gaston) and Jack Fincken, two agents sent to assist Lucas. Gaston had arrived the previous July, but was told to lie low during the Cat affair. He stayed in Normandy and carried out some successful sabotage actions; Fincken had been parachuted in January 1942.

Bleicher was called in to interrogate de Vomécourt. His first words to the man he had known as Lucas and whom he had helped escape to England were: "I have been betrayed. Our little cat has been playing a dirty game."

"Not at all," de Vomécourt replied. "If anybody has been betrayed by the Cat it's me."

Bleicher gave him some cigarettes, and on leaving his cell, he said, "Well, this time I can't help you. I feel sorry for you. You shouldn't have come back . . . ."

The interrogators who took over were less gentle than Hugo Bleicher. During de Vomécourt's questioning at Fresnes prison they knocked out almost all his front teeth and beat him mercilessly. But they were unable to extract any information from him, beyond what they already knew. De Vomécourt and the other agents, including Black, Abbott, and Redding, were treated as prisoners of war, tried at a German army court-martial, and sent to Colditz. They were liberated in April 1945 when the U.S. Ninth Army reached the Elbe River, occupied the town, and freed the prisoners. De Vomécourt died in Paris in 1965. Roger Cottin also spent the rest of

[3] Jouffret was tried by the French after the war and sentenced on 16 December 1949 to a long term in prison.

the war in German prisons and concentration camps. Some years after the war he went to America.

On Bleicher's advice the Germans kept secret the arrests of de Vomécourt and Cottin. But some weeks later a signal from the SOE *réseau* ADOLPHE, run by Pierre Culioli in the Sologne, informed London of their capture. The British intelligence chiefs assumed that de Vomécourt, under torture, might have told the Germans that the real nature of the Cat had been revealed in London.

In any case her usefulness had come to an end. She was taken from her comfortable apartment to a place of detention, and on 29 June, her thirty-third birthday, she was transferred to Aylesbury prison. A year later she was moved to Holloway prison, and after the end of the war she was handed over to the French authorities. She spent many months at the special prison in rue des Saussaies in Paris, in one of the cells that had been used as a torture chamber by the Gestapo during the war.

The wheels of French justice grind slowly. It took three and a half years before Mathilde Carré was put on trial. On 7 January 1949 she was sentenced to death. The following May the President of the French Republic commuted her sentence to life imprisonment. Mme Carré was released on 7 September 1954, having spent twelve years in captivity since her arrest in London, and now lives under an assumed name in a provincial town in France. In 1959 she published her memoirs [4] in which she tried to explain her wartime actions.

[4] *J'ai été la Chatte,* Editions Morgan, Paris, 1959.

5

Quarrels in the Sun

W I T H the destruction of INTERALLIÉ and the capture of their agents, British intelligence and SOE suffered a serious setback in Paris. But operations in the south of France began to look promising.

In August 1940 two officers who had stayed on to serve in Marshal Pétain's small French army of the armistice met for a talk in the officers' club at Marseilles. They were Captain Marcel Chevance and Captain Henri Frenay. Although not in sympathy with the Vichy regime, Frenay felt he must serve his country under Pétain, if only because the existence of the French State was, for the present, the sole guarantee that its colonies would remain under French rule.

Chevance was convinced Germany would lose the war once the United States could be persuaded to join Britain, and he insisted that everything possible should be done to speed up the process. They gathered around them a group of patriots who produced and distributed at irregular intervals a clandestine news-sheet. From this modest beginning grew the VÉRITÉ group, which in turn became the great Resistance organization COMBAT and eventually the backbone of the *Armée Secrète*.

Practical-minded Marcel Chevance bought an old furniture van and opened a remover's business at the Place d'Aix in Marseilles. The little office and the van proved of great value for underground work, but Agence Chevance became also a profitable company carrying goods and furniture, as well as clandestine leaflets, and providing funds for the secret organization. One of the leaders of VÉRITÉ was Guillain de Bénouville. In the summer of 1941 he introduced to his friends a man who had arrived from North Africa and who had made contact with the British.

This man was Henri Frager, a tall, good-looking, prematurely gray forty-four-year-old Alsatian, an architect by profession, who had served with distinction in the 1914–18 war, was badly wounded, and had won several decorations. In 1939 he had joined up again, and after the collapse of the fronts in June 1940 had gone to North Africa. There he made contact with British intelligence and offered to work for the SOE. In July 1941 a

British submarine put him ashore near Marseilles. Within a few weeks he set up several Resistance cells on the Côte d'Azur.

Before long it was Frager's turn to introduce someone of importance to the leaders of VÉRITÉ. "We call him Carte, but his real name is André Girard. You might have heard of him. He is a well-known painter," Frager explained to his friends. Carte already had established his own Resistance groups at Aix, Cannes, and Nice. Moreover, he was in touch with Emmanuel d'Astier de la Vigerie, who had founded an organization based in the industrial city of Clermont-Ferrand.[1] Even more important, he was in radio contact with London.

Negotiations between the VÉRITÉ leaders and Carte were soon completed and they sent a joint appeal to London for funds and arms. The SOE chiefs agreed to help and asked that one of the leaders of the French organization go to Geneva to meet a British representative. De Bénouville was selected by his friends, and in October 1941 he traveled to Annecy and across the mountains by night to Switzerland.

De Bénouville had memorized the code phrase *Louis XIV dira non a Vercingetorix,* which would introduce him to a man in an apartment at No. 60 Quai du President Wilson in Geneva.

After many months of perilous underground work, a secret journey through France, and a long march and climb across snow-covered Alpine passes, he arrived at the door of the apartment at 7 A.M. having spent a sleepless night at a railway station. He was in an understandable state of suppressed excitement.

"I rang the bell with a trembling finger," he recalls. "Several minutes passed until the door was opened by a tall, thin, fair-haired man with sleepy eyes, wearing an old dressing-gown and an expression of annoyance. 'What do you want?' he asked in very quaint French. I said: 'Are you *Louis Quatorze, monsieur?'* forgetting in my excitement the phrase I had memorized for so many days.

" 'No, I am Mr. Jackson, and I don't like canvassers calling at seven o'clock in the morning,' he answered, closing the door. I rang again and this time, Mr. Jackson opened the door and was really angry. I shouted: 'Please, *monsieur,* one moment.' I wanted to say *"Louis Quatorze dira non . . ."* Well, you said no, *monsieur,* so that's all right, isn't it?'

"Mr. Jackson gave me a long look. 'Why didn't you say immediately that you come from Marseilles? Well, come in. Have you had breakfast . . .?' "

They became friends over a real English breakfast—bacon and eggs, marmalade and toast—and got down to business.

Mr. Jackson took de Bénouville to the British legation. There the French-

[1] At that time the organization was called *Dernière Colonne.* D'Astier de la Vigerie later became leader of the great Resistance movement LIBÉRATION and eventually went to London, becoming minister of interior in de Gaulle's government.

man was told that a substantial sum of money would be placed with Swiss banks, which would in turn authorize French banks in Marseilles, Nice, and Cannes to pay out monthly allowances to agents of the CARTE organization. Many of the subsequent financial transactions were conducted by radio signals, after two radio posts were set up in the south of France and one at Annemasse, tuned to the receiving station at the British legation in Berne.

Olive Urchin

However, until the late autumn of 1941, Baker Street had been unable to establish a direct contact with CARTE. The chiefs of the French section of SOE decided to dispatch an officer to Cannes to take up the liaison and to set up a radio post.

They chose a Frenchman who had lived for many years in England. He was Francis Basin, a representative of French firms in London since 1925, whose wife, Marie Louise, had a well-known embroidery boutique in Kensington. Basin was born in Grasse—the town famous for perfume, north of Cannes—and his old mother still lived there. Thomas Cadett of SOE's French section prepared an involved new identity for him, but Basin suggested a more plausible one. He wanted to go under his real name, pretending to have been a soldier in one of the French units who had fought with the Chasseurs Alpins during the Anglo–French expedition in Norway in 1940. His story was that, after his return from Norway, he was stranded in Britain, had refused to join de Gaulle, and was now returning home. Baker Street provided him with the necessary forged army documents, and on 28 August 1941 he boarded the famous HMS *Fidelity*,[2] together with two fellow trainees of the SOE, another Frenchman, Raymond Roche, whose English alias was Bruce Cadogan, and Georges Dubourding (he assumed the name George Dolan while training in England), who became the famous Charles of Lyons. The three SOE men were landed on 21 September at Barcarès near Perpignan, where they parted. Basin went to Marseilles and eventually reached Cannes.

On his arrival, in order not to endanger his mother and relatives, he posed as Olive Urchin. But twenty-four hours later he was arrested at the Hotel de Bourgognes at Cannes as a suspected person. He was taken to the prison at Fort St. Nicholas, and it seemed his mission had come to an abrupt end. However, the officers who interrogated him were anti-German,

[2] Although the French tramp steamer *Fidelity* flew the White Ensign and had become one of HM ships, her crew was French. Their names appeared in the ship's manifest under assumed Scottish and Irish names, the sailors posing as Canadians. The fantastic exploits are described in Marcel Julven's *HMS Fidelity*, Souvenir Press, London, 1957.

and when he told them the story of his service in Norway and his escape from England, they let him go. A friendly police officer, Inspector Peretti, helped him and warned him not to go into the German-occupied zone.

Basin found Dr. Lévy and was soon working with CARTE. As Louis of Antibes, the Jewish physician became the reception chief of countless SOE officers. After having rendered great service for three years, Dr. Lévy was eventually caught and murdered during a forced march between two German concentration camps.

Within a few months Francis Basin set up thirty SOE *réseaux* from Marseilles to Grenoble and Cannes. For months he worked independently, without a direct radio link with Baker Street, relying solely on intermittent contact with Berne, maintained mainly by couriers. One of them was actor Claude Dauphin, who later went to London and became the chief of CARTE's BBC broadcasting station, *Radio Patrie*.

A chance meeting in a Cannes street suddenly changed Basin's situation. He met Captain Baron Henri Ravel de Malval, a former French naval attaché in London with whom Basin had worked during the first year of the war. The baron had returned to France just before the collapse and was living in retirement in his Villa Isabelle at Cannes.

Villa Isabelle

The baron immediately offered his help. His villa became the headquarters of the network OLIVE in which a number of remarkable men and women were enlisted. Basin had long urged London to send him a "pianist" but had received no response. There were many changes at the top in Baker Street, particularly in F section. Cadett and Marriott left and Major Maurice Buckmaster took over. OLIVE's Buckmaster paid greater attention to OLIVE's good work and sent out Isidore Newman (Julien), a trained W/T operator, who arrived in April 1942. Other agents sent to Basin were Denis Rake (Justin) and John Goldsmith (Valentin), a wealthy racehorse owner who had become a sabotage expert. After quarrels with Carte, Goldsmith returned to London. He later went back to France, taking part in the preparations for General Giraud's escape, under the supervision of General Mark Clark.

Baron de Malval (Antoine) had many connections among the local dignitaries and the police, and although he was suspected of helping British agents, he was not molested. At his house congregated the leading figures of the Resistance in the south: Emmanuel d'Astier de la Vigerie, Henri Frenay, André Girard, Henri Frager, Colonel Vautrin, General Cochet, and many others. Girard's beautiful young daughter acted as receptionist, secretary, and courier. After the war she became the celebrated film star Danièle

Délorme. Another of Basin's key agents was René Casale, now general manager of the Palm Beach Casino at Cannes. Casale, then a young croupier, provided safe hideouts for radio operators and escapees, acted as a courier, and took part in sabotage actions.

Francis Basin and Baron de Malval, very much contrary to their intentions, soon became involved in the quarrels that had broken out between the ambitious leaders of the various Resistance organizations. Frenay, Berthie Albrecht, Bertin-Chevance, and some of their friends had concluded an agreement on behalf of their VÉRITÉ group with the leaders of the rival organization LIBERTÉ, who included Georges Bidault, Pierre Henri Teitgen, and other politicians of the Christian-Democratic party.[3] This led to the emergence of the strong COMBAT organization. Meanwhile, Emmanuel d'Astier de la Vigerie and General Corniglion-Molinier, leaders of the *Habes Dernière Colonne,* aspired to the leadership of a united Resistance; while from Marseilles Léon Jouhaux, the veteran leader of the Socialist trade unions (CGT), forged ahead with his LIBÉRATION group, embracing Socialists and trade unionists. There were also many smaller rival groups as well as the extreme left FRANCS-TIREURS, the latter eventually growing into the most militant and strong organization under Communist control. André Girard, the leader of CARTE, which had close contact with SOE, stubbornly insisted upon his independence. Quarrels among the ambitious men who led these organizations resulted in many tragic incidents, including the betrayal of rivals to the Vichy police and the Germans.

Basin desperately tried to reconcile the warring patriots. He suggested that they form an action committee and appoint a trustee who would go to London on behalf of all the groups and negotiate with the SOE chiefs for more SOE instructors, liaison officers, money, arms, and explosives. But meetings he arranged often broke up after heated discussions, without any tangible results. Then one day Emmanuel d'Astier told Basin that at a secret meeting at Montpellier the leaders of the rival groups had appointed him— d'Astier—their spokesman, and he asked Basin to arrange his journey to London. He was collected by a boat at Antibes, taken to a British submarine, and brought to England.

No sooner did the other Resistance leaders learn of d'Astier's departure than they violently reproached Basin for having selected him as the man to negotiate with SOE in London. Henri Frenay insisted that it was he who had been elected the groups' spokesman to be sent to London.

Basin sent a signal to Baker Street, explaining that he had been misled and asked: SHALL I SEND FRENAY?

The reply from Buckmaster read: NO THANKS STOP ONE IS ENOUGH.

[3] After the liberation it became the MRP, and Bidault became de Gaulle's first premier. Bidault's activities as a leader of the OAS in 1961–63 led him into exile.

But Frenay never forgave Basin, and when Frenay finally did go to London, in September 1942, he joined de Gaulle and broke off his link with SOE. Safe in London, the two once-deadly rivals, Emmanuel d'Astier and Henri Frenay, made up their quarrels and both became ministers in de Gaulle's National Committee. It was not until Jean Moulin succeeded in establishing MUR (*Mouvements Unis de Résistance*) in March 1943 that a precarious unification of the many conflicting groups was achieved.[4]

Although inevitably hindered by these political intrigues, Basin neverthe-less accomplished some brilliant work. His reports were of utmost value and eventually reached Mr. Churchill, the War Cabinet, and the chiefs of staff in London. Basin recruited Philippe Rogue, secretary of former Fi-nance Minister Georges Mandel, as his informer in Vichy. He was able to send to London reports with copies of Pétain's cabinet documents and in-formation about Laval's intrigues with the Germans.

The SOE chiefs were greatly impressed with Basin's performance, and Buckmaster was told to send one of his senior officers to Cannes to find out how Basin did it all. Major Nicholas Bodington flew to Gibraltar, was brought in a felucca to Antibes, and was received by Basin, Dr. Lévy, and Henri Frager, who had become CARTE's deputy.

Equipped with papers in the name of William Brandt, an American citizen, Bodington arrived on 20 July 1942. Basin took him to the Villa Isa-belle, where he stayed until 9 September.

Basin had pulled off a particularly important coup. From members of an Italian anti-Fascist group, led by former Italian Foreign Minister Count Carlo Sforza, he had received documents about Italian and German defenses in Sicily and southern Italy. These documents, which included sketches of fortifications and lists of the units deployed, were of enormous importance for Allied plans for landing in Sicily and Italy. The documents were micro-filmed, and Basin suggested to Bodington that he should take them with him when returning to London.

But Major Bodington had no desire to burden himself with the micro-films. His refusal was understandable. If he were apprehended during the journey his situation would not have been enviable. Basin had, therefore, to find another way for dispatching the microfilms.

Some time before, Basin had enlisted a new courier who had made sev-eral successful trips to and from Switzerland for him. The courier was

[4] Characteristically, the distinguished French historian of the Resistance, Professor Henri Michel, blamed the British after the war: "The English played up this rivalry; they enticed away De Gaullist agents; they promised the Resistance arms and money which, they said, De Gaulle could never give them; they opposed more or less openly the unification of Free France . . ." (in *Histoire de la Résistance*, Presses Universi-taires, Paris, 1958).

Maurice Cogniat, a clerk at the Swiss consulate general at Marseilles. Cogniat had a diplomatic passport and traveled frequently on consular business between Marseilles and Berne, carrying sealed diplomatic bags. On several occasions he managed to slip Basin's films into the diplomatic valise before the Swiss consul, quite unaware of his clerk's spare-time job, sealed it with the sigil bearing the crest of the Helvetian Confederation. Cogniat, who was paid handsomely for this chore, was instructed to hand over the films in Switzerland to Marius, a British intelligence officer whom he was to meet at La Chaux de Fonds. Unfortunately, the Swiss clerk had more than one part-time job. On return trips he smuggled Swiss watches, which fetched very high prices in wartime France. Basin did not know, of course, that Cogniat was a smuggler; neither was Cogniat aware that the French customs men had for some time suspected him. When Cogniat arrived at the French customs house at Annemasse, he was arrested, the seals of his bags were broken, and the microfilms found. Italian and German field police officers were present, and they demanded that Cogniat be handed over to them. This the Vichy officials refused, and the man was taken to Lyons.

Cogniat had been turned in by a disaffected member of his smuggling syndicate. The discovery of the microfilms was only incidental, but it had disastrous results. Cogniat knew Urchin's real name, and realizing that he was now facing a much more serious charge than smuggling, he admitted everything. He told his interrogators that he had nothing to do with espionage but was taking the small parcel, not knowing its contents, to Switzerland for a friend in Cannes. He gave Basin's name and address.

One of the Vichy interrogators at Lyons was an underground member of the Resistance and he informed Colonel Vautrin of Cogniat's capture before the order for Basin's arrest reached the Cannes police. Colonel Vautrin hurried to the Villa Isabelle and warned Basin, who went into hiding. The villa was searched but Baron de Malval's good connections once again proved beneficial, and the policemen departed while the deputy chief of the SOE French section, Major Bodington, was pacing nervously in his room upstairs.

The Vichy police were now looking for Basin, and on 18 August he was arrested, through betrayal by an informer, and taken to the St. Rock barracks in Nice. There, the chief of the Vichy secret police, Cottoni, treated him kindly and told him he would try to let him escape. Although Cottoni had orders to send the prisoner to Lyons, he managed to keep him in Nice for twenty-one days, during which time Colonel Vautrin and Baron de Malval made frantic efforts to organize a rescue operation.

While Francis Basin was still in hiding, and even after his arrest, his friends of Villa Isabelle circulated freely on the Riviera. Bodington had several meetings with CARTE, and Julien carried on with his radio work.

Bodington had arranged with Buckmaster that another SOE officer should be sent to Cannes. When Basin was "burned," this officer was to become his replacement.

Peter Churchill

Buckmaster entrusted this mission to Captain Peter Churchill (no relation of Winston). Churchill, thirty-three (code name: Michel), knew France, where his father had been in the British consular service, and his French was faultless. Moreover, he had been on two missions to Cannes and knew Dr. Lévy and Francis Basin. Gifted with a sardonic sense of humor, he has described his adventures in three volumes.[5]

Although after the war Peter Churchill was criticized by some of his former comrades, his personal courage and self-sacrifice are beyond question. Before describing his third mission in August 1942, when he was sent to replace Francis Basin, his previous visits to France must be briefly recounted.

On his first mission, during the winter of 1941–42, he acted as a courier to Basin. He carried a large sum of money—about 2,000,000 francs—in a fat body belt, and because of this it was decided to send him by sea rather than drop him by parachute. He left Britain aboard the Polish liner *Batory* (which had escaped from Gdynia at the outbreak of the war, had reached a British port, and was subsequently used for war transport) for Gibraltar, where he was put aboard the British submarine P36. The submarine surfaced some eight hundred yards off Antibes and Churchill made the last part of his journey in a tiny canoe, in pitch-dark winter night.

Clutching his belt with the 2,000,000 francs, he made for the house of Dr. Lévy. The money was distributed among the SOE officers—400,000 francs to Francis Basin, 300,000 francs to Dubourdin at Lyons, another 300,000 to Edward Coppin (Olivier) of the Marseilles network, while the biggest share went to André Girard of CARTE. Basin then arranged Churchill's return journey, and on 4 February 1942 Churchill reached the Spanish frontier. After a long and strenuous mountain crossing, he arrived at Barcelona. The British consul general drove him to Madrid, thus avoiding unwanted encounters with the Spanish police. From Madrid Churchill was taken in a British embassy car to Gibraltar. On 14 February he arrived back in London.

Churchill had brought back Basin's urgent request for a radio operator. His first question to Buckmaster was: "When can I go back to France on a real mission?" Twelve days later he was off again, not only as the conducting officer of two "pianists"—Isidore Newman (Julien) and Edward Zeff

[5] *Of Their Own Choice; Duel of Wits; The Spirit in the Cage;* Hodder and Stoughton, London.

(Matthieu)—but also as the man who was to bring back to England an important Frenchman, whose identity he did not know. The man was Emmanuel d'Astier de la Vigerie, who had persuaded Basin to arrange this journey.

Peter Churchill and his two young companions were flown from Bristol to Gibraltar. At the Rock they received some bad news. The admiral in command at Gibraltar objected to putting his submarines at the disposal of SOE. Churchill was told that the Royal Navy officers "were not going to make a habit of using the meagre brood of submarines for cloak and dagger stuff, with the Malta situation giving everyone the jitters. . . ." [6]

It took all his ingenuity before Churchill succeeded in persuading the naval officers to provide the passage. In the end he was given the smallest submarine in the port, P42, commanded by twenty-five-year-old Lieutenant Alastair Mars. This was Mars' first patrol since he had brought the submarine from the Clyde yards. On 26 March she sailed with her secret cargo toward Antibes. Dr. Lévy and Henri Frager had prepared the landing operation ashore and had brought a reception committee to greet the arrivals, including Emmanuel d'Astier, ready to embark, and Guillain de Bénouville. Churchill asked Dr. Lévy: "What's all this mob doing here, Louis?"

The doctor grinned: "Some of the gang came to watch the fun. . . ."

"Louis, have you never heard about security?"

"No, you must tell me about it one day."

Guillain de Bénouville described that landing years after the war in a dramatic manner.

"From our little boat I watched the submarine surface slowly, with tears in my eyes. This little ship, these sailors and the three civilians on the bridge had come from England. They had come to fight on our side, to fight for France. And, please God, one day they might return home. To us Frenchmen the surprise in this was overwhelming, but to them it hardly seemed to be an adventure at all. The sailors threw a rope to us and pulled our boat alongside. The three civilians jumped down, shook hands, and stuffed packets of cigarettes into our pockets. We embraced them, patted their shoulders, their faces. You must remember that for us this was the first sign of action against the German conquerors of Europe by our friends, the free Anglo-Saxons. 'What a joy,' exclaimed Henri Frager, and we all repeated his words."

De Bénouville ended his recollections thus: "The three English officers brought with them a consignment of arms and ammunition. We felt very happy and proud."

A short while later d'Astier was nearly drowned when boarding the little boat in which Peter Churchill rowed him back to the submarine. But the

[6] Churchill, Peter, *Duel of Wits*, p. 17.

Englishman managed to get the French Resistance leader safely aboard, and a fortnight later d'Astier reported to the other Churchill at 10 Downing Street.

Back in England Peter Churchill went through a refresher course and made himself generally useful at Baker Street. Then one day Colonel Buckmaster called him to his office and said that the chiefs of staff wanted him to undertake "something of a specialized nature." Churchill immediately said he would take the job, whatever it was.

The proposition was to take two specially trained demolition agents to France, conduct them to the German radio station of St. Assise, and blow it up.

Tap-Dancing in Enemy Territory

The two saboteurs selected for the job by Buckmaster were Alfred and Henry Newton, sons of a former Lancashire jockey who had been a racing trainer in France and had lived there with his family for many years. The brothers had become well known on the Continent as variety artists, The Boorn Twins, performing a comic tap-dancing act. When the German invasion came, Alfred and Henry, who had both married French girls, decided to try and bring their families to England.

They trekked in nightmarish conditions along roads crowded with refugees to Penzon in the Vendôme. There the men were apprehended by the Vichy police, interned as enemy aliens, and put into a work battalion. After many difficulties the brothers escaped to Spain, were arrested by Franco's police, and taken to the internment camp at Miranda de Ebro. They were not released until Christmas 1941. Their families, meanwhile, were evacuated from France by the Red Cross and brought to Lisbon, where they boarded the *Avoceta* for the trip to Britain.

On 25 September 1941, during an Atlantic gale, the ship was torpedoed and the families of both men were drowned.

By the time the brothers arrived in London they had but a single thought between them: vengeance on the Nazis. They were given an opportunity almost immediately. Nearly all the volunteers for SOE came from the forces, but the story of the Newtons had become known to British intelligence officers at Gibraltar and was reported to headquarters in London. When they arrived aboard the destroyer HMS *Hesperus* in Liverpool, the brothers were taken to a field security officer, given tickets to London, and told to see a major at the War Office.

The officer gave them an address near Baker Street. The address was 6 Orchard Court, Portman Square, and the man who welcomed them was Major Louis Gielgud, the chief recruiting officer of F section.

Henry Newton spoke for them both: "Give us a couple of tommy guns and a bunch of hand grenades and we know bloody well what we're going to do."

Major Gielgud had some difficulty in explaining that it was not as simple as that. But he realized that he had two men who would shrink from no task, however dangerous or difficult. He decided they were ideal material for training as saboteurs. For several weeks, at STS No. 17 for industrial sabotage at Hertfordshire, the Newtons were put through their paces. When the chiefs of staff ordered the destruction of the St. Assise transmitter, Buckmaster had no doubt whom he wanted for the job.

The target was of utmost importance. The St. Assise station was used by the German naval command for directing U-boats in the Atlantic. Its destruction would cause a breakdown in these communications and probably save the lives of many Allied seamen. Many weeks of preparation preceded the dispatch of the two saboteurs. The Newtons were taken to SOE's big radio station at Rugby and shown all over its installation to learn what they had to look for at St. Assise. A safe house was prepared at La Pepinière, five miles from St. Leu, in the vicinity of the German transmitter. RAF reconnaissance aircraft brought back scores of aerial photographs of St. Assise, and the Newtons were briefed for hours.

On 28 May Buckmaster and Major de Guélis, the briefing officer, came to Wanborough Manor with the latest report of the meteorological department, which forecast perfect weather. But just as they were inspecting their parachuting gear, an SOE officer ran on to the tarmac. "The operation is off. Sorry, you'll have to get out," he told them.

The twins (as they were known in Baker Street) were livid. They never found out the true and farcical reason for the cancellation of their big venture. A day or two earlier a French Resistance man, in the habit of cycling past the St. Assise station, had stuffed some sticks of explosives into the handlebars of his cycle and those of two friends. They dismounted, leaned their bikes against one of the radio masts, and went looking for mushrooms. The explosives blew up but did not damage the mast badly. Within an hour German field police surrounded the St. Assise station and a regiment of the Wehrmacht was rushed to the area. The station was cordoned off, and neither the Newtons nor anybody else would have been able to get within miles of it for weeks.

However, a few weeks later, Alfred and Henry Newton were dropped on another mission—to teach sabotage to Resistance groups in the Lyons area. They were getting into their stride and were doing excellent work when through the betrayal of a V-man, an Alsatian named Robert Alesch [7] who posed as a priest and was known as The Bishop, they were caught by

[7] Alesch, a native of Luxembourg, was the former Abbé of St. Maur. He led a dissolute life, was unfrocked, and became a German V-man. After the war he was tried and executed.

[97]

the Gestapo. At Lyons, the twins underwent unspeakable torture at the hands of Gestapo commander SS Sturmbann-Führer Barbie and his thugs, but never gave any of their comrades away. They spent the last two years of the war at Buchenwald, had a miraculous escape from the gallows, and were freed in 1945.

Peter Churchill's Third Mission

It was on 27 August 1942, shortly after Basin's capture and during Bodington's stay at Cannes, that Captain Peter Churchill arrived there on his third mission. Although in many areas in north, southeast, and central France the French section had succeeded in setting up a number of effective networks, the situation in the south was becoming increasingly chaotic. The relations between the British government and de Gaulle's National Committee in London had gone from bad to worse.

To complicate matters, the first few American OSS agents began to arrive in France in the summer of 1942. This was before the integration of SOE and OSS, and the latter had established an office in London under Colonel Arthur Roseborough. The Americans had decided to go it alone as a result of Washington policy, which preferred General Giraud to General de Gaulle. A web of political intrigue soon covered the North African scene. A side effect in the south of France was the weakening of SOE *réseaux,* particularly after the loss of Basin, who had contrived to cope with political difficulties.

Although there were at that time several first-class SOE officers in the field in the south, most were young men with little experience and less diplomatic talent. They felt lost in the labyrinth of French Resistance dissensions.

Peter Churchill's mission was that of an organizer, and he tried to fulfill it against great odds. After the war Baron de Malval and some of the Frenchmen who worked with him took Churchill to task for alleged failures, particularly concerning the receptions of men and material in November at Vinon, in December at Chanoine near Arles, and in January 1943 at Périgueux. I inspected Baron de Malval's documents,[8] which allege that Churchill committed some grave errors of judgment. On the other hand, Churchill, in his book, *Duel of Wits,* admits his mistakes and gives reasons for them. He quotes the query from Buckmaster: WHAT ON EARTH WENT WRONG AT VINON? and the exchange of radio signals after the failure at Tournus, when Buckmaster asked: WHAT STOPPED YOU AT ARLES? and his reply: CULPA MEA STOP PROFOUND APOLOGIES ENDS. These honest admissions are certainly to his credit.

[8] *Le Journal de la Villa Isabelle,* printed for private circulation in 1956.

Other allegations in the documents concern Churchill's disregard of security regulations.

After Churchill and Odette Sansom were arrested at St. Jorioz in April 1943, Baron de Malval, who had been in hiding for some months, was himself arrested on 13 July 1943 in Paris.[9] During his interrogations at Gestapo HQ on the Avenue Foch, he was shown a sheaf of papers, from which one of the officers gave him a sheet to read. It was the copy of a signal that was found on Peter Churchill when he was arrested:

ON LANDING IN FRANCE THE SEVEN PASSENGERS WILL PROCEED STRAIGHT TO BARON DE MALVAL'S VILLA ISABELLE ROUTE DE FRÉJUS CANNES.

The baron and his wife were kept for many months at the prison of Fresnes. De Malval lost the sight of an eye as a result of tortures he had suffered. It is, perhaps, understandable that he bore a grudge. But there is no evidence that these arrests can be blamed on Peter Churchill's disregard of security. Postwar recriminations, however, published in reply to statements in Peter Churchill's books and in Odette's biography,[10] show that the climate in which they lived in Cannes in 1942 was far from healthy.

One of the allegations against Peter Churchill, made fifteen years after the war, was that he made no effort to rescue Captain Francis Basin. This is a little unfair since Churchill had only just arrived at Cannes and was still finding his feet. He certainly could not spirit Basin from his prison cell. He tackled Carte (Girard) about it, and in his book *Duel of Wits* he recorded Carte's reply:

Laurent [Basin's field name] is being taken to Lyons tomorrow. My rescue squad will board the same train and get him away from the gendarmes at the moment they think best. He will be then hidden away on a farm. We thought of snatching him at Nice, on the way to the station, but this is a bit too risky.

Although Carte's men boarded the train and traveled with the manacled prisoner and his guards to Lyons, they were unable to effect the rescue. Basin was kept at Lyons for three months, in a dark cell at Fort Montluc. Girard entrusted the plans for the rescue to his deputy, Henri Frager, and he and Colonel Vautrin traveled to Lyons, where they negotiated with the military commander of the Vichy army, Colonel Grenier. At this stage Virginia Hall (Marie) appeared on the scene. Colonel Grenier, though refusing to free Basin immediately, gave his word of honor to do so should German troops enter the Vichy zone.

[9] *Cf.* Bleicher's depositions before Commissaire René Gouillard of DST, October 1945.
[10] Tickell, Jerrard, *Odette, the Story of a British Agent,* Chapman & Hall, London, 1949.

On 26 November Lyons was occupied by the Germans, and Virginia Hall hurried to Colonel Grenier to remind him of his promise. The colonel was willing to help, but the prison commandant refused to release Basin without a written order from the CO of the region, General Maire. For ten hours the negotiations went on, until finally the president of the military tribunal signed the order. On 28 November Basin was free, but he had to disappear without delay; German patrols were already searching the town for him. With the help of Captain Lazare Racheline (Lucien), a DF section officer from Marseilles, Virginia Hall took Basin to Mont Dore. He was extremely weak and in need of medical treatment, but he had to be moved quickly. His friends took him to a safe house in the Auvergne, then to Nîmes, where a pickup by Lysander was to be arranged. In the landing area Basin broke his leg. At last, on 21 December, Henri Déricourt (Gilbert) put him on an aircraft and Basin reached London. For the rest of the war Basin was an instructor at Beaulieu and then on the headquarters staff in Baker Street.

André Girard had made every effort to help Basin, whom he greatly respected and with whom he was prepared to cooperate, but his relations with Basin's successor, Peter Churchill, were never more than diplomatic. Girard was not an easy man to work with, and Peter Churchill gives instances of Girard's temperamental outbursts. When relations between de Gaulle and the British government had reached the breaking point and, at about the same time, the Americans began to approach French Resistance leaders, Girard wondered whether he should go over to de Gaulle, accept American patronage, or continue his cooperation with SOE.

He made growing demands on London for money and arms and for radio transmitters to be operated by his own men and not by SOE officers. He accused Newman (Julien), who transmitted all his signals to London, of insubordination and even of scheming to have him arrested. Peter Churchill was compelled to send Newman back to England to pacify Girard.

One day, when Churchill brought him 650,000 francs, Girard threw the bundle on the table, exclaiming, "Here, you can take back your dirty English money!" He changed his mind, however, and kept the cash.

Shortly after Peter Churchill's arrival a young SOE radio operator was parachuted north of Grenoble, with orders to go to Paris. The pilot missed the prearranged dropping zone, and the operator found himself stranded after he reached the ground. He was twenty-six-year-old Alec Rabinowitch of whom Peter Churchill wrote in the dedication of his book *Duel of Wits:* "This book is dedicated to my beloved 'Arnaud'—the late Captain Alec Rabinowitch, a violent, difficult, devoted and heroic radio operator, and through him to all underground men and women of his supreme calibre who died, as they lived, in solitude."

Rabinowitch, unable to make contact with anyone, started south and was accidentally picked up by one of CARTE's men and brought to Cannes. Peter Churchill was so impressed by this young man that he sent a signal to Buckmaster asking to keep him. Arnaud proved himself a most valuable acquisition and a loyal friend, particularly in adversity. He was a giant of a man, had spent his childhood in Egypt (where his parents of Jewish-Russian origin had settled down), had been a junior wrestling and boxing champion, and had served in the French Foreign Legion before joining SOE.

In much the same way Peter Churchill acquired Odette Sansom. She and six other agents arrived at Cassis on 4 November 1942 by felucca; all of them came to Cannes in transit, being ordered to proceed to various *réseaux* in the north. Odette was to go to Auxerre, but Churchill, short-handed after Julien's departure, asked Buckmaster to be allowed to keep her in Cannes. She became his courier, and during the following weeks was entrusted with finding new dropping zones.

In November Peter Churchill had received a signal from Baker Street ordering him to keep himself ready for a journey to London. Buckmaster told him that he and Carte were required in London for consultations. The chiefs of staff wanted a firsthand report about the situation in the south of France prior to the imminent Allied landing in North Africa. Churchill, Girard, and five French officers were to be picked up by an RAF aircraft. To find a suitable landing ground Churchill sent out Odette and one of Girard's lieutenants, Meihac. The operation failed.

The result was a violent scene between Girard and Churchill. Girard accused Odette of incompetence while Churchill defended her, pointing out that one of Girard's own men had accompanied her. After several other attempts at finding pickup grounds failed, Girard refused to go to England because, as he put it, he "could not trust Churchill to make proper arrangements." This all but finished the already strained relations between the two men.

Peter Churchill was in touch with Colonel Vautrin, whom he had met through Guillain de Bénouville. With the news of the Allied landings at Casablanca, Oran, and Algiers, the colonel informed Churchill that General de Lattre de Tassigny, a divisional commander of the French army of the armistice under Vichy control, was prepared to go over with his men to the Allies.

The general's forces, some 12,000 fully equipped men, along with tanks and field artillery, were stationed at Montpellier and in camps in the valley of Hérault. General de Lattre offered to take his division to the Pyrenees and organize it as the first corps of the French army of the interior to fight the Germans inside France. This was a breathtaking proposal. The condition was that the British government (through SOE) would have to supply these troops from the air with provisions, ammunition, and any additional weapons required, and that RAF and American bombers would give full air support.

Peter Churchill immediately informed Baker Street. After hurried consultations in London, the Prime Minister gave orders to accept the general's offer. Peter Churchill was told to send one of his officers and a radio operator to Tassigny's headquarters at Montpellier. He entrusted Alec Rabinowitch with this mission.

General de Lattre moved his troops westward from Montpellier toward Toulouse. But, as the British and American troops went ashore in North Africa, Hitler ordered on 11 November the occupation of the Vichy zone. German troops crossed the demarcation line, swiftly occupied Lyons, Clermont-Ferrand, and Limoges, and drove toward Montpellier and Toulouse, while Italian troops moved into Savoy and the Côte d'Azur and occupied Corsica. Hitler sent a letter to Marshal Pétain stating that German troops would be withdrawn "as soon as the situation in the Mediterranean had improved and there was no question of endangering the interests of Germany and Italy." Pétain, in a desperate attempt to placate the führer, ordered strong units of his army (commanded by anti-Gaullist officers) and detachments of the *Garde mobile* (reinforced by the legions of Marcel Déat's pro-Nazi Fascist organization) to stop and surround de Lattre's division just as it was moving on the road from Béziers toward Narbonne and Perpignan. The division was disarmed when de Lattre refused to order Frenchmen to fight Frenchmen. The general and most of his officers were arrested and taken to Vichy's prison camps. The order for this action, although in the name of the old Marshal, was given by Pierre Laval, who had assumed the real power at Vichy in April 1942 and who had stated in June: *Je souhaite la victoire de l' Allemagne* (I desire a German victory). Any help the British government intended to give de Lattre would have come too late.

De Gaulle and his supporters, already enraged over the Anglo–American recognition of Admiral Darlan at Algiers, openly proclaimed that Free France had once again been betrayed by her allies.

At Baker Street frantic efforts were made to bring Girard, Frager, and Peter Churchill to London for consultations. Girard insisted on handling the arrangements for a flight himself, and RAF aircraft tried four times to make a pickup without success.

With the arrival of the German troops in the hitherto unoccupied Vichy zone, mass arrests among Resistance leaders began all over the area. In the south many of CARTE's members were taken, and Girard himself had a narrow escape. His wife was captured in February 1943. His disputes with Henri Frager, who remained loyal to the British, reached a paroxysm of hostility.

In the meantime Captain Heinz Eckert, the Abwehr officer who had stage-managed the escape of the Cat, had become chief of the newly estab-lished Abwehr post at Lyons. From some members of CARTE who had been enrolled as German V-men he received information as to Girard's where-abouts in Arles and of the setup of Peter Churchill's SOE groups on the Côte d'Azur. Girard was warned and moved to a country hideout in La Camargue. CARTE was rapidly breaking up, and Peter Churchill, now in peril himself, arranged for Girard's journey to London. In Britain he sought support from de Gaulle, from the chiefs of SOE, and from General Donovan of OSS, but was cold-shouldered by all. Eventually he went to New York and Washington, to secure assistance from the United States government. He settled in New York, working at his real profession—painting. André Girard's organization, which (according to his exaggerated claims) at one time had had "five thousand members and spread through ten departments of France," had finally collapsed.

Lyons, Marseilles, Cannes, and Nice became very dangerous after the German raids on the remnants of the CARTE *réseaux*. Some of the French officers who were associated with André Girard fled across the Spanish frontier.

Henri Frager moved to Montélimar with some of CARTE's reliable sub-commanders. There, encouraged by Peter Churchill, he began to build a new network in cooperation with SOE. Among the men who assisted him in creating the JEAN-MARIE circuit were André Marsac and Roger Bardet, two men who were destined to become tragic figures.

Peter Churchill and Odette Sansom, too, had to leave Cannes. They went to Toulouse, where the SOE network PRUNUS was headed by Cap-tain Maurice Pertschuk (Eugène). In spite of the German occupation of the Vichy zone, this area was fairly quiet during the winter of 1942–43. Captain Pertschuk had organized strong maquis units, was carrying out many sabotage actions, and helped to cover the escape routes across the Pyrenees. In the end he was caught, sent to Buchenwald, and hanged on 29 March 1945.

Into the Savoy Mountains

At Toulouse, Peter Churchill received more bad news from the Côte d'Azur. The Germans had raided his Cannes flat at 20 Quai St. Pierre, and many of his French friends had been arrested. Alec Rabinowitch hung around Cannes waiting to be told what to do with his radio. The situation was already critical and was not improved when Captain Ruffiol, one of Frager's operators, was captured while trying to install an emergency radio post at Montauban.

The only consolation was that Frager (Paul) was doing well. From his foothold at Montélimar he struck north and northeast, and the new JEAN-

MARIE circuit was growing rapidly, far beyond Provence and the Rhone Valley. Frager sent Marsac to the Savoy, where he established contact with the Resistance groups, which had remained little affected by the Italian occupation of the region.

Peter Churchill had sent a brave woman courier, Gisèle, to summon Frager and two of his top aides, Marsac and Jean Riquet, to a council of war at Toulouse. They arrived, and Frager was very insistent that Peter Churchill not return to the south of France.

"It is not just a question of your own survival, it is the question of the survival of our organization and all of us," he told Peter. But Churchill was anxious about Alec Rabinowitch and wanted to collect him and, if possible, the radio transmitters hidden at Cannes. Eventually he agreed that this dangerous mission should be entrusted to Riquet, who was not as well known in Cannes as Churchill and in less danger of being caught. Riquet returned safely after a few days with Rabinowitch and the radio equipment.

In the meantime Marsac suggested to Peter Churchill that he move his headquarters to a little village in the Savoy. This village, which Marsac knew from his reconnoitering for JEAN-MARIE, was St. Jorioz, situated high in the Haute-Savoie mountains, nine miles from Annecy and only twenty-five miles from Geneva, which would secure a convenient courier route to Switzerland. Marsac had made good friends at St. Jorioz and he developed a plan for organizing the new headquarters. Churchill and Odette would stay at the Hotel de la Poste, whose owner was a local Resistance leader, while Alec Rabinowitch would set up his radio post at Faverges, a little village in the neighborhood, where Marsac had already found a safe house. Frager suggested that Marsac should go with the British officers to St. Jorioz and become the liaison man.

At St. Jorioz all seemed as safe and comfortable as Marsac had promised. The owners of the hotel, Jean and Simone Cottet, were charming people and obviously completely reliable. The SOE men decided to change their identities. At Cannes Peter Churchill had been Monsieur Chauvet; now he became Monsieur Pierre Chambrun. He and Odette Sansom posed as a happy young married couple on a winter holiday in the Savoy. Alec Rabinowitch became Monsieur Guy Lebouton—*bouton* means a button or knob, and he had to do a lot of twirling on his radio transmitter.

Marsac and his wife were to live at Les Tilleuls, a small villa not far from the hotel. Roger Bardet and Jean Riquet, the twenty-five-year-old French air force sergeant who had collected Alec from Cannes, were to act as couriers to JEAN-MARIE.

Soon Arnaud was reporting cheerfully to Baker Street. Riquet was sent to Captain Pertschuk at Toulouse; Marsac was traveling to and from Paris, where Henri Frager had made contact with the PROSPER CIRCUIT and also established his own foothold for JEAN-MARIE; Roger Bardet was sent on many errands. The Hotel de la Poste, the villa Les Tilleuls, the farmhouse at Faverges, all hummed with activity, and St. Jorioz became one of SOE's important outposts in France. Couriers were now regularly traveling between the Savoy headquarters and Paris, Lyons, Clermont-Ferrand, Grenoble, Marseilles, Toulouse, Aix-en-Provence, Nice, Cannes, Antibes, and St. Raphaël.

Everything went according to plan; in fact better than expected. During February alone, forty new dropping zones were found, each with a well-organized reception committee. Churchill supervised the distribution of arms that began to arrive. They were used a year later by Tom Morel's maquisards, who fought bravely on the plateau of Glières.

Churchill and Odette undertook several journeys, inspecting the arrangements and recruiting new helpers. The radio link with Baker Street was good; Rabinowitch was pleased with the atmospheric conditions and the fact that the communication with London had been shortened by some 350 miles.

St. Jorioz might have become one of SOE's great successes were it not for a tragic mistake of a good man—Marsac—and for the shrewdness of another—Hugo Bleicher. As it happened, St. Jorioz, like INTERALLIÉ, became a disaster.

6

The Man Named "End"

THE CAUSE of the ensuing disaster of St. Jorioz lay deeper than simple betrayal. To understand it one must realize the moral and social conditions in France under the German occupation.

It was a time for heroism but not heroics. The general order of the day was self-preservation, usually at the cost of the community, sometimes at the cost of relatives and friends. By 1943, although a handful of Frenchmen did very well for themselves through collaboration with the enemy, France had become, in effect, a nation of slaves. Millions of men and women were deported or pressed into forced labor. The Germans systematically plundered the countryside to feed their armed forces and their people at home. Day after day, convoys of trucks rolled eastward carrying cattle and corn, coal and steel, textiles and wine, to the Fatherland, leaving the French cold and hungry. Inevitably a gigantic black market developed. The rigid and inadequate system of rationing became almost meaningless because the coupons could not be honored. Queues lined up all night for a loaf of bread. Soap, a cup of real coffee, a pat of butter, had become luxuries beyond the reach of all but a tiny minority. Families were thrown out of their homes to make room for German officers, Gestapo men, and a host of Nazi officials who descended on the country like a swarm of locusts.

Heavy Allied bombing raids, blackouts, curfews, and the strict curtailment of movement from one place to another made what was left of ordinary day-to-day life bewildering, frustrating, and dangerous.

Crime in the legalistic sense became commonplace. Men and women were denounced to the Germans by people they believed to be their friends. Some of those arrested on a paltry charge or who were innocent tried to save their lives or secure their freedom by denouncing others. Families were torn apart in disputes over their allegiance. The Germans and their collaborators embarked with relish upon a brutishly hedonistic way of life. The mass of the people, leading a life of gray despair and constant fear, abandoned the codes of behavior of an organized society that no longer existed.

It was out of this horror and humiliation that the spark of French Resistance grew into a flame that exorcised the evil memory of Nazi occupation and eventually restored the pride of a defeated nation. Perhaps it is well to remember this when reading about some of the following events.

The Trap Is Set for Marsac

On one of his journeys to Paris, from the Savoy mountains or the south of France, André Marsac (End), the deputy of Henri Frager, met a Gaullist Resistance group member named Marette. This man was introduced to him by a trusted comrade, Nicola Posniakoff, a Russian by birth, who had often been Marsac's driver. Posniakoff had known Marette for a long time; indeed, they had been members of the same Resistance group before the Russian had joined the JEAN-MARIE *réseau*. What Posniakoff did not know was that in the meantime, Marette had been arrested by the Germans, and to save his skin had agreed to work for them as a V-man. He was set free, ordered to continue working for his Resistance group, and put under the surveillance of one of the Abwehr's most skillful informers, Robert Kayser.

A native of Luxembourg, Kayser had spent several years in the United States and had worked for the Abwehr since 1937. Highly regarded by Colonel Oscar Reile, he was made the leader of a special *Sonderkommando,* in charge of informers whose job was to infiltrate the Resistance. At the Abwehr HQ Kayser was known as Gaston, and he reported directly to Colonel Reile.

Constantly threatened with arrest and deportation, Marette told Kayser that Marsac, whom he knew only by the code name End, was in contact with a Resistance organization that appeared to have connections with London. This was not much more than a shrewd guess, because End had told him nothing about his activities. Kayser decided that he needed a more intelligent go-between to ensnare the suspect. He ordered Marette to introduce Marsac to Helen James, a small, pretty, young Irish woman, with auburn hair and a zest for the good life. She had been a plaything of several Abwehr officers and was at that time Kayser's mistress. Kayser carefully briefed her before Marette introduced her to the intended prey.

On 21 March 1943 Colonel Reile called Hugo Bleicher to his office. With the Colonel was Gaston. The colonel informed his spy-catcher about the situation and ordered him to take over the case. Bleicher was to detain End and to try to win him over.

Helen informed Bleicher that she had told End she was British and an ardent anti-Nazi, that she knew German officers who trusted her because of her Irish nationality, and that she could give him some interesting information about the Germans. End had told her he would be away from Paris for a few days but would return on the 23rd. They had arranged a rendezvous at the Café Jacques in the Champs Elysées for the afternoon of that day.

Bleicher and two plainclothesmen of the *Feldpolizei* went to the café on the appointed day and sat in the balcony overlooking the entrance. Helen was already in position, pretending to read a magazine. Marsac arrived with his secretary, Lucienne Frommagot. Helen took a handkerchief out of her bag—the prearranged sign to the men on the balcony. The Germans went to the table, arrested Marsac and Lucienne, and drove them to Fresnes prison.

Of his conversations with Marsac in the prison cell Bleicher told me, "He was a brave man. For three days he wouldn't talk at all, even if I told him that I would have to hand him over to the Gestapo. Then the affair of the Cat gave me the idea of telling him that, having realized that after Stalingrad there was no chance of Germany winning the war, I decided to go over to the Allies. At first he did not trust me, but by and by he warmed up to me."

They had many long conversations. Bleicher told Marsac that he would get him out of prison if he, Marsac, would help him to contact the Allies. The best thing would be if they could go together to England. Marsac replied that this was a fantastic plan and, anyway, why should he trust a German Abwehr officer?

Such was Hugo Bleicher's power of persuasion that he succeeded in winning Marsac's confidence. He told him that he knew of several cases of anti-Nazi German officers escaping to England. The main thing would be to get in touch by radio with London, tell British intelligence that a German Abwehr officer was ready to defect to the Allies, and ask for a Lysander pickup for both of them. After several days of solitary meditation Marsac told Bleicher that he would try to arrange this, but that he would have to be released from prison in order to discuss the scheme with his friends.

This was not what Bleicher had intended. He explained to Marsac that he had to report to his colonel that Marsac had switched allegiance and was prepared to work for the Abwehr. Then he would be released and they could continue with their secret plan to go to England.

"I must have some names, addresses, and the location of your group's transmitters . . . some proof to convince my colonel that you agreed to cooperate. I'm not asking for a lot, just some information in order to justify your release," he told Marsac. But the Frenchman told him he must be crazy to imagine for one minute that he would betray his comrades. He said he would rather die in a concentration camp.

The trap was set but the spring seemed to be jammed. Bleicher, however, did not give up. He brought Marsac cigarettes and food and arranged to have him decently treated.

At last, after days of meditation and long sleepless nights, Marsac agreed to give Bleicher the address of his wife and two letters to some friends. Bleicher should go and see them, and if they agreed to the plan they would send a radio message to London. Marsac was still very cautious; he told Bleicher that his wife was on holiday in the Savoy mountains, at the villa Les Tilleuls at St. Jorioz. If she was not there a friend of his who was at St. Jorioz—Roger Bardet—would give her the letters. Marsac desperately tried to protect his comrades.

Bleicher said he would introduce himself to Mme Michelle Marsac, or to Roger Bardet, as Captain Henri of the German Luftwaffe, an anti-Nazi officer who wished to make common cause with the Allies. Marsac remarked with a wry smile, "You look more like a colonel than a captain," to which Bleicher replied: "Bon; Colonel Henri then."

On 4 April Bleicher traveled to St. Jorioz. When he arrived at Les Tilleuls, the place was littered with crates and suitcases. The inhabitants were clearly about to leave. They must have heard of Marsac's arrest. However, Mme Marsac seemed happy when Colonel Henri gave her the letter from her husband, informing her that the bearer was a friend and could be trusted.

Roger Bardet had gone to Annecy, and Colonel Henri met him later in the railway buffet. Bardet was tall, very thin, with jet-black hair and dark, fierce eyes.

"You're the man from Paris who saw Madame Marsac this morning?" he asked.

Colonel Henri gave him Marsac's other letter, and after Bardet had read it, suggested that he should come with him to Paris to see Marsac at the prison. "I hope to get him out of Fresnes within the next few days," he told Bardet.

Colonel Henri's Scheme

Bardet agreed to come to Paris but refused to travel with Colonel Henri. They arranged to meet next day, 3 April, at Marsac's apartment in Paris, to which Bardet had the keys. When Colonel Henri arrived at the apartment at the Porte d'Orléans, he found Roger Bardet in the company of two young men and suggested they go to visit Marsac at the prison.

"All right," Bardet said, "let's go." And turning to his two friends he said: "You stay here. If I'm not back within three hours give the alarm to our people at St. Jorioz. They know what they have to do."

When Bleicher and Bardet entered his cell, Marsac was overwhelmed with joy. Here was proof that Bleicher was a genuine friend. Marsac told Bardet that a pickup for himself and the German friend must be arranged very quickly. "It's the only way for me to escape and also to save our organization."

Bardet was doubtful. "But you know that Pierre [Peter Churchill] has gone. It may not be easy to get the message over and make such arrangements."

Marsac disagreed, pointing out that "because Pierre is there everything will be much easier. He will understand and arrange the pickup for us by a Lysander. Go back immediately and tell Arnaud to send a signal to London explaining the situation."

For many weeks Colonel Buckmaster had wanted Churchill and Henri Frager to come to London for consultations. The pickup was carried out during the night of the 22nd, with Marsac helping Churchill and Frager to guide the Lysander by light signals. The plane brought in two agents, Francis Cammaerts (Roger) and Georges Dubourdin, who exchanged their seats in the tiny plane with Churchill and Frager. Next morning the long-awaited Peter and Paul were in conference in Colonel Buckmaster's secret apartment at Orchard Court. They remained in London until 14 April.

After Churchill and Frager had taken off for England, Francis Cammaerts traveled to Paris. Marsac took him to his apartment in the rue Vaugirard, where he told him to have a rest while he went to meet a friend. Cammaerts never saw his host again. Marsac's meeting was with Helen—and Hugo Bleicher. Thus Cammaerts had a truly narrow escape.

The next day Cammaerts decided to make for St. Jorioz, hoping to meet Marsac again. Odette and Arnaud were surprised that Marsac had not come with Cammaerts, but they were not particularly worried. Cammaerts learned from Odette of the visit of the mysterious Colonel Henri and warned Odette to have no dealings with the German. Odette did not seem impressed by the warning from a "beginner," and Cammaerts left with a feeling that the St. Jorioz group was taking a somewhat lax attitude toward security.

Bleicher told me that he had never learned from Marsac of Cammaerts' arrival; nor had Marsac mentioned that he had dispatched Peter Churchill and Henri Frager to England. Although he had agreed to cooperate with Bleicher, Marsac was extremely careful in covering up for his friends.

No Love from London for Colonel Henri

At St. Jorioz, meanwhile, life seemed quiet enough. Bardet—after two or three days in Paris, during which he and Bleicher visited Marsac each day—

returned to St. Jorioz and kept the colonel informed of the progress in the exchanges of radio messages with London to arrange the pickup for him and Marsac. He telephoned Bleicher several times and eventually had to pass on some bad news. It seemed, Bardet reported, the chiefs of F section in London were not very eager to accept the proposals.

Indeed they were not. When Colonel Buckmaster received a more detailed report, transmitted by Alec Rabinowitch, of Bardet's visits to Marsac's prison cell he discussed the strange business with Peter Churchill and Frager. They decided to send the following signal to St. Jorioz:

COLONEL HENRI HIGHLY DANGEROUS STOP YOU ARE TO HIDE ACROSS THE LAKE AND CUT CONTACTS WITH ALL SAVE ARNAUD WHO MUST QUIT FAVERGES AND LIVE BESIDE HIS SET STOP FIX DROPPING GROUND YOUR OWN CHOICE FOR MICHEL[1] WHO WILL LAND ANYWHERE SOONEST

Although F section did not at that time identify the Luftwaffe Colonel Henri as Hugo Bleicher, their old adversary in the affair of the Cat and Pierre de Vomécourt, Colonel Buckmaster was extremely suspicious of the whole setup. Besides, Peter Churchill had never trusted Bardet.

Alec Rabinowitch shared Churchill's feeling. He, too, had grown increasingly suspicious of Bardet's repeated visits to Paris and told Odette that he would shoot Bardet. Yet there is no evidence that Roger Bardet did, or even intended to, betray his comrades at that time.

On 12 April Bleicher took Bardet and Mme Marsac to her husband's prison cell and discreetly waited outside during their reunion. That same evening Colonel Reile told Bleicher that the farce must end.

"Your plan to penetrate the St. Jorioz circuit by promising Marsac to escape to England was a first-class ruse. But will the Gestapo believe it? I have just heard from SS Sturmbann-Führer Kieffer that they have intercepted signals from an unidentified radio transmitter. Kieffer told me that some of these signals speak of a Luftwaffe officer trying to escape to England, together with a Resistance leader. So far Kieffer has not connected you with this business. But at any moment the Gestapo might discover the truth and we shall all be in trouble."

Bleicher hotly protested Reile's order that he arrest Bardet and Mme Marsac in Paris and then go to St. Jorioz and arrest anyone else he could find there. But Reile was not taking any more chances with the Gestapo, and Bleicher had to obey. He asked Bardet to come with all his Paris friends to Mme Marsac's apartment on the morning of 15 April to discuss the final plan for her husband's escape. Bleicher arranged for two squad cars of the secret field police to park in the Boulevard Brune near the apartment, and when the conspirators were assembled, eight Germans rushed the house and arrested them.

[1] Peter Churchill's code name.

Mme Marsac was completely taken aback. She had trusted the good German colonel implicitly. Roger Bardet remained calm when the handcuffs clicked on his wrists. He turned to Bleicher and said, "My congratulations, *mon colonel*. You played your game very well!"

Bleicher hurried to the Haute-Savoie before news of the arrests in Paris leaked out to the *réseau* and London. He took with him Kiki and two sergeants from Abwehr headquarters. They went to Grenoble to enlist assistance of the Italian intelligence; and Major Rancini, with a squad of *carabinieri,* accompanied Bleicher and his men to St. Jorioz.

The Golden Scarab

The St. Jorioz agents had been busy during the past twenty-four hours. At the farm at Faverges Alec Rabinowitch had been waiting by his set for the London signal announcing Churchill's return flight. Finally London came on the air: the pilot would make for the arranged dropping ground on the slopes of the 6,000-foot-high Semnoz peak. This was a bleak spot still under deep snow at that time of year. Rabinowitch and Odette decided to enlist the help of the maquisards in marking out the field. They still had to wait for the final BBC announcement that the aircraft was on its way. At 7 P.M., between items of music, they heard at last the eagerly awaited personal message: LE CARABE D'OR FAIT SA TOILETTE DE PRINTEMPS (The golden scarab is performing its spring toilet).

The party made off hurriedly. They marched eight miles to the slopes of the peak. The navigator of Churchill's aircraft, Colonel Livry-Lebel, knew the Haute-Savoie from his prewar skiing days and pinpointed the tiny dropping ground. The reception committee had made a line of small bonfires and they watched two parachutes descending, each bearing a container. At first there was no sign of Peter Churchill. Suddenly a smaller shadow appeared against the pale, moonlit sky. For a moment it looked as if he would land in a bonfire, but when he dropped he almost fell into Odette's arms.

Back at the hotel the party gathered round the fireplace for a celebration drink. After listening to an account of the strange events during his absence, Peter said firmly, "Tomorrow we'll clear out. Now let's go to bed and have some rest."

Alec Rabinowitch left the party to transmit a message to London:

FROM MICHEL STOP RAF AND RECEPTION PERFECT STOP ALL UNDER CONTROL

By 2 A.M. the hotel was in darkness when Bleicher and the *carabinieri* entered. The hotel owner came to the landing and saw the uniformed men in the hall. He began to talk loudly, desperately trying to warn Peter and Odette.

"What do you want, M'sieurs?" he asked. "Is this a police matter? Are you the police?" he nearly shouted, hoping that his friends would hear the ominous word. A door opened upstairs and Odette came out of her room.

Bleicher stepped forward. "German police. Don't move, Madame," he ordered. Then he asked Odette to show him her room. Silently she led the way. In one of the beds Bleicher saw a youngish, dark-haired man in blue-striped pajamas. On the coverlet was a book he had been reading. Bleicher asked him to get up.

"You are a British agent and a saboteur. You are under arrest. Please dress."

Bleicher had hoped to take Churchill and Odette with him to Paris, but Major Rancini insisted that the prisoners were under his authority, having been arrested in the Italian zone of occupation. The prisoners were taken to Annecy and locked up in the Italian military prison. The Germans thought their catch was even bigger than it was, for they believed Churchill when he said during his interrogation by Bleicher and the Italian intelligence agents that he was a relative of the British Prime Minister.

It took three weeks and an intervention by General von Stuelpnagel, the German commander in chief in France, before Churchill and Odette arrived under Italian escort in Paris, on 8 May. They were taken to Fresnes prison, where they remained for a year. The story of their sufferings— Churchill was subsequently held at the concentration camps of Flossenbürg and Dachau, while Odette spent a year in the extermination camp of Ravensbrück, which she miraculously survived—has been told in books[2] and films. They were both freed by American troops in May 1945.

The destruction of the St. Jorioz *réseau* was to have disastrous repercussions. Roger Bardet, whom Bleicher had used as a tool in his scheme for Marsac's escape to England, turned traitor. After his arrest Bleicher gave him the same choice he had given Kiki: "Either you cooperate with us, or I shall have to hand you over to the Gestapo." Bardet chose the easy way out. Bleicher says of him: "Like Kiki he volunteered to work for the Abwehr and, indeed, became the best assistant I ever had during my work in France." Eventually Bardet led the Germans on to the trail of other SOE networks and of Henri Frager, the leader of the JEAN-MARIE *réseau*.

Before employing Bardet, the Abwehr had to stage an escape so that the traitor could be restored to the Frager network. He was taken to Fresnes and kept there until May. One evening Bleicher collected him in an Abwehr car. On the road to Antony (a village near Paris) Bardet "escaped." German field police cars raced up and down the road, shots were fired, and

---

[2] Peter Churchill describes his imprisonment in his book *The Spirit in the Cage,* Hodder & Stoughton, London, 1954.

within minutes the whole district was awake. Everybody knew a prisoner had escaped during transport from Fresnes. News of "the escape of a dangerous terrorist" was published in the Paris newspapers, and a reward was offered for his recapture. Subsequently, Bardet was received by Frager and his friends as the escaped hero.

During the round up at St. Jorioz, Bleicher had missed one important member of the group—Arnaud, the radio operator Alec Rabinowitch. Bleicher later blamed it on the Italian *carabinieri* who made only a perfunctory search. A few other members of Peter Churchill's *réseau,* who were billeted at Duingt and at Taillaires, on the opposite shore of the lake, also managed to escape.

Rabinowitch was at his set at the Faverges farmhouse when he was told by a local Resistance member that all his friends had been arrested during the night. He immediately sent a signal to London, and taking his transmitter with him, left the area. During the next few days he managed to send a more detailed report to Baker Street. Then Colonel Buckmaster sent him a signal asking him not to take any more risks and to use the escape route to Spain. But Rabinowitch knew that Roger (Francis Cammaerts) had gone to Cannes. He decided to warn him of the events at St. Jorioz. He met Roger, told him the sad news, and then took the Spanish escape route to Britain. In 1944, before D day, he was sent on a second mission to France and was captured on arrival. Being a Jew, he suffered bestial treatment, and was eventually sent to the extermination camp at Rawicz in Poland. There, probably in the autumn of 1944, he was put to death in the gas chambers.

Roger

Francis Cammaerts, who was sent in March 1943 to France to reorganize the debilitated Resistance groups on the Côte d'Azur, had been absent from the struggle against Germany at the beginning of the war, having acquired deep convictions against war as an undergraduate at Cambridge. He was a schoolmaster in London when a tribunal for conscientious objectors directed him into agricultural work. Not until the end of 1941 did he decide, after much soul-searching, that the war against Nazi tyranny was just and deserved to overrule his pacifist convictions. When he volunteered for service behind enemy lines, Captain Selwyn Jepson, an F section recruiting officer, recognized that Francis Cammaerts possessed strength of character and a gift for leadership and was precisely the kind of man needed. No one, however, could foresee that this former "conchie" would become a war hero, perform deeds of extraordinary bravery, and finish

SOE top echelon in 1941. Brigadier Gubbins, Director of Operations (center), with Dr. Hugh Dalton, Minister of Economic Warfare (right), and Gladwyn Jebb, now Lord Gladwyn (left, background).

Col. Maurice Buckmaster, head of SOE's F section, 1941–1945.

Mathilde—Lily Carré, the Cat of IN-TERALLIÉ.

Hugo Bleicher (Henri), the Ace of the Abwehr.

Capt. Heinz A. Eckert, who dispatched the Cat to England. He infiltrated SOE networks by posing as Canadian Captain Harold Evans.

Major Francis Suttill, chief organizer of PROSPER. Executed at Sachenhausen.

Captain Pierre Culioli, organizer of *réseau* ADOLPHE. Survived Buchenwald.

Andrée Borrel (Denise), Suttill's chief assistant. Executed at Natzweiler.

Takeoff of an RAF airplane in England carrying SOE agents. Aircraft had to be over Allied territory on return journey before daybreak.

Packages ready for dropping over the DZ.

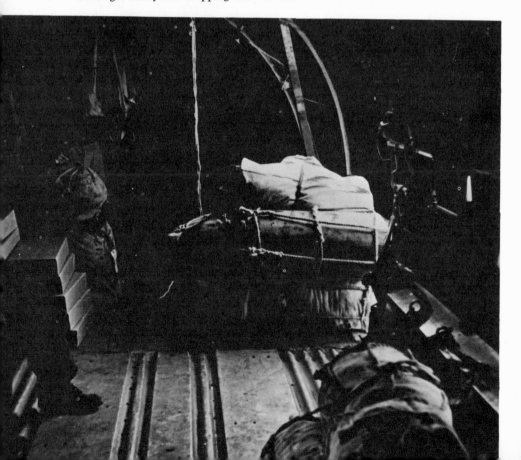

Containers with arms and explosives are dropped by parachute from an RAF aircraft to a Resistance reception committee.

Captain Harry Rée (Henri) of the Jura network in parachute kit.

An SOE agent drops into enemy-occupied territory.

Arms, ammunition, and explosives ready for packing in containers.

SOE officer at a maquis camp instructing Resistance members in handling weapons received from Britain.

Lt. Col. Francis Cammaerts (Roger), organizer of JOCKEY circuit, with his W/T operator Auguste Floiras (Albert), after the liberation.

Small Lysander aircraft were used for landing and picking up agents.

Some of the thousands of forged forms and rubber stamps manufactured by the SOE false documents section. Those illustrated include rubber stamps of French and Dutch municipalities, Registrars of Births, forced labor offices, police authorities, and the high command of the Wehrmacht, Gestapo, and *Sicherheitsdienst*.

his war service as a lieutenant colonel, with a DSO and the Legion of Honor among other awards.[3]

Within weeks of his arrival he set about rebuilding and establishing *réseaux* all over southeast France, from the Isère and Ardèche to the Alpes-Maritimes. Helped at first by only a handful of comrades and particularly by his radio operator, Albert (Auguste Floiras), he soon became the organizing officer of a region that stretched over 15,000 square miles. In June 1943 Colonel Buckmaster sent him two assistants, Alain (Pierre Rayneau), a young Frenchman, and Alice, forty-two-year-old Cecily Lefort, who became his courier. With members of the French Resistance whom he had enrolled, Roger carried out many sabotage actions. One of the most damaging was the destruction of the railway yards at Portes-les-Valances, where many locomotives and much rolling stock, about to be taken to Germany, were blown up.

In a raid on his headquarters at Montélimar, Alice was captured by the Germans, but Roger and Alain managed to escape and they established a new headquarters at Seyne-les-Alpes. From there, traveling all over his vast region, Roger organized many local groups and instructed their members in the handling of weapons, which had begun to arrive by parachute from Britain. He and his friends established more than seventy dropping grounds for the reception of containers. From these groups emerged strong and well-disciplined units of the FFI (French Army of the Interior,) which played an important part after the landing of British and American forces in the south of France in August 1944.

Recalled by Colonel Buckmaster to London for consultations, Roger was dropped by parachute on 9 February 1944 on his second mission, bailing out with the crew of the Lancaster, which had caught fire after being hit by German flak. He returned to his headquarters at Seyne and began to prepare his men even more actively for D day and Liberation. Shortly before D day, Roger was joined by a remarkable woman, known as Christine Granville (a Polish countess, whose maiden name was Krystyna Skarbek). Christine had worked for British intelligence since the beginning of the war, at first inside German-occupied Poland, smuggling out information through Hungary and Yugoslavia, and later through the Baltic and Sweden. Then, after an adventurous journey, she reached London and was sent once more into enemy territory, being parachuted into Hungary. Later she worked in Rumania, providing information that enabled Allied air forces to destroy the Ploesti oilfields. Next she went to Germany in the guise of a Polish collaborator. By 1942 she emerged in Turkey, trailing

[3] The story of Francis Cammaerts' service in France is told in my book *They Came from the Sky*, Heinemann, London, 1965.

Herr von Papen's activities in Ankara, and finally appeared in Algiers, where she was transferred to SOE.

By May 1944 Roger, in cooperation with General Henri Zeller, commander of the southeastern region of FFI, organized and trained units totaling more than six thousand men, many of them armed with infantry weapons, machine guns, and bazookas dropped to his reception grounds.

In the Beaujolais Country

Three weeks after Francis Cammaerts landed in a Lysander northeast of Paris, two other SOE officers arrived in France at a place some six hundred miles to the south. They were Harry Rée (Henri) and René Maingard (Dédé), a young native of Mauritius.

Buckmaster had selected Rée for a special task: to assist Squadron Leader Maurice Southgate (in charge of the SOE network at Clermont-Ferrand) in detroying the Michelin works, which manufactured tires and caterpillar treads for the Wehrmacht. Rée and Maingard had to jump "blind" into a meadow outside the town of Tarbes in the Hautes-Pyrénées, not far from the Spanish frontier, because their pilot missed the dropping ground where a reception committee was waiting.

When Harry Rée eventually reached Clermont-Ferrand—Maingard had gone on to Montauban—the plans to sabotage the Michelin works had been changed and he was ordered to go to the Jura region. The organizer of the HEADMASTER circuit, Brian Rafferty, had Resistance contacts at Lons-le-Saunier, and Rée took charge of a new network there.

It meant starting from scratch, but Harry Rée—or Henri Rehman, an itinerant watchmaker from Alsace, as he had now become—succeeded in establishing his STOCKBROKER circuit very quickly. Henri was fortunate in recruiting a number of excellent helpers from among local Resistance members, including the two Larsenieux brothers, Pierre and Jean; Raymond Lazerri, an ex-airman who had escaped from a German POW camp; Henri Clerc, a wine merchant; and Jean Simon, a young bank clerk from the cathedral town of St. Claude.

During the weeks following his arrival Henri crisscrossed the area, finding new helpers, establishing local groups, selecting dropping grounds, and preparing for the reception of arms and sabotage material. Lazerri took him to some of the secret maquis camps. The maquis was strong in the Jura; hundreds of young men had taken refuge in the mountains and forests from the threat of deportation and forced labor. Now they clamored for military instruction and weapons. Rée organized several more camps, but at first he had to be careful not to promise too much.

For many weeks he lacked a radio link with Baker Street and had to rely on the Clermont-Ferrand network for transmitting reports to Buckmaster and receiving instructions. Eventually, after he had reported that several dropping zones and reception committees were ready, the first supplies of arms and explosives began to arrive. By and by his large region, from Belfort and Besançon in the north to the villages in the valley of the river Ain in the south, was dotted with reception grounds and populated with many hundreds of men whom he had trained. In many a cave, lined with vats of Beaujolais wine, were now hidden the arms and ammunition that had arrived from Britain.

Early in May 1943 sabotage began in earnest. Some of the local Resistance men quickly became experts at that dangerous game: Robert Doriot, a former airman; Bothey, the baker at Dampierre who, with his small team, successfully sabotaged railways in the frontier region; Paupal, a little draper at Chaussin who blew up singlehanded a heavily laden troop train; Guth Granchet, a former journalist and air force pilot, now working in a toy factory at Point-de-Poite, to whom Henri entrusted many receptions of containers; André Jeanney, a young officer who had fought with de Gaulle's famous 5th Tank Division at Laon and Abbeville in 1940.

Rée devised many sabotage plans that were successfully executed, but there were bitter setbacks too. On 12 May one of the Larsenieux brothers was captured, and the Germans, enraged by the sabotage activities of the "terrorists," began to round up suspects in the Lons area. Many arrests were made and Lons became too hot for Henri. He moved his headquarters to Vallentigny, a village near Montbéliard, where André Jeanney found him a hideout in the house of Barbier, an accountant at the nearby Sochaux works of the Peugeot Motorcar Company. But Henri never stayed at Vallentigny for longer than a day or two at a stretch. He was constantly inspecting his groups—nearly always on his cycle—visiting the maquis camps, explaining the use of some new explosive gadget sent by London.

The Man Who Drove for the Gestapo

Brian Rafferty (Dominique) came once or twice from Clermont-Ferrand with instructions from London, otherwise contact had to be maintained by couriers. Rafferty's last visit, at which he met Raymond Lazerri at Lons-le-Saunier, ended in disaster. Both were arrested and taken to the Gestapo prison at Dijon.

Harry Rée tried to rescue them. But short of an armed attack on the heavily guarded prison there seemed to be no way of freeing his two comrades. Then Paupal the draper told him of Pierre Martin, who had escaped from Dijon prison and who boasted of good contacts with some warders there, and Paupal arranged a meeting with him. Martin was a huge man, strong and willful, with a certain amusing charm; and he was not reluctant to talk about his daring achievements. The Resistance men spoke of him with awe and respect. Martin told Henri that he was a former officer and had served with the *Deuxième Bureau* of French military intelligence.

Martin offered to take food and money to the Dijon prison for the two men, but he was unable to do anything more. Nevertheless he proved useful in many ways. He had a car and a Gestapo *permis de conduire,* which he said he had been given in order to drive Gestapo officers, who had never discovered that he had been in prison for Resistance activities. Martin found Rée a safe house at St. Jean-de-Lons, and together they destroyed the lock gates at the junction of two important canals. When several parachute drops were received near St. Amour and Dôle, Martin helped to transport the containers to hiding places.

At last news arrived from Isidore (Captain George Donovan Jones) at Clermont-Ferrand that two SOE officers would arrive from Britain to join Rée in the Jura and set up a radio post.

The two new arrivals were Captain John Starr (Bob) and Lieutenant John Cuthbert Young (Gabriel), the W/T operator. Guth Granchet collected them from Clermont-Ferrand, and Harry Rée, with the help of the Lons wine merchant, found them a safe place to stay: the Château Andelot, a moated castle near St. Amour.

Captain John Starr met Pierre Martin, the blustering Resistance leader and Gestapo driver, and apparently took a great liking to him. They became almost inseparable. By mid-June, however, Rée no longer trusted Martin. From Abbé Schwander, the leader of the Gaullist *réseau* at Montbéliard, and from other Resistance members Rée had discovered that Pierre Martin was a liar. He had never been an officer or a member of French intelligence. Before the war he had been a car salesman of dubious reputation. When Rée confided his suspicions to Captain Starr, his warnings were brushed aside with a casual "Don't worry old boy. I understand this type and I can handle him."

John Young, a pleasant Scot, proved to be a skilled "pianist," and Rée was able to use his transmitter for regular communication with Colonel Buckmaster.

The Peugeot Works

The great motorcar works of Peugeot at Sochaux had long been a priority target of the Ministry of Economic Warfare in London. Although Rudolphe Peugeot—unlike many other French industrialists and big-business men, who had either become German collaborators or jumped on the Pétainist bandwagon—secretly supported the Resistance, he was compelled to run his factories under German control. The Sochaux works manufactured tank turrets and vehicles for the Wehrmacht.

The RAF had carried out several bombing raids on the works, but the damage was slight; and production was stepped up after the Germans had brought their own technicians to Sochaux in the summer of 1943. The workers, constantly threatened with deportation or imprisonment, had to do their jobs. The problem of the Peugeot works was discussed by Ministry of Economic Warfare officials with the chiefs of staff and officers of Bomber Command. Eventually, it was suggested that the French section of SOE should be brought in. Colonel Buckmaster asked Rée to destroy the works by sabotage.

This was a tall order, but Henri was determined to carry it out. The motor works were heavily guarded day and night. A complicated system of passes had been introduced, and every worker, clerk, and visitor was searched on entering and leaving the factory area. Through his host at Vallentigny, Henri met Sire, the personnel manager of the Sochaux works. Sire secretly supported the Resistance, provided passes, and arranged for Henri to see Rudolphe Peugeot.

"Monsieur Peugeot, I'm a British officer," Henri said. "Your factories are producing gun-carriers and tank turrets for German Panzers. I know you don't like it, but you have to do it. We must put a stop to this business. We must blow up your works."

Peugeot looked at him quietly. Then he said with a smile, "I shall be delighted. But as the head of my family concern I find your suggestion a little . . . well . . . a little upsetting."

"I quite realize that, and I'm sorry," Rée replied. "But the Sochaux works is a major war objective. Air raids failed to destroy the factory. If sabotage fails we must expect more bombing. It will probably cause a lot of casualties among the workers and civilian population. None of us wants this to happen. In a direct sabotage action we could pinpoint the target, let's say the transformer hall, the power supply, the assembly workshops. But this is only possible if I have your help."

Rudolphe Peugeot agreed to organize the destruction of his own plant. Not only did he give the plans of the factory to Harry Rée and help to select the points for placing the explosives, but he also put him in touch with two trustworthy employees who could carry out the actual operation. One was the foreman Schorp, an Alsatian who worked in the upholstery workshop; the other, André van der Straaten, who became the contact between Schorp and Henri. Harry Rée told me it was largely due to these two men that the explosion was confined to the factory area and that the town was spared.

Preparations took several weeks. Then on 5 November, at ten minutes to midnight, five men selected by Rée entered the factory grounds. Schorp and van der Straaten had hidden themselves in clothes lockers on the office floor when the factory closed in the evening. The plastic explosives had been smuggled into the Peugeot works during the day and hidden in small boxes

[119]

in a cleaner's cupboard. Two members of the party who had passkeys freed the locked-in men and then left.

Schorp and van der Straaten placed the charges in the transformer hall, in the assembly plant, and on the steel presses—machines that were extremely difficult to replace. Knowing every nook and cranny of the factory, they avoided the sentries and let themselves out through the nightwatchman's room.

Ten minutes past midnight the Peugeot works were blasted by a series of heavy explosions. Fires started in a dozen places, and within minutes large parts of the plant lay in ruins. The fire brigades, rushed from towns and villages in the vicinity, could do little but keep the conflagration from spreading. Within minutes SS and army units arrived and the whole area was cordoned off.

Next morning hundreds of workers employed at Peugeot's stood around idly while frantic Gestapo officials began their investigations. Nearly all the presses had been blown up; there was no chance of restarting work for many weeks. The Germans arrested a few suspects, but Schorp, van der Straaten, and their helpers had escaped.

The German engineers were determined to restart production as quickly as possible. New presses for the tank turrets were sent from the Goering works at Fallersleben near Hanover. To get them to Sochaux the Germans had to use barges on the Rhine–Doubs canal. Rée and his friends had envisaged this possibility. The Canal du Doubs runs through a narrow artificial bed near Medière, behind some bombed factories and disused yards. There a party led by van der Straaten ambushed the first barge, opening fire from Sten guns. The French crew jumped ashore and ran for their lives; the German guards returned the fire, but were overpowered. Explosives were placed on the barge and it was blown up, blocking the narrow stretch of the canal.

This was a particularly gratifying success because the canal was used by the Germans to transport midget submarines from the east to the Mediterranean. Several weeks passed before the damage was repaired; then another shipment arrived—two new steel presses—this time from a factory near Stuttgart. It was heavily guarded and SS men patrolled the shores. An ambush was impossible, and Harry Rée's men decided to attack when the shipment reached Sochaux.

This was pulled off in broad daylight, as soon as the presses arrived on huge trucks in the factory yard. Hand grenades were lobbed at the trucks and several homemade bombs where thrown from the roof of one of the buildings. Even after several months and much effort on the part of the Germans to replace the damaged machines, the production of the tank turrets could not be resumed. The factory was not restored to its full capacity until the end of the war.

The Peugeot works, earmarked by the Ministry of Economic Warfare as "the third most important industrial target in France," which the Allied bomber raids failed to destroy, was thus successfully sabotaged by a handful of SOE men. Other targets sabotaged by Rée and his men included the Usines Marti, where thousands of gallons of oil were destroyed, and the factory of the Leroy Machine Company at St. Suz, which was badly damaged.

Betrayed

On 16 June 1943 a young WAAF officer, Diana Rowden (Paulette), was sent from London to act as Captain Starr's courier. Landed from a Lysander in the Angers area, she traveled to the Jura and joined Starr and John Young at the Château Andelot.

In July Starr told Rée that Pierre Martin had told him about a special train, carrying Field Marshal Rommel, that would pass through Mont-béliard on the 16th. He suggested that Henri's saboteurs derail the train. Starr said that he himself was otherwise engaged—he was to attend a *Quatorze Juillet* celebration—and Rée went to Dijon to organize the action with a group of railwaymen, led by Bothey. The plan proved to be a wet squib; the charges were laid but the train never passed that way. It seemed that Pierre Martin, for some reason of his own, had sent him on a wild-goose chase.

On the morning after the abortive attempt at the train, Rée was at Besançon. During the night there was a heavy Allied air raid. He made for a café whose owner had often acted as a contact between Rée and Starr and Pierre Martin. The man looked worried as he gave Harry a grubby piece of paper. The message was from Pierre Martin:

Bob and I were taken yesterday by the *frisés* [Germans] on the road to Dôle. I managed to talk myself out, but they took Bob to the prison of Dijon. Can't understand how they got me and Bob, nor why they released me and not Bob. Are you being followed? Take great care. Meet me on Friday afternoon in the waiting-room of Dijon station. Greetings, Pierre.

"Do you trust him?" asked the café owner. "I think he wants to get you, too!"

"Yes, it looks like it, doesn't it?" Henri replied. The news of Starr's arrest was stunning. Now the whole network was in imminent peril and he had to warn John Young, Diana Rowden, and a frighteningly long list of his Resistance comrades. Harry Rée was now convinced that Pierre Martin was a double agent. He recalls:

"I decided that I must avoid being arrested before I had warned my friends and done something to safeguard the arrival of a new man, due from

London. And I also decided that we must render Pierre Martin harmless . . . ."

He sent Jean Simon to tell John Young and Diana Rowden to go into hiding, and arranged a hideout for them at a sawmill at Clairvaux. Then he sent André Jeanney to Martin, asking him to come to a meeting at Maiche to discuss the situation. At this meeting Harry Rée and Jeanney were to kill Martin. Jeanney went to a café at Maiche to collect Martin while Harry Rée, armed with a blackjack and a revolver, waited for them in a wood. Martin, however, did not keep the date. Instead, Jeanney saw at the café several strangers who had arrived by car. He recognized two of them as Gestapo men from Dijon. Martin, too, had laid a trap.

When Harry and André returned to Vallentigny there was more bad news awaiting them. There had been a crop of arrests during their absence. The Germans had raided the Clercs' home at St. Amour, and although they failed to get Henri Clerc, they had arrested his father. They had also taken Starr's driver and the owner of the Café Strasbourg at Lons, who had been Rée's mail drop. Jeanney and other Resistance friends insisted that Henri must disappear if he was to save his life. But Rée was determined to make arrangements for the survival of his network. Not until he was satisfied that he had done what was humanly possible, did he get in touch with a *passeur,* and on 1 August he cycled to Hérimoncourt. Titi, the *passeur,* led him through mountain footpaths to the Swiss frontier.

The crossing was uneventful, but he was soon stopped by Swiss frontier guards and taken to Porrentruy police and internment. Harry Rée's enforced visit to Switzerland did not last very long. Four weeks later he was back, returning to adventures that nearly cost him his life.[4]

[4] See chapter 10.

7

"Prosper"

FOLLOWING the breakup of the INTERALLIÉ network, the most pressing need of Colonel Buckmaster's F section was a central network in the Paris area. Pierre de Vomécourt had been earmarked for this key position. But when he returned to Paris in April 1942, after his adventures with the Cat, he was arrested within a month—as was Roger Cottin, who had been holding the fort.

Buckmaster then decided to send Major Ben Cowburn to establish a new foothold in the French capital. After his narrow escape during the Cat episode, Cowburn had crossed France and reached Britain via Spain. Two months lated he volunteered for this second mission. Because Paris was a dangerous place for him, Buckmaster decided that Cowburn should go with another SOE officer, Ernest Wilkinson (Alexandre), introduce him to Paris contacts, and then leave the capital and concentrate on work in the unoccupied zone.

They departed on 1 June, but instead of being dropped near Bellac (Haute-Vienne) as arranged, an erratic navigator released them forty miles from the prepared dropping zone. On landing they lost each other and only after many adventures met again at a café at Tarbes, which had become, through French SOE agent Charles Rechenmann, a frequent rendezvous for "lost" agents.

They continued on to Lyons, where they met the ever-helpful Virginia Hall. Wilkinson, however, was arrested when he went with Robert Heslop (Xavier) to meet a radio operator, Denis Rake (Justin), at Limoges. Cowburn, without a radio operator, returned to Britain in October. But he had used the intervening time for some successful sabotage action.

Another attempt to form a Paris network was made at the end of June 1942. Raymond Flower (Gaspard), a restaurant chef who had worked for some years in Paris and had been a sergeant-cook in the RAF before joining SOE, was parachuted "blind" near Tours. His orders were to establish a pilot circuit and to make contact with Marcel Clech (Bastien).

Clech had been one of the very first agents of D department before SOE's F section made strides. A taxi driver from Brittany, he came to Britain with de Gaulle's first Free French units, enlisted in SOE, and was trained as a radio operator.

A plan to send him in February by motorboat to join Pierre de Vomécourt misfired, and he reached France by submarine from Gibraltar. After meeting Virginia Hall at Lyons, he eventually joined up with Gaspard at Tours, but the two never saw eye to eye. Flower also had been told in London to get in touch with Annette (Germaine Tambour), a middle-aged woman in Paris who had been one of the first contacts of the D section. But it seems he did little about it. It was hoped that Clech would later install the radio post for the intended Paris network. At Tours, Clech found he would hardly be overworked by Gaspard, who said they must wait for new instructions from London.

Clech became utterly frustrated, especially when signals he received from London expressed astonishment about the inactivity of the Tours *réseau*. He tried to contact local resistance leaders, but was quickly discouraged by his chief. Nevertheless he met several active Resistance men. Among them was the former member of the French Chamber of Deputies for Tours, M. Meunier, who introduced him to a remarkable young man, Pierre Culioli.

The Young Lieutenant

Toward the end of May 1940, the French Fifth Army Corps fought its last battle against the Germans near the forest of Mormal. The French sustained terrible casualties, and the remnants of the corps surrendered. Among the prisoners was a diminutive young lieutenant, Pierre Culioli.

In a German POW camp he became seriously ill and was allowed to go home. Although hardly recovered, he decided to go to England to join General de Gaulle. To this end he appealed to the American consul in Marseilles to help him get to Gibraltar, then tried to reach North Africa in a boat—all in vain. He traveled the length of France to Brest, seriously planning to cross the Channel in a rowboat. At that time he met the municipal architect of Chambery, M. Stephane, who was the chief of the first Resistance group in the district. Within weeks Pierre Culioli became the leading spirit of the group and helped fourteen RAF pilots, shot down by the Germans, escape to Spain.

Hunted by the Gestapo, he escaped to Tours, under the alias Pierre Leclair, to continue Resistance work. There he met Marcel Clech and made contact with SOE. Clech introduced him to Gaspard, who was not particularly interested until Culioli offered him a safe hideout with a family named

Bossard at Avaray, and a field at Boisrenard suitable for receiving agents and supplies. SOE had certainly acquired an enthusiastic and efficient agent, but Culioli's admiration for Gaspard diminished rapidly. He felt that his new chief regarded his stay in France as a holiday rather than a dangerous duty. Baker Street, too, began to wonder about Gaspard's suspended animation.

Culioli might have packed up and left to join a Resistance group, were it not for the arrival of a woman from London.

Yvonne Rudelatt, or Jacquelin, was the first woman agent sent by SOE into enemy-occupied Europe. She arrived in July from Gilbraltar, was received at Antibes by Peter Churchill and Marsac, and continued north to join Gaspard. Her instructions were to work for the Tours-Orléans outpost as a courier.

She was an extraordinary woman. The chief recruiting officer of F section, Major Lewis Gielgud, had been aghast when a middle-aged woman —a grandmother, no less—walked into his room. But he was so impressed by her bearing and intelligence that he recommended her. Mrs. Rudelatt underwent full training, including a sabotage course and the parachute course at Ringway. When the time came to send her into the field, Major Bodington was going to the south of France and she accompanied him on the flight to Gibraltar and then on the boat voyage to Antibes. Their plane was attacked by two Messerschmitts off Brest and landed at Gibraltar on one engine, having flown much of the way at fifty feet above the sea, with Luftwaffe fighters in pursuit. Finally, the felucca that took them to the Côte d'Azur was chased part of the way by an Italian corvette.

When she arrived at Tours, the forty-seven-year-old woman announced that she had come to fight. Gaspard had made no preparations to receive his new courier, and Jacqueline, as she was now called, had to find her own quarters in the house of a man who, she soon discovered, made no secret about his pro-German sympathies.

Neither was Gaspard particularly pleased with Jacqueline's fighting spirit. He became increasingly worried that the Germans were hot on his trail and decided to get rid of compromising evidence. Visiting Jacqueline's room when she was out, he deposited a loaded .38 Colt, a portable transmitter, a box of spare crystals, a large envelope full of broadcasting schedules of the BBC, and a coded list of the members of his *réseau*. When Jacqueline returned, she was horrified that all her comrades might have been put in jeopardy. She knew her landlord often went through her things when she was not in.

She told Pierre Culioli, who collected all the material and hid it with Professor R. P. de Solage at the Collège St. Gregoire. But it was too late. The landlord had already searched her room and had reported to the local police. When Jacqueline and Culioli approached the house they saw the gendarmes waiting. Together they fled. Culioli put Jacqueline on a train to Poitiers, where she hid for a few days. Thenceforth the young man and the grandmother became firm friends.

Culioli went to Gaspard and made a violent scene. He told him he would ask Bastien to report the incident to London. But of course he was not entitled to give any orders or messages to the radio operator, and in any case, Gaspard forestalled him. He sent a long signal to Baker Street saying that Pierre and Jacqueline had gone over to the Germans. He followed this signal with a request for a poison pill in order to "put the traitor Pierre away."

This request upset the Chiefs of F section at Baker Street. They knew nothing of Pierre Culioli. It was, of course, impossible for them to assess the true situation, and they could justifiably assume that Culioli was a German V-man who succeeded in infiltrating Gaspard's group. They trusted Jacqueline, but it was quite possible that, lacking experience, she had fallen into a trap. After all, Flower was a British officer, a trained SOE agent, and in command of the group.

It was decided to send a reliable officer with one of the L phials of cyanide of potassium. He would investigate, and if Gaspard was right, he was to give him the pill to make "the traitor Pierre" harmless. As it happened, two officers were to be sent within a few weeks to Paris to establish the long-planned new circuit. One was to carry the poison.

Before these officers were dispatched, Baker Street was shaken by another incident, which provoked doubt about Gaspard. Buckmaster had notified him that the first reception of agents in his area would be during the full moon in September. This was an important drop. The two agents were women, the very first to be parachuted into France by SOE: Lise de Baissac (Odile), on her way to join her brother Claude (David) at Bordeaux, and Andrée Borrel, who as Denise was to go to Paris to prepare contacts for the two officers who were to follow shortly.

Gaspard confirmed the instructions but made no preparations for the reception. The plane carrying the two women agents circled several times over the area where the reception was to take place, but having received no light signals, had to turn back. Gaspard, believing that the operation had been betrayed, had disappeared.[1]

Baker Street ordered a reception arranged for the following night, 25 September, without fail. Bastien, unable to find Gaspard, told Culioli. The young Frenchman prepared the field and received the two women safely, helped by the undaunted Jacqueline.

[1] Deposition before the Military Tribunal by M. Dutems, mayor of Mer and member of the Conseil Général, on 27 May 1948.

The days of Gaspard's activities were numbered. On 2 October 1942 the officer to whom Buckmaster had entrusted the establishing of the new circuit arrived in France. He was Major Francis Alfred Suttill, whose code name Prosper became the designation of the vast network that he created with astonishing alacrity and efficiency.

Suttill, a lawyer in civilian life, was born in Lille in 1910, the son of a Manchester man who had married a French woman and lived for many years in Lille. Educated in both France and England, Suttill enlisted in the East Surrey Regiment when war broke out, was commissioned, and in 1941 volunteered for service with the French section of SOE, spending seven months at five Special Training Schools.

He was dropped by parachute into a field prepared by Pierre Culioli in the Touraine and received by Culioli, Jacqueline, and the new woman agent, Andrée Borrel. Again Gaspard was absent. With Suttill came Jean Amps (Tomas), a French jockey who had ridden in France and England.

Suttill had been given wide powers. At about the time of his arrival, Henri Frager broke with CARTE in the south of France and, encouraged by Baker Street, was building up his JEAN-MARIE circuit, which later spread far north. Frager's second in command, Marsac, had established a Paris foothold for JEAN-MARIE before he fell into the trap set by Hugo Bleicher. But with Allied landings in North Africa imminent, Buckmaster felt more strongly than ever that SOE must have direct and absolute control of a Paris network.

Suttill was given instructions to establish it and to set up *réseaux* in northern, central, and eastern France. He was authorized to take over the group controlled by Gaspard and use the contacts made by Pierre de Voméart and Ben Cowburn. Buckmaster promised that a number of SOE officers would be sent to him.

For this Suttill needed all his ample resources of energy, leadership, and diplomacy. During his eight months as head of the PROSPER network he established nearly sixty supporting *réseaux* and groups, including Le Mans and Angers in the west; Orléans, the Sologne, Bourges, and Tours in the south; Troyes, Châlons, and St. Quentin in the east.

Suttill was provided in London with an identity that enabled him to travel widely without arousing too much suspicion. On his forged documents he was François Desprée, traveler in agricultural produce. Andrée Borrel found him quarters in Paris, but before long they set off into the country together. In October they visited Chartres, Melun, Orleans, Blois, Romorantin, and went north to Beauvais, Compiègne, and St. Quentin.

At Tours, Suttill met Gaspard and was not impressed; but he liked Pierre

Culioli and Jacqueline, whom he had first met in London and whose enthusiasm he admired. He told Culioli that he was expecting his deputy's arrival and asked him to prepare the reception for him.

Suttill's deputy was Major Gilbert Norman. Born of an English father and a French mother at St. Cloud, near Paris, in 1915, Norman had joined the army in 1940. Major Lewis Gielgud suggested a transfer to F section of SOE in 1942, and Norman readily agreed. He trained at Loch Ailort and became a skilled radio operator. He was dropped by parachute on 1 November near Boisrenard, along with Lieutenant Roger Landes (Stanislas; later Aristide of Bordeaux), and was received by Pierre Culioli and the two Dutems, sons of the mayor of Mer and brothers-in-law of the newly married Culioli.

Gilbert Norman's code and field name was Archambault. This is important because he later also used his real Christian name, Gilbert, which led to a mixup with another Gilbert, with unfortunate results.

It was Archambault who brought the poison phial requested by Gaspard for disposing of Pierre Culioli. The lethal dose was packed in a small cardboard box inside a sealed envelope bearing the inscription *Pour Gaspard.* Because Gaspard could not be found, Archambault gave the package to Culioli when the latter took him and Stanislas to the home of his brother-in-law. Archambault asked Culioli to give it to his chief.

Culioli walked around for several days with the poison phial in his pocket before handing it over to the elusive Gaspard. He did not know, of course, that he was carrying the means for his own extinction.

Having met Culioli and gained a good impression of the young man, Archambault became exceedingly worried, and even more so after his meeting with Gaspard at Tours. He told Suttill about the poison affair, and Suttill agreed that the plot must be foiled. He told Gaspard to forget about his plan: "If you have reasons to distrust Culioli you must ask London to send a Lysander for him and order him to go to England. There they will take any action they think appropriate, after proper investigation."

Eventually, Suttill sent a signal to Buckmaster, describing the situation, assuring him that he considered Culioli to be trustworthy and requesting the immediate recall of Gaspard. After Gaspard's departure on 18 March Suttill appointed Culioli as chief of the *réseau* in the Touraine and made Jacqueline his deputy and courier. The little ex-aviator, who had grown a small Hitlerish mustache, promptly named his sector *réseau* ADOLPHE.

He wasted no time. With Suttill's approval he moved from Tours to the Sologne. This is one of the most picturesque areas of central France. Bordered by the rivers Loire in the north and the Cher and Yèvre in the south, it is richly wooded, with some marshland. Much of it is covered by dense shrubs, which in spring produce a vast carpet of dazzling yellow flowers, while in autumn the lilac heather abounds. Main roads bypassed the Sologne and tales were still alive of people getting themselves lost in the forests and marshes. It is ideal hunting country; and the Germans, having discovered its food-producing potential, ordered the inhabitants to deliver three million rabbits a year to help alleviate the shortage of meat back home. But the peasants, normally quick to exploit their natural resources, were slow to comply, and the Germans had a bloody and bitter task in attempting to cow these sullen sons of the Sologne. To a man, the people of the Sologne joined Resistance groups, many of them formed by Culioli.

From the small towns and villages saboteurs emerged to wreck factories and installations of importance to the Germans at Blois, Bourges, Orléans, and as far afield as the banks of the Orléans Canal and the outer industrial belt of Paris.

Many of these raids were led by Yvonne Rudelatt. Freed from Gaspard's shackles, brave, middle-aged Jacqueline took part in innumerable sabotage operations. One was the destruction of the Chaingy power station, another the blowing up of the Bronzavia works at Blois, which manufactured components for the Luftwaffe. The sabotage actions carried out by Jacqueline and her young helpers, such as Gérard Oury and Marcel Sauvaget, also included the destruction of more than two hundred high-tension electricity pylons, the blowing up of several locomotive sheds, and at least fourteen serious derailments of German troop trains moving east to Germany and the Russian front. During March 1943 alone, the railway lines between Orléans and Tours and Orléans and Vierzon were put out of action six times. Cautious estimates show some two hundred German officers and men killed or wounded in these derailments.

A typically effective action of the Sologne saboteurs was the planting of time bombs aboard a train carrying agricultural loot to Germany and the Channel coast for the German garrisons. One of the trains arrived at Caen and was shunted into the center of a large yard full of German ammunition and armament stores. Exactly twenty-four hours after leaving the rural heart of France, the train erupted in a terrific explosion that razed a row of store sheds and ignited the ammunition stores, causing greater damage than a bombing attack from the air.

In the words of SS Colonel Mersch, "The Resistance terrorists in this area were the most dangerous and difficult in the whole of France." Several *Sicherheitsdienst* officers, including SS Hauptsturm-Führer Max Schneider and Ludwig Bauer, were sent to the Sologne in 1943 with strong units of the SS. From their headquarters at Blois the Germans made every effort to discover the hideouts of the "terrorists." All they discovered was that a woman was one of the leaders.

There were, of course, similar actions in other areas under Suttill's command. His PROSPER network quickly became so big and complex that an elaborate system of intercommunications had to be created. The public telephone could be used only sparingly and with the utmost discretion because the Gestapo tapped and monitored calls systematically. Many telephone exchanges were riddled with German V-men and informers, willing to betray for the price of a pack of cigarettes. Even if code phrases were used, enigmatic conversations were liable to arouse suspicion. Postal censorship rendered letters equally risky. Thus all SOE groups were compelled to use couriers—a perilous occupation.

Maintaining radio communication with Baker Street became increasingly difficult because the German wireless detection and direction-finding service operated efficiently and more and more D/F vans roamed the streets of French cities and town. Fortunately, in 1943 SOE began to supply greatly improved and much smaller transmitters, which could be moved as easily as portable typewriters. At the end of December a second radio operator, Jack Agazarian (Marcel), was sent, parachuted near Rouen.

A strict rule was that the chief members of a circuit should never live together or too near each other. This provided some protection from capture. Suttill quickly began to assemble a large decentralized network. He secured the cooperation of industrialists, civil servants, railway officials, employees in public utilities, postmen, and even police officers.

One of the most important safe houses that Suttill established was at the École Nationale d'Agriculture, the famous agricultural college and research institute at Grignon, northwest of Versailles, within easy reach of Paris. Its director, Professor Maurice Vanderwynckt, his family, and several members of the teaching staff worked for PROSPER.

The college stands in a magnificent park surrounded by a large experimental farm and plantations. Professor Vanderwynckt's house in the grounds became Suttill's second headquarters. There, he, Major Gilbert Norman, Andrée Borrel, Captain Garry, Henri Déricourt, the air movements officer, and Major France Anthelme, on his visits to Paris, met the heads of various *sous-réseaux*. Some agents later found a refuge there from the Gestapo.

Among the friends of Professor Vanderwynckt was Professor Alfred Serge Balachowsky, a distinguished biologist at the Institute Pasteur. He became chief of a PROSPER group in the Versailles district. From his villa at Viroflay, on the road from Versailles to Sèvres, Professor Balachowsky, his wife, Vanderwynckt's son-in-law, Jean Douillet, and his friend Octave Simon, a sculptor, undertook many operations.

Just outside the ancient town of Gisors, in a pleasant house at Triechâteau on the river Epte, lived Madame Renée Guépin. Her home became the outpost run by Captain George Darling, and it was often used by Gilbert

Norman for radio transmission. Darling was engaged to Renée, but they were unable to marry for fear that his forged documents might betray him.

Another PROSPER *sous-réseau* was in the northeastern part of Ile-de-France, organized by Captain Gustave Bieler (Guy), a French Canadian, who achieved success after a painful start. The first months in France he had spent under an assumed name as a patient in a Paris hospital, having sustained serious injury when he parachuted in November of 1942, along with Captain Michel Trotobas.

Most important of all was Suttill's cooperation with Henri Frager, who had developed his JEAN-MARIE into an organization that reached many parts of France. With Frager and his lieutenant, Marsac and Roger Bardet, were only a few British SOE liaison officers, maintaining radio communication with London.

Preparing for Overlord

By the early spring of 1943 PROSPER had become the largest and most powerful network. New and momentous tasks were assigned to SOE in France. After the Casablanca conference in January, Winston Churchill and President Roosevelt announced that the Allies were determined to enforce Hitler's unconditional surrender. The Prime Minister spoke of an invasion of Europe within nine months. SOE officers in France were aware that they and their Resistance comrades would play an important role in the great drama that was to unroll. The various Resistance organizations began to unite; in March MUR *(Mouvements Unis de Résistance)* was created, and in May the CNR *(Conseil National de la Résistance),* composed of representatives of the militant groups, political factions, and trade unionists. Liberation committees were appointed to take over national and local administration when the Allied invasion, code-named Overlord, came.

The foundations for Overlord were well laid. The buildup of PROSPER continued in a climate of comparative security. But the first dark clouds began to appear on the horizon. Soon they grew to a storm.

During April and May 1943 a number of puzzling arrests occured among PROSPER's French supporters. The first blow was the capture of Germaine Tambour (Annette) and her sister Madeleine. The two women had been in the fight since the early days of the Resistance. Annette had been working in Paris for Henri Frenay and Carte, and while she maintained connections with Frager and Marsac, she gave valuable help to PROSPER. She was Suttill's first contact in Paris when he arrived in October 1942 and had introduced him to many people, including the scientists at the agricultural college. Her arrest on 22 April was a backwash from the capture of Marsac (End), Peter Churchill, and Odette by Bleicher. She had assisted Marsac on his regular visits in Paris and most probably was betrayed by Roger Bardet—his first offering to his new German employers.

Suttill made a determined attempt to rescue the Tambour sisters. Disregarding his own security, he contacted a German V-man and through him two SD sergeants. He offered them a substantial sum to stop the prison van taking the sisters to Fresnes from the Gestapo headquarters, free the Tambours, and deliver them to his men. The two Germans did stop the van when it drove through the quiet Bourg-la-Reine, and released two women. Unfortunately, perhaps due to a genuine mistake by the Germans, they were not the sisters Tambour but two women arrested after a denunciation.

These and other arrests perturbed Suttill. He did not know the circumstances of Marsac's arrest, nor did he know that Roger Bardet had become a double agent. But Suttill realized that the Germans had become much more aggressive.

Until the spring of 1943 the Abwehr was in charge of the counter-espionage against British agents in France. The Gestapo and its *Sicherheitsdienst* concentrated on the French Resistance groups. This division of labor satisfied German logic in that the Gestapo, exercising the ultimate police authority in France, dealt with the French "terrorists," while measures against the belligerent enemy, Britain, were the responsibility of the German military intelligence.

Events inside the Third Reich, the growing suspicion of the Nazi leaders against their generals and the Abwehr in particular, wrought changes in this arrangement. Ultimately the Nazi leaders assumed control and the Abwehr knuckled under the thumb of the RSHA. All this was reflected in France, where Gestapo bosses Oberg and Knochen [2] achieved ascendancy over the Paris Abwehr.

Often the two organizations hunted the same men and spoiled each other's plans. The SD was much more crude and ruthless in its methods, but often more efficient. Many of its senior officers—for example, SS Sturmbann-Führer Hans Josef Kieffer, formerly chief of the Karlsruhe CID—were trained policemen. The Abwehr, like British intelligence, relied on regular officers, journalists, teachers, commercial travelers, who knew France and could speak French. Although few of the SD men knew the country or the language, this hardly proved a disadvantage. They had unlimited funds at their disposal and poured Judas money into the pockets of thousands of French V-men and informers. The SD dredged its way through muddy rivers of treachery and denunciation.

[2] SS General Karl Oberg and SS Major General Helmuth Knochen were the last two war criminals still kept in a French prison in 1962, after their death sentences were commuted. At Christmas 1962 they were released and returned to Germany.

A similar division of labor between the two German organizations existed in the Low Countries, where a plot was evolved that led to the total destruction of PROSPER.

Treachery in Holland

On 26 June 1942 a Dutch professor, George Louis Jambroes, was sent by the SOE Dutch section from London to his homeland to assume control of the Dutch secret army and prepare "Plan Holland," devised by the Allied chiefs of staff for the liberation of the Low Countries. Jambroes and his radio operator, Joseph Bukkens, were captured as soon as they set foot on Dutch soil, but London for many months remained unaware of this.

Using Jambroes' and other captured agents' radio transmitters, the Abwehr completely hoodwinked not only the Dutch section of SOE but also the Dutch exile government in London and its secret service departments. When after more than six months the British and Dutch, perplexed about Professor Jambroes' apparent inactivity, ordered his return to London, Major Giskes and SS Sturmbann-Führer Schreieder evolved a cunning scheme. Over the captured radio posts they informed London that Professor Jambroes was too busy to come to London, but would send a deputy, Captain Kist (Anton). This Dutch SOE officer had been captured by the Germans, but London was ignorant of this, too.

After many exchanges of signals over the *England Spiel* radio link, it was agreed that Captain Kist, accompanied by a French-speaking Belgian Resistance leader, would travel to Paris, where DF escape guides would arrange his journey to London. Naturally, the Germans could not send the real Kist, and the Abwehr embarked on a fantastic impersonation plot.

Sergeant Karl Boden, who spoke fluent Dutch, became Captain Kist. His companion, impersonating Arnaud, a Belgian Resistance leader, was Sonder-Führer Richard Christmann.

It has never been established exactly how the two impersonators, after their arrival in Paris on 18 May 1943, found the first four members of PROSPER with whom they made contact. But Helen James, her lover Robert Kayser (the German informer who had stage-managed Marsac's arrest), and Roger Bardet (who knew PROSPER members and Armel Guerne, Suttill's chief French adjutant, through Frager) all had a hand in arranging the first meeting.

Boden and Christmann apparently met Gilbert Norman, Jack Agazarian, and his wife Francine (who had arrived on 17 March by Lysander and as Marguerite became one of PROSPER's couriers), and Andrée Borrel at the Café Lorraine at Montmartre. They introduced themselves as two Dutch section agents and showed such good knowledge of DF's escape arrangements that they gained the confidence of the four PROSPER members. It is quite certain that the latter knew nothing about any arrangements that might have been made in London for the two would-be escapees, and that Buckmaster's F section was in no way concerned with this affair.

Christmann, the false Arnaud, was the spokesman, while the false Anton was prudently taciturn. Christmann seemed to believe that Gilbert Norman (Archambault) was "Gilbert" (Henri Déricourt), the air movements officer. Agazarian, who had worked for Déricourt as a radio operator, discussed with Christmann the possibilities of a Lysander pickup. He advised the two Dutch escapees to return to Holland or Belgium and to come back early in June. They pretended to do so, but they remained in Paris (though Christmann paid a brief visit to The Hague to confer with a superior there).

They had obtained from their new PROSPER friends an address where they could contact them—the apartment of Alain Bussoz, one of PROSPER's couriers.

Agazarian arranged a rendezvous with Arnaud and Anton for 9 June at the Café Capucines, having told the other three PROSPER members who had been at the Café Lorraine that he had asked Déricourt to arrange the pickup.

When Agazarian and the two "escapees" were at the Café Capucines, two German field policemen entered and asked the guests to show them their identity cards. This looked like one of the usual checks. Boden, playing the false Anton, whispered, "I don't want any trouble," got up and made for the door. Christmann (Arnaud) and Agazarian produced their cards, which one of the Germans inspected and found in order. The other policeman, however, went after the false Anton and arrested him. He was taken to a waiting car.

Agazarian was petrified and Christmann, still playing his part, seemed extremely upset. He told Agazarian that the pickup was now off and that he must return immediately to Holland. He also asked that he be given a radio transmitter so he could get in touch with his colleagues in Holland, saying they would accept as genuine only messages that were transmitted by him personally. Gilbert Norman produced a transmitter that was brought to Paris from Pontoise by Marcel Charbonnier, a member of PROSPER.

From Christmann's statements after the war to the interrogating judge of the 2nd Military Tribunal in Paris, it is clear that he and Boden obtained through their charade practically all the information about the PROSPER network they could possibly desire. Christmann reported his discoveries to SS Sturmbann-Führer Kieffer at Avenue Foch, taking great care not to be followed by members of PROSPER. His precautions were unnecessary; he was regarded as completely trustworthy.

The next day Arnaud (Christmann) appeared in Alain Bussoz' apartment, exhibiting proper anxiety, to inquire whether Anton's arrest had been reported to London. He asserted that the whole idea of putting Professor Jambroes through the escape route was now far too dangerous, and announced that he was returning to Holland. With a sense for irony, the German advised his SOE friends to be very careful lest Anton talked.

When Suttill received a report about the raid at Les Capucines he was seriously worried. He sensed disaster and confided in several people. He was angry with Agazarian for having been involved with the "two Dutchmen," and he told him that he was sending him to London "for a rest." On 16 June Agazarian and his wife left by Lysander in an operation that brought four new agents to France: Cecily Lefort (Alice) for Cammaerts' circuit; Diana Rowden (Paulette) to join John Starr and Harry Rée in the Jura; Noor Inayat Khan (Madeleine), who was to work for Émile-Henri Garry, head of PROSPER's subcircuit CINEMA; and Charles Skepper (Bernard) to organize MONK at Marseilles.

Jack Agazarian left under a cloud; he was soon to return—to his death

8

Pacts with the Gestapo

FRANCIS SUTTILL knew little about the meetings between the members of his staff with the two mysterious visitors from Holland. During the night of 13–14 May, a few days before Christmann and Boden staged their impersonation, he had gone by Lysander to Britain for consultations with SOE chiefs. He returned to Paris after the damage had been done.

The arrangements for his flight to London were made, as were all Lysander operations, by Gilbert—Henri Déricourt, the air movements officer of the French section. After the war Henri Déricourt became involved in a protracted investigation into the part he was alleged to have played in the destruction of the PROSPER network.

Déricourt arrived on 23 January 1943, three months after Major Suttill had begun to build his network. From the start he was one of the most important SOE officers in France, being in sole charge of all Lysander operations. As a former French airline pilot, member of the French air force, and pilot for SOE's Moon Squadron, he seemed ideally suited for this post. Although the Sologne became one of his main operational areas, he controlled fields in the Angers area, in the Touraine, and in the Ile-de-France. At his trial after the war it was stated that more than 250 people had traveled in and out of France under his arrangements. By the time he was accused of treachery in 1948, many of his "customers" had become famous and several testified that he had saved their lives.

To find suitable grounds and to attend pickup receptions he had to travel often and widely, using various aliases. But in Paris he lived with his wife and his family under his real name in his prewar apartment at 58 rue Pergolèse. Twenty years later Hugo Bleicher told me that he had lived next door at No. 56, and that he knew Déricourt by sight but never spoke to him.

"I heard that he was an agent of Gestapo chief Boemelburg, and my chief, Colonel Reile, strictly forbade Abwehr men to have any private dealings with Gestapo and SD officials and agents," Bleicher told me.

What was the truth of Déricourt's role as a double agent?

At his trial in June 1948 the president of the *Tribunal Militaire,* M. Déjean de la Batie, asked him whether he denied that he also maintained contacts with the Gestapo.

He replied that he never denied this, and that British intelligence had been fully informed about his contacts with the Germans. He said that on 2 June 1943 he was visited by two Germans whom he had known before the war as Lufthansa pilots. They took him to a car in front of his house. In the car were two other civilians, one who was addressed as "Herr Doctor." This German had told him that he knew his past and present history, had given him the correct dates of his arrival by parachute in France and his journeys to England, and had said that the Germans knew about his activities for SOE.[1]

"We can shoot you as a spy," the doctor had told him. "But you are an intelligent man and I hope that you will agree to work for us."

The president of the court asked the accused his reply.

"He knew all about me, and I did not know what to do. I am an aviator and not a spy," Déricourt replied at his trial.

He had accepted the doctor's offer to work for the Germans, but he was determined to fool the Gestapo. "I accepted, but not for money, neither because I was afraid to die. For a pilot, death is almost a natural thing and I do not fear it. But I accepted because I thought that it was the only way to save forty-eight agents of the British Intelligence Service whose lives depended on me."

There was one more life he was determined to protect, which he did not mention at his trial: that of his wife, Janine Déricourt.

After the war, when charged with treason and collaboration with the enemy, he said: "I had no choice but to accept the Gestapo demand. Even if I might have been able to abscond and escape to England, the Germans would have arrested my wife; a threat to this effect was made by the doctor at the very first meeting." [2]

The mysterious Gestapo agent was Dr. Josef Goetz, one of the top officials of the *Sicherheitsdienst* on SS Sturmbann-Führer Kieffer's staff and, like Kieffer, a former CID chief inspector of the Karlsruhe constabulary. Goetz was in charge of the *Funkspiel* at Avenue Foch.

From then on Gilbert became a double agent. But he insisted at his trial that he worked honestly for the British, and only "feigned to work for the Germans." He said he considered himself "a prisoner of the Germans, a prisoner at liberty" and that he had no alternative. He said he never gave the Germans information that could have endangered his comrades. He

[1] *Cf.* Trial transcript of the *Tribunal Militaire Permanent* at Reuilly Barracks, June 1948, and DST dossier of Déricourt's interrogations in 1946.

[2] Transcript of Déricourt's statement before DST (the French security police) on 22 November 1946.

admitted that he told the Germans the location of eight landing grounds in the Touraine, but these grounds were never again used for landing or pickup operations.

Gilbert remained in the field until the beginning of February 1944. During his service he was involved in many important operations. He dispatched Major Suttill to England in June 1943, received the Lysander that brought Madeleine (Noor Inayat Khan) on 16 June, and after the destruction of the PROSPER network he made the arrangements for the reception of Major Nicholas Bodington (Buckmaster's deputy), who arrived on 15 July to investigate the situation. Gilbert also sent Bodington back to England with several other SOE agents. Thus he had ample opportunity to betray these SOE officers, but he did not.

It cannot be verified whether Suttill suspected Gilbert of double dealing. Nor is it certain whether he was told in London that British intelligence chiefs had knowledge of Gilbert's contacts with the Germans. But I know that after his return to France on 12 June 1943 Major Suttill told his friends that "somebody who had enjoyed his trust must be a double agent." Surviving members of Suttill's network, such as Mme Guépin, Mme Balachowsky, and Armel Guerne, have confirmed my belief that this was Suttill's feeling.

Déricourt might not have been acquitted except for the testimony of Major Bodington. Appearing as a defense witness at Déricourt's trial, Bodington told the court: "I knew that Henri Déricourt was in contact with the Germans. He told me about it a few hours after I arrived at the landing ground at Cande on 15 July. I told him not to break off his contacts with the Germans. I remained in France for about a month and I saw Gilbert on a number of occasions."

The famous advocate Maître Moro-Giafferi, who defended Gilbert, asked Bodington whether he had felt safe. Gilbert had known his movements and the places he was staying in Paris and elsewhere. He could have had him delivered to the Germans, could he not?

"He certainly could," was Major Bodington's reply. "But if I had to start it all over again, I would start it with Gilbert."

With that reply the charges against Henri Déricourt suddenly collapsed and the military tribunal returned a unanimous verdict of "not guilty."

Déricourt's case was not unique. In 1948 Pierre Culioli also was tried—and acquitted—for collaborating with the Germans. During the first four postwar years 118,000 French men and women were prosecuted for collaboration with the enemy during the occupation. Of those, some 50,000 were brought to trial, but only 791 were executed. Of the remainder, 38,000 men and women were sentenced to various terms in prison and "loss of national dignity," which involved disfranchisement and ineligibility for public office. A very large number of the death sentences were commuted to imprisonment and most of those originally sentenced to death were released after a few years.

Considering the fact that he was found completely innocent and acquitted, Gilbert had suffered great hardship. He had been arrested on 26 November 1946 and was kept in custody for more than eighteen months until his trial.

A Mysterious Explosion

During his stay in London from 14 May to 12 June, Suttill conferred with the SOE chiefs. He left them in no doubt of his anxieties, stressing that he had reason to suspect that his PROSPER network had been infiltrated by the Germans. He cited details of the many arrests during April and May. One setback that badly upset Suttill was the capture of Captain Wilkinson (Alexandre), the SOE officer in charge of the *réseau* at Angers, who was arrested on a visit to Paris.

In fact the ultimate move made by Kieffer and the Gestapo against PROSPER was the result of the impersonation by the two Dutch "escapees."

At Baker Street, Suttill urged his chiefs to send him reinforcements, so that he could reshuffle some of the leading posts in his networks. He was still in London when Lieutenant Gaston Cohen (Justin) and Vera Leigh (Simone) were parachuted in.

Suttill also arranged at Baker Street for the pace of arms and explosives deliveries to be stepped up. The first drop in the new series took place on 12 June and several more followed. One was arranged near the hamlet of Neuvy, some eight hundred miles north of the road that leads from Neuvy to Neung-sur-Beuvron. Pierre Culioli and Jacqueline were entrusted with these operations and also with the reception of Frank Pickersgill (Bertrand) and John McAlister (Valentin).

Since 1 May Culioli had his safe house at a little forester's cottage called Cercle, at Veilleins in the Sologne, where Suttill had visited him and Jacqueline before going to England. On this occasion Suttill, Culioli, Déricourt, and Captain Armel Guerne, Suttill's liaison officer for the area, were guests of Count and Countess de Bernard at the Château Nanteuil. The count, an important Resistance leader in the Blois area, had been in touch with the British intelligence since 1941, when one of the members of CARTE, Valentin Rey, arrived in the Sologne from the south of France. Thus the château became known to Baker Street as a safe house. Archambault, after his arrival in November 1942, and Gilbert, in February 1943, as well as Major Suttill, contacted the count.

Only a few days before Suttill's departure for England, Count de Bernard introduced a new and valuable member to PROSPER—M. Bussière, the prefect of the department of Loir-et-Cher. A prefect is the highest administrative official of a department, in control of the gendarmerie and police and judicial powers. M. Bussière at first refused to cooperate with British intelligence officers, although he helped Culioli and Jacqueline organize many sabotage actions. Eventually, however, the prefect agreed to cooperate directly with SOE.

On the night of 12 June Pierre Culioli and Jacqueline drove to Neuvy with Count and Countess de Bernard. There they met several members of the local *réseaux:* Albert le Meur of the Chambord group, Georges Ferme, leader of the Montrichard group, and others waiting for a large drop of containers.

Three or four vehicles parked near the dropping ground were ready to convey the containers to hiding places. The RAF Halifax released the first containers without mishap. After twelve containers were dropped, one of them suddenly flared and exploded. One or two other containers caught fire and more explosions followed. Within seconds the whole dropping ground was enveloped by smoke. Two members of the reception committee, Caillard and Deck, were injured by flying debris. The situation became extremely dangerous. Although M. Bussière had arranged for French gendarmes to keep clear of the area, there was a German field police station at Fontaine-en-Sologne, only two miles away. The SOE agents and their helpers expected to be surrounded by the Germans at any moment. Nevertheless, they salvaged some of the containers, and then dashed to the cars. Strangely, no Germans arrived.

The next morning the owner of the field, a farmer named Massicart, discovered not only the smoldering debris but also two intact containers. To protect his family, Massicart reported the matter to the French gendarmerie post at Bracieux. The gendarmes, duty bound, passed on the information to the German field police. The Germans had been alerted during the night by the explosions, but for some unknown reason were unable to find the field. Now they arrived in strength, having reported the explosion to the Gestapo HQ at Blois. Five hundred SS men in squad cars from Blois and Orléans and a unit of infantry moved into the area between Bracieux, Neuvy, and Dhuizon, causing wild excitement throughout the quiet countryside by roaring along lanes in armored cars and firing at anything and nothing. Harassed for weeks by Culioli's and Jacqueline's sabotage actions, the Germans regarded this drop and explosion as the last straw and embarked on a punitive expedition throughout the Sologne. Within twenty-four hours a force of about two thousand men with tanks was concentrated in the area. Dozens of raids were made in the towns and villages and many people were arrested.

Culioli sent an urgent message to Déricourt asking him to tell the French section to cancel all air operations in the area for the time being. It is not known whether this message was ever sent to London.

The fact remains that from 12–20 June the most critical week in the history of PROSPER, all dropping operations from London continued according to the prearranged timetable.

Culioli received no reply to his message in which he had urged cancellation of further drops. So he prepared fields to receive the agents whose arrival had been announced previously by London.

On 13 June Culioli received Major Suttill. Culioli expressed surprise that Suttill was dropped in the Sologne, despite his warnings, but Suttill did not offer any explanation. Their only occasion to talk, and that briefly, was at dinner at the home of Guy Dutems, Culioli's brother-in-law. At the meal Suttill told Culioli of his anxieties about recent developments and said: "I asked you to receive me because I did not want to be received by anybody else." He did not elaborate, although his departure for London originally had been arranged by Déricourt. After dinner Suttill was driven to Amboise and caught a train to Orléans, where he changed for Paris.

On 16 June two SOE officers, Bertrand and Valentin, were dropped and received by Culioli. He took the two Canadians to the house of Mayor Dutems, where they stayed for two nights.

During the night of 20–21 June, a van loaded with containers, which had been collected after a drop at the Villeny field, was being driven to Dhuizon by André Habert, a Romorantin garage owner. In the van were Roger Couffrant, chief of PROSPER's subcircuit at Romorantin, and four of his men. They were caught at a German roadblock outside Dhuizon, and the containers, hidden under straw, were discovered. All the Resistance men were beaten up on the spot, bundled into a German truck, handcuffed behind their backs, and taken to the Gestapo prison at Blois. Another group, led by Marlot, a schoolmaster, succeeded in collecting other containers and unloading them at a farm; but they were also captured soon afterward. Significantly, the Germans told their prisoners: "We weren't looking for you or your stuff. We were looking for someone arriving from England." No one ever discovered how the Germans had knowledge of the parachute drop.

A Race With Death

In spite of these danger signs, Culioli and Jacqueline decided to carry out Suttill's order that they escort the two Canadians to Paris. At 7 A.M. the four drove in a Citroën on the Vernou road toward Dhuizon. They noticed German sentries standing on the roadside ten yards from each other. Culioli was at the wheel. They passed one roadblock safely; Culioli showed his papers, and the SS men motioned him on.

At the entrance to Dhuizon their car was stopped again. An SS Scharführer ordered the two men in the back to get out. Their seats were taken by two SS men, who ordered the driver to go to the town hall. The two passengers followed on foot, escorted by the SS sergeant and a storm trooper.

At the town hall the four prisoners were taken to the council chamber where they joined the sixteen other men arrested during the night. They were lined against the wall and guarded by SS men and field police. The four from the Citroën were searched but nothing was found to arouse the suspicion of the Germans, and their papers still seemed satisfactory.

At this point one of the German officers addressed the driver of the car: "Why were you on the road at such an early hour during the curfew?" Culioli replied: "I am a public servant on my way to a new position." In answer to further questions Culioli said that he was a forestry official and that this was borne out by his papers. The German officer called in the mayor, M. Montprofit, and asked him whether he knew the forestry official. After taking a good look, M. Montprofit said: "I do not know him personally, but I have seen him in the vicinity. I believe he works somewhere here on an agricultural job."

The officer then produced a small box that had been found in the car. It was sealed and the German asked Culioli, "What is in here?" "Oh, just a pork pie," said the little man with a disarming smile. The German handed back the box and made out a safe-conduct pass, which he gave the driver with a polite *"C'est à madame et monsieur."* The young forestry official and his middle-aged "wife" walked out of the town hall to wait in their car for their two passengers.

Suddenly an SS officer who was examining the Canadians' papers came into the street and asked them to get out again. Culioli realized the game was up. He put his foot down hard on the accelerator and the Citroën hurtled off.

As Culioli drove off with Jacqueline an SS man fired but did no damage. Culioli swung the car into a side street. A dozen SS men jumped into three powerful Fords and raced after the Citroën. Culioli forced his old car unmercifully. She responded with a speed of eighty miles per hour, but about eight miles from Dhuizon the leading Ford drew within a few yards of the Citroën, and the Germans opened fire again. The bullets ripped into the tires and body and smashed windows.

Jacqueline was hit twice and slumped down beside Culioli, who could no longer see the road through the cracked glass of the windshield. He drove on, but the Ford overtook them and forced the Citroën to ram a brick wall of the inn Mère Loulou. Culioli was knocked out in the crash. He was dragged from the car by the SS men and thrown to the ground; five of them set upon him with their fists, revolver butts, and boots. Jacqueline, covered with blood, was thrown to the ground by his side. But she had still enough strength to fire several shots at the Germans before she, too, lost consciousness.

Culioli came to and kicked the SS men savagely until one of them fired and smashed his knee with the shot. That ended the fight, and the prisoners were taken back to the town hall.

Culioli was dragged into an office. The Gestapo officer opened the pork-pie box; it contained two of the latest SOE miniature radio receiving sets— which ran on flashlight batteries—some radio crystals and four pieces of paper. One was inscribed "Pour Prosper," two "Pour Archambault," and one "Pour Marie-Louise" (the wife of Claude de Baissac, head of the Bordeaux circuit).

After examining the contents of the box, which had been brought to France by Pickersgill, the Gestapo officer turned to Culioli and said, "I think this will be sufficient, don't you, M'sieur?"

Culioli was given first aid and was driven to the Luftwaffe hospital at Blois. Jacqueline's condition was more serious and she was taken to St. Nicholas Hospital at Blois. Pickersgill and McAlister were taken to the Gestapo office, interrogated throughout the night by SS Sturm-Führer Ludwig Bauer, and beaten mercilessly by his men.

Tightening Tentacles

During the dramatic chase between Dhuizon and Bracieux, Suttill was with Major Gilbert Norman and Andrée Borrel in Armel Guerne's flat in Paris. Later he went to meet Madame Balachowsky at the Gare Montparnasse, where she took a train home to Viroflay. While seeing her off he remarked that he was deeply worried about a traitor within the circuit. He then went by *métro* to the Gare d'Austerlitz for the meeting with Culioli and the Canadians. With Andrée Borrel and Guerne he waited for two hours; but, according to Guerne—the only survivor of those two days in Paris—they were not particularly anxious, because Culioli had told them to wait again at the same place the next day should he be unable to make the journey on the 21st.

Suttill had spent the night at a small hotel in the rue de Mazagran, a side street off the Boulevard Bonne-Nouvelle. He registered with the proprietress, Mme Esther Fèvre, as "engineer François Desprée," and took a small room on the second floor.

When Culioli's party failed to arrive the next day, Suttill lunched in Guerne's apartment and said he would go to Triechâteau to see Captain George Darling. He hoped Culioli would contact Marcel Charbonnier and let him know when he would bring the Canadians to Paris. Suttill spent two nights at Triechâteau and had to be back in Paris on the morning of the 24th, having made a date for 10 A.M. with Claude de Baissac. On the 25th he was also to meet Michel Trotobas from Lille and Major France Anthelme (the itinerant SOE political emissary who had arrived on his second mission in May, to try once again to bring Édouard Herriot to Britain). At 8 A.M. on the 23rd Charbonnier arrived with the news that Culioli had neither appeared nor sent word. In Paris they were now anxious about what had happened in the Sologne. Suttill returned to the capital immediately, arriving in his hotel at about 10:30 A.M.

Nine hours earlier seven men in plain clothes had visited Mme Fèvre and inquired about François Desprée. Two of them sat down on the bed and one on the only chair. The other four went downstairs again and told Mme Fèvre to go back to bed, warning her not to say anything if Desprée appeared. When Suttill arrived he went straight upstairs. A few minutes later Mme Fèvre saw him brought down, handcuffed.

He was driven to Avenue Foch where long interrogations began in the office of SS Sturm-Führer Josef Placke, in the presence of Dr. Josef Goetz and SS Sturm-Führer Karl Langer.

In 1946, in depositions to French interrogating judges investigating Nazi war crimes, Placke maintained that Suttill was not harmed during his questioning, which continued for forty-eight hours, although Placke admitted he was not present the whole time, taking breaks for rest and food, which were denied to the prisoner. Another SD man, Sonder-Führer Vogt, said that as far as he could recall, Suttill's interrogation lasted sixty-four hours. It was sometimes conducted by SS Obersturmbann-Führer Kieffer and also by the chief of the SD in France, SS Standarten-Führer Dr. Helmuth Knochen.

None of the Gestapo men ever explained how Suttill's hotel address was discovered. This is perhaps the most puzzling feature of the whole case because he only stayed at Mme Fèvre's for one night and had never been there before. The Germans must have received the information from one of the very few people in whom Suttill had confided his address after his arrival from London. So we are forced to suspect that there must have been a double agent close to Suttill.

Suttill tried desperately to protect all his friends but in the end apparently broke down on at least one point. According to Placke, he told his interrogators that his circuit had an outpost at Triechâteau.[3] Why he admitted this single fact is a matter for speculation. It may well be that something was found on him at the time of his arrest that pointed to his visit to Gisors, possibly a railway ticket or a scribbled note he was unable to explain. The Germans learned of the existence of George Darling at Triechâteau; this disclosure was to have tragic results.

Archambault and Denise Are Taken

The arrests of Major Gilbert Norman and Denise (Andrée Borrel) presented no problem to the SD. The mystery is why they were not taken

[3] Depositions of Josef Placke and others, DST dossier No. 446/1/1946.

earlier, having been under constant surveillance ever since Sonder-Führer Richard Christmann (Arnaud) and the false Anton met them at the flat of Alain Bussoz.

French agents of the Gestapo, Mario Bay and Michel Bouillon, members of the Laffont–Bony gang, trailed them. In the early hours of 24 June three SD squad cars pulled up outside 75 Boulevard Lannes, the home of the Laurents where Norman and Denise were staying. Although fifteen men had come, no guard was posted at one entrance to the house, leading to the Boulevard Henri Martin.

A member of the squad rattled the garden gate and M. Laurent rose to open the door. Seeing only one visitor, who asked if "Monsieur Gilbert" was at home, Laurent hesitated. The man added, "I come on behalf of Archambault. This in itself was extremely odd: Archambault, Gilbert Norman's code name, was known to only very few agents. Members of the circuit knew him by his field name, Gilbert, which was his real Christian name (and also the code name of Henri Déricourt). Laurent had never heard of Archambault, and he went to Norman's room and gave him the message. Norman must have been puzzled that someone had come on his own behalf. When he came out into the hall he was seized by several men while others rushed into his room and found Andrée Borrel in bed. They ordered her to dress. Norman, Andrée, and Nicco and Maud Laurent were all driven to the Avenue Foch.

Meanwhile, a hundred miles from the capital, at Blois in the Sologne, Culioli's interrogations continued. Culioli described the scene to me as follows: "They put all my clothes and my hat in a heap, and I noticed there was a bullet hole in my hat. I must have had a very close escape from death. My arms were crossed over my head and chained to the bed railing. A doctor gave me three injections saying they would relieve my pain. SS Sturm-Führer Bauer and other Gestapo men began questioning me in this position, striking me with a heavy black leather belt, the buckle invariably hitting my nose, mouth, or eyes. They asked me where I stayed; and in order to protect the Dutems, my parents-in-law, I gave them an address of a boarding house in Orleans, where I did stay at various times. There was a postal order in my wallet bearing its address. The interrogation ended abruptly, I think, because the SS men decided they could not continue beating me in front of the Luftwaffe doctors who entered the room. I was then taken to the barracks of Duke Maurice of Saxe and put into a cell where the man-handling continued. Finally, they took me to the Gestapo building, where examinations proceeded in Bauer's office. Eventually, after Bauer told me they knew I was an important officer of PROSPER, and mentioned the names of Suttill, Archambault, Denise, Déricourt, Lequeux, and several others, I agreed to make a statement. Bauer knew all about our organization. I dic-

[145]

tated a statement to the interpreter, fabricating a story as I went along, hoping to protect myself and the others."

Bauer was not very impressed. He had already interrogated Pickersgill and McAlister and knew they had been received by Culioli. Asked about dropping zones and fields he had prepared, Culioli named two areas, one of them a site south of the Loire that had not been used for many months. He also explained the signals for landings, but outlined a system that had long been abandoned.

Half carried by SS men, Culioli was dumped into a car and driven with Bauer to Paris. On the way they halted outside Maves, where Culioli indicated a dropping field that had never existed. By extraordinary chance he saw his brother-in-law from the car as they drove through Mer. Jean Dutems was fishing in a river, and Culioli was reassured that the Germans had not yet caught up with him. They arrived at the Avenue Foch just before midnight on 24 June, and as he was being taken to Kieffer's office Culioli met Maud Laurent in the corridor.

He whispered to her: "Jacqueline has been killed by my side, I believe."

Madame Laurent replied: "Archambault and Denise have been arrested with my husband and myself."

Culioli just had time to add: "And Prosper?" before he was pushed on by the SS men.

Much was made of the two words "And Prosper?" at Culioli's trial in 1948. Some of his accusers insisted that he had completed Madame Laurent's phrase by adding ". . . and Prosper." They deduced that this meant he knew of the arrests and was a traitor. In fact, it was just a question and most understandable. Having been told of the capture of Major Norman and Andrée Borrel, he was anxiously asking about Major Suttill. This was believed by the court and eventually contributed to his acquittal.

The Trap for Darling

As soon as the SD men had extracted the Triechâteau address from Suttill, Kieffer personally organized an expedition to "clean out the nest." He prepared with pleasure and Teutonic elaboration.

Two truckloads of SS men, commanded by Sturm-Führer Keller, were accompanied by Placke and three SD interrogators. A squad of French Gestapo agents—"the scum"—including Roger Dupré, René Lefèvre, Jacques d'Arcangues, and Lucien Prevost (a notorious *agent provocateur* who rendered many similar services to Kieffer) traveled, fittingly, in a van.

The Germans obviously expected to find a large number of SOE officers at Gisors, the only place that Suttill had told them about. They were equipped with a letter, extracted from Suttill under duress, asking Darling to hand over hidden arms to the bearer. Outside Gisors, the van and Prevost, who was now riding a motorcycle, separated from the SS coaches, which were parked in a meadow.

At Madame Guépin's house Prevost presented Suttill's letter to Captain Darling, saying he and his Resistance men would like to collect the arms immediately. Darling did not suspect a trap. He invited Prevost in for a drink, and the V-man mentioned the names of several SOE officers and casually referred to Suttill's recent trip to London.

A little convoy of Darling and Prevost on motorcycles with the vanload of "the scum," posing as Resistance men, bringing up the rear, then proceeded to Darling's arms dump at the Bois d'Étoile. It took the French traitors nearly an hour to dig up all the containers of Sten guns, ammunition, and explosives. When the material was loaded, Darling offered to show them a road that avoided Gisors. Prevost declined this and insisted on leading the way.

To Darling, riding behind the van, the first sign of treachery was the sight of Prevost, dismounted by the side of the road, brandishing a revolver and yelling, "Hands up! German police."

Instantly Darling swerved off the road and accelerated along a rough footpath into the forest. The SS men ran out from their hiding place and SS man Keller and Prevost opened fire at the fleeing man.

Darling was hit several times, but he pushed on. His machine lurched and skidded along the rutted track. Eventually he collapsed on the saddle. Then he crept on all fours through the undergrowth. An hour later the SS men and French traitors found him lying in a pool of blood. Placke took him to the Municipal Hospital at Gisors and stayed by his bed all night. Captain Darling died the next morning without regaining consciousness.

Mme Guépin heard of Darling's desperate flight and left her home to hide in the hut of a friendly shepherd. When the German party returned to Triechâteau and found her house vacant, they stole many personal articles, including her jewelry. After lying low for a few days Mme Guépin stayed with friends at Rouen and later moved to Paris. She resumed work for the Resistance but was arrested in December 1943 and sent to Ravensbrück concentration camp. She survived and was freed after the war.

A German Pact of Honor

Placke, Langer, and Keller returned to Paris and reported Darling's death to Kieffer, who ordered Suttill to be brought to his office. There an extraordinary conversation took place.[4]

Kieffer told Suttill of Darling's death. The Englishman must have been tormented by self-reproach, as he had given the Triechâteau address to the

[4] Placke, Dr. Goetz, Vogt, and other men of Kieffer's referred in their depositions to this pact. Cf. DST dossier No. 446/46.

SD. Kieffer averred that such would be the end of all his comrades if he did not cooperate. He added that the Germans had known all about Major Norman and Andrée Borrel ever since the Christmann–Anton affair. Finally, he confronted Suttill with Norman.

Then Kieffer proposed a Pact of Honor: If Suttill and Norman would tell him the whereabouts of the other arms dumps, all members of the circuit arrested would be treated as prisoners of war. They would not be ill-treated, sent to a concentration camp, or executed.

"They will be held as soldiers and treated as prisoners of war. I give you my word as a German officer," concluded Kieffer.

Evidently Suttill and Norman independently decided that such a pact was the best they could hope to elicit. Their organization in ruins, the few remaining SOE officers and many hundreds, even thousands, of French supporters now leaderless and easy prey for the SD could, perhaps, be protected for the price of a few arms dumps.

Under this terrible pressure Suttill and Norman accepted the pact, although they did ask for a number of safeguards. Suttill insisted on having a document in which the *Sicherheitsdienst* stated that any PROSPER men, even if caught using a false name and bearing false papers, would still be regarded as soldiers and not civilians. Suttill tried to persuade the Germans to adhere to the terms of the Geneva Convention. Kieffer agreed, but said he must first obtain authority from the RSHA in Berlin. He said he was contacting Dr. Knochen and through him the chief of the *Geheime Staatspolizei,* Dr. Ernst Kaltenbrunner.[5]

Within four days Kieffer produced a document bearing the letterhead of the RSHA, Berlin, in which the Paris SD was given authority to treat members of SOE and their agents as prisoners of war. Kieffer explained in detail how this would work. Any captured member of the SOE and its suborganization—to which Kieffer invariably referred as the "*réseaux* of the War Office"—would, after interrogation, be handed over to the Wehrmacht provost authorities and sent to a *Stalag* for the duration of the war. Suttill accepted the pact. The document was countersigned by Kieffer and Suttill, probably the only time during the war a British officer added his name to that of a high SS Führer.

Then Kieffer ordered Major Gilbert Norman to be brought from his cell. He told him of the pact and said that he, too, should cooperate with the Germans, as this was the only way to save the lives of his comrades. Norman agreed.

At the end of the conference Kieffer said to Norman and Suttill: "Well, you will be the first prisoners to be treated according to this agreement. I have been ordered to send you to Berlin. You will be going in a few days and we will have another talk or two before you depart."

[5] Executed by the Allies in 1946 after the Nuremburg trial.

[148]

The agreement of cooperation was put into practice immediately. Sonder-Führer Ernst Vogt, an experienced CID inspector serving with the SD, was given the task of interrogating Major Gilbert Norman, who had already told Kieffer the position of arms and explosives magazines at Hirson, Méru, and Origny-en-Thierage. Vogt stated after the war that his work was easy. "I just had to write down what Archambault dictated."

Although Norman could name villages in the Sologne where dropping zones had been established, he did not know the exact positions and explained that Culioli had been laying out the fields. He also mentioned Gilbert—Henri Déricourt—but apparently the SD men were not interested for, according to Vogt, "they knew that Gilbert had been a German agent for a long time."

Major Norman probably assumed that since Culioli had been arrested, his relatives had also been caught. Therefore he mentioned that Culioli's two brothers-in-law, Jean and Guy Dutems, helped to organize the receptions. He also drew two small maps of the dropping zones in the Sologne. These disclosures led to the arrest of the brothers Dutems and their father, the mayor of Mer, who had not been suspected by the SD. However, Major Norman could not—or would not—give the names of the other members of the Sologne network, which the Germans were particularly keen to destroy. Vogt decided that a confrontation between Norman and Culioli would be useful.

Major Norman is dead, so I am dependent on information provided by official depositions and interviews with Culioli and surviving SD officers. Most of the information given by Culioli and the Germans tallies. Furthermore, several surviving French members of PROSPER, arrested through information supplied under the pact, corroborated these statements.

On 1 July Pierre Culioli was lying in a cell at La Pitié prison in Paris. Langer visited him and told him that the SD knew all the details of the PROSPER organization, including the arrival of Madeleine (Noor Inayat Khan) on 16 June, although he said they had not yet been able to find her. This he proved with horrifying thoroughness. First Langer produced a Michelin map showing sixteen dropping zones that, he said, were marked by Major Norman. He then produced a thick file of photostats. They were reports dispatched from the PROSPER circuit to London during the previous four or five months. They contained details of sabotage actions, including a plan to blow up two hundred pylons of the electric grid system, which had not been carried out because the PROSPER leaders had been arrested.

Finally, the SD man read out a precise list of parachute drops: "In May, at Chaumoint, 15 containers and two War Office agents; at Vallières, 10 containers; at Courmenin, 10 containers; at Mennetou, 10 containers; at

Neuvy, 4 containers; at Saint-Aignan, 10 containers; at Theillay, 10 containers . . . in June, at Vallières, 10 containers; at Guy, 4 containers; at Montrichard, two agents and 15 containers; at Huisseau-en-Beauce, 10 containers . . . ."

The following day Major Norman was led into Culioli's cell. He was handcuffed but apparently composed. His appearance was very much in contrast to that of Culioli, who, in addition to his leg wound, was covered with bruises and abrasions, including two black eyes.

Norman told Culioli about the pact signed between Kieffer and Suttill. He said: "They have known all about our activities for a long time; they are very smart but will not shoot anyone if they can recover the material. Prosper has agreed to deliver all the arms to them."

The two prisoners then discussed means of recovering the arms distributed in so many places. There were quite a few caches which neither of them could remember. Langer intervened: "We must get everything, down to the last pistol." There was some argument about the pact and Major Norman tried to explain that it would be impossible to find every Sten gun and revolver. Trying to soothe Langer, Culioli said: "Well, I did not distribute anything recently in my region because I wanted to avoid incidents, but I do know the whereabouts of some hundred containers." He realized the maps shown to him by Langer attested that at least four of the subcircuits had been "burned." With a heavy heart he decided to reveal the ammunition stores controlled by the four subchiefs, some of whom he knew had already been arrested: Roger Couffrant, at Romorantin, 30 containers; André Gatignon at Noyers-sur-Cher, 20 containers; Auguste Cordelet at Chaumont-sur-Loire, 25 containers; and Albert Le Meur at Chambord, 14 containers. Desperately he hoped this would be a sufficient sacrifice to save many other men and women and a large quantity of material.

Culioli's leg was still bandaged at the beginning of July when SS Sturm-Führer Langer took him on a tour of the Sologne. He was driven through the villages and confronted with the men who had fought so bravely with him. He was ordered to tell them about the PROSPER pact. At each place he repeated his message: Any Resistance men arrested would be treated as a soldier and no harm would come to their families or property.

A German Word of Honor

Culioli felt Kieffer would keep his word. He was encouraged in this belief by a message from Gilbert Norman brought to him by Langer: [6]

My old Pierre, according to my calculations there should be six radio trans-

[6] Guillaume, P., *La Sologne au temps de l'heroisme et de la trahison,* Orléans, 1950, p. 85 ff.

mitters in your possession. They have found only five at your place, the "gay brothel." Can you tell me where the sixth is?

Regards, Gilbert

In this way Culioli learned that his secret hideout, the tiny cottage at Veilleins, had been ransacked. He himself had never told the Germans about the place or the transmitters hidden there.

The missing sixth transmitter was with Count de Bernard at the Château de Nanteuil. But Culioli, determined to shield the de Bernard family, told Langer that as far as he could remember the sixth transmitter had been collected by Norman a long time ago. It was never found. Count de Bernard, hearing of the arrests, wrapped it in oilcloth and sank it in his ornamental pond. He retrieved it in 1945 after his return from a concentration camp.

At first the Germans were very correct. They arrested the subcircuit leaders named by Culioli, but during his tour they were released again; Pierre was glad to see that no harm befell them after they had surrendered their arms. But his concept of German honor was rather naïve.

A few days later the SS again descended on the Sologne villages. Cordelet was rearrested on 17 July, Caillard on the 15th, Culioli's brothers-in-law, Guy and Jean Dutems, on the 29th. They and scores of others, including the men who had retrieved the containers on the day of Culioli's car chase (Henri Daguet, André Habert, Prosper Legourd, Albert Mercier, Jean Sidney, and Marcel Thenot), were sent to concentration camps and executed. Their wives and children were also arrested, kept in prisons, or sent to Ravensbrück and Natzweiler. With a few exceptions, however, the women and children survived.

Thanks to Culioli's reticence, Count de Bernard remained at liberty for some time; but finally he, too, was caught. The circumstances of his arrest, yet again, involved the name of Gilbert. He was taken to Gestapo headquarters at Orléans and accused of hiding SOE officers in his home. His denials were met with the remark: "Gilbert has dined often at your château. He liked tripe and onions." This was indeed true, but the count was astounded when he was shown his own guest book, a fine volume in tooled leather. Obviously he had not been in the habit of asking SOE officers to sign it, yet there was a signature that the count had never seen before: "Gilbert."

The countess was arrested eight days later when she came to the prison with the prefect of Cher-et-Loire, M. Bussière, himself a secret member of the *réseau,* to visit her husband. Maurice Buhler, the count's second in command, was also arrested. The count was sent to Buchenwald, his wife to Ravensbrück, where she met Jacqueline. The de Bernards survived, but Buhler was executed. M. Bussière managed to keep his secret for a time.

He was later transferred to Marseilles as a regional prefect and continued to work in the Resistance until he was caught and executed in 1944.

The mighty PROSPER organization was dead. Very few of its leaders survived. Major Francis Suttill was hanged in the concentration camp of Sachsenhausen on 19 March 1945. Gilbert Norman remained for a while at Kieffer's office in the Avenue Foch. There he met Captain John Starr, who after his arrest in the Jura[7] was working as a draftsman and map maker. According to the depositions of several SD officers, Norman worked under Dr. Goetz as a radio operator for Kieffer's fake transmitters. When no longer useful he was handed over to the Gestapo and sent to the extermination camp at Mauthausen, where he was shot on 6 September 1944.

The two heroines of the circuit, Denise and Jacqueline, also perished. Denise (Andrée Borrel) was sent to the women's prison at Karlsruhe and on 6 July 1944 was transferred with three other SOE women—Vera Leigh, Diana Rowden, and Sonia Olschanesky—to Natzweiler, where they were killed by phenol injections. Andrée Borrel was twenty-five years old when she was murdered.

Jacqueline nearly survived. For weeks after the car chase, she lay gravely wounded in the hospital at Blois, but after several operations began to regain her strength. Countess de Bernard—then free—tried to organize her escape. She enlisted the help of one of the surgeons, Dr. Brun, two nurses, and M. Drussy, the hospital director. A Resistance man from St. Aignan, Georges Delille, manufactured a key to the door that led from the church of St. Nicholas to the hospital. Everything was ready for kidnapping Jacqueline from her bed, when Bauer suddenly ordered her transfer to Paris for interrogation. The conspirators were just twenty-four hours too late.

In Paris, Yvonne Rudelatt was kept first at La Pitié hospital, then at the prison hospital at Romainville; and, finally, she was transferred to the concentration camp of Ravensbrück. There she met her would-be rescuer, Countess de Bernard, who had been arrested in September. From Ravensbrück, Jacqueline was sent to the extermination camp at Belsen, where she was murdered in the gas chamber exactly a fortnight before the Allied forces arrived.

Pierre Culioli, after his tour with Langer through the Sologne, was finally returned to Paris to taste the Gestapo code of honor. From the Pitié prison he was taken to the special Gestapo prison at 13-bis Place des États-Unis, where he found Frank Pickersgill, one of the Canadians. On 20 November he was taken to Fresnes prison, where he met several other SOE officers awaiting transfer to Germany. Their destination was Buchenwald. There he remained until the end of the war.

Like Culioli, a few of the PROSPER team survived. One was Captain Maurice Lequeux, chief of the *sous-réseau* of the area north of the Orléans

7 See chapter 6, under "Betrayed."

Canal in the Touraine, who had to face a French tribunal when he returned. Lequeux had also surrendered to Kieffer's persuasion about the pact and had given the names of some of his helpers. His reward was a transfer to the extermination camp of Auschwitz. He survived, and after the war the French charged him with collaborating with the enemy. At Orléans in October 1945 he was sentenced to ten years' imprisonment, confiscation of property, and national "indignity." Later, however, the sentence was quashed. Having suffered so terribly at the hands of the Germans and his countrymen, Lequeux was a bitter man. He remembered Culioli's journey through the Sologne with Langer and firmly believed Culioli to be a traitor. It was his denunciation that led to Culioli's trial in June 1948. There were two charges against Culioli: "intelligence with the enemy" and "acts prejudicial to national security and defense."

At his first trial Culioli was acquitted of the first charge but found guilty on the second. Because of his heroism the court did not impose a sentence. He was not, however, the man to accept such a dubious verdict. He appealed to the higher military tribunal at Metz, and on 17 March 1949 was acquitted of all charges.

The two Canadians, Pickersgill and McAlister, were taken to the Gestapo torture chambers at the Place des États-Unis, where Culioli had occupied a neighboring cell. The Germans tried to induce them to operate the radio transmitter, which Pickersgill had brought with him and which was to be the Bertrand radio post. This the two SOE officers steadfastly refused to do.

In the spring of 1944 Pickersgill was brought back from Rawicz concentration camp and offered comfortable detention in Paris if he cooperated with Kieffer. So enraged was Pickersgill at the proposition, that at one "friendly" meeting he grabbed a bottle from his interrogator's desk, smashed it over his guard's head, and ran out into the hall. There he attacked two SS men with the broken bottle, killing one instantly and fatally injuring the other. Pickersgill then jumped from a second-floor window onto the street and ran toward the Avenue d'Iéna, with SS men in pursuit. Hit by four bullets, Pickersgill was recaptured and for weeks hovered between life and death. Finally he was earmarked for *Nacht und Nebel—Rückkehr Unerwünscht* (night and fog—return not required) treatment. On 8 August 1944 he was taken, with other SOE agents, on the infamous transport to Buchenwald.

The PROSPER circuit was ruined, but by July 1943 more brave SOE men and women were arriving in France to resume the fight.

9

Hide-and-Seek with Death

THE DISASTER that overtook PROSPER was a grievous but not mortal
blow to SOE operations in France. Twelve years after the war, some ill-
informed critics maintained that following the PROSPER debacle in June
1943 only four F section circuits were left—and that two of these were
almost certainly compromised. This statement does no justice to the more
than one hundred SOE agents who continued service and whose circuits
were completely unaffected by PROSPER's demise. Actually, in mid-1943
more than thirty circuits were in operation.

Among the more important of these was PIMENTO, organized during
the second half of 1942 by Anthony Brooks (Alphonse) in the south of
France. The members of this circuit were mainly railwaymen, truck drivers,
factory workers, and longshoremen. By the summer of 1943 PIMENTO
covered an area extending from the Garonne and the Bouches-du-Rhône
to the Lyonnais, the biggest network in what had been the unoccupied zone
of France. Its members received large quantities of weapons and explosives,
performed many sabotage actions, and, after D day, teamed up with FFI
units to liberate Lyons before the arrival of the U.S. Ninth Army.

Within the city of Lyons itself, several *réseaux* were active. The organizer
of the city's first circuit, SPRUCE, was Georges Dubourdin (Alain), a brave
and shrewd man who lacked the gift of getting along with people. Following his recall in October 1942, SPRUCE was commanded by Robert Boiteux
(Nicholas). Later, ACOLYTE was set up by Robert Lyon, DITCHER by Albert
Browne-Bartroli (Tiburce), and NEWSAGENT by Joseph Marchand, a leader
of FTP. Each of these groups worked successfully until the liberation.

New circuits were being established even at the height of the PROSPER
crisis. On June 13 Ernest Floegge (Alfred), a forty-five-year-old Chicago-
born American, parachuted in the Touraine. He set up his headquarters at
Mée, near Angers, where he had lived for twenty years and owned a truck-
ing business. Floegge and his "pianist," André Bouchardon (Narcisse),
recruited additional members for the *réseaux* and operated successfully
until Christmas Eve 1943, when the radio operator was arrested at Mée.

Resisting, Bouchardon was shot through a lung. The SD men failed to search the wounded prisoner, however, and during the drive to the SD office at Angers he pulled a revolver, shot his two guards and the driver, and escaped. Bouchardon and Floegge hid for a time in Paris, then went to Britain by way of the VIC escape route to Spain. In May 1944 they both returned, parachuting in the Jura to look after Harry Rée's network.

Other important circuits in operation during the latter half of 1943 included WHEELWRIGHT, established in Gascogny by George Starr (Hilaire); the MONK circuit, organized in Marseilles by Charles Skepper (Bernard) and Arthur Steele (Laurent); the Bordeaux circuit of Roger Landes (Aristide); the Rennes–Nantes circuit of Captain François Vallée (Oscar); and the circuits of Philippe Liewer (Staunton) at Rouen, Gustave Bieler (Guy) at St. Quentin, Michel Trotobas (Sylvestre) at Lille, Ben Cowburn (Benoit) at Troyes, Claude de Baissac (David) at Bordeaux, and Harry Peulevé in the Corrèze; Harry Rée (Henri) in the Jura and Francis Cammaerts in the southeast.

Even in Paris itself, SOE activity continued after the PROSPER disaster. As early as April 1943 Henri Frager (Paul) had successfully built up the DONKEYMAN network, which emerged from the original JEAN-MARIE organization. Even though some of his *sous-réseaux* were infiltrated by traitors, there were others, from Auxerre to Troyes, Bourges, and Le Mans and as far east as Châlons-sur-Marne, Nancy, and Yonne that remained unaffected by German efforts to destroy them.

Moreover, a shadow organization had existed in Paris since the autumn of 1942. Colonel Buckmaster stated that it had been formed "totally separate and beyond the knowledge of PROSPER, intended to take over, if anything should happen to Francis Suttill." Buckmaster gave in his memoirs no further details about it beyond remarking that there were three "set-ups, acting quite without knowledge of each other." [1] I can elaborate on this statement in regard to the ROBIN *réseau*.

It had its origin in a Resistance group founded in the autumn of 1940 by two wealthy Jewish businessmen in Paris, Jean Worms and Jacques Weil. They embarked on a sort of private war against the Nazis and refused to accept control by any of the French Resistance organizations. In 1942 they and their friends made contact with Virginia Hall and Francis Basin and were persuaded to work with SOE. Worms left in October 1942 for London, received SOE training and was parachuted on 22 January 1943 near Chartres. Although he was received by Denise (Andrée Borrel), he and Weil had orders to keep their ROBIN circuit separate from PROSPER. ROBIN had several safe houses in Paris—rue La Fayette near the Gare du Nord, rue Bleue, and rue Bergère, Montmartre—and in Châlons-sur-Marne, as well as a number of mail drops and at least three radio posts.

[1] Buckmaster, *They Fought Alone,* Odhams, London, 1958, p. 209.

After the arrests of Suttill and his comrades Weil warned Baker Street that all signals emanating from the Archambault radio posts were being sent by the Germans.

Early in June Buckmaster had sent Gaston Cohen (Justin), a skilled radio operator, to work for ROBIN. It seemed that despite the PROSPER disaster the other Paris circuit would survive. But Worms, trying to help the few PROSPER survivors, met Armel Guerne, Michel Trotobas, Gustave Bieler, and other agents, all already known to the SD; and on 1 July he and Guerne were arrested at a Paris restaurant. Nevertheless, ROBIN carried on under Jacques Weil, with Cohen maintaining the radio link, in Paris and in its other centers until the spring of 1944, although a setback was suffered at Christmas 1943. One of its couriers, a twenty-year-old former ballet dancer named Sonia Olschanesky, maintained contact between ROBIN and the SOE *réseau* of Canadian Captain Bieler (Guy) at St. Quentin. Sonia was lured by a V-man to a café near the Gare St. Lazare, and caught. Despite brutal torture she did not give away her comrades, but the Germans discovered the existence of ROBIN. Jacques Weil eventually ordered his friends to disperse and he himself escaped to Switzerland just before a Gestapo raid on his home.

ROBIN had survived PROSPER by six months. But in addition there were still several SOE agents in Paris and in the capital's vicinity. Some had organized small circuits; others worked in small groups, and although some of these had maintained contact with the ill-fated PROSPER, they managed to carry on. Among them was Émile-Henri Garry, a former French officer recruited by Philippe de Vomécourt back in the summer of 1942. He had never been in England and thus received no SOE training. He was a handsome man, slightly resembling Gary Cooper; hence his circuit, which operated south of Paris in the Chartres-Étampes district, was named CINEMA (after his code name).

Three Racing Drivers

The most important shadow organization set up in Paris went back to May 1942, when Buckmaster was anxious to establish a foothold there.[2] In addition to Cowburn and Wilkinson, he sent two other agents, with the strict order that they should keep away from any other circuit in or around Paris. They were Christopher Burney and Charles Grover-Williams (Sebastien). Burney was unlucky. He was given the address of a contact, Gaston (Noël Burdeyron), who had parachuted almost a year earlier, but having lost his "pianist," decided to dive under with his family in Normandy. Burdeyron was one of the victims of the trap into which Pierre de Vomé-

[2] See chapter 7.

court had fallen, and six weeks after his arrival Burney, too, was captured. But Sebastien made a getaway in time and went to Paris.

There he enlisted the help of two old French friends with whom he had often raced in peacetime: Robert Benoist and Jean-Paul Wimille. They lived unmolested by the Germans, who apparently respected them as well-known sportsmen. Benoist, a wealthy man who had raced in the Monte Carlo Grand Prix, had a fine estate at Auffargis near Rambouillet. Although neither Benoist nor Wimille had been interested in politics or had taken part in Resistance activities, they immediately responded to Grover-Williams' request. Benoist offered his château as a safe house. His wife and his brother Maurice, as well as Mme Wimille, became members of the new circuit.

For almost a year this small circuit worked quietly and successfully. In March a radio operator, Robert Dowlen (Richard), a London scoutmaster, arrived, and soon regular receptions of arms and ammunition were organized. The containers were stored in barns and cellars on Benoist's estate; these dumps were to be used to arm FFI units after an Allied landing. Grover-Williams conducted a few sabotage actions, but otherwise the small top-secret group sat tight, providing some excellent information for Baker Street gathered through Benoist's and Wimille's private connections in Paris.

Dowlen had set up the radio post at a farmhouse on the road to Pontoise northeast of Paris; Grover-Williams was determined to protect his hosts, and communications were maintained by couriers, using Benoist's car. Everything seemed to be set, but early in August Dowlen was spotted by a German DF van and captured while transmitting. His arrest led the SD to Maurice Benoist's apartment in Auteuil. Treated roughly, Maurice succumbed and led the Germans to his brother's estate, where they arrested his whole family and Grover-Williams, missing only Robert Benoist.

SS Sturmbann-Führer Kieffer, elated by the wonderful catch, started a hue and cry for Robert Benoist. On 6 August Benoist was recognized while walking on Boulevard Raspail, seized, and driven in a car to Avenue Foch. During the ride Benoist pushed one of his guards through the door. They both rolled into the street and the prisoner disappeared in the crowd before the SD men recovered from their surprise. This was one of Benoist's several daring escapes.

After hiding with friends he was put on a Lysander by Déricourt on 19 August, and reached England. Two months later he was back, landed from a Hudson aircraft with Albert Browne-Bartroli (Tiburce). He went to Nantes, where he had friends, and organized a number of successful sabotage actions against power stations and railway lines. He found Dubois (Hercule), the radio operator who had arrived in April with Frager (and was used as a radio link by Trotobas of Lille). Hercule had rendered splendid service for more than seven months for several circuits; now he set up his radio post at a farm near Le Mans. But three weeks after Benoist's return from London, Dubois was caught.[3] Once again the racing driver had to dive under. He went to Paris, renewed contact with Wimille, and worked until early February 1944, when he was forced to escape and return to England. A month later he was back in France.

The Daughter of an Indian Mystic

At the time of the PROSPER debacle, Henri Frager was enlarging his staff in Paris. In Simone (Vera Leigh), who had arrived from London a few days before the PROSPER arrests, he had acquired an excellent assistant.

Two nights after Simone's arrival, FANY Ensign Noor Inayat Khan was landed on 16 June by Lysander and received by Gilbert.

Noor (whose operational name was Madeleine) was twenty-nine. She was the daughter of an Indian mystic, Inayat Khan, the leader of the Sufi sect and a descendant of the sultans of Mysore, and Ora Baker, a niece of Mary Baker Eddy, the founder of Christian Science. Noor was trained as a W/T operator and in April 1942 was recommended for a commission. She might have spent the war in the comparative security of an RAF station's plotting room had she not heard of SOE. She was interviewed by Captain Jepson, who at first hesitated to recommend her for training. A shy young woman of very slight physique, she looked at the world with huge dark eyes. Her thin olive face, long dark hair, and gentle voice belied great courage and tenacity.

Her conducting officer at Wanborough Manor was FANY Commandant Jean Sanderson, who described Noor's reactions to a mock-Gestapo interrogation during training as follows: "She seemed absolutely terrified . . . the strong lights hurt her and she jumped when the officer shouted very loudly. Once he said: 'Stand on this chair!' Confused and overwhelmed, she nearly lost her voice and became practically inaudible. When she came out afterwards, she was trembling and quite blanched." [4] Yet, when confronted with real interrogation, torture, and solitary confinement in Gestapo prisons, Noor showed awe-inspiring courage.

When she reached Paris from the landing ground, Noor went to see Captain Émile-Henri Garry at his apartment in rue Erlanger at Auteuil. Garry did not want to expose a newly arrived, inexperienced woman to

[3] See chapter 10, under "Bleicher Meets Frager."
[4] The story of Noor was told in Miss Jean Overton Fuller's book *Madeleine*, (Gollancz, London, 1952). Some of the incidents described therein must, however, be seen in the light of fresh evidence and new documentary information obtained since that book was published.

undue risks; he suggested she go to the Agricultural College at Grignon, then regarded as a safe house.

Within a fortnight, mopping up PROSPER, eighty SS men surrounded the building on 1 July and arrested most of the members of the staff. Both the director, Maurice Vanderwynckt, and his son-in-law, Jean Douillet, were later executed in German concentration camps.

Garry succeeded in warning Noor to keep clear of the college on the day of the raid, and Professor Balachowsky found her a room at the home of Mme Germaine Agrain, director of the fashion house Toile d'Avon on the Champs Elysées, who lived in Square Malesherbes, not far from Garry's apartment. Major France Anthelme (Antoine) was staying with Garry. He had returned from one of his many missions in the provinces; had been to see Lise de Baissac and Roger Landes, the chief of the Bordeaux network. He sent reports of the PROSPER debacle to London and was now waiting for the arrival of one of the senior officers from Baker Street.

A few days after the raid at the college at Grignon, Professor Balachowsky was arrested. His wife was seriously ill when the Germans raided their apartment at Viroflay, and by order of SS Sturm-Führer Josef Placke the SS men ignored her. Ill though she was, Madame Balachowsky dragged herself to Grignon on 4 July to warn her friends there, only to find it was too late. But she did succeed in alerting Anthelme and Garry, who quickly moved in with Noor at Mme Agrain's flat.

Despite the situation becoming critical, the little group carried on as best they could. Garry went through with his plan to marry Marguerite Nadaud. On the great day, their apartment was raided by the Gestapo while they were being married at the town hall. Only the loyalty of their concierge, who waited at the corner of the street to warn them, prevented them going straight from their wedding reception into the arms of the Gestapo. They hurriedly left Paris for a secret honeymoon at Le Mans.

Noor, totally inexperienced in the field, was now almost on her own. She operated her radio transmitter for the SOE officers who had survived PROSPER and had remained in and around Paris, but Madame Agrain's apartment, which had served well as a PROSPER mail drop, had become too dangerous to be used as a radio post. Major Anthelme found Noor a room at 3 Boulevard Richard Wallace at Neuilly. During the past three weeks she had been compelled to carry her transmitter almost everywhere she went. Now she could at least operate it from a room that seemed safe for the present.

Anthelme went to Auffargis where Robert Benoist and Grover-Williams were still living in apparent safety. Noor visited them to transmit their messages to London. When Colonel Buckmaster received Noor's report, he decided to send Major Bodington to Paris. As mentioned, Bodington arrived on 15 July and was received by Gilbert. With Bodington came Captain Jack Agazarian, the only important survivor of the PROSPER disaster.

One unexplained point of Bodington's visit is that, in spite of the signals and messages sent to London—first by Gaston Cohen, the radio operator for ROBIN, then by Jacques Weil, by way of Switzerland, and finally by Noor on behalf of Major Anthelme—Baker Street was still confused about who had been arrested and who was still at liberty. Agazarian went to the apartment on the rue de Rome, where Archambault usually stayed, and was arrested there by SD men.

Agazarian was languishing in Fresnes prison in February 1944 when he met a French officer, Paul Philbée (who survived), and told him about the circumstances of his arrest. He not unnaturally felt he had been betrayed. In the spring of 1944 he was sent to Germany and executed in Flossenbürg concentration camp.

Bodington spent a month in France. He saw several SOE agents and had many meetings with Henri Frager. Frager's fate, of course was sealed by then: Roger Bardet was betraying all his movements to Bleicher. Fortunately for the SOE officers, the brief truce between the Abwehr and the Gestapo in the summer of 1943—shortly before the Abwehr was virtually taken over by the Gestapo—meant that there was a neat division of responsibilities. Kieffer was so preoccupied with mopping up the remnants of PROSPER that he left the Abwehr to concentrate on the other target: Frager's DONKEYMAN circuit.

Bleicher told me that he was "greatly amused" when he heard from Roger Bardet of Major Bodington's arrival in Paris. "I had no commitments in this affair. I just kept quiet and waited to see what Kieffer and the Gestapo would do."

Actually Bleicher and the Abwehr had other good reasons to leave Bodington alone. They preferred to let Bodington try and piece together the bits from the chaos resulting from the PROSPER debacle and watch him, rather than compel Baker Street to make a fresh start with new agents they did not know. They acted on the axiom that it is better to keep an eye on the devil you know than spoil his fun by arresting everybody in sight and putting yourself in the dark.

The Dieppe Raid

Strange events occurred during those summer weeks. Bleicher was preoccupied with other matters when Bardet told him of Bodington's arrival. His other French stool pigeon, Raoul Kiffer (Kiki), once a pillar of INTERALLIÉ, continued to operate the LISIANA network in the Lisieux-Caen area, which had spread throughout Anjou and Maine from Normandy. According to Bleicher, Kiki boasted in the summer of 1943 that three hundred members, 90 percent of them genuine Resistance fighters, were quite unaware that they were working for a traitor.

The remaining 10 percent were Kiki's cronies, who asked no questions as long as they were paid. They even carried out some small sabotage actions. Through Roger Bardet, Bleicher succeeded in linking the fake LISIANA network to DONKEYMAN. Frager never discovered that he was connected with a German-run organization; nor, of course, did he know that his trusted adjutant, Bardet, was a traitor.

The LISIANA organization still had its radio link with London and on several occasions received drops of arms and ammunition. Some material was left with the local groups, but most of it Kiki delivered, on Bleicher's orders, to the German field police in Caen.

Bleicher rarely visited Kiki in the north. But Kiki, who liked the night life and often visited Paris, did not know that Bleicher discreetly supervised his activities. The supervision was entrusted to the Rouen AST, where Captain Heinz Eckert was in charge.

When Major Bodington was still in France, Eckert, with Kiki's help, posed as a Canadian SOE officer. Kiki and another French traitor, André Lemoin,[5] who used the alias Moineau, had learned from LISIANA members that strong Gaullist réseaux existed at Le Havre, Duclair, and Veules-les-Roses and were supplied with arms from London.

Kiki, who knew the leaders of the réseaux, introduced Captain Eckert as a Canadian officer by the name of Evans. For a few days Evans stayed with a member of one of the réseaux, Jeannette Dumoulins, at Veules-les-Roses. She told him she had heard a personal message on the BBC from her husband, who had escaped to England. The message was: "Georges will very soon embrace Jeannette."

Jeannette naïvely asked the false SOE officer whether he knew the exact time and place of her husband's arrival. Evans promised to make inquiries in London. He was also told a great secret of the réseau: Its leader was in touch with a German officer of the Organization Todt (German labor force). The officer, a fervent anti-Nazi, had an important position at Dieppe and was supplying the information London had recently requested about dock installations, fortifications, positions of shore batteries, and deployment of German units at Dieppe.

"I nearly had a seizure when I heard this," Eckert said. "It was the very first case in my own experience and within my region that a German betrayed secrets to the enemy." He hurried to Paris, apprised his superiors at the Hotel Lutetia, and was ordered to return north and find the German traitor. For this task he employed three Frenchmen—André, Maurice, and Dupont—members of Kiki's fake réseau. They soon found the man.

5 Lemoin, a well-known marine painter, was tried after the war and sentenced to twenty years' imprisonment.

[161]

Eckert calls him Niemeyer, but this probably was not his real name. Eckert had been told not to arrest him but to watch all his movements.

On 19 August 1943 the Dieppe raid took place. The force, consisting mainly of Canadians, landed at dawn on six selected beaches east and west of the port. At Varengeville, four and a half miles from Dieppe, commandos succeeded in destroying the German fortifications, including a battery of six-inch guns. At Porville, the Canadian tanks penetrated to the center of town. Eckert watched the fierce fighting and wondered whether the Allied invasion of Europe had begun. He soon heard reassuring news: The attack at Berneval, east of Dieppe, had been repulsed. German E-boats and Flak-ships had inflicted heavy casualties on the Allied raiders before they even touched down, and shore batteries had added to the rout of the invaders. A destroyer, HMS *Berkeley,* was sunk. In the air the Allies suffered grievous losses: 98 British, American, Canadian, Polish, Free French, and New Zealand aircraft were shot down. On the beaches the Canadian force was all but wiped out. Out of the 5,350 officers and men engaged in the operation, 170 were reported dead, 633 wounded, and 2,547 missing, when the British communiqué was published. Many of the latter were, in fact, killed; the rest were taken prisoner. It was one of the most costly and controversial operations of the war.

When the Allied chiefs of staff examined the operation they came to the conclusion that the Germans were fully prepared for the attack.

Many years after the war, Captain Eckert gave me a clue to the Dieppe debacle. Information he had received—from members of the *réseaux* he had infiltrated—about persistent inquiries concerning Dieppe was duly conveyed to German military headquarters. Precautions immediately were taken to strengthen the defenses, and strong reinforcements were sent to Dieppe. The Germans were indeed fully prepared to meet an attack.

Eckert added a postscript: "I had lost my prey, Herr Niemeyer, in the raid." He is still convinced that the German escaped with the survivors of the Canadian units to England, and he says Niemeyer was employed after the war as an interpreter with SHAEF and later with the British Control Commission in Germany.

Kieffer Discovers Bodington

So far as Bleicher was concerned, the sooner Bodington left Paris for London the better; but the Englishman remained, and one day early in August Bleicher was called urgently to the phone in the Hotel Lutetia. Kieffer was on the line.

"Did you know that Major Bodington was in Paris?" asked the Gestapo man angrily.

"Really? So what?" replied Bleicher.

"What do you mean, so what!" shouted Kieffer, enraged.

He took quite a time to calm down. Eventually he told Bleicher that in his opinion Henri Frager must have arranged Bodington's visit, and therefore it was the Abwehr's business to act. A curious duel developed between the two German intelligence services. The Abwehr was convinced that Henri Déricourt (Gilbert) had asked Bodington to come to Paris. Having always assumed that Déricourt was one of SS Obersturmbann-Führer Boemelburg's double agents, they left the whole affair to the *Sicherheitsdienst*. Yet Kieffer's phone call proved that the *Sicherheitsdienst* knew very little about Bodington except that he was somewhere in France. Déricourt, however, was almost always with Bodington. If, as the Abwehr assumed, Déricourt was one of Boemelburg's agents, he would have been running a great personal risk by not informing the Gestapo about Bodington's movements. All this lends support to Déricourt's explanations at his trial that he had never been a genuine agent of the Germans but had only led them by the nose.

Bleicher, however, has another, rather ingenious, explanation for Déricourt's behavior. He told me he assumed that Déricourt aspired to the leadership of the JEAN-MARIE–DONKEYMAN circuit. Knowing that Henri Frager neither liked nor trusted him, he decided to save Bodington's life and in this way give SOE proof of his integrity. It must be emphasized that this was only Bleicher's, and possibly the Abwehr's, reasoning.

The threat to Bodington from the *Sicherheitsdienst* had become very real. Kieffer told Bleicher: "I must get Bodington, even if I have to arrest Frager and your lot." Bleicher asked him for time, forty-eight hours at least. Realizing the affair had grown far too big for him to handle, he consulted with Colonel Reile. He explained that arrests would destroy all his work; his double life as Monsieur Jean, if not already known to the British, certainly would be finished, and he would lose the fake *réseaux* he had built up through Kiki and Bardet.

"I told Colonel Reile that if Kieffer had his way I should ask to be relieved of my duties in Paris even if that meant sending me to the Russian front," Bleicher told me. Reile agreed that arrests would be pointlessly destructive, but said he was anxious not to enrage Kieffer and the Gestapo.

Such caution in espionage, however, can prompt surprising tactics. Colonel Reile suggested that Bleicher should warn Bodington and advise him to return immediately to England. Perhaps he thought this would enhance his own safety with the Allies . . . later. Bleicher had no intention of facing Bodington himself, but he assured Reile that he would warn Bodington through Roger Bardet. Accordingly, Bardet went to Frager and

[163]

said he had learned definitely that the Gestapo was aware of Bodington's presence in Paris and intended to arrest him.

Bodington and Anthelme Escape

When he first arrived in Paris, Bodington stayed with Major Anthelme, but after Agazarian's arrest he changed quarters every few days. Eventually he decided the safest hideout would be with Robert Benoist at Auffargis, because apparently the famous racing driver had not yet provoked German suspicion. During the second week of August, Bodington, Frager, and Anthelme gathered at Benoist's home for a long conference. In order to transmit Bodington's messages to London, Noor Inayat Kahn attended.

As a result of the raids at Grignon and on Garry's apartment, Noor and Anthelme were compromised, and Bodington told them they should get out of France as quickly as possible. One of his first orders to Déricourt was to arrange a pickup for them. He took Noor and Anthelme to a point between Beaufort and Longue on the north bank of the Loire, but heavy clouds forced the RAF aircraft to turn back and the plan had to be abandoned because of the bad weather, which lasted for a week.

At the Auffargis meeting, Bodington announced he would take Anthelme and Lise de Baissac, whose position in the Poitiers area had become precarious, with him to England. Benoist promised to look after Noor. Déricourt arranged Bodington's departure on 16 August. Bleicher, through the eyes of Bardet, watched the delay with anxiety. Through Bardet he had urged Frager to speed up Bodington's return. Now everything depended upon the inefficiency of Kieffer and the SD. The Gestapo's attempts to catch Bodington were intensified daily by Kieffer's conviction that Bodington held the rank of major general. Despite their frenzied efforts, the SD never caught Bodington, and he and Anthelme reached England safely.

After Garry and his wife had been forced into hiding, Benoist and Grover-Williams were the only persons Noor could turn to for help. But she had to be careful not to visit them too often. So Noor deliberately ignored one of the orders hammered into her during training: She approached some of her girlhood friends at Suresnes. Some of them, when they learned she had come from England, assumed she was an agent and refused to help; but others opened their homes to her. She wandered from one part of Paris to another with her transmitter in her suitcase.

Garry had introduced her to a Resistance group composed of French industrialists. Among them were Maurice Déspret, a director of the steel works at Hirson; Jacques Vaudevire, director of the *Société française radio-électrique;* Pierre Viennot, general manager of the same company; and two steel experts, M. Dagnaud and M. Coupault. The last was a director of a foundry at Le Cateau-Cambrai. Some of these men had been compelled to put their works at the disposal of the Germans, who regarded them as willing collaborators. They were entitled to Gestapo protection, which made their Resistance work fairly safe. When Noor's apartment in Neuilly-sur-Seine became too dangerous for radio transmissions, Vaudevire arranged for her to transmit from his home.

The sumptuous office of M. Dagnaud at 6 rue Cambacérès, just around the corner from the *Sicherheitsdienst* interrogation cellars, became the secret rendezvous for Garry, Benoist, Noor and the industrialists. At times she also used the home of Dr. Jourdan, a physician she had known as a child.

While Noor was establishing herself in Paris the Gestapo suddenly raided the villa at Auffargis. The French section was still unaware of the capture of the two Canadians, Pickersgill and McAlister, and signals were still being sent to Bertrand (Pickersgill), as well as to Madeleine (Noor), concerning arrangements for a proposed meeting between Pickersgill and M. Déspret. Baker Street wanted Déspret to help Pickersgill set up a radio post at Hirson. Of course this exposed Noor and the French industrialists to Kieffer, although he did not discover Madeleine's identity, or that she was Garry's radio operator.

Noor Meets the False Bertrand

Kieffer's main objective was to maintain London's faith in the fake Bertrand radio post and simultaneously infiltrate the industrialists' group. He concluded that Madeleine should meet Bertrand, and he had no difficulty in obtaining Baker Street's unwitting cooperation. Signals sent simultaneously to Noor and Bertrand suggested a meeting at the Café Colisée on the Champs Elysées.

But now Bertrand had to be produced promptly. Kieffer needed a Canadian. The right man was found at the Gestapo office in the rue des Saussaies: SS Hauptschar-Führer Karl Horst Holdorf, who had been a steward with a United States shipping line and spoke fluent English with an American accent. Holdorf was briefed and accompanied by Josef Placke, who posed as a French Resistance friend.

The meeting at the Café Colisée proved disastrous. Noor discussed the situation with Holdorf, alias Bertrand, not knowing that she was exposing her friends to the *Sicherheitsdienst*. Eventually Déspret and his two business partners were arrested.

Meanwhile Garry, whose circuit name had been changed from CINEMA to PHONO, had returned to Paris from Le Mans. Thus SOE now had three harassed representatives in Paris. One of Garry's tasks was to maintain contact with Gustave Bieler at St. Quentin and Michel Trotobas at Lille. In addition, he looked after agents passing through Paris. However, Garry was not content with desk work, as he called it. He embarked almost singlehanded on a number of sabotage actions. Noor and Marguerite Garry joined him on several of these dangerous nocturnal expeditions. The trio did not realize it, but by the end of September they had been "burned." Using an informer planted in the industrialists' group, Kieffer had at last found out that little Jeanne Marie Regnier (Noor) was a British agent and not just a Frenchwoman helping Déspret and his colleagues.

At this stage Noor was using a flat belonging to one of Garry's friends, named Solange, for her radio transmissions. It was at 98 rue de la Faisanderie, but Noor slept in her own room on Boulevard Richard Wallace, which she had rented in July. Rue de la Faisanderie seemed to have had a magnetic attraction for agents on both sides: Vera Leigh (Simone), Frager's courier, had an apartment at No. 134, and Hugo Bleicher lived at one time at No. 26.

After the arrests of Grover-Williams and the Benoist family Garry and his wife left Neuilly and took an artist's studio near the Observatoire in the 14th arrondissement. Garry changed his appearance and advised Noor to do the same. She dyed her dark hair to auburn and wore spectacles. Early in October, while Noor had a brief rest at a farm in Normandy, Baker Street made arrangements by radio for a pickup for her, Garry, and his wife.

The exact circumstances of Noor's arrest only became known after the war, when SD officers from Avenue Foch were interrogated by the DST. According to their depositions,[6] Noor was denounced by a woman informer who on 6 or 7 October telephoned the SD office and asked to speak to Kieffer. Because Kieffer knew little French, the call was taken by his interpreter, Vogt. The woman gave her name as Renée and said she could supply information about a Mlle Regnier who was "a spy of the War Office." She arranged to meet two SD men at the Jardin de Trocadero.

The woman told them that Jeanne Marie Regnier was English, that her real name was Norah Baker (the name used by Noor in the WAAF), and that she was operating a clandestine radio under the code "Poste Madeleine." She gave them the address 3 Boulevard Richard Wallace at Neuilly. The informer asked for a reward of 20,000 francs but the SD men said they would first need proof that the information was genuine. The next day Vogt went with three SD men to the address. They interviewed the concierge, Madame Jourdois, who told them she had not seen Mlle Regnier for some time. They searched the apartment, but found nothing incriminating. When the informer met the SD men again, she said that Norah Baker had another hideout, in the apartment of a women named Solange, at 98 rue de la Faisanderie. They took Renée to Avenue Foch, where she was

[6] *Cf.* Depositions of former SS Sturm-Führer Josef Placke and Sonder-Führer Ernst Vogt to DST, 1 and 9 April 1946.

interviewed by Dr. Goetz. She told him that Solange was entirely innocent and asked him not to harm her.[7]

Kieffer then ordered Vogt to go with V-man Pierre Cartaud to the second address. Cartaud was a member of Déat's RNP (*Rassemblement National Populaire*) and the Gestapo used him for work too despicable even for SD men. Their first visit was fruitless, but henceforth SD men were watching the place. In the meantime Noor had returned from Normandy and had visited Mme Agrain. She told her she expected to go to England on 14 October and said she knew she should not have come because her visit might endanger her friend, but she could not bear to leave without saying goodby. Soon after Noor left two SD men entered Mme Agrain's house and arrested her. She was sent to Fresnes prison and then to Ravensbrück. She survived and was freed in 1945.

Kieffer left Noor at large for a few days in order to have her movements watched and to keep account of her contacts. On 13 October, the day after Mme Agrain's arrest, Vogt and Pierre Cartaud went again to Solange's apartment. The V-man hid himself in a small back room, while Vogt returned to Avenue Foch. Cartaud waited in the apartment for six hours. At about 4 P.M. Noor arrived to collect her radio transmitter. Cartaud pounced on Noor, who struggled desperately. Later he reported that she bit him on his hands and wrist. He drew his pistol and telephoned Kieffer, who sent Vogt and two SD men to Cartaud's assistance. When they arrived they found Noor handcuffed and the V-man nursing his bleeding hands. At Avenue Foch Noor at first refused to talk. She was later confronted by Gilbert Norman (Archambault), who, according to Vogt's and Dr. Goetz' depositions, advised her to answer questions, as the Germans already knew everything about PROSPER.

Garry Goes into the Trap

Captain Garry was at Nantes when Noor was arrested. He returned to Paris with his wife on Saturday, 16 October, and was met by a member of his *réseau* who used Mme Agrain's mail drop; thus Garry learned of her arrest. He decided not to go to his apartment near the Observatoire and took his wife to the home of her sister, Mlle Nadaud. The following day Garry met a courier from Bieler (Guy), who brought news from Baker Street, received by Yolande Beekman's radio post at Fonsommes. It was to the effect that the French section was arranging a Lysander pickup for him and Noor during the moon period between 20 and 23 October. Garry

7 In November 1949 a woman relative of the late Captain Émile-Henri Garry was tried by a Paris court on a charge of collaboration with the enemy. She was accused of having betrayed Garry and probably also Noor. The court found the evidence not sufficient to convict, and she was acquitted.

decided to find Noor and ask her whether she had received a more precise message on her transmitter, and he went with his wife to Solange's apartment (watched, of course, by the SD). They stayed there overnight, waiting for Noor.

At breakfast time Cartaud called. He introduced himself as Peter, told Garry he was an SOE courier, and gave him a note written by Noor. He told Garry that Noor had gone under cover in the country because things had become hot in Paris. Marguerite Garry helped Solange make a parcel of clothes for Noor. Peter said he would return for it in half an hour. He did—along with three SD men.

They took Garry and his wife to Kieffer. Surprisingly Kieffer did not consider Garry a very important prisoner and did not order a confrontation with other SOE prisoners. On 22 October, the day they had hoped to reach England, Garry and his wife were taken to the Gestapo prison at Place des États-Unis.

In the same building was a branch of the *Corps d'autoprotection français,* an organization controlled by Amt IV of the *Sicherheitsdienst.* This auxiliary Gestapo concerned itself with French patriots, in particular "communists and terrorists." It was linked with the Bony–Lafont gang, which ran the profitable business of placing confiscated property on the black market. Kieffer's liaison officer with Bony and Lafont was Sturm-Führer Josef Placke. It seems that Captain Garry and his wife were treated as "French terrorists" rather than as SOE agents. Kieffer took pride in dealing with British agents himself.

Émile-Henri Garry was eventually sent to Buchenwald and hanged on 8 September 1944. Marguerite Garry was sent to Ravensbrück, where, among many other women prisoners, she met Mme Germaine Agrain. She survived and returned to France in 1945.

Noor Inayat Khan was kept at Avenue Foch for several weeks. She was confronted with John Starr, who had the next room to hers on the fifth floor; but they did not know each other, and Starr believed her to be a Frenchwoman. In a nearby room was Colonel Léon Faye, leader of the ALLIANCE *réseau,* who had been captured in September.[8] On 25 November Noor, Starr, and Faye made an attempt to escape. They got as far as the street but were recaptured. This exploit had immediate and tragic results.

Hitherto Kieffer had treated Noor reasonably, but her bid for freedom brought on one of his tantrums and he ordered Faye and Noor to be sent to Germany. Next day, 26 November, they were taken to the RSHA

[8] Faye succeeded to the leadership of ALLIANCE after the arrest of Loustenau Lacau in May 1941. With them worked an intrepid young woman, Marie Madeleine Méric (now Mme Foucade, OBE), who took over after Faye was caught. She and her comrades rendered vital service to the Allies before D day and after the landings in Normandy.

Leitstelle at Badenweiler, a reception center for prisoners destined for extermination camps. From there Noor was sent to Pforzheim and then to Karlsruhe women's prison, where she met other SOE women agents.

On 12 September 1944, Noor, Yolande Beekman, Eliane Plewman, and Madeleine Damerment were taken from Karlsruhe to Dachau by the head of the Gestapo *Leitstelle,* Rudolf Gmeiner.[9] They arrived in the camp at midnight. The next morning Noor and the three other women were shot.

Throughout the long winter of 1943–44 the *Sicherheitsdienst* continued to mop up with ruthless efficiency. They now controlled several transmitters that were in regular contact with Baker Street. Dr. Goetz improved on the fake Bertrand post by bringing Lieutenant Frank Pickersgill back from the Rawicz concentration camp and forcing him to operate. Noor's post, Madeleine, was also operated by the Germans for some time.

During October and November the Germans concluded their mopping-up operations by destroying the two northern *réseaux* of Guy Bieler at St. Quentin and Michel Trotobas at Lille.

The Burned Mill at St. Quentin

Captain Guy Bieler, the Canadian giant from Montreal, who had broken his back when he was dropped in November 1942, had not been able to begin building his *réseau* in St. Quentin for three months. But when he did get started, action soon followed.

In May 1943, for instance, he and his French helpers cut railway lines between Paris and Cologne thirteen times. They blew up the tracks, destroyed points, signal boxes, and shunting sheds between St. Quentin and Valenciennes, Maubeuge, and Belgian stations.

Besides its importance as an industrial and railway center, St. Quentin lies at the heart of the waterway system of northeast France. Several canals pass by, the most important being the north-south canal. These waterways carried military and industrial material for the German war effort, including pocket submarine components, which were transported to the Mediterranean by barges. The lock gates of St. Quentin were a favorite target for the RAF, but as soon as they were damaged they were repaired by German technicians and French forced labor. In the spring of 1943 the chiefs of staff named the canal system as a top-priority sabotage target for SOE in France. Guy Bieler was ordered to disrupt it.

The task would have been impossible but for the high quality of his helpers. Their leader was André Cordelette, a farmer in the nearby hamlet of Fonsommes. He was introduced to Bieler by Captain Darling, and gave Bieler a home and space for his radio transmitter and the storage of explosives and arms. Cordelette was a frail, retiring, middle-aged man, but he

[9] Tried and executed by the British in 1947.

was fired by Guy's enthusiasm. When the order came through for the destruction of the St. Quentin lock gates, Cordelette undertook the operation.

London had dropped containers with a large quantity of explosive limpet charges, to be attached to three of the main locks. But Cordelette decided to improve on instructions. With two assistants he paddled out in a little boat loaded with time-switch bombs. The men lay in the boat, which appeared to be drifting emptily on the calm water of the canal. Under the eyes of the German guards the little boat lay lazily alongside dozens of newly laden craft. That night more than forty barges erupted, causing havoc throughout a long stretch of the canals. This was just one of dozens of sabotage actions carried out by Bieler, Cordelette, and their helpers.

In the early autumn, Bieler was joined by a woman agent, quite his match in courage and determination: Yolande Beekman (Mariette). First ordered to go to Lille to join Captain Trotobas, she was parachuted near Tours on 17 September. She made a dangerous journey to Lille, posing as Mme Yvonne de Chauvigny, a war widow, carrying her radio transmitters and equipment in two suitcases.

When she arrived at Lille a signal was awaiting her from Baker Street ordering her on to St. Quentin where Guy Bieler needed a radio operator. Early in October she installed her transmitter at the house of Mme Odette Gobeaux, at 18 rue de la Fère, St. Quentin. Mme Gobeaux, a member of the local Resistance, worked at the Pharmacy Corteel. The proprietor and the dispenser, M. Camille Boury, both helped Bieler. Having set up her radio post, Yolande settled in with Mlle Lefèvre, a schoolteacher, on the Avenue de la Republique.

The outbreak of sabotage actions in the district spurred the *Funkhorchdienst* into such frantic activity that Bieler and Yolande decided to move the transmitter to Boury's house, and set up another radio post at Cordelette's farm at Fonsommes. Suddenly, on 13 December, the Germans pounced on the *réseau*. This was a follow-up of the arrests in Paris.

Guy and Yolande were together at the Café Moulin Brulé in St. Quentin sitting at a table with M. and Mme Thixier, the owners. There was only one other person in the café, a motor mechanic. Two Gestapo cars pulled up and a number of SD men rushed in. Guy and Yolande were taken to Gestapo headquarters. Despite severe torture, they refused to answer questions.

Bieler was one of the few SOE officers who did not have to endure long imprisonment before death. His sabotage had so enraged the Germans that he was executed a few weeks after capture. Yolande was sent to Fresnes, then to Karlsruhe, and finally to Dachau, where she was shot in September 1944.

The seizure of Guy and Yolande was the first of many in St. Quentin. The café owner, Thixier, was sent to Buchenwald, where he died of maltreatment. His wife was sent to Ravensbrück, survived, and returned in 1945.

Mme Lefèvre, Yolande's first hostess, was tortured and sent to Buchenwald, where she died. André Cordelette and his family also suffered, as did fifteen other Resistance men who had worked with Guy Bieler. Cordelette himself survived his imprisonment but came home a sick man.

The Germans had smashed another vital segment of PROSPER. But the memory of Guy and all his helpers remains alive in St. Quentin, and in the little hamlet of Fonsommes the main street is named rue du Commandant Bieler.

So far as Baker Street was concerned, however, the *réseau* Bieler continued to thrive during the winter of 1943–44. Once again the *Sicherheitsdienst* succeeded in duping London, which believed that transmissions from the St. Quentin radio post were coming from Pickersgill. Instead they were arranged and sent by Josef Placke.

Cradle of the Resistance

Bieler and Yolande worked in concert with FARMER, the Lille organization, which had emerged from one of the first Resistance centers set up in France. Lille is one of the great industrial cities with a tradition of militant trade unionism and strong Communist influence. Resistance organizations were controlled by left-wing leaders. After Hitler attacked the Soviet Union in June 1941 these men declared a holy war on the Germans.

Fortunately, the man to whom SOE entrusted the Lille outpost was as tough as the Resistance fighters with whom he cooperated. Michel Trotobas joined SOE when Marriott and Cadett were in charge of F section, and was dropped on 5 September 1941 with several other agents, including Ben Cowburn, near Châteauroux. With Cowburn he walked to Argenton-sur-Creuse and eventually reached Lille, where among the Resistance people he met a twenty-three-year-old French girl, Madeleine Damerment, who became one of his assistants.

Michel Trotobas was caught six weeks after his arrival by the Vichy police, during a journey in the unoccupied zone, and placed in the prison at Mauzac. After his escape with other SOE agents, he reached England and returned on his second mission to Lille. He was dropped with Guy Bieler and radio operator Albert Staggs in the Yonne area in November 1942. Many men in his Lille *réseau* were Poles working in factories and mines. The German policy in the Départment du Nord was ruthlessly oppressive. The whole economy of the area was driven to the limit for the German war effort. Sonder-Führers were put in charge of every industrial undertaking, and a horde of SS troops, field police, and Gestapo overran this densely populated area.

[171]

Probably the greatest single difficulty encountered by Trotobas was obtaining explosives for sabotage. It was almost impossible to find safe landing places or parachute dropping grounds in the region. He overcame this by mobilizing a large number of *routiers,* drivers of long-distance heavy trucks that rumbled back and forth on the N 17 motorway (linking the industrial north with Paris), carrying material for the Germans. Most of the *routiers* were Communists. Frequently they carried SOE containers to Lille for Trotobas, while armed SS guards sat beside them in their cabs. Because of the bravery of these men, containers could be dropped to grounds as far away as Melun and Meaux, and even in the Sologne.

These efforts were well worthwhile. Trotobas and his determined saboteurs used the explosives to inflict great damage upon industrial installations. Machine-tool factories at Armentières, textile mills at Roubaix, locomotive sheds at Tourcoing, the largest tannery at Cambrai, were among the plants annihilated. Trotobas arranged sallies, which he called *les excursions touristiques,* to Calais, Amiens, and Boulogne. Naval depots, railway yards, and wharfs attracted him just as much as factories did.

In December Trotobas lost his radio operator. Staggs was arrested on some paltry charge without the German police discovering he was an SOE man. For everyone's safety Staggs had to disappear after his release, and Trotobas used the radio post of Dubois (Hercule) and also PROSPER's radio links with London.

Competing with the RAF

In the spring of 1943 the chiefs of staff decided that the SNCF (French national railways) locomotive works at Fives, the second largest of its kind in France, must be destroyed. The bombing of Germany was now reaching its peak, and the Germans were relying increasingly on the production and repair facilities in France and Belgium to maintain their own railway system. Allied air raids failed to produce the required results at Fives, partly because the Germans had concentrated the heaviest antiaircraft defenses in northern France on the approaches to Lille.

At a meeting of the chiefs of staff in London, Brigadier Mockler-Ferryman, representing SOE, was asked whether his agents could carry out a direct action at Fives. The question was radioed to Trotobas. He decided he would do what he could, especially as his Resistance friends were upset by the effect of the heavy air raids on French working-class opinion. The locomotive sheds, in the eastern suburbs of Lille, were flanked by residential districts. Civilian casualties were mounting, and several hundred families were left homeless. The psychological effect was not helping the Allied cause, and German propaganda capitalized on this.

When Trotobas radioed London that he would undertake the sabotage attack on the locomotive works, the news was received by RAF bomber command with doubt bordering on derision. Brigadier Gubbins succeeded, however, in arranging a pause in the air raids and giving a chance to his men in Lille. The sabotage operation required large quantities of high explosives. Dropping of containers began northeast of Paris, and the *routiers* went to work. Some of them paid with their lives for attempts to transport the explosives to Trotobas. Buckmaster had to plead for a little more time. Sarcastic comments from bomber command filtered to Baker Street before Trotobas could signal: WE ARE READY.

During the night of 27 June he and twelve friends penetrated the locomotive works' security arrangements, with the help of a foreman, by joining a night shift. They worked feverishly from 9 P.M. to 2 A.M. placing eighteen large charges in carefully selected positions. The foreman gave the word to the workmen that it would be extremely unhealthy for them to remain on the job after 2 A.M. Trotobas and his comrades allowed themselves only a few minutes to quit the sheds. A series of explosions, which shook the whole city, began as the clocks struck two. Within minutes the whole area was a blazing inferno. The fires raged until the following afternoon, despite the efforts of fire brigades and forced-labor units ordered into the collapsing buildings by SS men.

Trotobas watched his handiwork for hours. When he returned to his hideout his eyes were red from the smoke and flames. He sent a two-word signal to London: OPERATION COMPLETED.

Triumphantly the message was run from Baker Street to the Ministry of Economic Warfare, to the chiefs of staff and the Air Ministry. It elicited the memorable response from Air staff headquarters: "Tell your man to send photographs of the operation area."

Doubtless this seemed a sensible enough request to an Air vice marshall sitting in a swivel chair at Ad Astra House (HQ of the RAF command). It was rather different in Lille, where SS men were rounding up railway workers by the score, racing through working-class districts in their squad cars, and smashing in the doors to drag out wives and children as hostages. The German commandant issued an order threatening to shoot every tenth man employed at the Lille-Fives locomotive works as a punishment for "the abominable terrorist outrage."

Baker Street tactfully tried to sugar the pill, but it still remained a pretty bitter one for Captain Trotobas. The message to him read: WELL DONE, PLEASE SEND PHOTOGRAPHS.

Dutifully Trotobas set about obtaining the required pictures. When he arrived back at the Fives works he found a mass of twisted steel and rubble still smoking and encrusted with foam and water. The officers of the German field police and the security guards who survived the holocaust were under arrest awaiting court-martial. The *Sicherheitsdienst* and detachments of the

SS had taken over. Trotobas was stopped several times by excited officers, but he managed to reach the SS officers in command. He produced a well-forged pass from the directorate of the SNCF that described him as a manager of the *Société Nationale d'Assurance Industrielle*. Calmly he explained to the SS officers: "My company will have to pay out hundreds of millions of francs in compensation. At the very least we must be allowed to see everything and take photographs if we are to assess the damage."

The SS commandant agreed this was *korrekt*. So Trotobas received the help of SS men in his photographing. Some obligingly held the lights to illuminate the smoldering ruins. Pictures were duly dispatched to a mail drop in Normandy and forwarded across the Channel. When the RAF opened the packet it found a small card: "With the compliments of the Resistance."

As the months passed and the sabotage failed to decrease, the Germans tried desperately to find the "terrorists." Trotobas himself had several narrow escapes. On one occasion he discovered that two men, who had been introduced by trustworthy but gullible members of his *réseau,* were Gestapo V-men. Made to talk, they confessed and were shot. The bodies were dumped near the back entrance of the Gestapo headquarters in the rue Léon Gambetta. Attached to their bodies were cards bearing the same message Trotobas had sent to London: "With the compliments of the Resistance."

In June 1943 Dubois sent him a tough young French engineer, Olivier, who was an efficient saboteur but who talked too much. Together they carried out many sabotage actions, including the Fives job, and Olivier felt too cocksure. He stayed with a baker, a local Resistance leader, and must have boasted of his exploits. On 27 November the SD raided the baker's house and caught Olivier. Under torture the young man confessed and told the Germans the address of Trotobas' safe house, hoping that Michel was away at Arras that night. The SD men went to the house and found Trotobas in bed. Trotobas did not surrender. In the ensuing gunfight he killed the leader of the raiding party, an SS Hauptschar-Führer, before he himself was killed.

In Lille today there is an association that calls itself OFACM *(Organisation française des amis de Capitaine Michel).* Differences of class and politics continue to bedevil France, but in this *amicale* there are wealthy industrialists, prosperous shopkeepers, railwaymen, miners, and laborers, as well as Gaullists, Christian Democrats, Socialist trade unionists, and Communists. They meet regularly and toast the memory of *ce garçon d'un courage merveilleux,* the Anglo–French hero of their Resistance *réseau,* Michel Trotobas.

10

The Balance of Treason

THE GERMANS had every reason to be pleased with their successes at impersonating SOE officers. It had worked in the case of the Jambroes affair, when Sonder-Führer Richard Christmann duped the PROSPER team, again when SS Hauptschar-Führer Holdorf played the part of Bertrand in the trap laid for Madeleine, and also earlier, when Captain Heinz Eckert impersonated a Canadian officer in Normandy.

At Avenue Foch Hans Josef Kieffer decided to employ a similar method after seeing reports from the Dijon SD about Harry Rée's network in the Jura. John Starr, after his arrest at Dijon in July 1943, had been brought to Paris. Having learned that Starr was a draftsman, Kieffer installed him in a room adjoining his own and ordered him to copy maps and draw pen portraits of himself and other SD and Gestapo officers. During the many weeks Starr spent in his studio in the Avenue Foch he watched a procession of captured SOE officers who were brought to Kieffer and his aides for interrogations. Starr himself underwent long interrogations, but he told as little as possible about the Jura *réseau;* in any case, nothing that Kieffer had not already learned through the reports of traitor Pierre Martin. Of Harry Rée's temporary absence in Switzerland and of John Young's and Diana Rowden's hideout at Clairvaux, Starr had no knowledge.

It was by a combination of unfortunate coincidences that the Germans eventually infiltrated the Jura *réseau.* Harry Rée, after his escape to Switzerland in August, was soon released from internment and allowed by the Swiss secret service to visit Berne, where he reported to British Military Attaché Colonel H. A. Cartwright at the British legation. His reports were transmitted to London and reached Baker Street. John Young, too, was able to maintain his radio link from the hideout Rée had arranged for him and Diana Rowden.

In September, Rée returned to the Jura, cautiously resuming some of his old contacts and relying mainly on his friend Claude (Jean Simon). While reorganizing his network Rée was determined to settle his account with

Pierre Martin. He decided not to get in personal touch with John Young and Diana Rowden in order not to endanger them if the Germans were still on his trail. He asked Buckmaster for reinforcements and was informed that an SOE officer would be sent to the Jura early in November.

The two ex-assistants of John Starr enjoyed comparative safety at the Clairvaux sawmill. John Young continued with regular "skeds" on his radio, while Diana Rowden was active with local Resistance groups. A few parachute drops of material were received by her during those weeks. She maintained sporadic contact with Harry Rée through couriers. Harry knew of her good work and admired her pluck.

The sawmill at Clairvaux belonged to the Janier-Dubry family. It comprised an isolated group of houses in the woods. The owner had a son and two daughters—one married to Marcel Juif, the other to M. Pauli—and the two young couples with their small children lived in separate houses on the small estate. There the two SOE officers found cordial hospitality and were able to continue their work and organize new local groups. Many months later when Xavier (Lieutenant Colonel Robert Heslop) became SOE's chief organizer of the region, he found a fine nucleus of a network, which under his command grew to a strength of 3,500 fighters in the Jura area alone. John Young, like Rée, had asked Baker Street for the dispatch of SOE officers; but it was not until mid-November that one was sent.

The False Maugenet Arrives

Baker Street had continued to exchange signals with the now German-controlled Madeleine post in Paris and also with Bertrand, believing that the latter was still worked by Frank Pickersgill, who had been caught more than four months earlier. Signals announcing the impending arrival of an SOE agent in the Jura were sent not only to Gabriel—John Young at Clairvaux —but also to the Madelaine and Bertrand posts. Because of the precarious situation in the Jura, Baker Street unfortunately decided on this duplication.

As in the case of INTERALLIÉ, the Germans had, on earlier occasions, succeeded in establishing a *Funkspiel* with London, using captured transmitters. Some of these attempts went back to the capture of Gaullist radio posts and those belonging to ALLIANCE, an organization that worked for the British Intelligence Service but not for SOE. The *Funkdienst* had established for this purpose two main posts—one at 64 Boulevard Suchet in Paris and another at Chartrette (Seine-et-Marne). Several agents had already been captured on arrival when their dispatch was announced by London over these *Funkspiel* links.

Moreover, by a stroke of luck, SD had just captured Albert Dubois (Hercule) at Le Mans, and Dr. Goetz was able to play back on this link, too. Thus the Germans knew everything about an important pickup prepared north of Angers for 16 November.

It was a remarkable operation. Ten SOE men were taken back, five arrived. Among those who returned to Britain were Francis Cammaerts, the organizer of the great JOCKEY circuit in the south; Denis Barrett, who had been dropped with Cowburn in April; Pierre Mulsant, who had been deputizing for Cowburn at Troyes; and the redoubtable Charles Rechenmann of Tarbes.

The Germans watched the Hudson land from a respectful distance. Kieffer allowed some of the most important and successful SOE agents to return to Britain unmolested. He was ready to make this sacrifice for the sake of capturing the agents arriving on the same aircraft, in order to use them in the impersonation game he wanted to play.

The five arrivals were Victor Gerson, on his third mission as organizer of the VIC escape line; Edward Levine (on his second, going to DONKEY-MAN); Jean Manesson, a young schoolmaster at the Lycée Français in Kensington, who had worked in 1942 with Dubourdin-Dolan in Lyons; Paul Pardi, on his way to join Claude de Baissac; and the expected new organizer for Rée's Jura network, Albert Maugenet (Benoit), whose dispatch had been announced in several signals from Baker Street.

They were allowed to disperse but were trailed by SD and V-men. Gerson, a cunning old hand, gave them the slip and disappeared. So did Levine, but he was eventually traced and arrested in a Paris hotel. The three others were all taken as soon as they arrived from Angers at the Gare Montparnasse. Kieffer was especially interested in Maugenet, who carried a personal letter from Mrs. Young to her husband at Clairvaux.

At the Avenue Foch Maugenet must have been petrified to learn that the German interrogators knew everything about his mission. It is unwise to pronounce a harsh judgment upon a man who finds himself in such a situation. But in contrast with those prisoners who endured brutal torture rather than betray their comrades, Maugenet quickly decided to cooperate with the Germans. After the war British authorities were reluctant to reveal the results obtained from investigation of his case. The French authorities, however, strove to catch up with Maugenet, who spent the rest of the war as a guest of his captors and in 1945 disappeared. Nine years later his trail was taken up in Canada, and in 1955 the French government began extradition proceedings in Ottawa. Then Maugenet disappeared again and was believed to have gone to South America. He was never traced.

After interrogations at Avenue Foch, Maugenet was taken to Lons-le-Saunier together with an English-speaking V-man who now assumed Maugenet's identity. The V-man put on Maugenet's *canadienne*, (a leather jacket with a fur collar) and took his imitation crocodile suitcase containing his personal belongings, a large sum of money, and his forged identity papers in the name of Raoûl Benoit, as well as the letter from John Young's wife.

The false Maugenet arrived early in the morning at the Janier-Dubry sawmill. He was well briefed. He went straight to the house of the Pauli family and asked for Gabriel. Young took one look at the letter the man gave him, recognized his wife's handwriting, and welcomed the new arrival with warmth. The impersonator then produced his credentials: instructions from Baker Street written in code on cigarette paper and concealed in a double-bottomed matchbox. He told Young that he had left his suitcase at Lons-le-Saunier and would like to collect it. He was driven there by young Janier-Dubry in the mill van. In the evening John Young was playing chess with Pauli and discussing with him and Diana where to put up Benoit, when three German field police cars drove into the yard. Eighteen soldiers and SS men jumped out and began to fire wildly from their machine pistols. They smashed the door of Juif's house, where the wife was cooking the evening meal, and finally dragged out Diana Rowden, John Young, and Mme Pauli in handcuffs, bundled them into the cars, and drove off.

During this raid the Germans did not search the place, but shortly after midnight the false Maugenet returned with a squad of SS men, this time without pretending to be a friend. With gun in hand he demanded Gabriel's radio transmitter be handed over. But by then the transmitter had gone. By a fortunate chance, which probably saved the lives of the whole Janier-Dubry family, Jean Simon (Harry Rée's courier) had arrived at the sawmill between the first and second raid. Advised of what had happened, he removed the radio set and made off with it on his bicycle.

Several SD men remained at Clairvaux for some days, continuing their interrogations and beating up everybody. They made no further arrests, but when they left they stole all the valuables: the family silver, jewelry, carpets, linen, even the children's trinkets and toys. Only Mme Pauli, who knew the least of her menfolk's clandestine activity, was imprisoned. Fortunately, she survived the terrors and was liberated by the Americans in 1945.

At Avenue Foch, John Young and Diana Rowden were confronted with John Starr. "Here is your chief," Kieffer told them with a smirk. On 5 December Diana was moved to Fresnes prison and on 13 May 1944 to the women's jail at Karlsruhe, en route to the extermination camp of Natzweiler. There, with other SOE women she was murdered by phenol injections on 6 July 1944.[1] There is no detailed record of John Young's sufferings. He

---

[1] At the two Natzweiler camp trials in 1946, the camp doctor, who supervised the murders and in several cases administered the poison, and several SS jailers were sentenced to death and executed. The camp commandant, Fritz Hartjenstein, sentenced to life imprisonment, was later sentenced to death by a French court; he died in prison of an illness before the impending execution.

was eventually taken to the concentration camp of Mauthausen and executed early in September 1944.

Amende Honorable

The Germans had succeeded in trapping Rée's SOE comrades in the Jura, but not Rée. After the Clairvaux captures, mass arrests occurred throughout the Franche-Comté and some seventy members of Resistance groups were rounded up. Rée, a hunted man, changed his abode almost every night but was never short of friends to offer him shelter at the risk of their lives. He had vowed to avenge his comrades whom Pierre Martin had betrayed. But the traitor moved with an escort of heavily armed SD men, and several attempts at ambushing him proved abortive. Rée organized several execution teams to follow him, including one led by Bothey, the baker of Dampierre, and another by Marcel Poète, the pastrycook and *"passeur"* of Grandvillars. But Martin proved elusive.

At last, another team, led by Jean Simon, spotted Pierre Martin in the dining room of the Terrace Hotel in Besançon. He was alone; he had finished his meal and was apparently waiting for somebody. The description of what followed is taken from an eyewitness report published in the newspaper *Le Pétit Comptoir*. In spite of German censorship, the report is correct:

Tuesday evening, at about 1950, guests dining in the restaurant of the Terrace Hotel in the rue Belfort, Besançon, were startled by the reverberations of a dozen revolver shots. Two young men, who had been sitting at one of the tables, had fired the shots at another diner sitting alone, Monsieur P. M., who had just finished his meal and got up to leave the salon. Hit by several bullets in the chest, abdomen, and head, the victim expired within 20 minutes, although guests and the staff of the restaurant did everything to assist him. Taking advantage of the general confusion after the shooting, the two assassins ran into the street and disappeared in the dark night. A German soldier chased them and fired. A woman, Madame Conraud, of Cité Rosemond, who happened to be passing by in the Avenue Carnot at the moment of the drama, was wounded in the leg by a stray bullet. She was taken to the Clinic Heitz in the rue de la Moulière. The body of the victim was taken to the morgue of the Hospital Saint-Jacques. The police were alerted immediately, as well as the appropriate German authorities. Their officers arrived at the scene within a few minutes. Commissar Buhr of the German Sicherheitsdienst is conducting the investigations in cooperation with Commissar Manton of the Besançon Police Judiciare.

The Gestapo, enraged by the execution of their most valuable V-man, redoubled their efforts to capture "the terrorists." A large reward was offered for their arrest. Harry Rée never saw Jean Simon again, though he received a few messages from him. The brave boy had "dived under"; and so had the other members of the execution team, though not for very long.

Soon Simon was active again, carrying out sabotage and organizing maquis units. Only after the war did Rée learn that his comrade was shot dead in a gun battle at the Café Grangier at Sochaux in January 1944. Surrounded by an SS squad, Simon sold his life dearly, killing one and wounding two SS men.

After Pierre Martin's assassination Colonel Buckmaster ordered Rée to quit his region and cross into Switzerland. But Rée, expecting the Allied invasion soon, refused to leave his comrades. On 27 November, a Sunday, he went to Audincourt to see Jean Hauger, a schoolmaster, who as Macout was the leader of the local Resistance group. The door was opened by a man with a pistol in his hand, who motioned Rée inside, ordered him to put up his arms, and told him that he was a sergeant of the *Geheime Feldpolizei*. Having searched Rée and found him unarmed, the German became quite friendly, although continuing to hold his gun pointed at Rée. They sat down at the kitchen table. The German said that Macout had been arrested —which was not true—and that his old mother had been taken to the Gestapo headquarters. Rée explained that he was a watchmaker who had come to collect a watch for repairs, and that he knew nothing of M. Hauger's clandestine activities. The German replied that in an hour or so an SD squad would arrive to relieve him, and Rée would be taken to the Gestapo office for a proper identity check.

Rée, not altogether looking forward to this little trip, suggested a drink. Mère Hauger always had some Armagnac in her cupboard. The German agreed and Rée poured a generous amount into a glass on the kitchen table. As the German reached for the glass Rée gripped the bottle by the neck, swung around, and struck him on the head as hard as he could. The German was thick-skulled. He jumped up, and as Rée closed in and tried to pinion his arms, the German dug his gun into Rée's ribs and fired. But Rée felt no impact.

"I tried to remember the dirty tricks taught us by the instructors at the Special Schools," Rée recalls. "But I could only remember *King Lear,* and I tried to gouge out one of his eyes, but it wouldn't come out." They fought in the kitchen with Mère Hauger's fine china crashing to the floor, into the hall, and onto the staircase. Rée heard several shots, but still felt no impact. At last he flattened the German and stumbled out of the house to his bicycle, which he had left by the wall. Too unsteady to mount the bicycle, he veered toward the back garden, staggered over a ditch and a stream, and crawled through a thick bramble hedge into the woods. Dazed but conscious, he headed for a village, four miles away, where he had friends. But his strength ebbed quickly and he slumped down, conscious of imminent unconsciousness. While his body flagged, his mind reiterated the thought that the SS men would soon find him. Rising unsteadily, he stumbled on. Only then did he notice that his raincoat and clothes were hot and splotched with blood, which was now streaming down his legs.

He had been hit by three bullets: two pierced his lungs; the third barely missed his heart. Somehow he managed to reach the house of Mme Bourquin at Etupes. When old Doctor Petréquin arrived from Seloncourt and examined the patient, he could not believe that a man so wounded could have walked for four miles across fields, streams, and woods. He paid a simple tribute: "Ah, *les Anglais . . . !*"

Rée was hidden at the Bourquin home, remaining for many days in a critical condition. When transport could be risked, he was taken by night to the château of Count d'Astier de la Vigerie near Belfort and eventually smuggled by Marcel Poète, that clever *passeur,* across the Swiss frontier to the hospital in Porrentruy, where a surgeon operated on him. Eventually he was brought to Berne, and the British legation arranged for his convalescence on Lake of Lucerne. Only partly recovered in May 1944, crossing France to the Pyrenees, he was caught by Spanish frontier guards and taken to the internment camp of Miranda de Ebro. At last, in July 1944, he reached London and worked until the end of the war at the F section office.

Donkeyman

Following PROSPER's demise in the summer of 1943, Frager's JEAN-MARIE network, renamed DONKEYMAN, became an important SOE foothold in northern France. Although Frager's adjutant, Roger Bardet, supplied Bleicher with regular reports about the network, he remained strangely devoted to his chief. He tried to protect Frager, keeping his movements secret from Bleicher and never disclosing Frager's real identity. He referred to him as Paul, and for many months Paul remained a somewhat mysterious figure to Bleicher. The Abwehr man was quite satisfied with this state of affairs; he did not want to prod Bardet too hard lest he lose his valuable services.

In the summer of 1943, however, relations between the Gestapo and the *Sicherheitsdienst* on one hand and the Abwehr on the other reached almost breaking point, reflecting the struggle between the Nazi leaders and the German general staff for the control of the secret services. Admiral Canaris, chief of the Abwehr, was already a marked man. The following winter he was removed from office and eventually was executed by the Gestapo. The officers of the Paris Abwehr had become aware of the catastrophe that was overtaking their service. Hitherto Colonel Oscar Reile had encouraged Bleicher in his sallies against the *Sicherheitsdienst,* taking personal delight in anything that upset Kieffer. But now he became wary. At a secret conference of senior Abwehr officers at the Hotel Lutetia, the chief of the Paris AST,

Colonel Friedrich Rudolph, declared that the Paris AST would have to be more accomodating to Messrs. Oberg, Knochen, and Kieffer.

Soon afterward Kieffer asked Colonel Reile about the plan to round up the JEAN-MARIE–DONKEYMAN network, which he referred to as the "British terrorist gang." He arrogantly lectured Reile about the contrast between the great successes he and the SD had scored in apprehending British agents and the meager achievements of the Abwehr.

In true military fashion Colonel Reile decided that the buck should be passed down the line. He told Bleicher to produce results. But this time Bleicher was not given a free hand and was ordered to submit detailed reports. Captain Schäffer was to supervise the clever sergeant. Bleicher was hurt but realized he must obey. In July, when Major Bodington was in Paris, Bleicher was able to persuade Colonel Reile that Bodington should be left unmolested in order not to endanger Bardet's position. But during the following weeks the situation changed, and the double game now became too dangerous to play.

Frager had three SOE officers working for him at this time. His chief radio operator was Bastien—Marcel Clech, who had worked for Gaspard and Pierre Culioli in the Sologne. In the spring of 1943 Clech had been picked up by a Lysander and returned to England. After a brief rest, he returned on his second mission on 13 May. With him came Vera Leigh (Simone) and Sydney Jones (Elie), a thirty-nine-year-old perfume merchant who, on his first mission in September 1942, had been landed from a felucca in the south of France and for six months had done a good job with CARTE (when he first met Frager) and at Marseilles. Clech, using his good knowledge of the Sologne, set up a radio post in a house belonging to Madame Bossard at Aulnay-sous-Bois. Later, when several of the Sologne hideouts were "burned," Clech moved to Les Essarts, south of Paris. Bleicher had a fairly good knowledge, through Roger Bardet, of the movements of Bastien, Elie, and Simone. He played with the idea of arresting them, even though he would forfeit a chance of discovering more information by watching their contacts and listening in on Bastien's radio communications.

Bleicher Meets Frager

Bleicher decided that the time had come to meet Frager. He asked Bardet to arrange a meeting and to introduce him as a German officer who wanted to defect to the Allies. They met on 12 August at the Café Monte-Carlo on the Avenue Wagram. Bleicher described himself as a Lieutenant Colonel of the Luftwaffe and impressed Frager with the disclosure that the Luftwaffe intelligence knew everything about Gilbert (Henri Déricourt) and his activities as SOE air movements officer. He also told Frager that Gilbert was an agent of the *Sicherheitsdienst* and had worked for SS Obersturmbann-Führer Karl Boemelburg. Frager, who knew nothing about Gilbert's double role or that Gilbert's contacts with the Germans were approved by British intelligence, was shocked. Bleicher then played his trump card and told Frager that he had known of Major Bodington's visit to Paris. Thus Bleicher gained Frager's trust.

In September Frager was away from Paris, inspecting several of his *réseaux* southeast of the capital; he had established a second headquarters at the Château de Petite-Ermite in Yonne. Although the Germans had infiltrated some of Frager's *réseaux* in the northwest, they did not discover for a long time the existence of many more in the east and southeast. Neither did they know of Frager's deputy, Lieutenant Colonel Jacques Adam, who was in charge of these *réseaux*.

During that time fairly large drops of material were received in the northwest, in the LISIANA area. Kiki had infiltrated a *réseau* at Caen, and many of its members were arrested. Subsequently the Abwehr learned, through Kiki and Bardet (and passed the information to the SD) of reception grounds in the Paris area: at Mantes, La Ferté-Alais, and Dourdan in the Départment Seine-et-Oise; at Donnemarie in the Départment Seine-et-Marne; and several others. All these were taken over and large quantities of material were captured.

The situation in the northwest became precarious for the Frager network. Bardet had also reported that, in addition to Bastien at Les Essarts, another radio post, in the charge of Hercule (Dubois), was working in Le Mans. The Abwehr chiefs, in order to please Dr. Knochen and Kieffer, decided to let the SD deal with the Le Mans post.

During the first week of November Kieffer sent an SD squad, headed by SS Sturm-Führer Scherrer and interpreter Ernst Vogt, to Le Mans. Hercule had his radio post in a farmhouse outside Le Mans. Baker Street had received reports from Paris warning that Hercule's radio signals appeared to have been intercepted by the *Funkhorchdienst*. Hercule was ordered to stop and prepare for a Lysander pickup. The Germans arrived a day or two before the Lysander operation could be arranged and found Hercule and his host, a tough Breton, barricaded in the farm. A gun battle ensued; Scherrer was killed and Vogt seriously wounded. The two Resistance men were finally captured, taken to Paris, and later executed.

After this unhappy incident Baker Street ordered Bastien (Marcel Clech) to abandon his hideout at Les Essarts and move to Paris. He established himself at Neuilly, in a house belonging to Madame Artus.

Meanwhile Frager returned to Paris and had another friendly meeting with Bleicher. This took place in early October at the buffet of Gare Saint-Michel. On this occasion Frager told the "Luftwaffe officer" that he would soon be going to London for consultations. Bleicher suggested Frager should tell Colonel Buckmaster about him and that he was prepared to come to London to work for the Allied intelligence. In fact, Bleicher repeated the game he had played with Marsac.

There was some delay in arranging the pickup. Eventually, on 21 October, Henri Frager was collected by a Lysander at one of Gilbert's landing grounds in the Angers region and brought to England. Significantly, Roger Bardet accompanied him to the pickup and bid him farewell. Frager intended to stay in London for only a fortnight, but dramatic events in Paris compelled him to postpone his return to France for several months.

Abwehr Loses the London Radio Link

When Bastien moved from Les Essarts to Neuilly, Bardet knew nothing about it and was unable to discover Bastien's new whereabouts. Bardet had previously been in fairly regular contact with Bastien. Twice Bardet had met him, bringing along Bleicher, whom he introduced, as with other Frager-*réseaux* members, as an anti-Nazi German officer. Now the contact had been severed, and the Abwehr had lost Bastien's London radio link.

Captain Schäffer became angry when he received Bleicher's report. "You're playing a dangerous game, Bleicher," he said. "You were shielding a terrorist and now he's slipped through our fingers. The SD is not going to sit back and watch idly while your friend Bastien sets up a new secret transmitter somewhere else!"

In order to find Bastien, Bleicher assigned two men to constantly follow Simone (Vera Leigh). She lived then at 134 rue de la Faisanderie, near the Boulevard Victor Hugo. But Simone apparently had no contact with Bastien; Bleicher's men reported no meetings between her and the missing radio operator. What the Germans did not know was that Bastien and Simone maintained contact through mail drops, unknown even to Bardet.

Bleicher, after a conference with Colonel Reile and Captain Schäffer, decided to arrest Simone. As he told me many years later, Simone had to be sacrificed because she had been the main SOE courier in Paris, and Bleicher hoped that if she were caught, Bardet would receive the badly needed information being withheld from him at that time.

Vera Leigh was lured to a rendezvous on 30 October at the Café Mas, Place des Ternes. The trap was laid (with Bardet's help, according to Bleicher, although Bardet asserted at his trial that he had warned Simone) by Jacky, a V-man and member of DONKEYMAN.

After imprisonment at Fresnes, Vera Leigh was transferred in May 1944 to the Karlsruhe prison. On 6 July she and Andrée Borrel, Diana Rowden, and Sonia Olschanesky were taken to Natzweiler. They arrived there at 3 P.M. and were put in single cells. Between 9:30 and 10:30 P.M. they were led singly to the crematorium. There each was injected with phenol and immediately put into the cremation oven.[2]

Next, Bardet persuaded Bleicher to liquidate Elie (Jones). Bardet had reasons of his own for eliminating Elie quickly. Evidently Captain Sydney Jones had become suspicious of him and had warned Frager that Bardet might be playing a double game. Bardet had queried Jones about some dropping zones, but Jones refused to tell him anything; this sealed his fate.

On 19 November Bleicher went with a sergeant to Elie's apartment early in the morning and found the SOE officer in bed. "He was a brave man," Bleicher told me. "He took his arrest calmly and only said, 'It's a pity, it's such a nice day today.' " Jones was turned over to the *Sicherheitsdienst*. Bleicher gave Colonel Reile a list of thirty dropping zones that Jones was alleged to have organized, and this was also passed on to Kieffer. Only twelve of these dropping zones had ever been used, but Kieffer was, for the moment, satisfied that Reile and Bleicher were adhering to the agreement.

Then it was Bastien's turn. He informed Baker Street of Elie's and Simone's capture, but soon afterward an officer of the *Funkhorchdienst,* Sonder-Führer Strassenschultze, located Bastien's radio post. An SD squad was sent to the house, and Bastien was caught literally with his finger on the Morse key. This was on 19 December 1943 and on the following day three other DONKEYMAN members were arrested. Their interrogations led to a number of further arrests and the seizure of arms dumps at Béthisy-St. Martin near Compiègne, Ermenonville near the forest of Chantilly, and other places around the capital.

But the capture of Bastien, a triumph for Kieffer and his SD, was a body blow to the Abwehr and to Bleicher personally. It broke the only radio link between DONKEYMAN and London known to the Abwehr just when Frager was expected to be sending important instructions from Baker Street.

Waiting for Paul

The arrests of the two SOE officers on Frager's staff and the numerous arrests among members of his network induced SOE chiefs to keep Frager in London. From reports received they were able to piece together the extent of the betrayals that led to these arrests, and they did not want Henri Frager to be captured. Through the rest of December 1943 and into January a lull was imposed upon activities of SOE groups in Paris and northern France.

Meanwhile, the Abwehr chiefs at the Hotel Lutetia, awaiting Frager's return, were not idle. Captain Schäffer and Bleicher were involved in in-

[2] *Cf. The Natzweiler Trial,* edited by A. M. Webb, William Hodge, London.

vestigations concerning a large Gaullist *réseau,* MITHRIDATE, which was not connected with SOE. Some months earlier Schäffer had won over a member of this *réseau,* a former radio operator in the French navy, Marcel Étasse. Bleicher became his control, and this new assignment took him to Clermont-Ferrand, Reims, and Lille, where MITHRIDATE had local groups. Throughout late 1943 and early 1944 the Abwehr almost succeeded in destroying the entire network. More than 150 members of MITHRIDATE, including its chief, Herbinger, were arrested.

At Christmas Bleicher was given leave and went to Tettnang, his home town in Württemberg. When he returned to Paris, on 17 January 1944, he found a dramatic change at the Hotel Lutetia: The Abwehr had been put under the control of Himmler's RSHA. This was the outcome of a long campaign that Himmler and Kaltenbrunner had been conducting against German military intelligence in general, and its chief, Admiral Canaris, in particular. Ernst Kaltenbrunner, the Austrian Nazi who in 1934 had been involved in the murder of Chancellor Dollfuss, had become the chief of the RSHA, and SS Gruppen-Führer Walter Schellenberg was now in charge of all counterespionage matters. The Abwehr had become a mere adjunct of the *Sicherheitsdienst.* A month later, on 14 February 1944, Hitler ordered the dissolution of the Abwehr. Some of its departments dealing with operational intelligence were attached to Hitler's OKW (High Command of the German Forces). The counterespionage sections were absorbed by the RSHA.

In the German-occupied countries the Abwehr ASTs were transformed into *Frontaufklärungskommandos* (Front Intelligence Units), designated FAK. In Paris, Colonel Oscar Reile, Bleicher's chief, survived in the new post as head of five of these FAKs for France, Belgium, and Holland: FAK 306 in Paris, under Major von Feldmann (who became Bleicher's immediate superior); FAK 307 in Brussels, under Lieutenant Colonel Hermann Giskes, for northern France, Belgium, and Holland; and FAKs 313, 314, and 350 (under Colonel Ehinger, Lieutenant Colonel Bernbach, and Major Weigand) for the rest of France. Nominally under the military C in C West, the FAKs had to take orders from the *Sicherheitsdienst.*

According to information obtained from Colonel Reile after the war, several hundred officers, NCOs, orderlies, clerks, drivers, and specialists (interpreters, code-clerks, radio operators, etc.) of the former Abwehr in France were ordered in February 1944 to return to units and were sent to the Eastern front. The special funds used by the Abwehr to pay their V-men and informers were almost completely withdrawn. Colonel Reile said that until the end of 1943 the Abwehr in France had had several hundred officers and NCOs and its own field security police, employing several thousand V-men. Now each FAK had only twenty-five to thirty-five officers and a few NCOs and Sonder-Führers; most of the V-men had to be dismissed. However, many of these informers and traitors quickly found more lucrative employment with the SD and the Gestapo.

Bleicher, who had lost his immediate superior, Captain Schäffer, soon discovered that his new chief, Major von Feldmann, was ineffective and frightened of the Gestapo. A few days after Bleicher's return to Paris, Kieffer summoned him to the Avenue Foch. The SD chief was as elated by the drastic changes as Bleicher was stunned. Kieffer told him:

"We left the Jean Marie organization and Paul (Frager) to you. This was foolish. You have lost track of them. I have given you and your Abwehr friends every chance. But make no mistake: You'll pay with your head if we don't get Paul quickly and clean up the entire terrorist nest . . . ."

With the new dominance of the SD and Gestapo, oppressive measures against the Resistance were intensified. Throughout France thousands of men and women, innocent of any clandestine activity, were rounded up and deported.

Baker Street received many reports from SOE officers in the field of the ruthless measures now employed by the Germans and their effect on the Resistance. In one way, however, these measures increased the fighting spirit of the French. Many more thousands of Frenchmen joined the maquis; many more training camps of the secret army were established in the mountains and forests. And the need for arms and equipment from Britain increased accordingly.

Bricklayer

In London, SOE chiefs decided to send to Paris one of their most experienced field officers, Major France Anthelme, to set up new headquarters in or near the capital and make a tour of inspection of the main networks. His code name, Bricklayer, was fitting, for in the course of two previous missions to France he had laid the foundations for several important networks. He had been on politico-military missions with leaders of Gaullist organizations, with ORA and OCM, and had accompanied Major Nicholas Bodington on his exploratory visit to Paris in July. On that mission Anthelme had established a *réseau* in Le Mans. He left it in charge of Émile-Henri Garry (Phono) and also arranged for a safe house for Madeleine (Noor Inayat Khan) at Auffargis.

While arrangements were being made for the dispatch of Major Anthelme's team, Henri Frager insisted on being sent back to France without further delay. He was becoming increasingly worried about DONKEYMAN. Because of Gilbert's recall early in February, no immediate arrangements for a Lysander landing could be made. So on 15 February Frager and his SOE radio operator were taken over by a Royal Navy MTB.

Four agents preceded Anthelme's mission to do the spadework: two

Frenchmen, Raoul Alexandre and Jacques Ledoux; a Canadian, Frank Deniset; and Robert Byerley, an American. They were, of course, captured on their arrival at the SD-controlled dropping zone.

Dr. Goetz immediately used Byerley's transmitter to confirm that the dropping of the Bricklayer team would be duly attended to. Although there was some doubt at Baker Street about whether this message was genuine (as Byerley never signaled again), Anthelme insisted on going ahead with his mission.

The dropping of the Anthelme team was set for 29 February, when the first quarter of the moon appeared at ten minutes to nine. The operation was code-marked "Phono 4," and signals arranging the reception of the team at a ground south of Poigny, five miles from Rambouillet, were sent from Baker Street to Garry's Phono and Noor's Madeleine radio posts. This proved a sad mistake.

The messages, which duly reached Kieffer's office, contained specific arrangements for the drop. The aircraft, a Halifax, was to arrive over Rambouillet at 2245 hours. Two small lakes, south and east of Poigny, and the course of the little river Droue would serve as landmarks. The dropping zone was within comfortable reach of Paris, enabling Kieffer to invite SS General Oberg, the chief of security in France, and SS Standarten-Führer Dr. Helmuth Knochen, the chief of the *Sicherheitsdienst,* to this reception of "a high British Military Intelligence officer." By 2115 hours the area was cordoned off, ensuring that local Resistance members would be kept away. The park of Rambouillet swarmed with SS squad cars. Such effort was hardly necessary.

The team consisted of Major Anthelme, radio operator Lieutenant Lionel Lee (Mechanic), and courier Madeleine Damerment (Martine). Eight large containers and six packages, including three radio transmitters of the latest small size, Eureka and S-phone equipment (for communicating with planes approaching a drop zone), and a large quantity of arms, were dropped first. Major Anthelme was the first to float down in the silvery moonlight. Kieffer had Vogt and several of his best V-men, posing as Resistance men, to form the reception committee. But once the three alighted, he did not consider ceremony.

Anthelme struggled to his feet and asked: "Where is Phono?"

The answer he received was a muzzle of a Luger automatic. The three SOE agents were driven to Avenue Foch. They were interrogated throughout the night, particularly Major Anthelme. Vogt stated after the war that Anthelme was "in a rage" when he entered Kieffer's office and that he repeatedly shouted, "I have been betrayed!" Vogt deduced that Anthelme meant he had been betrayed in London, or by someone connected with SOE. But Vogt made many wild statements in his depositions to the French DST, and his statement should be taken with a pinch of salt. In any case,

Kieffer and the other SD chiefs elicited little from Anthelme. Though tortured, he refused to talk.

On this occasion the Germans did not bother to observe the usual routine of imprisonment at Fresnes, transfer to a concentration camp in Germany, and so forth. The three prisoners were held in solitary confinement in the special cells at Avenue Foch until 12 May. The two men were then taken to the notorious torture cellars of the Gestapo at rue des Saussaies. According to one source, they were executed at Mauthausen; according to another, they were sent to the extermination camp of Gross Rosen and executed in September.

Madeleine Damerment was held at Avenue Foch, later sent to the prison at Karlsruhe, and then to Dachau concentration camp. There she was shot with three other SOE women agents on 13 September 1944.

Kieffer and Dr. Goetz had taken care to signal Baker Street that the Bricklayer team had been received. Knowing of Anthelme's important mission and not wanting to reply to complex queries, they informed London (using the Madeleine transmitter) that Anthelme had suffered serious head injuries on landing. Several signals followed, quoting doctors' opinions and saying that Anthelme was in a hospital. Replying to urgent demands for further details and questions about why Mechanic (Lionel Lee) did not himself report from his transmitter, the Germans used Lee's W/T set (code-named Daks) to inform Baker Street on 24 March that Anthelme was in a coma. Finally, on 20 April they sent a signal saying that Bricklayer had died. By then Baker Street was more or less aware that both teams had fallen into German hands.

How could a team, headed by a senior officer, entrusted with an important mission, drop straight into the arms of the Germans? Several years after the war there were accusations that Major Anthelme, Lionel Lee, and Madeleine Damerment "were deliberately sacrificed" by Baker Street in order to find out whether one or the other radio post—such as Bertrand, Madeleine, or Phono—was still genuine or controlled by the enemy. Even if one assumed, for the sake of argument, that Colonel Buckmaster and other officers of F section were capable of sacrificing a friend and two young people to ascertain the status of doubtful radio posts, the accusations are illogical. Major Anthelme, one of the most valuable officers of the section, had accomplished several major missions. He and his team were carefully selected for another one. Fourteen containers with radio transmitters, electronic equipment, S-phones, and arms were dropped with them at Rambouillet. It would not have been necessary to present the Germans with all this material if this were just a "guinea-pig" operation.

There is no doubt that a terrible mistake was made at Baker Street. But the fact is that in February 1944 the situation regarding the Paris SOE outposts was extremely confused. After the capture of Madeleine (Noor

Inayat Khan) and Phono (Émile-Henri Garry) the Germans were able to send most plausible signals to Baker Street, finally luring the Anthelme team into a trap.

Cat and Mouse in Paris

By the time Henri Frager returned to France on 15 February 1944, all the SOE officers who had worked with him before his departure—Hercule, Bastien, Elie, Simone—had been captured. Colonel Buckmaster had advised Frager to avoid Paris and make his headquarters at one of the maquis camps that his groups had established in Yonne. Frager went to Auxerre, where his deputy, Colonel Jacques Adam, was holding the fort.

Adam gave him good news. With the steady influx of Resistance men to the maquis camps during the spring of 1944, the *réseaux* had spread far beyond their original boundaries. Yonne, Brie, Aube, had always been DONKEYMAN strongholds, and Frager knew every *réseau* there. But now there were many *réseaux* and new camps in the Ardennes, Lorraine, Burgundy, and as far south as the Savoy mountains. Colonel Adam's largest camp, of several hundred well-armed men, was in the forest of Othe. Frager had brought good news, too. He could assure Adam and the group commanders that the Allied invasion was now only a matter of weeks.

Colonel Buckmaster sent Frager another liaison officer, a "pianist," and a woman courier, Peggy Knight (Nicole). Some of the adventures of this young girl are worth recounting if only to show that the latter-day agents of 1944 faced constant and unrelenting danger, too.

Peggy was dropped by parachute on 28 April 1944 to one of Frager's grounds in the Yonne. Within days of her arrival she arranged receptions of arms, now being parachuted thick and fast; taught newly arrived recruits to handle Sten guns; and was involved in an ambush on a German truck convoy, using her own Sten gun for the first time. Frager sent her to Paris with messages to some of his friends, a journey she repeated many times during the following weeks. Then came D day and Peggy bicycled from camp to camp, alerting the groups now mobilized into FFI units. She was at Frager's headquarters at the Château de Petite-Hermite when it was surrounded by the Germans, took part in the battle, and had a narrow escape with thirty maquisards, hiding in a wood for several days. When German divisions were moving to Normandy and Frager's Yonne and Loiret units attacked them, Peggy took part in an engagement on the road from Joigny to Montargis. This ended in the surrender of a German convoy, the capture of many motor vehicles, and a valuable cargo of arms, ammunition, and food. During the weeks before liberation Peggy was a courier between the FFI units under Colonel Adam and British SAS units dropped south of Paris, and finally with American tank forces. She crossed the German lines on several occasions. Twice she was stopped by German patrols, but the officers who interrogated her would not believe that the tiny girl could be a spy. Once she explained to a German officer that she was on her way to find a dentist, as she had a terrible toothache. The German, amused that a young girl dared to cross the firing line just to be relieved of toothache, gave her coffee and aspirin, and let her go. Thus Peggy learned the number of German units in the area and could enlighten the Allied commander.

Frager, since his return from London, had been staying with the Yonne maquis, regularly visiting Paris, Auxerre, Saint-Florentin, Troyes, and other centers of his networks. One day in March, Roger Bardet appeared at Frager's Château de Petite-Hermite. Colonel Adam did not trust him and during the winter months had seen him on only a few occasions. But Frager received Bardet with open arms. Bardet told him a long story of having been in hiding from the Gestapo, and suggested that Frager should meet again that friendly Colonel Henri (Bleicher).

Hugo Bleicher was living through anxious weeks in Paris. The SD chiefs of Avenue Foch inquired almost daily whether he knew where "the terrorist Paul" was hiding. Bleicher was doing some hard thinking about the wider implications of current affairs and his own uncertain future. Like most of the Abwehr officers he had concluded that Germany had lost the war. But in order to save his skin, he had to humor the *Sicherheitsdienst.*

Bleicher had relied entirely on Roger Bardet for information about Frager and his networks, but Bardet was very elusive. He came only when he needed money, telling involved stories of being watched by Resistance men who suspected him, and disappearing again as soon as Bleicher paid up. Bleicher began to suspect that Bardet was betraying him to the Resistance, and he was not far wrong. Bardet had also decided that the time had come to reconsider the situation and, in order to safeguard his future, to pay more attention to his Resistance friends. He went more often to Auxerre and began to travel extensively, renewing old contacts and making new friends among maquis leaders.

To restore his badly shaken reputation with the Gestapo chiefs, Bleicher took an SD squad to a house in the rue Cognacq Jay where, according to Bardet, an SOE officer named Segonzac used to stay. This off-the-cuff sortie produced a startling haul. The Germans found a group of French officers, headed by General Vernot, one of the chiefs of the *Armée Secrète,* and Colonel Cogny, his chief of staff.[3] The significance of these arrests was far greater than the Germans realized. Some time before, Pierre Brossolette,

[3] General Vernot died in a German concentration camp. Colonel Cogny was liberated in 1945 and was a witness at Bardet's treason trial.

one of the chiefs of General de Gaulle's BCRA, had come from London
with Wing Commander Yeo-Thomas of the RF section of SOE [4] to conduct
important negotiations with General Vernot and other Resistance leaders.
The capture of Vernot and his aides almost nullified the advantages of this
agreement.

At long last Bardet appeared again at Bleicher's apartment at 56 rue
Pergolèse. He was full of news, gloating over his scoops: Paul had returned
to France; Gilbert had been recalled; Major Bodington had been "sacked."
He proudly reported that Frager had made him his deputy again and gave
him all the news from London. He also told Bleicher that Frager had
agreed to meet him again. The meeting was arranged for 27 March at the
Bois de Boulogne.

Bleicher Receives a Testimonial

Frager was still convinced that Colonel Henri was a genuine anti-Nazi
friend. He told Bleicher that the invasion would take place within the next
few weeks; that he had five thousand men armed and trained to tackle the
Germans in the rear; and that they would prevent transport on the roads
and railway lines from Dijon, Paris, and Orléans to the north. He advised
his German friend to look after himself as the liberation was at hand.
Bleicher wished him good luck and then asked for a favor: Could Paul give
him a testimonial? If he were taken prisoner by the Allies after Germany's
defeat, it would be useful to show something in writing, a few words, saying that he had helped the Resistance.

Henri Frager, that magnanimous, brave, gullible man, readily gave the
testimonial the German requested. He also gave him the address of his
sister at Neuilly, advising Bleicher to go there and ask for shelter when the
Allied troops entered Paris. Frager promised he would tell his sister that
if a German called and told her he was Colonel Henri, she should receive
him as a friend.

Bleicher told me that he was sick at heart over his relationship with
Frager. He admired this brave Frenchman, whom he had deceived for
many months and whom he was to arrest and deliver to almost certain
death. There is in Bleicher's character that strange mixture of Teutonic
sentimentality, respect for his enemies, and a conviction that as a German,
he must do his duty.

For a while things turned out well for Bleicher. He told Major von
Feldmann that he knew Paul had returned, but pleaded to be left alone
for a time so that he could discover his *réseaux* and dropping zones. Bardet
had brought Bleicher a list of twenty-two dropping zones, but it proved of
little use. The grounds were watched, but no drops took place; apparently

[4] Indirectly this raid led to Yeo-Thomas' capture on 21 March 1944.

Bardet delivered a list of grounds that had long since been abandoned. April passed and Bleicher saw Bardet only once. Then Bardet disappeared again and Bleicher did not see him for many weeks. At his trial Bardet stated that he had decided to break with the Germans; he spent those weeks in Auxerre and in maquis camps.

D day came and Bleicher was hard pressed by the SD chiefs to deliver the long-wanted Paul. He gave them a list of some of Frager's camps in the Yonne, which Bardet had mentioned. On 16 June, by order of Paris Gestapo chief SS General Oberg, strong units of SS with SD squads were sent to Yonne. Since D day Frager had directed many sabotage actions and attacks on German troop convoys in Yonne, the Côte d'Or, and Nivernais. On the day of the raid he was at his command post at the Château de Petite-Hermite with Roger Bardet. The Germans had underestimated the strength of the maquisards, and after a pitched battle they were forced to withdraw. Frager and Bardet went to another camp.

After this abortive raid in Yonne, the enraged SD chiefs summoned Bleicher to Avenue Foch. Kieffer, who was usually more friendly than the others, told him, "You should have arrested Paul when you last met him. Now we might never catch up with him again. Well, you're responsible for it. I give you one week. Then I shall send a report to the RSHA. This means a People's Court trial for you, or worse . . . ."

Bleicher was in a turmoil. He had to find Frager, but how? On 28 June Major von Feldmann came to his apartment to discuss possibilities. They were having coffee when Roger Bardet arrived, quite unexpectedly. Bleicher asked him where Paul was; he wanted to see him again; he had some information for him. Bardet said he would arrange a meeting on 30 June at the Rond Point. Bleicher went to this rendezvous with two field policemen. But there was no trace of either Paul or Bardet. Bleicher was now convinced that Bardet had betrayed him.

The next day, 1 July, he went to Frager's sister at Neuilly. When he introduced himself as Colonel Henri he was received in the friendliest manner. "My brother told me about you; I know that you have helped him and if you're in trouble I can put you up," Mlle Frager said. They talked about the Allied landing, the fighting in Normandy, and agreed that it might not be long before the Allies entered Paris. Bleicher explained it was still too early for him "to leave his post with the Luftwaffe," but that he wanted to see her brother urgently. Did she know where he could be found?

She said her brother was away but would return the next day, and that she intended to collect him at 5 P.M. from the Gare Montparnasse. Bleicher thanked her for the information and left—as he told me years later—with a troubled mind. Now there was no escape for Paul. He consoled himself with the thought that at last the charade had ended, and that "it's either he or I."

[193]

He telephoned Kieffer and they made their arrangements for the arrest. On the afternoon of 2 July Bleicher went with six men to the Gare Montparnasse. Three were from the FAK office, three from Kieffer's SD office at Avenue Foch; this was the bargain with Kieffer. He posted two of them near the platform, two at the exit on the stairs leading to the street; two followed him at a short distance. When the train arrived a few minutes after 5, Bleicher saw Frager walking through the barrier of Quai 4. It struck him that the Resistance leader looked tired and drawn; his hair had become almost white since their last meeting a few weeks earlier.

Bleicher approached him, and when Frager saw him he stretched out his hand and said with a smile, "What are you doing here, Henri? Did you know I was coming?"

"Commandant Frager, I am sorry. I misled you. I am a German officer and I have come to arrest you." He made a sign to the two men behind him and they closed in. Frager looked surprised but did not say a word. They led him to a waiting car and drove to Avenue Foch. "Not a word was spoken during that drive," Bleicher recalls, "but I shall not forget the expression in Frager's eyes." Bleicher took Frager to Kieffer, who interrogated him through an interpreter. Kieffer was greatly impressed and, according to Bleicher, said afterward: "This man is a real patriot; I respect him. We shall try to do something for him. He will have to be sent to Germany, but it's not a *Nacht und Nebel* case. He won't be liquidated." Bleicher asked Kieffer for permission to visit Frager, who was taken after a few days to the Gestapo prison at rue des Saussaies.

I Bear No Grudge

He found Frager composed. He had not been manhandled; apparently Kieffer had ordered his men to refrain from violence. Frager told Bleicher: "I often suspected you might be a German counteragent, but one has to believe in one's fellow human beings. I believed you and I have only myself to blame."

Bleicher tried to explain that he had no choice. He told Frager it was Roger Bardet—whom he called a "despicable villain"—who had first betrayed him and he related Bardet's protracted intrigues and treachery. To Bleicher's surprise Frager shook his head. "Roger is not a villain, only a weakling, a foolish boy," he said. "I loved him like a brother. It hurts me deeply that he betrayed me, but I am a practising Catholic and I cannot hate. When the war is over, Roger will have to pay for his sins. But don't be too hard on him . . . I bear no grudge." He suggested that Bleicher tell nothing to the Gestapo about their dealings. "It will make things easier for you, too, and also for Bardet. Perhaps we shall all live and meet when the war is over," he said.

During the next few weeks events were hectic for Bleicher. His FAK unit was ordered to go to Auxerre; on 5 August it was moved to Nancy, and a few days later to Liège in Belgium. The Allies had reached Alençon and Angers, converging on Paris. In Belgium Bleicher met Kieffer with many of his officers from Avenue Foch. They had made their new head-quarters at Charleroi. He asked Kieffer what had happened to Frager and was told he was sent with other SOE prisoners to Germany on 8 August. "They were taken to a concentration camp, probably Buchenwald," Kieffer said. "But no orders for their liquidation have been issued, they are regarded as hostages. They have a good chance to survive, if Hitler comes to terms with the Allies."

Early in September Bleicher was ordered to report to FAK headquarters at Cleve in Germany, and later posted as an intelligence instructor in Cologne, where he remained until March 1945. Then he was transferred to a military intelligence office in Enschede, Holland. After the German surrender Bleicher remained in Holland, hiding in Amsterdam. He was arrested there by Canadian troops on 15 June 1945 and flown to London a month later. He was interrogated by Military Intelligence officers assisted by members of the French section of SOE. Among them was Vera Atkins, who was collecting evidence for the trial of German war criminals, par-ticularly those involved in the murders of SOE women agents at Natzweiler and Dachau. The British authorities decided not to charge Bleicher, and he was transferred to a French office in Paris that dealt with alleged war criminals and collaborators. In August 1945 Bleicher found himself in a cell in the rue des Saussaies, where he had visited Henri Frager a year before. In the next cell was Roger Bardet. They met when some prisoners were ordered to stoke boilers of the heating system. It was not a friendly meeting.

Bleicher went through many interrogations, but the French authorities decided that he was not guilty of war crimes. In September 1946 he was released and sent to Germany. Since his release Bleicher has visited France twice, the first time in December 1949 as a witness at the trial of Roger Bardet and Raoul Kiffer (Kiki), his two V-men. (Both were sentenced to death but later reprieved. Bardet's sentence was commuted to twenty years, but he was released in 1955 and now lives under a different name.) On the second visit Bleicher and his wife were guests at the Le Rouret villa of Peter Churchill—the SOE officer whom Bleicher had arrested with Odette Sansom at St. Jorioz in 1943.

I I

Toward Liberation

IF PROGRESS in SOE activities in France appears slow and studded with setbacks and debacles, consider the particular difficulties SOE chiefs encountered in dealing with France. While the struggles in the field continued unrelenting, SOE had to fight a separate battle of its own at the top—in London. Politics played a major role. General de Gaulle had raised the standard of Resistance in 1940 in London, but this was a one-man show for a very long time. Neither the Allies—particularly the Americans—nor his own countrymen, at first, recognized him as the unquestioned leader of France. Until the end of 1942 France was divided into two zones—occupied and unoccupied; many Frenchmen accepted the Vichy regime, and others acquiesced in collaboration with the enemy. Not until the Allied invasion of North Africa and total German occupation of France, did the many warring factions of French Resistance unite. Meanwhile, de Gaulle insisted that he alone should be the arbiter of how the Resistance and an underground army in France should be organized; and he impeded SOE activities at every stage.

For all its operational activities, its supply of aircraft, and its arms, SOE was dependent on the chiefs of staff, who until 1943 had serious doubts about the value of French Resistance and regarded France as a sideshow. For three years SOE chiefs pleaded for more transport and arms, usually in vain. When early in 1944 the situation dramatically improved, it was because of the new emphasis on Overlord and the increased participation of the United States Army Air Forces.

At Baker Street every effort was made to persuade the powers that be—from Churchill to the air marshals—of the great upsurge in French Resistance activities. SOE chiefs submitted detailed reports proving that tens of thousands of able-bodied Frenchmen (whether from patriotism or from the desire to escape deportation and forced labor) had formed. maquis bands in the mountains and forests. These, SOE insisted, represented the cadres of a guerrilla army, if only they could be trained and armed.

Churchill read these reports and in January 1944 ordered the Air Ministry to make additional aircraft available to SOE's two Special Duties Squadrons. He also wrote a special minute ordering that, in view of the plans of an Allied invasion of southern France, the maquis groups in that region should be armed first.[1] His orders were carried out, but only after many delays and strong objections on the part of the air marshals, who disliked diverting to SOE planes that could be used in bombing operations against German industrial targets.[2]

During the second quarter of 1944, which included D day, the Americans carried out a large proportion of the operations. Even so, the chief of U.S. Special Operations, Colonel Joseph P. Haskell, expressed his concern over the small scale of the American contribution, stating that American–French political relations might suffer if the British were allowed to continue carrying the main burden of supporting the Resistance.[3] General Donovan, the chief of OSS, supported Colonel Haskell's views and sent a report to President Roosevelt. The State Department warned the joint chiefs of staff that the impression was gaining ground among the French that, whereas the British were doing everything possible to arm the French Resistance, the United States was holding back for political reasons.[4] The outcome was that twenty-five more American aircraft, mainly B-17s and B-24s, were allocated to SOE/OSS.

Although it was not until after D day that the Special Duties Squadrons were equipped with long-range Stirlings, the number of deliveries increased dramatically during the first six months of 1944. Until the third week in May, in addition to considerable quantities of explosives and ammunition, these weapons were parachuted into France:

Sten guns	45,354
Pistols	17,576
Rifles	10,251
Bren guns	1,832
Bazookas	300
Antitank weapons	185
Mortars	143

On D day these supplies and previous deliveries meant that 20,000 men were fully armed and some 50,000 additional men were armed in some degree.

A comparison of the figures for the last quarter of 1943 and the first two quarters of 1944 speaks for itself:

[1] SOE Progress Report, dated 7 March 1944.
[2] Memo, SOE Aircraft Requirements, 14 January 1944.
[3] Report from Colonel Haskell to General Donovan, chief of OSS, dated 22 February 1944.
[4] Memorandum from Joint Chiefs of Staff to General Eisenhower, 17 April 1944.

1943 4th quarter	101 sorties
1944 1st quarter	557 (plus 52 U.S.A.A.F.); total 609 sorties
1944 2nd quarter	1,197 (plus 521 U.S.A.A.F.); total 1, 718 sorties

The Trail of Destruction

SOE, constantly on the defensive and compelled to prove to Allied military chiefs that the French Resistance was worth its salt, provided in its monthly reports convincing evidence. Widespread sabotage was carried out at the cost of many lives and untold hardship. Reports of destruction of the French railway system, of canals, bridges, roads, telephone and telegraph communications, all vital to a German strategic counterthrust against the Allied invasion, were impressive.

During the months between June 1943 and May 1944—and in 1943 the supplies of explosives were scarce—1,822 locomotives were destroyed or badly damaged; 200 passenger cars were destroyed and 1,500 damaged; 2,500 freight cars were destroyed and 8,000 damaged.[5] These statistics are incomplete and on the conservative side. A report of the Vichy police covering only one month, between 25 October and 25 November 1943, stated that during that period more than 3,000 separate attempts were made by Resistance saboteurs to wreck the railway system. Of this number, 427 resulted in very heavy damage and 132 caused derailment of trains with serious loss of life of German troops.[6]

During the first three months of 1944, when supplies of explosives were stepped up, Resistance saboteurs destroyed 808 locomotives, more than twice as many as were damaged (387) by Allied bombers in continuous, heavy, and costly air attacks. Within the first week of the Allied invasion in June 1944 no less than 960 railway demolitions were officially listed by SHAEF; many more were never reported.

Aware that many acts of sabotage involved French railwaymen, the Gestapo arrested thousands of them. Eventually the Germans were forced to bring 20,000 German railwaymen to France to run troop transport and freight trains and to repair damage. Army and SS units were diverted from combat at the front to guard duty at the rear, patrolling stations, loco sheds, workshops, and thousands of miles of track, day and night.

SOE agents and Resistance men also destroyed many industrial plants vital to the German war effort. The annihilation of the Ratier propeller works, the extensive damage to the Schneider-Creusot armament works,

[5] Cf. *Les Résultats de l' Action de la Résistance dans la SNCF* (History of the FFI), pp. 1364 ff.
[6] Report of the Vichy Ministry of the Interior.

the demolition of the Gigny *barrage* (dam) on the river Saône, the destruction of innumerable power stations, transformers, high-frequency pylons and cables, and Nazi radio stations hit the Germans very hard. Agents also helped pinpoint targets for Allied bombers. For example, Maurice Southgate, head of the STATIONER network, after an unsuccessful attempt at sabotaging the Michelin rubber works, made the arrangements for a raid by RAF and USAAF bombers that left the great plant a gutted ruin.

French patriots were fully aware of the fact that they were destroying vital assets of their country's economy and that France would suffer hardship for a long time after liberation. But they readily accepted this as the inevitable cost of defeating Nazi tyranny.

Elaborate plans were made by the French Committee of National Liberation (of which General de Gaulle had become sole president after the resignation of General Giraud on 9 November 1943) for the role the Resistance and its armed units would play before and after D day. In addition to the plans evolved by BCRA in cooperation with SOE/OSS, which were approved by SHAEF (such as *Plan Vert* for the sabotage of the railway transport, of *Plan Tortue,* for blocking enemy road movements), a general plan, based mainly on ideas submitted by General Revers, the chief of ORA, was devised for grouping the Free French forces into three main groups. Group A embraced units that would participate in the Allied landing operations across the Channel; Group B, those for the Allied invasion from North Africa; Group C, the Resistance units and maquis of the interior.

Within this framework, SHAEF assigned an important role to the SOE circuits and maquis units in central France. German road and rail communications were to be cut to prevent the movement of troops to the invasion fronts; maquis units—becoming the French Forces of the Interior (FFI)—were to harass and, if possible, to attack German troops. On 1 July 1944 SOE/OSS became part of EMFFI *(État-Major des Forces françaises de l'interieur)* and its officers were supposed to take orders from General Marie-Pierre Koenig, de Gaulle's commander in chief. In practice it did not work out quite like this.

The change in command, the designation "Special Forces" for SOE/OSS (which had been cooperating since the fall of 1942 and were officially merged on 1 May 1944) caused much confusion. SOE officers in the field were not sure whether they were now subordinated to SHAEF, to EMFFI, or to a new headquarters in Algiers named SPOC (Special Projects Operations Center), from which British, American, and French officers were supposed to direct SOE/OSS agents and Jedburgh teams throughout the southern part of France.

Not that it really mattered, apart from radio communications and supplies of arms. SOE officers went about their business as before, except that everything had become more complex and confused. Also, they had to deal more than ever with political jealousies and intrigues.

On the Channel Coast

Until the spring of 1943, SOE activities in the coastal regions of northern France were limited by an agreement that left Brittany and Normandy to General de Gaulle's BCRA. The famous Colonel Rémy (Gilbert Renault) had established a number of networks from the mouth of the Loire to Brest, St. Malo, Cherbourg, Caen, and the Seine estuary. These networks, such as CENTURIE and CONFRÉRIE DE NOTRE-DAME, later spread much farther south and were the most successful of all Gaullist circuits.

But with the approach of the Allied invasion and in view of the strained relations between BCRA and the British and American organizations, it became necessary to establish SOE circuits also in these parts of France. Colonel Buckmaster decided to set up a circuit to cover Le Havre and Rouen, where the Germans had built submarine pens for refitting their U-boats.

As organizer for this task he chose a remarkable man, the twenty-seven-year-old French journalist Philippe Liewer, who had joined SOE under the name of Charles Staunton. Recruited by Jacques de Guélis during his visit in the summer of 1941, Staunton organized some of the very first circuits in the south of France. Caught by the Pétain police, he was one of the participants in the famous escape from Mauzac prison. He reached Britain via Spain and went through the STS training. In March 1943 Staunton, who had refused to take parachute training, was landed from a Lysander with a French-Canadian agent, Jean Chartrand (Dieudonné). Staunton knew the Malraux brothers, the novelist André,[7] Roland, and Claude; the last became his second in command when Staunton set up his SALESMAN circuit in Rouen. In April Buckmaster sent them a W/T operator, Isidore Newman, the Julien who had worked with Peter Churchill and CARTE and who now was named Pepe. With the radio link established, supplies of arms and explosives began to arrive.

A few weeks later Staunton and Newman were joined by Robert Mortier (Maloubier). Staunton soon found that Bob Mortier, only twenty years old, was an excellent assistant, and put him in charge of supply receptions. Staunton had set up several local groups, had recruited ninety-six members, and Bob helped him instruct Resistance men in handling arms and in carrying out a number of successful sabotage actions.

After nine months in the field, Staunton was collected by a Lysander for consultations and a short rest in London; he left Mortier in charge of the

[7] He later worked with an SOE circuit in the Lot, while Roland worked with Harry Peulevé's circuit in the Corrèze.

Rouen network. Before Christmas 1943 Bob received material at a dropping zone near Elbeuf. He went there on a motorcycle with a Resistance man on the pillion. After midnight, riding along the Seine toward Grande Couronné, they were overtaken by a German field police car. The Resistance man jumped off and ran into a wood. The Germans arrested Bob and told him that he must go with them to the field police station at Oissel where his identity would be checked. One of the Germans mounted the pillion, with his machine pistol stuck in Bob's back. Arriving at Oissel, Bob decided to take a chance, and ran into a side street behind the German police station. The Germans pursued, firing, and Bob was hit by three bullets; two perforated his lungs. Although gravely wounded, he continued to run and dived into a ditch in the dark. The Germans brought dogs but did not find him, and Bob somehow managed to drag himself to a house. His host, a local Resistance member, called a doctor.

The doctor offered little hope after he had examined the patient. He said that Bob would not survive the night. The good Samaritans were faced with the problem of what to do with a body. A death had to be reported, the funeral arranged, a grave ordered. This would involve formalities with the authorities. The police, or even the Gestapo, would hear about it, and having discovered that the dead man was the suspect who had escaped at Oissel, would arrest all the people who had helped him. The men decided to put Bob's body into two potato sacks—he was very tall—which were stitched together, weight the sacks with stones, and drop it into the Seine, hoping the body would not be found. The sacks were duly prepared. But Bob survived the night. The doctor explained that the recovery was miraculous but temporary, and advised proceeding with the plan for sinking the body. After several days Bob began to recover, to sit up and clamor for a square meal. After a fortnight he was able to join in a little New Year's celebration and drink a few hearty toasts to the liberation.

Baker Street had been informed of Bob's misfortune by signals from Newman, and Staunton wanted to return immediately. But bad weather prevented a Lysander flight until mid-January. After Staunton's arrival, a Lysander picked up Bob, and in view of his condition Staunton was asked to accompany him. They returned to England on 7 February. Staunton had repented and decided to take parachute training. It was at Ringway, when Bob was recovering in a London hospital, that Staunton met a young girl who was to become one of the heroines of SOE, Violette Szabo.

Violette

Gay, very pretty, and intelligent, a sportive tomboy, Violette Szabo had an unusual hobby for a young girl: shooting. After a long day at training school shadowing ersatz "Gestapo spies," she and Lieutenant Cyril Watney would visit shooting galleries in London, where Violette would hit the bull's-eye every time and win cigarettes to replenish their ration.

When she was ready for the field, Staunton asked Colonel Buckmaster if she could go as his courier to Rouen. The Lysander operation was fixed for mid-March; but just before their departure a signal arrived from a *réseau* connected with André Malraux, reporting that his brother Claude, Pepe Newman, and many members of the Rouen circuit had been captured. Buckmaster canceled the flight; Staunton might be compromised if he returned to Rouen now. Instead, it was agreed that Violette should reconnoiter in Rouen while he waited for her in Paris. They landed from a Lysander on 15 April near Châteaudun and went to Paris. Next morning Violette traveled to Rouen equipped with papers in the name of Corinne Leroy and a permit to enter the prohibited coastal zone. She found Rouen plastered with Gestapo posters offering a reward for the capture of "two wanted terrorists" and bearing fairly good photographs of Staunton and Bob Mortier. It was clear that a traitor had been at work. Apart from Claude Malraux and Newman some eighty members of the circuit had been arrested. Staunton sent a report to Baker Street and Colonel Buckmaster ordered him and Violette to return to London. A Lysander was sent on 30 April to pick them up in a field near Chartres.

Back in London Staunton was more determined than ever to return to the field. But weather was extremely bad in May and he had to wait for the June moon. Bob Mortier, now recovered from his injuries, also begged to be sent back. After much heart-searching Buckmaster finally agreed that Staunton, Bob, and Violette should go as a team to the Limoges area to take charge of a maquis group whose SOE instructor had been assigned elsewhere for D day. An American OSS officer, Lieutenant Jean Guyet, the fourth member, was Staunton's radio operator. The four were parachuted during the night of 6–7 June—D day plus 1—and only on the airfield did they hear that the invasion had started. They were dropped near Sussac in Haute-Vienne, in the heart of the Limousin maquis—which numbered some two thousand members—and not very far from the area where Cyril Watney, Violette's shooting-gallery companion, had landed in January.

The leader of the local maquis was Anastasie, actually Jacques Dufour, whose daring sabotage actions had elicited a Gestapo reward for his capture. He had six hundred men, but not all obeyed his command. Some were local farmers and landworkers; others, Communist workers from Limoges, banded together in FTP units. There were Spanish Republicans—refugees of the civil war—and Polish miners from the north. It was not easy for Staunton to effect some order among the motley crew; most were neither trained nor properly armed. The only bright news was that 185 gendarmes from Haute-

Vienne and Creuze had joined the maquisard when they learned of the Allied landing.

Two days after their arrival, the SOE officers heard that advance units of the Das Reich SS Panzer Division, commanded by SS General Heinz Lammerding, moving from Toulouse to reinforce the German army in Normandy, were only twenty or thirty miles to the south of Staunton's headquarters.

The maquis leader declared: "The Germans will never get through here!"

Staunton warned him that their small and poorly armed units could hardly equal a crack panzer division of the Waffen SS. Anastasie agreed that reinforcements should be requested from other maquis units in the Corrèze and Creuze, and that the regional FFI commander in Châteauroux should be alerted.

Violette accompanied Anastasie in a car. Near the village of Salon-le-Tour they were ambushed by an advance unit of the Das Reich Division. They ran across a field toward a farm. Violette fell and wrenched her ankle, which she had hurt in a parachute jump at Ringway. Anastasie carried her for a stretch with the soldiers in pursuit and firing. Violette told Anastasie to let her go and save his own life. The maquis leader hesitated; finally he ran to the farm. The farmer hid him under a pile of logs while the Germans searched the place. Violette took cover behind a cluster of trees in a cornfield and for two hours held off some four hundred Germans and two tanks, until she ran out of ammunition for her Sten gun. The farm people saw several German soldiers fall, though it was never established how many Violette killed or wounded. Finally she was overwhelmed and taken to Limoges prison.

After the Germans left, Anastasie,[8] nearly suffocating under the logs, freed himself, hurried to Staunton's headquarters at Croiselle, and told him of Violette's capture. Staunton immediately planned a rescue operation. He and Bob Mortier went to Limoges and watched the prison for several days. They found that twice a day Violette was led from the prison to the Gestapo office nearby, apparently for interrogation. Staunton decided to kidnap her on one of these walks. The rescue operation was staged for 16 June, six days after her capture.

Bob Mortier and four Resistance men were to come in a car and snatch Violette while Staunton and six heavily armed men—all volunteers—were to provide cover and, if need be, shoot it out with the SS guards. But at dawn on the day set for the rescue, Violette was taken from Limoges to Paris.

[8] Anastasie (Jacques Dufour) was a brave man. He played his part in the liberation of Limoges and the Limousin, enlisted in 1945 in the French army. He was sent to Indochina and was killed there a year later.

At Avenue Foch, Violette Szabo was interrogated by Kieffer and his assistants, but she refused to talk. On 8 August 1944 Violette and two other SOE women, Denise Bloch (a French Jew who had escaped from France, joined SOE as Danielle Williams, and arrived in March 1944 to be Robert Benoist's radio operator) and Lilian Rolfe (who in April 1944 had become a courier to a *réseau* at Orléans, headed by George Wilkinson) were put on a train carrying a large group of British and French prisoners—including SOE agents—to Germany.

Violette, Denise, and Lilian were taken to Ravensbrück, the concentration camp in the marshes of the Mecklenburg lake district. Built in 1939 for 7,000 prisoners, it contained 40,000 women from every country of Nazi-subjugated Europe when the three girls arrived. They remained there for three weeks, then were sent to Torgau, a labor camp, where conditions were much better and where the three began to plan their escape. But some weeks later they were returned to Ravensbrück. On 26 January 1945, when the Allied armies had already penetrated Germany and the Russians had captured Warsaw and entered Eastern Prussia—Violette Szabo, Denise Bloch, and Lilian Rolfe were taken from their cells to the yard behind the crematorium. Lilian, who suffered from lung trouble, and Denise, who had been badly manhandled, were carried on stretchers; only Violette walked.[9]

The camp commander, SS Sturmbann-Führer Fritz Suhren, read out an order from the RSHA in Berlin that the three prisoners "were condemned to death," and then ordered SS Schar-Führer Schulte to carry out the executions. Schulte shot each girl from behind in the neck. The camp doctor, SS Sturm-Führer Dr. Trommer, certified their deaths. The bodies were immediately cremated.

By the time Violette was shot at Ravensbrück, the war in France had been over for several months. Staunton, Bob Mortier, and their Resistance comrades of the Limoges circuit had contributed their part to the liberation of France. The Das Reich Division was cut to pieces by the FFI on its progress toward Normandy. In July 1944 the situation at Limoges and the Limousin had become extremely serious, partly because of disagreements between leaders of Communist and Gaullist groups and partly because 4,000 heavily armed members of the *milice,* the pro-Nazi organization formed by Pierre Laval's security chief, Joseph Darnand, were in the area. The *milice,* who had used their auxiliary police powers to terrorize the population, knew they would have to fight for their lives when FFI units laid siege to Limoges.

At the beginning of August the German garrison commander, General Gleininger, was ready to surrender. The Limoges Gestapo chief, SS Haupt-

[9] The scene was described by an eyewitness, Mrs. Julie Barry, who survived her imprisonment.

sturm-Führer Meier, who had ordered the mining of the main buildings, threatened to arrest him and blow up the city if Gleininger should desert the Führer. Staunton brought his maquis groups, now incorporated into the FFI, to the outskirts of the city; Colonel Guingouin did the same with his Communist FTP troops. There was now real danger that the Gestapo chief would carry out his threat.

On 18 August, when the situation came to a head, Staunton sent a note to General Gleininger demanding a meeting to discuss the surrender. On 20 August Major Staunton, accompanied by American OSS Captain Charles E. Brown (who had been parachuted with a Jedburgh team) and two officers of the FFI, went to General Gleininger's headquarters. The German commander offered capitulation but asked Staunton to give "his word of honor as a British officer that the German garrison would be treated as prisoners of war and not handed over to the French guerillas." The Allied officers agreed to this, but excluded the pro-Nazi French militiamen and traitors from the agreement. Gleininger raised no objection. Staunton persuaded Guingouin to promise that the Communists would refrain from illegal acts of vengeance. In the evening the FFI units marched into Limoges, and Gleininger formally surrendered his eight thousand officers and men. Within minutes the FTP seized the huge German arms stores.

Thus by cool-headed action Staunton and his comrades saved Limoges from destruction, as well as many lives.

The Bordeaux Network

Farther to the west and southwest, in the departments of Vienne, Charente, Corrèze, Dordogne, and Gironde, several strong SOE networks had been functioning since 1942. The Germans had not succeeded in destroying them, though not for lack of trying. Some of these circuits were set up by three men who had trained together in the SOE Special Training Schools: Claude de Baissac, Roger Landes, and Harry Peulevé. Other trainees in this vintage team had been Francis Suttill and Gilbert Norman, who had built up the PROSPER network and had been executed; and Arnaud, Alec Rabinowitch, who served with Peter Churchill and escaped the St. Jorioz debacle only to be caught on a later mission.

Claude de Baissac, the son of a French landowning family in the British colony of Mauritius, and Harry Peulevé—in spite of his French name, an English engineer who had already fought with the BEF in France in 1940—were dropped together in August 1942 near Châteauroux. Harry, breaking his leg on landing, had to be smuggled into a hospital and eventually returned to England. He went to France on his second mission in the summer of 1943.

Claude went on to Bordeaux and soon had a strong network there. He asked Buckmaster to send Roger Landes, a young London architecture student, who had joined the army in 1940 and had been trained as a radio telegraphist with the Royal Corps of Signals before joining SOE. He was parachuted on 2 November 1942 (with Archambault, Gilbert Norman) in the Sologne. There he met Claude's sister, Lise, en route to Poitiers to establish a *réseau*. Landes joined Claude de Baissac at Bordeaux and set up a radio post that, frequently changing location, functioned until the end of the war.

Bordeaux, Gironde, and most of southwestern France was a stronghold of the OCM, a Resistance organization composed mainly of right-wing patriots, such as former officers and civil servants. The regional chief in Bordeaux since March 1942 was a former regular officer, André Grandclément, the son of an admiral. A royalist, he had been a follower of Colonel de la Rocque, the leader of the French Fascists, and later a supporter of Pétain. Grandclément had been de la Rocque's adjutant in Vichy after the armistice, but he changed his allegiance, turned against the Pétain regime, joined the Resistance. Alas, his conversion proved only temporary.

Claude de Baissac, who became David in Bordeaux, contacted Grandclément, and soon the two cooperated in setting up local Resistance groups all over Gironde, and the departments of Dordogne, Landes, Lot et-Garonne, and Basses-Pyrénées. Bordeaux and La Rochelle, the two important Atlantic ports, and the U-boat base of Arcachon, were vital targets for sabotage. Grandclément, however, remained inactive, although he did bask in his role as *Le Chef* of the Resistance in the vast area from the Pyrenees to the Loire.

Some weeks after his arrival Roger Landes (Aristide) was fortunate in making friends with the family of an inspector of the Bordeaux police, Charles Corbin, who in his spare time was an ardent Resistance leader. He not only provided information obtained through police contacts but also procured genuine identity cards and other documents for members of the SCIENTIST circuit. His eighteen-year-old daughter, Ginette, became one of Aristide's couriers and, after the war, his wife. Two other Resistance leaders who became Aristide's close friends were an ironmonger at Dax, Léonce Dussarat (who became an outstanding FFI commander and liberated large areas of the southwest in a series of battles with crack German units), and Inspector André Bouillard of the Bayonne police (known to the Resistance as Dédé le Basque), who organized escape routes across the Pyrenees and several subcircuits in the Basses-Pyrénées.

In March 1943 Claude de Baissac was recalled to London (he later returned to France to take charge of a circuit in the north), and Buckmaster appointed Aristide to command the network based at Bordeaux. Already in December Buckmaster had sent Captain Charles Hayes (Victor) to instruct Resistance men in the handling of weapons and explosives, which were now parachuted in increasing quantities to many new dropping zones found by Aristide and his helpers, among them Mary Herbert (Marie-Louise), a courier, who had come by felucca from Gibraltar. After Aristide took sole command, Buckmaster sent him a young Scottish dock engineer, Marcel Deffence (Dédé), whose French father had settled in Glasgow, as radio operator.

Sabotage Against U-boats and Luftwaffe

During 1943 members of the Bordeaux network executed important acts of sabotage assigned to SOE by the chiefs of staff and the Ministry of Economic Warfare. They blew up the huge German radio sender at Quatre Pavillons, which provided the main communication between Admiral Doenitz' headquarters and the German U-boats raiding Allied shipping in the Atlantic.[10] They destroyed the power station that fed the installations at the Mérignac Luftwaffe airfields, and the Belin power station, which supplied the German antiaircraft batteries and radar establishment at Deux Poteaux. Many successful actions were carried out against railway, road, and telephone communications, isolating, often for days, Group G (1st and 19th armies, 56th Corps, and two SS divisions under the command of General Blaskowitz in the area from the Gulf of Biscay to Avignon and the Mediterranean) from contact with the German high command. Such actions were repeated on a much greater scale just before and after D day.

Although during the summer of 1943 many SOE networks had been "burned" and mass arrests occured throughout France, the Bordeaux circuit remained uncontaminated by treachery. Then, suddenly, several of its members were arrested, arms dumps uncovered by the SD, and on 12 October the Germans raided the house of café-owner Deboué at Lestiac, where Charles Hayes (Victor) was staying. After a gun battle in which Hayes was wounded, they took him and the whole Deboué family. To Aristide it became clear that a traitor was at work, and he suspected Grandclément, who had known the safe house at Lestiac and the location of some of the arms caches.

Unknown to Aristide, Grandclément had been arrested when visiting Paris in September. In a pact with the Gestapo he gave them a list of many members of the OCM and SOE groups and the location of 132 arms dumps. During the following weeks the Germans collected almost 2,000 Sten guns

[10] In the spring of 1943 Admiral Doenitz expressed alarm that the Allies seemed to have exact knowledge of the disposition and, in some cases, of the number of U-boats in operational areas. (Cf. extracts of documents of the U-boat Division of the German Navy Command, published after the war by the British Naval Intelligence Directorate.) At least some of the information came from the Bordeaux SOE circuit in 1943.

and large quantities of pistols, ammunition, and explosives. A very large portion of the supplies, still stored in parachute containers, was seized: 45 containers at Sabres, 260 in various caches around La Brède, 300 more at Blaye, Temple, Saint-Médard, Lacenau. The traitor had told the Germans of Aristide, but the SOE officer, a stickler for security, changed his domicile several times and thus avoided capture. However, 300 members of the Resistance throughout Gironde, Saintonge, the Médoc country, and right down to the Basses-Pyrénées were rounded up.

There was only one duty for Roger Landes: obey Colonel Buckmaster's order and escape across the Pyrenees. With him went Inspector Corbin, whose name Grandclément had also given to the Gestapo.

Arrested by the Spanish police, interned at Miranda for many weeks, and bailed out by the British embassy in Madrid, the two fugitives reached London from Gibraltar on 14 January 1944. Colonel Buckmaster told Roger Landes that he had been awarded the Military Cross. But Landes had only one thought: to return to Bordeaux quickly.

Six weeks after his arrival in England he was back in France, parachuting on 2 March near Auch. He sprained his leg on landing, but after a short rest and still limping, pressed on for Bordeaux. Inspector Corbin, who returned by Lysander, had left his wife and daughter to an uncertain fate; they were, in fact, arrested and kept in custody for several months. Eventually, the two women were released but watched. The Germans hoped they might lead them to the two fugitives.

Bordeaux had become too dangerous for Inspector Corbin, and after his return he moved to Angoulême, where he set up a *réseau* with another SOE officer, Allyre Sirois, who had been parachuted with Roger Landes. The Angoulême *réseau* worked in close cooperation with the Bordeaux circuit.

When Aristide returned to Bordeaux he found that some of his old friends had maintained a nucleus of the circuit. But they lived in constant danger. Grandclément, having agreed to work for Bordeaux Gestapo chief Dhose, had been set free, had returned to the city, and drawing his Judas pay from the Germans, had surrounded himself with shady characters while pretending to serve the Resistance. He had succeeded in bamboozling many genuine Resistance men and in infiltrating V-men into several OCM groups. Thus he delivered to the Gestapo many of his former OCM comrades, including General Jouffrault.

At last, on 28 July 1944, Grandclément fell into the hands of the Resistance. He was taken to a farmhouse at Belin and tried by FFI court-martial in Aristide's presence. He confessed to his treachery, which had cost the lives of more than three hundred. Sentenced to death, Grandclément, his wife, and his adjutant, Marc Duluguet, were shot in a wood near the farm and buried there.

The Bordeaux network came out into the open when the Allies invaded

Normandy. On D day Aristide mobilized five companies of his Corps Francs. These men, under the command of Léonce Dussarat, André Bouillard (who was killed in the fighting at Royon), and Alban Borge, took Dax, Mont-de-Marsan, Bayonne, Belin, and many towns in the Gironde and the south, capturing more than ten thousand Germans. Together with the FFI under Colonel Druilhe, Aristide's units liberated Bordeaux on 27 August.

If it had not been for a ruse devised by Aristide and General Koenig's military delegate, Triangle (Colonel Charles Gaillard), the port installations and the city center of Bordeaux might have been left in ruins when the Germans withdrew, and thousands might have perished. The commander of the German 64th Corps, General Nake, had ordered the mining of port installations, many public buildings, the three railway stations, and the bridges over the Garonne. Fuses and electric charges were stored in a magazine in rue de Raze. With the help of an anti-Nazi sergeant-artificer, Stahlschmitt (a Socialist trade unionist before the war), the Resistance men blew up the magazine only a few hours before the fuses were to be connected to the mines.

When General de Gaulle triumphantly entered Bordeaux on 17 September, Major Landes, together with FFI commanders, was introduced to the leader of Free France. Realizing that Landes was an SOE officer, the general said: "You are English? Your place is not here," and turned on his heel. Landes was asked by one of de Gaulle's aides to leave Bordeaux within twenty-four hours. He went to Paris and later to London. One would have thought that he now had had enough of war. But he asked SOE chiefs to be sent to the Far East. In March 1945 he was parachuted into the Malayan jungle, served in Special Force 136, and commanded sabotage units against the retreating Japanese.

General de Gaulle's insult was rectified in 1950, when his successor, President Auriol, awarded Major Landes the Legion of Honor, and the city of Bordeaux made him an honorary citizen at a ceremony attended by hundreds of his Resistance comrades from all over the southwest of France.

The Ratier Works

On his second mission Captain Harry Peulevé (Paul) established his circuit at Brive in the Corrèze. He was parachuted on 8 August 1943 into this mountainous region of the Limousin, which had become the major stronghold of the maquis in central France. Since January several thousand *réfractaires,* fugitives from the forced-labor conscription, had set up camps there. Many of them were factory workers from Limoges, Socialists and Communists, and they formed strong groups eager for action. The Communists were first to organize themselves into FTP units, but there were also groups adhering to MUR, forming companies of the *Armée Secrète.*

One of their leaders, Colonel Royer (who later became chief of Region 5), had contacted SOE in the spring of 1943; and the first arms were parachuted to his groups on 17 May near Beaulieu.

Peulevé's task was to act as liaison officer to these groups, arrange dropping zones, and instruct the maquisards in the handling of the arms. He was also his own W/T operator. This involved a great deal of cross-country traveling. He was fortunate in meeting Jean Arnouil, a Resistance leader who had a small factory at Brive, where he manufactured *bloc-gazo,* charcoal burners (used as a substitute for gasoline) for motorcars and trucks. Arnouil held a German permit for the manufacture of this ersatz engine fuel, and Harry Peulevé became his representative. This enabled him to travel in the Corrèze, Cantal, and Lot without arousing suspicion and with a *permis de circulation.*

He established his headquarters above Arnouil's Brive workshop at 26 Avenue de la Gare, where he also set up his radio post. The workshop was visited by German army drivers and field policemen, but they regarded Arnouil as a "good Frenchman" and the place proved quite safe.

His guise and his own engineering knowledge enabled Harry to reconnoiter industrial establishments controlled by the Germans, and he initiated many successful sabotage actions. Life, however, was not all serene. As soon as a fair quantity of arms had arrived—most of them from SOE, but some also sent from Britain by the Gaullist organization to the clandestine COPA *(Centre d'opérations de parachutage et d'atterrissage)*—some of the militant groups, particularly the FTP, began to clamor for action and engaged small German garrisons and troop convoys in guerrilla attacks. Between 15 September and 15 November, soon after Peulevé's arrival, many such skirmishes resulted in German retaliatory arrests. These led to the discovery of arms dumps and drew the attention of the Gestapo to the presence of a British agent in the area. The Gestapo chiefs at Bordeaux and Limoges cast about for the wanted man. Peulevé evaded capture on several occasions.

He had a number of meetings with Roger Landes, who advised him to ask Colonel Buckmaster for SOE officers who could take charge of the Lot area, where strong maquis had been formed by the VÉNY groups of Socialist trade unionists. The VÉNY organization was composed mainly of Socialist partisans (but not of Communists); though based at Cahors, and with maquis camps in Lot, Corrèze, and Tarn, its *réseaux* spread as far as Limoges in the north and Toulouse and Marseilles in the south. Its military leaders were Colonel Collignon and Jacques Chapou (a schoolmaster and district secretary of the Teachers Union). Many local groups were led by trade unionists of ability and courage. The most remarkable of the maquis leaders, however, was André Malraux, the famous poet and novelist, who had fought in the Spanish civil war and since 1959 has been de Gaulle's minister of culture and arts.

Buckmaster promised Peuleve that two first-class men would be sent. In the meantime Harry Peuleve had yet another narrow escape, when the Bordeaux traitor Grandclément informed Gestapo chief Dhose that the wanted British agent had a hideout at Tulle. Grandclément had his informers in Corrèze, where he maintained, for the benefit of the Gestapo, two small fake *réseaux* composed of the remnants of the OCM. Fortunately the information was wrong, and the Germans did not discover Harry's safe house at the Brive workshop.

On 7 January 1944 the two SOE officers—Captain George Hiller (Maxime) and radio operator Lieutenant Cyril Watney (Michel)—were parachuted. They had been told they would be received by a Monsieur Chevalier, and were pleasantly surprised to recognize their respected instructor from Beaulieu STS—Harry Peuleve. He had brought his old Chevrolet, running on charcoal burners, and when Cyril Watney suggested—according to the strict rules Peuleve had always insisted upon during training—that they bury their parachutes on the dropping ground, Harry laughed. "Yes, that's the rule, according to the book. But we need the silk for the girls."

So they drove to a farm, Cyril and George sitting on their parachutes. Later they moved to the *Fromagerie de Quatre Routes* near Martel, whose owner, Jean Verlhac, combined cheese making with being the leader of the VÉNY group in the area.

Two days later Hiller and Watney were at work, attached to the headquarters of the VÉNY group at Cahors. Cyril set up his radio post in the safest house in the area—the town hall of Creysse. The town clerk, Gouygou, was one of the Resistance leaders. Cyril's link with Baker Street functioned, though from different places, until the liberation.

Ten days after their arrival Hiller and Watney were involved in one of the major actions organized by SOE in France: the sabotage of Usines Ratier, one of the world's largest manufacturers of airplane propellers. The company's three plants—at Montrouge and Chatenay near Paris and Figeac, northeast of Cahors—under German control, manufactured propellers for Messerschmitts and Heinkels. The Figeac works produced equipment for fifty Heinkels weekly. Allied bombing raids had hitherto caused little damage.

Cyril Watney was in charge of communications for the sabotage action, timed for 19 January. But he also found time for relaxation. His new friends taught him how to catch fish with nets in the Dordogne; and he had the proverbial beginner's luck, netting the largest broach ever caught in this river. It can still be seen, stuffed, in a glass vitrine at the town hall of Creysse.

Hiller had been doing the planning, and when London sent a large supply of explosives, they went to work. Plastic explosives were fashioned into small limpet mines at Verlhac's *fromagerie*. Then they had to be taken to the other end of town, to the garage of Charles Gamade, who was to drive them to the Ratier works. Crossing the town, which was patrolled by the German field police, was a problem. A VÉNY member, Dédé St. Chamant, dressed up as a pastry cook—white overalls and a tall chef's hat—and crossed the town several times, carrying the mines on a large tray covered with a fresh napkin.

The night of 19 January was almost moonless. Jacques Chapou, Yves Ouvrieu (another schoolmaster),[11] and St. Chamant were driven to the factory in Gamade's van. They entered with keys obtained from a foreman, placed their charges, and left without attracting attention, although the factory was heavily guarded.

Shortly afterward Figeac was shaken by a terrific explosion. Although the Ratier works stood well outside the built-up area, hardly a window in town remained intact. The five thousand inhabitants gladly endured the loss when they realized what had happened. A thirty-ton press was lifted twenty-five feet and smashed to pieces; several machines that produced the precision blades of the aircraft propellers were destroyed; within minutes the whole factory was in flames. Wailing sirens summoned fire brigades and German field security police from neighboring towns. They arrived in time to witness utter destruction. Production at the Ratier works was not resumed again during the war.

Buckmaster sent Hiller and Watney a congratulatory signal, adding that the chiefs of staff had commended their success. But the sabotage of the Ratier works instigated savage retaliation. The Gestapo carried out raids throughout Lot and Corrèze. Cyril Watney had to pack up his radio post and disappear. For four days he slept in a derelict house, having lost contact with George Hiller but still working his transmitter. Then they met at Souillac and within a few days returned to Figeac, where Cyril set up his radio post at Labastrou's farm. Soon afterward Hiller was told by Baker Street to arrange receptions for new SOE teams.

Several teams were dispatched from London to assist the VÉNY groups. Perhaps the most remarkable was the team of three young SOE officers, all Jewish. They were Captain Gaston Cohen (who on previous missions was a radio operator for PROSPER and ROBIN in Paris), Robert Boiteux, and Bernard Aptaker. They were received by Hiller's helpers near St. Céré. On 8 March the two Mayer brothers arrived. On 22 March came young Maureen O'Sullivan, a pretty girl who had trained at Thame Park as a

[11] In May Yves Ouvrieu was caught in a German ambush when driving near Saint-Girons with two other Resistance members. In a pitched battle he killed two Gestapo men and the traitor who had set the trap, but was himself mortally wounded, as was one of his comrades. The third man, Guillemot, was executed at the prison of St. Michel.

W/T operator with Cyril Watney; everybody called her Paddy. The Mayer team moved to Limoges; Cohen, Boiteux, and Aptaker to Marseilles.

The MONK Circuit

Marseilles circuits had long, checkered, and often tragic histories. During the earliest stages of SOE, Gerry Morel reconnoitered there with Frenay's COMBAT *réseau*; the ill-fated CARTE had a foothold; and both Henri Frager (after the foundation of JEAN-MARIE) and Captain Basin (Olive) had maintained cells in Marseilles, the latter through Gisèle (Mme Experton, who was eventually executed at Ravensbrück). Lazare Racheline (Lucien) and Captain Coppin (Olivier), who was caught and executed, served there; and Ben Cowburn and Philippe de Vomécourt had used Marseilles for passing fugitives to the escape centers of Virginia Hall and Robert Lyon, working with a relief organization run by American Quakers.

SOE officers always regarded Marseilles as a difficult and dangerous place; some Frenchmen dubbed it "the Chicago of France," which perhaps was unjustified, even though the city and port teemed with strange and desperate people, refugees from the unoccupied zone, smugglers, and blackmailers who extorted Jews.

Yet there were strong Resistance groups in Marseilles. One was the SFIO Socialists and trade unionists, led by Félix Gouin (who in 1946, after de Gaulle's retirement, became head of the French government) and Gaston Deferre (who after the liberation became the mayor of the city). Before D day they had some three thousand armed underground fighters in the FROMENT and VÉNY groups. ORA, politically more to the right, had about two thousand; and in the Bouches-du-Rhône the Communist FTP could muster even larger and better armed groups.

After the Allied landings in North Africa, Marseilles became one of the main centers of clandestine traffic and communications between Algiers and occupied France. The Gestapo redoubled their efforts to destroy the Resistance organizations in the city and all along the south coast.

The most important SOE circuit was established at the end of 1942, with the special task of safeguarding these communications. Captain Sydney Jones (Felix), who later worked as Elie in Paris, did the spade work, contacting a group led by Pierre Massenet. He met some of its remarkable members: Mme Suzanne Goutte, who had been a famous aviator and had competed in many international flying rallies with her friend Mme Marysia Hilcz; Jean Hellet, a former French air force officer; and Julien Villevielle. When Sydney Jones was recalled to work for Frager in Paris he introduced his contacts to two SOE officers, sent from London, who established the MONK circuit in Marseilles.

They were Major Charles Milne Skepper (Bernard, Henri) and Arthur

Steele (Laurent), his radio operator. Their first safe house at Marseilles was near the convent of Les Dames de Saint-Charles; it was disguised as a commercial office, where Skepper worked under the name of Henri Truchot, and Steele as his assistant, Arthur Saulnier. They induced neighbors to think they were engaged in black market deals, supplying German naval officers with coffee. This ill repute made them "good" Frenchmen in the eyes of the Germans and provided protection from the Gestapo for a time.

But radio reception in the center of the city was poor, and in September 1943, Steele asked Mme Goutte for the use of her home. She lived in an isolated villa, La Cavalière, some seven miles from Fréjus. Steele arrived at Mme Goutte's villa with four transmitters and worked there undisturbed for many months, until the Germans set up a *Funkhorchdienst* at Anthéor and began to prowl for clandestine senders. Suspecting a radio post, the Germans raided the old Camaldules monastery, a stone's throw from the villa, and finding nothing, beat up the monks. Steele continued to transmit from La Cavalière until after Christmas 1943.

Eliane

In the early autumn of 1943 MONK received a woman courier. She was twenty-five-year-old Eliane Sophie Plewman, who had joined SOE with her brother, Albert Browne-Bartroli. As Tiburce he was parachuted into France with Robert Benoist, the racing driver. She followed him after several abortive flights, was dropped on 14 August near Lons-le-Saunier, and was received by Diana Rowden and John Young of Rée's Jura network.

Eliane (Gaby) was a valuable addition to the MONK team. She was at home in Marseilles and had some trusted childhood friends there, particularly Mme Chaix-Bryan, who was in touch with Skepper before Eliane's arrival. She maintained the contact between Skepper's headquarters at 8 rue Mérentié, and Steele's radio post at Mme Goutte's villa, carrying the coded signals on many dangerous journeys. Skepper worked amicably with Resistance organizations, controlled by both Socialists and ORA, and Eliane helped to organize many receptions of arms and ammunition in the Vaucluse and Gard.

During the months preceding D day and the Allied landing from Africa, MONK provided important information about the deployment of German forces and the coastal fortifications in the south of France. Indeed, it is not too much to say that the swift success achieved by the Allied forces under General Alexander Patch, in August 1944, was at least partly due to the intelligence received from MONK.

Skepper, Steele, Eliane, and their Resistance comrades were straining every nerve to collect and convey this intelligence and to help arm the groups of VÉNY, ORA and FTP in readiness for Anvil.

In the spring of 1944 a German V-man, Jean Bousquet,[12] infiltrated the circuit and betrayed it to the Gestapo. On 24 March Skepper was alone at rue Mérentié, waiting for Julien Villevielle and two Resistance leaders, returning from the Vaucluse where they received parachuted arms. Bousquet knew about this meeting and led the SD men to the house. Skepper and his visitors were overwhelmed and taken to the prison of Les Baumettes.

Steele and Eliane learned of the raid a few hours later. Believing that Skepper was still at the apartment, they tried to rescue him. Eliane, pistol in hand, tried to force the entrance, which was guarded by two SD men. But there were many more in the house, and she and Steele were taken. Julien Villevielle (who was sent to Buchenwald and was freed in 1945) recalls the courage of his comrades, who, in spite of torture, refused to divulge the names of their friends.

Skepper had asked Mme Goutte and Jean Hellet to come to his place on the following Sunday, 27 March. Sensing treachery, he wanted to discuss with them the removal of his headquarters to a place in the country. On Sunday the two came from Aix, but the barber who had a shop beneath Skepper's apartment told them of the raid and warned them that there were Gestapo men upstairs, disguised as gas workers. Mme Goutte and Hellet escaped and went into hiding.

The prisoners were taken to Paris but were eventually separated. After the war surviving prisoners reported that Skepper was for a time at the Compiègne concentration camp, in very poor health. He was then sent to a Gestapo prison in Hamburg, where he was executed in August 1944. Steele was taken from Paris to Buchenwald on the infamous transport of 8 August 1944 and hanged there on 9 September. Eliane Plewman was sent with other SOE women to Karlsruhe prison and was executed on 13 September in Dachau.

The MONK circuit was destroyed in March, but its work was to bear fruit. Baker Street was notified of the captures almost immediately, and within three weeks the Boiteux teams arrived in St. Céré en route to Marseilles, to replace the captured SOE officers.

Between D day and 15 August, when the Allies landed between Cap Nègre and Estérel, Boiteux and Aptaker received several Jedburgh teams and arms drops, and Cohen maintained the radio link with Algiers, conveying intelligence to the commanders of the U.S. 7th Army in their rapid advance toward Toulon and Marseilles. Eventually the three SOE officers took part in the fighting that ensued prior to the entry of the Allied forces

12 After the war, French intelligence officers found Bousquet in the American zone of Germany, working as an agent for the Americans. He was taken to Marseilles, tried, and executed.

into Marseilles on 27 August. The liberation of the city cost 4,000 French lives and many thousands wounded. The port and the basins of La Joliette were in ruins. But the Germans suffered heavy casualties, until General Schaffer surrendered with his 700 officers and 37,000 men.

The Gardener of The Butcher of Lidice

The reception by the Hiller–Watney circuit of the Marseilles team was only one of many. Realizing how smoothly and safely drops were received in the Lot department, Baker Street directed more agents to this area. One, Lieutenant Richard Pinder, had probably the most fantastic experience of any SOE officer. An instructor of sabotage, he stayed for a while with the Hiller circuit, and was then sent to the department of Tarn to train a maquis group.

At Montauban, together with several young Frenchmen, he was arrested by the German police rounding up evaders from forced-labor conscription. Pinder had forged documents stating he was a *horticulteur* by trade. Thus the Germans deported him for forced labor. Some weeks later he found himself in Prague as a gardener at the palace of Gestapo chief Karl Hermann Frank, the deputy of the Reichs-Protector of Bohemia, who had acquired the richly deserved epithet of "Butcher of Lidice." After Heydrich's assassination in March 1942 Frank ordered and personally supervised the execution of 1,700 hostages in Prague, and 1,300 in Brno. On his orders the village of Lidice was annihilated, its entire male population shot, the women taken to Ravensbrück, and all children sent to an orphans' camp at Gneisenau. At his trial after the war, Frank admitted to having signed orders for 23,000 executions, many of which he attended in person (he was accused of more than 70,000).

This was the man who became the "master" of SOE agent Richard Pinder, the "French landscape gardener." With his truly German mixture of brutal cruelty and gooey sentimentality, Frank loved flowers. He was very pleased with Pinder's green thumb, a talent Pinder himself never understood; he admits he knew nothing about gardening. In order to survive he had to serve Frank; he was freed when Prague was liberated in 1945.

Another SOE officer sent to a dropping zone near St. Céré, Lieutenant Peters (Guguste), a Frenchman whose real name was Jacques Poirier, had been trained with Cyril Watney at Inverie and Wanborough Manor. He joined Harry Peulevé at Brive, and after Harry's capture in March 1944, took charge of the circuit, assisted by two new arrivals, Jean-Pierre Lake (Basil) and Robert Beauclerc (Casimir), running it successfully until liberation.

For many months the Germans had been searching for Harry Peulevé, the leader of the Corrèze network. Twice Bordeaux Gestapo chief Dhose had tried to set a trap for him at Libourne, assisted by the traitor Grandclément. But Harry had slipped through his fingers. His capture was the result of an incident in which he had risked his own life to save the lives of two Jews hunted by the Gestapo. On 21 March Harry, with Roland Malraux, was sitting at his radio set above Arnouil's workshop at Brive, transmitting to London. There was a knock at the door, and when he opened it he saw a trembling, elderly man, supporting a woman. The man told him they were Jews who had escaped from a raid by Darnand's *milice;* and he begged Harry, apparently a French householder, to shelter them. For a moment Harry hesitated. It was a risk he could not really take. The man raised his hands as in prayer, imploring him. Harry looked up and down the street. All seemed quiet; no pursuers in sight. He motioned to the fugitives and led them to his bedroom. He gave them coffee and told them to rest.

Half an hour later there was another knock. This time the callers were *miliciens* and SD men. They must have found out that the two Jews were hiding somewhere in the Avenue de la Gare. When they were discovered at Harry's place, he was arrested and, at first, charged with harboring fugitives. Only later, through a V-man, did the Germans realize what an unexpected catch they had made. Harry Peulevé was taken to the Gestapo in Tulle and then sent to Paris. Finally, on 8 August 1944 he was put on the train to Buchenwald. At the time of Harry's capture, Poirier was in the Basses-Alpes, expected to return within a few days to the safe house at Brive, now watched by the Gestapo.

Cyril Watney was at Bannes and learned what had happened from a Resistance man, named Bru, who had been to Brive. Bru warned him that the Germans were looking for him. Cyril knew he must disappear, but first he sent a signal to London, reporting Harry's misfortune and asking Baker Street to warn Guguste by radio not to return to Brive. Then, carrying his transmitter, Cyril moved to Figeac, where Mme Odette Bach put him up and hid his set.

A few hours after Cyril's arrival, SS men came to Odette's home asking for Michel, the terrorist from St. Céré. They stood on the threshold while Cyril was hiding behind the open door. Odette Bach, with her five-year-old daughter, Pierrette, in her arms, assured the SS men that she had not noticed a stranger in the street. They went away, knocking at other doors. Cyril said he would leave at once; he did not want to endanger the good woman's life. But Odette insisted on accompanying him. Arm in arm, leading the child by hand, they walked down the street, passing the SS men—just a local couple on a stroll. Odette brought Cyril to Mère Marie, an old schoolteacher who let rooms to single women and was known at Figeac for never allowing a man to enter her home. There Cyril stayed for a few days and once again escaped capture, though SS men came to the house. The raid on Figeac had a tragic sequel: the Germans found three Resistance men, and though they knew nothing of Michel, they were shot on the spot.

Cyril had several transmitters hidden with comrades in the district. He went to Villefranche-de-Rouergue where he radioed a full report to Buckmaster. But D/F vans appeared on the scene and he had to move on. Eventually he went to the maquis camp near Carregnac. André Malraux (Colonel Berger), whose brother Roland was captured with Peulevé, was in command of the FFI region and he and Hiller also came to the camp. On D day in Normandy Cyril Watney and two French W/T operators received the instructions for the mobilization and, using twelve maquisards as couriers, alerted all Resistance units in the area.

The Massacres of Tulle and Oradour

The SS division Das Reich was now on the move from Toulouse, along Route Nationale 20, having been ordered on D day as reinforcements to Normandy. On 7 June it passed Cahors and reached the river Dordogne at Souillac. Colonel Collignon, André Malraux, and other FFI commanders went into action. In a series of ambushes and skirmishes, the long German tank columns were halted and forced to abandon the main road. In a four-hour battle at the bridge of Bretenoux, small FFI units sacrificed themselves, forcing some of the panzer squadrons to disperse. The news of this fighting reached Tulle, 35 miles north, and to the inhabitants came out into the streets, supporting local FFI men in the attack on the German garrison, barricaded in the *Manufacture d'Armes,* the École Normal, and the Hotel Lattremolière. The school and the hotel were taken by storm, and Colonel Bouty, the mayor of Tulle, proclaimed the liberation of the town.

But at dawn on 9 June the advance units of Das Reich, bent on vengeance, had battled their way to Tulle and entered the town. Their commander, SS Lieutenant General Heinz Lammerding, proclaimed Tulle would pay with "blood and ashes" for the rebellion. More than five hundred men and several women were rounded up. Lammerding ordered all to be publicly hanged. Strangely enough, one of his officers, SS Sturm-Führer Walter, disobeyed this order and selected only 120 hostages for the execution. When Abbé Espinesse pleaded with him for the life of an eighteen-year-old backward boy, saying that he was innocent, Walter replied: "I know, they are all innocent, but they have to pay for the guilty . . . ." He finally released twenty-one prisoners, and then the hangings of ninety-nine men, boys, and women began. The victims were lined along the main street, rue Pont Neuf, where most houses have balconies, and they were hanged from these balconies, the executions continuing from 5 P.M. until dusk. Lammerding,[13] his officers, and German women who had worked at the garrison offices watched the executions from the terrace of the Café Tivoli, drinking, smoking, and listening to recorded music.

André Malraux and his men had followed the Das Reich Division, but could not risk an open battle against Lammerding's eighty tanks and motorized infantry. Leaving a rearguard behind, the SS division moved northwest, constantly attacked by the FFI, who forced the Germans to split up—the heavy panzers going to Périgueux, the motorized units, under SS Major General von Brodowsky, toward Limoges. Battling through a series of ambushes, these units reached Oradour-sur-Glane, north of Limoges, where von Brodowsky[14] perpetrated the most terrible massacre of the war. Almost the entire population of this small town was murdered. Most of the women and children were burned alive in a church, which the Germans set afire. The massacre was in retaliation for the killing of a German officer. Compounding the tragedy, the people of Oradour-sur-Glane were innocent of even this "crime." The officer had been killed in Oradour-sur-Vayres, and by mistake the Germans wreaked their vengeance on the wrong village.

During the fighting with the FFI in the Limousin, the SS murderers of Tulle and Oradour suffered heavy losses too. The Das Reich Division arrived in Normandy, ten days behind schedule, completely disorganized, leaving many disabled tanks behind and its men hardly able to fight. They could not be included in Rundstedt's and Rommel's defense plans. On Malraux's orders Cyril Watney had asked London to send RAF bombers, and the German division was bombed throughout its progress north.

[13] Lammerding later hurriedly left France and was given a command on the Eastern front, where he committed more atrocities. Taken prisoner, he disguised himself as a sergeant and managed to return home to Düsseldorf in 1945, where he lived under an assumed name. In 1953 twenty-one of his SS officers were tried at Bordeaux for the Tulle and Oradour massacres; he sent them a letter of encouragement. The French government asked the British for his extradition, but by then he had disappeared from the British zone. He went to the American zone in Austria, disappeared again, and was never apprehended.

[14] SS General von Brodowsky did not escape justice. On 16 September men of the French 1st Tank Division near Jussey in Haute-Saône, saw a German prisoner pushing a child's perambulator. Inside, under a blanket, they found Colonel von Alweyeden, von Brodowsky's chief of staff. A search in the vicinity yielded the SS general; he was found asleep in a barn. He was taken to the HQ of General Sudre and later imprisoned at the Citadel of Besançon, where he was shot.

Between the end of May and mid-July, with the radio link firmly established, large quantities of arms were parachuted to the Corrèze, Dordogne, and Limousin, FFI averaging one drop daily. Then came the greatest parachute operation staged by SOE and OSS in France.

On 14 July, France's national holiday, in the bright light of a fine summer day, two hundred Flying Fortresses and Liberators, escorted by sixty Spitfires, appeared over the plateaux of Causse de Loubressac. For six hours the aircraft came and went in relays, dropping their cargo, so impatiently awaited and so joyously received by the maquisards. Defying German garrisons and patrols, 1,500 Resistance men under the command of Colonel Collignon surrounded the dropping grounds covering almost eight square miles. Women brought bed sheets and spread them out into huge white Z-signs for every dropping zone. Farmers and tradesmen emerged from the villages with every available vehicle to collect the containers; the improvised transport included 180 oxen-drawn farm carts.

Cyril Watney and a French W/T operator, Gineste, maintained radio and S-phone contact. More than 600 containers were dropped with 1,200 Sten guns, 150 Bren guns, several hundred Tommy guns, 3,000 pistols and small arms, a large quantity of antitank weapons, bazookas, and Piats, several million rounds of ammunition, as well as plastic explosives, limpet bombs, and other material. Throughout the evening and night the carts and vans trundled to the villages and maquis camps; in all, 7,000 men were armed.

Resistance men, now assembled in FFI companies, paraded through the villages to the rejoicing of the populace. The joy was marred only by the news that Jacques Chapou, one of the VÉNY commanders, who had led the saboteurs at the Ratier works, was killed on 16 July in a battle with retreating German troops near Bourganeuf. Although many places had been liberated, and most of the German soldiers thought only of how to reach the Fatherland quickly, there were still pockets of strong German resistance, particularly in towns occupied by SS units.

The Ambush of Gramat

On 24 July Colonel Collignon, André Malraux, and George Hiller left Carregnac by car to inspect FFI units in the department Tarn. Three days later, driving near Gramat, they were ambushed by an SS platoon. Their car had a Tricolor flag and the SS fired from bushes along the road. The driver was killed and the car overturned. When the three passengers scrambled out they were sitting ducks. Nevertheless Collignon returned the fire from his Sten gun and then ran into a wood. André Malraux, hit twice in the leg, crumpled on the road. Hiller, although hit in his stomach and seriously wounded by a dum-dum bullet, managed to crawl into a ditch and hide.

The Germans, afraid of FFI units in the vicinity, picked up Malraux, sent a few men to search the wood, and departed with their prisoner. André Malraux was taken to Tulle, beaten and tortured, and eventually sent to the St. Michel prison in Toulouse.

At 4 A.M. the following morning Colonel Collignon arrived at the camp of Carregnac. Emerging from the wood, he had killed two German sentries with a small Spanish pistol (which his friends had always regarded as a useless toy) and, after walking for more than three miles, had reached the camp. He told Cyril Watney that his SOE comrade "Commandant Georges" had disappeared, but might have found a woodman's hut in which to hide. Cyril Watney asked for two volunteers (a dozen Resistance men immediately stepped forward). Selecting nineteen-year-old Pierrot Méjanés, whom he was training as a wireless operator, and Dr. François Lacheize, he drove with them toward Gramat in his old Bugatti, with a Bren gun on the roof.

At dawn they found George Hiller behind a cluster of trees, not far from the scene of the ambush. His abdomen was torn open. Hiller had stuffed two handkerchiefs and his tie into the wound to stop the bleeding, but he was in critical condition. Cyril took him to the deserted village of Magnagues, to the house of the curé. The two Resistance men drove to Cahors, which was full of Germans, and at pistol point kidnapped a doctor and a nurse from the Hospice hospital. The doctor brought neither surgical instruments nor anaesthetic to perform the operation. Cyril forced George Hiller (a teetotaller) to drink half a bottle of brandy, and held his head and shoulders, with the two Resistance men gripping his legs, while the doctor operated.

The doctor told Cyril that the patient had suffered grave injuries to his intestines and could not be moved. For eight days Hiller remained at the curé's house. Marie Verlhac, wife of the cheese-making véNY commander, Dr. Lacheize, and nurse Pervanche Camboul came to the village to tend him. Then Hiller was taken to the Château de Loubressac, where he remained for six weeks and received proper medical attention. By then France was liberated, and Hiller was taken to Toulouse and flown to London.

After Hiller's rescue, Cyril Watney assumed command of the SOE circuit. By mid-August his area had been liberated, and with an FFI battalion recruited from his véNY comrades, Watney led five hundred men to Toulouse, determined to free André Malraux from the prison of St. Michel.

While marching through the Guyenne and Tarn, Watney's unit mopped up several pockets of Germans and took many prisoners.

Hilaire

Although young Cyril Watney showed brave initiative, his efforts were, of necessity, modest compared with the exploits of his seasoned neighbor to the southwest. George Starr, the redoubtable Hilaire, with two years' experience in the field, had spread his circuit, WHEELWRIGHT, from the Pyrenees to the Guyenne. By the beginning of 1944 he had several *sous-réseaux* under his command and a number of assistants, including Jean-Claude Arnault (Neron), an SOE-trained sabotage instructor, and Anne-Marie Walters (Paulette), a most astute courier and W/T operator.[15]

While a team led by Jean-Claude Arnault undertook several important sabotage actions (including the blowing up of the Empalot gunpowder factory on a heavily guarded island in the Garonne outside Toulouse, earmarked as a priority target by MEW but hitherto left intact despite several RAF bombing attacks), Starr and Anne-Marie Walters organized the escape of several SOE agents, including Major Charles Hudson and Philippe de Vomécourt, from Eysse prison. Starr had several efficient escape lines to Spain, and many safe houses where he often could accommodate large parties of escapees. On occasion, as many as twenty or thirty crossed the mountains at once.

Starr recruited and trained many groups of maquisards, and during the four months preceding D day his circuit was given priority by Buckmaster for supplies of arms. The RAF undertook about a hundred drops to his well-organized reception grounds, and some 1,200 containers were parachuted.

After D day Hilaire's saboteurs blew up scores of fuel dumps, forcing German armored units, on the move to Normandy, into prolonged suspended animation. His units attacked the 2nd Panzer Division all the way from Toulouse, particularly after it reached the area of Bergerac, where Starr had an excellent *sous-réseau*, commanded by the Baron Philippe de Gunzbourg, a prewar racing-horse owner and playboy.[16]

Eventually, Starr marched on Toulouse at the head of a thousand maquisards from Gers and the Armagnac country. In a pitched battle they threw the Germans out of the western suburbs of Toulouse, and would have succeeded in liberating the city without much further bloodshed if unity could have been established between the leaders of rival Resistance groups.

[15] In her book *Moondrop to Gascony* (Macmillan, London, 1946) she gives a vivid description of the atmosphere in Starr's circuit.
[16] Baron de Gunzbourg's exploits are described in Bergeret and Grégoire's *Messages personnels* (Bière, Bordeaux, 1945).

The irony of their tragicomic struggle for power was that politically they all belonged to left-wing organizations. Inside the city was Colonel Ravanel in command of Communist FTP units. His position was disputed by another left-wing leader, Jean Cassou, whom General de Gaulle in Algiers had appointed *Commissaire de la République* for Toulouse. There were other pseudo-leaders who quarreled with both Ravenel and Cassou. During the night of 19 August, Cassou, returning by auto from a meeting, fell into a German ambush. His driver was killed and he himself badly wounded. Believing him dead, the Germans left him lying on the road. A Toulouse schoolmaster, Pierre Bertaux, proclaimed himself Commissaire. With a handful of armed men he occupied the prefecture and took command of eight hundred gendarmes, who were not at all certain who was in charge. Ravenel's Communists then threatened to storm the prefecture.

Meanwhile German troops were withdrawing from the city, terrorizing, shooting inhabitants, and burning down public buildings. On the morning of 20 August the main post office, the Cafarelli barracks, the Collège Saint-Aubin, the great stores of the Magazins Généraux, were ablaze. When firemen arrived they were machine-gunned by German troops. There was no gas, electricity, or water in the city, and no bread or foodstuffs, because shopkeepers had boarded up their shops and fled. But the rival leaders still quarreled and tried to arrest or oust each other.

The chaotic situation during the liberation of Toulouse was described by Professor Aron, the Resistance historian, who states that there were thirty-seven self-appointed leaders and commanders, each with his own secret service, and threatening one another.[17] It was, in fact, with the help of the men Hilaire led into the city that Commissaire Bertaux succeeded in restoring some semblance of order. At last, on 15 September, long after the Germans had gone, General de Gaulle could visit Toulouse.

Captain Cyril Watney had arrived with his men from Guyenne at Toulouse at the height of the chaos. He learned that the prisoners of St. Michel, organized by André Malraux, had overwhelmed their guards and freed themselves. Seeing Malraux free, and preferring not to be involved in the conflicts of the warring Resistance leaders, he took his men down the Garonne. They liberated Montauban and Agen and took two thousand German prisoners.

Starr and Watney had completed their missions.

17 Aron, R., *Histoire de la Libération de la France,* Fayard, Paris, 1959.

12

Climax in France

To Allied planners preparing for the invasion of France, one large SOE circuit was of particular importance. Code-named STATIONER, it was located in the Auvergne, through which ran vital north-south railway lines and roads.

STATIONER was set up by Major Charles Hudson and later directed by Brian Rafferty and George Donovan Jones. Since the spring of 1943 the circuit had been under the command of Squadron-Leader Maurice Southgate (Hector). He and his courier, Jacqueline Nearne, had originally been sent to France in January 1943 to take over from Ben Cowburn the nucleus of a *réseau* at Châteauroux. After Brian Rafferty's capture, Buckmaster asked Southgate to assume command of the circuit in the Auvergne.

Southgate's revived STATIONER spread far and wide. In addition to heading the circuit, Southgate became the chief organizer of receptions for new agents within a perimeter that encompassed areas as far apart as Châteauroux, Périgueux, Agen, Tarbes, Le Puy, Clermont-Ferrand, and Montluçon. He was fortunate in having inherited W/T operator George Donovan Jones (Isidore), who had been dropped with Charles Hudson in September 1942.

After repeatedly changing the location of his radio posts, Jones found a safe house at Rochefort-Montagne, where he transmitted undisturbed for many weeks. One day he went by bus to Clermont to take some important London messages to Southgate. The bus was stopped by *miliciens,* who searched all passengers and found a few coded notes on Jones. He was taken to the headquarters of the Pétain police at Vichy.

Worried that he might endanger the whole network, Jones decided to sacrifice himself. He told his interrogators he was an escaped British soldier, that his name was Watson, and that he was helping a Resistance group of which he knew only three or four members. He gave some imaginary addresses at Moulins and concocted such a plausible story that the Vichy officials believed it and told him he would be interned at Castres. But one of the *miliciens* reported "Watson's" arrest to Vichy Gestapo chief SS Sturmbann-Führer Geissler. Jones was collected by SD men and taken to the notorious prison at the Château de la Malcoiffée. Although the Germans discovered the names and addresses he had given were false, Jones stuck to his story and denied any knowledge of a British intelligence circuit—even after the Germans found his two radio transmitters at Rochefort.

After three weeks of brutal interrogations at the prison he was taken to the Gestapo headquarters in Vichy; for two months, constantly handcuffed and chained to the wall, he was beaten every night. SS men stabbed him with daggers, burned him with cigarettes and gas pokers, and held an open flame to his eyes until he could see no more. On one occasion Jones underwent gymnastics—knee-bends and push-ups—for thirty-six hours, with SS men watching in relays. At last, on the second night of this exercise, the SS men left the interrogation room, bored and tired, having attached their victim to a chair by his handcuffs. Incredibly, Jones still had enough strength to smash the chair, shake the splinters off his handcuffs, and jump from the third-floor window to a flat roof and then to the street.

On the street he saw a man walking toward him. With his manacled hands he snatched the man's cap from his head, put it on, and said, "Please forgive me; the Gestapo is after me." He then calmly walked down the street—a worker returning from the night shift.

Finding a house that was apparently empty, he entered the garden and hid in a small shed, where he could observe SS men running up and down the street looking for him. He stayed in the shed for two days, bruised, bloody, and exhausted. He ate some raw vegetables and slept; then he decided to move on. He walked twelve miles through the night, always in danger of meeting a patrol, hiding in bushes from passersby. At last, on the outskirts of a village he saw a fat, jolly-looking man and decided to ask him for help. Luck was with Jones: the man turned out to be the village blacksmith and a Resistance member. He broke Jones' handcuffs on his anvil, and his wife tended Jones' wounds. Eventually the blacksmith contacted Hector's *réseau*; Jones was collected and taken to a safe house at Puy-de-Dôme.

After Jones had recovered somewhat, Southgate arranged for a guide to take him across the Pyrenees. Jones, who had lost the sight of one eye as a result of the Gestapo interrogations, at first refused to leave and obeyed only when Buckmaster sent an order, adding that his further presence would endanger the network. Two months later, after internment in Spain and a journey from Gibraltar, he reached London. Eight months after that Captain George Donovan Jones, wearing a glass eye, was back in France, dropped by parachute near Issoudun. He was now Claude and preparing the ground for a new circuit in the Sologne.[1]

---

[1] See later in this chapter, under "St. Paul."

Southgate, a born leader and probably the best organizer the French section had, quickly built up STATIONER. By the winter of 1943–44 he was in close communication with Resistance groups in the departments of Allier, Creuse, Puy-de-Dôme, Cantal, Lozère, and Haute-Loire. Some had strong maquis camps. However, the political allegiance of several of these groups differed. It was not until April 1944, after a meeting at Montluçon between Southgate (who at that time used the *non de guerre* of Commandant Philippe) and Gaspard (Colonel Émile Coulaudon), that a conference of leaders was held at a farm near Paulhaguet in order to unite for action, as Southgate had suggested.

The outcome of the Paulhaguet conference—at which Coulaudon and Ingrand (Rouvres) represented COMBAT; Roger Vallon, the FTP; Raymond Périer, LIBÉRATION; Aufouvre (Carlos) and Eldin (Charles), the Communist and Socialist party organizations and trade unions—was the setting up of a Grand Council. It was agreed to concentrate maquis units in the area of Mont-Mouchet, in the mountains and forests of Margeride, between the valleys of the rivers Loire and Allier. The plan foresaw a concentration of 15,000 to 20,000 men, many already armed with British-supplied weapons.

Southgate made arrangements with Baker Street to step up parachute deliveries of arms and material, and in addition to the dropping zones the network had already been using during past months, he prepared with leaders of COPA for several other DZs, particularly at Villelonge and Tence. The Communist FTP provided separate dropping zones, the most important at Felines (Chaise-Dieu). Massive supplies of arms, including machine guns, mortars, bazookas, and Piats soon began to arrive from Britain.

Detailed plans were made for the mobilization of all units, which were to converge in April or May (the final date depended on the Allied invasion) at three redoubts: Mont-Mouchet; Truyère, in the area of Chaudesaigue; and Lioran, in the heart of the Cantal massif. The headquarters of the general staff was set up at the Château la Trinité at Mont-Mouchet with Colonel Garcie (Gaston) at its head.

The military regional delegate of R-6 (Clermont-Ferrand), Colonel Vivier, called a meeting of several members of the general staff for 8 February in a café at Brioude. Three days later he and several of the men who attended the meeting, including Lhomenède, a pioneer of the Resistance in Haute-Loire, and Colonel Henri Billot, one of the chiefs of MUR, were arrested by the Gestapo. They had been denounced by the V-man Albert Schmitt (alias Batissier). Vivier was executed in April; the others were deported to Germany. This was a blow; but the Germans were unable to extract any information from the captured leaders, who withstood severe torture. In spite of these arrests preparations continued, and on 1 April Southgate received instructions, having informed Baker Street of the progress. At the same time, from London, the newly appointed chief military delegate for the French Forces of the Interior, General Marie-Pierre Koenig, issued detailed orders to the maquis commanders.

During these weeks Southgate hardly removed his clothes. He had to organize scores of receptions, supervise the distribution of the parachuted material, remain in constant radio communication with London, and confer with dozens of Resistance group leaders, which proved the most difficult task of all. Baker Street told him that several SOE and OSS Jedburgh teams would be parachuted into the maquis areas to take up liaison with the commanders of the redoubts and to provide reinforcements of instructors and radio operators. Large-scale arms supplies were also promised.

Two members of the first SOE team were parachuted on 8 March in a field between Cérilly and Herisson, north of Montluçon. They were Captain John Farmer (Hubert) and FANY Ensign Nancy Wake-Fiocca (Andrée). Captain Denis Rake (Justin) and Alex Shaw (whose real name was Szokolowski) arrived by Lysander.

Rake's Progress

This was Rake's second mission to France. In April 1942 he had been sent to Cannes to serve as Captain Francis Basin's W/T operator. When Basin later received another radio operator, Isidore Newman (Julien), Buckmaster asked Rake to go to Lyons, find Virginia Hall, and set up a radio post there. Denis worked in Lyons and established the first regular radio link with London for the Lyons circuit. Then he was ordered by Buckmaster to take a sum of money to an SOE agent in Paris, "a man with a Roman nose." On 3 May 1942 Denis set out. Virginia Hall had given him 78,000 francs and told him she would arrange for his radio transmitter to be taken by courier to a villa at Auteuil, belonging to a Russian princess.

Denis' adventures on this mission took several weeks and were wild. Pursued by Vichy gendarmes in Lyons, he hid in a brothel, then escaped in a horse-drawn cart with a young girl and posed as her lover when stopped by German field police. Subsequently he was arrested at Chalon-sur-Saône, accused of being a black marketeer, and relieved of most of his money. He escaped and hid under a pile of coal in the yard of a *charbonnier,* Jean Aimé; was caught again but released (the Gestapo man, listening to Denis' voluble assurances that he was going to the funeral of his aunt and must not be late, declared: "This fellow could never be a terrorist . . .").

[227]

Denis finally reached Paris and the sumptuous villa at Auteuil, crowned with a cupola and turrets, where he was warmly greeted by an enormous old woman—the widow of a Russian prince—who told him she knew nothing of a package for him (his radio transmitter!), but expected he would make love to her. He gently managed to ward her off, was nevertheless regally entertained, sleeping in a fourposter and having wonderful breakfasts in bed (a rather welcome change from the cell at the grimy Chalon prison).

One day he had a drink with an SS officer at the Boeuf-sur-le-Toit, just behind the Gestapo building at rue des Saussaies; the German became amorous and invited him to his apartment, just as a waiter (who had recognized Denis as an old prewar guest) warmly welcomed him, addressing him in English "Oh, it's nice to see you again, Meester Rake . . . I thought you were in England . . . !" Luckily, the German, preoccupied with other thoughts, did not grasp the import of the remark, and Denis quickly excused himself and left.

Arriving in Paris, he tried to find his contact at the Bar Napoleon in the Arcades des Champs Elysées. Denis had been told the man would be there, reading *Le Figaro,* at a certain hour in the afternoon. Five visits to the bar proved fruitless, but the sixth time he espied his contact. The man with the Roman nose was Xavier (Robert Heslop), who had recently arrived to set up a circuit at Angers and who was to accomplish four separate missions.

When Denis told him that most of the money he was to bring him had been seized at Chalon, and that his radio transmitter had got lost somewhere between Lyons and Auteuil, Heslop was not amused. Saying he would make his own arrangements about the transmitter, Heslop ordered Denis to go to Limoges and wait there for him and another agent, Ernest Wilkinson (Alexandre), who had arrived on 1 June with Ben Cowburn.

On his third day in Limoges, while closeted in his hotel room anxious not to miss Xavier's and Alexandre's arrival, Denis heard a scuffle in the hall. A few moments later Xavier and Alexandre were pushed by French gendarmes into his room. With horror, Denis saw that they were handcuffed. What shocked him even more was that the two SOE officers looked at him with hate and contempt. He realized they believed he had betrayed them. The three prisoners were taken to the central prison at Lyons and put into a single cell.

Virginia Hall soon discovered what had happened. She sent a parcel containing canned meat, chocolate, condensed milk, and cigarettes to the prison. Xavier and Alexandre now enjoyed excellent meals, but they decided that the traitor Denis deserved nothing. They did not even speak to him. Denis, drinking his thin prison soup and munching the dry black bread, looked hungrily at his accusers but was too proud to beg a favor.

At last Heslop relented and, without saying a word, pushed a tin of condensed milk and some cigarettes toward Denis.

This continued for days. Then Alexandre tried to bribe a guard to procure a file for an escape attempt and was put into solitary confinement. Eventually the three SOE officers were taken to the prison of Castres. Their fate was now in the balance: If they were handed over to the Germans they would be treated as spies. Then, at the end of October and only a fortnight before the Germans entered the unoccupied zone, they were released. A Vichy official told them: "You're lucky; we have decided to let you go, but get out of France quickly and don't come back, or else—" The three stood outside the prison gate and Heslop now spoke the first words to Denis he had uttered since their arrest at Limoges: "Push off!"

Heslop and Wilkinson were convinced that Denis had caused their arrests. With bitterness in his heart, Denis traveled to Marseilles, then to Toulouse, hoping to find Hilaire (George Starr). After more adventures he contacted him, and Hilaire arranged his escape across the Spanish frontier. However, Denis was caught by Spanish frontier guards, spent five months in the camps of Miranda de Ebro and Garaba, until finally his appeals to the British embassy in Madrid—after careful checking of his *bona fides* with Baker Street—were answered, and he was bailed out and taken to Gibraltar. On 14 May 1943, almost thirteen months after his odyssey had begun, he was put on a plane. But the aircraft had engine trouble and returned to base. Eventually Denis sailed to England aboard a frigate from Lisbon.

When he reported to Colonel Buckmaster he insisted that he had failed in his mission. But Buckmaster knew that Denis had done his best and had been the victim of a combination of unfortunate circumstances. Denis begged to be sent back into the field, but he was in a poor state of health and Buckmaster told him to spend a spell as an STS instructor. Thus he became Nancy Wake's conducting officer.

Reward: One Million Francs

In the spring of 1944 Maurice Southgate, the head of the great STATIONER network, was completing his preparations for D day. At the end of April, Colonel Buckmaster asked him to come to London for consultations and bring Jacqueline Nearne with him. She had been in the field for more than a year and certainly deserved a rest. Besides, she had just received news that her younger sister, Eileen, also an SOE agent, had been captured by the Gestapo a few weeks after her parachute landing in the Paris area.

STATIONER had suffered some losses and Buckmaster, anxious that nothing untoward should happen to them, urged Southgate and Jacqueline to return to England for a while. But they pleaded with him to be allowed to stay on; they did not want to miss D day. When a Lysander with two new agents was sent to one of Hector's grounds, Buckmaster ordered Jacqueline to return; but Jacqueline gave her seat to a French political refugee. Only after another urgent order from Buckmaster, and the words "Jacqueline MUST come" chalked on the fuselage of the Lysander that on 9 April brought Philippe de Vomécourt and two other SOE officers, did the brave young woman obey and return to England.

On 1 May Southgate arrived from Châteauroux at Montluçon. He had come to confer with leaders of his groups in Bourbonnais. A safe house was arranged for him, but a few days earlier some of the Montluçon Resistance leaders had been betrayed by a V-man who had infiltrated one of the groups. Among them was Southgate's host.

On the day of Southgate's arrival two members of the *réseau* discovered that the safe house was being watched by SD men. They hurried to the station, hoping that the train from Châteauroux, which rarely arrived on time, would be late. But for once the train arrived punctually, and they missed Hector by a few minutes. He went to the safe house and was captured. The Gestapo had been searching for many months for the elusive Hector and a reward of a million francs had been offered for his arrest. Now he was taken in triumph to Kieffer at the Avenue Foch.

His capture was a grievous blow, but the STATIONER network was immediately reorganized. The command was divided between Captain René Maingard (Dédé), who had worked with Southgate since he was parachuted to him in April 1943, and Pearl Witherington, each of them taking over about half of the groups.

Pearl, who had arrived by parachute on 23 September 1943, soon became one of the main pillars of the network. Not only did she act as chief courier, she also trained saboteurs and arranged many receptions. Of her service in the Cher area after Southgate's capture she gave this account, which in its honest simplicity needs no comment.

On D day I was without detailed instructions because my radio operator had been forced to go into hiding. With a handful of maquisards we attempted to cut all rail and road communications in our area. Five days after D day, a hundred and fifty of us were surrounded and attacked by twenty-five hundred German troops on the move to Normandy. Near Romorantin a battle ensued that lasted for fourteen hours. After being cornered, I dived into a cornfield and had to remain hidden there for eleven hours in the scorching sun. The Germans were taking potshots into the field, where they imagined my comrades and I might be lying, but they finally gave up. The Germans took terrible reprisals against the people of the district. Nevertheless, many hundreds of Frenchmen poured into our maquis camps to join in the fight. Ten days later our radio operator returned to me; he had received instructions from London, and with the influx of Resistance men we were able to reorganize our units, which had grown to a strength of fifteen hundred men. It was not my official mission to command guerilla fighters, but events were beyond me and I had to make the best of my modest abilities. Finally, at the end of July, we received a French regular officer to take military command of the units, which went on expanding to thirty-five hundred men.

To the credit of these units were one thousand Germans killed, and many more wounded, and the continuous sabotage of main railway lines (particularly in the area between Dijon, Bourges, and Paris). Last but not least, they were responsible for the surrender of twenty thousand German troops.

Mont-Mouchet

The maquis in the STATIONER area had begun to come out in force shortly before D day. On 20 May 1944, Colonel Coulaudon (Gaspard), convinced that the Allied invasion was imminent even though the SOE officers warned him that his hopes might be premature, issued his Order No. 1 announcing that the time of a *levée en masse* had come and asking all maquis leaders of the Auvergne to converge with their men on the plateau of Mont-Mouchet. The appeal was only partly answered. The Communist FTP leaders refused. "The Gaullists are running into the mountains; we are staying in the towns where we shall fight the enemy and seize power," they said.

Between 2 and 10 June more than twelve thousand men assembled in the Massif Central. They came from all the adjacent departments, and as far as the Lyonnais and Bourbonnais: steelworkers from St. Étienne, firemen and policemen from Clermont-Ferrand, railwaymen from Lyons, thousands of farmers and landworkers, miners, shopkeepers, tradesmen, schoolteachers. They carried with them anything they considered useful: tents, blankets, spare boots, picks and shovels, Sten guns, hunting guns, stout sticks, and kitchen knives. The men of Corps Franc Laurent brought six thousand leather jackets, "liberated" in a raid on a factory producing uniforms for Pétain's *milice*. Men from Montluçon, more than 125 miles away, came with a ton of tins of sardines, confiscated from a warehouse.

Colonel Garcie set up logistic and ordnance services, a medical unit, engineering squads, a mess corps, appointed officers to direct sabotage actions and an intelligence service. Captain Denis Rake became the chief radio operator; two or three more radio posts were operated by French telegraphists. The men were formed into fourteen companies, and although at first only 30 percent of them were properly armed, urgent signals from Denis Rake to Colonel Buckmaster resulted in several drops of containers with Sten guns, machine guns, bazookas, and mortars. Not until 20 June did a mass drop from one hundred American Liberators provide arms for some six thousand men. By then the battle of Mont-Mouchet was almost over.

Before D day the Germans had greatly underrated the strength of the Auvergne maquis. When they discovered the movements in the Margeride country, an SS battalion of eight hundred men was sent on 2 June from Mende to Paulhac. It was immediately engaged by the 2nd Company of the newly formed FFI. The SS men, though they outnumbered the Resistance fighters, suffered heavy casualties and were thrown back in disorder, a signal victory over crack SS troops. Then came D day, and Gaspard and his commanders went to the attack. The maquis drove the German troops out of Clavières, Lorcières, Pinols, Monistrol, and many villages, inflicting heavy casualties on the enemy while suffering slight losses and replenishing their armament with the capture of three tanks, several field guns, vehicles, and stores of ammunition.

The Germans now brought up heavy reinforcements. Some ten thousand motorized infantry troops, tanks, field artillery, and assault units of the Waffen SS moved hurriedly from Clermont-Ferrand and other towns against "the fortress of the Auvergne."

On 11 June a pitched battle at Clavières lasted all day and night: three thousand FFI men, under Colonel Thomas, faced an enemy three times their strength that employed heavy artillery, mortars, and fifty tanks. At least thirty aircraft of the Luftwaffe bombed the FFI emplacements and mercilessly strafed small towns and villages, dropping incendiaries on houses, farms, and crops. Nevertheless, when the FFI withdrew to their redoubt of Truyères, they had lost only 160 dead and 200 wounded compared with 1,400 dead and nearly 2,000 wounded Germans. The town of St. Flour was full of German wounded. All public buildings, schools, and many private houses were converted into field hospitals, and German patrols raided homes for bed linen to provide dressings.

The Germans brought more reinforcements, and between 18 and 20 June some twenty thousand men, with strong artillery and air support, attacked the Mont-Mouchet redoubts in strength. The battles in the heart of the Auvergne, which lasted for three weeks, bear every comparison with the famous epics of Vercors or Gliers. Indeed the Resistance fighters were much more successful at Mont-Mouchet. Although they had to evacuate many of their positions and disperse, they did so in good order and remained in control of many villages.

During the battle of Auvergne, several SOE/OSS Jedburgh teams were dropped in the area. There were now thirty British, American, and French officers with the maquisard commands. Nancy Wake, John Farmer, and Denis Rake arranged many receptions; Denis maintained a regular radio link with London from the command posts of Colonels Coulaudon (who, incidentally, promoted himself to general), Fournier, and Garcie throughout the fighting. When one SOE/OSS Jedburgh team arrived at Nancy Wake's post, she was delighted to find that one of its members, Anselm, whose dispatch had been announced by a signal to Denis' radio post, turned out to be René Dusacq, an OSS agent and former Hollywood stunt man with whom she had trained in England. He had come as an antitank weapons instructor and was promptly christened Bazooka by the Resistance men. Two other American officers, Reeve Schley and John Alsop, joined the SOE team.

Attack on Vichy

Colonel Coulaudon ordered that the withdrawal should be made in small groups. Nancy and Bazooka joined his unit, while John Farmer and Denis went with other FFI groups. They arranged to meet at the village of Saint-Santin. Denis' unit was attacked by a German SS company, but succeeded in battling its way out. Fearing that he might be taken prisoner, Denis burned his radio code. When he arrived at Saint-Santin, he had a mute transmitter. An old leg wound had opened and Nancy gave him a bottle of Eau de Cologne, a most treasured possession, as a disinfectant. Next morning Denis looked much brighter, and Nancy asked him whether the Eau de Cologne had helped. "It definitely did," Denis replied, "I drank the whole bottle."

During July the SOE team survived many adventures. Nancy went to Châteauroux and secured another transmitter; Denis received a new code and set up a radio post near Ygrande. They took part in many hit-and-run attacks on German troop convoys moving through the Auvergne toward Normandy; carried out sabotage actions against railways and roads; destroyed the synthetic gasoline plant at St. Hilaire; blew up forty-seven pylons of high-tension cable; escaped an ambush and received several Jedburgh teams.

At the beginning of August, Captain Farmer, Nancy, and Denis were in the forest of Tronçais with an FFI unit ordered to blow up the bridges over the river Allier. Isolated and disorganized, German columns were trying to escape from the pursuing FFI toward Burgundy and through the Belfort Gap to the Fatherland. The bridges at Cosne d'Allier were blown up by Nancy Wake and a few Resistance men. Cut off and surrounded by the FFI, several German battalions surrendered, with tanks and artillery. After a battle into which the Germans had thrown heavy panzers, Coulaudon's little army liberated Montluçon and Moulins. The SOE officers set up a radio post at the Château de Fragne, while Colonel Coulaudon led his men toward Clermont-Ferrand. He then turned south again, determined to be the first FFI commander to enter Vichy, "the capital of shame."

Colonel Coulaudon established his headquarters near Mont-Dore. On 17 August he received an emissary from Marshal Pétain. The Head of the French State, by the Grace of Hitler, offered to surrender himself to the Free French forces. Already on 13 August, the Swiss minister in Vichy, Dr. Stucki, had come to Gaspard's HQ, offering his mediation for the surrender of Vichy. Coulaudon agreed to collect Pétain, but on condition that he would be accompanied by only one adjutant, or his physician, Dr. Menetrel. He offered to guarantee Pétain's personal safety, but not that of the "traitors of Vichy." Pétain was prepared to surrender himself, but at dawn on 20 August he was taken under heavy SS guard to Germany. Avoiding towns in the hands of the Resistance, this cavalcade reached Belfort, crossed the Rhine, and brought the marshal to Sigmaringen.

To save French blood, Colonel Coulaudon waited before ordering the attack on Vichy. By 24 August German troops began to evacuate the town; but Darnand, with five thousand of his pro-Nazi *milice,* was still in Vichy, making bombastic statements that he would defend it to the last man. A day later he fled, in disguise, together with his Gestapo friends and a rearguard of SS troops. During their last hours at Vichy, Gestapo men and *miliciens* shot at civilians and looted shops. Order was quickly restored by Resistance units within the town; and shortly after mopping up German marauders Gaspard took his troops into Vichy. More than a thousand *miliciens* and collaborators were rounded up at the racecourse of Concours Hippique. Understandably there were some excesses, and a number of alleged traitors and German V-men were killed.

The Tragedy of Vercors

In stark contrast to the successful rising of the Resistance in the Auvergne was the three-week battle of Vercors. Francis Cammaerts (Roger), reorganizer of the networks on the Côte d'Azur following Peter Churchill's departure, had always insisted upon avoiding premature action. His orders to his men were to operate in small units, behaving like mosquitoes—harassing enemy troop convoys, destroying communications, attacking German military establishments—but avoiding heavy engagements. His men ambushed and dispersed German road convoys; blew up railway lines, bridges, and roads; destroyed telephone and telegraph communications, power stations, and cables, thoroughly disorganizing German troop movements and logistic supplies. A SHAEF report issued after D day stressed the importance of this work: "The actions of the Resistance groups in the South resulted in long delays in the movement of German reinforcements to Normandy. The enemy was facing a battlefield behind his lines."

By June 1944 some of the leaders of the Resistance were no longer able to control their impatience for action. In Roger's own area this led to an uprising in the Valley of Ubaye, which was brutally put down by overwhelmingly stronger German forces. Then the Germans staged an all-out attack upon the plateau of Vercors where several thousand maquisards were encamped. Roger and Christine Granville accompanied General Henri Zeller when the latter hurried with a handful of other FFI officers to the aid of the

Vercors defenders. There they witnessed the terrible onslaught of several German divisions, supported by heavy artillery and Luftwaffe bombers. The battle of Vercors ended in tragedy. Thousands of the Resistance men were killed and wounded, prisoners were massacred, and such aid as was given by the Allied Command in Algiers—sending aircraft and dropping supplies—came too late. Roger, Christine, General Zeller, and a few of their comrades managed to escape from what became known as "the hell of Vercors." Roger reached his old foothold at Seyne-les-Alpes, where he was joined by another SOE officer, Major Ian Fielding, who had arrived from Algiers and had already seen long and distinguished service behind enemy lines in Greece.

On a car journey from Seyne to Digne on 12 August, two days before the Allied landings on the Côte d'Azur, Roger, Major Fielding, and a French officer, Commandant Sorensen, were captured by a German patrol. They were taken to the Gestapo prison at Digne, and their execution by firing squad was fixed for 16 August. But Christine whisked the three men from prison on the eve of their execution by bribing a Gestapo man with two million francs (which were dropped to her by parachute in a pouch from SOE headquarters in Algiers).

Saint Paul

On 26 March Monsieur Bonnin, a fruit grower at Issoudun, who for a long time had worked with Southgate and Pearl Witherington, came to see his friend Antoine Vincent at his garage at Salbris. "I have received a British parachutist," he said. "He needs a place where he could put up his radio transmitter." They installed the officer at the house of the former town clerk of Salbris, Souriou. The officer had introduced himself to his new friends as Claude and told them he had come to prepare the ground for a team of British officers who would arrive within the next few days.

He seemed to know all about underground work, though he was very secretive about his past. Claude was none other than Isidore—Captain George Donovan Jones—Southgate's former radio operator. After his fantastic escape from the Gestapo [2] he had returned, determined to get his own back. Vincent introduced him to Colonel Dufour (Colonel Vésine de la Rue), a former leader of OCM who founded his own organization in the Sologne; the VPO *(Volontaires paysans et ouvriers)* and other Resistance leaders in the Loir and Cher region; and General Koenig's newly appointed military delegate, Formule (Colonel Marc O'Neill). Soon everything was ready for the reception of the new team.

The man to whom Colonel Buckmaster had entrusted the task of rebuilding and commanding a new network in the five departments of Cher, Loir-et-

[2] See beginning of this chapter.

Cher, Loiret, Sarthe, and Indre—where once PROSPER had its strength and which bordered on Henri Frager's network in the east and Pearl Witherington's area in the south—was Philippe de Vomécourt. He was one of three brothers who had been in the front line of underground work since 1940: Pierre, the famous Lucas, one of the first three SOE agents parachuted in May 1941, was involved in the Cat case, and was caught through betrayal on his second mission in April 1942; Jean, who lived near Besançon, organized escape routes to Switzerland in 1940, established SOE *réseaux* in Nancy and the Vosges, and was caught in the summer of 1942 and later put to death at the concentration camp of Oranienburg; Philippe, having helped Pierre during his two missions in 1941 and 1942, organized *réseaux* in the unoccupied zone, was arrested by the Vichy police on 13 November 1942 near Limoges, and was sentenced to ten years in prison by a Vichy judge.

Philippe de Vomécourt was kept for six months at the St. Paul prison at Lyons. In July 1943 he was transferred with two hundred other prisoners to the Eysse prison in the Lot-et-Garonne. He escaped from there in January 1944, crossed the Pyrenees to Spain, and eventually arrived in Britain. Having worked for three years for SOE, he was now officially recruited and given a British army commission with the rank of major. Colonel Buckmaster introduced to him three or four agents, and Major de Vomécourt selected as his radio operator a twenty-two-year-old, small, dark-haired Jewish girl named Muriel Byck. "She looked so young, but I had seen enough in France to know that courage knew no barriers of age," he recalls. He was proved right. Her field name was Michèle. The two other members of this team were Captain Stanislas Makowski (Maurice), a handsome, charming, and impulsive young Pole, and George Wilkinson (Étienne), who was to set up a circuit in Orléans.

Vomécourt, whose new field name was Antoine, chose as his *nom de guerre* "Major St. Paul," after his prison at Lyons. Setting up his first headquarters with Antoine Vincent at Salbris, St. Paul organized many groups in the Sologne. Before and after D day he received several Jedburg teams, and later, uniformed units of SAS. Étienne was put in charge of the Loiret area, and Claude (George D. Jones), relieved as a radio operator by Muriel Byck, trained maquisards of Le Mans and Vendôme.

The Arsenal of Michenon

Within a month of his arrival St. Paul organized one of the most spectacular sabotage actions ever carried out in France, a combined ground-and-air-raid on the German arsenal at Michenon. Believing it to be fairly safe from Allied bombing attacks, the Germans had established a huge arsenal between the marshland of the river Sauldre and the forests of the Sologne. Bombs for the

Luftwaffe, artillery shells, infantry and tank ammunition were stored there for the garrisons in northwestern France and on the Atlantic wall. The arsenal covered fifty acres; it was heavily guarded by SS troops and field police and was enclosed by electrified wire.

For a long time Resistance men had eyed this arsenal hungrily, but direct sabotage was impossible. St. Paul devised a plan. He had learned that on 6 or 7 May several trains would arrive at Salbris to collect large supplies from the dumps. He notified Buckmaster and asked that Michenon and the railway yards of Salbris be bombed by the RAF. His men, meanwhile, prepared to mine roads and stage ambushes. On Saturday, 6 May, when the trains arrived at Salbris and began loading, St. Paul sent the go-ahead signal.

On Sunday at 2330 hours RAF and U.S. bombers appeared over the area, preceded by Pathfinder planes that pinpointed the targets St. Paul had described. Incendiary bombs were dropped in relays while German fighters took off from airfields as far away as Paris to engage the raiders. A few minutes after the incendiaries ignited fires in Michenon, the main bombing attack was delivered. "Standing on a roof miles away I watched as great explosions scorched the sky . . . . The trains packed with explosives blew up, almost simultaneously, causing a sort of volcanic eruption of twisted, burning metal . . ." de Vomécourt recalls. There was chaos as German soldiers and SS men, trying to save themselves from the inferno, ran out of the camp only to encounter mines, tripwires, and roadblocks planted by St. Paul's men.

At least two hundred Germans were killed or wounded; losses among French civilians were slight because the people of Salbris had been forewarned. German losses of ammunition and materiel were crippling. Indeed, the destruction of the Michenon arsenal had a serious effect on the German operations in Normandy after D day.

This was only one, though a very important, exploit of St. Paul's network. Others quickly followed. In May St. Paul received Maurice Lostrie (Alex), who specialized as a "Bombiste," and around D day performed some extraordinary feats. Almost singlehanded—helped by only two or three inexperienced young men—he blew up thirteen bridges, a huge lock on the Loire, blocked the canal (which was used to ship grain to Germany) with a fifty-ton crane, carried out thirty sabotage actions against the railway system, and destroyed twelve locomotives and thirty-four diesel engines at the SNAC factory near Bourges. SHAEF later sent a special signal commending Alex's work.

But May was also a month of sorrow. Little Michèle had toiled hard as a radio operator, maintaining an hour-to-hour link with London, and (between "skeds") as a courier, alerting sabotage teams. But she was shaken by the bombing raid and the explosions. She appeared very tired to her friends. Since her arrival she had been working in a shed behind Vincent's garage, which was often visited by Germans needing repairs to their vehicles. This became very dangerous after the Michenon raid; retaliations were savage.

Michèle moved to the house of blacksmith Jourdain at Vernou, where she became seriously ill. Dr. Andrieux, a Resistance doctor, diagnosed meningitis and told St. Paul that she must go immediately to a hospital. It was a risk, because hospital admissions were controlled by German police. But Philippe de Vomécourt decided that the risk must be taken. He drove Michèle to the hospital at Romorantin and introduced himself as Monsieur Philippe de Courcelles, Michèle's uncle, explaining they were evacuees from Paris. The nuns admitted the patient and did all they could to save her life. But Muriel Byck died on 23 May, in the arms of Philippe de Vomécourt, who had visited her daily.

Souesmes to Beaugency

The maquis of Souesmes was one of the strongest groups in the Sologne. St. Paul sent Maurice (Stanislas Makowski) there to organize the men for attacks on German troops moving toward Normandy. On 17 June Maurice's units, using only Sten guns and a few machine guns, fought a battle with seven hundred Germans between Souesmes and Monetroel. The battle lasted for many hours, and when the maquisards withdrew the German column had been scattered, leaving many casualties behind. The maquisards lost only nine dead in the fighting, but many were wounded. Four prisoners taken by the Germans were stabbed to death with bayonets. The next morning, when the Germans returned for their dead and dying, local inhabitants and St. Paul (who had come disguised as a gamekeeper to see for himself) counted 121 dead Germans and 65 seriously wounded.

Maurice laid many ambushes during the following weeks, then joined St. Paul at Saint-Viatre. There they took their men to attack a camp of pro-Nazi *milice*. On 15 August Maurice led another big attack on two German columns, which had arrived battered and disorganized at Neung-sur-Beuvron. As perhaps happened in only a few other areas of France, the SOE officers in the Sologne worked in perfect cooperation with FFI units, now emerging from the maquis. On 17 August Maurice was driving with two FFI officers in a car from Romorantin toward Neung. They carried packets of printed proclamations from General Koenig's military delegate to the FFI. Near Neung they met a German troop transport. Maurice tried to charge on, knowing there was no other way to escape. The Germans opened fire on the car.

While the car was taking a corner at great speed, a door opened and one of the passengers, Bernard Rohmer, was flung out. Maurice drove on for fifty yards, but seeing several German cars nearing the spot where Rohmer lay, he stopped, and both he and his other passenger, Auguste Maundy, began to fire, hoping to keep the Germans off and to pick up Rohmer. But more German armored cars with mounted machine guns arrived. Rohmer, although injured, fired from his Sten gun and then ran to the river, intending to swim to the other side. He was killed in midstream by hand grenades. Maurice and Maundy had taken cover behind their car and were firing, but they could not defy German machine guns.

Maundy was killed; Maurice was hit in the shoulders, stomach, and legs. He was taken to the Gestapo office at Romorantin and tortured for hours. Then the SS threw his corpse on a rubbish heap in the rue du Four. It was mutilated, with every bone broken, the skull bashed in, and the face bearing many bayonet or dagger wounds. The body was secretly removed and buried at the cemetery.

On the day Captain Stanislas Makowski was murdered, the American 3rd Army under General George S. Patton entered Orléans and Chartres; three days later the people of Paris rose, and on 23 August General Leclerc's Free French tank division arrived at the outskirts of the capital. But while General Dietrich von Choltitz, the German C in C in Paris, had begun negotiations for the capitulation, and German divisions, aimlessly fleeing and utterly disorganized, began to surrender in many parts of France, an army corps of some twenty thousand men under General Elster, harassed by St. Paul's units, drew back from the Sologne and the Cher into a triangle formed by lines between Châteauroux, Vierzon, and Bourges. General Elster's intention was to battle his way out in the direction of Nevers and Chalon-sur-Saône, in a desperate attempt to reach the Swiss frontier. Philippe de Vomécourt held a council of war with his subcommanders at Romorantin. He had only two thousand men, not all adequately armed, and a few small units of the British and Free French SAS. But de Vomécourt said: "If the Germans make the dash, we shall slaughter them!"

Plundering villages, setting fire to farms, killing peasants, the farthest point General Elster's division reached was Sancoins, southeast of Nevers. By then the Germans were frightened almost out of their wits by Philippe de Vomécourt's maquisards. Many were convinced that if they surrendered to the French they would be killed. Some tried to reach Germany on their own; they threw away arms and uniforms, stole civilian clothes, and ran. Having heard that American troops had reached Briare on the north bank of the Loire, General Elster sent emissaries to the commander of the U.S. 83rd Division and offered to surrender with honor. In the end, the St. Paul men had to provide escort for the German division, or what was left of it, in order to protect the weary, dejected, and utterly demoralized mob of once-arrogant Nazi soldiery from the wrath of the local population.

For three days and nights the Germans crawled toward Beaugency, where they were finally disarmed, and General Elster formally surrendered to U.S. General Macon and Commandant Philippe de Vomécourt of SOE.

The Final Hours

During August and September this scene was re-enacted in many parts of France. In the southwest the Corps Francs, organized and armed by Major Roger Landes and his SOE comrades, had ripped German divisions moving toward Normandy, and with FFI units, liberated five departments without the help of the Allied armies. Lieutenant Colonel George Starr (Hilaire) and his men attacked the Das Reich Panzer Division and the Hermann Goering SS Division; the latter never reached the battlefront to the north. In the Provence, Ardèche, and Drôme, Lieutenant Colonel Francis Cammaerts, after his narrow escape from a firing squad, could now drive through the towns and villages where parents and children swarmed over his car to shake his hand and offer wine. A few of them were at first a little embarrassed at the sight of his uniform, addressing him as *"mon colonel,"* but he quickly made it clear that he was still their *"vieux Roger"* who fought beside them on the plateau of Vercors.

In the Jura and the Ain departments, bordering on Roger's old battleground, Colonel Heslop, the redoubtable Xavier—who had served two years in the field on missions in the Limousin and the Massif Central and finally in the Franche-Comté—also played a key role in liberating a large area before Allied forces appeared on the scene.

In March 1944 Heslop had done his best to help the eight hundred maquisards who, under the command of brave but impetuous Tom Morel, had gathered on the plateau of Glières and were attacked by five thousand German troops and Vichy *miliciens*. Heslop supplied them with arms and ammunition, but it was an unequal struggle, and on 26 March it ended with a massacre after Tom Morel was killed.

Throughout his campaign in the Savoy mountains Heslop could rely on some splendid assistants—men such as Jean Rosenthal, with RF section, and Dr. Geoffrey Parker, a London surgeon, who arrived in July and set up a secret hospital where wounded maquisards were tended.

Leading two thousand men toward Besançon in an attempt to split two German divisions trying to battle their way to Alsace, Heslop joined forces with FFI units of Savoyard maquisards. After his men captured a German field artillery battery, Heslop ordered the gunners to instruct his men in the handling of the guns, which were turned on the fleeing enemy. This action produced a rumor among German commanders, whose troops made a last stand on a line between Belfort and Metz, that the maquisards were being supplied with field artillery by parachute drops.

During the last few weeks preceding the liberation, SOE and OSS dropped great quantities of arms, including mortars, bazookas, and machine guns to the FFI. Several experienced SOE organizers arrived on their second and third missions.

According to French sources, ninety Jedburgh teams were parachuted to the maquis after D day, with three hundred French, British, and American officers to provide commanders and instructors. According to SHAEF, the number of French, British, and American officers thus employed was almost twice that figure. In addition, many units of Special Air Service, each consisting of thirty to sixty heavily armed, commando-trained men, were dropped to aid the FFI units.

Among the many SOE agents who arrived during the final stages of the war in France was a young count, Maurice Gonzagues de St. Geniès (Lucien), who parachuted with Yvonne Baseden (Odette), an English W/T operator. They set up a small circuit in the Jura, next to Heslop's, and their main task was the reception of arms for the maquis. While storing a large supply, dropped from U.S. Flying Fortresses, they were surprised by a German raiding party, and hid in a loft. At first the Germans found nothing. Then one of the SS men, giving vent to his frustration, began to fire at random. A bullet went through the trap door of the loft and hit de St. Geniès in the head, killing him instantly. Blood trickled through the trap-door frame and was spotted by the SS men. They found the dead organizer and arrested everyone present, including Yvonne Baseden. She was sent to Ravensbrück, from which she was eventually freed by U.S. troops—one of the few SOE inmates to survive this extermination camp.

Robert Benoist returned in March 1944, with Denise Bloch, to revive his Paris–Rambouillet circuit. He found his old colleague Jean-Paul Wimille, and they soon had a good *réseau* going west of the capital, with almost two thousand armed FFI men. Shortly before the liberation of Paris, Benoist learned that his mother was dying and hurried to the family château—straight into the arms of the Gestapo. He was hanged at Buchenwald. Denise Bloch, also caught, was killed at Ravensbrück.

Several agents fell victim to the *Funkspiel,* still functioning in the spring of 1944, after the Germans had captured some new transmitters. One was the redoubtable Alec Rabinowitch (Arnaud), who arrived on 2 March with Roger Sabourin to start a new circuit at Nancy. They were dropped into a reception zone controlled by Kieffer. Alec, recognized as the long-wanted "pianist" of St. Jorioz, was killed at the extermination camp of Rawicz; Sabourin was hanged at Buchenwald.

It is impossible to give more than a fleeting glimpse of this final period in France: the rejoicing of the population in the flag-bedecked towns and villages, the triumphant welcome given to the British and American liberators, the endless columns of German prisoners being marched to camps, and the hunger and hardship caused by the destruction of transport and public services during the fighting.

The *Herrenvolk,* who had moved about so arrogantly only a few days before, were now completely cowed. Here and there barefoot youngsters, no taller than the rifles they held, guarded hundreds of prisoners. Even blackshirted SS men saluted the urchins, asking for permission to relieve themselves at the side of the road, or picking up cigarette butts thrown to them by American soldiers.

The SOE men and women—those who survived until victory—felt gratified when General Eisenhower announced:

I consider that the disruption of enemy rail communications, the harassing of German road moves, the continual strain placed on German war economy and German security services throughout Occupied Europe by the organized forces of the Resistance, played a very considerable part in our victory . . . .

And some of the SOE organizers and saboteurs, reading further, may have perceived their own personal actions in the following:

Sabotage caused effects beyond the capacity of the Allied air effort, delaying all German divisions moving from the Mediterranean to Normandy, and forcing extensive enemy detours, with the consequence that they arrived, if at all, too late and not in fighting condition, or in a state of extreme disorganization and exhaustion.

The Reckoning

But many SOE men and women who served in France never read this. Many perished almost in the sight of liberation and freedom. On 8 August 1944, just two weeks before the liberation of Paris, 180 prisoners, all selected for extermination, were herded on a train bound for Germany. Between Paris and Châlons-sur-Marne the train was attacked by Allied aircraft, probably because a British pilot assumed it was a German troop transport. The engine and the track were damaged, and near Châlons the prisoners had to change to army trucks.

One of the prisoners was Wing Commander F. F. T. Yeo-Thomas. His recollection of the journey is limited to that of two of the trucks, one containing thirty-seven SOE and French prisoners, the other a number of women, including several SOE agents. The following passage is taken from Bruce Marshall's book *The White Rabbit,* the story of Tommy's service in the field in France and imprisonment in Buchenwald. The two army trucks stopped at Châlons and again at Verdun. Then the trucks continued to Saarbrücken, where the prisoners were taken to a prison camp for "refitting."

The men were chained in groups of five. The chains were in the shape of an

X, in the centre of which was a ring fitted to a pair of handcuffs, which were fixed round the ankles of one prisoner so as to force him to take short, shuffling steps. At the extremities of the chains were more handcuffs which were fastened to the ankles of the four others in the group. To prevent them from using their hands to keep their balance, the prisoners were no longer attached to one another in pairs by their wrists, but each man's hands were shackled separately. In these cumbersome fetters they were marched to the distant latrines and, as they tripped and stumbled, were kicked and beaten with truncheons, coshes and fists by the SS men. In the latrines, where fat, slimy worms crawled among the overflowing faeces, they were forced to relieve themselves in these chained groups. After this humiliating and awkward procedure they were marched across the camp under the gaze of scared white faces crowding the dirty windows of the huts round the square. It is not surprising that their hearts were filled with anger and hatred . . . .

Yet this was only a transit camp at Saarbrücken. The journey ended in Buchenwald, the concentration camp near Weimar, the *Kultur* town, where Goethe had lived. Next to Belsen, Buchenwald was probably the worst of all concentration camps. The suffering caused by overwork and hunger was aggravated by typhus epidemics and the use of prisoners as guinea pigs for "biological research." The camp commandant, SS Colonel Koch, was a demented sadist; his deputy, SS Colonel Roedl, a cold-blooded sadist; and among the guards were some of the most brutal ever produced by the SS.[3]

The SOE officers who arrived with Yeo-Thomas were Denis Barrett, Robert Benoist, Pierre Culioli, Henri Frager, Émile-Henri Garry, Desmond Hubble, Kane, John A. Mayer, John McKenzie, Harry Peulevé, Maurice Southgate, Arthur Steele, and George Wilkinson. Already in Buchenwald were several other SOE officers, including Christopher Burney, Maurice Pertschuk, and Alfred and Henry Newton.

On 24 August 1944 Allied aircraft bombed the Gustloff armament factory outside the camp, where many prisoners worked. Several bombs fell on the SS barracks, killing eighty and injuring three hundred SS men. There were also heavy casualties among the prisoners. According to German sources, four hundred were killed and fifteen hundred wounded, many of whom, receiving no first aid or surgical treatment, died.

As a retaliation for the Allied bombing raid, the camp commandant, SS Obersturmbann-Führer Pfister (who had succeeded Koch when he became

[3] A truthful description of conditions in the camp can be found in *Buchenwald*, by Walter Poller (Souvenir Press, London, 1961). There are other books about Buchenwald and German concentration camps, but I may be biased in favor of Poller's story. He worked as an orderly at the so-called medical block, and he saved my life when I was badly injured while a prisoner at Buchenwald. Poller, a German Socialist journalist, had been in Buchenwald since 1938 and miraculously survived six years of imprisonment.

chief of German concentration camps at the RSHA), ordered executions of British and French "terrorists," all of them officers of SOE and BCRA. On 9 September sixteen prisoners were hanged, including SOE agents John McAlister and Frank Pickersgill (who had spent a year at the Rawicz concentration camp, had been taken to Paris for the *Funkspiel,* and were eventually sent to Buchenwald), Émile-Henri Garry, Robert Benoist, Arthur Steele, John McKenzie, John Mayer, Charles Rechenmann, and François Garel. On 4 October twelve more men were hanged. Among them were Denis Barrett, Henri Frager, George Wilkinson, Albert Dubois, and Pierre Mulsant.

Wing Commander Yeo-Thomas told me that all were hanged from hooks in the wall of the crematorium and left to die by slow strangulation. Harry Peulevé, too, was called on the loudspeaker to report. But he had exchanged his prison garb (as had Yeo-Thomas) for that of a dead French prisoner and had become No. 76,635, Marcel Seigneur. The dead Seigneur was sent to the crematorium as Peulevé.

Executions took place at regular intervals and many thousands of prisoners were hanged (or later shot in large groups) right up until the end of the war. Maurice Pertschuk, who had commanded the Toulouse circuit at the age of twenty-three in 1942–43, was hanged on 29 March 1945, less than six weeks before Germany's surrender.[4]

Other SOE agents perished in the concentration camps of Dachau, Sachsenhausen (where Francis Suttill, the commanding officer of PROSPER, was hanged on 21 March 1945, having been held as a possible hostage until almost the end of the war), Oranienburg, Torgau, Blankenburg, Lutzkendorf, Ravensbrück, Natzweiler, Rawicz, Mauthausen in Austria, and Gross Rosen in Silesia.

Dachau, originally an all-male concentration camp, contained a compound for women prisoners. On 13 September 1944 Noor Inayat Khan, Yolande Beekman, Eliane Plewman, and Madeleine Damerment were executed there. The camp had been used for German political prisoners since 1933. Huts designed to hold 200 to 250 prisoners housed 2,000 each in 1943, and up to 3,000 at the end of 1944, in spite of continuous executions.

The Mauthausen camp was built in 1938, soon after the German occupation of Austria. It was used mainly for Jews and, during the war, by the head of Section IV-B of the RSHA, SS Obersturmbann-Führer Adolf Eichmann, for the "final solution of the Jewish problem." Later it became an extermination camp for Allied secret agents and Resistance leaders also. Among those executed there whose names will be remembered were

[4] His co-prisoner Christopher Burney dedicated his book *Dungeon Democracy* thus: "To the memory of Maurice Pertschuk hanged in Buchenwald crematorium on March 29, 1945, who fought more gallantly than any of us and died more sadly."

Gilbert Norman, Sydney Jones, and John Cuthbert Young, as well as most of the SOE officers captured in Holland. Himmler, Heydrich, Kaltenbrunner, and other visiting Gestapo chiefs watched the death agonies of prisoners in the gas chamber through a glass-covered spy hole. On one occasion in 1944, three different methods of execution were used on the same day for the benefit of Kaltenbrunner: hanging, shooting (bullet in the neck), and gas poisoning.[5]

In all the camps biological, physiological, and medical experiments were conducted by German doctors and scientists, which in many aspects were similar to vivisection, the only difference being that they operated on human beings.[6]

According to the records of SOE F section, 480 agents served in France; of these 130 were captured. Only 26 survived and returned, having been liberated in concentration camps; 106 were executed and killed in combat. French sources[7] give different figures: 393 agents dispatched; 119 executed or killed. The reason for this might be that the French historians deducted some 90 agents from the over-all figure of 480, because they considered them French nationals. There is no apparent explanation for the two different figures of executed agents.

The number of circuits and *réseaux* established by organizers of the SOE Buckmaster section—geographically separate networks (not all, of course, operating at the same time)—was between seventy and eighty. Many of the circuits had several subcircuits and often as many as thirty local groups and cells, sabotage teams, and reception committees.

Today, more than twenty years after the end of the war, there are still forty-six "Amicales Buckmaster," clubs of former members of SOE circuits of F section, each with a chairman (sometimes a woman), a secretary, or a *liquidateur*. Plotting the places where these honorary officers reside (although some have meanwhile moved to other localities), provides a rough picture of the French section's wartime coverage: Paris (eleven), Aix-en-Provence, Anglet (Basses-Pyrénées), Antony (Seine), Arles (Gard), Bagnolet, Besançon, Brive, Bordeaux (two), Bourbonne (Haute-Marne), Cannes, Chartres, Château-du-Loire (Sarthe), Clermont-Ferrand, Égry (Loiret), La Celle-St. Cloud (Seine-et-Oise), Lans-en-Vercors (Isère), Le Mans, Le Perreux (Seine), Lille, Longvic (Côte d'Or), Lyons (two), Marseilles (two), Mayenne, Montbazon (Indre-et-Loire), Nice, Nogent-sur-Marne, Poitiers, Romorantin, Toulouse (two), Vec-sur-Seille (Moselle), and Villefranche-sur-Saône. The list is not nearly complete; it contains only those "amicales" of former members of SOE networks, registered with the federation of *Amicales des Anciens Réseaux de la Ré-*

---

[5] *Cf.* Delarue, J., *Histoire de la Gestapo,* Fayard, Paris, 1962.
[6] *Ibid.*
[7] Michel, H., *Les Mouvements Clandestins,* Presses Universitaires, Paris, 1961, p. 77.

sistance, which comprises some thousand separate clubs and societies. Many have never registered with the federation, and in many places throughout France there are informal gatherings of men and women who served with SOE officers.

I have tried to give a few details about SOE agents in France and of the losses suffered. I cannot even attempt this concerning the tens of thousands of brave men and women of the French Resistance who sheltered SOE agents, served as couriers, mail drops, receptionists at dropping zones, saboteurs; and, above all, those who fought and were killed.

At least 24,000 Resistance fighters, men and women, were executed by the Germans in France; and of the 115,000 deported to German concentration camps only 40,000 returned home, most of them skin-covered skeletons in an appalling state of health. These figures do not include people deported for forced labor, or the losses of the maquis and FFI in actual battles with the enemy; the latter were estimated to exceed 30,000 killed.

French patriots paid a terrible toll. But they restored the honor and freedom of their homeland and helped to defeat a tyranny that threatened all mankind. British members of the SOE *réseaux* in France will never cease to admire their courage and sacrifice, and to cherish the comradeship which bound them to these brave and devoted people.

13

Dutch Tragedy

O n 1 0 M a y 1940 Germany attacked the Netherlands and Belgium without warning. The Belgian army surrendered after a fortnight, on King Leopold's order; the Dutch offered brief resistance, until Rotterdam was laid in ruins by the Luftwaffe and west and northwest Holland seized within a few hours by German paratroops.

By 17 May the whole country was occupied. Queen Wilhelmina and Crown Princess Juliana, Prince Bernhard, and their children—with members of the government, some hundred officials and military men—escaped aboard two British destroyers to England. Several Dutch warships, with 3,100 men, and the entire merchant navy also escaped and brought 1,500 Dutch officers, soldiers, and gendarmes to Britain.

Before leaving, the queen empowered the commander in chief of the Netherlands armed forces, General H. G. Winkelman, to make any decision necessary to avoid further bloodshed. On 14 May the general ordered a cease-fire; but he never capitulated, and the Netherlands never officially surrendered to the German invaders.

Hitler appointed the Austrian Nazi party leader, Dr. Seyss-Inquart, as Reichs-Kommissar for the Netherlands, proclaiming that there was no intention of oppressing "the kindred Dutch people"; but he also appointed SS Obergruppen-Führer Hans Rauter, a ruthless Gestapo man, as general commissar for public security, lest the Dutch kinsmen failed to embrace their German cousins with proper enthusiasm.

Almost immediately a Resistance movement sprang up. Within a few weeks the first organized groups were formed, among them the Beggars' Action (after the Dutch patriots who rose in 1566 against the Spaniards and whom the Duke of Alba had called "just beggars"; nevertheless, they liberated the country from the Spanish oppression). The leader of the modern Beggars was Bernard Ijzerdraat; their headquarters, a sailing club near the Hook of Holland; and most of their members, sportsmen, students, and officers. They had only a vague idea of how to organize an underground movement, but by creating the first clandestine broadsheet they contributed a great deal toward drawing the Dutch people out of the stupor and confusion brought about by the sudden invasion and the German promises. The Beggars hoped to establish contact with Britain but in November, through treachery of some Dutch Nazis who infiltrated the group, Bernard Ijzerdraat and all his subleaders were arrested. Eventually, during the general strike in February 1941, fifteen of them were executed by a German firing squad.

Other Resistance groups were organized during 1940–41, mainly among members of the Social Democrat and Catholic youth leagues. The Communists joined the Resistance actively only after Hitler's attack on the Soviet Union. Officers of the disbanded Dutch armed forces, who managed to avoid internment, secretly gathered together. Two high-ranking officers, Major General H. D. S. Hasselman and Colonel J. P. Bolten, assembled a number of younger men to collect information and convey it to London. The leader of this group was Dr. Johan Stijkel, a young Rotterdam lawyer. He was fortunate in finding a skilled radio expert, Cornelis Drupsteen, who succeeded in establishing the first radio link with England. His signals were picked up by chance a receiving station of the Royal Corps of Signals. For several months the Stijkel group exchanged radio messages with the SIS.

Dutch Secret Service in London

Into exile with Queen Wilhelmina had come the former commissioner of the police at The Hague, F. van 't Sant, who had been responsible for the security arrangements during the escape of the royal family. In London he became the queen's secretary and began organizing a secret service bureau. Colonel G. P. Rabagliatti was the liaison officer of the SIS.

Although some officers of the intelligence branch of the Dutch army had reached Britain with the queen and the cabinet, they, as well as the British, were entirely groping in the dark. The Dutch intelligence had made no preparations to leave behind secret networks, nor had they established any secret radio posts before they fled. The SIS fared little better, for not only had its Dutch network been destroyed after the Venlo incident, but also one of its important Dutch agents, when leaving the country in a hurry, left behind a suitcase with information on all his contact addresses, which was found by the Germans.[1]

Superintendent van 't Sant's *Centrale Inlichtingendienst* (Central Intelligence Service) was in operation in London by July 1940—long before the Dutch section of SOE was formed. With the cooperation of Colonel Rabagliatti, the first secret agent was sent to Holland.

[1] De Jong, Dr. Louis, director of the Netherlands State Institute for War Documentation, editor, *Britain and Dutch Resistance* (Unpublished report).

[248]

He was a young lieutenant of the Dutch navy, Lodo A. R. J. van Hamel, who was dropped by parachute near Leyden on the night of 28 August 1940. For six weeks he worked tirelessly, often under depressing circumstances—many of the people he appealed to refused to help—and sat up four groups, which he equipped with radio transmitters. He had brought one W/T set with him; three more were constructed in Holland and tuned to the British receiving station. Trying to return to Britain with a dossier of valuable information and microfilmed maps of German establishments and newly erected coastal defenses, he was instructed by London to go to Zurig, a little village on the dikes in Friesland, near the embankment that divides the salty water of the North Sea from the fresh water of the Zuider Zee. There, on a date that was to be fixed by radio signals, a Royal Navy seaplane was to land and collect him.

Van Hamel had suggested that a leader of the newly created *Orde Dienst* (OD) organization[2]—consisting mainly of officers and men of the former Dutch armed forces—Professor Baas Becking, should accompany him. The two men traveled on 14 September to Friesland, the professor carrying a fat briefcase stuffed with reports, codes, microfilms, and photographs. At Harlingen they were joined by two couriers of the OD to guide them to the lonely rendezvous with the seaplane.

That night a gala performance took place in the Deutsches Theater in The Hague, the famous City Theater (seized by the Germans and renamed), where shows were now given in the German language, as one of the *Kultur* instructions for the Dutch people. In the royal box were Arthur Seyss-Inquart, Hans Rauter, and other high officials; while in other boxes and in the stalls sat German officers, Gestapo officials, and the whole throng of German functionaries with their *frauen*. Among them was the newly arrived chief of the SD Amt IV, SS Sturmbann-Führer Joseph Schreieder. He had arrived in Holland from Austria only a month before and was still waiting to catch his first "British spy."

During the interval an adjutant asked him to come to the box of the commander of the *Sicherheitsdienst,* SS Standarten-Führer Dr. Wilhelm Harster, who gave Schreieder a small piece of paper. On it was a teleprinter message, which had just reached Harster's office and had been rushed to the theater.

FROM SD AST LEEUWARDEN TO DR. HARSTER. TODAY AFTERNOON A BRITISH AGENT WHO CALLS HIMSELF VAN DALEN WAS APPREHENDED ON THE EAST COAST OF FRIESLAND NEAR THE TJEUKEMEER IN COMPANY OF THREE OTHER PERSONS WHILE AWAITING A BRITISH SEA PLANE TO TAKE THEM TO ENGLAND EXPECTING YOUR INSTRUCTIONS.

[2] *Orde Dienst*—Order Service; its originally envisaged task was to maintain law and order after the liberation.

Harster ordered Schreieder to go immediately to Leeuwarden and investigate the case. With two of his men Schreieder drove north.

The four people arrested by the German field police at Zurig were van Hamel, Professor Baas Becking, and the two OD couriers, a man and a woman. They had been denounced by a local V-man, who had become suspicious watching them strolling on the dikes.

After Schreieder's arrival at Leeuwarden the prisoners were put through the third degree by the SS men. Nothing incriminating was found on them because Professor Becking managed to throw his briefcase into the water. After many salvage attempts the Germans later recovered it on a small island.

Eventually, after long interrogations at Schreieder's office in The Hague, van Dalen admitted to being Lieutenant Lodo van Hamel; he also admitted that he had arrived some time before from England. He never gave away any of his comrades. The OD leader whom he appointed in charge of his radio post, van Hattum, was not caught by the Germans until two years later. Van Hamel saved Professor Becking by telling Schreieder that Becking had nothing to do with the Resistance but only wanted to get a lift to England, to go to the Dutch East Indies where his family lived. Van Hamel also saved the lives of the two couriers, whom he described as "two local people whom he hired as guides and who never knew of his intentions to wait for a British plane." Van Hamel was held in prison many months, tried by a court-martial, sentenced to death, and executed in June 1941.

His capture prompted the Germans to redouble their vigilance on the coast and eventually led to the capture of the Stijkel group.

For several weeks no more agents were sent from Britain to Holland, mainly because of the confusion at the Dutch secret service headquarters in London and because the Dutch section of the newly founded SOE was still embryonic. But the radio link had been established through van Hamel's sacrifice, and for a time it was also maintained by the Stijkel group.

The People's Rising

Holland was in an extremely disadvantageous geographical position to establish regular communications with Britain. France, Norway, and—across a short stretch of sea—Denmark all bordered on neutral countries. Couriers could reach Switzerland, Spain, or Sweden, however perilous such journeys. Holland was isolated, the Dutch coasts closely watched by the Germans. In France it was possible to land and take off with small Lysander aircraft. Holland was often covered for weeks by mist or haze, which precluded such landings. Moreover the country, densely populated and crisscrossed with roads and railway lines, completely flat and sparsely wooded, was easy for German patrols to control.

[251]

All this made the dispatch of agents by air or sea extremely difficult. Between November 1940 and June 1941 only three agents were sent. Two were soon caught; the third managed to work on for a year. Such Resistance groups as existed were still preoccupied with problems of organization. There were a few cases of sabotage, but on the whole life was normal during the winter, when the first sign of popular discontent and resistance became apparent. There were demonstrations against the rapid rise in the price of food and the new, stringent rationing regulations. Attacks took place on trains carrying industrial goods and foodstuffs from Holland to Germany.

Until the German invasion there was no "Jewish question" in the Netherlands. Of 140,000 Dutch Jews, some 70,000 were residents of Amsterdam, and most Jewish families could trace their Dutch ancestry back for several centuries. They were regarded as Dutchmen and respected by their fellow countrymen. In October 1940 Reichs-Kommissar Seyss-Inquart imposed the first restrictions upon Dutch Jewry. The Dutch authorities were ordered to dismiss all Jews employed in municipal offices, health services, universities, and schools. When students at the famous universities of Leiden and Delft refused to attend lectures given by their non-Jewish successors, Seyss-Inquart responded by closing the universities.

When Jewish civil servants were suspended on German orders, senior Dutch officials called on the Nazi overlord and informed him that this measure would greatly impair the administration. This only increased the Nazi ire, and Seyss-Inquart gave orders that Jews were forbidden to use public transport, visit public libraries, attend theaters and cinemas. Jewish doctors were prohibited from treating non-Jews. The registration of all Jewish businesses and shops was followed by confiscations.

Thousands of Dutchmen responded to the Nazi persecution by queuing in front of Jewish doctors' surgeries, by trading at the Jewish shops still open, and by inviting Jews to their homes. Roman Catholic and Protestant organizations, normally distant in their relations, cooperated with social and scientific institutions and prominent Dutch public figures "in defense of Jewish compatriots." Resistance groups turned the anti-Jewish measures into a weapon against the Nazis.

The Germans were enraged. Rauter, anxious to show that there were anti-Semitic Dutchmen, gave the leader of the small Dutch Nazi party, Adriaan Mussert, a free hand to deal with the Jews. Most of the members of Mussert's party in Amsterdam were hooligans known only too well to the local police. On 10 February 1941 the streets of north Amsterdam, where most of the Jews resided, filled up with groups of these toughs. They beat up men, women, and children, broke into and looted Jewish homes, and set fire to many shops and houses. Several hundred Jews were seriously injured.

[252]

Using this stage-managed, anti-Jewish riot as an excuse, Rauter ordered all Jews to be confined to a ghetto in Amsterdam. That same week the Germans ordered several hundred Dutch workers, mainly from the shipbuilding yards of Amsterdam and Rotterdam, to be shipped to Germany for war work.

On Saturday, 15 February 1941, spontaneous strikes broke out among the workers of Amsterdam. For the first time since the invasion, tens of thousands of Dutchmen marched through the streets, shouting abuse at the Nazis, carrying placards expressing sympathy with the Jews, and promising them protection "by the workers of Amsterdam."

To punish the Dutch for their "impudent demonstrations," Rauter ordered the execution of three Communist strike leaders and fifteen members of the Beggars' Action. Many thousand Jews were deported to concentration camps and perished there. Collective fines were imposed on the cities of Amsterdam ($6,000,000), Hilversum ($1,000,000), and Zaandam ($200,000), where the most violent anti-German demonstrations had occurred. Their municipal councils were dissolved and replaced by Gestapo commissars.

The pro-Jewish rebellion in Holland had no parallel in any other German-occupied country, and it had an important bearing on all German activities against secret agents from London. Seyss-Inquart, Rauter, and Nazi propagandists accused—on the radio and in a flood of leaflets and posters—Winston Churchill, "the notorious servant of World Jewry," of having instigated the events in Holland by sending "terrorists and saboteurs" from London. The Nazi leaders announced that they would "deal mercilessly with these terrorists."

The Specialists

Until the February uprising, the Germans had maintained comparatively few Gestapo and SD personnel in Holland. Pursuing his kid-glove policy, Reichs-Kommissar Seyss-Inquart had come to an arrangement with Himmler that the Gestapo would exercise restraint. Similarly, the German Military Intelligence (Abwehr) had only a small office at The Hague, headed by Colonel Hempel, attached to the headquarters of the German C in C, General of the Luftwaffe Friedrich Christiansen. The military commander, a bluff, elderly officer of the old school, although amiably disposed toward the Nazis, insisted that his own military courts should try cases of sabotage.

It was not until late autumn of 1940 that the Gestapo began to handle counterespionage matters. In March 1941, following the people's rising, the Gestapo and SD were greatly reinforced; and Schreieder, much to the discomfiture of the Abwehr, asserted himself as the specialist to cope with the anticipated influx of agents from Britain.

[253]

The Abwehr, regarding counterespionage as its prerogative and concerned with the Gestapo interference, decided to recruit a specialist, too. He was to establish in The Hague a branch of the III-F section, the military counterespionage department, which was headed in Berlin by Lieutenant General von Bentivengi, under Admiral Canaris' direction.

The specialist selected by Berlin was Major Hermann Giskes of the Abwehr headquarters in France. Giskes, nearly forty-six, was a man of more than medium height, well-cut features, a strong hooked nose, and thinning hair. The Dutch intelligence officer, Major Kees de Graaf, who after the war interrogated Giskes when he was an Allied prisoner of war, said of him:

> The first impression Giskes made, as he sat there in civilian clothes, with his spectacles alternatively on and off, middle-aged, bald and sturdy, was of an average German. However, within five minutes, an acute observer would have changed his opinion. For it did not take long to realize that Giskes possessed characteristics rare among the Germans, particularly those in higher functions— a pleasant mixture of culture, intelligence and a sense of humor. However, this did not alter the fact that these valuable qualities had been devoted— voluntarily or involuntarily—to the Nazi system.[3]

On his arrival, Giskes established his office at the Hoogeweg at the famous seaside resort of Scheveningen on the outskirts of The Hague. It was a secluded building, requisitioned from its wealthy owner. Visitors were admitted by a back entrance hidden by a row of lime trees, which bordered on premises occupied by the headquarters of the German navy. Giskes recalled that he had seen a film produced by the German counterespionage before the war, in which the entire staff of the British intelligence office in The Hague appeared.[4] He was determined that nothing like that should happen to his office.

Giskes originally expected an easy assignment in Holland. But he soon discovered that he was supposed to work closely with the SD and the Gestapo. His opposite number at the SD headquarters at the Binnenhof, Joseph Schreieder, was a professional police officer, then thirty-nine years old. Giskes, the aristocratic army officer, felt only contempt for the Gestapo officer; he described their first meeting thus:

> A small, almost bald man with a heavy round head, in the uniform of an SS Sturmbann-Führer, entered my office. He extended a flabby, well-manicured little hand. With a series of small bows he preceded me into the sun room, where he placed himself in a chair and crossed his short legs. During the exchange of conventional platitudes which followed I had leisure to observe him more closely.

[3] K. de Graaf (under the pseudonym of Noel Degaulle), *Carnaval der Desperados,* Bezige Bij, Amsterdam, 1952.
[4] See chapter 1, under "The Venlo Incident."

[254]

His age was difficult to judge—perhaps forty. Slightly protruding, rat-like eyes gave lift to a pasty face, and the nose betrayed the delights of the bottle. The whole well-fed man exuded joviality, his slightly provincial accents emphasizing the note of southern warmth, as though he was immensely pleased to have found in me an entirely unexpected and beloved old friend. He radiated the well-known benevolence of certain criminal investigators, before which Edgar Wallace's murderers are supposed to have dissolved in tears . . . To judge from his intimate manner and the friendly *"Lieber Kamerad Giskes,"* with which he continually addressed me, I realized it was not going to be very difficult. I was quite sure that he had had my background investigated and that he was fully conversant with my private and political pedigree.[5]

Thus began a partnership fraught with jealousy and intrigue. Yet, during the following two years, Giskes and Schreieder between them succeeded in destroying almost all the efforts of the SOE Dutch section and the Dutch secret service in London. At first Schreieder was much the more successful. After the capture of van Hamel, using several V-men and members of the NSB (the Dutch Nazi party) as informers, he had smashed the Stijkel group of the Dutch Resistance.

In March 1941 Dr. Stijkel suggested to London that he, his deputy Jan Gude, and two of his helpers should come to Britain and bring important material, accumulated after van Hamel and Professor Baas Becking's mission had failed. The Dutch and British intelligence agreed, but warned Stijkel of great difficulties in arranging a pickup. Stijkel suggested he and his comrades would sail from Holland in a small cutter, at their own risk.

The Germans permitted Dutch fishermen to fish in coastal waters, provided their movements were checked. This was often left to the harbor police. Dr. Stijkel knew two policemen who had secretly done some work for the Resistance; he enlisted their help. He did not know that the two men were, in fact, Gestapo V-men. As soon as they realized that this was not a fishing expedition they reported to the local Gestapo chief, SS Sturmbann-Führer Lorenz. During the night of 2 April, Dr. Stijkel, Gude, and the brothers van der Plas boarded the cutter, while some of their friends stood on the jetty, bidding them farewell.

A detachment of SS men appeared on the jetty, and motorboats manned by SS emerged from the darkness and surrounded the cutter. The whole party was taken to the Gestapo headquarters at The Hague. Eventually all members of the Stijkel group were captured and sent to Berlin, where they were tried by a German tribunal. All but one of the accused were sentenced to death and were later executed by firing squads in Berlin. The lone man who was sentenced to life imprisonment never returned from Germany.

The Stijkel group became a symbol of national heroism in Holland;

[5] *Abwehr III-F,* pp. 64 ff.

their leaders were the first to be caught in a brave, if hopeless, attempt to reach England without any help from the secret service in London.

Quarrels in London

The relations between the British and Dutch secret services in London in the early summer of 1941 steadily worsened. British intelligence chiefs demanded that all communications between the Dutch CI (Central Intelligence) of van 't Sant and its few agents and Resistance contacts in Holland be controlled by the British. The Dutch were denied the right to operate their own radio transmitters, and after the Dutch section of SOE began functioning, the British insisted that all agents be enlisted into and trained and dispatched by SOE.

In order to come to an understanding with the British, the Dutch exile government in London set up an office for matters concerning the dispatch of agents and communications with Resistance groups. The department was named *Bureau Militaire Voorbereiding Terugkeer* (Bureau for the Military Preparations for the Return), or MVT for short. Colonel M. R. de Bruyne, a Dutch Royal Marines officer, became its chief.

Relations between the Dutch and British secret services, however, hardly improved. Colonel de Bruyne constantly complained that he was being left in the dark by the British. Despairing of these quarrels, the Dutch prime minister, Professor Gerbrandy, created a private secret service at his own office. Its chief was Dr. R. P. J. Derksema, a young lawyer from Zutphen who had escaped to Britain after the German invasion. Dr. Derksema's "shadow intelligence," with an office in Chester Street, worked independently of the official Dutch secret service departments.

This only aggravated the discord, but Dr. Derksema, a man of great ambition, turned it to his advantage. He made his own arrangements with some of the chiefs of British intelligence and he selected the first agents sent from Britain to Holland. While the chiefs of the British intelligence did not see eye to eye with Commissioner van 't Sant and Colonel de Bruyne, they approved of Derksema and his somewhat eccentric schemes.

A daring enterprise was started by a group of students of Leiden University, led by Hazelhoff Roelfzema, who had escaped to Britain. He knew that every Friday night German officers held a boisterous party at a hotel on the Esplanade of Scheveningen. The plan was to send a motorboat from the coast of East Anglia and arrive off Scheveningen between midnight and 2 A.M. At a short distance from the shore one or two agents would transfer to a dinghy and land. They would wear evening dress, carry champagne bottles, and pretend to be tipsy. If challenged by a German sentry, they would say they were guests from the hotel party. The scheme sounded like a students' prank, and Colonel de Bruyne objected strongly when he heard of it. It was, however, approved by Prime Minister Gerbrandy, a man with a lively sense of humor.

Cooperation between the various official departments had become so strained that Commissioner van 't Sant offered his resignation. Shortly afterward the head of the SOE Dutch section, Richard Valentine Laming, who had spent most of his life as a businessman in Holland, also relinquished his post and was succeeded by Major Blunt (Blizzard).

The Roelfzema scheme for landing agents at Scheveningen proved extremely difficult. No less than seven attempts were made, and each time the motorboats carrying the agents in evening dress had to turn back. At last, during the night of 21 November 1941, the eighth attempt succeeded; but only one agent, William van der Reyden, was disembarked, and he lost his radio transmitter and nearly drowned when the dinghy carrying him to shore capsized. He was not challenged on landing, and the carefully rehearsed champagne charade was never enacted.

On 23 November agent Lieutenant Pieter Tazelaar was put ashore by the Roelfzema ferry. He did well and got in touch with the Socialist leader Dr. Wiardi Beckman, whom Prime Minister Gerbrandy wanted to come to London and join his cabinet. Tazelaar tried to arrange a pickup for him, but although a motor-gunboat was sent several times, the plan was dogged by misfortune. Finally, on 15 January 1942 Dr. Beckman, waiting on the shore for yet another rendezvous with the boat, was betrayed by a V-man and arrested. Tazelaar managed to escape and returned to Britain by the Spanish escape route.

The discord between the Dutch and British secret service chiefs continued until the end of 1942, when, by a decree of Queen Wilhelmina in November, the Dutch secret services in London were completely overhauled. But for two years the dispute in London had continued, particularly during 1942, when an ugly quarrel developed among Dutch ministers and officials over the control of their secret service departments. Nevertheless, inside Nazi-subjugated Holland the Resistance movement was growing to a formidable strength, despite debacles and mass arrests, and owing little or nothing to the various organizations in London.

The Archtraitor

In July 1941 Schreieder learned from one of his informers of the existence of a clandestine radio post in regular contact with Britain. The man who brought this news was Antonius van der Waals. He was to become Schreieder's best and most trusted helper, an archtraitor who during three and a half years sent several hundred of his compatriots to German prisons and firing squads.

Van der Waals was the son of a respectable Rotterdam decorator and church sidesman. In 1934, at the age of twenty-two, he had broken away from his pious Protestant family and joined Mussert's Dutch Nazi party, becoming a squad leader of the jackbooted *Afdelingen,* the Dutch equivalent of the German storm troopers. After the invasion he worked for Gestapo chief Moeller in Rotterdam, denouncing Jews. He succeeded in taking over the electrical business of his employer de Hoop, and although he prospered as a subcontractor for the German army, his ambition was to work for the Gestapo and he became Moeller's full-time V-man.

One day van der Waals discovered that A. P. van der Meer, the director of an electrical firm, was connected with a Resistance group. The director knew van der Waals only slightly, having met him as the proprietor of the de Hoop firm; he did not know about van der Waals' Gestapo work. Van der Waals showed him blueprints of a mechanism that would drive combustion engines and was applicable to aero-engines. The blueprints had been given to the traitor by his Gestapo masters and came from the German marine works in Kiel.

Van der Waals suggested that the director introduce him to people who had connections with Britain. Being a patriot, he said, he wanted to prevent the invention from falling into German hands; rather it should be used for the British war effort. Van der Meer, impressed by the young man's patriotic sentiments, took the bait. He introduced him to Professor R. L. A. Schoemaker, a scientist connected with the Resistance group led by Dr. Otto Verdoorn, which had a radio link with London. One of its safe houses was at the shop of the tobacconist Knape in Bergweg. The Dutch patriots were enthusiastic about van der Waals' offer and asked London to arrange the inventor's trip to England. When London showed little interest, the patriots still encouraged van der Waals, who, realizing his good luck, demanded 10,000 guilders (about $4,000 at that time) to buy machinery and tools to perfect his invention. Eventually, he was given 5,000 guilders by van der Meer.

Meanwhile van der Waals collected details about the organization and compiled a dossier for Moeller's successor, SS Hauptsturm-Führer Hammer. On 30 April 1941 Hammer introduced him to Schreieder, who, in his own words, realized that "this was the man I had been waiting for." Schreieder offered van der Waals a salary of 225 guilders and generous expenses.

In July he told Schreieder of a secret radio post somewhere near Bilthoven. He had already betrayed several Resistance groups, including one led by Father Joseph Klinge of the Heemstede Monastery. The twenty-six-year-old monk, two theological students, C. van Last and J. G. Tillema, and other members of this group, were later executed. He had also betrayed a man named Jan Bierhuys, who had shot a German officer in a Haarlem street. For this, van der Waals collected a reward of 5,000 guilders, offered by the Gestapo.

However, van der Waals was unable to tell Schreieder the exact location of the Bilthoven radio post. The Abwehr's *Funkhorchdienst* was alerted and for several weeks German radio detection vans cruised through Utrecht and Bilthoven. On 31 August the search narrowed to the vicinity of the villa of a businessman named Jan Sickinga, who was not suspected of sympathy with the Resistance. The villa was raided and the Germans found a young, fair-haired man staying with the Sickinga family. They also found a complete radio transmitting station in a garden shed and a warning system installed between the shed and the villa, by which a bell would ring if unwelcome visitors entered the house.

The young man was Dutch naval cadet Hans Zomer, an agent sent to Holland by the Dutch section of SIS. Zomer, a brave man, refused to talk even under torture. The Germans tried everything to extort information and even summoned a hypnotist, Major von Wedel, from the Abwehr headquarters in Paris, but failed to elicit anything of value.

However, in Zomer's possession were found signal codes used for his transmissions. Zomer denied any knowledge of them, insisting they were given to him for safekeeping by a Resistance member whose name and address he did not know.

Schreieder gave the papers to one of his subordinates, Ernst May, a sergeant of the *Sicherheitsdienst*. Although May was not a trained cipher clerk, he spent many hours trying to decode the notes and eventually succeeded. The most valuable prize won by Sergeant May for his homework was the knowledge that the London code contained a security check—jumbled up figures that made no sense in themselves but indicated at the receiving end that the signal was genuine. Thus May discovered the most important key that was to lead to SOE's downfall in Holland. Like Sergeant Bleicher in Paris, Sergeant May in The Hague in many ways surpassed his superiors' performance.

Sergeant May tried to explain his discovery to Schreieder, but the Sturmbann-Führer apparently did not attach much importance to it, even when May told him that the code and the security check could be used to penetrate radio transmissions between enemy agents in Holland and their headquarters in Britain by using the captured transmitters.

The Broken Code

On 13 February 1942, six months after the Germans obtained the first SOE code, an SD squad raided the house of a Dr. Krediet, a physician in Wassenaar near Leiden. This was a routine matter. A V-man had reported that the doctor might be connected with the Resistance. The SD men found two strangers at the doctor's home. After going through the experience of Gestapo interrogations, the two men admitted being secret agents from Britain.

One was a former officer of the Dutch army, Johannes ter Laak. He had parachuted in September 1941 in North Holland as an agent of the Derksema organization and had been given Dr. Krediet's address as a safe house. Ter Laak's radio transmitter was badly damaged on landing and he was unable to set up a radio post.

The other man was William van der Reyden, the Derksema agent who swam ashore on 21 November 1941 in the remarkable "evening dress" enterprise. The agent, soaked and half frozen, somehow reached Dr. Krediet's house at Wassenaar. He was dejected about the loss of his transmitter, but the doctor had some good news; He was harboring another agent—ter Laak—who had a damaged transmitter. If van der Reyden could repair it, all would be well.

Van der Reyden was a former signalman and radio operator of the Dutch Royal Navy, and a skilled mechanic. He told the doctor his story—though not all of it. After completing his naval service in 1935, he had joined the Dutch Nazi party, but became only a lukewarm supporter. Shortly before the war he enlisted in the Dutch mercantile marine and sailed to the Dutch East Indies. His Nazi sympathies were known to his shipmates, and after the invasion of his homeland he was interned in Batavia. In 1941 he was released on the understanding that he would sail as a radio operator aboard a Dutch ship to England. He went through the Patriotic School in London and eventually was asked to report to Dr. Derksema.

The chief of the unofficial Dutch intelligence service told van der Reyden he would be interned by the British for the duration, because of his Nazi past, but that this could be avoided if he agreed to serve as a secret agent. He wanted van der Reyden to take a new set of codes to another agent who had been working in Holland for some months, but whose code had been compromised after the capture of Hans Zomer. This agent, whose field name was Claas, was Aart Hendrik Alblas. Colonel de Bruyne of the MVT strongly objected to the selection of van der Reyden to carry the new code, but was overruled by Dr. Derksema and his friends of the S.I.S.

Dr. Derksema assured van der Reyden there was no great danger in this assignment. Even if the Germans captured him, they would treat him kindly because of his Nazi past. Van der Reyden agreed and was put on the Roelfzema ferry. At Dr. Krediet's house he repaired ter Laak's set, and they started to exchange signals with London. Van der Reyden also found Claas and gave him the new code.

With the capture of ter Laak and van der Reyden, SS Sturmbann-Führer

Schreieder was now in possession of a radio transmitter and crystals tuned to the London reception station, and of copies of the codes van der Reyden had brought for Claas. Sergeant Ernst May skillfully analyzed the codes, but at first Schreieder did not know what to do with them. He decided to consult Major Giskes. Van der Reyden was given the choice of being handed over to the Gestapo in Berlin or of agreeing to work for the Germans. Giskes suggested that he should send a test radio message to London.

Van der Reyden, whatever his Nazi past, was not a traitor. When he sent his first and only radio signal to London, with Giskes, Schreieder, and Sergeant May watching and waiting for a reply, no answer came. Van der Reyden had omitted from his message one of the security checks, and London had noticed the omission. The Germans accepted van der Reyden's explanation that he had only an incomplete knowledge of the code, and ter Laak's patched-up set was of little use to them thereafter.

For a time van der Reyden and ter Laak were held at the Cellenbarakken prison at Scheveningen; then they were taken to the Gestapo prison at Haaren. Eventually both were sent to German concentration camps. Van der Reyden survived and was liberated in 1945; ter Laak was put to death at the extermination camp of Mauthausen in September 1944.

After the war the disaster that had overcome the agents sent to Holland by the SOE Dutch section and the Dutch secret service in London was investigated by a Dutch Parliamentary Commission of Inquiry [6] headed by Dr. L. A. Donker, who later became Minister of Justice. The case of William van der Reyden was thoroughly investigated and the Commission stated in its report:

From W. J. van der Reyden's information, Sergeant May was in a position to increase his knowledge of the code, used by British SOE agents, by an appreciable degree. Van der Reyden revealed not only the general code, but also details relating to his particular case. Moreover, van der Reyden put May in possession of facts concerning a special security measure, the so-called test question. Furthermore, van der Reyden . . . also disclosed the new code which he was to supply to Alblas (Claas), whose transmitter the Germans had already gauged and whose messages they were recording.

Van der Reyden, however, revealed only two of his three "security checks," and also succeeded in omitting part of the code. He knew that Alblas was still free, and that he could undoubtedly inform England about the arrests. Alblas later told him in prison, where they met, that this had indeed been the case.[7]

Agent F 2087

Giskes said that among the staff of his Abwehr office—which he called the Citadel—he had "only one man on whom, in character and ability, I could

6 Subsequently referred to as Inquiry Commission.
7 Inquiry Commission, Vol. 4a.

completely rely," Captain Richard Wuhr, a sixty-year-old, red-faced and rheumatic Swab, who became his alter ego. Apart from Captain Wuhr and Sergeant Willy Kupp, whose Dutch was fluent and who acted as an interpreter, Giskes says "there was scarcely anyone in the crew who fitted into my scheme of things." It was Sergeant Kupp who helped Giskes achieve the success to which he had so long aspired.

In November 1941—some three months before the raid on Dr. Krediet's house—Kupp brought to Giskes a professional criminal, George Ridderhof, who boasted of having been a diamond smuggler, a gun-runner, and a sometime opium peddler in Singapore. He had got into trouble with the German police in Amsterdam about black-market deals. On 27 November 1941 Giskes made the following entry in his log book:

> At 1300 hours meeting with Ridderhof, American Hotel, Amsterdam. Ridderhof says he is in contact with a Dutch reserve officer who works for two English agents, operating probably in The Hague. Ridderhof needs money. Also asks for protection against *Devisen Überwachung-Stelle* (German currency control office) who held him temporarily in custody.

Ridderhof was a large, fat, bloated fellow, lame in the left leg, who spoke a mixture of Spanish, English, and Dutch when he was drunk.

Soon he was supplying ample information. Giskes gave him the code name George and the registration number Agent F 2087. His reports began to fill the steel safe for top-secret papers. But 2087's reports appeared so fantastic that Giskes concluded the man was concocting lies in order to earn his pay. On 10 December one of the reports read:

> British agent No. 2 at The Hague is looking for suitable sites for dropping of weapons and sabotage material by parachute. The timing will be arranged with London by radio and a reception committee detailed by him. A widespread organization is being planned, which will be systematically trained and armed.

How did Ridderhof obtain this data? Posing as a Resistance man, he had gained the confidence of Captain van den Berg, the leader of an important *Orde Dienst* group, one of the first to make contact with SOE. Early in November 1941 two SOE agents, Hubertus Lauwers and Thijs Taconis, were dropped by parachute at Stagerveld, near Ommen in east Holland, not far from the German frontier. Taconis had been sent to work as a liaison officer with the *Orde Dienst* and, with Lauwers as his radio operator, had accomplished excellent work during the past four months. Lauwers had a room at 123 Second Schuytstraat, a safe house at The Hague belonging to a Mr. Nakken. He manned his radio post in the home of former army Lieutenant Teller, at 678 Fahrenheit Street, while Taconis traveled in the country, visiting *Orde Dienst* commanders.

Ridderhof's information was quite accurate. He had hit upon nothing less than the initial preparations for the Plan Holland and the organization of the secret army of the interior.

But Giskes found this report so absurd that he wrote on the margin: "Go to the North Pole with your stories! There is no radio communication between Holland and England. F 2087 has three days to clear up the matter!"

Ridderhof realized that his position had become extremely precarious. He knew that if he were to lose Giskes' favor, he would be put in prison for his black-market deals. He decided to put his cards on the table and told the Germans that he had managed to infiltrate the Resistance group of Captain van den Berg. To prove this he reported a few days later that the Berg group was to send three escapees to England on a MTB which would pick them up at the second dike north of Scheveningen pier.

Giskes did not believe this either, but informed the *Sicherheitsdienst* and the naval intelligence, in case there was some truth in Ridderhof's claptrap. On the night in question three men were arrested on the spot described by Ridderhof, and they admitted to having tried to escape by a boat that was to pick them up.

Shortly afterward, Lieutenant Heinrich, in charge of the radio control service, using azimuth direction-finding appartus, reported that his D/F station had picked up a series of radio signals that left no doubt about the existence of a regular radio link between London and Holland.

The Germans had also been monitoring all broadcasts by BBC's Radio Orange. Ridderhof informed Giskes that the Berg group was receiving instructions in the form of personal messages on that radio program. Ridderhof now appeared in Giskes' eyes as fully rehabilitated, and the Abwehr chief began to pay serious attention to the reports of Agent F 2087.

At the end of January Ridderhof brought news that Captain van den Berg was expecting a drop, either of agents or of containers of arms. The drop was to be in the vicinity of Hooghalen, and was to take place at the end of February. The signal announcing the departure of the RAF aircraft from England would be given by Radio Orange in a cipher, expressed by an even, or positive, number; a postponement of the flight by an odd, or negative, number. On 27 February Radio Orange repeated the number 783 several times; the Germans rightly assumed that the operation was off. The following afternoon and evening BBC's Radio Orange repeated several times the number 962.

Giskes, believing this was the positive signal, asked the field police to watch all roads going north and south from Arnhem, Apeldoorn, Zwolle, and Meppel. But he had no intention of interfering with the Resistance men preparing the ground for the reception, because Ridderhof was to be a member of the party and make a full report of the events. Giskes ordered the field police to make no arrests, even if men were parachuted. He was anxious to follow their trail, which he hoped would lead him to the clandestine radio post. The RAF plane arrived over Hooghalen after midnight and dropped two containers. The Resistance men retrieved only one; the other was carried off by the strong wind.

Next morning Ridderhof reported that the salvaged container was filled with explosives, fuses, Colt revolvers, and ammunition. The other container had drifted toward the road from Assen to Beilen, and the men gave it up when they saw field police patrolling the road. Once again Ridderhof's information had proved genuine.

Giskes was even more interested to learn that the reception had been directed by a tall man, addressed by his comrades as "Long Thijs," whom Ridderhof believed to be an SOE instructor. More information about Long Thijs (Tamonis) came from another traitor, Johnny Droog, who had succeeded in penetrating the *Orde Dienst* and had met Taconis at Arnhem.

Giskes toyed with the idea of arresting this man. It occurred to him that if he could seize one of the secret transmitters and secure the code he could establish a link with SOE headquarters. Giskes did not know that Schreieder was thinking along the same lines, the only difference being that the Gestapo chief was, through van der Reyden, already in possession of the Bristish codes and two-thirds of the security check.

From confidential information he had received from Abwehr officers in Berlin, Giskes knew that it would be dangerous to bypass the *Sicherheitsdienst,* which was growing increasingly suspicious of Abwehr's loyalty to Nazi ideals. On the morning of 6 March he went to the Binnenhof, the headquarters of the Gestapo, for a long conference with Standarten-Führer Wolf, Schreieder's superior. Schreieder, called in, listened to Giskes' story with a sour expression. The SS officers were greatly annoyed that Giskes had kept Ridderhof's activities from them, but assumed that the Abwehr chief was now repentant and forgave him.

"All right," said Schreieder. "Tonight we will stage the raid on The Hague transmitter and during the night take in the van den Berg boys and Long Thijs at Arnhem."

Through Ridderhof the Germans knew of Captain van den Berg's hideout in Sweelinckstraat. They also had a shrewd idea, from prolonged D/F work, that the RLS transmitter with the code call "Ebenezer" was being operated in a nearby block of flats. They had been tailing seven members of the Berg group, whom Ridderhof had betrayed, and soon noted that some of them paid surreptitious visits to a flat on Fahrenheit Street. It was a fair guess that the transmitter was hidden there.

Ebenezer Calling

The day of 6 March 1942 was a frosty one in The Hague. In the evening snow began to fall, covering the city with a white blanket. People shivered in their homes; the grates were empty because the stringent fuel rationing allowed but a handful of coal weekly.

It was very cold in the Teller family's small parlor. Hubertus Lauwers sat at his transmitter in his winter coat, a blanket over his knees. As on every Friday night he was trying to tune the set to the English wavelength. The curtains were tightly drawn to shield the glow from the tubes of the transmitter. On the table lay three messages ready for dispatch.

Lauwers waited with his eyes on the clock for the "sked time" to start. A few minutes after 6 P.M. Lieutenant Teller came home. He told Lauwers that he had just seen three large cars drawing up at the corner of Oleander Lane and Fahrenheit Street.

"Do you think it's a raid? Have they found us out?" asked Teller. Lauwers went to the window and peered into the street from behind the curtain. The street was deserted.

For weeks Lauwers had been reflecting on the possibility of being spotted by the German D/F. But only one of the places available to him was practicable for operating—the flat of the Teller family, where a long aerial could be rigged. Only there had he succeeded in getting through to the English receiver. He had tried to transmit elsewhere, but he always had to return to the Teller home. He was aware that continued transmissions from the same spot must eventually attract the attention of the German radio control; still, the link with headquarters had to be kept open. Although the Germans had located the street, they were not yet certain of the exact location of the radio post, otherwise they would have broken in at once. Lauwers felt sure he and Teller could get away safely.[8]

"Let's pack up," he told Teller. "Tell your wife to throw the transmitter into the back garden and then leave the house. Be quick!"

Outside, in Oleander Lane, Giskes and Lieutenant Heinrich, with his D/F men and apparatus, had arrived on the scene first. Their meeting with Schreieder's SD men had been fixed for 5:50 P.M. Giskes alighted from the car and looked down Fahrenheit Street. He could see his interpreter, Willy Kupp, whom he had sent ahead, lurking in the dark entrance of a house.

Willy ran toward him excitedly. "I know the place," he said breathlessly. "The operator is in. I trailed him from Berg's place. Ridderhof's description fits him exactly—about thirty, blond, medium height, small, pale face, spectacles . . . He's our man, all right. He came in at about four o'clock."

"You have done the trick, Willy," Giskes said approvingly, "but we shall wait until the fellow gets on the Morse key and tries to establish communication. Then we shall strike."

They were still talking when one of Heinrich's men gave them a sign. Giskes returned to the car where the radio expert was fumbling with the knobs of his D/F apparatus.

[8] Lauwers' and Giskes' own accounts. E. H. C.

[265]

A soft piping note became audible, repeated at brief intervals.

"RLS is working," said Heinrich, deftly turning the knobs. "The operator is trying to make contact, but the receiver has not yet been tuned to the exact frequency," he explained. Suddenly the piping noise stopped.

"Well, he must have given up," said Giskes. "Perhaps he has spotted our cars. We must pounce before he gets away." He turned to Heinrich. "In two minutes at the front door . . . I am going to Willy."

There was still no sign of the SD men, and Giskes wondered for a moment whether Schreieder had hoodwinked him. Arrests were a matter for the Gestapo. Did Schreieder intend to let the Abwehr burn their fingers if anything went wrong? But as soon as Giskes turned the corner three large cars swept into Fahrenheit Street, and a number of SS men jumped out.

In the parlor Teller and his wife packed the radio set as fast as they could and Mrs. Teller lowered the box from the window to the garden on a rope, to avoid any noise. Lauwers had stuffed his papers into his pocket. While Mrs. Teller was still tidying up the flat to leave nothing incriminating behind, Lauwers told her husband to come with him.

They walked down the street, in animated conversation—just two friends going for an evening drink—their senses strained to detect whether anyone was following. They walked the length of Fahrenheit Street toward the Laan van Meerdervoort without noticing anything unusual. They turned into Cypress Street and at the corner glanced back. It seemed that their departure had passed unnoticed.

They now began walking quickly, believing that the danger was over. Perhaps, they thought hopefully, it was a false alarm.

Suddenly they were overtaken by two large cars at high speed. A third mounted the pavement and drove straight at them. A dozen men jumped out, brandishing revolvers and yelling, "German police! Hands up! You're under arrest!"

They were pushed to the wall and searched. Lauwers was bundled into one car, Teller into another. It was the last time the SOE man saw the brave young Dutch officer.

For Lauwers it was a short drive back to Teller's home. The flat was now full of Germans. Several of them were examining the radio transmitter, which they had retrieved without much trouble from the garden. Lauwers then was taken to the special Gestapo prison at Alkemadelaan in Scheveningen.

When Giskes returned to his office more good news awaited him. Another SD squad had arrested Captain van den Berg and most of the members of his group. A telephone call from the Arnhem Gestapo told him that the arrest of Long Thijs, the other SOE officer, was expected at any moment. His hideout had been found by V-man Droog, and the SS men were waiting for him to come home.

After a brief interrogation, Lauwers was left in solitary confinement for a week. Only then did Giskes begin the brainwashing. In contrast with Gestapo methods, he did it gently and cunningly. He described his conversations with his prisoner thus:

"After a few enquiries touching his health and living conditions in prison, I put to him forcefully that he alone could save himself and Thijs, who had meanwhile been arrested, from a death sentence by a German military court. I used every kind of appeal to his intelligence and emphasized how pointless it would be to throw his life away. I told him he must at least help me to produce one single argument which would enable me to avert the death sentence that would otherwise certainly be passed on both Thijs and himself. To do this he would have to transmit today at noon the three messages which he had been unable to pass on when he had been arrested by us."

Hitherto Lauwers had spoken scarcely at all. At last he began to show interest. "What, I must pass my last three signals?" he asked.

"You can't object to that, and you can do it with a good conscience into the bargain," Giskes reassured him.

As Lauwers later told the Inquiry Commission, he was startled by this proposition. The messages contained information dangerous to the Germans. Why did they want London to receive it?

Lauwers did not realize then that Giskes needed his cooperation if the German plan to penetrate the SOE radio system was to succeed. Giskes and his signal experts were, of course, aware that on the Morse key every W/T operator had his own special touch and rhythm, as individual as handwriting. They were afraid that if Lauwers' transmitter were operated by one of their own men, the British would realize it was not Lauwers' touch and discover the deception.

But Giskes did not know that the Royal Corps of Signals and FANY telegraphists, who were usually careful to identify the style of the operators in the field, had been given new instructions to disregard small deviations from the known style, because much depended on the conditions in which SOE agents worked. If an operator in the field was in a hurry or under great strain, his style might vary anyway. As long as the message included security checks and the operator replied to the test question, the signals were to be regarded as genuine.

Lauwers at first refused to comply with Giskes' offer. He did not believe that Long Thijs (Taconis) had been arrested and hoped that Taconis would be able to warn London of Lauwers' capture. But he was badly shaken when he saw Taconis and Jacob van Dijk, one of the leaders of the Berg group, pass the door of the interrogation room in handcuffs. Next he was confronted with Lieutenant Heinrich and Sergeant May, who told him they had decoded the three messages found on him. Lauwers did not believe this either. He was therefore astounded when Giskes told him with a smile:

"There is no harm in letting London know that the *Prinz Eugen* is lying at Schiedam. . . ."

Only then did Lauwers realize that the Germans really knew the code. One of the messages he had prepared for transmission on that Friday night at Teller's flat in Fahrenheit Street read:

GERMAN BATTLESHIP PRINZ EUGEN LYING UNDER REPAIR IN SCHIEDAM DOCK.

When he finally agreed to transmit messages to London under German control he did not completely reveal his security checks, and on many occasions he desperately tried to include warnings in his signals, deliberately scrambling the five or ten key numbers that preceded the coded text. Several times he included the English word "caught" in the Dutch text of the messages, thus risking his life again and again.

It is incomprehensible that all these warnings were disregarded by Baker Street. Lauwers' "errors" were simply accepted as hazards of poor or hurried transmission. For two years the chiefs of the SOE Dutch section were to accept the cleverly fabricated signals from Giskes, Schreieder, and their subordinates as genuine messages from SOE agents and Resistance leaders.

After the war SOE chiefs tried to explain the laxity in security regulations. In October 1949 the Dutch Inquiry Commission obtained statements from several SOE chiefs in London. The director of the SOE Western directorate, Brigadier Robin Brook, declared that the fact that Lauwers had not used his security check had not passed unnoticed. He said: "This fact was established and it was weighted against other arguments which testified to the conclusion that this agent was still at liberty. In view of this consideration it was decided to continue the traffic." [9]

From 12 March to November 1942 Lauwers operated his "skeds" from his "Ebenezer" transmitter in a comfortable apartment on Park Street, Scheveningen, under the control of Giskes and officers of the Radio Interception service of the Abwehr and the SD. He transmitted many fabricated messages and, what was far more damaging, received scores of signals from the chiefs of the Dutch section of SOE and the Dutch secret service in London. These announced the dispatch of new agents and arms and sabotage material, as well as instructions, referring to Allied strategy, intended for the secret army and the *Orde Dienst*.

[9] Inquiry Commission, Vol. 4a, p. 852.

Giskes tried to enroll Long Thijs into his *England Spiel,* too, but Taconis staunchly refused. Contemptuous of his captors, he attacked one of his SS guards and beat him up. He was given the usual Gestapo treatment and kept in chains and handcuffs for many months. In November 1944 he was executed at Mauthausen concentration camp.

Although Taconis did not talk, Giskes discovered—from captured notes and from signals sent by London to Lauwers—that Taconis had suggested that Baker Street prepare a new dropping zone for SOE agents. It was to be south of Zoutkamp, near the banks of the Reitdiep Canal. This area was not convenient for the Germans; there were too many Resistance groups in the vicinity. Giskes feared that his own reception committees of Dutch traitors might be identified or captured by genuine Resistance men.

He ordered Lauwers to suggest to Baker Street another DZ, in the moorlands north of Steenwijk. But this site did not suit Baker Street, and on 25 March they told Lauwers to prepare to receive an agent, code-named Abor, within forty-eight hours at a DZ near Assen. The signal read:

PREPARE DZ KEEP HELPERS READY TO RECEIVE BODY AND SEVERAL CONTAINERS STOP PLACE LIGHTS IN THE FORM OF A TRIANGLE STOP WHITE TOP LIGHT AND GREEN END LIGHTS END

Blond Rita

Two days later Abor—Lieutenant Arnold Baatsen—was dropped by parachute to the ground selected by Giskes. He was a photographer by trade, a gifted amateur actor and singer, and had been nicknamed Blond Rita by his comrades in England because of his mane of golden hair.

On the ground a posse of the fake Resistance men—led by V-men Ridderhof, Leo Poos, and Martin Slagter—shined flashlights for the pilot, who could not at first pinpoint the zone. Four or five times the RAF aircraft flew over the ground, circling for twenty minutes, until Abor dropped, followed by six containers stuffed with revolvers, Sten guns, ammunition, and explosives.

Schreieder and Giskes, sitting in a car parked on a nearby road, watched with growing excitement the approach of the RAF plane, saw the man jump from the aircraft, and the containers float to the ground. The three traitors went through all the motions, shook hands with Baatsen and helped him bury his parachute. Then, after taking away his revolver—under the pretext that it would be dangerous for him should a German patrol stop them—they led him to the Germans' car. Ridderhof stuck his revolver into the man's back while the others put handcuffs on him. Baatsen did not understand the situation at first, believing that his comrades were pulling his leg.

Giskes returned to his office and a signal was sent from Lauwers' trans-

[269]

mitter to London reporting Abor's safe arrival. The Germans were jubilant. Abor was the first SOE agent to fall into the trap prepared by the Ebenezer radio post.

Two days later the Germans were confronted with an urgent signal from Baker Street inquiring about two other "bodies" dropped on 10 March; no confirmation of their arrival had been received. Giskes and Schreieder knew nothing about this drop and realized they must reply convincingly if the radio link was to be preserved.

Luck solved the problem. On 3 April the German field police reported that the body of an enemy parachutist had been found near Holten. From the forged documents found on the dead man, he was identified as Henk Martens. It appeared he had fractured his skull when landing on a concrete water trough. Further investigations revealed that he had landed with another parachutist, who had disappeared.

Giskes fabricated a message to Baker Street, reporting the regrettable accident, rightly assuming that the dead man must have been one of the two missing agents. But the Germans had not found his companion. The missing man was Akkie, Lieutenant Leonard Andringa, who made his way to Amsterdam. He was looking for someone to replace his dead radio operator so he could communicate with London. He eventually arrived at the cigar shop of F. J. Martens in Haarlem, and was put up there by the owner, who acted as a go-between and provided a safe house for many SOE agents from Britain.

There Akkie met Jeffers, Lieutenant Hendrik Jordan, and his comrade Gerard Ras, who had arrived—unknown to the Germans—on 29 March. Jordan acted for a while as Akkie's radio operator and conveyed his request to London for another "pianist," as Akkie would not be working in the same area as Jordan and Ras.

On 5 April two more SOE agents, Barend Kloos (Leek) and Hendrik Sebes (Heck) were dropped by parachute in North Holland. They reached their safe house, the home of Dr. Kees Bolle, in the garden town of Pijnacker. They were followed on 19 April by Lieutenant Hendrik Jan van Haas, who was landed from a motorboat at Castricum to join Akkie. Van Haas had already proved his mettle. In the summer of 1941 he and his friend Piet Homberg enlisted as sailors on a fishing trawler, whose skipper was permitted by the German coastal guards to fish outside the territorial waters in the North Sea. On one voyage Haas and Homberg forced the skipper at gun point to sail to England, reached Harwich, and after passing through the Patriotic School in London were both enrolled as SOE agents. They were nicknamed Boog (Bow) and Pijl (Arrow). Homberg (Boog) returned to Holland by parachute in the autumn of 1941, was betrayed soon afterward, arrested, and taken to the Cellenbarakken prison at Scheveningen. From there he escaped after a month and was still at large when his friend van Haas arrived in April 1942.

Van Haas (Pijl) had brought an S-phone and the Eureka apparatus, which made it possible to communicate from the ground with an aircraft in flight. He was the first SOE agent sent to Holland equipped with this device. To avoid damage to the apparatus from a parachute drop it was decided to dispatch him by sea.

By the end of April things were looking up for the Dutch section. In Holland they had at least ten agents—Andringa, Homberg, Jordaan, Ras, van Haas, Sebes, and Kloos—as well as Lauwers, Taconis, and Blond Rita, the last three still believed to be free. Moreover, there were several of the Derksema–British Secret Service agents, such as van der Reyden (also believed to be free), Aart Alblas, and George Dessing.

Dessing, a South African, was dropped "blind" on the night of 6 January 1942 near Ermelo. His was undoubtedly the most fantastic blind drop ever made: he landed on the roof of a hut in the middle of the Ermelo SS camp. Only after a while did he realize where he was. He folded his parachute, slid down the roof, and coolly walked through the camp to the gate, where he gave a resounding "Heil Hitler!" salute to the SS sentries. The sentries, believing he was a VIP civilian, smartly returned the salute as Dessing walked away.

London Leads the Gestapo to the Safe House

London now had a regular radio link with at least three SOE posts—including the German-controlled Ebenezer, worked by Lauwers. Although Jordaan was operating his set efficiently, Baker Street preferred to send signals and instructions to Ebenezer, thus providing the Germans with clues to the still-free agents.

The chiefs of the Dutch section particularly wanted Pijl to be in charge of future receptions, as he could operate the S-phone and guide the aircraft. In a message sent to Lauwers' Ebenezer post, London asked Taconis to get in touch with Pijl through the cigar shop at Haarlem.

Schreieder, having received the message from Giskes, sent V-man Leo Poos to Haarlem. Posing as a Resistance member, Poos ferreted out all the information he needed from the gullible tobacconist. He met Akkie and on the following day, Pijl.

In quick succession all the agents, except George Dessing, Aart Alblas, and Boog Homberg, were arrested: on 28 April 1942, Akkie and Pijl; on 1 May, Kloos and Ras, who were lured by Poos to a date at Utrecht's Terminus restaurant; and on 9 May, Jordan and Sebes at Rotterdam, where the SD also captured Jordaan's transmitter.

Giskes now opened a second communication link with London, using Jordaan's transmitter. Pijl's transmitter provided link number three.

London had been making frequent inquiries about George Dessing, whom Akkie had been asked to contact. Now Schreieder decided Dessing must be pulled in. Following a signal from London, Poos took Akkie (with SD policemen in plain clothes following at a discreet distance) to the Bodega bar at the Leidse Poort for the rendezvous. Akkie saw Dessing sitting in a corner of the bar, but gave no sign of recognition. Eventually, by frowning and shaking his head, Akkie managed to warn him off. The Nazis waited for a long time in vain. Captain Dessing calmly read his newspaper and finally walked past Akkie, who whispered, "Gestapo . . ." Dessing brushed past, murmuring, "Excuse me, *mijnheer* . . . thank you very much." He went to the lavatory and escaped through a window.

Dessing remained in Holland for several months and tried to warn London. Eventually he crossed Europe, took the Spanish escape route, was interned in Spain, and arrived on 3 September 1943 in London. Only then could he make a full report about the arrests, fifteen months earlier, of the agents in Holland. The chiefs of the Dutch section felt that Dessing's account was much too pessimistic. As incredible as it may seem, they believed that some of the radio links were still genuine; so the *England Spiel* continued for some time.

Shortly before his capture Jordaan had asked London's permission to train a Dutch Resistance member as a substitute W/T operator. After his arrest Jordaan, despite severe pressure, maintained he had not been given a security check and thus was unable to comply with Giskes' demands to disclose it. He hoped that, when forced to transmit signals on his line, Baker Street would realize that his radio post had been "burned." Then came London's instruction:

ARRANGE FOR NEW OPERATOR TO SEND TEST SIGNAL

This Giskes immediately did, employing a German telegrapher, but he could not add Jordaan's security check. Another signal from Baker Street was startling:

INSTRUCT NEW OPERATOR IN USE OF SECURITY CHECK

The signal contained the secret number combination. Jordaan could not now cling to his story, and under threats of execution he revealed his security check to the Germans.

Meanwhile, through the tobacconist Martens, Poos met Boog Homberg's brother, who told him that he and eleven Resistance fighters intended to charter a fishing boat and escape to Britain. Poos promised them help. With Schreieder's assistance, he hired a small trawler lying in the harbor of Ijmuiden. On 17 May the escapees boarded the ship, with Poos waving farewell from the jetty. While the boat slid smoothly into the sea, German motor-boats appeared from nowhere. A hail of hand grenades and machine-gun bullets hit the trawler. Homberg and his eleven comrades, many of them wounded, were taken to the Scheveningen prison, and all of them were eventually executed.

Two weeks later, on the night of 29 May, SOE agents Herman Parlevliet (Beetroot) and Antony Steen (Swede) were dropped with orders to blow up the Juliana Canal locks. Notified of the saboteurs' impending arrival via the Ebenezer radio post, the Germans were waiting for them. The agents had brought along radio transmitters and Eureka apparatus, which gave the enemy two more radio links with London, only one of which was apparently ever used.

In the meantime van der Waals was not idle. Having worked his way into the Resistance group led by Kees Dutilh, the son of a prominent Rotterdam city councilor, van der Waals delivered, on 22 May, three of Dutilh's lieutenants—Ernest de Jonge, who had been landed at Katwijk in February, Leen Pot, and Lex Althoff. Dutilh himself succeeded in evading arrest and continued working for another year. When the three prisoners were taken to the Gestapo offices at the Binnenhof, Pot made a daring escape through an unguarded back door. He later joined his friend Dutilh and they accomplished a great deal until, in the end, they fell victims to more treachery.

On 23 May one of the Dutilh group's radio operators, Felix Ort, was taken in The Hague, and on 29 May the Germans arrested the group's other operator, Evert Radema. On 30 May the Germans also took Jan Emmer, a friend of Dr. Bolle. Schreieder expressed his satisfaction by raising van der Waals' pay from 225 guilders to 1,150 guilders ($575) per month.

London learned nothing of this series of disasters. During the night of 23 June two SOE agents, Lieutenant Jan Jacob van Rietschoten (Parsnip) and radio operator Johannes Cornelius Buizer (Spinach), were dropped by parachute to the DZ near Assen, which Giskes had selected and London had approved.

Buizer was to operate a new radio post in central Holland. Met by Schreieder's reception committee on arrival, the two were taken to the prison at the theological college at Haaren. With the capture of Buizer's transmitter Giskes had added a sixth radio link with London.

On the night of 23 July Lieutenant Gerard John Hemert was parachuted with his transmitter, like his predecessors, into a reception committee provided by the Gestapo, and the Germans opened another link with Baker Street. The success of Giskes' *England Spiel* can be gauged from the fact that Hemert carried a message for Taconis—who had been in captivity for nearly five months, since 9 March—ordering him to destroy the German navy's radio station at Kootwijk, which served as the main communication center in Holland for U-boats.

The Germans had made their biggest catch a month earlier. It was to have an important influence upon some aspects of Allied strategy. British and American war leaders had been discussing Plan Roundup, which envisioned an Allied landing west and east of Le Havre, followed by a thrust across the Meuse into Belgium and Holland. Roundup bore little relation to the ultimate Overlord—the landing in Normandy. War historians have called the summer of 1942 "the time of Allied indecision."

But in view of Britain's weakness, fighting alone on the edge of Hitler's Europe, and of America's unpreparedness and her bitter struggle in the Far East, it was significant that planning for a second front in Europe took place at all in the spring of 1942. Plan Roundup was at that time closely linked with Plan Holland, which presupposed the creation of a secret army of the interior in the Netherlands.

The secret army, recruited from among former soldiers and sailors and members of the Resistance, was to be supplied with arms parachuted from Britain. Members of the *Orde Dienst* would provide the nucleus of the secret army. Holland was divided into military districts, which were commanded by former officers of the Netherlands armed forces, with SOE agents as instructors and liaison officers.

Its main task would be to cut communications between Germany, Holland, and Belgium, block the Rhine passages, and prevent German reinforcements from being brought up to the west when the Allies landed in northern France. Elaborate plans for sabotage were made, and the Allied chiefs of staff were confident that even partial paralysis would be of great assistance to the invading forces.

The British CIGS, Field Marshal Sir Alan Brook (later Lord Alanbrook), took a personal interest in Plan Holland. So important was Plan Holland that the chiefs of staff ordered SOE to concentrate on the dispatch of instructors and radio operators to the Netherlands. These orders were carried out, often to the detriment of other SOE theaters in Europe, particularly France. When the SOE French section clamored for more aircraft and material, its officers were told that supplies promised to them had to be diverted to Holland.

SOE and the British Secret Service were constantly prodded by the chiefs of staff to provide more information about the situation in the Low Countries. SOE was ordered to bring some of the leaders of *Orde Dienst* to London. In April 1942 Major Gerard Dogger, adjutant to Colonel Schimmelpenninck, the C in C of OD, arrived in London and reported that the organization of the military sectors was progressing very well and that the men of the secret army were there and ready. He was unaware that shortly after he left Holland many OD groups had been rounded up and several

Violette Szabo, GC. Captured after a gunfight; executed at Ravensbrück.

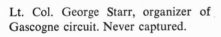

Lt. Col. George Starr, organizer of Gascogne circuit. Never captured.

Lt. Col. Robert Heslop (Xavier), organizer of circuits in Ain and Jura.

Major Roger Landes (Aristide), organizer of Bordeaux circuit. Never captured.

Noor Inayat Khan, W/T operator in Paris. Executed at Dachau.

Major Philippe de Vomécourt (Gauthier), early agent and organizer of ST. PAUL.

Staff of the Paris Gestapo and *Sicherheitsdienst*, 1943. Front row, left to right: SS Hauptsturm-Führers Fritz Bittner and Karl Döring, SS Sturmbann-Führer F. Sattler, SS Obersturmbann-Führer Karl Boemelburg, chief of the Paris SD; SS Sturmbann-Führer Hans Josef Kieffer, chief of SD IV/E at Avenue Foch; SS Hauptsturm-Führers Albert Reisser, Fritz Mohr, and Alfred Katzenmich. Second row, extreme right: SS Sonder-Führer Ernst Vogt, Kieffer's interpreter and interrogator.

Destruction of eight 150,000-volt high-tension pylons on the Paris–Hendaye line on Hitler's birthday, 20 April 1944, in anticipation of D day. (The photograph was found on the body of a German officer.)

Major Henri Frager (Paul), chief of the JEAN-MARIE network.

Captain Peter Churchill (Michel) of the south of France and St. Jorioz networks.

Odette Sansom (Lise), courier for Peter Churchill.

Dutch traitor Anton van der Waals. The German SD circulated false reports of his assassination to help van der Waals disappear and assume another identity.

SS Sturmbann-Führer Joseph Schreieder, chief of the SD IV/E counterespionage in The Hague, as a prisoner after the war.

Lt. Col. Hermann J. Giskes, chief of Abwehr III/F counter-espionage in Holland and Belgium. (Photo taken when a prisoner of the Allies.)

Professor George Louis Jambroes, bearer of Plan Holland. After his capture he was impersonated by a Gestapo agent. Executed at Mauthausen.

Theological College at Haaren, North Brabant, the special prison for SOE agents.

Lofoten raid, March 1941. A British landing craft collected many Norwegian volunteers.

Lorens Duus Hansen, who established the first radio link in Denmark and organized V-rocket intelligence.

Major Flemming Muus, SOE chief organizer in Denmark.

district commanders and their staffs captured, including Colonel Schimmel-penninck. The British chiefs of staff, working on Plan Sledgehammer (whose limited objective of large-scale raids across the Channel in the autumn of 1942 was designed to placate the Russians, who urged the open-ing of a second front), seemed satisfied with the news Major Dogger brought. Assuming all was well with the OD cadres of the secret army, but realizing that more organizing was urgently needed, they agreed with the Dutch exile government that a prominent member of the National Resistance Council in London, Dr. George Louis Jambroes, should be sent to Holland. He was to be the chief representative from London to the secret army and adviser to the leaders of the Dutch Resistance on Plan Holland. At that time there was no centralized body of Resistance leadership. The first national council, the *Raad de Verzet* (Council of Resistance), was not constituted until the spring of 1943. In view of the lack of central direction, the mission of Dr. Jambroes as the representative of the Dutch exile government, with Allied blessing, was of particular importance.

Dr. Jambroes, professor of physics at the college of Zaandam before the war, was an officer of the reserve. Before his departure he was briefed by Prime Minister Gerbrandy and Minister of War Admiral J. T. Furstner. He also conferred with members of the Dutch cabinet, the Dutch general staff, chiefs of the British intelligence, and military experts of the British chiefs of staff. He carried, in code, detailed plans and instructions for setting up sixteen military areas of the secret army.

Preceding Jambroes' dispatch, London sent a series of signals expressing anxiety over the preparations for his reception. Five different dropping zones were considered. Giskes and Schreieder were amused. They were ready to send their own reception committee to any of the grounds London cared to choose. In the end, London decided on the Apeldoorn DZ. The night of 27 June was fixed for Jambroes' drop. He was accompanied by Lieutenant Joseph Jan Bukkens, a skilled radio operator, equipped with one of the new small and selective transmitters with which SOE had begun to supply their agents. The Jambroes operation bore the code name Marrow.

The reception committee assembled by Giskes and Schreieder, who themselves went to Apeldoorn, comprised their most efficient V-men: van der Waals, Leo Poos, Slagter, Veefkind father and son, van der Vaart, Wijmenga, Leemhuis, and Vietor. The traitors were masquerading as a deputation of the Resistance to welcome the new chief organizer. Van der Waals, as their leader, was the first to shake hands with the professor and his companion, helping them out of their parachutes. A moment later they were handcuffed and taken in Schreieder's car to the Gestapo office at the Binnenhof.

There Professor Jambroes was subjected to a twenty-four-hour *Dauer-*

verhör (nonstop interrogation). In the containers dropped with Jambroes, Schreieder and Giskes found five bulky parcels of documents. After they were examined, a special courier carried the papers to Himmler's RSHA in Berlin. Plan Holland caused much ruminating among the Nazi leaders and German war lords.

Professor Jambroes and his radio operator were taken to the prison at Haaren. Bukkens' transmitter, a very special prize, was installed at Giskes' office. Soon Radio Jambroes was in full operation. With Hemert's radio, the Germans now had eight links to London.

14

The Great Impersonation

THE *England Spiel* and the capture of Dr. Jambroes destroyed Plan Holland. In the opinion of some Dutch writers, the failure to put it into practice and thus coordinate Allied and Resistance military actions was one of several reasons for the delay of the liberation of the Low Countries in 1945.

Although Giskes did not know the full extent of Plan Holland, he had learned enough from the information received by Lauwers' Ebenezer and Jordaan's Trumpet radio posts to recognize that matters of high strategy were involved. He found this opinion confirmed by a number of highly disturbing instructions over his London radio links. Some concerned the assassination of German and Dutch Nazi leaders. One such signal read:

IN OUR OPINION THE TIME HAS COME TO BEGIN ACTIVE HOSTILITIES AGAINST POLITICAL OPPONENTS IN HOLLAND STOP REPORT WHAT MEASURES YOU CONSIDER POSSIBLE FOR CARRYING OUT ATTEMPTS AGAINST LEADING MEMBERS OF THE NSB STOP WHEN YOU ARE READY WE WILL SEND YOU A FIRST LIST OF THESE INDIVIDUALS END

The list the *England Spiel* radio posts subsequently received included death sentences for Colonel Feldmeyer, commander of the SS; Zondervan, commander of the WA (*Weer Afdelingen,* the storm troopers of the Dutch Nazi party); Rost van Tonningen, president of the Netherlands Bank and an ardent Nazi since 1936; Adriaan Mussert, leader of the Dutch Nazi party; his deputy van Greelkerken; Ernst Voorhoeve, propaganda chief of the Dutch Nazi party; Woudenberg, chief of the Labor Front in Holland, and several other Nazi officials and Dutch collaborators.

After a conference, Giskes and Schreieder decided to pass on the responsibility to higher authority. Schreieder submitted a long report to Dr. Wilhelm Harster, chief of the SD in Holland, who in turn informed SS General Hans Rauter. Giskes submitted his report to the Abwehr headquarters in Berlin. Just how far Admiral Canaris—involved in intrigues against the Hitler regime—was prepared to pursue the matter can only be surmised. In any case, RSHA was determined not to let the Abwehr steal its thunder. Himmler himself, bypassing Canaris, took a hand in devising the countermeasures against the "British plot."

SS Standarten-Führer Dr. Harster was put in charge of the case. After the war, when he was imprisoned by the Allies, he discussed his role before the Dutch Commission of Inquiry.

To persuade the other side that all was in order, it was necessary to produce results. One could either signal across really important information to London, in which case it would have meant self-betrayal, or give the enemy false or useless information, in which case the game would soon have been exhausted. But a high degree of deception was possible and this was particularly so in the Jambroes Case. London sent Jambroes to organize the "Plan Holland" for the invasion. Jambroes had a *carte-blanche* for all practical purposes, and London was unable to verify the details of his organizing activities, which obviously had to be shrouded in the greatest secrecy. If, for instance, we sent a report (purporting to come from Jambroes) that the new organization in the Groningen area had 127 members, that each of these members had been supplied with a machine-pistol (Sten guns dropped in SOE containers), that arsenals and munition dumps were in such and such places, it was virtually impossible for the British to check up.[1]

At first, for the Germans, the affair was easy. That Jambroes had been captured on arrival was, of course, unknown to the British. They had to allow him time to organize his work, and had to wait patiently for his reports. Then his reports began to arrive from Harster, Giskes, and Schreieder. The radio network of the *England Spiel* had been greatly expanded. Before Jambroes' capture the Germans transmitted from five captured sets located at The Hague, Rotterdam, Amsterdam, Gouda, and Noordwijk—the cities where SOE operators were to have set up their radio posts. Giskes now added transmission points at Eindhoven, Utrecht, Hilversum, Arnhem, Driebergen, and 's Hertogenbosch. London readily accepted the explanation that some of the SOE operators had to relocate their radio posts from time to time to avoid discovery.

Driebergen had a special advantage for Giskes, as the town was the headquarters of the German Luftwaffe night fighters in Holland. The Luftwaffe commander was ordered to give every support, and German pilots flew all over Holland looking for suitable dropping grounds. By the summer of 1942 the Germans had thirty such dropping zones, several of them in the heathland of the Veluwe, others east and north of Steenwijk, near Assen, near Hoorn in the Polder, and south and east of Utrecht.

Into these dropping zones—and the arms of the Gestapo—landed the unsuspecting SOE officers and hundreds of containers with arms and supplies. The Germans carefully listed all these items, which never reached Jambroes' secret army. According to Schreieder, the Germans received 570 containers

[1] Inquiry Commission, 4a/XV, XVI (Samenvatting, p. 153).

and 150 parcels with 15,200 kilograms of explosives of every kind, 3,000 Sten guns, 5,000 small arms, 300 Bren guns, 2,000 hand grenades, 75 radio transmitters and spare parts; 100 Aldis lamps, flashlights, and signal apparatus; 3 Eureka sets, 3 S-phones, about 500,000 rounds of ammunition, 40 bicycles, bicycle tires, clothing (particularly raincoats), shoes, boots and Wellingtons, tobacco, cigarettes, canned food, coffee, and chocolate. More than 500,000 guilders (about $200,000) in Dutch currency and several thousand pounds, dollars, and French and Belgian francs were found on captured agents, or in containers dropped by parachute.[2]

German fighter planes and AA batteries kept interfering with the plans of Giskes and Schreieder. Again and again they asked the Luftwaffe to be gentle with enemy aircraft spotted at certain dates, particularly during moonlit nights. Nevertheless, according to Giskes' records, 12 four-engine British and U.S. bombers were shot down on flights to or from the dropping zones. After Jambroes' capture the Germans knew that many more SOE agents would be flown over to assist him in the Plan Holland work, and Giskes wanted them caught alive.

The Germans busily built up the fictitious Plan Holland organization, always aware that London might discover the truth through an agent still at large.

One major threat to the German scheme was the elusive Aart Alblas (Claas), the Derksema–SIS agent for whom van der Reyden had brought the new code. Alblas had already had one narrow escape. In the early autumn of 1941 he had set up a radio post at the home of the Hoogevoorst family in Paulina Street in the Hague. The German *Funkhorchdienst* soon picked up his signals. By October the SD narrowed the search to a row of houses in Paulina Street. Schreieder sent one of his men, disguised as an employee of the electricity works, to remove the main fuses at every house, while a radio detection van waited outside for the bleeps to stop.

While the "electrician" was going from house to house, a girl, carrying a suitcase, came out of one of the houses and pedaled off on her bicycle. Twenty-year-old Kok Hoogevoorst, who worked as a shop assistant at the Bijenkorf (Beehive) department store and acted as Alblas' courier, had saved Alblas and probably her family as well.

Moving his transmitter from place to place, Alblas remained for almost a year in fairly regular contact with London. Because he had been a secret service agent and not an SOE operator, Baker Street did not communicate to him the dispatch of the agents who followed in 1942, using instead the radio posts captured by the Germans. Had Alblas been informed he might have saved many lives. He sent several warnings of arrests, but working alone, he did not know the details. By the spring of 1942, after van der Reyden's arrest, the Germans knew Claas' call sign, OTB, and for months

[2] Schreieder, J., Das war das Englandspiel, Walter Stutz Verlag, Munich, 1950.

searched for him. They were able to pick up his coded signals warning London of arrests among Resistance members. Although the warnings were vague, Schreieder and Giskes became increasingly worried that Claas might learn of the capture of Jambroes and other agents and of the German take-over of their transmitters. Claas had to be silenced, but he remained elusive. Finally, through betrayal, Schreieder learned that Pam Hutting, a young nurse who worked at the Zuidwal hospital, had a boy friend who was believed to be operating a secret radio post. Pam was arrested, but Schreieder was unable to extract information from her.

Holding her in prison would have warned off her boy friend, so Schreieder took her to her home, with two Gestapo women, and ordered her to go to bed. One of the women rang up the hospital and said that her friend Pam had had a slight accident and was laid up. Schreieder hoped that Claas—if it was Claas—would ring the hospital to talk to his girl friend. He did, two days later, and was told Pam was ill. Love proved stronger than caution. Alblas went to the girl's home on 17 July and into the trap.

During his long imprisonment and brutal interrogations Alblas never gave anything away. He refused Schreieder's offer of freedom and money in ex-change for working his transmitter for the Germans. Eventually he was put to death at Mauthausen.

"Erica Arrived Safely"

The prolonged silence from Professor Jambroes eventually prompted the chiefs of the Dutch secret service in London to send a special mission to Holland, led by Ralph Christian Jongelie, a former colonial administrator in the East Indies. With him were Captain Carl Beukema-toe-Water, Cornelius Drooglever-Fortuyn, and Adrian Mooy.

Jongelie (code name Arie), the personal emissary of Prime Minister Gerbrandy, carried a message to the leaders of all political parties in Holland to form a coalition and establish a national council of resistance in alliance with *Orde Dienst*. The mission was to coordinate and unite the Resistance movement. There was enmity between the Communists and trade union lead-ers and the *Orde Dienst,* commanded mainly by right wing former regular officers. Neither did the leaders of the Social Democratic party, the conserva-tive Anti-Revolutionary party, the Catholic State party, and the right wing Calvinist party, see eye to eye, even though their rank and file followers worked amiably together in the Resistance groups.

The members of the Jongelie mission (Operation Erica) were dropped on the night of 24–25 September—after signals had announced their dispatch —and were duly received by Schreieder's SD men.

Jongelie, in particular, was subjected to long interrogations. With Giskes and Schreieder were Dr. Harster and SS Standarten-Führer Wolf. Giskes described the questioning thus:

He told us that he was supposed to send a radio message over the Jambroes or Ebenezer transmitter, informing London of the safe arrival of his Erica team. He said he must pass the message "The express left on time" by 11 A.M., or London would realize that he and his friends had fallen into German hands.

I said that we would send the message at 11 A.M. Then, as I raised my eyes quickly and looked straight at him, I noticed a gleam of triumph appearing in his. So this was treachery! [3]

The Germans decided that this confirmatory message was, in fact, a warning. They were right. The message expected in London was simply "Erica arrived safely." Any other would have alerted London. Giskes sent a very different one:

ACCIDENT OCCURED IN OPERATION STOP ARIE LANDED HEAVILY AND IS UNCONSCIOUS STOP HE IS SAFE AND IN GOOD HANDS STOP DOCTOR DIAG-NOSED SEVERE CONCUSSIONS STOP FURTHER REPORT WILL FOLLOW STOP ALL MATERIAL SAFE END

When the Dutch secret service in London inquired about Jongelie's condition two days later, the Germans replied that Arie regained consciousness for a brief period; but on 4 October they reported his death:

ARIE DIED SUDDENLY YESTERDAY STOP WE WILL BURY HIM ON THE MOOR STOP HOPE TO GIVE HIM WORTHY MEMORIAL AFTER VICTORY IS WON END

Ralph Jongelie survived the interrogations. Like many of his comrades, he was killed in the autumn of 1944 at Mauthausen.

Although Jongelie's superiors now believed he was dead, glowing reports from the German-controlled radio posts assured them that Beukema and the other two members of Erica were safe and active. After a while London asked Carl Beukema to return to England for consultations and suggested arrangements as in the case of Professor Jambroes. One of Major Bingham's proposals was that a British MTB could be sent to collect him. Another conference was held at the Gestapo office at The Hague, with Giskes' chief Colonel Hempel, Dr. Harster, and the two *England Spiel* managers attending. Giskes advised against any attempt to capture the British vessel, and it was agreed to stage another accident. They decided that Beukema's demise should be "by drowning while waiting for the pickup on the coast."

London swallowed this too, and sent a signal appointing Cornelius Drooglever-Fortuyne the political coordinator. Like the others, he was in the Gestapo prison at the theological college in Haaren.

[3] *Abwehr III-F,* p. 178.

Agents continued to drop into the waiting arms of Giskes and Schreieder. On the night of 2 October 1942 a young Dutch naval lieutenant, Aat van der Giessen, arrived. He had gone to England in 1940, and after naval service had volunteered for SOE as a saboteur. He was sent to join Jan Jacob von Rietschoten (who had been captured on his arrival in June). Van der Giessen carried 10,000 guilders (about $5,000) and new identity documents for British Secret Service agent William Niermeyer, who had arrived in the spring of 1942 and was still at large.

Van der Giessen was received by SD men as soon as he touched Dutch soil, and the money and documents were found. One of the documents bore Niermeyer's photograph. In the message announcing van der Giessen's impending arrival to the well-used Jambroes–Marrow radio post, London sent instructions directing van der Giessen to an address at Okeghem Street in Amsterdam. This was the house of Niermeyer's aunt, where he had set up his radio post.

Schreieder sent van der Waals to the address. Niermeyer was out, but he telephoned while the visitor was there. The traitor told him he "had just arrived from a long journey and had brought him a nice present."

"I shall be with you in ten minutes," replied Niermeyer, and he arrived breathlessly to greet the comrade from Britain. They left the house together, and Niermeyer was not seen alive again. Like the other captured agents he was taken to Haaren prison and put to death at Mauthausen a year later. Schreieder's men collected both his transmitter and his aunt. Giskes now had a ninth link to London, but realizing that it was an SIS link, he used it for only a few messages, afraid he might not be able to supply the information required.

On 22 October three more SOE agents were sent (to strengthen Jambroes' staff)—Peter Kamphorst, Meinart Koolstra, and W/T operator Michael Pals. This was Operation Tomato, followed two nights later by Operation Celery, with organizers Jan Hofstede and Horst Steeksma and W/T operators Max Macare and Charles Pouwels. All dropped into the arms of the Gestapo; all brought radio transmitters. Giskes got his tenth, eleventh, and twelfth links. The thirteenth radio link was provided by Operation Cucumber on 28 October, when Captain Jan Dane and "pianist" Jacob Bakker were received by the Germans.

Giskes became so bored with the receptions that he stopped going to the dropping grounds and delegated this to his deputy, Major Kiesewetter. But Schreieder never missed these pleasant occasions. "Our kitchen garden," he recorded in his diary, "is thriving marvellously." But he also complained that the constant flow of SOE agents meant a terrific amount of work for him and his men. "The business did not end with the reception and interrogation of the British agents. Once they were safely at Haaren, we had to play back their transmitters and reply to many queries and instructions from London which were pouring in. Sergeant May and Sonder-Führer Huntemann [one of Giskes' men] worked seven days a week to decode the messages; we had to compose replies and reports of imaginary sabotage actions and activities of prisoners, the signals had to be put into the SOE code . . . and all this meant hard work—particularly as we had to be careful to compose the messages in phrases which the individual captured agents were likely to use. Some were intelligent and well-educated men, others were former sailors and artisans, and would express themselves very differently from their colleagues."

By November 1942, when thirty British and Dutch agents had fallen into the hands of the Germans and there was still no end of the influx in sight, the offices of Schreieder and Giskes were full of card indexes, maps, and files containing descriptions of each captured agent, his character, education, foibles—and his imaginary progress in Holland. London must have been impressed and satisfied with this progress, because agents continued to arrive. After a pause due to bad weather, two teams were dropped at the end of November. The arrival of Lieutenant Johann de Kryuff and radio operator George Russell on the 28th gave the Germans their fourteenth radio link. The following night organizers Hermann Overes and Johan Bernard Ubbink were received by Schreieder's men.

The Golf Team

With this much traffic, Giskes and Schreieder had to face the possibility that an agent might slip through their grasp, learn that the *Orde Dienst* leaders had not met Jambroes, and radio the news to London. This would mean the end of the *England Spiel*. To minimize this danger, the Germans decided to isolate Jambroes. Messages via Ebenezer and Trumpet asked London to allow him to make his own arrangements, without following day-to-day instructions. In some messages Giskes explained that Jambroes was moving from one place to another and that he would be unable to get in touch with the radio operators. In others, some of the *Orde Dienst* leaders were described as "unsuitable in character to advance the plan," and eventually Giskes informed London that Jambroes would in future "only maintain distant contact with OD commanders."

For a while this worked out satisfactorily. But after some months London became restive. Many teams of agents had been dropped to provide assistants and instructors for Jambroes. But in spite of soothing reports London was receiving, SOE and MVT chiefs sensed that there was little coordination of the effort in the field. Moreover, they received inquiries from the chiefs of staff committee and from Major Morton, Churchill's representative on the Committee for Allied Resistance, asking for progress reports on Plan Holland.

Eventually London asked Professor Jambroes to return to London for consultation. The *England Spiel* managers tried to stall: Jambroes was too busy to come; the time was inopportune; it was too dangerous to risk a sea or air pickup in Holland. But London insisted on Jambroes' return. The SOE chiefs suggested he should use the Spanish escape route and offered to provide facilities with the help of DF section agents in Paris. The radio exchanges about Jambroes' return went on for many weeks, and the Germans were running out of ideas to explain his strange reluctance to go to London.

By Christmas 1942 London's patience seemed exhausted. The Germans received a series of signals announcing that a special team would be dispatched to Holland to arrange Jambroes' journey.

Early in 1943 this team was carefully selected by Major Blunt (Blizzard), chief of SOE Dutch section, and Colonel de Bruyne, head of the Dutch MVT. It consisted of Captain John Kist (Anton), Lieutenant Gerard van Os, and the brothers Peter and William van der Wilden, both SOE trained radio operators. The operation was given the code name Golf. This was Blunt's last major decision at the Dutch section; in March he was promoted and took over the SOE Italian section. He was succeeded by his deputy, Major Seymour Bingham, who until 1940 had worked at the British consulate in Amsterdam. Major Bingham thus became responsible for all further developments concerning the Golf team and Jambroes.

The Golf team dropped on the night of 18–19 February 1943, and all four were taken by the Germans as soon as they landed. Schreieder immediately used the two transmitters to inform London of the Golf team's safe arrival.

The Thatched Barn Laboratory at Barnet had outdone itself in providing the four SOE men with documents, concealed compasses, escape-route maps, and other equipment needed for guiding Professor Jambroes through Belgium and France to the Spanish frontier. Captain John Kist had some $25,000 in guilders, francs, and pesetas. The Germans found in the prisoners' suitcases excellently forged forms for Dutch, Belgian, and French identity cards, Dutch passports, frontier traffic passes, dies for forging German passes, swastika rubber stamps of the Wehrmacht and Gestapo, and even ink pads in the correct colors for stamping the forged documents.

Within a few days London was informed that the preparations for Jambroes' journey were going ahead slowly but smoothly. A little later Giskes signaled that it might take some weeks before Jambroes could be sent on his way.

As Giskes put it: "I was anxious to prove to London that the Golf team was seriously at work on the task assigned to them, that it was not an easy matter to carry it out, and I noted with satisfaction the growing prestige of the Golf group as we continued to send London reports of their imaginary activities." London accepted the inevitable.

At the time the Jambroes case came up, van der Waals told Schreieder that the National Committee of the Resistance was anxious to smuggle a group leader named Knoppers to England, because the Gestapo was on his trail. Having made sure that Knoppers knew nothing of Jambroes' arrest, Schreieder decided that here was a chance to impress and placate the SOE chiefs, who were growing more impatient every day. London was informed that Knoppers was coming under the auspices of the Golf team, and that his escape should be regarded as a trial run for Jambroes' journey. The sergeant was put on the Spanish route—the escape organization was already being controlled by the Abwehr and SD—and he safely reached England.

Major Bingham commended the Golf team for extricating Knoppers from danger, but said that headquarters had decided Jambroes was too important to be sent off blindly across Belgium and France. Major Bingham therefore ordered Captain Kist to go to Paris and contact members of an SOE network who would tell him of their arrangements for a Lysander pickup for Jambroes from France.

This was not what the Germans had bargained for, but they realized Bingham's order must be carried out. Obviously someone had to impersonate Captain Kist. Giskes reckoned that if he sent one of his men to Paris, the SOE officers there might accept him as the genuine leader of the Golf team. There was, however, the risk that one of the Paris agents might have met Captain Kist in England. Giskes made sure of this by sending a signal to Baker Street, asking Major Bingham whether Anton (Kist) was known to any of the Paris officers. The answer was a regretful no, and that Anton would have to identify himself by a prearranged password—which Baker Street duly supplied.

To impersonate Captain Kist it was necessary to find a man who spoke Dutch, looked Dutch, and had some knowledge of English. For this job Giskes found Sergeant Karl Boden of the Abwehr office at Driebergen, who spoke fluent Dutch. But Giskes considered Boden not too bright and decided he should be accompanied by someone who could do the talking. He selected one of his most efficient men—Sonder-Führer Richard Christmann.[4]

[4] In official documents Christmann has been variously described as a sergeant or a captain in the Wehrmacht, and as an SS and Gestapo officer. His rank, however, was Sonder-Führer (special leader). This rank was given to interpreters, cameramen, military clerks, particularly those attached to intelligence; they wore military uniform and were subject to military law but held no substantive officer's rank. (*Vocabulary of German Military Terms,* H.M.S.O., 1943.)

Christmann had come to Holland in November 1941 with orders to infiltrate the Dutch and Belgian Resistance as an *agent provocateur*. While attached to Giskes' office at Scheveningen, he had the good luck to meet a Resistance leader, one G, who had known him before the war. Christmann showed G a passport issued by the consul general of the Republic of Haiti in the name of Herman Eberle, and told him this was his alias as an agent of the French secret service of de Gaulle in London. He told the Resistance man that he was engaged on an important mission for the Free French and British intelligence.[5]

Through G, and V-man George Ridderhof, he met leaders of several Resistance groups and contacted two escape organizations. One was a group led by Dr. Maurice de Voss, operating from Paris; the other was PAT, the efficient escape organization established by Captain Ian Garrow and later led by Commander Pat O'Leary (Dr. Albert Guérisse). Harold Cole, known as Paul, a British soldier who had remained in France after Dunkirk, had helped Captain Garrow set up the first escape routes to Spain. In December 1941 Christmann persuaded Cole to work for the Germans. Christmann's infiltration into the escape organization and Cole's treachery resulted in many of PAT's members, Allied agents, escapees, and Jewish refugees being delivered to the Germans. Christmann and Cole were plying the Brussels escape route, and Christmann also infiltrated several Belgian Resistance groups.

Christmann later moved his headquarters to Amsterdam. Under the name of Henk Jandoel, he opened a shop in Cornelis Kruseman Street, trading in surgical appliances, medical dressings, trusses, and the like. It provided an excellent cover. Visits of German officials could be easily explained away by Mr. Jandoel: he was, after all, compelled to supply the German army with dressings and surgical appliances. He employed as representatives Harry Rouwendaal, Jan Solomons, Kamps, and Visser. All were Giskes' or Schreieder's V-men; all posed as Resistance men.

Christmann frequently traveled to Belgium, where his gang had penetrated several Resistance groups. Eventually Giskes ordered George Ridderhof to take up permanent residence in Brussels, and Sergeant Willy Kupp was posted to the Brussels Abwehr III-F office to supervise his work, in the absence of Christmann.

At one time the Christmann–Ridderhof gang was virtually in control of the RINUS network, a Belgian Resistance group in contact with the SOE Belgian section and the Action office of Deuxième section of the Belgian

---

[5] Kaptein, A., Also in dossier of Christmann's interrogation by U.S. Army Field Security, September 1946. *Tussen Verraders en Spionen,* De Eendracht, Pijnacker (Z.H.) 1948, pp. 104–107.

Ministry of Defense in London. Since the summer of 1941 a number of SOE and Action agents had arrived in Belgium, having been preceded by SIS agents who had established the WHITE LADY, CLEVELAND, and CLARENCE networks. Until Christmann took a hand, the Belgian networks were free of enemy infiltration, and several radio posts were in operation. In the spring of 1942, thanks to Christmann's activities, several of these groups were rounded up, including the important Antwerp network headed by a former Belgian officer, van Serveyt.

Posing as a Resistance man, Christmann even organized his own escape line. He was so highly regarded by the SOE Dutch section in London that he regularly was sent large sums of money, much of it dropped in packages to his fake reception grounds.

To prove to London how smoothly his escape line worked compared with other (legitimate) lines, Christmann on several occasions sent V-men and even Abwehr sergeants as escapees to Spain. Obviously, he also had genuine escapees (Knoppers was one) to pass along his line, and thus saved quite a few lives.

Christmann also wanted to run his own *England Spiel* over some of the Belgian transmitters. For a while he conducted a successful exchange of messages with the Belgian section and Action in London. Giskes soon stopped this, however, and further transmissions from the German-controlled groups in Belgium were directed through Giskes' well-developed radio network.

The British Decorate a Nazi

Some SOE chiefs were greatly impressed by the exploits of Richard Cholet (Christmann's alias as the Begian Resistance leader, whose code name was Arnaud), and in September 1942 he was informed that he had been recommended for a British gallantry decoration. Shortly afterward Christmann received a message from the Belgian section suggesting that he come for consultations to London and receive the award. He parried this invitation by pretending that his presence in Brussels was imperative because of the "burning" of several Resistance groups and possible dangerous repercussions to his own network.

In the spring of 1943 the chief of the SOE Dutch section consulted his colleagues of the Belgian and French sections in Baker Street about the plans for extricating Professor Jambroes and the mission of Captain Kist (Anton). When Giskes suggested in a signal to London that Anton should be accompanied to Paris by Belgian Resistance leader Arnaud to act as his French interpreter, the Belgian section confirmed that Arnaud was well known to them and could be trusted.

It was at this juncture, apparently to encourage Arnaud about his impending special mission, that he was informed the War Office had confirmed the award of a military Cross for him.[6]

The citation of this award was that Arnaud had been instrumental in arranging the escape of four SOE Action agents. In fact they were four *Feldpolizei* sergeants from Giskes' office. Near the frontier, at Ronse (Renaix), Christmann arranged for one of the escapees to be arrested by the German police, then continued the journey with the other three.

In Paris, on the morning after the three escapees had departed, Christmann arranged another raid at the hotel where they had been staying. German field police and SD men cordoned off the street, causing great commotion. An official communiqué was issued by the German police and published in Paris newspapers, announcing that three dangerous Belgian or Dutch terrorists had succeeded in evading arrest, and a reward for their recapture was offered. This story, duly conveyed by Giskes to Baker Street, greatly enhanced Arnaud's reputation in London. He had also been given credit for the escape of Knoppers and several Allied airmen whom he had previously put on the Spanish escape route.

This led to Christmann's most astonishing feat of the war—the award of a British gallantry decoration for his services to the Allied cause, surely a unique achievement for a German spy.

At the end of the war most of the members of the Christmann–Ridderhof gang met their deserts. British traitor Harold Cole, who lived in Berlin during the final months of the war, presented himself at a U.S. Army Corps headquarters posing a a liberated British intelligence officer. Declaring he knew of caches of Nazi loot, he was employed for a while by the U.S. art recovery section of OSS. He was finally traced by British security officers and shot dead when resisting arrest.

Another of Christmann's cronies, Dutch V-man Nico Johannsen, was shot dead on 16 August 1944 by a Resistance man whom he tried to arrest in a village in Friesland. The V-man Kamps was killed by machine-gun bullets from a diving Allied plane near Arnhem, during the British parachute operation in September 1944. V-man Visser died by accident; his machine pistol went off when he stumbled in drunken stupor from a car.

Christmann fared better. When the German collapse came, he left hurriedly for France, an expert of escape routes. He had made enough money to live comfortably. For a year he went into hiding in the south, using his forged French documents and posing as an ex-maquisard. On 9 May 1946 he was arrested by the police in Cannes. After several years in French prisons, Christmann was freed and deported to Germany. He moved to North Africa in 1960, and was later reported working for President Nasser of Egypt.

This, then, was Arnaud, the Belgian Resistance leader who stage-managed

[6] Kaptein, *op. cit.,* pp. 106 ff.

the impersonation of Captain Kist (Anton) in Paris. That episode is related in Chapter Seven.[7]

Jambroes "Dies"

Following the fake arrest in Paris of the bogus Captain Kist, which enabled Christmann to penetrate the PROSPER network, Schreieder and Giskes left it to the SOE men in the French capital to inform Colonel Buckmaster, and through him the SOE Dutch section, of the misfiring of the plan for Jambroes' return. They had not many days to wait before news came from Baker Street, informing the remaining members of the Golf team, Gerard von Os and the brothers van der Wilden, that their chief, Captain Kist, had been taken by the Gestapo in Paris.

London advised the remaining Golf members to be extremely careful, because Kist might have been forced by the Gestapo to talk. Giskes sent London a reassuring reply, saying that, while they deeply regretted Kist's misfortune, they were quite safe. This was true: Captain Kist and his team were safe behind bars at the Gestapo prison at Haaren.

Although the Anton mission had failed, London was still determined to retrieve Professor Jambroes from Holland. Giskes later said he received innumerable messages from Major Bingham, urging the Golf team to explore possibilities. London finally returned to the original idea of using the Spanish escape route. By then Giskes was sick to death of the whole Jambroes affair.

Once again, Giskes, Dr. Harster, and Schreieder pooled their ideas for a plan to mystify London and dispose of the Jambroes case. A signal was sent, informing Baker Street that Jambroes had left for Spain. This time Karl Boden—the Dutch-speaking Abwehr sergeant—assumed the identity of Professor Jambroes. He traveled in the company of a Dutch V-man, who posed as his Resistance bodyguard. Giskes and Schreieder hoped that Boden would be able to contact some French groups of the SOE, or at least arouse attention among French Resistance men. But by the end of June 1943, in the midst of the misfortunes that began with the destruction of PROSPER, many of the SOE officers in France had gone underground.

Boden thus had no opportunity to discover more French *réseaux,* though not for lack of trying. Captain Roger Landes (Aristide), who was in command of the SOE network in the departments of Gironde, Landes, and Basses-Pyrénées, told me that a mysterious Dutchman tried to contact some of his men. Landes, a stickler for security, discouraged his men from associating with strangers, and nothing came of Boden's efforts.

In Toulouse, Boden, as the false Jambroes, visited several *bistros* and cafés suspected by the Gestapo of being meeting places of Resistance men, and talked loudly about his wish to cross the Pyrenees and escape to Eng-

[7] See chapter 7, under "Treachery in Holland."

land. Satisfied that some local people were at least aware of his existence, Boden and the V-man set about ending it by staging a fake car accident on the road from Tarbes to Pau.

The local SIPO put in an appearance and "a gravely injured motorist" was whisked away in bandages to a German military hospital, where he cheerfully sat down to a good meal. The next day the German police announced that the man, "apparently a Dutch national suspected of illicit activities and attempting an escape to Spain," had died from injuries suffered in a car crash.

The accident was reported in the local press and reprinted in the clandestine newspaper *Libérer et Fédérer*, published by the Resistance organization in Toulouse. The story was copied by other clandestine news-sheets, and Baker Street soon received messages from several sources in France about the tragic accident that had befallen the Dutch Resistance man near Tarbes. To give an authentic touch to the story, the Germans "leaked" the information that the dead man was identified as one Jambers, leaving little doubt in London that Professor George Louis Jambroes was dead.

Giskes followed through with a signal from Ebenezer, reporting Jambroes' tragic death. The news caused consternation in London. The Dutch newspaper *Vrij Nederland*, published in London, carried a long obituary of Jambroes and extolled his work for the Resistance. Professor Jambroes, though in poor health, was very much alive in his prison cell. In 1944 he was removed to Germany and, with a group of SOE officers, executed at Mauthausen.

I5

"In Defeat—Defiance"

D U R I N G the winter of 1942–43, while using the *England Spiel* to round up SOE agents as they landed in Holland, the Germans also infiltrated and rendered totally ineffective the most important of the Dutch Resistance organizations. To understand the situation in Holland at that time, it is necessary to go back to February and March 1942.

Agent George Dessing was sent to Holland to contact leaders of the political parties who had formed a national committee. After his arrival Dessing contacted a man whose code name was Vinus.

Vinus was Levinus van Looi, former news editor of the Socialist newspaper *Het Volk,* and in 1942 chief assistant to Koos Vorrink, president of the Social Democratic Labor Party. Vorrink was one of the few prominent politicians who had avoided capture by the Gestapo. Special precautions were taken in London to arrange Dessing's meeting with van Looi and Vorrink. He was given a photo of Marijke, the young daughter of Meyer Sluijser, a friend of van Looi who had escaped to Britain. Dessing was to go to the house of the Lelie sisters in Amsterdam, show the photo, and ask for Vinus. The agent met van Looi, and through him Vorrink and other leaders of the clandestine committee. They were waiting to establish a radio link with the Dutch exile government. The SIS requested SOE to provide radio operators.

Leonard Andringa (Akkie) and Jan Molenaar (Martens) were selected for this assignment. Akkie had trained Dessing, so recognition was no problem. But Molenaar was given a copy of Marijke's photo to be used as a credential in case he should meet Dessing alone. The meeting between them was arranged by a personal message broadcast by the BBC Radio Orange program. Dessing was to go to the Leidse Poort Bodega in Amsterdam, where Akkie and Martens would wait for him on 11 March. The two agents were dropped on 9 March, but Molenaar met with a fatal accident on landing; Akkie had to go into hiding and missed the date. Eventually he was captured by the Germans.

After Akkie's arrest London sent several signals to the German-controlled radio posts urging Akkie to meet Dessing on 11 May. Akkie was collected from prison and taken to the Bodega bar, where he managed to warn Dessing.[1] But the plan to provide the Vinus group with a radio post misfired. By October Dessing discovered he was being trailed by the Gestapo; he fled to Belgium and later to Switzerland, and after a long trek through Europe eventually reached England.

On 29 November 1942 Giskes received a signal from London urging Akkie and Martens to meet Vinus, and mentioning a photograph as a credential.

That Baker Street sent this instruction seven months after Akkie's capture and nine months after Martens' death, may seem unbelievable. There are two explanations for it—apart from the inefficiency that pervaded the Dutch section. One is that the Germans worked so many fake radio stations, including Jordaan's Trumpet, which had originally provided a genuine link with Vinus, that they succeeded in causing utter confusion in London. The other is that SOE officers at the Dutch section had only a vague knowledge of the movements of agents selected by the British Secret Service, such as Dessing. The same applied to the Dutch MVT. Its chief, Colonel de Bruyne, stated after the war that he had no control whatsoever over these operations. "Between 2,000 and 4,000 signals passed between London and Holland and vice versa during the *England Spiel,* but the Dutch secret service received only paraphrased copies of no more than 200 messages." [2] The Dutch thus laid the blame for the *England Spiel* disaster on the British organizations.

The message on 29 November instructed the agent "who had the small photo" to go to an address in Amsterdam and contact Vinus. Giskes asked Schreieder whether he could make any sense of this. Schreieder could. On a few occasions photos of sweethearts or relatives (although forbidden by SOE) had been found on captured agents. Schreieder consulted his files and produced a small photo of a little girl that had been found on the body of Henk Martens in March. He decided to take a chance with it.

Schreieder gave the photo to Anton van der Waals and sent him to the address as a newly arrived SOE parachutist. Van der Waals showed the photo to the woman who opened the door—it was Mrs. van Looi—and he was warmly received. She asked him when he had arrived from England.

"Yesterday," he said. "I was dropped near Holten and I've made my way to Amsterdam in easy stages. When can I see Vinus? It's urgent."

He was told to come a little later, when a friend would take him to Vinus. When he returned he found Mrs. van Looi with a man who began to ask questions. Van der Waals answered them all without arousing suspicion. Finally the man offered to take him to Vinus. They walked through blacked-out Amsterdam for almost an hour. His guide led van der Waals through

[1] See chapter 13, under "London Leads the Gestapo to the Safe House."
[2] Netherlands State Institute for War Documentation, No. 109, p. 15.

the center of the city and back to the port area, assuming that he was unfamiliar with the city's topography and obviously trying to conceal Vinus' hideout. In the end they arrived at a café, not far from their starting point.

In a small back room a middle-aged, bald man with a haggard face rose from a chair. For a while he stared at the arrival with a quizzical look. Van der Waals introduced himself as Anton de Wilde, a native of Brabant, and said he had escaped to Britain in 1940 and had been trained in SOE Special Training Schools. Then he produced the little photo. Vinus scrutinized it carefully.

"Yes, that's the credential," he said slowly, "but I must have a double check. You see, there have been many arrests recently and I must be quite sure you're a friend. I assume you can install your transmitter and send signals to London. Or do you need help?"

"No," said agent de Wilde, he did not need any help. What was the signal he was supposed to send?

"I want Radio Orange to broadcast, tomorrow or the day after, the names with which I signed the second letter I sent to London. If your mission is genuine, your superiors will understand. If the names are mentioned in the broadcast, I shall meet you again and introduce you to the people you want to meet. Come after tomorrow in the evening to that same address."

Giskes signaled London that Vinus was a little awkward and informing London of his request. It caused a flutter at Baker Street, but with Sluijser's help the letter was found and the names broadcast on the BBC Radio Orange program and repeated four times on two successive evenings:

KOERT EN FIA—HEBT VERTROVUEN
(Kurt and Fia—trust us)

When Anton de Wilde arrived the evening following the broadcast he was warmly welcomed by Vinus, who was now convinced that he was the long-expected radio operator. The traitor was taken to a house at Haarlem and introduced to Koos Vorrink and other members of the National Committee.

Allied Top Secrets in German Hands

From then on de Wilde became a trusted helper of the Resistance leaders. Soon the Morse keys at Giskes' office were kept busy with a host of messages exchanged between the National Committee and the Dutch exile government in London. De Wilde carried the messages—all carefully edited by the Germans, who sent copies of the original texts to Berlin.

The Germans had no intention of arresting the members of the National Committee. In prison they would have been useless, and soon replaced by other men to be trailed and watched. By keeping them active, the Germans were assured of a steady flow of valuable information. De Wilde's work for the National Committee proceeded to the complete satisfaction of both the Resistance leaders and the German counterintelligence. Koos Vorrink, the big, bearded Socialist leader, trusted him implicitly, and the traitor was admitted to the inner sanctum of the committee. He could soon report to Schreieder about his meetings with prominent politicians such as the former cabinet minister and leader of the Anti-Revolutionary party, Jan Schouten; the chairman of the Democratic party, Dr. A. M. Joekes; the leader of the Catholic State party and former cabinet minister, Dr. T. J. Verschuur; the seventy-year-old former war minister J. J. C. van Dijk; and the leader of the Socialist Youth League, Klaas Toornstra. The Germans quickly had the complete list of the top committee members.

It is a matter of conjecture what knowledge Hitler and his advisers gained in the winter and spring of 1943 about Allied political and strategical plans and decisions. The Resistance leaders meanwhile were sending London reams of material: long memoranda about the political and economic situation, about German administration, military deployment, and industrial production; day-to-day reports about the organization of Resistance groups, the *Orde Dienst,* its training and armament, plans for action when the Allies invaded, and so on. Among reports that aroused excited interest at Giskes' office were descriptions of German fortifications at the Hook of Holland, radar installations at the Peel, Luftwaffe airfields; the production at the Fokker aircraft works and at the Philips factories; and other top-secret material. Of course London never received them.

This traffic held Giskes and Schreieder constantly on tenterhooks. They knew that van der Waals had little education and limited intellect; they were worried he would make a fatal mistake that could destroy the *England Spiel.* But the former house painter managed to move among the Dutch statesmen, treating them almost as equals, and retaining their trust. One day Vorrink suggested to de Wilde that he move his radio post to the home of Levinus van Looi. Vorrink and his friends felt it would speed up the transmissions.

To Giskes the move was out of the question. He could not allow the Resistance leaders to transmit and receive unedited messages to and from London. However, when Vorrink insisted, Giskes evolved an ingenious plan. A set was brought to van Looi's home, but it was tuned to Giskes' office at Driebergen, not to London. De Wilde also provided an operator, a young V-man named Wolters. From now on the reports were radioed first to Driebergen, and then censored versions were transmitted to London. Similarly, all London replies were first received at Giskes' office, then relayed to the receiver at van Looi's home. The leaders of the National Committee never discovered the deception.

The Germans were extremely clever in creating the impression in London that all was going well. When London inquired about the Jambroes mission, replies, purporting to come from the National Committee, assured London that Professor Jambroes was continuing his work. This was another reason why London was so incredibly patient for so long, why demands for Jambroes' return were delayed for many months, and why the Golf team was not dispatched until February 1943.

Between the end of November 1942 and April 1943 few SOE agents arrived. None was dropped until February, partly because of bad weather and partly because London was apparently so satisfied with the establishment of a direct radio link with the National Committee that it was thought unnecessary to dispatch more agents for a while.

During this period the Dutch secret service in London was overhauled. A new *Bureau Inlichtingen* (Intelligence Bureau) was set up by a decree of Queen Wilhelmina, dated 22 November 1942, and Major Broekman became its chief. After a few months Broekman was succeeded by Major J. M. Somer, a former general staff officer, who had spent nearly two years in the underground movement in Holland. He proved to be expert, and under his control the Dutch secret service for the first time became effective. Dr. Somer decided to isolate his department from both the SOE Dutch section and Colonel de Bruyne's MVT and to cooperate more closely with the SIS.

Assassinations

Giskes and Schreieder certainly needed a respite. Events in Holland now required all their attention. Back in May 1942, when van der Waals had infiltrated a Resistance group led by Kees Dutilh [3] and delivered several members of the group to the Gestapo, Dutilh himself had evaded arrest. Dutilh continued his underground work, and during the following nine months he organized an efficient espionage network covering many areas. He and his friends photographed German military installations and gathered information about Germany's armament industry, making several daring trips across the frontier to the Rhineland and Ruhr. They organized a courier service to Switzerland and a number of valuable microfilms reached Britain in this way.

One day when de Wilde was at the office of the National Committee, Dutilh arrived, and the two men, who had never met, were introduced. Like many young Resistance fighters, Dutilh believed that party politics had lost its meaning. Among his friends were Conservatives, Communists, Catholics, and Calvinists. One of his closest collaborators was a young neurologist, Dr. Gerrit Kastein, a convinced Marxist who had fought with the International Brigade in the Spanish Civil War.

Van der Waals, with Schreieder's approval, offered his help to Dutilh and Dr. Kastein. The latter did not, at first, trust de Wilde; but one day, perhaps to test him, Kastein asked de Wilde if he could get him a revolver. Schreieder told him to give the doctor a gun; it would show the doctor that de Wilde

[3] See chapter 13, under "London Leads the Gestapo to the Safe House."

could be trusted. It was a 7.65 mm. Luger, the kind used by SS men of the *Sicherheitsdienst*.

On the evening of 5 February 1943 a man rang the bell at a house in Van Neck-Straat in The Hague. This was the home of General Seyffardt, one of the few Dutch officers who had gone over to the Nazis. Now he was the commandant of the so-called Netherlands Legion against Communism. Usually his house was guarded, but on this bitter-cold evening the guards must have nipped to a bar for a glass of gin. A maid opened the door and the visitor asked to see the general. When Seyffardt entered the hall the man fired, and the general fell to the floor, dead.

The Gestapo began a hunt for the assassin. Two nights later a stranger came to the house of former Conservative politician Reydon, who had joined the Dutch Nazi party and was in charge of the department of propaganda. The visitor wore the party badge on his lapel, and was admitted. In the salon he fired two shots at Reydon and his wife, killing the woman outright and fatally injuring her husband. Once again the assassin disappeared without leaving a clue.

Van der Waals was sure the assassin was the doctor to whom he had given the Luger, but he did not know his real name or his hideout. The traitor was now afraid to keep a date with the doctor, which had been arranged for 19 February at Delft. However, he was placated by Schreieder, who increased his pay to £100 a week and promised a special bonus if the assassin were caught. Anton went to Delft, but arrived too late. A local V-man had informed the Delft Gestapo chief, Munt, that some Communists were to hold a meeting that evening at the Café Kroon. The café was raided and three men arrested. One of them was Dr. Kastein. Led away in handcuffs, he still managed to draw a gun hidden between his legs. But before he could fire he was nearly beaten to death by the SD men. The gun was the 7.56 Luger that van der Waals had given him. At Gestapo headquarters the doctor, in spite of injuries, fought like a madman, suddenly ran to a window, smashed the glass with his manacled hands, jumped to the street, and fell to his death. Dr. Kastein took his secret with him, but there is little doubt that it was he who had killed the two Dutch Nazis.

While Schreieder was still preoccupied with the two assassinations, which coincided with increased sabotage activities by Communist and *Knockploegen* groups, Giskes told him of the dispatch of another agent, Felix, announced in a signal from London. The reception was arranged for 13 February, and Schreieder went to watch. After six containers flumped on the ground, he saw the agent descending. Felix had a rough landing when a gust of wind drove the parachute across the field. SD men who hurried to the spot were astonished to find that the parachutist was a woman. They helped her to her feet and noticed that she had injured her face. When one of the

Germans tried to handcuff her, she laughed and said, "Don't make silly jokes. You think I'll be frightened because I'm a woman?" Only slowly did she realize that it was not a joke. With her manacled hands she desperately tried to put two oblates (which contained coded addresses) and the lethal "L" pill in her mouth, but her captors prevented her.

This woman of exceptional courage was Beatrix Terwindt, a former stewardess of the KLM airline. She was a British Secret Service organizer of escape routes, sent to extricate some Dutch Resistance leaders. Schreieder promised her she would not be sent to a concentration camp if she cooperated. But Beatrix Terwindt told him nothing. Schreieder, however, was lenient. The young woman was imprisoned at Haaren, survived, and was one of the very few agents to testify after the war before the Dutch Commission of Inquiry.[4]

Two days after Miss Terwindt's arrival, SOE agents Klaas Bor, Cornelius van Hulsteyn, and Cornelius Braggaar jumped into the arms of an SD reception committee and Giskes got his fifteenth radio transmitter tuned to Baker Street. This operation bore the code Netball. On 18–19 February it was followed by the Golf team: Gerard van Os, the brothers William and Peter van der Wilden, and Captain John Kist, mentioned earlier. By capturing their two transmitters Giskes obtained his sixteenth and seventeenth radio links and, as we know, later made great use of the Golf radio when staging the Jambroes impersonation. The eighteenth link with London was provided by radio operator Peter Arendse, dropped on 9 March 1943 with SOE agents Peter Dourlein and Peter Bogaart.

The Gloves Are Off

The German defeat at Stalingrad has often been described as a turning point of the war. In the Russian winter campaign some 500,000 Germans were killed, wounded, or captured, and during the short space of three months a stupendous amount of German armament was destroyed and lost. By February 1943 British victories in Africa and the threat of Allied invasion in Europe persuaded many Germans to realize that Hitler was losing the war. Defeatism was now widespread throughout the German officer corps, and particularly among Abwehr officers, who were in a better position than field officers to know the real situation. Himmler, always suspicious of Admiral Canaris and his Abwehr, had discovered the first anti-Nazi plot at its Berlin headquarters. Although Canaris was not dismissed until a year later, the Abwehr was subordinated to the Gestapo, when SS General Ernst Kaltenbrunner became Reich-Chief of Security and SS General Walter Schellen-

---

[4] Inquiry Commission (Samenvatting) pp. 156, 161–164.

berg—the Dr. Schemmel of the Venlo incident—was put in charge of counterespionage and actions against terrorists in occupied Europe.

In Holland, tougher men replaced the chiefs of Giskes and Schreieder. Colonel Reuter, whom the Nazis trusted, took over the command of the Abwehr, SS Ober-Führer Naumann, a ruthless Gestapo man, replaced Dr. Harster as chief of the *Sicherheitsdienst*. Both the newcomers considered the intellectual cat-and-mouse play, which Giskes and Schreieder had so immensely enjoyed, a waste of time. One of Nauman's first orders to Schreieder was to liquidate the National Committee.

Oppressive measures, meanwhile, reached a new peak as the Nazis brutally suppressed a series of strikes called to protest the deportation of workers to Germany. Railway traffic and telephone communications were sabotaged, and German establishments and individuals were attacked. But when the actions gained momentum, the Resistance fighters had become leaderless.

On 1 April—"Fools' Day," as Schreieder gleefully remarked—all members of the National Committee were arrested. Koos Vorrink and Vinus van Looi were lured by de Wilde (van der Waals) to a meeting at Eindhoven. Both Vorrink and van Looi fought fiercely with their Gestapo captors, but were quickly overwhelmed. One by one the members of the National Committee were rounded up in The Hague, Amsterdam, Den Helder, Utrecht, and elsewhere. By 9 P.M. that day Schreieder could report to the chief of the *Sicherheitsdienst* that the *Gross Aktion* had been successfully accomplished.

In the cells of the Scheveningen Gestapo prison were some fifty leaders of the Resistance, former government officials, and leaders of the political parties and trade unions.

The complete success of this grand action was made possible not only by van der Waals' prolonged treachery, but also by a vital catch the Germans had made a fortnight earlier. In December Koos Vorrink had asked de Wilde to send a signal to London requesting a pickup for the director of the Fokker aircraft works, van Tijen. While working under German control and posing as a willing collaborator, van Tijen had procured important information for the National Committee. He was to go to England with a collection of blueprints and microfilms revealing closely guarded secrets of German aircraft and V-rocket production and containing information about the preparations to install V-rocket ramps in Holland. The plan had to be postponed many times, but by March the National Committee insisted that van Tijen must go, and a series of signals for transmission to London were given to de Wilde. Although the messages never left Giskes' office, de Wilde brought the good news that a British seaplane would be sent to pick up van Tijen during the night of 10 March near Enkhuizen in the IJsselmeer. The Fokker works director and de Wilde traveled to Zaandam; from there, at dusk, they were to go to the coast.

At Zaandam they were joined by two men—Schreieder and V-man Johannsen—whom de Wilde introduced as his helpers. All four walked to a waiting car. The two V-men pounced on van Tijen, who, realizing he had been betrayed, tried to shoot himself. He was disarmed, tied up, and taken to Schreieder's office at the Binnenhof where he was searched. An "L" pill was found in his possession, and Schreieder put it on his desk, next to the contents of the prisoner's pockets. In van Tijen's suitcase were files of blueprints, photographs, and descriptions of the Fokker works production, reports from the National Committee, and a complete list of its members.

Schreieder was in a generous mood when he began the interrogation, well satisfied with his splendid catch. He offered van Tijen a cigar. Stretching out his hand, van Tijen instead snatched the pill, put it into his mouth, and bit through the tiny glass phial. Johansen, who was standing behind him, grabbed his head with one hand and thrust the other into van Tijen's mouth. With bleeding fingers the V-man extricated the still half-filled phial. Van Tijen had swallowed only a few drops of the poison. A Gestapo doctor, always on call during interrogations to revive manhandled prisoners, administered antitoxin. Van Tijen was brought back to life, only to be removed to the Haaren prison and later to a concentration camp. The list of members of the National Committee proved of great value for subsequent arrests.

Six more agents were sent over in April and May, providing Giskes, when all were captured on arrival, with his nineteenth radio link.

By May, after the drastic overhaul of the Dutch secret service in London, the new chief of *Bureau Inlichtingen,* Dr. J. M. Somer, decided to stop further dispatch of Dutch agents in cooperation with SOE. Reports of the capture of the members of the National Committee and of mass arrests among Resistance members, which began to reach London through Switzerland, created great uneasiness, although the SOE Dutch section still maintained regular radio contact with the German-controlled radio posts and continued dropping supplies until the late summer of 1943.

Wim and Rinus

Among the signals from the SOE Dutch section received by Giskes at the end of March 1943 was an instruction to Gerard van Os (one of the Golf team members) to go to a house in Bergen op Zoom. A password was provided, and Anton van der Waals was sent to the address, where he found one of the leaders of the SERVICE WIM organization, Juten.

London had once again put the Germans onto the trail of a network that had thus far escaped detection. Cooperating with SERVICE WIM was the Belgian RINUS network, established in 1942 by a twenty-three-year-old student, Gaston van der Meersche, who had escaped from Ghent to Britain and was sent back by the British Secret Service. He proved a most efficient agent, spreading the RINUS network across Belgium, northern France, and southern Holland; during 1942 he sent many important reports to London, where "they were gathering dust on the shelves of the Belgian intelligence office in London until, about one year later, they were at last discovered by the Dutch." [5]

Both WIM and RINUS had managed to smuggle out important information and microfilms to Sweden. There was a certain amount of coastal traffic between the port of Delfzijl and Swedish ports. Strictly controlled by the Germans, it served mainly to carry cargoes of Dutch chemicals to Sweden in exchange for Swedish ore, ball bearings, and timber, which the Germans needed. A Delfzijl physician, Dr. A. L. Oosterhuis, was instrumental in organizing a regular channel of communications between Dutch Resistance leaders and the Dutch consul general in Stockholm, Adriaan de Jong, while Captain Roossien, the skipper of the *Hollandia*, and sailors of other cargo ships acted as couriers. The material smuggled out of Holland was handed over to the SOE office in Stockholm [6] and sent by air to Britain.

The WIM and RINUS networks were destroyed in July 1943. In another grand action, Giskes and Schreieder rounded up more than eighty members of these organizations in Holland and Belgium, including the leaders: Juten, Schortinghuis, van Tuyl, Lam, Stienstra, Vermeulen. Gaston van der Meerssche was caught in Paris, trying to escape to Spain. On 23 June 1944 forty-eight of the prisoners were sentenced to death at a special court-martial at Haaren.

The contact between the SOE Dutch and Belgian sections and Giskes' radio posts continued even after the destruction of these two networks. Giskes sent George Ridderhof to Brussels, where he established a fake Belgian Resistance network, working its own radio post. At the end of July London signaled a Giskes radio post that because of the series of disasters in Holland, agents would in future be dropped only in Belgium. Their code names would be taken from Roman mythology and history, the first two being Apollo and Brutus. In quick succession four were dropped "blind" near Mechelen in Belgium: Captain G. Zembsch-Schreve, A. J. Cnoops, J. D. van Schelle, and Hans Gruen. The latter, who was Brutus, was lured by Ridderhof to a lending library at Doorn and arrested, but the Germans were not so lucky with the other agents. Indeed, the tables had at last begun to turn.

The Escape of Dourlein and Ubbink

Haaren is a small town in the province of North Brabant. Before the war it

[5] Dr. Louis de Jong, *op. cit.*, p. 10.
[6] See chapter 16, under "The Stockholm Office."

was best known for its theological college. The Gestapo converted this religious institution to a prison for special prisoners and *Todeskandidaten* (prisoners to be executed without a trial). The four-story building stands in a large park. Some thirty rooms were converted into cells; windows were heavily barred and doors reinforced with double locks. To the existing high walls were added two fences of barbed and electrified wire. SS men patrolled the park round the clock, and by night searchlights from several guard towers played upon the building and its approaches. Corridors and staircases were guarded by armed SS sentries. It was a most unlikely place from which to escape.

Schreieder never referred to the college as a prison; he called it a detention house, and took some pains to make the prisoners comfortable. Prisoners slept in beds, three or four to a cell; food was fairly plentiful and the men were given a weekly tobacco ration. The idea behind this unusually lenient treatment was that some of the prisoners might yet be persuaded to work for the Gestapo as V-men.

Sergeant Ernst May often visited the inmates. He never maltreated them; indeed he was polite and friendly. "You can have all the cigarettes you want, if you answer my questions sensibly," he would say. "You didn't expect such fair treatment from the Gestapo? Well, you see we are not monsters; we just do our duty."

May was extremely well informed about the organization of SOE, and told stories about Major Blunt and Major Bingham, the Patriotic School in London, and even funny tales about the young women who served as telegraphists and cipher clerks. He must have gained his knowledge from some of the more talkative prisoners.

Peter Dourlein and Peter Bogaart (SOE agents who had been captured on their arrival on 9 March 1943) shared a cell with SOE agent Klaas Bor (caught on 15 February—also on arrival). Peter van der Wilden and Captain John Kist (of the Golf team) were on one side, and agents Johan Ubbink and Hermann Overes (dropped together—and caught—on 29 November 1942) on the other. Soon they were all talking to each other, by knocking on the walls in Morse code. Their conversation centered on one subject only: escape. But they realized that it was an idle hope. Only Dourlein insisted that it could and should be attempted.

From his very first day at Haaren his mind was bent on escape. Of his coprisoners only Johan Ubbink, a young sailor like Dourlein, agreed to join him. They chose Sunday, 29 August, the 45th anniversary of Queen Wilhelmina's accession to the throne. On Sundays there were fewer guards at the prison. At 6 P.M. two SS men unlocked the door, pushed in a tray with the supper, and continued with the trolley along the corridor. For a fortnight, with fork and spoon, Dourlein and Ubbink had each loosened the bars of the little fan-windows above their doors. Now each one pushed apart two bars, but the space was no wider than ten inches. Both men were of slight build and they managed, with help from their comrades, to get through. In the corridor in front of their cells, they met face to face for the first time and shook hands in silence. Around the corner they heard the clatter of the supper trolley; the SS men might be returning at any moment. They dashed to one of the lavatories and spent several hours inside. Once an SS man tried the handle, but noting it was occupied, went away with a muttered curse. How they accomplished their fantastic escape, Dourlein vividly describes in his book.[7]

Ubbink had been given a safe address in Tilburg by Captain Kist, and the two agents walked all night to reach the town. The address turned out to be a chemist's shop; it was closed when they arrived there at 7 A.M. They walked to a Catholic church. Although they were both Protestants, they knew that priests often helped the Resistance. The priest put them in touch with Police Inspector van Bilsen, a local Resistance leader, who took them to his house, fed them, gave them two bicycles, and told them to go to a farm at Moergestel. There the farmer hid them for two weeks.

The escape roused the Germans to frenzy. An intensive manhunt got under way. Roadblocks were set up and SS search parties with dogs were sent out around Tilburg and as far as 's Hertogenbosh. Giskes recalls: "Everybody at the Abwehr and Gestapo offices was in great agitation. It was clear to me that the bottom had been knocked out of the whole *England Spiel*. Even if the fugitives did not succeed in reaching Switzerland or Spain, they would report their experiences to some Resistance men and the report would somehow cross the Channel. My anxiety was only equalled by my admiration for the audacity of these two determined men."

Schreieder wavered between fear and hope that the two escapees might be recaptured. He had always assured his superiors that escape from the college was impossible. He dreaded that the two men would tell how it could be done. The breakout led to a sharp conflict between Himmler and Canaris. The Nazi boss accused the Abwehr of interfering with security arrangements, and gave orders that all matters concerning SOE agents should become the sole responsibility of the Gestapo. The *England Spiel* radio posts, hitherto run by Giskes' Abwehr office, were put under the control of the Gestapo's *Funküberwachung* (radio surveillance), headed by SS Sturmbann-Führer Kienhardt.

Having failed to track down the two escapees, the Gestapo offered a reward for their capture, in the hope they would be reported by local people if described as fugitive criminals. All over southern Holland posters were distributed:

[7] *Inside North Pole*, Kimber, London, 1953.

REWARD 500 GUILDERS
WANTED
by the Criminal Investigation Department for
ROBBERY WITH VIOLENCE
two men
JOHAN BERNARD UBBINK
born 22nd May 1921 at Doesberg
last domiciled at Arnhem, former officer
in the Mercantile Marine
and
PIETER DOURLEIN
born 2nd February 1918 at Veere
last domiciled at Amsterdam, bricklayer

Their real last domicile at the Haaren prison was carefully omitted. Although some of the people they met during their ensuing wanderings in Holland might have suspected them as the wanted criminals, no one came forward; and after changing their hideouts many times, they reached Switzerland by the middle of November 1943. At Berne they made a detailed report to the Dutch military attaché, Major General van Tricht, who immediately conveyed it by radio to London. The *England Spiel,* it appeared, was unmasked at last.

Giskes and Schreieder, however, were prepared for such an emergency. They sent an urgent signal over two of their radio links to the SOE Dutch section:

DOURLEIN (CODE DAVIDS) AND UBBINK (ULDENHOUT) RECENTLY CAP-
TURED BY GESTAPO STOP TURNED ROUND AND WORKING FOR GERMANS
STOP THEY ARE SENT TO ENGLAND PRETENDING TO HAVE ESCAPED
FROM HAAREN STOP GERMANS TRYING TO CAUSE CONFUSION END

When the two escapees reached Spain, by way of France, they were received with suspicion by Dutch diplomats in Madrid, who had been notified by London of the warning. They were taken to Gibraltar and arrived at an RAF airfield near Bristol on 1 February 1944. Their journey from Haaren took five months. Although by then the British and Dutch secret service authorities suspected the truth about the *England Spiel,* Dourlein and Ubbink were not fully trusted and were kept for many months at Brixton prison. It was not until the Dutch Inquiry Commission investigated the whole fantastic story of the German deception that they were completely cleared. Belatedly, in October 1950, Dourlein and Ubbink were awarded the Knight Cross of the Military Willems Order, one of the highest Dutch decorations for gallantry.

[303]

On 23 November 1943 three other prisoners, Jan Jacob van Rietschoten, Aat van der Giessen, and Anton Wegner, escaped from Haaren and subsequently managed to send warnings and reports to England. But it was not until the early spring of 1944 that a clean sweep was made in London. Major Seymour Bingham, chief of the SOE Dutch section, was succeeded by Major Dobson, who soon reorganized the section and established more cordial relations with the new chiefs of the Dutch secret service.

In the Dutch secret service in London far-reaching changes had taken place. Colonel de Bruyne's office was dissolved; Major Somer's office was entrusted with military intelligence matters, while a new organization, BBO *(Bureau voor Bijzondere Opdrachten*—bureau for special services), was set up to deal with all matters concerning the Resistance and the dispatch of agents. Its nominal head was elderly Major General J. W. Oorschot, who had been head of Dutch intelligence before the war, but the operations of BBO were controlled by two officers who had been active in the Dutch Resistance and had only recently escaped to Britain: Major Cornelius de Graaf and Major F. J. Klijzing.

After four years of disaster and frustration, after many brave men had been senselessly sacrificed and large quantities of arms destined for the Dutch secret army captured by the Germans, the cooperation between the British and Dutch in London became close and successful. But it was too late to repair the terrible mistakes of the past.

The escape of the Haaren prisoners—the three men involved in the second escape remained at large for many months—convinced Giskes that London must have discovered the truth at last. Although the exchange signals still went on over eight of the original nineteen radio links, messages from London seemed to Giskes now as fabricated and meaningless as those which he had been sending. By the end of March 1944, the two managers of the *England Spiel* decided there was no point in continuing it. Giskes composed a final signal to London which, he believed, was full of biting sarcasm:

TO MESSRS BLUNT, BINGHAM AND SUCCESSORS LTD. STOP YOU ARE TRYING TO MAKE BUSINESS IN THE NETHERLANDS WITHOUT OUR ASSISTANCE STOP WE THINK THIS RATHER UNFAIR IN VIEW OUR LONG AND SUCCESSFULL COOPERATION AS YOUR SOLE AGENT STOP BUT NEVER MIND WHENEVER YOU WILL COME TO PAY A VISIT TO THE CONTINENT YOU MAY BE ASSURED THAT YOU WILL BE RECEIVED WITH SAME CARE AND RESULT AS ALL THOSE YOU SENT US BEFORE STOP SO LONG [8]

During the winter and spring of 1944 only a few agents were dropped into

[8] This is the original version (occasionally misquoted in other publications) published by the Inquiry Commission (Vol. 4a, p. 878).

Holland; most of the dispatches were directed to Belgium, where the Resistance was not so badly disrupted by German infiltration. Several of the agents succeeded in setting up radio posts, which for several months escaped German detection. Among them were the Heintje transmitters, set up by SOE agent Peter Gerbrands, who had arrived in the spring of 1943, and the Barbara radio post of Captain Tonnet, working from Escharen.

The Gestapo offered a high reward for the recapture of van Rietschoten, van der Giessen, and Wegner, but all efforts of Schreieder's V-men to find their trail were fruitless. Wegner left Holland for Belgium; the other two escapees went to Rotterdam, where they joined an OD group. Later, a local Resistance leader put them in touch with one of the Heintje transmitters. Signals were sent to London informing the SOE Dutch section of their escape and suggesting a pickup be arranged for them. But Major Dobson was not convinced that the two men were genuine. After the experience of the *England Spiel* he was careful not to fall into another German trap. Several signals were exchanged and a somewhat vague arrangement was made by which the two men were to go to the Walcheren coast and wait for a British MTB, whose dispatch was to be announced by a BBC message.

The Dutch Resistance historian A. Kaptein, who investigated the Rietschoten–Giessen case says "London had been informed, but no effective measures were taken by either the Dutch secret service or the SOE to arrange a pickup and bring back the two men, who could have given vital information."

Exterminations

At that time Schreieder was trying to ferret out the secrets of the Heintje radio posts. The Germans were well aware of their existence, because the Funkpeildienst had picked up their signals, but they were unable to locate them. On a farm at Malden, shortly before Christmas, a German patrol found a few containers that had been dropped from an RAF aircraft and hidden by the farmer. This discovery resulted in arrests of several Resistance members and put the Gestapo on the trail of Jaap Webster, a member of the Barbara group. His capture led to the arrest of Captain Tonnet, and by February 1944, the agents Grisnigt and Letteboer were nabbed. These arrests nullified all four Heintje radio posts. Van Rietschoten and van der Giessen had lost their radio contact with London.

A Resistance member, Jan Nauta, advised them to take the Spanish escape route. He told them that he knew a *passeur,* Christian Lindemans, who had helped many hundreds of escapees. What Nauta did not know was that Lindemans had turned traitor and was working for Giskes. Lindemans met the two men, promised to help them, and then reported to Giskes that he had found the two escaped prisoners.

[305]

Giskes gleefully informed Schreieder that he had traced the two fugitives for whom the Gestapo had been hunting for months. Lindemans now set a trap, telling them to go to Bergen op Zoom where he would arrange their journey to England. There, on 2 May 1944—five months after their escape—Lindemans led them into the arms of an SS squad. They desperately fought their captors, were wounded, and taken back to Haaren.

After the capture of van Rietschoten and van der Giessen, the Germans were still looking for Anton Wegner. He had gone from Maastricht to Belgium, where he was trying to find a *passeur* to put him on the Spanish escape route. On 6 or 7 June Lindemans traced him, with several other would-be Belgian escapees, to Liège, and they were all arrested. Wegner was later sent to Germany and executed in a concentration camp.

At Haaren van Rietschoten and van der Giessen were tortured, after microfilms were found on them, which, according to Giskes, "gave an almost complete picture of the German V-rocket launching sites erected for the bombardment of London." In spite of the terrible torture they refused to tell from whom they had received these microfilms, which they were supposed to take to England. Dr. W. H. Nagel, a judge of the Special Tribunal at Leeuwarden, who after the war investigated German war crimes, gave the following description of the execution of Jan Jacob van Rietschoten and Aat van der Giessen: [9]

On 9 June 1944, three days after the Allied landing in Normandy, a conference was held at the Binnenhof in The Hague at which SS Obersturmbann-Führer Deppner, SS Sturmbann-Führer Schreieder, and other Gestapo officers were present. Deppner told them of SS General Rauter's order that Rietschoten and Giessen should be liquidated forthwith. Schreieder protested, saying he needed them for further interrogations. Deppner angrily interrupted and said that the "kid glove" policy had to end. He ordered the two prisoners taken to the extermination camp at Vught near 's Hertogenbosch and executed on the following day.

The two men, who had suffered serious injuries during the torture, were taken to Vught by car. They were handcuffed and manacled, though they certainly were in no condition to attempt escape. On the morning of 10 June they were murdered by SS men, by the notorious *Genickschuss* [shot in the neck] and buried at the Vught camp.

Schreieder was notified. On receiving the report he said to his assistant Ernst May: *Diese Hinrichtung is eine Schweinerei!* (This execution is a swinish business.)

A few days later Rauter ordered that all SOE prisoners kept at Assen, Haaran, and Vught be sent to Germany. Schreieder and Giskes managed to keep at Haaran three of the fifty-four prisoners—Hubert Lauwers, the man

[9] Nagel, Dr. W. H., *Verantwoording te de duitse contraspionnage in Nederland,* Amsterdam, 1949.

who started the *England Spiel,* Hendrik Jordaan, and William van der Reyden. They told SS Obersturmbann-Führer Deppner that they were still using them for the radio game. These three prisoners were later sent to a German concentration camp, where Jordaan died from exposure. Lauwers and van der Reyden survived and were liberated in 1945.

The other fifty-one prisoners were sent to the concentration camp of Rawicz in Poland, where several died from exposure. The survivors were transferred to Mauthausen in upper Austria. The story of their liquidation has been reconstructed by eyewitnesses and through investigations of the Dutch Inquiry Commission.[10]

On 5 September 1944 a transport of 47 persons arrived at Mauthausen. It consisted of Dutch and British SOE agents, 40 Dutch and 7 British. They came from Rawicz. On entering Mauthausen they were ordered to deliver their civilian clothes and possessions at the *Effektenkammer* [depot of the quartermaster], their hair was cropped and their bodies shaved, and they were bathed and disinfected. This was the usual procedure before prisoners were taken to a *Block* [hutment compound] and enrolled into an *Arbeitskommando* [labor unit]. The 47 were not, however, marched to a *Block* but to a *Bunker* [an underground concrete shelter]. There they spent the night. Next morning, 6 September, they were marched at 8 am to the building of the Kommandatur. They were paraded before the camp commandant, SS Standarten-Führer Ziereis. With the commandant were SS Hauptschar-Führer Heider and SS Oberschar-Führer Trum. Ziereis ordered that a broad strip should be shaved on each prisoner's already closely-cropped head. [This was done in order to recognize the "special prisoners" when their corpses were taken to the mortuary]. Then Hauptschar-Führer Heider registered each of them and wrote the number of each on the men's bare chests with an indelible pencil, remarking: "That's to recognize you, if you ever get the idea to try and escape. Anyway, the only place you can escape to is the ditch . . . !"

The prisoners were then marched to the Wienergraben, a quarry inside the camp, and put to work as *Steinträger Kolonne* [stone-carrier unit]. They were barefoot and clad in a shirt and trousers. In charge of the unit was SS Unterschar-Führer Gogl; the *Capo* [foreman] was the "green" [professional criminal] prisoner Joseph Pelzer. The 47 prisoners carried on their backs a crate, like a chair with very short legs, upon which large stones were loaded. The men had to carry them up the 186 steps from the bottom of the quarry to the top. SS men were placed on the steps at short distances and beat the prisoners with steel rods or kicked them when they passed them. At the top the prisoners had to carry the stones a fairly long distance and drop the load on to a heap. By 12:30 pm many of the prisoners were exhausted and had suffered injuries. Some of them collapsed.

The SS men now devised an elaborate method by which the prisoners were driven to their death. When a man collapsed, he was told to drop the large stones and collect smaller stones. To do this the prisoners had to walk to a

[10] Inquiry Commission, Vol. 4a, pp. 645 ff.

[307]

heap, where lighter stones were piled up. This heap was near a footpath that led to the gate of the camp. The prisoners had to advance towards the *Postenkette,* a line of SS sentries surrounding the entire working area. [Inmates of a concentration camp knew that it was forbidden to approach a *Postenkette* nearer than about 20 yards. The newly arrived prisoners, however, did not know this rule, any violation of which was always regarded by the SS men as "an attempt to escape."]

Whenever a prisoner overstepped the distance in order to reach the stone pile one or two of the SS sentries fired at him. In this way by 5 pm thirteen of the prisoners were killed, or died from bullet wounds, without any attendance. Several of the prisoners, seeing what was happening walked voluntarily towards the *Postenkette* and were shot dead. After 5 pm the SS men thought that their day's work was done and the surviving prisoners were not ordered to walk in the direction of the prohibited boundary. Eventually they were taken back to camp.

On the following day, 7 September, the procedure was repeated during the morning. Several prisoners were shot when ordered to walk towards the *Postenkette,* two were shot after refusing to walk, and those remaining were lined up at a stone wall of the quarry and shot by a salvo from a squad of ten SS men, ordered to fire by Unterschar-Führer Gogl.

Such was the end of the men who left Britain full of enthusiasm, determined to help free their homeland from Nazi oppression. There were many other lives lost as a result of the *England Spiel.* Dr. de Jong estimates that one in every three RAF aircraft sent to the Low Countries to drop agents and supplies was shot down on the return flight, because the Germans could correctly plot the route, having observed the planes over the dropping zones. Because of the detailed instructions and information received in the radio signals from London, the Germans were able to infiltrate many Resistance groups and the National Committee. Effective organization of the Resistance was destroyed and many hundreds of its most experienced and active members captured and executed.

Rebirth of the Resistance

"A catastrophe which assumed proportions far in excess of any failure in any of the other German-occupied countries in Western Europe." This was how the Dutch Parliamentary Commission of Inquiry described the results of the combined activities of the SOE Dutch section and the Dutch secret service in London between 1941 and 1943.

It is a harsh verdict, but the Dutch investigators, as well as German Abwehr and *Sicherheitsdienst* officers who were employed in Holland in counterespionage, have given ample evidence that it was fully justified. The Commission heard testimony from, among others, Giskes and Schreieder. (Neither man was charged with crimes after the war; van der

Waals, however, was tried as a war criminal by a Dutch court in 1948, found guilty, and executed.)

To this day some Dutch politicians, public figures, and former leaders of the Resistance maintain that the activities of the SOE Dutch section and its Dutch counterparts in London achieved nothing until the very late stage of the war, and in fact greatly weakened the Resistance between 1941 and 1943. Owing to the capture of so many leaders who walked into the mouse-traps provided by the *England Spiel,* after the capture of almost all SOE agents on their arrival, the Resistance suffered disproportionate losses.

The failure to carry out Plan Holland prolonged the fighting in Holland until Germany's surrender, and brought untold tragedy, hardship, and famine to the Dutch people.

If total reliance had been placed upon the efforts of the Dutch section of SOE and the Dutch secret service in London, there would have been no Resistance movement in Holland. The heroism of the Dutch people, how-ever, enabled them to survive the attentions of their friends in Britain and their German enemies, and to create and maintain a Resistance movement that, though temporarily weakened, became one of the most militant and courageous in Western Europe.

So dismally had the SOE Dutch section failed to discharge its tasks that it is not surprising that even many years after the end of the war some responsible Dutchmen are still convinced that all this was due to treachery within the London headquarters.

Accusations of treachery against SOE officers in London were rejected as being without foundation. The Inquiry Commission did find that grave mistakes had been made at the London headquarters "caused by lack of experience and by utter inefficiency and disregard of elementary security rules," and that these mistakes led to "catastrophic results and the loss of many lives." But the Commission completely rejected the allegations of treachery and, although repudiating a statement by the British government that the disaster had been caused by mere "errors of judgment," excluded any suggestion of treasonable activities on the part of SOE officers in charge of the Dutch section in London.[11]

Among the specific allegations that were investigated and rejected by the Commission was the charge that Major Seymour Bingham, the chief of the Dutch section of SOE, had acted as a double agent for the Germans. It was revealed in the course of this investigation, however, that a Dutch V-man, Albert Brinkman, had betrayed a number of Resistance members while posing at times as Major Bingham.

The Commission also considered charges that British and American in-telligence chiefs made a "secret pact" with the Russians, the terms of which provided that Dutch agents would be sacrificed in order to lead the Germans

[11] Inquiry Commission, Vol. 4a, pp. 902 ff.

to believe false radio messages purporting to describe plans for an invasion of Holland in 1942. Although the existence of an elaborate Soviet espionage network in Holland and Belgium was known at the highest British and American levels, there is no evidence that the heads of the SOE Dutch section were aware of it. A statement by the British Foreign Office after the war, while not mentioning directly the allegations about the "secret pact," denied in the strongest possible terms "that British authorities departed from the objectives on which they had agreed with their Dutch colleagues and, in particular, the suggestion that the lives of Dutch patriots were deliberately sacrificed *in the interest of other objectives.*"

Despite the clouds, real and imagined, which surrounded SOE operations in Holland, the Resistance not only survived but became more determined and militant as oppression increased. Deprived of arms supplies from Britain, after most of the parachuted containers were dropped to German reception committees, Resistance men armed themselves by raiding Wehrmacht arsenals and by capturing weapons from police stations. Often they carried out raids armed with dummy revolvers carved out of wood, or using clubs and knuckle-dusters. From the summer of 1943 sabotage greatly increased; and after D day, particularly from August 1944 on, the Resistance carried out large-scale railway sabotage in the Dutch–Belgian and Dutch–German frontier regions, which greatly aided the British–Canadian thrust into Holland and prevented rail transport of German reinforcements.

Not long after the arrests of the members of the National Committee, leadership was assumed by new men of a reorganized National Resistance Council, who succeeded in re-establishing radio and courier contact with SOE and the Dutch BBO in London. All Resistance groups united under the council. The *Orde Dienst, Knokploegen,* and other militant units were fused into a single organization, the Army of the Interior (*Binnenlandse Strijkrachten,* or BS), under the command of Major General H. Koot, with secret heaquarters at Amsterdam.

To many Dutchmen it seemed that within a matter of days the BS units would link up with the advancing Allied armies. On 8 September 1944 Canadian troops entered Ostend and Bruges, and British tanks crossed from Belgium into Holland. At last, the combined SOE/OSS could render the long-awaited assistance to the Dutch freedom fighters. Mass drops of arms began, with the help of the U.S. Army Air Forces. But the Allied offensive soon came to a halt, and the Germans turned a large part of the country into *Festung Holland,* successfully repulsing Allied attacks.

Nevertheless, after four years of continuous disaster, cooperation between SOE/OSS and the Dutch organizations at last achieved perfection. More than forty SOE/OSS agents and teams were parachuted into Holland within a short period. Major Somer's office offered thirteen agents to OSS, and they were all successfully parachuted into southern Holland.

[310]

On 13 September, when the U.S. First Army entered the southern tip of the province of Limburg, its intelligence officers discovered with surprise that they could talk by telephone to commanders of the Dutch forces in German-occupied Amsterdam and The Hague. This was achieved by one of the most incredible though little-known feats of the Dutch Resistance. Dr. de Jong, the director of the State Institute of War Documentation, has given details of this astonishing operation. Several months before the Allied invasion, two engineers at the central Telephone Exchange at The Hague, J. P. Posthuma and J. R. Schuilenga, assisted by former Police Officer W. E. Sanders, set up a secret telephone network covering the whole country. Using the existing automatic telephone system, they maintained connections between Resistance leaders and BS commanders in every town, and by skillfully tapping German telephone lines and teleprinter circuits were able to pick up German military orders and conversations between German commanders.

The contact between the headquarters of the Army of the Interior and the command of the U.S. First Army at Limburg was maintained for several days, until the Germans discovered it and cut all lines between the western and southern parts of the country. Even so, Dutch secret agents were able to use the telephone system of the Provincial Electricity Company in the south, which remained unknown to the Germans. A secret information center was installed at Geertruidenberg, and from there reports of German troop movements were telephoned to Eindhoven when the British Second Army entered the town on 17 September.

The telephone communications were maintained even during the battle of Arnhem, when airborne troops were dropped in a fruitless attempt to outflank the West Wall. Again, in March and April 1945, during the final Allied offensive, the secret telephone system was used by Dutch and British agents to transmit tactical intelligence reports.

The Battle of Arnhem at first roused the highest hopes, and many Resistance fighters came into the open, attacking German military establishments. This and a railway strike, ordered by SHAEF at the beginning of the Arnhem operation to hamper German transport, provoked the Germans to retaliation. At Amsterdam, Rotterdam, The Hague, and other cities, there were indiscriminate mass arrests, and many hostages were shot. The railway strike added to the already grave food shortage. Famine was aggravated by a total lack of fuel and the breakdown of public utilities. Beetroot and tulip bulbs became the mainstay of many, and furniture was burned to boil this unappetizing fare. The famine claimed 15,000 lives in the western part of the country.

In spite of hunger and cold, the Dutch Resistance persevered. Between September 1944 and April 1945 British and American aircraft carrying supplies made 600 flights over Holland, but owing to extremely bad weather, containers could be dropped in only 200 sorties. Nevertheless, some 20,000 weapons were delivered, rifles, Sten guns, pistols, bazookas, and Piats, plus several million rounds of ammunition and quantities of explosives. Teams of SOE, BBO, and OSS agents—more than one hundred men—were parachuted behind enemy lines. The Albrecht group organized the crossings of agents and couriers through the water maze of the Biesbos, east of Dordrecht, which divided the liberated territory from German-held territory. Under cover of darkness small boats plied to and fro, bringing weapons and wireless transmitters to the besieged Resistance, and carrying intelligence reports to the Allies.

At the end of March 1945, when the Canadian First Army pushed from Nijmegen toward the north, cleared Arnhem and Zutphen, and within ten days reached the Zuider Zee and liberated North Holland, the units of the Dutch Army of the Interior could at last render active assistance. The Germans, though still holding the western areas and the three largest cities, were harried incessantly by Resistance units. During the last weeks before the surrender, the Germans carried out more savage retaliation. Bridges, roads, locks, and docks were blown up, railway stock destroyed, and public buildings set afire. To crown it all, the Germans opened the dikes of the Polder and flooded large areas of the Wjeringermeer north of Amsterdam. This was their final act, aimed at the destruction of an important asset of Dutch economy, for the Wjeringermeer had been reclaimed from the sea by hard toil and at great expense. When completed in 1930 it was the largest cultivated polder in the world. Scores of villages, agricultural and industrial establishments, and wharves were devastated. This took place on 17 April. Three weeks later Germany surrendered, and Canadian troops entered Amsterdam, Rotterdam, and The Hague. The Netherlands was free.

16

Quest for Atom

THE SCANDINAVIAN peninsula, stretching from the mouth of the Baltic to the Arctic, was of enormous strategic importance to both Britain and Germany.

Long before they invaded Norway on 9 April 1940, the Germans had infiltrated Scandinavia with hundreds of secret agents. They could also rely on a small but well-organized and financed fifth column—Vidkun Quisling's *Nasjonal Samling* and his armed *Hird* storm troopers in Norway, and Clausen's Nazi formations in Denmark. On the other hand, there were British intelligence outposts in Norway in 1940. At shipping offices in Stavanger, Bergen, Ålesund, Trondheim, and Narvik, British intelligence officers were interested in landing facilities, transport and communications, and cooperation with the Norwegian general staff, if an Allied invasion should take place. They reported to the naval section of the British Secret Service.

At the end of March 1940 they were reinforced by a small group of officers of Military Intelligence R section: Captain J. Watt Torrance was sent to Narvik, Major Palmer to Trondheim, Captain Andrew Croft to Bergen, and Captain Malcolm Munthe to Stavanger. One of their tasks was to maintain radio communications with Britain. London was to send the signal "Beltor," announcing the impending arrival of Allied troops, and these men were to act as liaison officers with local Norwegian commanders at the ports of landing. These four officers of MI(R) can be regarded as the forerunners of agents of the Norwegian section of SOE. Major Palmer was taken prisoner by the Germans during the short (20 April to 7 June) and futile campaign by the British Expeditionary Force in Norway, but the three others were to play an important part in organizing Norwegian Resistance.

The west coast of Norway is 1,200 miles long, but because of its thousands of fjords, firths, and indraughts of the sea, its actual shoreline length exceeds 10,000 miles. Geographically, Norway provided seemingly little difficulty for maintaining sea communications with Britain and for landing secret

[313]

agents and material with local help. The Germans could not watch every fjord and cove. Norwegian Resistance was thus more fortunate than Resistance organizations in any other enemy-occupied country. Nevertheless, clandestine traffic was perilous because the Germans soon established a coastal watch by sea patrols, U-boats, and particularly from the air. This did not prevent hundreds of Norwegians from escaping to Britain, or in many cases returning to their homeland as secret fighters. The Shetland Bus [1] later played a vital role, carrying agents and arms from Britain.

During the Norwegian campaign raiding operations were carried out, such as Operation Knife at the end of April 1940. A group of officers under the command of Lieutenant Colonel Brian Mayfield—many of whom were, like their leader, former Finland volunteers—were to be landed from the submarine *Truant* in Sogne Fjord, establish contact with Norwegian guerrillas, and blow up the Bergen–Oslo railway line. In miniature, this was the kind of assignment SOE agents were given during the next four years. But en route to Norway the *Truant* was attacked by a U-boat, hit by two torpedoes, and limped back to Rossyth.

The next undertaking, in May, was more successful. Twelve men were put ashore to destroy telephone communications and railway lines in the area of Sognefjord and Hardangerfjord. Two of the turbines of the Alvik power station were blown up, and the expedition returned safely on 18 June to Lerwick aboard a Norwegian trawler. Other small raids followed, but until the Norwegian section of SOE began work in earnest, they were rather haphazard affairs.

The Scandinavian section was one of the first SOE established. Sir Charles Hambro became its head, with Colonel Harry N. Sporborg as his deputy. Captain P. W. T. Broughton-Leigh and Lieutenant J. L. Chaworth-Musters, RNVR, who had been attached to the British legation in Oslo, joined them, as did Commander Frank Stagg, RN, after his return from Copenhagen.

During the summer and autumn of 1940 a number of Norwegians escaped to Britain, making perilous journeys in small boats. Among the arrivals in September was Martin Linge, a well-known actor of the Oslo National Theater. As a lieutenant in the army reserve, Linge had fought the German invaders and had been wounded. In Britain, he became the leader of a group whose exploits were to become famous. Linge had been a neighbor of Lieutenant Chaworth-Musters, who owned a small farm in southern Norway. At the SOE Norwegian section office at Chiltern Court in Baker Street, these two selected the first six agents from several Norwegian volunteers.

Three of them, Odd Starheim, Konrad Lindberg, and Frithjof Pedersen, had arrived in Aberdeen in August in a 21-foot motorboat, aptly named *Viking*. The other three were Ruben Langmo (who had taken part in the raid at Alvik), Nils Nordland, and Gunnar Fougner. They were the first

[1] See chapter 17, under "The Shetland Bus."

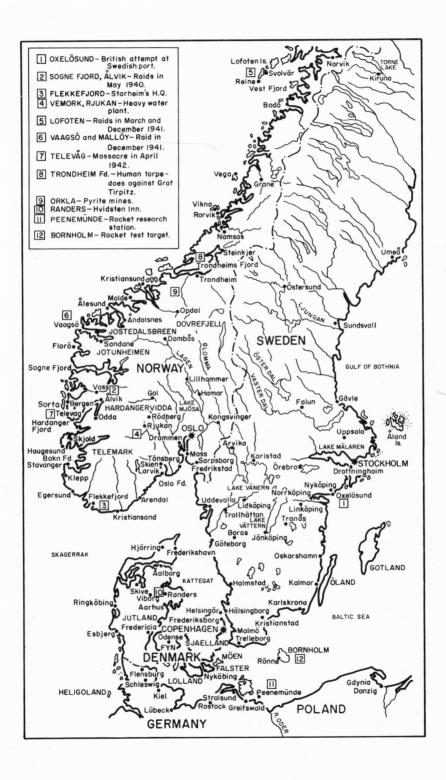

1 OXELÖSUND – British attempt at Swedish port.
2 SOGNE FJORD, ÅLVIK – Raids in May 1940.
3 FLEKKEFJORD – Starheim's H.Q.
4 VEMORK, RJUKAN – Heavy water plant.
5 LOFOTEN – Raids in March and December 1941.
6 VAAGSÖ and MALLÖY – Raid in December 1941.
7 TELEVÅG – Massacre in April 1942.
8 TRONDHEIM Fd. – Human torpedoes against Graf Tirpitz.
9 ORKLA – Pyrite mines.
10 RANDERS – Hvidsten Inn.
11 PEENEMÜNDE – Rocket research station.
12 BORNHOLM – Rocket test target.

to be trained by SOE. Later, about a hundred young Norwegians, including some who had joined Colonel Gubbins' Striking Companies and had been evacuated with the British troops, were formed into the Linge Company.

At first the Norwegian exile government in London stood aloof, and it was not until July 1941 that the Linge Company was renamed Norwegian Independent Company No. 1, as a unit of the Royal Norwegian Army in Britain, although it remained under the control of SOE.

Some of the SOE volunteers went to the STS at Fawley Court near Henley, where they trained as saboteurs. Others underwent commando training in Inverness-shire, Scotland, where the countryside resembled Norway's landscape. In November 1940 Lindberg and Pedersen, having received brief training as W/T operators, were sent to Norway to set up radio posts; but they were soon captured by the Germans and executed on 11 August 1941.

The Stockholm Office

In October 1940 Sir Charles Hambro flew to Stockholm, where he met Norwegian and Danish politicians, officers, and Resistance leaders. In Stockholm also were a few British intelligence officers, who had made their way to Sweden after the end of the Norwegian campaign in June. Among them was Malcolm Munthe, now a major, who was badly wounded fighting at Dirdalsfjord and narrowly escaped capture. He had become the British assistant military attaché in Stockholm and, helped by Captain Hugh Marks, Consul Nielsen, and Mrs. Ann Warring, had established a combined office of SOE and the British Secret Service.

This Stockholm office became a vital pivot of SOE operations. Through it communications were maintained between London and SOE and British Secret Service agents, as well as with the Resistance movements in Norway and Denmark, in Eastern Europe, and even in France and the Low Countries. Munthe's office also became the clearing house for financing Resistance movements and SOE circuits in several German-occupied countries, a planning base for sabotage operations, and a directing center for couriers and escapees in Scandinavia. It arranged regular traffic of men, arms, and ammunition across the Swedish frontier, particularly after the establishment of the Central Leadership *(Sentral-ledelsen)* of the Norwegian Resistance and *Milorg* (Military Organization). Many Norwegians and Danes found refuge in Sweden and were trained there as saboteurs, radio operators, or instructors before returning to their countries. Swedish authorities closed their eyes to these activities and often gave direct assistance.

During the winter of 1940–41 Norwegian Resistance gained momentum. Sverre Kjeldstadli, the historian of Norway's fight for freedom, said it was not until the German Reichs-Kommissar Terboven had proclaimed the deposition of King Haakon, and he had brought Vidkun Quisling to power, that the Norwegian people united in resistance against the invaders and traitors. "Improvisation, trial and error were characteristic of the first two years of the movement. The British were right in their criticism that the Norwegians were too trusting, too talkative toward friends and even strangers. They had to learn the hard lesson of security through bitter experience." [2] And he added that "the Norwegian military resistance was started by the British, who already during the campaign in the spring of 1940 had contacted Norwegian officers."

After the end of the campaign, these officers built up from small groups of former servicemen an organization called *Milorg*. Among its founders and leaders were Major Olaf Helset, Captain John Rognes, Professor Johan Holst, Colonel Ole Berg, Colonel Johan Beichman, Captain Jacob Schive. They were joined by a number of business and professional men, including Arne Krogh-Johanssen, Theo Platou, Dr. Bjoern Hansen, Dr. Carl Semb, and editor Baard Krogvik.

The Norwegian exile government considered *Milorg* a "private enterprise of the British" and for a long time refused to recognize it as a representative national movement. Its leaders were themselves not sure whether they had a right to organize a militant organization without the consent of the king and the exiled government and without a mandate from the Norwegian people.

A delicate problem arose from the fact that Norwegian officers, soldiers, and sailors, released from German POW camps under the initial German kid-glove policy, had given their word of honor not to take up arms against the invaders or to engage in subversive activities. When SOE embarked upon coastal raids and sabotage actions, using Norwegian volunteers from Britain without the foreknowledge of *Milorg,* some of *Milorg's* leaders became disenchanted. Thus protracted controversy ensued between the British and the Norwegian exile government in London, and between SOE and *Milorg*. This lasted until the summer of 1941 and delayed many plans and actions. In the meantime, many young Norwegians, unaware of, or unconcerned with, these problems, were eager to accept British help. The Munthe office in Stockholm reported that thousands of Norwegians were forming local Resistance groups, that hundreds had crossed into Sweden and, being cold-shouldered by the Norwegian legation, had turned for help to the British legation and the SOE office.

The Sinking of the Bismark

After the misfortune that had overtaken his friends, Odd Starheim insisted on being sent alone to Norway. He was taken over by a British submarine, and on New Year's Eve 1940 he stepped ashore from a rubber dinghy in

[2] Kjeldstadli, *Hjemme Styrkene,* Aschenhoug, Oslo, 1959.

a fjord on the southwest coast of Norway. He had brought along a radio transmitter, and his orders were to establish contact with a Resistance group at Kristiansand, Norway's third largest port, which the Germans were using as a naval base. There Starheim met two men who enjoyed the special trust of the Germans. One was ship chandler Viggo Axelssen, who was permitted to enter the port, to supply stores, and to help German naval guards check the outgoing and incoming fishing boats. The other was a young journalist, Johannes Seland, secretary of the National Relief Fund. Although both were regarded by the Germans as harmless and even useful, they were active members of the Resistance. Arne Mohn, a truck driver whom the Germans employed for transporting supplies, joined them. With the help of this clandestine group Starheim set up his radio post in the small port of Flekke-fjord, some sixty miles northwest of Kristiansand, at the house of a local grocer. Starheim's mission was code-named Cheese.

Outside Flekkefjord lived a farmer, Gunwald Tomstad, who before the war had been an amateur radio operator. He looked after the transmitter when Starheim traveled around the country to make more contacts; Tomstad's fiancée, Sofie Rorvig, became a courier for the group. Under the noses of the Germans a stream of reports about German naval movements, especially about the U-boat traffic, began to reach London.

At Kristiansand Axelssen was not idle either. Scanning the surrounding fjords through his binoculars one day in March 1941, he spotted four German warships, cleverly camouflaged in a narrow fjord situated in the *Sperr Zone* (the coastal area Norwegians were forbidden to enter). Axelssen sent a message to Starheim. It reached him just when a Gestapo squad, using radio direction-finding apparatus, was trying to locate the Cheese post at Flekkefjord. Starheim decided to risk transmitting the message about the warships. It reached the SOE Norwegian section in London and was passed on to Naval Intelligence, where its importance was quickly recognized. For some time the Admiralty had suspected that the German battleship *Bismarck* and the cruiser *Prinz Eugen* were in a Norwegian fjord, ready to come out and prowl the Atlantic.

Several weeks passed before Starheim reported that the German warships, accompanied by four destroyers, had left their hideout and were steaming in a northerly direction. Coastal Command reconnaisance aircraft began to search. On the evening of 23 May the enemy warships were sighted, and on the next morning they were engaged by HMS *Prince of Wales* and HMS *Hood* in the straits between Iceland and Greenland. The old dreadnought *Hood* received a hit in her magazine and blew up; only three members of her crew survived. The 1,700-mile chase of the *Bismarck* by British naval forces, determined to avenge the *Hood,* became one of the most dramatic naval actions of the war. After being attacked by aircraft from HMS *Ark Royal,* the *Bismarck* was finally destroyed west of the French Atlantic coast on 27 May by torpedoes fired from HMS *Dorsetshire,* while the badly damaged *Prinz Eugen* managed to reach the port of Brest. To the small group of men in a remote fjord goes the initial credit, although their part is rarely mentioned in history books.

By now the Germans were pretty sure that the British were being informed of the movements of their Norwegian-based warships. Mysterious signals, which German radio detectors had picked up, convinced them. Gestapo and SS squads encircled the valley of Flekkefjord; houses and farms were searched, and although the transmitter was not discovered, Starheim and his friends were now in a precarious position. As the only stranger in the area, Starheim might have attracted attention, and his friends persuaded him to go into hiding at a farm at Helle in Hardanger.

One day Sofie Rorvig came to warn him that the Germans had circulated his description as a wanted terrorist. While she was telling him this an SS patrol arrived. Starheim and Sofie left the farmhouse, their arms entwined in tender embrace—just a couple making for lovers' lane. The SS men let them pass and went on searching houses, barns, and haystacks. Starheim had to disappear. He traveled across Norway, reached Stockholm, and reported at Munthe's office. After a short respite he was flown to London. But this was not the end of Operation Cheese. Tomstad, who had joined the Quisling organization as a pseudo-collaborator—and thus remained unmolested by the Germans—was able to resume regular radio transmission to London. His group established contact with *Milorg,* and a network based on the Cheese radio post at Flekkefjord spread over a wide area of south and southwest Norway.

The Barren Mountain

Exactly a year after starting his first mission, Odd Starheim, now a captain, returned to Norway. Several SOE agents—some sent by sea, others through Sweden—had preceded him. Starheim parachuted into a snow-covered field on 31 December 1941, and was received by his friends. He had come on a highly important mission.

Back in London, experts of the Ministry of Economic Warfare and British and Norwegian scientists were conducting secret investigations. They knew that before the war *Norsk Hydro Elektrisk* (Norwegian State Hydro-electric Board) had established a plant near Vemork on the Barren Mountain north of Rjukan for the production of heavy water, deuterium oxide, a requisite for experiments dealing with atomic energy. In May 1940 information had reached London that the Germans had occupied the plant even before the conclusion of the Norwegian campaign.

The Germans ordered the *Norsk Hydro* managers to increase the output of heavy water to 3,000 pounds a year. British government experts knew why the Germans wanted heavy water so urgently: their scientists had been conducting research into the production of atomic bombs. A Norwegian exile in London, Professor Leif Tronstad, knew the Vemork plant and its capacity intimately. In October 1941 the SOE chiefs reported to the Ministry of Economic Warfare and the chiefs of staff that Reichs-Kommissar Terboven had ordered that the heavy water production at Vemork be increased to 10,000 pounds within the next twelve months.

Odd Starheim was asked to go and find out the details of what was happening on the Barren Mountain and, if possible, bring to England Norwegian engineers who were forced to work there. Starheim went first to Oslo, where he hid out at the home of a family named Rasmussen. Three days after his arrival Mrs. Rasmussen woke him up in the middle of the night.

"For God's sake, get out," she whispered. "The Gestapo are here; they've arrested my husband."

Starheim slipped into his trousers and moved to the window. But it was too late. Five armed Germans burst in and he was pushed downstairs into the parlor, where he found his host and other members of the family already handcuffed. Before the handcuffs were snapped on his wrists, Starheim asked to go to the bathroom, feigning stomach pains. After some argument he was allowed to do so, and a sentry was placed at the door, which Starheim bolted behind him. He knew there was a second door, opening into the grandmother's room. In one long leap Starheim darted through grandma's room, gesturing to her to keep quiet, and jumped from the window into the ice-covered yard. He sprained his ankle, but managed to limp into a back street and on to the main road. A truck was passing. He jumped on the running board and called to the driver: "Are you a good Norwegian?"

The driver asked who was chasing him. "The Gestapo," Starheim told him truthfully. The driver helped him into the cab and drove off without asking more questions.

The next day Starheim was at Flekkefjord, where Tomstad hid him for a while. Then Starheim went to Kristiansand, where he stayed with Axelssen. He changed his abode every few nights, never short of friends who would risk their own lives to give him refuge, food, and money. At last he reached his destination: the Barren Mountain of Hardangervidda.

The Pirates of the Galtesund

In London Starheim had been given the name of an engineer at Rjukan, Einar Skinnarland, who had worked on the construction of the heavy water plant. Skinnarland not only knew the layout of the factory and laboratories, but being a native of Hardanger, he also was well acquainted with the surrounding territory. When Skinnarland agreed to go to England, Starheim devised a bold plan.

No arrangements had been made by SOE to bring Starheim and Skinnarland back. It was left to the agent to work out his own plan and report it to London by radio. Starheim realized that a pickup was impossible by air and difficult by sea. So he decided on a truly Viking-like expedition. All he needed was a ship, preferably a fairly large one, because several of his Resistance friends wanted to go with him to Britain to be trained by SOE and to return as professional saboteurs.

Viggo Axelssen told Starheim of a 620-ton coastal steamer, the *Galtesund,* which made regular runs from Kristiansand along the southwestern coast to Stavanger and Bergen. Starheim recruited a small crew—an engineer, two stokers, several sailors—and trained them to use firearms. Some of the men boarded the *Galtesund* as passengers at her various ports of call; Starheim went aboard at Flekkefjord. When the ship was at sea, he went to the bridge, pulled out a pistol, and ordered the captain to head for Scotland. Most of the regular crew agreed to join the pirates, although some feared their families might suffer.

Starheim maintained radio silence during the journey as a precaution against pursuit by German aircraft, but he had given Tomstad a message to radio to London.

HAVE STOLEN A BOAT AND MAKING FOR SCOTLAND STOP PLEASE GIVE
AIR PROTECTION CHEESE

Because of bad weather British aircraft could not at first find the little ship, but eventually a Hudson bomber saw her Aldis lamp signals and guided her into Aberdeen. The *Galtesund* arrived on 17 March 1942.

At Chiltern Court in London, Colonel Wilson and Professor Tronstad were soon planning with Einaar Skinnarland one of the most secret operations of the war: the destruction of the *Norsk Hydro* heavy water plant at Vemork. Skinnarland volunteered to go back and undertake the preparations. After only eleven days of training, which included parachute jumping, the engineer was dropped on 29 March from a Halifax aircraft into the icy waste of Hardangervidda. Less than three weeks after his disappearance he was back at work, and when he explained his absence was due to illness, the German managers suspected nothing. Colonel Wilson recalls: "It was the quickest turn round and the quickest and most important bit of training that the Norwegian section ever achieved. Only two or three people in London knew the real reason for it."

Skinnarland's task was to prepare the ground for a party of saboteurs to be dropped. These men were specially trained for the operation, which was given the code name *Grouse*. Skinnarland was told not to use radio transmission for his reports. Instead, his reports were written in an elaborate code, microfilmed, sent by courier to Oslo, then to Malmö in Sweden, and finally forwarded by Major Munthe to London.

"The Germans depend too much on the natural defenses. The guards are billeted in hutments situated between the main engine halls and the electrolysis plant. Inside the plant are fifteen armed men; change of guard is at 18.00 hours. There are sentries on the suspension bridge between Vemork and Rjukan, and the road, the only approach to the plant, can be floodlit in an alarm . . ." Skinnarland reported.

In his undercover work he was helped by only one man in whom he had confided, twenty-five-year-old Per Longum, who later became the commander of all *Milorg* forces in the Hardanger area.

Grouse

Hardangervidda is one of the wildest places in Europe. When Colonel Wilson and his Norwegian experts prepared the plans, they arrived at the following evaluation: "Weather usually appalling, foggy and unpredictable, sudden air currents of gale force spring up during autumn; terrain inaccessible, mountain peaks with hundreds of dangerous glaciers and precipices, marshes, swamps, impassable streams; hardly any landing strips and dropping grounds."

Four volunteers, all trained at SOE special schools, were selected by Colonel Wilson for this mission: Claus Helberg, Jens Poulson, and Arne Kjelstrup, all born in the Rjukan district, and Knut Haugland, who knew it. Poulson was the leader, Haugland his second in command. For several months the group went through additional training, the toughest that British commando instructors could provide. From Sergeant Harry Court they learned twenty different ways of killing a German sentry silently. Helberg, the radio operator, was trained to transmit twenty words a minute in Morse. Special ski equipment was sent from Canada.

By September 1942 they were ready. Colonel Wilson and Professor Tronstand went with them to the Wick RAF station. Twice their Halifax returned to base because of fog over Hardanger. On 18 October their third try was lucky. They parachuted onto a small rough mountain plateau at Flarfeit above the Sogne valley, many miles and several high peaks and glaciers from Vemork.

A few days later a radio signal arrived from Skinnarland:

GERMANS ORDERED TO PACK AND SHIP TO GERMANY ENTIRE STOCK OF HEAVY WATER STOP QUANTITY BELIEVED SUFFICIENT TO SATISFY PRESENT DEMANDS FROM BERLIN

This perturbed the scientific advisers of the Ministry of Economic Warfare. Churchill was informed and he called a Cabinet meeting attended by the chiefs of staff, his science adviser, Professor Frederick A. Lindemann, and the chief of combined operations, Lord Mountbatten. It became clear that time was running out and that the operation could not be entirely left to four young men, however well trained and enthusiastic. The outcome of the war might now depend upon the success or failure of the destruction of the Vemork plant and stores.

Brigadier Gubbins and Colonel Wilson drew up new plans for an operation on a much larger scale. A commando of Royal Engineers and men already seasoned in raids on Norway was formed. Thirty men were to be landed near Rjukan from gliders in a full-scale armed attack.

Meanwhile, the four *Grouse* saboteurs were skiing, marching, and climbing toward their target. They had with them six containers of explosives, arms, and food. Eventually they had to abandon most of them. Discarding food rather than explosives, they kept iron rations and some dried reindeer meat, and on 30 October they reached Reinar, the first inhabited mountain hamlet. By 6 November, after fifteen days, nearing exhaustion and living on a daily ration of reindeer meat, four biscuits, and a bar of chocolate, they set up their base at Sandvatn, in an abandoned ski-hut. The only life was petrels, which swooped low from the ice-covered peaks. On 9 November, from their base 4,500 feet above sea level, they made their first radio contact with London; their signal was: "Three pink elephants." Colonel Wilson now knew his men were in sight of Rjukan.

The Disaster of the Gliders

In Scotland, Operation Freshman began. Thirty-four British officers and men in two Horsa gliders, towed by two Halifax bombers, each with a crew of seven, took off from Wick on 19 November: the first Halifax, A for Apple, at 17:15 hours, the second, B for Bertie, thirty-five minutes later, their glider caravans crowded with Royal engineers, sappers, commando men, and two W/T operators.

The pilots were to shed the gliders over a flat strip of country near Mjösvatnet Fjord, some twenty miles south of Rjukan. The raiding party was to be met by the four SOE saboteurs, who had visited the proposed landing zone and had minutely described it in their radio signals. They had warned that the aircraft's magnetic compasses might deviate because of the ore-loaded mountains the planes had to cross.

Six hours and twenty-six minutes after the take-off, the first signal from Apple came through:

REQUEST COURSE BACK TO BASE STOP GLIDER DROPPED INTO SEA

Interrogated at the base after their return, the crew of Apple could give only a vague account of the disaster. Their Halifax had flown into thick, low clouds, thirty-five miles from the point where the glider was to be released.

The pilot decided to turn back because the tow and the glider had rapidly begun to cover with ice. When he turned the tow snapped. The Halifax crew briefly glimpsed the glider spiraling down into the fog. They believed it had hit the sea.

In fact the glider crashed on snow-covered ground, and of the seventeen men, nine survived. German ski patrols soon arrived and four badly injured survivors were taken to the hospital at Stavanger. There they died. According to investigations conducted after the war by Lieutenant Colonel Haukelid, they were killed by a quisling doctor who injected air bubbles into their veins. He did not escape justice; in 1945 he was executed by *Milorg* men.

The five other survivors were taken to the concentration camp Grini. There they were executed, along with a number of Norwegian Resistance men arrested in reprisal raids.[3]

No signal had been received at Wick RAF station from the other Halifax, Bertie, and its glider. But twenty-four hours later a communiqué from the headquarters of the German C in C Norway, General von Falkenhorst, was picked up in London:

Two British bombers, each towing gliders, loaded with saboteurs, flew yesterday over southern Norway. They were forced down by fighter aircraft of our Luftwaffe. The crews of the enemy bombers and gliders were annihilated to the last man in the air fight.

The truth of what had happened to the second air train soon became known from signals received from SOE agents. Halifax Bertie crashed (in the fog) into a hill, some ten miles inland, not far from Egersund. The Halifax crew members were killed on impact, the glider was torn off and crash-landed surprisingly gently in the snow. Only three of its crew were killed, though several were wounded. They were rounded up by German field police and taken to Egersund.

There the prisoners were shot by a firing squad after only cursory interrogation. All the prisoners were in British Army uniforms. This was a textbook case of a war crime.

The operation had been a tragic failure. The four SOE men waited in vain in the icy desert of Hardanger. But not for long. Colonel Wilson began to plan a new operation, code-named *Gunnerside*.

A team of six SOE agents, led by Joachim Ronneberg, was to be parachuted to join the four *Grouse* men, whose code name, with the advent of spring 1943, was changed to *Swallow*.

[3] The executions were carried out on 18 January 1943 by an SS squad under the command of SS Hauptsturm-Führer Oskar Hans. After the liberation, Norwegian Resistance men forced Vidkun Quisling to help exhume the bodies at Trandum cemetery. The former Nazi premier vomited and whined for mercy at the sight of the corpses of the British soldiers, whose hands were tied behind their backs with barbed wire.

In the meantime other SOE agents were dispatched by air and sea to Norway, and by the end of 1942, Colonel Wilson had nineteen men in the field, operating in various parts of the country, most of them in direct radio link with London and Stockholm.

Gunnerside

The planners of the Rjukan job were now greatly helped by the former chief engineer of *Norsk Hydro,* Professor Jomar Brun, who had escaped to Sweden and was flown to Britain. He provided up-to-date information about the plant and German security measures, which had been greatly tightened up. Professor Brun brought photographs of the factory buildings, power stations, and stores, and a large model of the installation was built for Ronneberg and his men to study. They were sent for training to an SOE school near Southampton, a special sabotage course known as "the gangsters' school."

Ronneberg's teammates were Knut Haukelid, Kasper Idland, Fredrik Kayser, Birger Strömsheim, and Hans Storhaug.

Haukelid, whose twin sister is the film star Sigrid Gurie, was at Trondheim during the invasion of 1940. He took part in the fighting and when it was over he went into hiding in the western lake district. An old friend, Captain Sverre Midtskau, found him when he landed from a British submarine as a courier for the Norwegian exile government. Together they went to Oslo. Midtskau became one of the outstanding pioneers of the Resistance, shuttling by sea and air between Norway and Scotland. In November 1940 he reurned to Norway aboard a fishing smack with a large sum of money for *Milorg.* He could not take Haukelid with him on the return journey, but promised to collect him soon. A few weeks later Midtskau was dropped by parachute and was received by Haukelid. With several other patriots they set up a network based in Oslo. One of their comrades was Max Manus (Mardonius), who was to become SOE's most resourceful saboteur. Manus suggested they blow up a few German U-boats berthed at Trondheim. They accomplished this, but disaster struck the little group; Midtskau and Manus were captured, Haukelid managed to escape to Sweden. Manus later escaped through the window of the train while being taken to a German concentration camp and subsequently carried out many daring acts of sabotage.[4]

Haukelid had come from Sweden to Britain, and now he was the most experienced of the six men of *Gunnerside.* Colonel Wilson and his Norwegian opposite number, Colonel Bjarne Öen, chief of the intelligence section of the Norwegian general staff in London, thought the six saboteurs, plus the four *Swallows* and Skinnarland at Rjukan, might succeed.

Although Skinnarland's reports in October had told of impending ship-

[4] See chapter 17, under "SOE Sabotage."

ments of heavy water to Germany, SOE chiefs knew destruction of the heavy water plant was still of vital importance. Although scientists had advised the Allied governments that, despite possession of such quantities of heavy water as they had secured, the Germans were still two years away from producing an atomic bomb, it was imperative to prevent further shipments in the spring of 1943.

The winter 1942–43 was one of the most severe in Norway in the memory of the oldest inhabitants. *Gunnerside,* planned for late autumn, had to be postponed again and again. Finally, on 16 February 1943, the six men of *Gunnerside* parachuted near Skrykenvann, some twenty-eight miles from the eerie hideout of the *Swallows,* by then half-starved and frustrated by their fourteen-month wait in the vastness of Hardangervidda.

On 23 February, after a forced mountain march, the *Gunnerside* men met the four *Swallows.* The newcomers, themselves half-frozen, were in a sorry state. Their ragged beards were encrusted with ice and blood from cracked flesh. They had suffered badly from frostbite, and under normal circumstances would have been considered hospital cases. But they all decided that no time should be lost. Ronneberg and his men had brought their own containers: there was enough explosive to blow up the entire plant.

Ronneberg and Poulson drew up the final order. It included the following points: "All men to wear uniform. Positions will be taken at midnight, 500 meters from the fence. Attack at 00:30 hours, after guards are changed. If alarm is sounded, covering party to attack guards immediately, while demolition party is to proceed. Demolition party to destroy high-concentration plant in the cellar of electrolysis factory. Entrance by forcing cellar door; failing this by using ground-floor door; failing this, through the cable tunnel. Each man carrying out demolition to be covered by one man with .45 pistol. Sentry with Tommy gun to guard entrance. If fighting starts before demolition party reaches target, men of covering party to take over placing explosives. If anything happens to the leaders of the party, everybody is to act on his own initiative to ensure success of operation."

The order ended with this sentence: "If any man is about to be taken prisoner, he undertakes to end his own life." For this, two "L" pills of potassium cyanide, which every man carried, were to be used.

To identify each other in the dark or in confusion, passwords were issued: the call was "Piccadilly"; the reply, "Leicester Square."

On Saturday morning, thirty-six hours before flashpoint, an unexpected incident occured. Four young skiers, two boys and two girls, suddenly appeared near the hut. They had chosen this difficult area for a skiing excursion, and they were frightened to see a group of wild-looking bearded men, armed with tommy guns. Realizing something important was happening, they allowed themselves to be locked up in the hut until Sunday.

The descent to Rjukan was not easy. The heavy explosives had to be carried and moved carefully when they reached the inhabited valley. Helberg had done some reconnoitering and reported that the Germans had sent SS reinforcements to the Mösvatn area only the day before. When they reached the Mösvatn road they saw German patrols. On the Vaer bridge they saw two workmen's buses, guarded by German sentries, going to the nightshift at the plant.

At last, on that moonless frosty night, the SOE men reached their positions. Forbidden to smoke or use flashlights, they crept like cats toward the fence. At exactly thirty minutes past midnight the advance party reached the fence gate, which was padlocked with a chain. They cut this and slipped into the compound. Six men—Poulson, Haukelid, Haugland, Helberg, Kjelstrup, and Storhaug—took up positions to cover the operation.

Ronneberg led the demolition party—Kayser, Strömsheim, and Idland. They had to make a detour, passing two German sentries, which denied them the use of the cellar door. In the darkness they were separated and only Ronneberg and Kayser remained together. The leader decided to use the cable intake to enter the cellar. It was a narrow tunnel, full of ice and snow and a tangle of cables and pipes. The two crept through it and emerged into a large cellar full of fuse boxes and transformers.

They reached the door to the cellar of the high-concentration plant and saw a night watchman dozing over a book. Kayser crept up behind him and poked his pistol into the man's ribs. The man, a Norwegian workman, said nothing. He did not even look astonished. A few moments later Strömsheim, who had also come through the cable tunnel, appeared; and with his help, Ronneberg began to place the charges.

The workman watched Ronneberg. Suddenly he whispered: "Be careful, or you'll blow up the place."

"That's just what we're going to do," replied Ronneberg with a grin. The charges were now in position, the fuses connected. Ronneberg turned to the night watchman.

"You have exactly twenty seconds to get out of here after we've left."

The night watchman nodded. He was an elderly man and looked shaken. He said to Kayser: "Look here, I don't know what happened to my spectacles. I'm lost without them. I shan't be able to get out."

"They're at the end of your nose, Dad," Kayser answered. "Getting a bit rattled, aren't you?"

The three men went to the tunnel, Ronneberg last. He lit the fuses and called to the night watchman: "Now run as quickly as you can!"

Outside, their comrades waited, huddled in the black shadow of the seven-story building, only twenty yards from the nearest German guard's hut. Haukelid took six hand grenades from his pockets and said: "I'll cover the exit—go!" They reached the bridge where two sentries were talking and laughing.

Then from the building came a whistling noise, which was followed by a deep but not very loud rumble. There was no fire and no smoke visible. The noise was heard in the guard room, and an SS sergeant came out, looked round the yard, and then headed for the main gate. Against the light of the open hut door the SOE men could see his silhouette. The sergeant tried the gate, was apparently satisfied that it was locked, and ambled back to the hut.

The men moved toward the fence. There they found Kjelstrup with a tommy gun in his hand. "Everything quiet," he said. "A Jerry came and went; he saw nothing."

After several hours' march they reached their hideout. They were tired, but so excited that they could not sleep. They were not sure whether they had been successful. The explosion seemed to have misfired. Haukelid called it "an insignificant little bang." Yet the high-concentration installations had been completely demolished and vital electrical apparatus destroyed. Even after six months of frantic repair work the Germans could never again use the Vemork plant to full capacity.

Five of the saboteurs, all in British battle dress, traveled more than 250 miles across Norway to the Swedish frontier. Haugland, Haukelid, and Kjelstrup were joined by Skinnarland, and they remained in the Hardanger area to watch the results of the operation. Poulson and Helberg went to Oslo.

In London, after reports of the operation had reached Downing Street, Winston Churchill wrote a note: "What has been done for these brave men in the way of decorations?"

The Germans went berserk. Reichs-Kommissar Terboven, General von Falkenhorst, and members of the Quisling government hurried to Rjukan. Himmler ordered special retribution measures; and under the command of SS Ober-Führer Henrich Fehlis, 200 Gestapo men, 400 men of the *Geheime Feldpolizei*, units of the Wehrmacht, and ski squads of Quisling's *Hird* storm troopers—a total of 2,800 men with armored cars—were brought to Hardanger. The whole area was cordoned off. Every farm and village was searched, homes were raided and set afire, and hundreds of innocent people were driven away. More than 150 Norwegians were taken as hostages to prisons and concentration camps.

Vital Cargo

When Haukelid and Skinnarland, some months later, discovered that the Germans had repaired the worst damage, they reported to London, and the chiefs of staff ordered the RAF to bomb the area. A series of heavy air raids caused little damage to the plant, but twenty-one Norwegian civilians were killed and twenty-two British and U.S. airmen were lost.

The chiefs of staff asked Colonel Wilson to prepare another sabotage raid. But Haukelid, with heavy heart, advised against it. German security measures made it impossible. He suggested that instead, the drums with heavy water be attacked in transit. The precious cargo was being loaded onto railway trucks at Rjukan and carried to the north end of Lake Tinnsjo, then by train ferry to Skien and Larvik, from where it was shipped to Germany.

It was not until a year after the *Gunnerside–Swallow* operation, in February 1944, that Haukelid learned that the Germans were to transport a half-year's output of heavy water from Vemork. During the night of 20 February Haukelid and two SOE/*Milorg* men, Knut Lier-Hansen and Rolf Sorlie, persuaded a crew member to let them board the ferry. Disguised as mechanics they managed to place high-explosive charges. The electric fuses were set for the following Sunday noon, when the ferry would be over the deepest part of the lake. They left with mixed feelings, knowing that some of the Norwegian crew might die.

The ferry blew up, and its cargo of nearly 4,000 gallons of heavy water was destroyed. Four German guards and four Norwegians were killed and several more badly injured. Haukelid and his comrades could take comfort in knowing that previous operations had cost the Allies eighty-four lives: forty-one in the glider disasters of 1942 and forty-three in the air raids.

These SOE operations delayed German preparations for the manufacture of atomic bombs in 1943, and by depriving them of the vital supply in 1944 foiled Hitler's plan to use rockets with atomic bomb warheads against Britain as a final desperate weapon. This was clearly borne out by secret German documents examined after the war. Thus the men of *Grouse* and *Gunnerside* and the planners in London played an important part in the Allied victory.

In contrast to the misfortunes that struck SOE networks in France and the Low Countries, the Norwegian operations caused comparatively few casualties among SOE agents. Nearly all the actors in the heavy water drama survived the war. Claus Helberg returned after the liberation to his home town of Rjukan. Knut Haugland, the first man to establish radio contact with London from the Barren Mountain, is now a colonel in the Norwegian army. Knut Haukelid, also a colonel, is the commanding officer of the Telemark Infantry Regiment, stationed not far from the scene of his war exploits. Jens Poulson is a Norwegian general staff officer.

Einar Skinnarland became, in the final stages of the war, a leader of the SOE/*Milorg* SUNSHINE group, assigned by SHAEF in 1945 to rescue Norwegian hostages and to protect industrial plant and railway installations from German destruction.

Two men of the heavy water enterprise did not survive the war. Professor Tronstad, one of the chief planners, was killed by a traitor when he returned to Norway shortly before the liberation. Odd Starheim, the hero of the *Galtesund,* who brought Skinnarland to Britain, died fighting. On 1 March 1943, on his third mission, during which he carried out many successful sabotage actions in Norwegian ports, he repeated another daring act of piracy. He seized the sister ship of the *Galtsund,* the coastal steamer *Tromosund,* and headed for Britain with several comrades. Halfway to Scotland an aircraft dived on the ship. This time it was not a friendly Hudson but a Messerschmitt. There were no survivors of the *Tromosund.* Starheim's body was washed ashore many months later.

17

The Vikings

WHILE the SOE saboteurs were busy on Barren Mountain, sharp friction between British and Norwegian leaders in London flared up and kindled for a long time. In 1942 Winston Churchill considered Norway a prime target for an Allied invasion. Neither the British chiefs of staff nor the Norwegian exile government in London shared his opinion. The Americans, who favored the cross-Channel invasion of France, were strongly opposed to an attack on Norway, and Churchill was compelled to drop the idea.

Because of Churchill's predilection for invading Norway, however, SOE was ordered early in the war to produce a document entitled "Norwegian Policy." This was submitted 11 December 1940 to the chiefs of staff and seen by Churchill. It began with a discussion of the general strategic position and the likely developments in the future, and went on to analyze the tasks of SOE thus: (a) to organize Resistance groups and secret army units to assist an Allied invasion; (b) to furnish the directorate of Combined Operations with saboteurs and landing parties; and (c) to provide information for Allied air bombardment.[1]

The authors of this document concluded that an invasion of Norway was feasible, provided that the organization and arming of military Resistance groups would start without delay on a large scale, and sabotage raids and propaganda would be intensified at the same time. But the document stressed that an invasion would have to be delayed for a long time and that the efficacy of an early Norwegian uprising must be discounted. The immediate tasks were to counteract defeatism and keep up the morale of the Norwegian people, and to do everything to make the Germans realize that they could never feel safe. "Norway must become and remain a thorn in the German side," the document stated, while the ultimate aim must be a Norwegian *levée en masse*. Thus in each district of Norway it was necessary to have an organization under effective leadership in close contact with SOE.

In southern and central Norway secret army groups would be set up in Bergen, Trondheim, Stavanger, Kristiansand, Skien/Drammen, Sarps-

[1] Norwegian General Staff War Archives, Vol. 28, 8/9.

borg, and Elverum/Lillehammer. A strong Oslo group was described as being of utmost importance. It would be unnecessary to have separate groups in northern Norway—apart from sabotage and intelligence units—with the exception of Bodö, where volunteers must be trained in guerilla warfare to help cut Norway in half. Instructions would be issued by SOE regarding recruitment and training, and SOE would provide some of the instructors and radio operators. During commando raids units of the secret army would help to isolate German troops from the areas of operation.

The document was shown to the Norwegian exile government in London and immediately produced a sharp protest, even though it stressed that the secret army organization would be under Norwegian command and that SOE would only send instructors, radio operators, and saboteurs trained in Britain.

Claymore

At about this time the first small-scale raid, carried out in the Sognefjord area, though resulting in comparatively little damage, provoked German reprisals against the local population. Although SOE never intended to embark upon actions that would result in futile sacrifices, a bitter controversy ensued, which for many months frustrated all plans. The Norwegian exile government, then almost completely deprived of home news, naturally assumed that the British, and particularly the SOE chiefs, wanted exclusive control over Norwegian Resistance movements. Moreover, Resistance leaders in Norway later sent a letter to King Haakon in London protesting against British coastal raids and pointing out that reprisals taken by the Germans had made a deep impression upon the Norwegian people "not yet immunized against German threats and Gestapo terror." The leaders also rejected "hazardous sabotage actions," insisting that "every action should be carefully thought out with our cooperation before young Norwegians are asked to carry out such dangerous work."

Conferences between Norwegian ministers and Dr. Hugh Dalton, the minister of economic warfare, dissolved the worst misunderstandings. On the Norwegian side, Foreign Minister Trygve Lie[2] proved more conciliatory than most of his colleagues, and an improvement in the relations between the Norwegian and British authorities was achieved when the newly arrived Resistance leaders, John Rognes and State Councilor Ljundberg, agreed that guerilla groups without assistance from Britain and without proper training—which SOE had offered—would be useless and "mere military Sunday schools."

Shortly after a compromise was reached in London, the first large raid, Operation Claymore, took place (4 March 1941) in the Lofoten islands.

[2] Secretary-General of the United Nations 1946–1953.

Accompanying British commando troops were fifty-two members of SOE's Linge Company, led by Captains Martin Linge and Andrew Croft. At Reine and Svolvär 11 German and Norwegian ships, totaling 19,000 tons, were sunk; herring and cod liver oil factories were blown up; and 213 Germans and 12 Norwegian quislings, including the police chief of Svolvär, were brought back as prisoners. The raiders returned to Britain with 314 Norwegian volunteers, many of whom enlisted in Captain Linge's company.

The Lofoten raid was regarded by SOE chiefs as an unqualified success. But the Norwegian government and many Resistance leaders in Norway saw it in a different light. In the barren far north two small factories and a number of fishing trawlers, on which the local population depended for its livelihood, had been destroyed. The Gestapo retaliated with mass arrests and the execution of several hostages.

SOE maintained, however, that the raid greatly strengthened the spirit of resistance in Norway. In a letter to the Norwegian government, dated 16 April 1941,[3] Sir Charles Hambro expressed the surprisingly optimistic view that "the liberation of Norway by a landing of Allied troops could come before Christmas." He also informed the Norwegian government that systematic recruitment of Norwegians for SOE had been decided on, at a rate of twenty-five to fifty a month.

The precariously patched-up quarrels began anew. The Norwegian leaders now felt that Britain was determined to assert "hegemony over Norway and control the Resistance by recruiting, training, and paying agents among Norwegian citizens, controlling all radio communications, and running the so-called Shetland Ferry by excluding cooperation with the Norwegian government." [4]

Two events in 1941—a document entitled "Looking Ahead in Scandinavia" (on 15 April) and a suggestion made by Soviet Foreign Minister Molotov to Sir Stafford Cripps in Moscow that Russia and Britain should prepare a plan for a joint occupation of northern Norway—did not improve the mood of the Norwegian cabinet in London.

The Claymore operation had been somewhat melodramatic, and a British war historian summed up this and some later raids thus: [5]

These small attacks can scarcely be regarded as conforming to the conception of the Prime Minister [Churchill] who noted that he considered it "unworthy of the British Empire to send over a few cut-throats." But, for some months the few cut-throats represented very nearly all that we could do in the way of offensive action and, if the German Wehrmacht remained contemptuous of such gnat-bites, no other means existed at the time operating offensively out of Britain.

[3] Norwegian General Staff War Archives, Vol. 20, File 4–B2/1942.
[4] *Cf.* Kjeldstadli, *op. cit.,* pp. 89 ff.
[5] Buckley, C., *Norway—The Commandos,* London, 1951.

In October 1941, when Lord Louis Mountbatten succeeded Admiral Keyes as chief of Combined Operations, the whole concept of raids in German-occupied Europe changed, as the raids in Norway and at Bruneval, St. Nazaire, and Dieppe were soon to prove. The object of these raids was not only to destroy military and industrial installations, but also to engage the enemy and probe his coastal defenses.

The Lofoten Raids

On 26 December 1941 a considerable Royal Navy force, commanded by Rear Admiral (later Admiral Sir Louis) Hamilton, appeared off the Lofoten islands. If a foothold could be gained at Bodö, Norway would be cut in half and an operation against Narvik would then be feasible. But in Operation Anklet only a halfhearted attempt was made in this direction. Three hundred men were landed, the main towns of Reine and Moskenes occupied, the small German garrison wiped out; and Admiral Hamilton contemplated establishing a beachhead in the southern Lofoten islands. He had sufficiently strong forces and could count on reinforcements by sea and air from Scotland. But on the 28th a Luftwaffe aircraft dropped a bomb near HMS *Arethusa,* and enemy radio signals were intercepted indicating that a German force was being assembled at Narvik to counterattack the invaders. Admiral Hamilton ordered the withdrawal of the landing parties, and sailed home.

With the British Commandos and Royal Marines were 77 SOE Norwegians of the Linge Company, and they were joined by 266 new volunteers. The effect of the hasty retreat on the morale of the people of Reine and Moskenes was disastrous. Commander Frank Stagg, of the SOE Scandinavian section, wrote in reports dated 5 and 10 January 1942:

The population had been told that the British Force had come to stay, and as they believed it was feasible, the voluntary evacuation of the place was nearly complete, as it was realized that the district would be relentlessly bombed by the Germans. The local population was very patriotic-minded; the town of Reine was nicknamed London! All these people were hoping that the moment had at last come when the fight would be taken up once more, although the majority were rather sceptical as regards present operations developing. None were, however, prepared for the news that the forces were to flee without even having tried to fight; therefore when the notice came about retreat it did not cause only deep disappointment, but also indignation and fury. The general opinion was that once more propaganda had been successfully achieved with nearly 100 per cent security for the military, whereas the landing would once more bring upon the heads of the remaining population the horrors of German reprisals.

I believe that unfortunately the bitterness which came through this opinion made several good patriots stay behind, although they had helped the British;

also others who had helped could not come over as the short notice of departures would not allow them to collect their evacuated families . . . . The population of Reine were strongly pro-British, but I feel that henceforward this attitude may be less marked.[6]

At the same time as the second Lofoten raid, Operation Archery took place (27 December) on the coast of Måløy and Vågsö. The raiding force consisted of 51 officers and 525 men, including 16 men of the SOE company commanded by Captain Martin Linge. More than 15,000 tons of shipping and the large oil factory at Vågsö were destroyed by British sappers. The two small towns were occupied and the entire German garrison killed or taken prisoner. At Vågsö Captain Linge was killed while leading an attack on the German headquarters. Norwegian volunteers who sailed to Britain with the raiders were saddened; they shared the grief of the Linge men over the loss of their beloved leader.[7]

Reprisals for the two December raids were savage. Family members of the men who had gone to Britain were taken to concentration camps, though some fled before the SS squads arrived. The town of Reine and many villages became almost depopulated. But worse was to come.

The Televåg Tragedy

On 21 April 1942 SOE agents Arne Vaerum (Penguin) and Emil Hvaal (Anchor) were landed near Nesvik from the cutter *Olaf,* which had sailed from Shetland. Penguin was to blow up Luftwaffe installations at Stavanger; Anchor was to engage in sabotage in eastern Norway. They went to Sotra, where they contacted a local *Milorg* group. On Sunday, 26 April, they were at the house of a Resistance leader at Televåg.

Through a quisling, the Gestapo chief of Bergen, SS Hauptsturm-Führer Behrens, learned of their presence and led an SD squad to Televåg. When the Germans came to the farm, Vaerum and Hvaal barricaded themselves in the loft and opened fire. The gun battle lasted for four hours. Vaerum was fatally wounded, but not before he had killed Gestapo chief Behrens and his deputy, SS Sturm-Führer Bernhardt. The severely wounded Hvaal was dragged from the farm and taken to Trandum.

Reichs-Kommissar Terboven ordered that the entire population of Televåg pay for the crime of the terrorists. The village became a Norwegian Lidice. All 300 houses were burned to the ground; 260 men and boys between the ages of sixteen and sixty-five were rounded up and taken to German concentration camps, and 76 of them eventually perished at Sachsenhausen. The wounded Emil Hvaal, his host Lars Telle, and 18 men

[6] RVPS reports.
[7] Linge was buried with British casualties at Måløy; his body was exhumed in 1946 and reburied with military honors at Vestre Akers.

suspected of being members of *Milorg* were tortured, then executed.

More arrests were made in Bergen, Stavanger, and the Hardanger area. Among the captured was Leiv Lea, a Resistance pioneer and *Milorg* commander at Stavanger. He was tortured to death at the Gestapo office in Bergen. Two SOE men, Erling Marthinsson and Christian Aall, who had arrived on 8 April and had set up radio post Mallard near Bergen, also fell victim to the roundup, betrayed by a quisling. They were put to death at Trandum.

The Televåg tragedy caused great resentment in Norway. Even *Milorg* members felt the price paid by the innocent civilian population was too high for the meager results of individual SOE actions. "No more Televåg!" demanded the Norwegian exile government in London.

But Norwegian Resistance continued in spite of all these setbacks, and 1942 became "the great year," even though military operations played only a minor part from then on. The great improvement in the British–Norwegian relations during the second half of 1942, which developed into a wholehearted and fruitful cooperation and endured until the liberation in 1945, was the result of several factors.

At the beginning of 1942, Colonel John Skinner Wilson became head of the Norwegian section of SOE. At the offices of the Norwegian exile government, the new Defense Minister, Oscar Torp, and the new chief of the Norwegian secret service in London, Thore Boye, were much more inclined to cooperate with SOE than were their predecessors. The commander in chief of the Norwegian forces in Britain, General Carl G. Fleischer, who understandably resented the British "hegemony," was placated when SOE conceded the *Milorg* should be put under his over-all command. Nevertheless, SOE retained control of all agents sent to Norway and of all radio communications with them and with *Milorg* leaders. It was mainly to the credit of Colonel Sporborg and Colonel Wilson that relations became cordial, after an Anglo–Norwegian Joint Committee was established. Colonel Sporborg produced a document entitled "Anglo Norwegian Collaboration regarding the military organization in Norway," which bolstered agreement about the future of *Milorg*.[8] Until then the Norwegian government and the British authorities were somewhat suspicious of *Milorg*, though for different reasons. The Norwegian Socialist ministers in London were doubtful about possible political ambitions of some *Milorg* leaders; the British were not entirely satisfied with *Milorg*'s militant spirit and doubted whether it was properly organized and could cope with the growing infiltration by Gestapo V-men and quislings.

Until the beginning of 1942, SOE had given only limited assistance to *Milorg*. With the conclusion of the new Anglo–Norwegian collaboration

[8] *Cf.* Norwegian General Staff War Archives, Vol. 20, *Samarbeidet med SOE.*

agreement, and after Captain Jacob Schive, a *Milorg* leader, visited London, detailed plans for organization, training, and supplies of arms were evolved. Subsequently, *Milorg* was completely reorganized. It became a nationwide movement, joined by farmers, workers, and trade unionists, most of whom supported the Social Democratic party, which had for many years provided Norway's governments.

Two other factors contributed to the general improvement in the relations between SOE and Norwegian leaders in London. One was the excellent work of the Stockholm office under Major Malcolm Munthe; the other, the Shetland Ferry initiated by SOE.

The Shetland Bus

The Shetland Bus had made its first trip from Scotland to Norway on Christmas Eve 1940. The secret ferry started modestly, with its initial base at Flemington House, north of Lerwick, under Major L. H. Mitchel, a British intelligence officer. He was soon joined by Commander David Howarth,[9] three British sergeants, and a few Norwegian fishermen, all volunteers. Their skipper was thirty-four-year-old Leif Larsen, whose subsequent exploits became almost legendary.

To start, there were four old and not very seaworthy fishing boats. The first journey to Norway was made by the *Vita*. She and *Aksel, Siglaos,* and *Igland* later made many trips until they were gradually replaced by Arctic whalers, British MTBs, and finally by modern American submarine chasers. The fishing boats were utterly defenseless and at the mercy of U-boats and German air patrols. All were manned by Norwegians. They laid mines, carried arms, ammunition, and explosives for *Milorg* and the Resistance, conveyed SOE agents to Norway, and invariably returned with Norwegian volunteers for training in Britain, and often with Norwegian VIPs.

The Shetland Bus base was later greatly improved, after it was moved to Lunna Voe on the magnificent sweep of Yell Sound. Mitchel and Howarth were joined by Captain Rogers (whose real name was Arthur Sclater; he used a *nom de guerre* because he had relatives in Norway). There were never more than one hundred sailors at the base, forty sailing, others resting. The many losses never discouraged Norwegian sailors from re-embarking on the perilous journey. One of them, Jan Baalsrud, the sole survivor of the *Brattholm* (which was attacked and sunk by a German warship in the Arctic Circle), had been hunted across Lapland during his escape to Sweden. Suffering from frostbite, he lost nine toes, but reported for duty as soon as he was repatriated to Britain by the Swedish Red Cross. Such

[9] The full story of the ferry service is told in David Howarth's *The Shetland Bus* (Longmans, London, 1953).

[337]

was the spirit of the modern Vikings who sustained the Shetland Bus.

When American submarine chasers were added to its fleet, work became much more efficient. The tough sailors gladly accepted the gadgetry and luxury of the American ships—central heating, oil-fired galleys, refrigerators, ice-water fountains, comfortable beds, hot and cold showers—and never grew tired of cracking jokes about it.

By the spring of 1942 the old fishing boats had made more than forty trips, had landed 43 SOE agents and picked up 9, brought 46 refugees to Britain, and delivered 150 tons of equipment to Norway. Then the traffic greatly expanded. During the winter of 1943–44 alone, eighty sailings were made without a single loss, although winter sailings were always more perilous. During the summer months the Shetland Bus service was busier than that of most British country buses.

Operation Title

In autumn 1942 a daring attempt was made to blow up the battleship *Graf Tirpitz,* the pride of Hitler's navy. She had been completed only two years before and had taken refuge at Trondheim Fjord, after being chased in the North Sea by the Royal Navy. The operation, code-named Title, had been in preparation for many months by the Admiralty, whose research scientists had developed new "human submarines," the Welman chariots.[10]

SOE agents—one disguised as a Lutheran clergyman—reconnoitered near the *Graf Tirpitz* base and brought back photographs of the dock. Additional reconnaissance was made by RAF Spitfires. Skipper Larsen volunteered to take three chariots to Norway aboard the boat *Arthur.*

The *Arthur* was disguised as a fishing vessel registered at Trondheim. German fishing permits and registration papers were forged at the SOE laboratory. Larsen and his crew were supplied with forged papers and a crew list certified by the Gestapo, as well as food specially brought from Norway—black bread, hard sausage, German ersatz coffee. Thus equipped, the *Arthur* sailed with six British Royal Navy artificers and the chariots hidden under layers of peat in the hold. The precautions proved wise. The vessel was stopped by a German patrol boat at the entrance of Trondheim Fjord. The registration documents and the crew's papers were carefully examined, and the *Arthur* was passed as a coastal fishing boat.

Larsen sailed to a small island off the mouth of the fjord, where his

---

[10] A chariot looked like a midget submarine or a torpedo, about 20 feet long, and was driven by electric motors. The crew of two sat astride in diving suits. At the nose of the chariot was the large, detachable warhead. The crew could steer the chariot submerged below the target, unscrew the warhead, set a time fuse, and then make their escape.

men lowered the chariots and took them in tow. With the submerged chariots hanging from steel wires, the *Arthur* had to pass another German examination ship. As the two vessels lay close together a German naval lieutenant jumped on board, and all the documents were inspected once again. Although several German sailors stood at the rail of their ship and watched the scene, they did not notice the wires or the chariots, which the initiated could spot in the clear water. At last the *Arthur* approached the *Tirpitz*. Then, in despair, the men discovered they had lost the chariots. Apparently the special attachments holding the tows had snapped off; the chariots had sunk, irretrievably.

Larsen had to make a heart-rending decision. There was no chance of sailing back through all the controls; the only solution was to scuttle the *Arthur* and escape by land to Sweden. All but one of the men, Able Seaman Robert Evans, eventually reached Sweden and safety after a long and dangerous trek. Near the Swedish frontier they were stopped by two German field policemen. In the ensuing gunfight Evans was badly wounded and captured. He was taken to the hospital, and after he recovered, he was executed by order of Admiral Karl Doenitz, at that time the German naval commander in Norway. When captured, Evans was wearing his uniform under his mackintosh. That murder was one of the charges against Doenitz at Nuremburg. He was sentenced to ten years' imprisonment for war crimes.

The five Britons and Larsen and his men were flown from Sweden to England, and the Norwegians rejoined the Shetland Bus base to take part in more dangerous journeys.

The Resistance Grows

By the end of 1942 both the civilian Resistance organizations and *Milorg* had vastly improved. From a nucleus of five military districts, *Milorg* grew to eleven at the end of 1942 and forty-one at the beginning of 1944, with an effective strength of 33,000 disciplined and armed men. It was not *Milorg's* task to engage in sabotage. Such sabotage as was thought necessary to weaken the German war effort was performed by SOE saboteurs and small Resistance groups, particularly the extremely militant Communist *Norge Fritt*. The main task assigned to *Milorg* was to set up a military organization which, at the hour of Germany's defeat, could be relied upon to mop up German pockets of resistance and assume the role of an army of liberation, thus relieving the Allies from having to land large forces in Norway. This task was completely fulfilled in the spring of 1945.

Meanwhile the strong *Milorg* units compelled the German high command to maintain a disproportionately large number of troops in Norway. The Germans were in constant fear of armed uprisings in remote sections of the country. On 7 November 1943 General Alfred Jodl, the chief of staff of the Wehrmacht, reported to Hitler that 380,000 troops must be kept in Norway; a few weeks later he gave the strength of Wehrmacht garrisons in Norway as 430,000.[11] At that time the Germans were in dire need of reinforcements for the Eastern front. But to occupy Norway they had to use thirteen Wehrmacht divisions and 150,000 naval and Luftwaffe personnel; 6,000 SS men; 12,000 men in paramilitary groups, including Quisling's *Hird;* and many more thousands in the motley *Volksdeutsche* units, recruited from all over Europe. This huge force was needed to control a population of less than 3,000,000.

Compare this with the force of about fifty divisions that Germany maintained in France and the Low Countries—to man the Atlantic Wall and the coasts, to face the threat of Allied invasion from both the north and the south, and to combat the Resistance activity produced by a population twenty times that of Norway—and the significance of the Norwegian Resistance becomes apparent.

As in Holland, in the person of Anton van der Waals, the Gestapo acquired in Norway a master traitor—Henry Oliver Rinnan, a former truck driver from Levanger, who recruited teams of informers and denunciators, called the Rinnan-Banden (Rinnan gangsters). They served not only as V-men but also as interrogators, employing tortures often worse than those used by SS men. Rinnan had been enrolled by SS Sturmbann-Führer Herbert Noot, the chief of Section III (counterespionage) of the SD, on Vidkun Quisling's personal recommendation. He was paid at first 500 kroner (about $125) weekly, but his pay was greatly increased after he had infiltrated a few Resistance groups and betrayed SOE agents. Alone during the second half of 1941, Rinnan and his "gangsters" were responsible for the execution of twenty-nine SOE men and *Milorg* members.

SS Sturmbann-Führer Noot gave Rinnan a special task to infiltrate the export organizations, which dispatched Norwegian volunteers to Britain by the Shetland Bus, and to locate SOE agents arriving from Britain. Rinnan worked closely with SS Hauptsturm-Führer Siegfried Fehmer, head of Section IV of the Gestapo, and SS Hauptsturm-Führer Oskar Hans, who was in charge of special squads (*Sonderkommandos*) dealing with SOE saboteurs. Although Rinnan and the Gestapo succeeded in arresting several SOE agents, they failed to achieve anything remotely resembling the successes scored by Kieffer in Paris or Schreieder in Holland. There was no *England Spiel* from Norway, and the few radio transmitters that fell into German hands could not be used because their capture was usually discovered by the SOE Norwegian section in London within days.

[11] Cf. *Nazi Conspiracy and Aggression,* Vol. 7, pp. 936 ff., Washington, 1947.

The Anglo–Norwegian agreement foresaw that sabotage should be limited to essential targets and that all actions should be executed by SOE agents. It was hoped that if only a few Resistance and *Milorg* members were involved, the Germans would not retaliate against innocent members of the public. This purpose was partly achieved.

Unlike SOE agents in France or the Low Countries, SOE saboteurs in Norway were not members of networks because no such networks existed; organization of the secret army was a prerogative of *Milorg*. Therefore, independent SOE teams were dispatched, assigned to undertake specific actions, and instructed to return to Britain by the Shetland Bus or to find their way to Sweden. In some cases members of such teams remained for several months in Norway, making contact with local *Milorg* groups.

One of the outstanding organizers of sabotage teams was Captain Birger Sjöberg, who led the first three important operational teams—*Archer* (16 December 1941), *Heron I* (10 March 1942), and *Heron II* (12 April 1942). For two and a half years Sjöberg's operations went without a hitch, although he and his friends had some narrow escapes from the Gestapo. But in the early summer of 1944 one of Rinnan's V-men infiltrated a local Resistance group in Oladalen and the Gestapo learned of the impending arrival of yet another team led by Sjöberg. He arrived with five SOE agents, and split them into two groups: Ensign Baarnes and two men went to Hattfjelldalen; Captain Sjöberg and two men went to Stavassdalen, where they stored a large quantity of explosives in a hut.

There, on 9 June 1944 they were surrounded by an SD squad. In an exchange of fire a Gestapo officer was killed. Sjöberg was mortally wounded but detonated a charge in the hut in order to prevent the explosives and arms from falling into enemy hands. The hut and all its contents were destroyed. Sjöberg died before the SD men could take him. One of the SOE men, Johan Gundersen, escaped; but Ole Casperen, badly injured, was captured and tortured to death. This was not the end of the *Archer–Heron* team; it continued under Sjöberg's second in command.

Some of the most remarkable exploits in 1942 were carried out by members of the *Knotgrass* and *Unicorn* teams, who arrived with a commando unit of Combined Operations. SOE men Magnus Djupdraet and Sverre Grandlund, with ten commandos, blew up the power station at Glomfjord, which supplied electricity for a large aluminum factory; the total output had been used for the manufacture of Luftwaffe aircraft. This was in September 1942.[12] Seven members of the *Knotgrass–Unicorn* group were later captured and executed. On 5 October *Kestrel* arrived; its two members were Per Getz and Thor Grong, who previously had taken part in an

[12] The full story is well told in Stephen Schofield's *Musketoon*, Cape, London, 1964.

operation against the Orkla power station. The *Kestrel* team succeeded in destroying a large part of the ore mining installations at Fosdalen in Nord-Tröndelag. These mines supplied iron ore for the Hermann Goering works armament factories in Germany, and the sabotage reduced production by 75 percent.

The Tröndelag action prompted savage retaliation. Reichs-Kommissar Terboven, declaring he would "bring the terrorists to their knees," ordered a state of emergency. An SD *Sonderkommando*, led by SS Hauptsturm-Führer Oskar Hans, descended on the district. To prevent escapes, Terboven ordered the frontier with Sweden closed. Mass arrests were carried out by SS squads assisted by men of Quisling's *Hird*. Between 9 and 12 October thirty-five Norwegian civilians, none connected with sabotage actions, were executed without trial by German firing squads at Majavatn.

A special OKW order, signed by Hitler, announced that "in future all members of British terrorist and sabotage groups, and their helpers, will be treated by the German Wehrmacht as bandits [*Banditen*] and not as fighting soldiers and, wherever captured, whether in uniform or civilian clothes, put to summary execution."

The German threats did not deter volunteers from even more daring sabotage operations. In 1943 they were greatly intensified. In the Operation Cartoon, on 25 January, SOE saboteurs were landed under the cover of commando units of Combined Operations at Lileboe and Stord, and blew up mine installations and stores with 150,000 tons of ore. Unfortunately, this action provoked more retaliations; some two hundred arrests were made by the Gestapo in Bergen, including the harbor-master, two town councilors, four masters of the cathedral college, several police officers; and, for some unknown reason, all the members of a teetotal society. They were taken to a new concentration camp near Espeland. In February the *Seagull* team concentrated on the ore mines of Sulitjelma, causing much damage. At Eydehavn the Arendal smelt works were blown up by the SOE team *Company*, led by Edward Tallaksen, and 2,500 tons of ferrosilicate were destroyed. The same team carried out sabotage actions against the Lysaker chemical works and the Norsk sulphur factory near Engene.

But the heavily guarded Orkla pyrite mines—after Rio Tinto the largest source of the mineral used in radar and W/T apparatus—remained the coveted target. Four SOE teams were sent against Orkla: *Redshank* in May 1942, *Granard* in December 1942, *Feather I* in October 1943, and *Feather II* in April 1944. The first three teams carried out small sabotage actions that reduced the output of the mines, but they were unable to destroy the main target. Finally, in a series of operations during the last two weeks of May 1944, all four teams, assisted by Gunnar Sonsteby's

Oslo Gang, completed the assignment. At a crucial stage of the war, just before D day, the Germans were deprived of vital supplies for their aircraft.

There was widespread sabotage against shipping and harbor installations. In many instances these operations were performed singlehanded by Max Manus, the famous Mardonius, who arrived in Norway from Britain by parachute on 12 March 1943 with three SOE comrades. His exploits are recorded in his own fascinating books.[13] Manus used limpet mines, and within a month of his arrival he sank several ships in Oslo harbor. The German transport steamers *Ortelsburb* (3,800 tons), *Tugela* (5,600 tons), and several others followed. His achievements were crowned by the sinking of the German troopship *Donau,* with 1,200 men aboard.

In the spring of 1943 SOE had begun to train squads of "limpeteers," who were sent from Scotland in a series of Vestige operations. The first took place on 3 September 1943 at Gulenfjord; many more followed.[14]

A substantial amount of German shipping was destroyed, including the troopships *Hartmuth, Sanev,* and *Fritzen.* Chariots of the Welman type—an improvement over those used against the *Graf Tirpitz*—with warheads containing 250 kg of high explosives, were also used.

A number of teams were assigned to sabotage railways, among them *Grebe, Lapwing, Fieldfare,* and *Woodpecker.* At first SHAEF explicitly forbade railway sabotage—against *Milorg's* advice—but changed its mind during the Ardennes offensive in September 1944. Railway sabotage was then greatly intensified, particularly around Oslo, Bergen, and Skien.

The Oslo Gang

If Manus was a master underwater saboteur, Gunnar Sonsteby certainly matched him on land. He had been an accountant but became a James Bond character in many disguises and under many aliases: No. 24, Kjakan, Broch, Erling, Field. Sonsteby had joined the Resistance soon after the invasion, later went to Britain, was trained by SOE, and returned with Knut Haugland (of Barren Mountain fame). Colonel Wilson said of him: "Gunnar Sonsteby, in all probability, was the most efficient and most productive secret agent in Norway."

Sonsteby assembled a group of young men who proudly called them-

[13] *Det vil helst ga goth,* and *Det blit alvor,* Oslo, 1946; also *Underwater Saboteur,* Kimber, London, 1953.

[14] The dates of the more important Vestige operations were: Vestige II, 5 September 1943, Askvoll; Vestige III, 9 September 1943, Alesund; Vestige IV, 5 March 1944, Egersund; Vestige V, 31 March 1944, Sagvag; Vestige VIII, 12 April 1944, Sovdefjord and Skorpen; Vestige XII, 16 March 1944, Malm and Jossundfjord; Vestige XIV, 31 March 1944, Fredrikstad.

selves the Oslo Gang. With bombs they attacked the Oslo Gestapo headquarters, the SS barracks at Korsvoll, destroyed the Luftwaffe establishment at Tonsberg and the armament factory at Kongsberg. They helped
the *Company* team blow up the Lysaker chemical works and the plant and
stores of the Norsk Sulphur Company. These were but a few of their many
actions.

After German attempts to enlist Norwegian technicians and workers for
German war factories on a voluntary basis had utterly failed, Reichs-
Kommissar Terboven ordered compulsory mobilization of labor in Norway (*Arbeitseinsatz*), and 80,000 engineers, fitters, and skilled workers
were ordered to report. For their records the Germans used punched cards
that were run through tabulating machines. Only one firm in Norway, the
Norsk Watson Company, had these machines. The Oslo Gang attacked
the office in broad daylight, and the machines were destroyed. But the
Labor Office, headed by the quisling Christian Astrup, still had an index
with the names of the forced-labor conscripts.

Sonsteby led six abortive attacks on the Astrup office until, on the
seventh attempt, the office was demolished by bombs and the archives and
records destroyed. The Germans, unable to round up the conscripts, de-
creed that men eligible for the *Arbeitseinsatz* would have to produce their
conscription cards when applying for food ration books. They had now
the choice of starving or reporting for deportation.

On the morning of 26 July 1944 a large van carrying boxes of 75,000
newly printed food ration books left a plant in Oslo to be distributed
to district food offices. The Oslo Gang staged a holdup, overwhelmed the
driver and four guards, and drove the van outside the city. At a safe house
Milorg members collected the ration books and distributed them to nearly
all the men threatened by deportation. The entire *Arbeitseinsatz* in Norway
collapsed as a result. The Germans could trace only a few hundred of the
men, although they deported several thousand, rounded up at random.
At least 60,000 technicians and skilled workers were saved from forced
labor in Germany.

The crowning coup of Sonsteby's gang was the capture of the archives
of Quisling's Department of Justice and the Nazi-controlled police headquarters. These archives contained the records of all members of the
Nasjonal Samling, the *Hird* militia, traitors, collaborators, and Gestapo
V-men. Resistance leaders wanted these records to bring the quislings
to justice after liberation. But they knew that quisling officials and Gestapo
chiefs had prepared to destroy them. Assisted by officials in the Justice
department and in the police headquarters who secretly worked for the
Resistance, Sonsteby secured passes to enter the building. Several members of the gang, wearing uniforms of high-ranking police officers, arrived

at the two offices. Sonsteby presented a forged order from SS Gruppen-Führer Heinrich Fehlis, the chief of the Oslo Gestapo, demanding the delivery of all records. At the Department of Justice the gang collected two tons of documents, which were loaded into a van and driven away. At the Oslo police HQ the officer on duty had no keys to the safe containing the files. Sonsteby, arrogantly ordered the safe to be removed; it was lowered from a second-story window and driven off in a German van which the gang had stolen beforehand. This happened only a few days before the German C in C Norway, General von Falkenhorst, surrendered. The records captured by Sonsteby's gang provided all the evidence needed at the trials of Vidkun Quisling and other traitors and German war criminals, which began soon after the liberation.

Arms for Milorg

Norway was the only enemy-occupied country in Western Europe that liberated herself from the Nazi invaders. Although Field Marshal Montgomery had accepted Germany's unconditional surrender on 4 May 1945 at his headquarters on the Lüneburger Heide, the surrender terms applied only to German armies in Western Germany, Holland, and Denmark. In Norway the Germans remained in power until 8 May, when General von Falkenhorst decided to capitulate after a show of force by armed units of *Milorg,* which began to occupy Oslo and all the larger towns. Allied troops arrived by air, mainly units of the British Special Air Forces, but they were so few that they could not possibly cope with the German army of occupation, which still exceeded 400,000 men. *Milorg* men also freed 85,000 Russian, 2,000 Yugoslav, and 4,000 British, Danish, French, and Belgian prisoners of war, who had been brought by the Germans to Norway to work on fortifications and coastal defenses and in ports.

The 45,000 *Milorg* members were able to liberate their homeland, round up and disarm the German troops, and maintain law and order because they had been adequately armed by SOE and OSS during the preceding year.[15] SOE liaison officers, instructors, and W/T operators played a vital role in organizing and training *Milorg* and in maintaining an unbroken and regular radio link with the headquarters of SOE, the Norwegian high command in London, and finally with SHAEF. That two SOE instructors, Olav Doublong and Torbjorn Hoff, alone trained fifty-nine potential *Milorg* commanders indicates the successful efforts of many more SOE men in organizing Norwegian patriots. It must be stressed that,

[15] Allied Special Forces arrived by air on 7 and 8 May 1945 only at Oslo, Stavanger, Kristiansand, and Bergen. A British military mission, headed by Brigadier Hilton and Lt. Colonel Hampton, arrived on 8 May in Oslo.

with very few exceptions, all SOE agents sent to Norway were Norwegian citizens, who trained in the Special Training Schools of SOE but remained in contact with their own national headquarters in London. Colonel Bjarne Öen, chief of Section IV of the Norwegian general staff in London, was the senior officer, who, with several other Norwegian officers, worked with Colonel Wilson at the SOE Norwegian section between 1942 and 1945.

The following figures of SOE supplies to *Milorg* are taken from the records of the Norwegian general staff [16] and are not complete, because other deliveries were made to groups under the control of other organizations, including the British Secret Service.

In 1942: 67 containers with arms, explosives, and other material

In 1943: 272 containers with arms, explosives, plastic charges, and other material

In 1944 (until 2 May): 3,659 containers and packages with Sten guns, Bren guns, rifles, bazookas, mortars, plastic explosives, and other material

In 1944 (after 2 May and until liberation): 8,434 containers and packages of every kind of arms, including heavy equipment.[17]

In 1,241 air sorties, 12,524 containers were parachuted. In addition, 445 tons of supplies were delivered by the Shetland Bus from Scotland. Millions of rounds of ammunition, arms, and limpet and R-mines were brought by sea. *Milorg* also secured arms at home. In daring raids on German dumps and on arsenals of the disbanded Norwegian army seized by the Germans, Norwegian patriots captured substantial quantities of rifles, small arms, and ammunition. Moreover, arms were manufactured in sixteen clandestine workshops. Two Oslo gunsmiths, the With brothers, and their helpers, produced more than a thousand homemade Sten guns.

More than 400 SOE agents were parachuted or landed from boats; others came from Sweden. Many were saboteurs or radio operators, but by the autumn of 1943 a large percentage were instructors, badly needed by *Milorg* because of the mass arrests of its commanders and officers. In August 1943 Terboven ordered the arrest of 1,100 former officers and NCOs of the disbanded Norwegian forces, with the explicit purpose of destroying *Milorg* by depriving it of military leaders.[18]

Although in 1942 SOE controlled only about a dozen radio posts, there were more than eighty in operation during the last year of the war; and 289 separate code-named operations took place using this radio link. From the end of 1943, the American OSS (which had established Norwegian

[16] Norwegian General Staff War Archives, Vols. 9–12.
[17] A large percentage of these later supplies came from the U.S. Army.
[18] Norwegian General Staff War Archives, Vol. 20 (SOE Progress Reports).

offices in London and Stockholm) played an increasing role in helping the Norwegian Resistance. From the London OSS office Commander Vetlesen joined Colonel Wilson and Colonel Öen at the SOE Norwegian section.

On 7 June 1945, a month after liberation, Colonel J. S. Wilson stood beside King Haakon and General Wilhelm Hansteen, commander in chief of the new Royal Norwegian Army, reviewing the parade of 15,000 *Milorg* men in Oslo. Like all of them, throughout long and bitter years, the chief of SOE's Norwegian section had striven his utmost to help free Norway. It was an immensely gratifying day.

18

Redoubtable Danes

WHEN the Germans invaded Norway and Denmark on 9 April 1940, British naval units attacked them two days later at Narvik and occupied the port. A few days later the first British brigade landed in southern Norway. But no assistance could be given to the Danes. Their flat and open country, bordering on Germany, offered no prospect of any effective defense as did the snow-covered mountains and remote fjords of Norway.

During the initial stages of the occupation the Germans tried to coax their northern cousins to collaborate. Hitler sent a note to the king, assuring him that "Germany would respect in full measure the existence of the Kingdom, the freedom of the Danish people, and the future independence of the country," but added that "any resistance would be broken with all our power." He did not appoint a German *Statthalter,* as in other occupied countries, but made the German envoy von Renthe-Fink (who had Danish family relations) his personal plenipotentiary. Even the Social Democrat government, in power since 1929, was allowed to function until it was later reformed into a coalition of all parties.

The Nazis had good reasons for assuming that they could take over control by subterfuge while adopting a policy of conciliation. Long before Denmark attracted Hitler's military attention, she had suffered the distinction of being the center of German espionage and subversion in Scandinavia. Captain Horst von Pflugh–Hartung, a veteran of the Nazi Free Corps, was the chief of the German spy center in Copenhagen. Since 1936, offering lavish funds, he supported the tiny Danish Nazi party of Frits Clausen and enrolled a handful of Danes who admired Hitler's racial theories. Among them were Inspector Max Pelving of the Danish Police Aliens Department and Eiler Pontopiddan, a lawyer.

The German spy center had no difficulty in maintaining communications with Berlin. The facilities of the Danish branch of the German-owned Telefunken Radio Company were used to establish several secret radio posts in Copenhagen and elsewhere.

On the other hand, the Danish Foreign Office and Danish Military Intelligence had cordial relations with the British and French authorities and kept British diplomatic and secret service representatives in Copenhagen informed about German activities. After the German attack on Poland and the outbreak of the war, the Danish government did not flinch from arresting Pflugh-Hartung and several of his agents. They were put on trial and two Danish agents were sentenced to eight years' imprisonment for treason. Berlin reacted to this "provocative action" with threats of retaliation, which were fulfilled sooner than the Danes anticipated.

There were a British legation and military and naval missions in Copenhagen, and the Danish government obtained permission from General Luedke, the commander in chief of the occupation forces, for them to leave unmolested. On 13 April 1940 a sealed train set off from Copenhagen through Germany for Belgium. In it were the British minister, Howard Smith, his diplomatic staff, and British subjects who had represented shipping and commercial interests in Denmark.

By the time the forlorn Britons arrived in Brussels, Commander Frank Stagg of the British naval mission decided to prepare plans to help Danish patriots who had told him that they were determined to set up clandestine Resistance groups. At his room at the Hotel Gallia in Brussels, Stagg assembled seven or eight members of the British legation staff and the naval and commercial missions and asked them whether they would be willing to work in an Anglo–Danish office in London for Denmark's liberation.[1]

Their immediate response was enthusiastic. But after their arrival in London, Stagg and his friends soon discovered that they had misjudged the attitude of Chamberlain, Lord Halifax, and the Foreign Office. When Stagg submitted his plans to them he received a very cool response. On 16 April he turned to Brendan Bracken, the parliamentary private secretary to Winston Churchill, then first lord of the Admiralty. Bracken jumped at the idea.

Unfortunately, Churchill was immersed in preparations for the Norwegian campaign. When Bracken approached the Foreign Office he received short shrift. A few days later he telephoned Commander Stagg to say the Foreign Office had turned down any suggestion of becoming involved in the affairs of Denmark, which technically was "neither an ally nor a belligerent, but a neutral country whose government had accepted German occupation." As for the officials who had arrived in London from Copenhagen, the Foreign Office—according to Bracken—decided that "if

[1] Commander Stagg's articles in *Politiken*, 27 September 1948.

there was anybody who knew Denmark, they would post him quickly to South America . . . !" [2] The Foreign Office was as good as their word. The little group that wanted to help the Danes resist the Nazis was hastily dispersed.

Even among Danes in London there was a division of opinion on the merits of establishing a Resistance organization in exile. Two men, however, had no doubts. Werner Michael Iversen, a former rubber planter in Malaya, and Carl Johan Bruhn, a young doctor studying in London, began to create a Danish organization that could align itself with Britain. They encountered opposition from the Danish ambassador in London, Count Eduard Reventlow, who had decided to wait and see. Denmark had declared herself a neutral country; Hitler had reassured King Christian that he would respect Danish neutrality. Any premature move by the Danes abroad, it was argued by Count Reventlow and some other Danes in London, could only worsen the situation at home.

It was not until early in 1942, after the United States had entered the war and the Danish government, headed by Eric Scavenius, had signed the so-called Anti-Komintern covenant with the Axis powers, that Count Reventlow and his friends abandoned that argument. In the meantime, in October 1940, a group of Danes established the Free Danish Council in London.

As the months wore on these Danish patriots in London desperately canvassed members of Parliament and junior ministers for help. Usually they were brushed off. Nevertheless, their efforts and those of a few British friends succeeded in bringing many Danish ships, which had been on the high seas at the time of the German attack, to British and American ports. As a result, some two hundred Danish ships and five thousand Danish sailors served in the Allied merchant navy for the duration.

Danes Join SOE

Undaunted by the opposition, Iversen was eager to enroll young Danes into a Danish voluntary corps, which would serve with the British army. He and his like-minded countrymen regularly met at the Danish Club in Knightsbridge, London. Neither they nor the newly established Free Danish Council received support from the British government; indeed their activities were viewed with misgivings.

In the autumn of 1940 Iversen heard of Churchill's order to carry subversion and sabotage into German-occupied Europe, and while SOE was

[2] This was told to the author by Commander Stagg, who also mentioned it in his articles in *Politiken,* September 1948.

still being formed, Commander Stagg introduced him to Sir Charles Hambro. Iversen submitted a plan for a Danish section of SOE. Sir Charles was impressed and decided to incorporate the plan into his Scandinavian section. In November 1940 Hambro flew to Stockholm where he met the leader of the Danish patriotic movement in Sweden, Ebbe Munck, a distinguished journalist. During the autumn of 1940 Munck sent England microfilms of important German documents depicting the deployment of the German fleet in the Baltic, plans for U-boat operations in the North Sea, and the location of German military installations in Denmark. Danish officers managed to supply Munck with other valuable information, which he relayed to London; and finally the realization dawned that Danish Resistance could assist in the war against Hitler.

When Sir Charles Hambro returned to London, the Danish section of SOE became active. Ronald Turnbull, who had been press attaché of the British legation in Copenhagen, was sent to Stockholm to join Munck as SOE's liaison officer. He did not reach the Swedish capital until February 1941 after a wide detour forced on him by the unreliability of a direct air journey. He traveled by sea to South Africa, flew from the Cape to Cairo, then to Turkey, and on by rail to Moscow, Leningrad, and Finland for the final voyage to his destination. Turnbull was ordered to take this route following Sir Charles Hambro's adventures on his return flight from Sweden; he was flown in an RAF aircraft by an erratic Polish pilot, who lost his way, went too far south, and was fired on over the German island of Silt.

Brigadier Gubbins asked Dr. Dalton to help him enlist for SOE some of the other South Americans (as the former British officials in Copenhagen were nicknamed, after having been banned from work for Danish Resistance). Thus Lieutenant Commander Ralph Hollingworth, a former member of the naval mission in Copenhagen, was retrieved from a post in Iceland and appointed head of the new Danish section, a post he filled with great distinction until the end of the war. Commander Stagg, one of very few Britons who spoke fluent Danish, became the guiding hand in the complex preparations for recruiting and training Danes and Norwegians as SOE saboteurs, instructors, liaison officers, and W/T operators.

Three other veterans of the diplomatic train were given important appointments: Reginald Spink became Hollingworth's deputy, Captain R. L. Taylor was entrusted with recruitment and training, and Albert Christensen was sent to Göteborg, Sweden, with instructions similar to those of Ronald Turnbull in Stockholm. SOE also gained the services of Werner Michael Iversen, who was commissioned as a captain in the Royal East Kent Regiment, The Buffs, whose honorary colonel in chief was King Christian X. It was agreed that The Buffs should become the cadre for all Danish volunteers, and that those suitable for SOE should be sent on from the regiment to the Special Training Schools.

Recruitment proved difficult. Quite apart from the shortage of young Danes in Britain qualified for the dangerous work, Whitehall had yet to be convinced of the wisdom of supporting a Danish Resistance movement. By dint of great effort, however, the first fifteen recruits had begun SOE training at Gumley Hall by the end of January 1941. Even so, the War Office insisted that no volunteer should be told he might be sent to Denmark to engage in sabotage or subversive activities.

Captain Iversen, who became the chief recruiting officer for the Danish section, soon ran afoul of the Free Danish Council, whose leaders were filled with understandable resentment at not being told what was happening to the men they were supposed to help recruit. Iversen, disliking the impossible position in which he had been placed, left SOE in the spring of 1943 to serve in the 21st British Army Group. After the war Commander Hollingworth admitted that "security regulations were such that few Free Danish leaders in London were allowed to know what was being planned." Once again the unwillingness of Whitehall and the War Office to trust the exiled leaders of anti-Nazi Resistance produced frustration and, on occasion, outright hostility.

The redoubtable Commander Stagg solved the problem of recruitment. He nurtured an unofficial working arrangement with Captain C. L. Heel, who presided over the Danish department of the merchant navy reserve pool in Newcastle-on-Tyne. Behind the backs of Whitehall this department forwarded many men to SOE.

One achievement was the formation of a home school for Danish and Norwegian volunteers at Hetherop Castle in Gloucestershire. It gave those responsible for encouraging the Resistance in the two countries a chance of producing agents with proper training. It did not, however, do much to mitigate the confusion prevailing between the British Secret Service, Military Intelligence, and SOE. The extent of that confusion may be judged by the following incident.

In May 1941 SOE, with the cooperation of the Political Warfare Executive, embarked upon a program of "black propaganda" in Denmark— mainly the dropping of subversive leaflets from aircraft. PWE needed a man with detailed knowledge of German measures in Denmark and chose Sten Gudme, the assistant editor of the Copenhagen newspaper *Politiken,* who had become one of the leaders of the underground movement. Sir Charles Hambro ordered Gudme to be brought to England. Turnbull in Stockholm arranged Gudme's escape to Sweden, and after many difficulties he reached London. No sooner did the RAF aircraft touch down in England than Gudme was arrested by the field security police on suspicion of being a German spy. Commander Hollingworth succeeded in obtaining Gudme's release from custody, but he spent another spell under house arrest at the Patriotic School in Battersea.[3]

The Germans Find a Body

The first two Danish SOE trainees selected for parachuting into Denmark were Dr. Carl Johan Bruhn and Mogens Hammer. Bruhn was to be the chief of the first SOE network, and Hammer was to operate the radio link with London. Until then the only contact with the Danish underground movement was by courier to Sweden.

Denmark is a small flat country and the dropping of agents was a much more difficult task than in France or Norway. After several attempts, Bruhn and Hammer were dropped "blind" on 27 December 1941 in the hope that German patrols would be slack at Christmas.

They jumped at Torpeskov near Haslev, forty miles south of Copenhagen. Bruhn was killed; his parachute failed to open. When Hammer landed he looked round for his comrade, who had carried the radio. He never found Bruhn's body or the radio set, but the Germans did. They also discovered Hammer's parachute, and the SD issued an order to all German troops: "The first parachute drop of British agents on Danish soil took place during the night of 27/28 December near Köge. One of the agents is dead, but the other succeeded in escaping. As further parachute drops are to be expected, all troops are warned to observe special attention."

Hammer reached Copenhagen with little money and only a vague idea whom to contact, as Bruhn had been the man in charge. Although strictly forbidden by Commander Hollingworth to approach his own relatives, Hammer decided he would have to. He told a reasonably credible story about leaving his ship at Archangel in Russia and traveling home through Norway and Sweden. Fortunately his brother, Svend Eric, already a member of a Resistance group, could put him in touch with Christmas Möller, the chairman of the Danish Conservative party and former minister of commerce.

The subversive movements in Denmark were as yet weak and without central direction. Officers of the Danish army had established their own group and were known as the Princes. Among their members were several officers of the intelligence department of the Ministry of Defense. Like the French *Deuxième Bureau* at Vichy, this group had approached British Military Intelligence. They did this through the British embassy in Stockholm, and were supplying important information to London.

The Danish Communist party, suppressed by the Gestapo, had gone underground. By the winter of 1941 many of its members had formed the most militant and disciplined of all Resistance organizations, carrying out many acts of sabotage and producing the first clandestine newspaper, *Land*

[3] *Cf.* Muus, F. B., *Ingen taender et Lys,* pp. 14–16 (Copenhagen, 1950).

og Folk (Country and People). The Communists were fully engaged in direct action. Their spearheads were the shock troops of the *Bopa,* regarded as terrorists not only by the Germans but also by many conservative Danes. *Bopa* men burned factories and farms and inflicted more damage on the Danish economy than on the German war effort.

It was not until the middle of 1942 that strong non-Communist organizations, such as *Ringen,* under Social Democratic leadership, and *Dansk Samling* (Danish Unity) came to the forefront of the Resistance movement.

In Stockholm, Ebbe Munck maintained a link between Denmark and London, and although operating by remote control, he established himself as one of the most important leaders of Denmark's struggle against the Germans. He enlisted the support of some Swedish politicians, industrialists, and officers and began to smuggle arms and explosives across the narrow Öresund in fishing boats from the Swedish ports of Malmö, Landskrona, and Hälsingborg. Some of these supplies fell prey to German motorboat patrols, but most of the fishing craft got through. Munck also organized a weekly courier service to London, and it was through him that Hammer finally received a radio to replace the one lost when Dr. Bruhn was killed.

On 26 April 1942 Munck was able to make the following entry in his diary: "First direct radio communications from Arthur [Hammer's code name]." Within a few weeks Commander Hollingworth and Major Taylor were complaining that Hammer's radio signals were very weak. They asked Munck to provide him with more powerful equipment. The problem was taken care of by Hammer himself, who realized the deficiencies of his radio only too well. He persuaded a radio engineer, Lorens Arne Duus Hansen, manager of the firm of Bang and Olufsen, to build a replacement in that company's laboratory. Duus Hansen was to become SOE's key man. But all this was somewhat belated for, although SOE knew nothing about it, London had been receiving important information over the air from Copenhagen for a long time. Their ignorance was due to interdepartmental jealousy in the British Secret Service.

A Do-It-Yourself Plane

Shortly after the German invasion, a young Danish officer, Thomas Sneum, and two friends, Kjeld Petersen and Christian Michael Rottböll, made up their minds to go to England. They attempted to sail across the North Sea in a small fishing boat during the winter of 1940–41, but were forced to abandon the enterprise because of bad weather.

Undeterred, the youthful trio embarked upon a more audacious enterprise: They began to build an aircraft in a lonely barn at Sanderum near Odense. Somehow they acquired the frame of a tiny two-seater sporting plane, and using an automobile engine and an exotic selection of scrap, they assembled a flying machine, which they named Elseminde. On the night of 21 June 1941 Sneum and Petersen dragged the plane out of the barn, swung the prop, and took off for Birtain. (Rottböll had gone to Sweden some weeks before, eventually reached Britain by sea, and joined SOE.)

Predictably, their arrival in Britain was met with profound suspicion. How could two men take off in an aircraft without the knowledge of German authorities? M15 swung into action and long investigations were conducted in great secrecy. After the *bona fides* of the two Danes had been established, they were asked by the British Secret Service whether they would return to Denmark as secret agents. In September 1941, Sneum and a Dane named Christoffersen, a former ship's radio telegrapher, were dropped near Brofelde. They contacted Duus Hansen, who supplied them with a transmitter. Thenceforth they were able to give the C department of the British Secret Service many reliable reports. The value of their work greatly increased after they began receiving regular information from a Danish police officer, Roland Olsen, who later worked for SOE.

At that time, however, SOE was kept in complete ignorance about the SIS link with Denmark. Before long the Germans became aware of the men's activity and they had to separate. Sneum, warned by Olsen of his imminent arrest, escaped across the ice of the Öresund to Sweden.

In the spring of 1942 Hammer became involved in a Danish Resistance group that Baker Street believed to be Communist controlled. SOE chiefs were justifiably upset when they learned, through Stockholm, that Hammer was connected with the production and distribution of clandestine Resistance news-sheets, a laudable activity but quite unsuitable for an SOE agent.

This incident persuaded Hollingworth to abandon the principle that all SOE agents must be trained in Britain. He ordered Hammer to hand over the transmitter and codes to Duus Hansen, the radio engineer, who had already proved his reliability. For the next three years, Hansen was one of SOE's most efficient and successful agents. He maintained the radio link with London and provided the Danish section with a veritable running commentary on events in his country; using microfilms, photographs, and reports, which were reliable and apposite, although he had never received any training by SOE.

But the Danish section needed trained men in the field to serve as liaison officers with Resistance groups, to establish SOE circuits, and to direct sabotage actions.

New Leaders

In April Hollingworth selected Christian Michael Rottböll, the young man who had helped Sneum and Petersen build their makeshift aircraft, as the chief of SOE's circuits in Denmark. Two Danish sailors, Paul Johannesen and Max Mikkelsen, were chosen to accompany Rottböll; both were radio telegraphers who had served in the merchant navy before they enlisted in SOE.

Two attemps to drop them from an RAF aircraft were foiled by Messerschmitt attacks; but on 17 April they jumped into a field near Aggersvold, where the reception had been prepared by Mogens Hammer. Rottböll landed safely, but the other two landed in a group of trees two miles from the DZ and were injured. Neither was found by the reception committee, but they succeeded in dodging German patrols and, despite their injuries, reached Copenhagen, where they contacted Resistance friends and joined Rottböll.

Rottböll arrived in Denmark just as a new leader of the scattered Danish Resistance groups was emerging: wealthy forty-two-year-old Eigil Borch-Johansen. As the managing director of a shipping line with regular service to Swedish ports, he had day-to-day dealings with the Germans, whom he treated with outward courtesy; the Nazi *Landes-Führer,* Dr. Gustav Meissner, considered the shipowner a friend of the Third Reich.

One of Rottböll's assignments was to coordinate the various Resistance groups and to persuade Borch-Johansen to pool his resources with the Princes group of Danish army officers. Rottböll's mission was exceedingly difficult for someone who was only twenty-four.

Rottböll had been told to try and find a prominent Danish politician who would be prepared to escape to England and become the head of a Free Danish Council in London. The Foreign Office felt that the existing organization was insufficiently representative. The natural choice for this post was the Conservative party's Christmas Möller.

Borch-Johansen introduced Rottböll to Möller and they began to plan the escape of the politician and his family. A secret cabin was built in one of Borch-Johansen's ships for the Möllers and their son. They were brought to Limfjorden singly by car, whisked into the concealed compartment, and taken to Göteborg. There they were received by Albert Christensen, the SOE liaison officer who was nominally the British vice-consul. The Möller family arrived in London in May, and Christmas Möller was elected chairman of the Free Danish Council, which in practice became the Danish government in exile.

Back in Copenhagen, Rottböll was having a difficult time. Hammer, mindful that he was the first SOE agent on the scene, refused to take orders from him, and the Princes leaders also resented taking orders from the young "civilian amateur." Moreover, when Rottböll asked London for increased supplies of explosives with which to launch a series of sabotage raids, he was quickly pulled up. The British chiefs of staff had ordered SOE to refrain from any drastic action in Denmark.

On 1 August 1942 three more SOE agents, Hans F. Hansen, Peter

Nielsen, and Knud E. Petersen, were dropped in a field prepared by Rottböll and a few Resistance men, near Farsö on Jutland. The containers that were dropped with them, however, landed miles away near Ranum and were recovered by the German field police.

During 1942, the Germans became increasingly concerned as sabotage and assaults on German soldiers became more frequent and the hostility of the Danish people mounted. The Germans grew so jittery about reports of "mass descents of British agents and saboteurs" that Copenhagen trolley conductors were moved to announce: "All British saboteurs change here," or "Gothersgade; British agents jump here." But in May 1942 there were exactly seven SOE agents in Denmark, and not all were effective.

Paul Johannesen, Rottböll's chief operator, had set up his radio post in an apartment at 8 Vinkelager in a suburb of Copenhagen, and maintained regular "skeds" with Baker Street. Two other transmitters were operating, beamed to Stockholm and Göteborg. The Abwehr was aware of their existence, and direction-finding vans began patrolling the streets.

On the night of 4 September one of these vans located Johannesen's post. This was the first time the Germans had discovered a British radio post in Denmark, and Abwehr officers were so excited that they cordoned off the entire district with *Feldgendarmerie,* German troops, and Danish police. One of the Abwehr officers ordered a Danish policeman to lead the way into the house and several Germans followed, with Alsatian dogs.

Johannesen was ready to sell his life dearly. When the door of his room burst open, he fired, fatally wounding a Danish policeman, Ostergaard Nielsen, and injuring several Germans. Unfortunately, Nielsen was himself a member of the Resistance and was acting under German orders he could not evade.

Before the Germans opened fire, Johannesen dashed into another room, shouting, "You won't get me alive!" Then he swallowed his cyanide pill.

The Abwehr officers found little material in Johannesen's room, but some of it incriminated Hammer. Borch-Johansen volunteered to get Hammer out of Denmark, much against the latter's wish. He had been having a lively time disguising himself as a Protestant parson and on occasion preaching at a German military service. While he was organizing the parson's getaway Borch-Johansen was warned by the Danish police that he, too, had incurred the Abwehr's suspicion. As a major in the Danish army reserve, Borch-Johansen also had a good disguise for subversive activity—his uniform. He arranged a rendezvous with Mogens Hammer in the Grib forest; they traveled to Hilleröd and paddled across to Sweden in a *kajak* (canoe), Borch-Johansen in his uniform and Hammer in his clerical collar.

They had left just in time. Later that month the Abwehr discovered Rottböll's identity and whereabouts. On 25 September Abwehr and Gestapo officers went with seven Danish policemen to Rottböll's headquarters at 29

Öresundgade, in Copenhagen. Again a Danish policeman was ordered to lead the raid. Inspector A. F. Orst entered first and asked Rottböll to surrender. Seeing the Germans hovering in the doorway behind the inspector, Rottböll fired. The shot hit Ost's belt buckle without wounding him. The Germans retaliated with their machine pistols. Fatally wounded, Rottböll fired twice as he fell, but missed.

With Rottböll and Johannesen dead, the small SOE circuit in Denmark broke down. Only four agents were left in the field and none of them could take over the leadership. They had no radio connection with London or contact with each other, no material, no money or ration cards and did not know how to get them.

Commander Hollingworth's problem was solved by the arrival in London of Mogens Hammer and Borch-Johansen.

"I saw Hammer almost immediately after his arrival in London," Hollingworth recalls. "I told him of Rottböll's death and asked him whether he would return to Denmark. He was surprised and he knew the great difficulties which would face him. Yet he agreed at once, which shows what a courageous man Hammer was . . . ."

He was instructed to contact only one of the SOE agents who remained in Denmark, Peter Nielsen. Hammer and Nielsen did not know each other, but Hollingworth feared the other agents might be known to the Germans. Hammer was told to introduce himself to Nielsen as Lindberg.

A Drop into the Sea

It was not going to be easy to land Hammer in Denmark, as the radio link was broken and Baker Street had lost all direct contact with the Resistance groups. Major Taylor suggested to Hammer that he drop into the sea. This type of parachuting had never been attemped before by any SOE agents, but at Ringway Colonel Newnham had conducted a series of successful experiments in water jumping.

Hammer was dropped into the Kattegat off the coast of Tisvilde, Sjaelland on 20 October, wearing an experimental waterproof suit over his ordinary clothing. The new suit served its purpose, and he reached the coast and Copenhagen.

In Copenhagen Hammer (Lindberg) found that Nielsen had already contacted Dr. Mogens Fog, a thirty-nine-year-old professor of medicine, who had taken over from Borch-Johansen. Dr. Fog had been a leading spirit in the underground since the beginning of the German occupation and, with Christmas Möller, had founded the clandestine newspaper *Frit Danmark,* which became a rallying point for several Resistance groups. He also had given a helping hand to Rottböll and occasionally acted as a special courier for SOE using his professional activities as a cover: He was able to travel to Stockholm on the pretext of attending medical conferences.

One of his helpers, Ole Killerich, a member of the editorial committee of *Frit Danmark,* also became an important SOE contact man with Stockholm. Hammer invoked Killerich's aid in dispatching the three hunted SOE agents, Hansen, Petersen, and Mikkelsen, to Sweden. Toward the end of November the three men and Mrs. Mikkelsen were assembled in a flat belonging to Mrs. Emmy Valentin in Höje Skodsborg, a village on the coast of the Öresund, opposite Landskrona, Sweden.

The plan was for the party to row across on 2 December, but there was much drift ice in the sea, and after several attempts they returned to Mrs. Valentin's house. This part of the coast was heavily guarded and apparently the Germans discovered their footprints in the snow.

A *Feldgendarmerie* squad, with Danish policemen surrounded Mrs. Valentin's house. As they did so one of the policemen was able to give a warning, and Killerich and Mrs. Valentin managed to escape. The three SOE agents, however, were captured.

Danish Police Chief Eivind Larsen insisted that the men be remanded in the custody of the Danish authorities. After protracted negotiations, the German C in C, General von Hanneken, promised that if they were handed over to the *Sicherheitsdienst* he personally would guarantee that they would not be shot. For once the Germans kept their word, and Hansen, Petersen, and Mikkelsen were sent to German concentration camps and survived the war.

Hammer and Nielsen, left to their own devices, found there was very little they could do. Even Resistance leaders who had helped SOE agents wholeheartedly up to now had become disenchanted with the benefits of cooperation with Baker Street. Although they continuously asked the Stockholm office for supplies of arms and explosives, very few drops took place, partly because the Danish section remained the Cinderella of SOE and partly because of the general shortage of aircraft and material. Moreover, the SOE chiefs were well aware of the weakness of the organization in Denmark.

When the bitter complaints of the Danish Resistance were passed on to London by Munck and Christensen, it appears Hammer was nominated as the scapegoat. Hammer was a brave man but neither easy to get on with nor very conscious of security. Complaints were made that he was endangering the Resistance movement, and in February 1943 Commander Hollingworth decided to recall him.

As the tempo of Allied planning for the invasion of northern France increased, the importance of the Scandinavian countries became more apparent. The Danish section was given higher priority, but it still remained the smallest at Baker Street, its tiny staff—Hollingworth, secretary Maisie Defries, Major Taylor, and Reginald Spink—squeezed into three small rooms.

In preparation for greater activity, Major Taylor visited Stockholm and discussed plans with Ebbe Munck and others. Eigil Borch-Johansen, after his arrival in London, was put in charge of operations at Baker Street, a post he retained until the end of the war.

In the spring of 1943 RAF Bomber Command was ordered to attack targets in Denmark for the first time. German installations and barracks were bombed and a heavy raid was made on the large shipbuilding yards of Burmeister & Wain in Copenhagen. Although the Danes suffered casualties and heavy property damage, they welcomed these signs of Allied interest. After each raid hundreds of V-signs appeared on the walls and pavements of Copenhagen.

It was at the ebb of its fortune that the Danish section of SOE found a new and vigorous leader to command the circuits in the field.

Table Talk

To replace Hammer, Hollingworth chose Flemming Bruun Muus, a big hearty man with a ready smile and an indefatigable zest for adventure, who before the war had tramped around the world as a sailor, engineer, and prospector. After coming to London in 1942, he was enlisted by the British Secret Service; but having learned that there was "a much more interesting joint," he finally found his way to Iversen and Hollingworth, and was sent to the STS at Hatherop Castle.

Muus felt uneasy about replacing Hammer, a man who, Hollingworth told him, "had taken a terrific risk in returning to Denmark on his second mission after being hunted by Gestapo." But Hollingworth assured him that Hammer was a marked man and had to be withdrawn.

Two new teams were selected to be dropped in Denmark. The first consisted of Ole Geisler, Hans Henrik Larsen, Gunnar Christiansen, and Adolf Larsen; the second was Flemming Muus, Einar Balling, Vener Johansen, and Poul Jensen. The new circuit was code-named TABLE. Hammer, while he was still in charge, was Table Top; Duus Hansen, the chief radio operator, was Table Napkin; Gunnar Christiansen, the other "pianist," was Table Mat. The ebullient Flemming Muus was Table Talk. Other agents were Table Salt, Pepper, Marmalade, and so forth.

Muus was given a new identity as Carl Moeller, salesman, for Valentinervej, Copenhagen; his English shirts bore the label of the well-known Copenhagen Andersen Brothers store; on his jacket (bought in Regent Street) was the name of a Danish tailor. Borch-Johansen briefed him about contacts and safe houses. At last, on 12 March 1943, Muus and his team jumped near Lake Nordum on Jutland.

The drop was unusual in that the team took bicycles with them, which were dropped in special containers. They were supposed to be met by a reception committee, but the pilot missed the dropping zone, and they decided to cycle to Stovring. There the safe house was the school; headmaster Robert Staermose was a Resistance leader who had given great assistance to Rottböll and other SOE agents. As Paul Jensen was injured on landing, the cycle cavalcade proceeded slowly. When they saw German patrols on the road they dumped their cycles in one of the many lakes and continued on foot. At last they reached the safe house. Next morning one of the cycles was found by a German patrol, and the hunt for the "British terrorists" started sooner than Muus had expected.

They had to leave the school quickly, and separated. Muus went to Aalborg to contact Resistance leaders whose names he had been given in London, and eventually reached Copenhagen, where he met Hammer. The other men went to Terndrup to wait for orders.

The first meeting with Hammer was rather painful for Muus. He had to explain that he was to take over the leadership. Hollingworth, of course, had notified Hammer about this in a signal: "You have had a long run in a most risky and exposed position. It is better for you to come back, and you could be of very great value to us here." At the same time Hollingworth sent a signal to Duus Hansen that explained his decision in plain words: "Hammer will never again be sent back and will never be given a position of authority in London. As far as Denmark is concerned Hammer is finished until the end of the war."[4] The bravest of agents is expendable. Having become too great a liability in the field, Hammer was no longer useful. Even after he arrived in London he was never offered the post of planning officer at the SOE Danish section, for which he had hoped. Bitterly disillusioned, he enlisted in the Royal Army Service Corps and was killed in a motor accident in 1945, when commanding a transport unit in Hamburg.

Flemming Muus took over the reins soon after his arrival in Copenhagen. He established good relations with such prominent leaders of the Resistance movement as Stig Jensen, Flemming Juncker, and Professor Fog; soon he had regular contact with the three large Resistance organizations—*Ringen, Dansk Samling,* and the Communists. While Duus Hansen continued to occupy an important position as chief of radio operations, Muus relied to a large extent on his friends Gunnar Christiansen and Ole Geisler (with whom he had been trained). The radio post that Christiansen operated continued without a break until spring 1944.

[4] Haestrup, J., *Kontakt med England,* Thanning, Copenhagen, 1959, p. 187.

The choice of his headquarters was characteristic of Flemming Muus' sense of humor. He had an elderly aunt in Copenhagen, Mrs. Gudrun Zahle, who lived in the Damenhotellet which provided accommodation exclusively for women. Muus persuaded the hotel owner, Mrs. Else de Neergaard, to turn it into the headquarters of SOE's TABLE. Soon Auntie Zahle, under the code name Daphne, and the matronly hotel owner were immersed in clandestine work, and Herr Moeller, the traveling salesman, had become the only resident male guest at the Damen Hotel.

During the late spring and summer of 1943 several new SOE agents arrived by parachute in Denmark. Muus worked tirelessly enlarging his organization and TABLE was now richly laid.

19

V-Rocket Secrets

A GOOD DEAL of nonsense has been written since the war about V-rocket spies and the discovery of the German rocket-testing station at Peenemünde. One romantic story was about a White Russian engineer who worked for the Germans and, plagued by his conscience, revealed the secrets to the British. Another writer ascribed the discovery of German rocket and atom bomb experiments to a blond double agent, Lilly Sergeyev (another Russian), who is supposed to have popped up in most unlikely places between London and Madrid, Paris and Berlin, or Warsaw and Lisbon, spilling the secrets of the flying bombs on her travels. Then there was a glamorous French woman spy, *la Souris* (the Mouse), who is said to have smuggled out the plans of the V-rockets developed by Wernher von Braun.

A claim also has been made on behalf of young Englishwoman, Flight-Officer Constance Babington-Smith, who in May 1943 drew the attention of her superiors to recurring unidentifiable objects on some aerial photographs taken during RAF reconnaissance flights. The objects were rocket ramps, but I am sure that she would be the last person to claim that she had discovered the secrets of Peenemünde. The Germans began experiments with unmanned rockets before 1933; the work was concentrated at Peenemünde in 1936. British intelligence received information about it before the war, even though some air marshals were inclined to dismiss the reports as a propaganda plan invented by Goering and Goebbels.

Early in 1941 British Secret Service and Air Intelligence knew many details about the Peenemünde research station. By the winter of 1942 detailed reports were reaching London from the French MARCO POLO group in Paris. This group, led by Pierre Montrose and Jacques Bergier (who called himself Verne, after author Jules Verne), included two scientists, Professor André Heilbronner and Dr. Alfred Eskenazy, the latter a pioneer of the electronic brain. Both worked for the French general staff before 1939 on rocket research. Being Jews, they took a grave risk by remaining in France to continue their work after the German occupation. The MARCO POLO Resistance scientists were mainly responsible for the information about V-rockets and Peenemünde received by Allied Intelligence and SHAEF.[1]

But Danish SOE agents also made an important contribution. They provided vital information about German efforts to perfect the V-rockets, which were later used for the bombardment of London and southern England.

On 16 July 1943 Duus Hansen, who had worked for the SIS since December 1941, long before he was asked to assist SOE, received a message from a British intelligence department known to him as Hannibal. He maintained regular contact with Hannibal by radio and by courier service to the Stockholm office. The message received by Hansen on 16 July 1943 read:

CAN YOU REPORT ON ACTIVITY AT PEENEMUNDE REPEAT PEENEMUNDE NEAR GREIFSWALD WHERE ENEMY ARE PRODUCING AND EXPERIMENTING WITH LONG RANGE ROCKETS REPEAT ROCKETS STOP BELIEVE NEW RADIO REPEAT RADIO APPARATUS ON BORNHOLM CONNECTED WITH THESE EXPERIMENTS STOP WE WOULD LIKE DESCRIPTION OF ROCKET AND EMPLACEMENT AND SCALE OF ROCKET AND PROJECTOR PRODUCTION AT PEENEMUNDE REPEAT PEENEMUNDE END

This was a tall order. The Danish island of Bornholm, which had become the target area for the German rocket tests, is only 25 miles from the southernmost tip of Sweden and 50 miles north of the German coast, but more than 120 miles from Copenhagen. Bornholm had been virtually sealed off by the Germans from the outside world; people in Copenhagen used to say that each of its 40,000 inhabitants was guarded by a German SS man. Several thousand islanders had been deported. In peacetime the small town of Rönne and the seaside villages on Bornholm were holiday resorts, and there was frequent steamer service from Denmark. But in 1943 the only regular connection between the island and the mainland was by German warships and E-boats from and to Kolberg and Stettin.

Hansen asked a former Danish naval officer, Commander Christian Hassager Christensen, a member of the Princes Resistance group to go to Bornholm and find out what he could about the German rocket installations. Christensen's assignment was extremely dangerous. Nevertheless, he got to Bornholm on a fishing boat, and succeeded not only in photographing the German rocket establishments and radar installations but also in making detailed plans of the test target area. He brought all this material safely back to Copenhagen.

[1] Jacques Bergier recounted the story in *Agents secrets contre armes secrètes* (Editions Arthaud, Paris, 1955). Also *cf.* Illingworth R., *The Flying Bomb;* and Air Chief-Marshal Sir Roderick Hill, *German Flying Bomb and Rocket Offensive.*

Hansen was reluctant to risk dispatching such sensational intelligence through couriers to Sweden. Moreover, he had received queries from Commander Hollingworth about Peenemünde and was not certain whether his reports should be sent to Hannibal or to the Danish section of SOE. As on so many occasions, work of the SIS, Military Intelligence, and SOE appeared to overlap—confusing agents in the field. He sent a message to Ronald Turnbull in Stockholm, asking him to inform Hannibal and requesting instructions. Turnbull replied:

MY HEADQUARTERS [2] ARE PREPARED TO GUARANTEE ABSOLUTELY FULL SECRECY OF YOUR SPECIAL MESSAGES STOP I HAVE BEEN INSTRUCTED TO FORWARD ANY SUCH MESSAGES TO MY HEADQUARTERS UNDEVELOPED STOP I ENTIRELY AGREE THAT SUCH MATTERS ARE SO ALL-EMBRACING AND SECRET THAT IT IS NECESSARY TO TAKE STRICTEST PRECAUTIONS END [3]

Thus, after some delay, Hansen forwarded the microfilms and diagrams to the Stockholm office of SOE and sent explanatory radio signals to Hollingworth. SOE was able to steal the British Secret Service's thunder. The significance of the Bornholm and Peenemünde material may be judged from a signal sent by Commander Hollingworth to Duus Hansen, received on 27 August:

PLEASE TELL BANNOCK [Christenen and his friends] THAT HANNIBAL IS DELIGHTED WITH THE VAST AMOUNT OF INTELLIGENCE MATERIAL THAT THEY HAVE BEEN ABLE TO SEND STOP IT IS GREATLY APPRECIATED BY ALL DEPARTMENTS CONCERNED END

On this occasion rivalry in London was forgotten and the vital information from Denmark was shared by all the secret departments and submitted to Churchill and the Allied chiefs of staff. RAF and American aircraft carried out the famous raids on Peenemünde; on 18 August 1943 the heaviest Anglo–American raid ever concentrated on such a small area destroyed much of the research station. V-1 rocket operations began during the night of 13–14 June 1944, but Hitler's plan to plaster London with 5,000 V-rockets every day was never fulfilled. The destruction at Pennemünde, together with the heavy bombing of Bornholm and the rocket ramps in France and Holland, broke the back of Hitler's vengeful offensive. It is a common belief in Britain that the "V" of the V-weapons stood for "victory"; in fact it stood for the German word *Vergeltung*—vengeance.

Danish SOE agents and Resistance men contributed much other information concerning rockets. For instance, they produced answers to queries like this:

[2] Meaning SOE headquarters. E. H. C.

[3] This and subsequent messages are from the Duus Hansen Archives, files 9–12.

Rugen is the German island opposite Peenemünde. Again, the Danish SOE
agents succeeded in accomplishing the almost impossible by finding out what
was going on in the immediate vicinity of the rocket research station.[4]

The Inn in the Forest

Although Duus Hansen was being kept busy with these assignments, he did
not neglect to provide Flemming Muus, the newly arrived leader of the
SOE circuit, with regular radio links with London and the Stockholm office.
Muus had left his safe house at the Damen Hotel and moved to the Hvidsten
Inn in the midst of a pine forest near Randers. It proved an excellent
hideout from the intensified searches of the *Sicherheitsdienst* after more
SOE agents arrived from Britain.

Landlord Marius Fiil and his family had devoted themselves to the cause
of Resistance from its early days, working with Flemming Juncker, one of
the Resistance leaders, who had a large estate near by. When Ole Geisler
and his SOE team arrived in February, they found a refuge at the inn. Many
more receptions were later arranged near Hvidsten.

Between May and August 1943 eighteen SOE agents arrived there, in-
cluding Preben Lok-Lindblad, who became Flemming Muus' personal
assistant. Using Hvidsten Inn as his headquarters, Flemming Muus within a
very short time organized a number of circuits covering the whole country.
He placed his SOE comrades in strategic places: Poul Jensen in Aalborg,
Andy (Adolf) Larsen in Frederikshavn, Verner Johansen in Randers, Einar
Balling in Esbjerg, with Ole Geisler later in command of all Jutland circuits.
Peter Nielsen in Copenhagen was in charge of Sjaelland and set up the first
sabotage college which trained SOE sabotage groups led by Lars Landorph.

Muus treated Baker Street in the same forthright way as he did his
subordinates. A recurrent complaint in his signals to London was the un-
satisfactory manner in which some RAF pilots made their runs and effected
drops. In May Muus signaled: "In both last cases the aircraft flew far too
high, probably between 1,000 and 1,100 feet, and the dispatch of the containers could very well have been observed for miles. Furthermore, it is
dangerous for aircraft to fly straight towards the DZ, drop the cargo, and
return in a beeline. This was the case when Table Lamp [Kai Lund] was
dropped. In the case of Habit [Lok-Lindblad] the aircraft spent far too
much time over the DZ, making huge circles, first dropping the containers

[4] Duus Hansen Archives, files 9–12; and *cf.* La Cour, V., *Danmark under Besaettel-
sen,* Vol. III, pp. 483–484, Copenhagen, 1947.

(which could have been observed by German patrols) and then returning after six minutes and dropping Habit. Our lights were already removed when Habit jumped . . . ."

In another signal Muus described how SOE agents Tripe and Margarine were dropped by an apparently erratic pilot. Margarine was dispatched over Madum Lake, landed in the water some 60 feet from the shore, and nearly drowned; his radio transmitter fell into the middle of the lake and sank. These were normal vagaries of parachuting, and Muus did not fully appreciate the difficulties of the pilots and dispatchers. Drops of men and material in Denmark were carried out with far fewer losses than in any other enemy-occupied country.

Muus also frequently complained about the quality of some of the agents sent to him. A very tough man himself, he only wanted agents who could live up to his standards. Adolf Larsen, who had done good work in Frederikshavn, was caught by the Gestapo when, flouting security rules, he had a love affair with a woman and boasted to her that he had come from England. This woman was a Gestapo informer, Grete Lorte. Worried that Larsen might talk under torture, Muus first tried to arrange his escape from Aarhus prison; when the attempt failed, he tried to smuggle an L pill into Larsen's cell, knowing that he would swallow the poison rather than betray his comrades. Police Inspector Roland Olsen, who secretly worked for the Resistance, undertook to give the pill to Larsen. But this plan was foiled, too. Larsen was taken to a German concentration camp.

His comrades decided to avenge him. At that time the SOE agents received a consignment of 808 plastic explosives, which they called "marzipan" because of its pleasant smell. Poul Jensen made a small bomb with a detonator that would go off when the string round the box, containing a generous portion of the marzipan, was detached. The parcel, disguised as a box of candy, was sent to Grete Lorte. She was out when it was delivered, and it was opened by her lover, a V-man. The explosion killed the man on the spot. Although Grete had escaped, the SOE agents consoled themselves with the thought that at least they had succeeded in disposing of another traitor.

There was another incident that, from the point of view of the SOE men, was more tragic. An agent, whose code name was Table Tennis, was killed by his own comrades. By his careless behavior he had endangered the whole circuit of Sjaelland. On Muus' order—confirmed by Baker Street [5] —he was shot on 2 May 1943 at Sjaelse.

Muus and his friends either carried out themselves, or organized a great many sabotage actions. At first they were extremely short of explosives, but

[5] Hollingworth replied: "The reports re Table Tennis are extremely disturbing. We regard his indiscretion as criminal treachery. We blame it on ourselves for not picking the right material."

by the summer of 1943 increasing supplies of containers reached them at the dropping zones of Jutland, and particularly around the Hvidsten Inn.

The Danish Council in London was worried that a large amount of these arms and explosives would reach Communist groups. This was inevitable, as they were by far the most active saboteurs of the various Resistance organizations. But Muus was careful not to let the Communists dominate the Resistance movement. In July he reported to Hollingworth: "I have made Table Jelly [Captain Paul Hansen] sabotage chief for Copenhagen. He has under him various groups, but I do not want Jelly to become entangled with the Communists who are attended to by yours truly and Orange [Professor Fog]. It is my aim to collect all sabotage groups under one hat."

Muus' careful supervision of the Communist saboteurs was wise. The Russians, who had agents in Denmark, were trying to exert as much influence as possible.

Initially sabotage was performed almost exclusively by the Communist *Bopa* groups. But from the autumn of 1943 a new non-Communist sabotage organization, *Holger Danske,* came into its own. While before, actions were hit-and-run affairs, often rather senseless, SOE instructions, and saboteurs trained by them, began to select targets whose destruction would inflict real harm on the Germans and the German war effort. In 1942 only 122 major sabotage actions were successfully carried out; the number increased to 969 in 1943. Among the SOE men, Ole Geisler and Einar Balling were particularly responsible for organizing actions against port installations at Esbjerg and the railway system in Jutland. Many factories under German control were destroyed or badly damaged. In 1943, from May to August, 398 major sabotage actions took place in Copenhagen alone.

An End to Correctness

Until 1943 the Germans had adopted a lenient attitude toward the Danes. There were few arrests; the Gestapo, although firmly established, was not much in evidence. The Danish authorities, the courts of law, and the police were allowed to function almost normally. For once it seemed the Germans were content not to provoke aggressive resistance by tyrannical behavior. They swallowed their pride to a surprising extent. In the streets of Copenhagen it was not uncommon to see Danes displaying little badges in their buttonholes with the letters "SDU," standing for the popular slogan *Smid den ud* (Throw them out); the letters were also painted on many walls. Some Danes even wore Union Jack badges, and this symbol also appeared in windows, particularly when the BBC found some good news to broadcast. Boys and girls wore knitted caps with blue, white, and red circles resembling the RAF insignia. Movie audiences were especially lively, greeting the frequent appearance in newsreels of Hitler with cries of "Who is this guy?" and making comments on Dr. Goebbels' harangues. A typical exchange between a Nazi film commentator and a Danish audience would go like this: "Here are one hundred bombers on their way to attack England!" And the reply in unison: "And two hundred returned safely to base!"

As late as March 1943 the Germans allowed the Danes to hold a general election. They tried everything—promises, bribes, intimidation—to win votes for candidates of the Danish Nazi party. The result was overwhelming defeat. The Social Democrats won 66 seats, the Conservatives 31, the Agrarians 28, and the Liberals 13; the remaining 11 seats were split up among several minor parties, with the Danish Nazis scraping up just 3 of them.

Hitler's wrath was aroused by the election results, and the days of German correctness were over. The Führer's special plenipotentiary, Dr. Werner Best, summoned some of the toughest RSHA officials to Copenhagen. The Gestapo took over. The first measures were to impose a curfew and to carry out mass arrests at Odense and Esbjerg, sites of major sabotage. The Danes responded with street demonstrations and attacks on German establishments. German troops quelled the riots by firing into the crowds of demonstrators, killing and wounding many people.

This in turn prompted a wave of strikes in Copenhagen and other cities. German officers and soldiers, particularly SS men, were set up in the streets, military vehicles were attacked and set afire.

By August 1943 the strikes had spread throughout the country. SS Ober-Führer Best proclaimed a state of emergency and a general curfew, 8:30 P.M. to 5 A.M., and introduced summary courts to pronounce death sentences upon terrorists. Capital punishment had been abolished for many years in Denmark, and the Danes were shocked and enraged. Unrest increased, and in September the German SD began to take hostages. The first ten Danish civilians were executed at Odense.

Best sent an ultimatum to seventy-three-year-old King Christian, who was recuperating from a serious illness at the castle of Sorgenfri, demanding that he and the Danish government approve the hostage system and that Danish police cooperate with the Gestapo in handing over suspected terrorists. On 28 August the ailing king replied with a message of one word: "Never."

The Danes displayed the fighting spirit of their proud and brave nation. German troops patrolled every town and through Copenhagen rumbled panzers and armored cars. Many prominent Danes were arrested, the Social Democratic party and the trade unions were suppressed. To humiliate the Danes, the German *gauleiter* demanded the surrender of the tiny Danish fleet, which had remained under Danish command, confined to ports. Again King Christian refused. German SS units appeared at the gates of Sorgenfri.

The royal guards refused to admit them and fired a few shots. The German commander gave the order to open fire. Machine guns sprayed the castle walls and hand grenades were lobbed into the palace yard until the king ordered his guards to cease fire.

A German general, with his aides, entered the castle, went to the king's study, and asked: "Do you now surrender?"

"Good morning, my brave general," replied King Christian. "You have won a splendid victory."

This was the memorable 29 August 1943. The king was now a prisoner. German sentries were put at the palace of this formidable monarch. At the same time German army and navy units attempted to seize all Danish naval installations and ships. Vice-Admiral Vedel, the C in C of the Danish navy, gave all his captains the following order: "Escape to Sweden or scuttle your ships." The largest of them, the 3,500-ton *Peter Skram* erupted soon after, and within the next few hours twenty-seven ships of the Royal Danish Navy lay, honor intact, on the sea bed. The government—headed by Eric Scanvenius, a member of the Radical party, who had, much to the annoyance of the people, tried to come to terms with the Germans—resigned. Parliament was adjourned, and Denmark was without a constitutional government.

Planning Liberation

On Saturday, 16 September 1943, the leaders of all parties met in secret and established The Freedom Council of Denmark, which became, for all practical purposes, the nation's underground government. It embraced all political parties, from the Conservatives to the Communists, as well as three co-operative members representing the Free Danish Council in London, the student organizations, and the SOE circuits in Denmark. It was the only time an SOE delegate sat in what amounted to the cabinet of an enemy-occupied country.

On 7 October Flemming Muus went to Sweden and then to Britain. In London he had many conferences with SOE chiefs, members of the British government, and the Free Danish Council. He also was promoted and decorated. Detailed plans for the reorganization of Danish Resistance and the creation of a home army were made. Muus was impatient to return to Denmark, but the discussions dragged on. On 2 December he attended a conference at Baker Street with Brigadier Mockler-Ferryman, Colonel Wilson, Commander Hollingworth, and other SOE officers.

"Mockler-Ferryman let the bombshell burst," Muus recalls. "He told me that the War Office had given orders for all activity in Denmark, Holland, and Belgium to cease without further notice. At ten o'clock next morning,

Whitehall wanted assurance that the order had been received, and also wanted a draft plan for recalling all SOE personnel. If the door had opened to admit Hitler and Mussolini arm in arm I doubt whether our surprise could have been greater . . . ."

The reason for the extraordinary order was the collapse of the SOE organization in Holland. Only in December 1943 had the British government and the War Office learned of the full effects of German infiltration in Holland and of the terrible damage caused by the *England Spiel*. The cessation of further SOE activities in Holland, Belgium, and Denmark was regarded as inevitable if further catastrophe was to be avoided. But subsequently the order was rescinded. Muus had little difficulty proving that, as far as Denmark was concerned, there was no danger of a repetition of the Dutch debacle.

On 11 December Muus took off in a Halifax, piloted by Flight-Lieutenant Peter Barter with a crew of seven. They were heading for the DZ near the Hvidsten Inn. Over the Kattegat the aircraft was attacked by Messerschmitts and set afire. Somehow Barter managed to fly on until he was over Denmark. Then he ordered everyone to bail out. When they landed, Muus was asked: "What do we do now?" "Don't worry," he told them. "You are in Denmark among friends." The eight RAF men were conducted to Sweden by Resistance men; ten days later they were back in Britain.

In Copenhagen Muus reported to the Freedom Council. Measures were taken to implement the London agreement. Denmark was divided into six military districts, each under the command of a former colonel of the Danish army, supervised by a Military regional committee appointed by the Freedom Council and including SOE representatives. A national M committee was made responsible for over-all military leadership.

Shortly before D day, after Hollingworth visited Stockholm and had meetings with delegates of the Freedom Council, a general staff for the secret home army was set up. It had four members: Frode Jacobsen, Captain C. V. Hjalf, Commander Lundsteen, and Flemming Muus. The Chair, as this new command was named, was approved by SHAEF and entrusted with the direction of all actions.

General Eisenhower sent orders outlining the principles upon which the Chair was to act:

(1) To carry out harassing and delaying tactics against enemy troop movements to and from Denmark; (2) to assist in any operations carried out by Allied troops on Danish soil, following Allied invasion; (3) to take action in such diversionary operations as SHAEF would consider necessary; (4) in the event of the enemy withdrawing from Denmark before the arrival of Allied Forces, the Chair will prevent destruction by the enemy of public services and other installations, and maintain law and order.

These arrangements were designed partly to prevent the Communists from embarking on premature action, which they advocated, and partly to avoid chaos at the hour of Germany's surrender.

By early 1944 Flemming Muus and his SOE comrades were performing prodigies of organization. Several hundred dropping zones were established for the reception of arms, ammunition, and explosives, which began to arrive in increasing quantities. Thousands of men were trained for the home army.

A regular canoe ferry was started to the Swedish coast. Resistance men had watched German rubber boats with envy for a long time; if only they, too, had such convenient, collapsible craft, which could be carried to the shore without arousing attention. When Muus heard that the British also produced such boats, he asked Baker Street to send as many as possible. Muus soon had quite a fleet of rubber boats. He put all his naval operations under the command of Gylding Sabroe at Frederikshavn. Fishermen from Saeby conducted the crossings to Sweden. So great was the demand for the rubber boats that Muus ordered that all the craft must be returned to base for repeat trips.

A fruitful alliance also was established between the SOE agents and the Danish police. Until the Germans put the king under house arrest, the police force, although sympathetic to the Resistance, tried to maintain a neutral attitude as the only means of preventing or delaying a take-over of police authority by the Germans. When SS Ober-Führer Best began his ruthless persecutions, the police, with very few exceptions, joined the Resistance. Notable leaders of the underground police were Inspector Roland Olsen (later compelled to escape to Sweden) and Inspector Haakon Lauritzen at Aalborg.

Uninvited Guests at the Inn

There were, of course, setbacks and casualties. But in marked contrast to other enemy-occupied countries, particularly France and Holland, where the Germans succeeded in enlisting thousands of collaborators, traitors, and informers, there was hardly any treachery. Even some Danish Nazis became disillusioned. On the rare occasions when members of Frits Clausen's Nazi party infiltrated SOE circuits, they were discovered before harm was done and quickly liquidated. The Danes, normally peaceful and friendly, were implacably opposed to their enemies and traitors.

Yet throughout their suffering they never abandoned a wintry sense of humor. For instance, one evening a Hvidsten group sat in Marius Fiil's inn waiting for a personal message on the BBC concerning the departure of an aircraft from Tempsford airfield with several agents and a batch of containers. There was nothing very unusual about this; during the previous few weeks Hvidsten had received eleven SOE agents and forty-two containers. Suddenly Fiil's son entered and said German soldiers and SS men were patrolling near by. They had with them some apparatus that might be radio direction-finding equipment.

Fiil sent Peter Carlsen with other men to the dropping zone and went to meet the Germans halfway. He invited them to the inn and plied them for more than three hours with schnapps, sausage and coffee, and the Danish pastries his wife made so well. This required a good deal of *sangfroid*. The inn's cellars were full of explosives and arms, and two radio transmitters were in the attic. The drop proceeded as planned, and the new SOE arrivals from Britain trooped into the warmth of the Hvidsten hostelry minutes after the Germans' departure. The Germans, a little dazed by the lavish hospitality they had received, were quite unmindful of the task on which they had set out.

Such cool daring was fully shared by Danish women. Many housewives hid agents and escapees, nursed the wounded, acted as couriers, and participated in sabotage raids. Edith Bonnessen was typical. Aged thirty, she joined the Resistance in its very early days and worked for the clandestine newspaper *De frie Danske*. She then became personal assistant to Duus Hansen, the radio chief. Known to her comrades as Lotte, for more than two years she did nearly all the cipher work for the messages between London, Stockholm, and Göteborg.

Hansen operated from the offices of a Copenhagen textile company. One morning Lotte went there after collecting a parcel of radio transmitter crystals that had just arrived from London. The SD, who had been watching the offices for some time, chose that morning to raid them. Lotte and several others were taken to the SD headquarters at Shellhus, which the Gestapo had requisitioned from the famous petroleum company, using the cellars as torture chambers.

After a check and a fair amount of manhandling, most of the textile firm's clerks were released; but when Lotte was searched the parcel of crystals, bearing the label "For Lotte," was found in her handbag. The Germans had been searching for the elusive Lotte for two years and the Gestapo officer who found the parcel ran out of the room shouting, "Now we have got her!"

Edith Bonnessen denied she was the wanted Lotte but knew that her chances were very slight. She was left in the room with a Gestapo man who was slightly drunk. He tried to become intimate and Lotte kept him in a good humor for a while. Then she asked for permission to go to the bathroom. The man wanted to accompany her, but in his alcoholic state he posted himself before the wrong door and didn't notice Lotte when she came out the right one.

Lotte found herself alone in the corridor. She calmly trotted down the stairs, passed several guards and officers, and reached the main hall at ground level. There she discovered that to get out of the building one had to show a pass. So she calmly began a solitary tour of the Shellhus. In one Gestapo office she equipped herself with a few files, which she took under her arm to lend strength to her role as a secretary. In one of the corridors she saw two high-ranking SS officers heading downstairs. She walked one step behind them and passed the guards at the front door, who snapped to attention in deference to Lotte's companions. For the benefit of the sentries, as the two SS officers ducked into their car, she called out: *"Auf Wiedersehen,* Herr Hauptsturm-Führer, I shall see you in the afternoon!" and walked briskly down the road to freedom.

Inside the Shellhus, SS men were frantically searching every room, desk, and cupboard, unable to believe that Lotte had simply walked out of the heavily guarded Gestapo headquarters. Ultimately Edith Bonnessen became too well known to the Germans, and in September 1944 she had to flee to Sweden.

At Grips with the Oppressors

Before D day London unbridled Resistance sabotage activities. The Chair gave a free hand to the sabotage groups, and many actions followed in quick succession, crowned by severe damage to the German-controlled Standard Electric factory, which turned out items for the Luftwaffe.

On D day itself, a group of fifty saboteurs attacked the Globus factory outside Copenhagen, which manufactured aircraft parts for the Germans. The factory was completely destroyed. Most of these sabotage attacks in Copenhagen were made by the *Holger Danske* groups, but the Communist *Bopa* did not lag far behind. On 22 June *Bopa* men attacked the Rekylriffel Syndikatet works, Denmark's only armament factory, which manufactured antitank guns and artillery equipment for the Germans. The *Bopa* men took pride in the fact that they did not depend entirely on supplies from London. On 13 July, in broad daylight, they raided the Jaegersborg barracks and made off with a huge haul of arms, ammunition, and explosives. On 24 July saboteurs placed explosive charges in the Danish Citroën works, destroying the main assembly line. On 28 August the Forum factory was ruined by explosives. These are but a few instances of the widespread sabotage.

The Germans retaliated savagely. Following the attack on the Rekylriffel Syndikatet, hostages were executed. Hooligans of the Danish Nazi party's auxiliary SS, the Schalburg Corps, were unleashed in an orgy of counter-sabotage. The famous Tivoli Pleasure Gardens were set on fire and almost completely destroyed, as was the equally famous Royal Copenhagen Porcelain factory Schalburg men, led by the German SS, blew up Citizen House

—Copenhagen's community center—and wrecked the Student Union building, which the Germans regarded as one of the nerve centers of the Resistance.

On 26 June SS Ober-Führer Best proclaimed a state of emergency, martial law in the capital, and a curfew from 8 P.M to 6 A.M. More hostages were executed.

The Danes replied to the terror by laying down their tools. Ten thousand workers of Denmark's largest shipyard Burmeister & Wain, went on strike. Best declared the strike illegal and threatened all strikers with arrest and deportation to Germany. The Danes knew it was an empty threat. The German plenipotentiary for economic questions and labor, Duckwitz, had warned Best that Gestapo measures would only wreck Denmark's industrial life, which was of great importance to the German war effort. The shipyard workers were joined by tens of thousands of factory workers. In spite of Duckwitz' protests, Best retaliated by cutting all electricity, gas, and water supplies in Copenhagen, in the vain hope of forcing the strikers to return to work.

But now the Danes were determined to accept any hardship. On 27 June Copenhagen rebelled. Thousands of demonstrators thronged the streets, attacked German soldiers and SS men, and began to erect barricades. Trolleys and buses were overturned, pavements were ripped up, and for the first time since the invasion days young Danes appeared in the streets carrying rifles and British Sten guns. All railway traffic stopped. Telephone exchanges were out of action. At night the city was plunged into darkness and food was running short.

Street fighting began in several districts. Resistance men dug up cobblestones, improvised trenches, and lit huge bonfires in the main streets to stop German armored cars and tanks, which rumbled through the capital firing indiscriminately at windows. More than one hundred Danes were killed and over six hundred seriously wounded. The hospitals, without water and without light at night, were full. The Germans, too, suffered casualties, and on many lampposts hung German uniforms and steel helmets—trophies of the Resistance fighters.

The general strike was not called off until the Germans complied with the demands of the National Freedom Council: that the martial law and curfew must end; that all vital supplies must be restored; that the Schalburg Corps be removed from Denmark, and that no reprisals be taken by the Germans.

SS Ober-Führer Best wanted to reject these demands, but the German military commander, General von Hanneken, fearing epidemics and realizing that some of his officers and men were sympathetic to the Danes, overruled him. Like many German officers, he knew that Hitler had lost the war. Electricity, gas, and water supplies were restored. It was announced that the Schalburg corps would be sent to the Russian front. Although the curfew remained, it was to start at 11 P.M. instead of at 8. Slowly the capital returned to normal life. But the unrest had spread to the provinces, and the revolt continued for several days in twenty towns where the Germans had only small garrisons.

The revolt, quite apart from the sabotage, caused serious difficulties for the German high command. Several German divisions, some from Norway, were being moved to France to repulse the Allied invasion. Some were held up by the Danish railway strike for nearly a week. German troops and Waffen SS units had to be disembarked in Denmark to reinforce the garrisons. Danish railway tracks and roads had to be guarded by two sentries stationed every two hundred yards, to protect military transport.

The fury of the Gestapo turned upon the Danish police, who had not only observed suspended animation during the revolt when ordered by the Germans into action against the terrorists, but in many instances had openly assisted the rebels. SS Ober-Führer Best ordered the Danish police to be disbanded and the SS to take over their duties.

On 19 September, SS and German army units swooped on every police station in Denmark. The Gestapo had drawn up lists of the most unreliable policemen beforehand, and more than two thousand of them were seized and deported to German concentration camps. Altogether nearly ten thousand policemen were arrested. Some seven thousand were interned in Denmark; many hundreds of them, suspected of underground work for the Resistance, were savagely beaten up and imprisoned in Gestapo cellars of the notorious Shellhus in Copenhagen. Later, when the Germans discovered that they were quite unable to cope with the many routine duties of the police, such as traffic control and day-to-day petty crimes, they reinstated a number of Danish policemen. They were ordered to serve unarmed and under supervision of SS officers. Many of the deported policemen died in Germany.

The Gestapo headquarters at the Shellhus did not escape its deserved fate. After SOE officers in Denmark had drawn up detailed plans, SHAEF approved a special RAF raid. On 31 March 1945 a small force of Mosquitos made a pinpoint attack on the building. The pilots had been told that many Danish prisoners were inside. The bombing was accomplished with extraordinary accuracy; the upper floors containing the Gestapo offices were machine-gunned, and eighty Gestapo and SD men were killed and wounded; whereas casualties among the prisoners were light, and many of them escaped in the ensuing chaos.

During this period the flow of supplies to the secret army was greatly increased. Before D day, deliveries had been relatively small. In February, in addition to explosives and ammunition, 400 Sten guns and 125 pistols were dropped; in March, 600 and 250; in April, 710 and 290. From May onward deliveries were stepped up and by June reached seventy to eighty containers a month, weighing about eight tons. During the first quarter of 1945, 2,043 containers, weighing 214 tons, were dropped; in the last month of the war, drops totaled 2,349 containers, weighing 251 tons. At first nearly all the arms were delivered from British stocks. Between August 1944 and February 1945, 2,272 containers were British and only 284 American. Later, the American contribution increased. In March 1945 there were 713 British and 627 American containers received by the Danes.

Monica and Inkie

The aftermath of the uprising during the summer of 1944 and the subsequent savage retaliations gravely endangered the SOE circuits. The Germans regarded the "British terrorists" as ringleaders of the insurrection. Muus and his friends had to abandon some of the more exposed dropping grounds and safe houses on Jutland and Sjaelland. They decided to move some of their work to the small southern islands of Lolland and Falster. Some months earlier Muus had met the Wichfield family, who had a large farm at Engelstofte near Maribo on Lolland. The area was ideal for dropping zones. Mrs. Monica Wichfield was an Englishwoman who had married a Dane, Jorgen Wichfield, and had three grown-up children—two sons, Ivan and Viggo, and pretty, vivacious Varinka, called Inkie. The whole family had worked in the local Resistance for a long time, and when Muus approached them, they immediately agreed to organize reception teams, with Monica as their leader. Inkie longed to take an even more active part in the fight. She went to Copenhagen and became assistant to Captain Rantzau, in charge of distributing SOE and PWE propaganda material and clandestine Resistance newspapers. Later Inkie was Muus' chief courier and, being bilingual, did the coding and decoding of signals to and from London.

Mrs. Wichfield was doing excellent work in her own sphere and, with Carl Larsen, was also looking after SOE finances. On 13 January 1944, shortly after Muus returned from London, she and her husband, their two sons, and several Resistance workers were arrested—following the capture of an SOE agent who had arrived by parachute in Lolland in the autumn of 1943. Disregarding security rules he had used the public telephone—tapped by the Germans—to convey a message. Under torture at the Aarhus Gestapo office, he gave away the names of forty-four Resistance members, including the Wichfield family and Carl Larsen.[6]

---

[6] Larsen had for two years performed feats of ingenuity to provide funds. He was killed on 21 May 1944, after being tortured at Dagmarhus, without giving information to the Gestapo.

The Wichfields, father and sons, somehow managed to convince the Germans that they had nothing to do with the Resistance, and in due course were released. But the Gestapo held Monica Wichfield on the charge of assisting "terrorists from Britain." Being British-born was sufficient evidence. Muus and Inkie were determined to save her. A German woman, married to a Dane, was manager of the Gestapo canteen at Dagmarhus; although her employers considered her loyal, she was violently anti-Nazi and supplied information to the Resistance. Muus enlisted her help and bribed a Gestapo official named Renner with 30,000 kroner (about $13,500). Renner promised to take Mrs. Wichfield to another prison. During the drive Muus, Inkie, and SOE men Jens Peter and Hans Johansen were to stage a holdup and free the prisoners. On 31 March the four arrived in an ambulance, driven by a Resistance man, at the arranged point on the route, but the German car never came. The evening before, Renner had brought suspicion upon himself by throwing about his ill-gotten money and standing drinks for other Gestapo men, and was taken off duty. Mrs. Wichfield was eventually sent to a German concentration camp and perished there in February 1945.

After the capture of her mother, Inkie was hunted by the Gestapo. But this did not prevent her from continuing to work for Muus, whose wife she became in June. Both were now in constant peril. The Resistance had suffered other severe losses. Among those forced to flee to Sweden were Flemming Juncker and Svend Truelsen, prominent leaders of the Resistance from its early days. Truelsen represented the London office of the Danish secret service in Denmark and had worked closely with the SOE circuits. In September there were many arrests. Muus' assistant Preben Lok-Lindblad was caught, and also several of his closest helpers: Aage Schoch, Flemming Larsen, Poul Justesen, Kate Fleuron. At the interrogations the Gestapo men reiterated the same question: "Where is Flemming Muus?"

The net was closing rapidly, and Muus and Inkie changed their hideouts almost daily. Although the danger of harboring them was evident—the Gestapo had offered a high reward for Muus' capture, and Copenhagen was plastered with "wanted" posters bearing his description—there were always people ready to give him shelter. Even as a hunted man, Muus never stopped directing the circuits. He rejected all suggestions to escape to Sweden.

Then disaster struck the command committee. On 14 October 1944 Professor Mogens Fog was captured. With the Gestapo hot on their trail, some of the national council's other members decided to go to Sweden; but Muus still insisted that he would stay on until liberation. He remained in regular radio contact with London and was repeatedly urged by Hollingworth to leave Denmark. Eventually, London sent an order: "You must leave immediately." By then Muus knew that two hundred SS men were raiding homes of all his acquaintances, going from hotel to hotel, watching cafés and taverns, in search for him.

The Removal Men

To reach Sweden, Muus and his wife used an escape organization, the *Speditoren* (removal men), which he himself had helped set up in October 1943. From March 1944 until liberation more than two thousand men and women, including prominent Danish politicians, Resistance leaders, SOE agents, and couriers, had been safely conducted to Sweden. The *Speditoren* ran a formidable fleet of small boats, but on several occasions they seized trawlers, packet boats, and even cargo vessels, with German naval guards aboard.

A group of *Speditoren* would board a ship plying between the ports of the Danish islands. They presented German travel permits and posed as genuine passengers. Once at sea, they would order the captain, at pistol point, to sail to Malmö or Trelleborg in Sweden. In the autumn of 1944 one of these groups, led by an eighteen-year-old student, Arne Seyr, planned the capture of five German navy cutters anchored at Vordingborg. After a gun battle, they managed to seize one, the *Adler,* and sailed her to Sweden. Two of Seyr's fellow students paid with their lives for this enterprise, but a large group of refugees safely reached Sweden. The *Speditoren* saved many Danish Jews and Jewish refugees from Germany, Austria, and Eastern Europe, and more than two hundred Allied airmen and soldiers who had escaped from POW camps or were shot down and reached Denmark from Germany. One of the heroes of the escape organization was Robert Jensen (Tom). He had made innumerable trips himself and had saved many lives. On 24 February 1944 Tom was traced by the SD to his hideout in Copenhagen and, after a gunfight, shot dead.

Flemming Muus and Inkie finally went to Sweden on 11 December 1944, and two days later arrived in London by air. Muus had handed over command to Ole Geisler, who was later replaced by Captain Ole Lipmann, sent from London at the end of January 1945. In London, Muus was received by King George VI at Buckingham Palace, feted by his SOE chiefs and compatriots, and promoted to the rank of major in the British army.

The German Surrender

Like the Norwegians, the Danes did much more than fight for the liberation of their own country. They made an important contribution to Allied strategy and final victory—as the case of the V-rocket intelligence showed.

Danish agents also reported on the deployment of German troops in North-western Europe and in Germany itself and on the Wehrmacht's logistic potentials before D day.

Danish SOE officers and Resistance men traveled in disguise to Hamburg, Bremen, Kiel, and Wilhelmshaven in search of information and brought back invaluable material. Just before D day Hollingworth sent, on behalf of SHAEF, this signal to Svend Truelsen, one of the organizers of these extraordinary sorties:

WE HAVE BEEN VERY PLEASED WITH THE SPLENDID WORK YOU HAVE BEEN DOING STOP THE MAPS OF GERMAN TROOP LOCATIONS ARE EX-CELLENT AND YOUR VARIOUS W/T REPORTS VERY USEFUL STOP YOU ARE DOING A VERY IMPORTANT JOB

SOE operations in Denmark were the last to be concluded, because the country remained occupied by the enemy to the very last moment of the war. Denmark was still a sideshow when the Allied armies had crossed the Rhine and were deep into Germany. Although the Danish home army and the Resistance could not play as dramatic a part as the maquis in France or *Milorg* in Norway, it rendered good service to the Allies. The Germans were compelled to maintain several divisions in Denmark, though they badly needed them elsewhere. Two divisions, which Hitler ordered to be moved to Germany during his last desperate attempt to halt the onrush of the Allied armies, were so greatly delayed by railway and road sabotage and direct attacks that they never reached the front.

It was to the Danish home army that the German commander in chief, General von Hanneken, capitulated a few hours before the spearhead of a British armored division of Montgomery's army entered Denmark.

The Danes paid dearly for their hard-won freedom. Their country was ruined. For years the Germans had ruthlessly looted the country, carrying thousands of head of pedigree cattle and tens of thousands of pigs to Germany, and confiscating industrial output and dairy produce. In May 1945 the Danish railways were at a standstill. Innumerable sabotage actions had destroyed almost all locomotives, several hundred carriages and trucks, sixty railway bridges connecting the many islands, scores of power stations, and a large portion of railway track.

Operations in Denmark were probably the most satisfying to SOE chiefs and section officers in London. There was none of the bitterness that existed between SOE and the other secret services of the exile governments. In the field, the SOE men served in complete accord with the Resistance, which was rarely undermined by treachery. Denmark provided a happy ending to the work of SOE in Western Europe.

Glossary and Abbreviations

ABWEHR	German Military Intelligence
ANVIL	Code name for Allied invasion of southern France
AS	*Armée Secrète*
AST	Abwehr *Leitstelle*, offices of the Abwehr in occupied countries
ATB	Advisory Committee on Trade Questions in Time of War (U.K.)
BBO	*Bureau voor Bijzondere Opdrachten*, Netherlands Secret Service Office in London from 1943
BCRA	*Bureau Central de Renseignements et d'Action*, Intelligence and Operations service of General de Gaulle in London, 1940–44
BI	*Bureau Inlichtingen*, Netherlands Intelligence Service in London from 1942
BNV	*Bureau Nationale Veiligkeit*, Netherlands Secret Service after the war
BOPA	Danish left-wing Resistance organization
BS	*Binnenlandse Strijkrachten*, Netherlands Secret Army of the Interior
CFTC	*Confédération Française de Travailleurs Chrétiens*, Federation of Christian Trade Unions in France
CGT	*Confédération Générale du Travail*, Federation of Socialist Trades Unions in France
CIGS	Chief of the Imperial General Staff
CND	*Confrérie Notre-Dame*, Gaullist network led by Colonel Rémy
CNR	*Conseil National de la Résistance*, National Council of French Resistance groups
COMAC	*Comité d'Action Militaire*, military committee of the National Council of French Resistance groups
COSSAC	Chief of Staff to the Supreme Allied Commander
DF SECTION	SOE section for organizing escapes
DGSS	*Direction Général des Services Spéciaux*, Free French Command of Special Forces in North Africa

DMI	Director of Military Intelligence (U.K.)
DMO	Director of Military Operations (U.K.)
DMR	*Délégué Militaire Régional,* regional commander of FFI, appointed by EMFFI
DST	*Direction de Surveillance du Territoire,* French security service
DZ	Dropping zone (for parachuting of agents and supplies)
EH	Electra House committee; precursor of PWE
EMFFI	*État-major des Forces Françaises de l'Intérieur,* general staff of FFI (under General M.-P. Koenig)
FAK	*Frontaufklärungskommandos* (Front intelligence units) in German-occupied countries
FANY	First Aid Nursing Yeomanry, a woman's auxiliary service in Great Britain
FFI	*Forces Françaises de l'Intérieur,* French army of the interior
F SECTION	SOE French section
FTP	*Francs-tireurs et partisans,* Communist-led Resistance organization in France
FUNKDIENST	W/T service of the Wehrmacht
FUNKHORCHDIENST	W/T listening and interception service of the Abwehr, SD and Gestapo
FUNKSPIEL	Radio "game" using captured Allied W/T transmitters
GESTAPO	*Geheime Staatspolizei,* German Secret State Police
IIC	Industrial Intelligence Centre (U.K.)
ISRB	Inter-Services Research Bureau (U.K.), also used as a cover name for SOE
JPC	Joint Planning Committee of British chiefs of staff
KP (LKP)	*Landeliijke Knokploegen* (literally, *bone breakers*), left-wing Resistance organization in the Netherlands
MEW	Ministry of Economic Warfare (U.K.)
MI	Military Intelligence
MI(R)	Military Intelligence, research section
MID	*Militaire Inlichtingen Dienst,* Netherlands Military Intelligence
MILORG	*Militaerorganisasjonen,* Norwegian Resistance organization, developed into the secret Army of the Interior
MUR	*Mouvements Unis de la Résistance,* first council of the large Resistance groups in France in 1943
MVT	*(Bureau) Militaire Voorbereiding Terugkeer,* Netherlands office of Military Preparation for the Return (in London)
N SECTION	Netherlands (Dutch) section of SOE
OCM	*Organisation Civile et Militaire,* French Resistance organization composed mainly of former officers and civil servants

OD	*Orde Dienst,* Netherlands Resistance organization, at first composed mainly of former members of the armed forces and police, later developed into the secret Army of the Interior
ORA	*Organisation de Résistance de l'Armée,* French Resistance organization, composed mainly of right-wing officers
OKW	*Oberkommando der Wehrmacht,* High Command of the German forces
OSS	Office of Strategic Services, American counterpart of SOE
OVERLORD	Code name for the plan of Allied invasion of northwest Europe in 1944
OVRA	*Organizzazione Volontaria Repressione Antifascismo,* Italian secret political police, recruited from members of the Fascist party
PIANIST	SOE slang for W/T operator
PWE	Political Warfare Executive (U.K.)
RF SECTION	SOE French section for liaison with BCRA
RSHA	*Reichssicherheitshauptamt,* Reich Security Office, government department in control of the Gestapo, SD, SIPO, etc.
SAS	Special Air Service
SD	*Sicherheitsdienst,* Security Service, originally of the National Socialist party in Germany; later a department of RSHA, correlated to the Gestapo and concerned mainly with counterespionage and measures against the Resistance in German-occupied countries
SF	Special Forces (particularly SOE/OSS)
SHAEF	Supreme Headquarters, Allied Expeditionary Force
SIPO	*Sicherheitspolizei,* Security Police, executive organ of SD and the Gestapo
SIS	Secret Intelligence Service (U.K.)
SNCF	*Société Nationale des Chemins de Fer,* French national railways
SO	Special Operations
SOE	Special Operations Executive
SPOC	Special Projects Operations Centre at Allied Headquarters in North Africa
SS	*Schutzstaffel,* originally the elite guards of the National Socialist party, developed into units of special police under the Gestapo and SD. Waffen SS were militarized units of the SS employed in the fighting line
STS	Special Training School(s)
V (SIGN)	Used in Germany for *Vergeltung* (vengeance)
V-MAN	*Vertrauensmann,* trusted man, or informer, recruited from among nationals of German-occupied territories by the Gestapo and SD
W/T	Wireless telegraphy

[383]

Relative Ranks in the SS (SD) and German Army

SS Gruppen-Führer	Lieutenant General
SS Brigade-Führer	Major General
SS Ober-Führer	Brigadier General
SS Standarten-Führer	Colonel
SS Obersturmbann-Führer	Lieutenant Colonel
SS Sturmbann-Führer	Major
SS Hauptsturm-Führer	Captain
SS Obersturm-Führer	Lieutenant
SS Sturm-Führer	Second Lieutenant
SS Hauptschar-Führer	Sergeant Major
SS Schar-Führer	Sergeant
SS Unterschar-Führer	Corporal

Documentation and
Selected Bibliography

Primary Sources

SOE Monthly Progress Reports; Reports from Special Forces HQ; SOE memoranda on Present Value and Tempo of Resistance; SOE and SIS memoranda on Aircraft Requirements; Analysis of the Resistance Movement. (All in SHAEF files, available in the Historical Records Section, Adjutant General's Office and the Archives of the Chief of Military History, U.S. Department of the Army, Washington, D.C.)

History of FFI (and SOE circuits) compiled under official aegis by Major R. A. Bourne-Paterson, Captain Lucien Galimand, and Captain Marcel Vigneras (unpublished manuscript).

Memoranda and papers of the Combined Chiefs of Staff, the Joint Planning Staff, the Joint Intelligence Committee, the British Chiefs of Staff, COSSAC, SHAEF Memoranda from Joint Chiefs of Staff to General Dwight D. Eisenhower; Reports of the Supreme Allied Commander to the Combined Chiefs of Staff (in SHAEF files); Reports on Evaluation of Allied Air Attacks (U.S. Air Force Historical Section, Air University, Maxwell Field, Montgomery, Alabama).

Documents at the Historical Division of the U.S. State Department, and at the Federal Record Center, Alexandria, Virginia.

Captured German documents (including the collection at the Hoover Institution and Library, Stanford University, Palo Alto, California), particularly *Tätigkeitsberichte der Befehlshaber der Sicherheitspolizei und des Sicherheitsdienstes* (SD), 1940–41 complete, 1942–45 incomplete; *Abwehr* archives (captured in France, the Netherlands, Norway, Denmark, and Germany); *Oberkommando West* documents (so-called Rundstedt papers).

Reports of trials of German war criminals (Proceedings of the International Military Tribunal at Nuremberg; trials in the British, American, and French zones of Germany).

Nazi Conspiracy and Aggression (Office of U.S. Chief of Counsel for Prosecution of Axis Criminality).

Archives of Commission d'histoire de l'occupation et de la libération de la France (Ministère de la Education nationale, Paris) and of Comité d'Histoire de la 2-e Guerre Mondiale (Office of the Prime Minister of the French Republic).

[385]

Reports of the Commission des Comités de la libération au Conseil National de Résistance; Bibliothèque de documentation (France occupée; Résistance maquis); Archives militaires des Régions; documents and memoirs of Association de maquis; bulletins of FFI (État-Major National, 2-e bureau); Statutes of the Comités départementeaux du Conseil National de la Résistance; reports of *Commission d'enquête parlementaire sur les événements survenue en France de 1933–1945*, vols. I–IX. Paris, 1951–52.

Transcripts of depositions before interrogating officers of Direction de la Surveillance du Territoire; transcripts of trials of German war criminals and collaborators before Tribunal Militaire Permanent (at Reuilly Barracks, Paris) and other French military tribunals.

Transcripts of interrogations of German prisoners of war (PWIS, 269 files).

Reports of Commission d'enquête sur les violations du droit des gens, des lois et des coutumes de la guerre, vols. I–II. Liège, 1945–47.

Report of *Enquêtecommissie Regiringbeleid 1940–45* of the Second Chamber of the Netherlands Parliament, vols. I–VIII, 1948–56; and the summary of these investigations, *Samenvatting*, ed., H. C. P. Meyjes. Amsterdam: Van Loghum Slaterus, 1958.

Archives of the Netherlands State Institute of War Documentation (Rijkinstituut voor Oorlogsdumentatie, Amsterdam), including *Geschiedschrijving van Nederland in Oorlogtijd*, ed., Dr. Louis de Jong (British and Dutch Resistance) 1940–45, no. 109 (in manuscript).

Investigations as to the Military Resistance in the Netherlands, ed., Lieutenant Colonel S. P. van 't Hof, and *Military Operations in the Netherlands*, ed., Lieutenant Colonel P. L. G. Doorman (Netherlands Government Information Service).

Civil Resistance in the Netherlands, a survey by Dr. L. de Jong (State Institute for War Documentation, Amsterdam, 1950).

Documents at the Royal Norwegian State Archives, Oslo; and reports *German Crimes against Norway* (prepared by the Royal Norwegian Government for the International Military Tribunal at Nuremberg).

Witness reports of the Gestapo work in Norway (compiled by the Royal Norwegian Information Office).

Report of the Inquiry Commission of the Norwegian Parliament (Stortinget), vol. I–II. Oslo, 1946–47.

Archives of the Royal Norwegian General Staff, Oslo (including *Samenarbeidet med SOE* (cooperation with SOE) and reports on Swedish-Norwegian cooperation *Kontakt over gränsen;* reports of SOE Norwegian section; F.O. IV and M.I. IV departments of the Royal Norwegian General Staff in London, 1940–45; messages exchanged between SOE HQ in London and the *Stockholmkontorer* (Stockholm Office); documents relating to *Milorg* in Sentralledelses Mikrofilm arkiv, Oslo (Archives of the Central Leadership of the Norwegian Resistance).

Kompani Linge arkivs, Oslo.

Domsarkivet, Oslo (the Archives contain captured *Abwehr* and SD documents and papers relating to Quisling's *Nasjonal Samling, Hirden*, etc.).

Transcripts of interrogations and trials of German war criminals and collaborators in Norway, including the trial of Vidkun Quisling.

Report of the Commission of Inquiry of the Danish Parliament (*Folketinget*), vols. I–XIV. Copenhagen, 1945–49.

Archives of the Danish Freedom Council (*Denmarks Frihedsraad*), Copenhagen.

Archives of Danish Resistance groups and SOE organizers in Denmark (particularly Lorens Arne Duus Hansen's arkiv, Ebbe Munck's arkiv, Flemming B. Muus' arkiv, Erik Seidenfaden's arkiv, Dansk Hjaepetjeneste arkiv, and Spediteren's arkiv).

Archives of the Office of the Resistance, Ministry of National Defense, Brussels.

Collection of German documents of Verband der Verfolgten des Naziregimes (VVN), Frankfurt/Main.

Nagel, W. H., *Verantwoording te de duitse contraspionnage in Nederland.* Amsterdam, 1949. Dutch Inquiry Commission, vol. 4a.

The author obtained, in addition, extensive and unpublished material from the Archives of Associations des anciens réseaux and from records of many Amicales des Forces Françaises Combattantes (in France), as well as from many associations of former Resistance members in the Netherlands, Norway, and Denmark. Many eyewitness reports in this book are based on interviews and tape-recordings taken with former SOE officers and leaders and members of Resistance groups, and affidavits taken from former *Abwehr*, SD, and Gestapo officers and officials. These statements were in most cases corroborated by personal documents, diaries, and copies of original wireless telegraphy signals, and carefully checked with official documents examined at the various archives.

Selected Bibliography *

ALSOP, S., and BRADEN, T., *Sub Rosa: The O.S.S. and American Espionage.* New York: Harcourt, Brace & World, 1964.

AMERY, J., *Explanation of De Gaulle.* New York: Harper & Row, 1965.

———, *Explanation of De Gaulle.* New York: Harper & Row, 1965.

———, *France; Steadfast and Changing.* Cambridge, Mass.: Harvard University Press, 1960.

———, *France Reborn.* New York: Charles Scribner's Sons, 1964.

———, *Sons of the Eagle.* London: Macmillan, 1948.

ASHCROFT, E., *General De Gaulle.* New York: Transatlantic Arts, 1962.

Assessment of Men (*Selection of Personnel for the Office of Strategic Services*). Washington, D.C.: Government Printing Office, 1948.

ASSMAN, K., *The Invasion of Norway.* Annapolis, Md.: U.S. Naval Institute, 1952.

ASTIER DE LA VIGERIE, E., *Seven Times Seven Days.* London: McGibbon, 1958.

AVON, LORD, *The Eden Memoirs.* Boston: Houghton Mifflin Co., 1965.

* Only English language publications are cited.

BARRY, R. H., *European Resistance Movements*. Oxford: Pergamon, 1960.

BELL, L., *Sabotage*. London: Laurie, 1957.

BELOFF, M., ed., "On the Track of Tyranny," *Wiener Library Bulletin*, 1965 (London).

BENTWICH, N., *I Understand the Risk*. London: Gollancz, 1950.

———, *Mandate Memories 1918–48*. New York: Schocken Books, 1965.

———, *My 77 Years*. Philadelphia: Jewish Publication Society of America, 1961.

BEST, S. P., *The Venlo Incident*. London: Hutchinson, 1940.

BOAS, H. S., *Religious Resistance in Holland*. London: Allen & Unwin, 1945.

BOOLEN, J. J., and VAN DER DOES, J. C. *Five Years of Occupation*. The Hague: David, 1945.

BRADDON, R., *Nancy Wake*. London: Cassell, 1956.

BROME, V., *The Way Back*. New York: W. W. Norton & Co., 1958.

BRYANS, J. L., *Secret Communications*. London: Skeffington, 1951.

BRYANT, A., *Triumph in the West*. London: Collins, 1959.

———, *The Turn of the Tide*. London: Collins, 1957.

BUCKLEY, C., *Norway—The Commandos—Dieppe*. London: H.M.S.O., 1951.

BUCKMASTER, M. J., *Specially Employed*. London: Batchworth, 1952.

———, *They Fought Alone*. London: Odhams, 1958.

BULLOCK, A., *Hitler: A Study in Tyranny*. New York: Harper & Row, 1964.

BURNEY, C., *The Dungeon Democracy*. London: William Heinemann, 1945.

———, *Solitary Confinement*. New York: St. Martin's Press, 1961.

BUTCHER, H. K., *My Three Years with Eisenhower*. Garden City, N.Y.: Doubleday & Co., 1948.

BUTLER, E., *Amateur Agent*. New York: W. W. Norton & Co., 1964.

CARLYLE, M., ed., *Documents on International Affairs, 1939–1946*. Vol. II. London: Royal Institute of International Affairs, 1954.

CHAMBERLAIN, J., "O.S.S.," *Life*, vol. XIX, no. 21 (New York).

CHAPMAN, F. S., *Duel of Wits*. London: Hodder, 1953.

———, *The Jungle is Neutral*. London: Chatto & Windus, 1948.

CHURCHILL, P., *Of Their Own Choice*. London: Hodder, 1952.

———, *The Spirit in the Cage*. London: Hodder, 1954.

CHURCHILL, W. S., *The Second World War*. 6 vols. Boston: Houghton Mifflin Co., 1948–53.

COLLIER, R., *House Called Memory*. New York: E. P. Dutton & Co., 1961.

COLVIN, I., *Chief of Intelligence*. London: Gollancz, 1951.

———, *The Unknown Courier*. London: Kimber, 1953.

———, *Vansittart in Office*. London: Gollancz, 1965.

COOKRIDGE, E. H., *The Net that Covers The World*. New York: Holt, Rinehart & Winston, 1955.

———, *Soviet Spy Net*. London: Müller, 1955.

———, *Sisters of Delilah*. London: Oldbourne, 1959.

———, *They Came from the Sky*. London: Heinemann, 1965.

———, *Traitor Betrayed*. London: Pan, 1962.

COOPER, A. D. (Lord Norwich), *Old Men Forget*. London: Davis, 1953.

COWBURN, B., *No Cloak, No Dagger*. London: Jarrolds, 1960.

CRESSWELL, J., *Generals and Admirals*. London: Longmans, 1952.

CROSSMAN, R., "Psychological Warfare," *Journal RUSI*, vol. XCVII, August 1952 (London).

DALLIN, D., *Soviet Espionage*. New Haven, Conn.: Yale University Press, 1955.

DALTON, H., *The Fateful Years*. London: Muller, 1957.

———, *Hitler's War Before and After*. London: Penguin, 1939.

DATTNER, S. W., "Espionage," *Mufti*, vol. XVII, 1952 (London).

DE GAULLE, C., *Complete War Memories of Charles de Gaulle*. New York: Simon & Schuster, 1964.

———, *Discours et messages*. Paris: Berger-Levrault, 1946.

———, *Edge of the Sword*, trans., G. Hopkins. New York: Criterion Books, 1960.

DE GRAMONT, S., *The Secret War*. New York: G. P. Putnam's Sons, 1962.

DELARUE, J., *Gestapo*. New York: William Morrow & Co., 1964.

DERRY, T. K., *The Campaign in Norway*. London, H.M.S.O., 1952.

———, *Short History of Norway*. New York: Hillary House Publishers, 1955.

DONOVAN, Y. W., "Intelligence Key to Defense." *Life*, vol. XXI, no. 14.

DOORMAN, P. L. G., *Military Operations in the Netherlands*. London: Netherlands Information Office, 1942.

DORNBERGER, W., *V-2*. New York: Viking Press, 1954.

DOURLEIN, P., *Inside North Pole*. London: Kimber, 1953.

DOWNES, D. C., *The Scarlet Threat*. London: Verschoyle, 1953.

DULLES, A., *Craft of Intelligence*. New York: Harper & Row, 1963.

———, *Germany's Underground*. New York: The Macmillan Co., 1947.

DUNFORD-SLATER, J., *Commando*. London: Kimber, 1955.

EISENHOWER, D., *Crusade in Europe*. Garden City, N.Y.: Doubleday & Co., 1948.

ESSAME, H., and BELFIELD, E. M. G., *The North-West Europe Campaign 1944–1945*. London: Gale, 1962.

EVANS, J., *Confessions of a Special Agent*. London: Hale, 1951.

EVANS, JACK, and DUDLEY, E., *Face of Death*. New York: William Morrow & Co., 1958.

EVANS, JEAN, *Three Men*. New York: Alfred A. Knopf, 1954.

FARAGO, L., *Age of Scoundrels*. New York: Ivan Obolensky, 1965.

———, "British Propoganda," *United Nations World*, 1948 (New York).

———, *Burn After Reading*. New York: Walker & Company, 1961.

———, *It's Your Money*. New York: Random House, 1964.

———, *Patton*. New York: Ivan Obolensky, 1964.

———, *Spymaster*. New York: G. P. Putnam's Sons, 1964.

———, *Strictly from Hungary*. New York: Walker & Company, 1962.

———, *Tenth Fleet*. New York: Ivan Obolensky, 1962.

FIELDING, X., *Hide and Seek*. London: Secker & Warburg, 1954.

FOOT, M. R. D., *S.O.E. in France*. London: H.M.S.O., 1966.

FOOTE, A., *Handbook for Spies*. London: Museum Press, 1949.

FORD, C., and McBAIN, A., *The Secret Story of the O.S.S.* New York: Harper & Row, 1946.

FULLER, J. O., *Double Webs*. London: Putnam, 1958.

————, *Madeleine*. London: Gollancz, 1957.

————, *The Starr Affair*. London: Gollancz, 1954.

GARBY-CZERNIAWSKI, R., *The Big Network*. London: Ronald, 1962.

GAULLE, C. DE, *see* de Gaulle, C.

GAVIN, C., *Liberated France*. London: Cape, 1955.

GEORGE, W. D., *Surreptitious Entry*. New York: Appleton-Century, 1948.

GILBERT, F., ed., *Secret Records of Hitler's Conferences*. Philadelphia: University of Pennsylvania Press, 1950.

GILMAN, W., *The Spy Trap*. New York: MacFadden-Bartell (Bartholomew House), 1945.

GLAHN, G. VON, *see* von Glahn, G.

GOFFIN, R., *The White Brigade*. Garden City, N.Y.: Doubleday & Co., 1946.

GRAAF, K. DE, *see* de Graaf, K.

GRAMONT, S. DE, *see* de Gramont, S.

Grand Strategy, History of the Second World War. London: H.M.S.O., 1952–62.

GREE, W. F., "With the O.S.S.," *U.S. Marine Corps Gazette,* vol. XXIX, no. 12 (Washington, D.C.).

GUBBINS, C. McV., "Resistance Movements," *Journal RUSI,* vol. XCIII, May 1948.

GUDME, S., *Denmark—Hitler's Model Protectorage*. London: Gollancz, 1943.

HABER, H., *Adolf Hitler,* trans., L. Wilson. Chester Springs, Pa.: Dufour Editions, 1961.

HACKETT, J. W., "The Employment of Special Forces," *Journal RUSI,* vol. XCVIII, February 1953.

HARRISON, D. I., *These Men Are Dangerous*. London: Transworld, 1958.

HAUGE, E. O., *Saltwater Thief*. London: Duckworth, 1958.

HAUKELID, K., *Skis Against the Atom*. London: Kimber, 1954.

HAYES, C. J. H., *Mission to Spain*. New York: The Macmillan Co., 1946.

"Heroines of the War," in *Stand-To*. (Vol. I, no. 1.) 1950.

HIBBERT, C., *The Battle of Arnhem*. New York: The Macmillan Co., 1962.

HILLS, R. G. T., *Phantom Was There*. London: Arnold, 1951.

History of the Second World War, ed., J. R. M. Butler *et al.* Vols. II, III, V. London: H.M.S.O., 1956–62.

HOARE, S. (Lord Templewood), *Ambassador on Special Mission*. London: Collins, 1946.

'T HOF, S. P. VAN, *see* van 't Hof, S. P.

HOWARTH, D., *Across to Norway*. New York: William Morrow & Co., 1951.

————, *D-Day*. New York: McGraw-Hill Book Co., 1959.

————, *The Shetland Bus*. New York: W. W. Norton & Co., 1953.

————, *Sledge Patrol*. New York: The Macmillan Co., 1957.

————, *We Die Alone*. New York: The Macmillan Co., 1955.

HULL, C., *Memoirs*. New York: The Macmillan Co., 1948.

HUTTON, C., *Official Secret*. London: Parrish, 1960.

HYDE, H. M., *The Quiet Canadian*. London: Hamish Hamilton, 1962.

INGERSOLL, R. A., *Top Secret*. New York: Harcourt Brace, 1946.

ISMAY, H. L., *Memoirs of General Lord Ismay*. New York: Viking Press, 1960.

JAWORSKI, L., *After Fifteen Years*. Houston, Texas: Gulf, 1961.

JOHNSON, T., "Battle Underground," *Combat Forces*, vol. III, no .11 (New York).

JONG, L. DE, *Civil Resistance in the Netherlands*. Amsterdam, 1950.

———, *The German Fifth Column in the Second World War*. London: Routledge, 1956.

———, *Holland Fights the Nazis*. London: Drummond, 1942.

JULVEN, M., *HMS Fidelity*. London: Souvenir Press, 1947.

KEMP, P. K., and LLOYD, C., *Brethren of the Coast*. New York: St. Martin's Press, 1961.

KENNEDY, J., *The Business of War: The War Narrative of Major General Sir John Kennedy*, ed., B. Fergusson. New York: William Morrow & Co., 1958.

KENT, S., *Strategic Intelligence for American World Policy*. Princeton, N.J.: Princeton University Press, 1948.

KOEHLER, H., *Inside the Gestapo*. New York: Pallas, 1950.

LANGER, W., *Our Vichy Gamble*. New York: Alfred A. Knopf, 1947.

LEAHY, W. D., *I Was There*. Toronto: McGraw-Hill, 1950.

LEASOR, J., *Passport to Oblivion*. Philadelphia: J. B. Lippincott Co., 1965.

———, *Uninvited Envoy*. New York: McGraw-Hill Book Co., 1962.

LEEUW, A. J. van, *see* van Leeuw, A. J.

LEVERKUEHN, P., *German Military Intelligence*. London: Weidenfeld & Nicholson, 1954.

LIDDELL-HART, B. H., *Defense of the West*. New York: William Morrow & Co., 1950.

LOCKHART, R. B., *Comes the Reckoning*. London: Putnam, 1957.

———, *Friends, Foes and Foreigners*. London: Putnam, 1947.

MACLEAN, F., *Eastern Approaches*. London: Cape, 1949.

MANUS, M., *Underwater Saboteur*. London: Kimber, 1953.

MARSHALL, B., *The White Rabbit*. Boston: Houghton Mifflin Co., 1953.

MARTELLI, G., *The Man Who Saved London*. Garden City, N.Y.: Doubleday & Co., 1960.

MARTENS, A., *The Silent War*. London: Hodder, 1961.

MASCHWITZ, E., *No Chip on My Shoulder*. London: Jenkins, 1957.

MAUGERI, F., *From the Ashes of Disgrace*. New York: Reynal & Co., 1950.

MEDLICOTT, W. N., *Congress of Berlin and After*. Hamden, Conn.: The Shoe String Press, 1963.

———, *The Economic Blockade*. 2 vols. London: Longmans, 1959.

———, *From Metternich to Hitler*. New York: Barnes & Noble, 1963.

MENTZE, E., *Five Years of Occupation of Denmark*. Malmö: Allhems, 1946.

———, *International Conference on European Resistance Movements*. Vol. I: *European Resistance Movements 1939–1945*, ed., H. Michel. 2 vols. New York: Pergamon Press, 1960.

MIKES, H. G., *The Epic of Lofoten*. London: Hutchinson, 1941.

MIKSCHE, F. O., *Secret Forces*. London: Faber, 1950.

MILLAR, G., *Horned Pigeon*. London: Heinemann, 1946.

———, *Maquis*. London: Heinemann, 1945.

MINNEY, R. J., *Fanny and the Regent of Siam*. Cleveland, Ohio: The World Publishing Co., 1962.

———, *No. 10 Downing St.* Boston: Little, Brown & Co., 1963.

MITCHELL, V., ed., "From Weimar to Hitler," *Wiener Library Bulletin*, 1965.

MORGAN, W., *The O.S.S. and I.* New York: W. W. Norton & Co., 1957.

MOSS, W. S., *A War of Shadows*. London: Bordman, 1952.

MUNTHE, M., *Sweet Is War*. London: Ackworth, 1954.

"The Netherlands During German Occupation," *Annals of the American Academy of Political and Social Science*, 1946.

NEWNHAM, M., *Prelude to Glory*. London: Sampson Low, 1947.

NICHOLAS, E., *Death Be Not Proud*. London: Cresset, 1958.

OGDEN, M., *The Battle of North Cape*. London: Kimber, 1962.

OLSEN, O., *Two Eggs on My Plate*. London: Allen & Unwin, 1952.

PAPE, R., *Boldness Be My Friend*. London: Elek, 1953.

PAPEN, F. VON, *see* von Papen, F.

PAWLE, G., *The Secret War: 1939–1945*. New York: William Morrow & Co., 1957.

PENDAR, K., *Adventure in Diplomacy*. New York: Dodd, Mead & Co., 1945.

PERRAULT, G., *The Secret of D-Day*. Boston: Little, Brown & Co., 1965.

PIQUET-WICKS, E., *Four in the Shadow*. London: Jarrolds, 1957.

POLLER, W., *Medical Block Buchenwald*. New York: Ballantine Books, 1961.

PRATT, F., *How To Run a Spy System*. New York: Harper & Row, 1947.

REITLINGER, G. R., *The Final Solution*. New York: Barnes & Noble, 1961.

RIBBENTROP, J. VON, *see* von Ribbentrop, J.

SAUNDERS, H. A. ST. G., *The Green Beret*. London: H.M.S.O., 1950.

SCHELLENBERG, W., *Memoirs*, ed. by L. Hagen. London: Deutsch, 1962.

SHERWOOD, R., *Roosevelt and Hopkins: An Intimate History*. New York: Harper & Row, 1950.

SIMPSON, W., *I Burned My Fingers*. London: Putnam's, 1950.

SINGER, K. D., *Spies and Traitors*. Englewood Cliffs, N.J.: Prentice-Hall, 1948.

SKODVIN, M., "German and British-French Plans for Operations in Scandinavia," *The Norsemen*, vol. IX, 1951 (London).

SPEARS, E., *Assignment to Catastrophe*. Vol. I: *Prelude to Dunkirk*. Vol. II: *Fall of France*, 2 vols. New York: Hill & Wang, 1955.

SPEIER, H., *Psychological Warfare*. Stanford, Calif.: Stanford University Press, 1952.

STACEY, C. P., *The Canadian Army*. Ottawa: Cloutier, 1946.

STALIN, J. V., *Correspondence with Churchill, Attlee, Roosevelt and Truman*. New York: E. P. Dutton & Co., 1958.

STEAD, P. J., *Second Bureau*. London: Evans, 1959.

STIMPSON, H. L., and BUNDY, McG., *On Active Service in Peace and War*. New York: Harper & Brothers, 1948.

SWEET-ESCOTT, B., *Baker Street Irregular*. London: Methuen, 1965.

TERKELSEN, T. M., *Frontline in Denmark*. London: Free Danish Publishing, 1944.

THOMAS, J., *No Banners*. London: W. H. Allen, 1955.

TICKELL, J., *Hunt for Richard Thorpe*. Garden City, N.Y.: Doubleday & Co., 1959.

———, *Moonsquadrons*. London: Wingate, 1956.

———, *Odette*. London: Chapman, 1949.

TOMPKINS, D. C., *Sabotage*. Berkeley: University of California Press, 1961.

VANSITTART, R. G., *Lessons of My Life*. London: Hutchinson, 1947.

VAN 'T HOF, S. P., *Investigations as to the Military Resistance in the Netherlands*. Amsterdam, 1950.

VEYSEY, A., "Queen of the Underground," in *Chicago Sunday Tribune*, March, 1953.

Vocabulary of German Military Terms. London: H.M.S.O., 1944.

VOMÉCOURT, PHILIPPE DE, *An Army of Amateurs*. Garden City, N.Y.: Doubleday & Co., 1961.

———, *Who Lived to See the Day*. London: Hutchinson, 1961.

VON GLAHN, *The Occupation of Enemy Territory*. Minneapolis: University of Minnesota Press, 1957.

VON PAPEN, F., *Memoirs*. London: Deutsch, 1952.

VON RIBBENTROP, J., *Memoirs*. London: Weidenfeld & Nicolson, 1954.

WALKER, E. E., *Lunch with a Stranger*. London: Wingate, 1957.

WALTERS, A.-M., *Moondrop to Gascony*. London: Macmillan, 1946.

WARD, I., *FANY Invicta*. London: Hutchinson, 1955.

WASE, D. A. L., "A Survey of the Trials of War Criminals," *Journal RUSI*, vol. XCVI, February 1951.

WEBB, A. M., ed., *The Natzweiler Trial*. London: Hodge, 1950.

WEEKS, R., *Organisation and Equipment for War*. London: Cambridge University Press, 1950.

WHEELER-BENNETT, J. W., *Nemesis of Power: The German Army in Politics 1918–1945*. New York: St. Martin's Press, 1964.

WIGHTON, C., *Pin-striped Saboteur*. London: Odhams, 1959.

———, and GUNTER, P., *Hitler's Spies and Saboteurs*. New York: Holt, Rinehart & Winston, 1958.

WILMOT, C., *The Struggle for Europe*. London: Collins, 1951.

WOLFE, L., *Sabotage*. London, Nicholson.

WOLFF, I. R., ed., "Persecution and Resistance under the Nazis," *Wiener Library Bulletin*, 1965.

WOODHOUSE, C. M., *British Foreign Policy Since the Second World War*. New York: Frederick A. Praeger, 1962.

———, *New Concert of Nations*. Chester Springs, Pa.: Dufour Editions, 1964.

WOODWARD, L., *British Foreign Policy in the Second World War*. London: H.M.S.O., 1962.

YOUNG, GORDON, *The Cat with Two Faces*. London: Odhams, 1958.

ZACHARIAS, E. M., *Secret Missions*. New York: G. P. Putnam's Sons. 1949; paperback, 1965.

[393]

Index

[397]

[398]

Etasse, Marcel, 186
Etienne, *see* Wilkinson, George
Eugène, *see* Perschuk, Maurice
Evans, Harold, *see* Eckert, Heinz
Evans, Robert, 339
Experton, Gisèle, 104, 213

Falkenhorst, General von, 324, 328, 345
FAMILLE, *see* INTERALLIÉ
FARMER, 171
Farmer, John, 227, 232, 233
Faye, Leon, 168
Fehlis, Heinrich, 328, 345
Fehmer, Siegfried, 340
Felix, *see* Jones, Sydney; Terwindt,
    Beatrice
Ferme, Georges, 140
Fèvre, Esther, 143, 144
Field, *see* Sonstbey, Gunnar
Fielding, Ian, 235
Fiil, Marius, 366, 372–373
Fincken, Jack, 85
Fischer, Franz, 8
Fleischer, Carl G., 336
Fleuron, Kate, 378
Floegge, Ernest, 154–155
Floiras, Auguste, 114
Flower, Raymond, 123–129, 182
Fog, Mogens, 358–359, 361, 368, 378
Formule, *see* O'Neill, Marc
Fougner, Gunnar, 314
Frager, Henri, 87–88, 90, 92, 95, 99,
    102–104, 107, 110, 111, 113,
    114, 127, 131, 133, 155, 157,
    158, 160, 161, 163–164, 166,
    181, 182–185, 187, 190–195,
    213, 236, 243, 244, foll. 274
France, 1, 2, 4, 5, 10–11, 14–16, 18,
    24, 26, 34, 41, 43, 45–46, 50–246
Frank, Karl H., 216
Frenay, Henri, 87, 90–92, 131, 213
Frommagot, Lucienne, 108
Furstner, J. T., 275

G, 286
Gabriel, *see* Young, John Cuthbert

Gaby, *see* Plewman, Eliane
Gaillard, Charles, 209
Gaitskell, Hugh, 13
Gamade, Charles, 212
Gamwell, Hope, 28
Garcie, 226, 231, 232
Garel, F., 244
Garrow, Ian, 52, 286
Garry, Emile-Henri, 130, 135, 156,
    158–159, 164, 165–168, 187, 188,
    190, 243, 244
Garry, Marguerite, 159, 164, 166–168
Gaspard, *see* Couladon, Emile;
    Flower, Raymond
Gaston, *see* Burdeyron, Noël; Garcie;
    Dayser, Robert
Gatignon, André, 150
Gauthier, *see* Vomécourt, Philippe de
Gavin, James, 27
Geisler, Ole, 360, 361, 366, 368, 379
George, *see* Ridderhof, George
George VI, King (England), 379
Gerbrands, Peter, 305
Gerbrandy, Professor, 256–257, 275,
    280
Gerson, Victor, 52, 68, 177
Getz, Per, 341
Gielgud, Lewis, 57, 96–97, 125, 128
Giessen, Aat van der, 282, 304–306
Gilbert, *see* Déricourt, Henri;
    Norman, Gilbert
GILBERT, 53
Girard, André, 58, 88–94, 99–103
Giraud, H. H., 18, 90, 98, 199
Gisèle, *see* Experton, Gisèle
Giskes, Hermann, 10, 133, 186, 254–
    255, 261–273, foll. 274, 275–276,
    277–290, 292–300, 302–306, 308
Glenconner, Lord, 13
Gmeiner, Rudolf, 169
Gobeaux, Odette, 170
Godfrey, J. H., 11 fn.
Goebbels, Paul Joseph, 12, 363, 369
Goering, Hermann, 240, 342, 363
Goetz, Josef, 137, 144, 147 fn., 152,
    167, 169, 176, 188, 189

[401]

46, 50, 102, 131, 171, 186, 195, 233, 247, 248, 274, 294, 297, 329, 338, 340, 342, 348, 350, 351, 365, 369, 371, 375, 380
Hjalf, C. V., 371
Hoff, Torbjorn, 345
Hofstede, Jan, 282
Holdorf, Karl Horst, 165, 175
Holland, 1, 2, 8–12, 14, 16, 37, 41, 43, 66, 133–135, 247–312, 370, 371
Holland, John, 6
Hollingworth, Ralph, 351–355, 358–361, 365, 367 fn., 368, 370–371, 378, 380
Holst, Johan, 317
Homberg, Piet, 270–273
Hoogevorst, Kok, 279
Howarth, David, 337
Hubble, Desmond, 243
Hubert, *see* Farmer, John
Hudson, Charles, 222, 224
Hulsteyn, Cornelius van, 297
Humphreys, Leslie, 52, 53
Hutchison, James, 62
Hutting, Pam, 280
Hutton, Clayton, 42
Huxley, Julian, 41
Hvaal, Emil, 335
Hymans, Max, 67, 69

Idland Kasper, 325, 327
Ijzerdrast, Bernard, 247–248
Inayat Khan, Noor, 135, 138, 149, 158–160, 164, 169, 187, 188, 189–190, 244, foll. 274
INTERALLIÉ, 53, 72–85, 87, 105, 123, 160, 176
Isidore, *see* Jones, George Donovan
Ismay, Lord Hastings Lionel, v, 2, 4
Iversen, Werner Michael, 350–352, 360

Jacky, 184
Jacobsen, Frode, 371
Jacqueline, *see* Nearne, Jacqueline; Rudelatt, Yvonne

Jambroes, George Louis, 133–134, 175, foll. 274, 275–276, 277–285, 287, 289–290, 294–295, 297
James, Helen, 107–108, 110, 133
Jandael, Henk, *see* Christmann, Richard
Janier-Dubry family, 176, 178
Jean, Monsieur, *see* Bleicher, Hugo
JEAN-MARIE, 103–105, 107, 113, 127, 131, 155, 163, 181, 182, 187, 213
Jeanney, André, 117, 122
Jeffers, *see* Jordaan, Hendrik
Jensen, Poul, 360, 361, 366, 367
Jensen, Robert, 379
Jensen, Stig, 361
Jepson, Selwyn, 57, 114, 158
JOCKEY, 177
Jodl, Alfred, 340
Joekes, A. M., 294
Johannesen, Paul, 355–458
Johannsen, Nico, 288, 299
Johansen, V., 360, 366
Jones, George Donovan, 118, 224–225, 236
Jones, Sydney, 182, 185, 190, 213, 245
Jang, Adriaan de, 300, 308, 311
Jong, Louis de, v
Jonge, Ernest de, 273
Jongelie, Ralph C., 280–281
Jordaan, Hendrik, 270–273, 277, 292, 307
Jouffret, Claude, 85
Jouhaux, Leon, 91
Juif, Marcel, 176, 178
Juliana, Crown Princess (Netherlands), 247
Julien, *see* Newman, Isidore
Jumeau, Claude, 69
Juncker, Flemming, 361, 366, 378
Justesen, Poul, 378
Justin, *see* Cohen, Gaston; Rake, Denis

Kaltenbrunner, Ernst, 148, 186, 245, 297
Kamphorst, Peter, 282

Levine, Edward, 177
Lévy, Louis, 90, 92, 94, 95
LIBERATION group, 91, 226
LIBERTE, 91
Lie, Trygve, 332
Lier-Hansen, Knut, 329
Liewer, Philippe, 70, 155, 200–205
Lindberg, see Hammer, Mogens
Lindberg, Konrad, 314, 316
Lindemann, Frederick A., 323
Lindemans, Christian, 305–306
Lindsay, Martin, 25
Lindsay, Thomas, 36
Linge, Martin, 314, 333, 335
Linge Company, 316, 333, 334
Lipmann, Ole, 379
Lise, see, Sansom, Odette
Lloyd, Lord, 3
Lockhart, Robert Bruce, 12
Lok-Lindblad, Preben, 366–367, 378
Long Thijs, see Taconis, Thijs
Longum, Per, 322
Looi, Levinus van, 291–294, 298
Lorte, Grete, 367
Lostrie, Maurice, 237
Lotte, see Bonnessen, Edith
Louis of Antibes, see Lévy, Louis
Lovat, Lord, 26
Lucas, see Vomécourt, Pierre de
Lucien, see Gonzagues de St. Geniès,
    Maurice; Racheline, Lazare
Lund, Kai, 366
Lyon, Robert, 70, 154, 213

McAlister, John, 134, 141, 143, 146,
    153, 165, 244
Macare, Max, 282
Mackenzie, Compton, 7
McKenzie, John, 243, 244
Macout, see Hauger, Jean
Madeleine, see Inayat Khan, Noor
Maingard, René, 116, 230
Makowski, Stanislas, 236, 238–239
Maloubier, see Mortier, Robert
Malraux, André, 200, 202, 210, 218–
    221, 223
Malraux, Claude, 200, 202

Malraux, Roland, 200, 217, 218
Malval, Henri Ravel de, 90, 91, 93,
    98, 99
Mandel, Georges, 92
Manesson, Jean, 177
Manus, Max, 325, 343
Marcel, see Agazarian, Jack
Marchal, Marc, 73
Marchand, Joseph, 154
MARCO POLO group, 363
Mardonius, see Manus, Max
Marette, M., 107
Margarine, 367
Marguerite, see Agazarian, Francine
Marie-Louise, see Herbert, Mary
MARIE MADELEINE, 53
Marie of Lyons, see Hall, Virginia
Mariette, see Beekman, Yolande
Marks, Hugh, 316
Marriott, Harry, 53, 55, 90, 171
Mars, Alastair, 95
Marsac, André, 103–122, 125, 131,
    132, 133
Marsac, Michelle, 104, 109, 111–112,
    184
Marshall, Bruce, v
Martens, F. J., 270
Martens, Henk, see Molenaar, Jan
Marthinsson, Erling, 336
Martin, Pierre, 117–118, 121–122,
    175–176, 179, 180
Martine, see Damerment, Madeleine
Massenet, Pierre, 213
Matthieu, see Zeff, Edward
Maugenet, Albert, 177–178
Maugham, Somerset, 7
Maundy, Auguste, 239
Maurice, see Makowski, Stanislas
Maxime, see Hiller, George
May, Ernst, 259, 261, 268, 283, 301,
    306
Mayer, John A., 243, 244
Mayfield, Brian, 26, 314
Mechanic, see Lee, Lionel
Meer, A. P. von der, 258
Meersche, Gaston van der, 299–300
Meissner, Gustav, 356

[404]

Sanders, W. E., 311
Sanderson, Jean, 158,
Sansom, Odette, 28, 98, 101, 103–105, 110–118, 132, 195, foll. 274
Sant, F. van 't, 248, 256–257
Saulnier, Arthur, see Steele, Arthur
Sauvaget, Marcel, 129
Scavenius, Eric, 350, 370
Schäffer, Captain, 182, 184, 185, 186, 187, 216
Schelle, Jan van, 300
Schellenberg, Walter, 9, 186, 297–298
Schemmel, Dr., see Schellenberg, Walter
Schive, Jacob, 317, 337
Schley, Reeve, 233
Schmitt, Albert, 226
Schneider, Max, 129
Schoch, Aage, 378
Schoemaker, R. L. A., 258
Schouten, Jan, 294
Schreieder, Joseph, 250–251, 253–255, 257–259, 261, 264–266, 268–273, foll. 274, 275–276, 277–286, 289, 292, 294–303, 305–306, 308, 340
Schuilenga, J. R., 311
SCIENTIST, 206
Sclater, Arthur, 337
Scott, J. M., 25
Sebastien, see Grover-Williams, Charles
Sebes, Hendrik, 270, 271
Seigneur, Marcel, 244
Seland, Johannes, 318
Selborne, Lord, 4, 21, 58, 84
Semb, Carl, 317
Senter, John, 24
Sergeyev, Lilly, 363
SERVICE WIM, 299–300
Sevemet, Henri, 67
Seyr, Arne, 379
Seyss-Inquart, Arthur, 247, 250, 252, 253
Sforza, Carlo, 92
Shaw, Alex, see Szokolowski
Shetland Bus, 314, 337–338, 339, 340, 341, 346

Sickinga, Jan, 259
Sidney, Jeaan, 151
Simon, André, 64
Simon, Jean, 116, 122, 175, 178–180
Simon, Octave, 130
Simone, see Leigh, Vera
Sinclair, Archibald, 45
Sinclair, Hugh, 7, 8
Sirois, Allyre, 208
Sjoberg, Birger, 341
Skepper, Charles, 135, 155, 213–215
Skinnarland, Einar, 320, 322, 325, 328, 329, 330
Slagter, Martin, 269, 275
Sluijser family, 291, 293
Smith, Howard, 349
Sneum, Thomas, 354–355
Solage, R. P. de, 125
Solange, 166–168
Solm, Captain, see Travaglio, Johannes
Solomons, Jan, 286
Somer, J. M., 295, 299, 304, 310
Sonsteby, Gunnar, 342, 343–345
Sorlie, Rolf, 329
Southgate, Maurice, 116, 199, 224-227, 229, 230, 235, 243
Spinach, see Buizer, J. C.
Spink, Reginald, 351, 360
Spooner, Frank, 32
Sporborg, Harry, 61, 314, 336
SPRUCE, 154
Staermose, Robert, 361
Stagg, Frank N., vi, 314, 334, 349, 351–352
Staggs, Albert, 171–172
Stalin, Josef, 25
Stanislas, see Landes, Roger
Starheim, Odd, 314, 317–321, 330
Starr, George, 155, 222–223, 229, 240, foll. 274
Starr, John, 118, 121, 122, 135, 152, 168, 175–176, 178
SATIONER, 199, 224–225, 229–231
Staunton, Charles, see Liewer, Philippe
Steele, Arthur, 155, 213–215, 243, 244
Steeksma, Horst, 282